Learning Intervention Manual

Second Edition

Goals, Objectives, and Intervention Strategies

Samm N. House

© 2019 Hawthorne Educational Services, Inc.

Printed in the
United States of America.
6/22

H A W T H O R N E
Phone: (800) 542-1673 Fax: (800) 442-9509 Website: www.hawthorne-ed.com
800 Gray Oak Drive, Columbia, MO 65201

Table of Contents

B. Math

Behavior
Number

C. Reading

Behavior
Number

D. Writing

**Behavior
Number**

E. Spelling

**Behavior
Number**

F. Communication

**Behavior
Number**

G. Listening

Behavior
Number

H. Speech

Behavior
Number

I. Early Childhood Learning Problems

Behavior
Number

I. *Learning Intervention Manual - Second Edition*

The *Learning Intervention Manual - Second Edition* (LIM-2) is a compilation of goals, objectives, and intervention strategies for 194 behaviors grouped by categories. It was developed to respond to the most typical learning problems exhibited by students in educational settings. The interventions are appropriate for any student exhibiting the learning problem. The student need not be identified as disabled in any way. The appropriateness of the interventions relates directly to the learning problem and not to classification labels. The interventions selected reflect positive teacher behavior, contribute to a positive classroom atmosphere, and facilitate student success in the educational environment.

The interventions contained in this manual represent solutions which are both preventive and reactive. Preventive interventions are environmental modifications used to reduce variables (e.g., noise, movement, another student, etc.) which may contribute to unsuccessful learning performance. Reactive interventions teach the student ways to manage his/her behavior. These strategies include increased self-control, problem-solving skills, etc.

Some interventions in this manual apply to most students and should be implemented first to provide a more general approach to facilitating learning. Other interventions are more specific and should be individually selected for a student based on the appropriateness of the intervention for that student and the situation.

For any learning problem exhibited by students, it will be of value to assess the extent to which institutional variables influence and possibly contribute to the problem. Limited supervision in learning areas and during extracurricular activities, as well as arbitrary groups and seating arrangements are examples of factors which are inherent in the educational setting and often contribute to learning problems. As a first step in improving a learning environment, institutional variables should be evaluated and reduced. To appropriately respond to individual situations, all related variables in the educational setting which influence student learning should be identified and considered when choosing appropriate interventions to facilitate a student's success. Professional judgment should guide the choice of interventions for any particular student. The student's age, gender, grade level, local community standards, and disability, if one exists, are all to be considered in selecting appropriate intervention strategies. In order not to overlook any historical or contemporary determinants of educational performance, other variables to consider are vision, hearing, general health, nutrition, and family case history.

The goals and objectives in this manual are examples which may be used in writing IEPs. Criteria for measuring the success of the student's attainment of the goals and objectives must be determined by those professional educators and parents who are aware of the student's current abilities and program recommendations.

Interventions may be chosen by a team of professionals, a special educator in a self-contained class or functioning in a resource or consultant capacity, or by a regular education teacher. The interventions have been found to be appropriate for special education, as well as regular education classroom environments.

Use of the same interventions in all settings by all teachers and instructional personnel working with the student facilitates the likelihood of student success in the educational environment. The interventions included in this manual are appropriate for all educational environments and lend themselves particularly well to creating continuity across all the educational settings in which the student functions.

II. Goals, Objectives, and Interventions

1   Does not demonstrate problem-solving skills in new or unique situations

Goals:

1. The student will demonstrate problem-solving skills in new situations.
2. The student will demonstrate problem-solving skills in unique situations.

Objectives:

1. The student will solve problems by withdrawing from conflict situations on _____ out of _____ occasions.
2. The student will solve problems by reasoning in new or unique situations on _____ out of _____ occasions.
3. The student will solve problems by apologizing in conflict situations on _____ out of _____ occasions.
4. The student will solve problems by talking in a quiet, controlled manner in new or unique situations on _____ out of _____ occasions.
5. The student will independently solve problems in new or unique situations on _____ out of _____ occasions.
6. The student will solve problems in conflict situations by allowing others the benefit of the doubt on _____ out of _____ occasions.
7. The student will rely on verbal cues to solve problems in new or unique situations on _____ out of _____ occasions.
8. The student will rely on visual cues to solve problems in new or unique situations on _____ out of _____ occasions.
9. The student will solve problems by requesting clarification of information not understood in new or unique situations on _____ out of _____ occasions.
10. The student will solve problems by considering the consequences of his/her behavior in new or unique situations on _____ out of _____ occasions.
11. The student will react in a consistent manner in similar situations on _____ out of _____ occasions.
12. The student will seek teacher assistance when he/she is experiencing difficulty in a new or unique situation on _____ out of _____ trials.

Interventions:

1. Reinforce the student for demonstrating the ability to appropriately solve problems in new or unique situations: (a) give the student a tangible reward (e.g., classroom privileges, line leading, passing out materials, five minutes free time, etc.) or (b) give the student an intangible reward (e.g., praise, fist bump, smile, etc.).

2. Speak to the student to explain (a) what he/she is doing wrong (e.g., fighting, name calling, etc.) and (b) what he/she should be doing (e.g., withdrawing from personal interactions, reasoning, etc.).

3. Reinforce those students in the classroom who demonstrate the ability to appropriately solve problems in new or unique situations.

4. Reinforce the student for demonstrating the ability to appropriately solve problems in new or unique situations based on the number of times the student can be successful. As the student demonstrates success, gradually increase the length of time required for reinforcement.

5. Write a contract with the student specifying what behavior is expected (e.g., making logical decisions in new or unique situations, reasoning, etc.) and what reinforcement will be made available when the terms of the contract have been met.

6. Have the student question any directions, explanations, and instructions he/she does not understand.

7. Communicate with the student's parents (e.g., notes home, phone calls, etc.) to share information about the student's progress. The parents may reinforce the student at home for demonstrating the ability to appropriately solve problems in new or unique situations at school.

8. Choose a peer to model the ability to appropriately solve problems in new or unique situations for the student.

9. Evaluate the student's problem-solving ability and limit his/her exposure to new or unique situations to a level he/she can manage appropriately.

10. Teach the student a variety of ways to solve problems in new or unique situations (e.g., withdrawing, reasoning, relating previous experiences to the current situation, compromising, etc.).

11. Model for the student a variety of ways to solve problems in new or unique situations (e.g., withdrawing, reasoning, compromising, etc.).

12. Provide the student with hypothetical situations and ask him/her to suggest appropriate solutions to the situations.

13. Have the student role-play ways to solve problems in new or unique situations with peers and adults (e.g., withdrawing, reasoning, relating previous experiences, etc.).

14. Use cause-and-effect relationships as they apply to nature and people. Discuss what led up to a specific situation in a story or picture, what could happen next, etc.

15. Make sure the student understands that natural consequences (e.g., embarrassment, peers may not want to interact, teachers may have to intervene, etc.) may occur if he/she reacts inappropriately in new or unique situations.

16. Teach the student to solve problems in new or unique situations before the situation becomes too difficult for him/her to solve.

17. Explain to the student that it is natural for new or unique situations to occur. What is important is how he/she reacts to the situation.

18. Identify new or unique situations which may occur (e.g., being asked to participate during an assembly, peers encourage him/her to engage in inappropriate behavior to be accepted, etc.) and discuss appropriate ways to react to specific situations.

19. Discuss with the student his/her inappropriate response to a new or unique situation. Explore with him/her appropriate solutions which could have been used to handle the problem.

20. Maintain mobility throughout the classroom to supervise and intervene during new or unique situations in which the student is unable to successfully solve problems.

21. Each day provide the student with problem-solving situations which require logical thinking (e.g., What do you do if a stranger takes you by the arm in a department store? What do you do if you see smoke coming out of a neighbor's house?).

2   Does not demonstrate problem-solving skills in typical situations

Goal:

1. The student will demonstrate problem-solving skills in typical situations.

Objectives:

1. The student will solve problems by withdrawing from conflict situations on _____ out of _____ occasions.
2. The student will solve problems by reasoning in typical situations on _____ out of _____ occasions.
3. The student will solve problems by apologizing in conflict situations on _____ out of _____ occasions.
4. The student will solve problems by talking in a quiet, controlled manner in typical situations on _____ out of _____ occasions.
5. The student will independently solve problems in typical situations on _____ out of _____ occasions.
6. The student will solve problems in conflict situations by allowing others the benefit of the doubt on _____ out of _____ occasions.
7. The student will rely on verbal cues to solve problems in typical situations on _____ out of _____ occasions.
8. The student will rely on visual cues to solve problems in typical situations on _____ out of _____ occasions.
9. The student will solve problems by requesting clarification of information not understood in typical situations on _____ out of _____ occasions.
10. The student will solve problems by considering the consequences of his/her behavior in typical situations on _____ out of _____ occasions.
11. The student will react in a consistent manner in similar situations on _____ out of _____ occasions.
12. The student will seek teacher assistance when he/she is experiencing difficulty in a typical situation on _____ out of _____ trials.

Interventions:

1. Reinforce the student for demonstrating the ability to appropriately solve problems in typical situations: (a) give the student a tangible reward (e.g., classroom privileges, line leading, passing out materials, five minutes free time, etc.) or (b) give the student an intangible reward (e.g., praise, fist bump, smile, etc.).

2. Speak to the student to explain (a) what he/she is doing wrong (e.g., avoiding typical situations, overreacting, etc.) and (b) what he/she should be doing (e.g., relating previous experiences, reasoning, etc.).

3. Reinforce those students in the classroom who demonstrate the ability to appropriately solve problems in typical situations.

4. Reinforce the student for demonstrating the ability to appropriately solve problems in typical situations based on the number of times the student can be successful. As the student demonstrates success, gradually increase the length of time required for reinforcement.

5. Write a contract with the student specifying what behavior is expected (e.g., withdrawing from conflict situations, reasoning, etc.) and what reinforcement will be made available when the terms of the contract have been met.

6. Communicate with the student's parents (e.g., notes home, phone calls, etc.) to share information about the student's progress. The parents may reinforce the student at home for demonstrating the ability to appropriately solve problems in typical situations at school.

7. Choose a peer to model appropriately solving problems in typical situations for the student.

8. Have the student question any directions, explanations, and instructions he/she does not understand.

9. Evaluate the student's problem-solving ability and limit his/her exposure to situations requiring problem solving to a level he/she can handle appropriately.

10. Teach the student a variety of ways to solve problems in typical situations (e.g., withdrawing, reasoning, calling upon an arbitrator, apologizing, compromising, drawing upon previous experiences, etc.).

11. Model for the student a variety of ways to solve problems in typical situations (e.g., withdrawing, reasoning, asking for assistance, compromising, drawing upon previous experiences, etc.).

12. Provide the student with hypothetical situations and have him/her suggest appropriate solutions to the situations.

13. Have the student role-play ways to solve problems in typical situations (e.g., withdrawing, reasoning, compromising, drawing upon previous experiences, etc.).

14. Make sure the student understands that natural consequences (e.g., peers may not want to interact, teachers may have to intervene, he/she may become embarrassed, etc.) may occur if he/she reacts inappropriately in typical situations.

15. Teach the student to solve problems in typical situations before the situation becomes too difficult for him/her to solve.

16. Explain to the student that it is natural for conflict situations to occur. What is important is how he/she reacts to the situation.

17. Discuss typical situations with the student and appropriate solutions to specific problems (e.g., peers taking things from him/her, peers hitting or grabbing, forgetting required materials, losing supplies, etc.).

18. Discuss with the student his/her inappropriate response to a typical situation. Explore with him/her appropriate solutions which could have been used to handle the problem.

19. Set aside time each day for problem-solving games, analogies, decision-making activities, assigned responsibilities, etc.

20. Maintain mobility throughout the classroom to supervise student interactions and intervene in situations in which the student is unable to successfully solve problems.

21. Teach the student acceptable ways to communicate displeasure, anger, frustration, etc.

22. Teach the student to think before acting by asking himself/herself questions: *What is happening? What am I doing? What should I do? What will be best for me?*

23. Each day provide the student with problem-solving situations which require logical thinking (e.g., What do you do if a stranger takes you by the arm in a department store? What do you do if you see smoke coming out of a neighbor's house?).

24. Make sure the student experiences the consequences of his/her behavior (e.g., appropriate behavior results in positive consequences while inappropriate behavior results in negative consequences).

25. Provide the student with a list of questions involving logic, which he/she answers verbally (e.g., Why do we post wet paint signs? Why do we have stop signs at intersections? Why do we wear seat belts?).

26. Give the student situations/pictures and have him/her explain what variables are related (e.g., Snow is falling; the wind is blowing. Is the temperature hot or cold? What should you wear outdoors?).

27. Use cause-and-effect relationships as they apply to nature and people. Discuss what led up to a specific situation in a story or a picture, what could happen next, etc.

28. Make sure that the student can verbalize the reason for real-life outcomes of behavior (e.g., why the student had to leave the class line on the way to recess, why he/she earned the privilege of being line leader, etc.).

3   Has difficulty understanding directions and/or carrying out instructions and often requires repetition or rephrasing

Goal:

1. The student will improve his/her listening and direction-following skills.

Objectives:

1. The student will identify and define key words from verbal directions and/or instructions in _____ out of _____ trials.
2. The student will restate and carry out verbal directions in _____ out of _____ trials.
3. The student will follow individual or group directions in everyday situations in _____ out of _____ trials.

Interventions:

1. Have the student's hearing checked if it has not been recently checked.

2. Evaluate the appropriateness of the task to determine (a) if the task is too easy, (b) if the task is too difficult, and (c) if the length of time scheduled to complete the task is adequate.

3. Explain the importance of understanding directions and/or carrying out instructions.

4. Discuss with the student what behavior is expected (e.g., following one-step directions, etc.).

5. Reinforce the student for following directions and/or carrying out instructions: (a) give the student a tangible reward (e.g., classroom privileges, line leading, passing out materials, five minutes free time, etc.), or (b) give the student an intangible reward (e.g., praise, fist bump, smile, etc.).

6. Write a contract with the student specifying what behavior is expected (e.g., following directions without repetition or with one cue, etc.) and what reinforcement will be made available when the terms of the contract have been met.

7. Reduce distracting stimuli when directions are being presented. Move the student away from other students who may interfere with his/her ability to attend to directions, explanations, or instructions.

8. Seat the student near the teacher and away from noisy or visually distracting areas.

9. Make sure that directions, explanations, or instructions are delivered loudly enough to be heard by the student.

10. Teach the student to recognize key words and phrases related to directions/instructions to facilitate his/her ability to accurately follow directions.

11. Stand close to or directly in front of the student when delivering verbal instructions.

12. Maintain mobility to provide assistance to the student.

13. Draw the student's attention to key aspects of auditory communications as they occur (e.g., repeat important points, call the student by name, tell the student which information is particularly important, etc.).

14. Make sure the student is attending to the source of information (e.g., eye contact is being made, hands are free of materials, student is looking at assignment, etc.).

15. Use simple demonstrations and reduce abstractions by giving concrete examples and firsthand experiences.

16. Informally assess the student's auditory and visual short-term memory skills to determine which is the stronger. Utilize the results when presenting directions, explanations, and instructional content.

17. Provide the student with auditory cues when he/she is required to recall information, to help him/her remember the information previously presented (e.g., Remember yesterday when I said . . .?).

18. Have the student audio record directions, explanations, and instructions to replay needed information.

19. Provide information visually (e.g., wall-mounted board, pictures, projections, gestures, etc.) to support information the student receives auditorily.

20. Provide the student with written directions and instructions to supplement verbal directions and instructions.

21. Deliver information in both verbal and written form.

22. Write stories, directions, etc., so the student may read along as he/she listens.

23. Teach the student to visualize the instructions as if they were a movie, then play it back (e.g., student sees himself/herself opening an English book then turning to page 212, etc.).

24. Establish a routine for the student to follow in performing activities, assignments, etc., (e.g., listen to the person speaking to you, wait until directions are given before starting the assignment, make sure you have all needed materials, etc.).

25. Use multiple modalities (e.g., auditory, visual, tactile, etc.) when presenting directions, explanations, and instructional content.

26. Have the student carry out directions as soon as they are given to minimize the effect of irrelevant and distracting information on his/her ability to follow the instructions.

27. Teach the student how to organize information into smaller units or segments (e.g., divide the number sequence 132563 into units of 13, 25, 63, and point out that phone numbers are learned as small units of numbers).

28. Tell the student what to listen for before delivering auditory information.

29. Use a predetermined signal prior to delivering verbal questions and directions (e.g., clap hands, turn lights off and on, call the student by name, etc.).

30. Have the student read ahead on a subject to be discussed in class so that he/she is familiar with new vocabulary and concepts that will be used during instructional periods. If the student cannot read, have a peer/parent/sibling read the information to him/her or audio record the material, with emphasis on the vocabulary.

31. Deliver directions, explanations, and instructional content in a clear, concise manner and at an appropriate rate.

32. Deliver verbal directions prior to handing out materials.

33. Stop at key points when delivering directions, explanations, and instructions to determine student comprehension. Ask questions about what he/she needs to do.

34. Deliver information to the student on a one-to-one basis. As the student demonstrates the ability to listen successfully, gradually include more students in the group with the student.

35. Decrease the steps and/or stages involved in a series of directions until the student meets with success. As the student demonstrates success, gradually increase expectations

36. Give the student one task to perform at a time. Introduce the next task when the student has successfully completed the previous task.

37. Print the day's schedule on the board and refer to it frequently.

38. Establish assignment rules:
- Listen to directions.
- Wait until all verbal directions have been given.
- Ask questions about anything you do not understand.
- Begin the assignment only when you understand the requirements.
- Make sure you have all the materials necessary.

Review rules often. Reinforce students for following the rules.

39. Have the student ask questions about directions, explanations, instructions he/she does not understand.

40. Reinforce those students in the classroom who follow directions appropriately.

41. Choose a peer to model following directions for the student.

42. Choose a peer to model delivering and/or repeating verbal questions and directions for the student.

43. Review the schedule of the morning or afternoon activities with the student and have him/her repeat the sequence. As the student demonstrates success, increase the length of the sequence.

44. Provide the student each day with a schedule of daily events and activities at school.

45. Have the student physically perform directions (e.g., have the student go to the door and then stand near the teacher, etc.).

46. Have the student sequence the activities which occurred on a field trip or special event.

47. Have the student practice following directions by engaging in sequential activities which are purposeful to him/her (e.g., operating equipment, following recipes, opening a combination lock, etc.).

48. At the end of the school day, have the student recall three activities in which he/she was engaged during the day. As the student demonstrates success, gradually increase the number of activities the student is expected to recall.

49. Use the calendar every day and discuss what the student did yesterday, is doing today, or will do tomorrow.

50. Have the student repeat/paraphrase directions, explanations, and instructions after receiving them.

51. Provide the student with environmental cues and prompts designed to facilitate his/her success in the classroom (e.g., posted rules, schedule of daily events, steps for performing tasks, etc.).

52. Teach the student to make reminders for himself/herself (e.g., notes, lists, etc.).

53. Provide the student with written lists of things to do, materials he/she will need, etc.

54. Have the student practice making notes for specific information and directions he/she wants and/or needs to remember. Encourage him/her to use these notes as a checklist to make sure that he/she has completed all the steps.

55. Teach the student information-gathering skills (e.g., listen carefully, write down important points, ask for clarification, wait until all information is received before beginning, etc.).

56. Have the student pretend he/she is a waiter/waitress and recall the items from an order given to him/her.

57. Make sure the student is not engaged in activities that interfere with listening to directions, explanations, and instructions (e.g., looking at other materials, putting away materials, talking to others, etc.).

58. Reduce the emphasis on competition. Competitive activities may cause the student to hurry and carry out instructions without listening carefully.

59. Have the student practice repetition of information to facilitate short-term memory skills (e.g., repeating names, phone numbers, dates of events, etc.).

60. Have the student play barrier games. Place a screen between two students so they cannot see each other's paper, objects, etc. Have one student give the other student directions (e.g., Mark an **x** below an **o**.). Check to see how accurately the instructions were followed.

61. Have the student be a classroom messenger. Give the student a verbal message to deliver to another teacher, secretary, administrator, etc. As the student demonstrates success, increase the length of the messages.

62. Teach the student to use associative memory clues.

4 Has difficulty with short-term and long-term memory

Goals:
1. The student will improve his/her short-term memory skills.
2. The student will improve his/her long-term memory skills.
3. The student will improve his/her information retrieval skills.

Objectives:
1. The student will independently follow one-step directions on _____ out of _____ trials.
2. The student will independently follow two- or three-step directions on _____ out of _____ trials.
3. The student will memorize a short poem and recite it word for word on _____ out of _____ trials.
4. The student will immediately remember information that was presented visually and removed from his/her sight on _____ out of _____ trials.
5. The student will recall information at intervals of 10-15 minutes on _____ out of _____ trials.
6. The student will recall information at intervals of several hours or more on _____ out of _____ trials.
7. The student will recall information at intervals of several days or weeks on _____ out of _____ trials.

Interventions:

1. Have the student complete fill-in-the-blank sentences with appropriate words (e.g., objects, persons, places, etc.).

2. Present concepts following the *Who, What, Where, When, How,* and *Why* outline.

3. Review the morning and afternoon schedule of activities with the student and have him/her repeat the sequence. As the student is successful, increase the length of the sequence.

4. Have the student help a peer remember sequences.

5. Have the student develop a flow chart of the steps necessary to complete a task.

6. Have the student be a classroom messenger. Give the student a verbal message to deliver to another teacher, secretary, administrator, etc. As the student demonstrates success, increase the length of the messages.

7. Encourage the student to ask for clarification of any directions, explanations, and instructions before beginning a task to facilitate his/her comprehension.

8. Reinforce the student for demonstrating short or long-term memory skills: (a) give the student a tangible reward (e.g., classroom privileges, five minutes free time, etc.) or (b) give the student an intangible reward (e.g., praise, fist bump, smile, etc.).

9. Assign one task at a time. Give the student adequate time to complete it.

10. Consider carefully the student's ability level and experience when assigning responsibilities for him/her to complete.

11. Involve the student in activities to facilitate his/her short-term memory skills (e.g., deliver verbal messages from one location to another; act as group leader or teacher assistant, etc.).

12. Provide the student with adequate repetition of information through different experiences to facilitate his/her memory.

13. Have the student listen and take notes for *Who, What, Where, When, How,* and *Why* when concepts are presented.

14. Assign short-term projects that can be quickly completed.

15. Reinforce the student for demonstrating short-term or long-term memory skills based on the length of time the student can be successful. As the student demonstrates success, gradually increase the length of time required for reinforcement.

16. Have the student question any directions, explanations, and instructions he/she does not understand.

17. Instruct the student to ask people to repeat parts of a conversation he/she was unable to follow.

18. Establish a specific time at the end of each class period for the student to take care of responsibilities (e.g., copying homework assignment, collecting materials, clarifying directions, etc.).

19. Informally assess the student's auditory and visual short-term memory skills to determine which one is stronger. Utilize the results when presenting directions, explanations, and instructional content.

20. Evaluate the visual and auditory stimuli in the classroom and remove or reduce extraneous environmental stimuli.

21. Use multiple modalities (e.g., auditory, visual, tactile, etc.) when presenting directions, explanations, and instructional content.

22. Provide the student with auditory cues to help him/her remember information when he/she is required to recall it (e.g., key words, a brief verbal description to cue the student, etc.).

23. Encourage the student to avoid ingesting any substance (e.g., drugs, alcohol, cold remedies, etc.) that might further alter his/her ability to remember.

24. Present directions following the *What, How, Materials*, and *When* outline.

25. Gain the student's attention before telling him/her to do something. Have the student make eye contact and repeat the information to check for understanding.

26. Have the student carry a notepad with him/her at all times and write information down he/she needs to remember.

27. Give the student specific categories and have the student name as many items as possible within that category (e.g., objects, persons, places, etc.).

28. Have the student's hearing checked if it has not been recently checked.

29. Reduce the emphasis on competition. Competitive activities may increase the student's anxiety and reduce the student's ability to remember information.

30. Help the student develop an awareness of himself/herself and the environment. Instruct the student to periodically step back and ask himself/herself: *Am I on task and paying attention? What could I do to remember this information?*

31. Use sentence dictation to develop the student's short-term memory skills. Begin with three-word sentences. As the student demonstrates success, increase the length of the sentences.

32. Instruct the student to develop a checklist/chart to follow to facilitate him/her in completing all assignments. Assist the student in developing the checklist/chart if appropriate.

33. Stop at various points during the presentation of directions, explanations, or instructions to check for the student's comprehension of the information presented.

34. Encourage the student to eat a balanced diet and get plenty of rest to facilitate his/her ability to remember.

35. Provide the student with environmental cues and prompts designed to facilitate his/her success in the classroom (e.g., posted rules, schedule of daily events, steps for performing tasks, etc.).

36. Encourage the student to establish a routine for himself/herself by maintaining a weekly schedule and a weekend schedule.

37. Instruct the student to establish a timeline for completing a project and meet each deadline to complete the project on time.

38. Describe objects, persons, places, etc., to the student and have him/her name the items described.

39. Label objects, persons, places, etc., in the environment to facilitate the student's ability to recall their names.

40. Use concrete examples and experiences in sharing information with the student.

41. Deliver all directions, questions, explanations, and instructions in a clear, concise manner and at an appropriate rate for the student.

42. Have the student ask for help when he/she needs it.

43. Have the student prepare for tests using the *Who, What, Where, When, How*, and *Why* format.

44. Establish a regular routine for the student to follow in performing activities, assignments, etc., (e.g., listen to the person speaking to you, wait until directions are completed, make sure you have all the materials necessary, etc.).

45. Provide a demonstration and hands-on learning when teaching new skills.

46. Have the student outline, highlight, underline, or summarize information he/she needs to remember.

47. Provide the student with information from a variety of resources (e.g., texts, discussions, films, slide presentations, etc.) to facilitate the student's memory/recall.

48. Allow the student to highlight important information in written materials.

49. Encourage the student and his/her parents to establish a regular daily routine to follow to help him/her remember to take care of responsibilities. For example:

- 6:30 a.m. - get up, make bed, get dressed
- 7:00 a.m. - eat breakfast
- 7:30 a.m. - leave for school
- 3:30 p.m. - return from school
- 4:00 p.m. - feed pets
- 5:00 p.m. - set the table for dinner
- 5:30 p.m. - eat dinner
- 7:00 p.m. - do homework
- 8:00 p.m. - go to bed.

Post the schedule in a central location (e.g., on the refrigerator, in the student's room, etc.) to remind the student of what to do and when to do it.

50. Reward the student (e.g., homework pass, visit briefly with a peer, etc.) for remembering information for a specific length of time.

51. Have the student rehearse in his/her head information just heard to help him/her remember the important facts.

52. Actively involve the student in learning to remember sequences by having the student physically perform sequential activities (e.g., operating equipment, following recipes, solving math problems, etc.).

53. Have the student participate in memory game activities with a limited number of symbols. As the student demonstrates success, gradually increase the number of symbols.

54. Highlight or underline important information the student reads (e.g., directions, reading assignments, math word problems, etc.).

55. Instruct the student to keep necessary materials for specified activities together (e.g., gym clothes in a gym bag in the car, backpack with all school-related materials by the door, etc.).

56. Write down verbal directions. Instruct the student to mark each step off as it is completed.

57. Deliver directions, explanations, and instructional content in a clear manner and at an appropriate rate.

58. Present an assignment that involves immediate, short-term responses.

59. Make sure the student is attending to the source of information (e.g., eye contact is being made, hands are free of materials, student is looking at assignment, etc.).

60. Instruct the student to keep needed information in a readily accessible location (e.g., backpack, wallet, folder, locker, etc.).

61. Instruct the student to keep a master calendar. Encourage the student to write family activities, project due dates, upcoming tests and quizzes, homework assignments, school events, etc., on the calendar.

62. Provide audio-recorded information from lectures and assemblies. Allow the student to supplement his/her notes from these recordings.

63. Instruct the student to maintain attention to the source of information by maintaining eye contact, keeping hands free from other materials, and reducing other distractions.

64. Encourage the student to make notes of phone conversations.

65. Have the student practice making notes for specific information he/she wants and/or needs to remember.

66. Assess how meaningful the material is to the student. He/she is more likely to remember the material if he/she can relate it to real experiences.

67. Relate the information being presented to the student's experiences.

68. Encourage the student to put items that should be taken to work/school in a designated place (e.g., in front of the door, at the bottom of the stairs, etc.).

69. Help the student use memory aids to recall words (e.g., link a name to another word such as, Mr. Green is a colorful person).

70. Have the student take notes when directions are being given following *What, How, Materials*, and *When* format.

71. Show the student an object or a picture of an object for a few seconds and remove it. Ask the student to recall specific attributes of the object (e.g., color, size, shape, etc.).

72. Allow natural consequences to occur (e.g., personal possessions being lost, failing a homework assignment, etc.) due to the student not taking care of responsibilities.

73. Make a written list of procedures the student is to follow.

74. Maintain a consistent sequence of activities to facilitate the student's success (e.g., the student has math every day at one o'clock, recess/break time at two o'clock, etc.).

75. Provide directions on a one-to-one basis before beginning a task.

76. After a field trip or special event have the student recall and sequence the activities which occurred.

77. Have the student repeat/paraphrase directions, explanations, and instructions.

78. Have the student practice short-term memory skills by engaging in activities which are purposeful to him/her (e.g., delivering messages, being in charge of room cleanup, being a custodian's helper, operating equipment, etc.).

79. Choose different people (e.g., peer, counselor, paraprofessional, etc.) to help the student improve his/her memory.

80. Require the student to perform tasks, assignments, homework, etc., even though he/she did not do so at the established time.

81. Encourage the student to play word games such as Hangman®, Scrabble®, Password™, etc.

82. Teach the student to recognize key words and phrases related to information to facilitate short-term or long-term memory skills.

83. Have the student audio record directions, explanations, instructions, lectures, etc., and replay the information as needed.

84. Teach the student the relationship between inappropriate behavior and the consequences which follow (e.g., not picking up possessions may result in their damage or loss, not doing homework may result in a failing grade, etc.).

85. Teach the student to rely on resources in the environment to recall information (e.g., notes, textbooks, pictures, etc.).

86. Assist the student in remembering responsibilities. As the student demonstrates success, gradually decrease the assistance and have the student to independently assume responsibilities.

87. Have the student repeat directions, explanations, and instructions after they have been given to reinforce retention.

88. Have the student practice repetition of information to facilitate short-term memory skills (e.g., repeating names, phone numbers, dates of events, etc.).

89. Give the student a series of words describing objects, persons, places, etc., and have the student identify the opposite of each word.

90. Give the student a series of words or pictures and have the student name the category to which they belong (e.g., objects, persons, places, etc.).

91. Teach the student listening skills (e.g., stop working, look at the person delivering information and directions, have necessary note-taking materials, etc.).

92. Teach the student direction-following skills (e.g., stop doing other things, listen carefully, write down important points, wait until all directions are given, question any directions not understood, etc.).

93. Teach and practice information-gathering skills (e.g., listen carefully, write down important points, ask for clarification, wait until all information is presented before beginning a task, etc.).

94. After reading a short story, have the student identify the main characters, sequence the events, and report the outcome of the story.

95. Teach and practice different strategies to remember information:
- repetition,
- mnemonic,
- acronym, and
- association.

96. Review periodically with the student the daily calendar of events, notes, or tasks that need to be completed.

97. Do not require the student to learn more information than he/she is capable of learning at any time.

98. Do not punish the student for legitimate forgetting, for accidents that interfere with doing things, etc.

99. Audio record a message. Have the student write down the message after he/she has listened to it. As the student demonstrates success, increase the length of the message.

100. Maintain a consistent daily routine in the classroom.

101. Provide information in the student's preferred learning style (e.g., visual, auditory, etc.) to facilitate memory.

102. Teach the student to recognize main points, important facts, etc.

103. Provide written reminders of task sequences.

104. Give the student one task to perform at a time. Introduce the next task after the student has successfully completed the previous task.

105. Demonstrate for the student the correct way to perform a task. Assist the student in performing the task several times before having him/her perform the task independently.

106. Reduce distractions to facilitate the student's ability to remember.

107. Have the student tell the schedule of daily events to other students.

108. Be specific when telling the student what he/she is supposed to do.

109. Have the student memorize the first sentence or a line of a poem, song, etc. As the student experiences success, require him/her to memorize more lines at a time.

110. Write a contract with the student specifying what behavior is expected (e.g., following two-step directions, etc.) and what reinforcement will be made available when the terms of the contract have been met.

111. At the end of the school day, ask the student to recall three activities in which he/she participated during the day. As he/she demonstrates success, gradually increase the number of activities the student is required to recall.

112. Have the student deliver the schedule of daily events to other students.

113. Have the student sequence the activities which occurred during a field trip or special event.

114. Evaluate the appropriateness of the memory activities to determine (a) if the task is too easy, (b) if the task is too difficult, or (c) if the length of time scheduled to complete the task is adequate.

115. Have the student identify the main characters, sequence the events, and report the outcome of a short story he/she has just read.

116. Reduce distracting stimuli in the environment when information is being presented, the student is studying, etc.

117. Organize assignments by dividing them into small segments. Set deadlines and provide the student with a reward after completing each segment of the assignment.

118. Choose a peer tutor to participate in short-term memory activities (e.g., concentration games, following directions, etc.) with the student.

119. Reinforce students for remembering to have materials such as pens, pencils, paper, textbooks, notebooks, etc.

120. Use written/verbal repetition to aid retention of information.

121. Do not give directions to the student from across the classroom. Go to the student, get his/her undivided attention, and tell the student what he/she is to do.

122. Teach the student how to organize information into smaller units (e.g., divide the number sequence 132563 into units of 13, 25, 63).

123. Evaluate the responsibilities given to the student and make sure they are appropriate for his/her level of development and ability.

124. Have the student quietly repeat to himself/ herself information just heard to help remember the information.

125. Encourage the student to use visual reminders (e.g., attach a note to a backpack, place a self-adhesive note on the inside of his/her locker, etc.).

126. Explain to the student when he/she forgets to do something exactly what he/she did wrong, what should have been done, and why.

127. Teach the student to use associative memory clues.

128. Encourage the student to use an electronic organizer to record the day's homework assignments, general reminders, and messages.

129. Provide the student with written lists of things to do, materials he/she will need, etc.

130. Teach the student to use associative cues or mnemonic devices to remember sequences.

131. Tell the student what to listen for when being given directions, receiving information, etc.

5   Has limited test-taking skills

Goal:

1. The student will improve his/her test-taking skills.

Objectives:

1. The student will have necessary materials available for test-taking on _____ out of _____ trials.
2. The student will have a clear work area when taking a test on _____ out of _____ trials.
3. The student will remain on task when completing a test on _____ out of _____ trials.
4. The student will follow directions for completion on the test on _____ out of _____ trials.
5. The student will take his/her time when completing a test on _____ out of _____ trials.
6. The student will engage in a relaxation activity prior to taking a test on _____ out of _____ occasions.
7. The student will perform classroom tests with _____% accuracy.
8. The student will meet a _____% level of mastery on classroom tests.

Interventions:

1. Make sure the reading level of the test is appropriate for the student.

2. Make sure directions are completely understood by the student (e.g., have the student paraphrase the directions).

3. Have the student read all multiple-choice answers before responding to the question.

4. On true-false items, have the student underline key words before responding.

5. On true-false items, teach the student the whole statement must be true for an item to be true.

6. On matching items, teach the student to read all choices prior to responding.

7. On matching items, teach the student to respond to known items first and mark off used choices.

8. Teach the student to pace himself/herself on timed tests.

9. Have the student use a place marker on a standardized test's response sheet.

10. Teach the student mnemonic devices to remember information.

11. Have the student list important points prior to taking the test.

12. For spelling tests, have the student practice writing spelling words five times each while saying them aloud.

13. For spelling tests, have the student take a pretest one day prior to the final test.

14. Teach the student not to spend too much time on any one item on timed tests.

15. Teach the student to proofread all answers on a test.

16. On essay tests, have the student include *Who, What, Where, When, How,* and *Why* in the answer.

17. Have the student study with a peer.

18. Allow the student additional time to take the test.

19. For standardized tests, give the student sample test questions to familiarize him/her with the format.

20. Allow the student to take the test in another place in the building (e.g., resource room, counselor's office, etc.).

21. Have the student study for tests according to the *Who, What, Where, When, How,* and *Why* format; then test according to that same information.

22. Provide the student with sample test questions.

23. Make sure the student knows what topic/ areas will be covered by the test.

24. Provide a review session in which test topics and typical questions are reviewed.

25. Have the student check all answers on tests/quizzes for accuracy.

26. Give the student a practice test in class.

27. Allow the student to verbally respond to test items/questions.

28. Provide time for the student to study for tests/quizzes at school.

29. Provide the student with multiple opportunities to master information that will be covered on a test/quiz (e.g., listening to presentations in class, reading assigned materials, studying with a friend, playing games using the information to be tested, etc.).

6   Is unprepared for tests

Goal:

1. The student will be prepared for tests.

Objectives:

1. The student will study for _____ out of _____ tests.
2. The student will study for _____ out of _____ quizzes.
3. The student will study and perform classroom tests with _____% accuracy.
4. The student will study and perform classroom quizzes with _____% accuracy.
5. The student will be prepared for assigned activities by reading the assigned material for _____ out of _____ activities.
6. The student will complete his/her assigned tasks, such as book reports, projects, etc., by the due date on _____ out of _____ trials.
7. The student will complete his/her homework prior to coming to the assigned activity on _____ out of _____ trials.
8. The student will correctly answer questions covering the assigned reading material on _____ out of _____ trials.
9. The student will read necessary information prior to coming to the assigned activity on _____ out of _____ trials.

Interventions:

1. Provide the parents with specific instructions for how the student should study for tests/quizzes.

2. Provide the student with the information that will be included on a test (e.g., textbook pages, lecture material, charts, graphs, tables, etc.).

3. Have the student write down all information that will be included on tests/quizzes.

4. Have the student use a daily *Assignment Sheet* or *Schedule of Daily Events* to write down assignments and dates of tests/quizzes to facilitate early preparation for tests/quizzes.

5. Have the student use the *Outline Form* when taking lecture notes.

6. Teach the student several note-taking formats. Encourage the student to use the most efficient format for him/her.

7. Have the student study following the *Studying for a Test* steps.

8. Teach the student mnemonic memory strategies (e.g., to remember the Great Lakes have the student memorize **HOMES** - **H**uron, **O**ntario, **M**ichigan, **E**rie, **S**uperior).

9. Choose a peer to model preparing for tests/quizzes for the student.

10. Have the student question any directions, explanations, and instructions he/she does not understand.

11. Provide the student with a list of necessary materials to be prepared for tests/quizzes.

12. Give the student a practice test in class.

13. At the end of the day, remind the student which materials are required for tests/quizzes to be given the next day (e.g., send a note home, verbal reminder, etc.).

14. Provide the student with structure for all tests/quizzes (e.g., specific directions, routine format for tests/quizzes, time limits, etc.).

15. Provide the student with verbal reminders of materials required to be prepared for tests/quizzes.

16. Provide the student with time at school to prepare for tests/quizzes (e.g., supervised study time).

17. Present concepts following the *Who, What, Where, When, How,* and *Why* outline.

18. Reduce the number/length of tests/quizzes. As the student demonstrates success, gradually increase the number/length of tests/quizzes.

19. Provide individual assistance to the student to help him/her prepare for tests/quizzes (e.g., set aside time during the day, study hall, or after school, etc.).

20. Identify other personnel in the school who may be able to assist the student in preparing for tests/quizzes (e.g., aide, librarian, other teachers, etc.).

21. Provide a review session in which test topics and typical questions are reviewed.

22. Have the student study for tests according to the *Who, What, Where, When, How,* and *Why* format. The teacher should then test on this information.

23. Have the student check all answers on tests/quizzes for accuracy.

24. Provide the student with multiple opportunities to master information that will be covered on a test/quiz (e.g., listening to presentations in class, reading assigned materials, studying with a friend, playing games using the information to be tested, etc.).

25. Provide the student with written directions to follow in preparing for all tests/quizzes.

26. Choose a peer to help the student prepare for tests/quizzes.

27. Provide the student with sample test questions.

7   Performs classroom tests or quizzes at a failing level

Goals:

1. The student will improve his/her performance on classroom tests.
2. The student will improve his/her performance on classroom quizzes.

Objectives:

1. The student will perform classroom tests with _____% accuracy.
2. The student will perform classroom quizzes with _____% accuracy.
3. The student will meet a _____% level of mastery on classroom tests.
4. The student will meet a _____% level of mastery on classroom quizzes.

Interventions:

1. Establish classroom rules:
- Concentrate while working.
- Work quietly.
- Remain in your seat.
- Finish task.
- Meet task expectations.

Review rules often. Reinforce the student for following the rules.

2. Present concepts following the *Who, What, Where, When, How,* and *Why* outline.

3. Communicate with the student's parents (e.g., notes home, phone calls, etc.) to share information about the student's progress. The parents may reinforce the student at home for improved test or quiz scores.

4. Have the student maintain a performance record for each subject in which he/she is experiencing difficulty.

5. Provide the student with a set of prepared notes that summarize the material to be tested.

6. Have the student take a sample test or quiz before the actual test.

7. Have the student question anything he/she does not understand while taking tests or quizzes.

8. Deliver all directions, questions, explanations, and instructions in a clear, concise manner and at an appropriate rate for the student.

9. Reduce the emphasis on competition. Students who compete academically and fail may cease to try to succeed and do far less than they are capable of achieving.

10. Reinforce those students who demonstrate improved test or quiz scores. (It may be best to reinforce privately rather than publicly.)

11. Identify the student's most effective learning mode and utilize it when giving tests or quizzes.

12. Have the student prepare for tests using the *Who, What, Where, When, How,* and *Why* format.

13. Teach the student skills for studying for tests/quizzes.

14. Develop tests and quizzes for the student using the *Who, What, Where, When, How,* and *Why* format.

15. Reduce the emphasis on formal testing by grading the student on daily performance.

16. Teach and encourage the student to practice basic study skills (e.g., reading for the main point, note taking, summarizing, highlighting, studying in an appropriate environment, using time wisely, etc.) before taking tests or quizzes.

17. Assess the student's performance in a variety of ways (e.g., have the student give verbal explanations, simulations, physical demonstrations of a skill, etc.).

18. Provide the student with increased opportunities for help or assistance on academic tasks (e.g., peer tutoring, directions for work sent home, frequent interactions, etc.).

19. Modify instructions to include more concrete examples to facilitate student learning.

20. Provide parents with information on test and quiz content (e.g., the material that will be covered by the test or quiz, the format, the types of questions, etc.).

21. Provide a variety of opportunities for the student to learn the information covered by tests or quizzes (e.g., films, visitors, community resources, etc.).

22. Provide the student with opportunities for review before taking tests or quizzes.

23. Prior to the test, provide the student with all information that will be on the test (e.g., list those items he/she will need to know).

24. Remove the threat of public knowledge of failure (e.g., test or quiz results are not read aloud or posted, test ranges are not made public, etc.).

25. Have the student listen and take notes following the *Who, What, Where, When, How,* and *Why* format when concepts are presented.

26. Have the student verbally answer tests or quizzes.

27. Reinforce improved test or quiz scores: (a) give the student a tangible reward (e.g., classroom privileges, line leading, passing out materials, five minutes free time, etc.) or (b) give the student an intangible reward (e.g., praise, fist bump, smile, etc.).

28. Provide the opportunity for the student to study daily assignments with a peer.

29. Teach the student test-taking skills.

30. Make sure the student has mastery of skills at each level before testing a concept.

31. Arrange a time for the student to study with a peer before taking tests or quizzes.

32. Give shorter tests or quizzes, but give them more frequently. As the student demonstrates success, gradually increase the length of tests or quizzes and give them less frequently.

33. Allow the student to respond to alternative test or quiz questions (e.g., general questions which represent global understanding).

34. Teach the student test-taking strategies (e.g., answer questions you are sure of first, learn to summarize, check each answer, etc.).

35. Allow the student to take tests or quizzes in a quiet place to reduce distractions (e.g., study carrel, library, etc.).

36. Make sure that the test questions are worded exactly as the information was given in either verbal or written form.

37. Have the student take tests or quizzes in the resource room where the resource teacher can clarify questions, offer explanations, etc.

38. Make sure that the tests or quizzes measure knowledge of content and not related skills, such as reading or writing.

39. Review with the student the *Test-Taking Skills* and *Additional Suggestions* located in the *Appendix* of this manual.

40. Evaluate the appropriateness of the task to determine (a) if the task is too easy, (b) if the task is too difficult, or (c) if the length of time scheduled for the task is adequate.

41. Have the tests or quizzes audio recorded. Allow the student to replay questions as often as necessary.

42. Speak with the student to explain (a) what he/she is doing wrong (e.g., not attending in class, not using study time, etc.) and (b) what he/she should be doing (e.g., attending during class, asking questions, using study time, etc.).

43. Give tests and quizzes when the student is likely to be successful (e.g., after he/she has had adequate time to learn the information).

44. Have tests or quizzes read to the student.

45. Write a contract with the student specifying what behavior is expected (e.g., improved test or quiz scores) and what reinforcement will be made available when the terms of the contract have been met.

46. Monitor the student's performance to understand errors and determine where learning problems exist.

47. Teach the student skills to use when taking notes.

8   Remembers information one time but not the next

Goals:

1. The student will improve his/her short-term memory.
2. The student will improve his/her long-term memory.
3. The student will improve his/her visual memory.
4. The student will improve his/her auditory memory.
5. The student will improve his/her skills in logical thinking.

Objectives:

1. The student will immediately remember information presented visually and removed with _____% accuracy.
2. The student will remember information at intervals of 10 to 15 minutes with _____% accuracy.
3. The student will remember information at intervals of several hours with _____% accuracy.
4. The student will remember information at intervals of days or weeks with _____% accuracy.

Interventions:

1. Have the student audio record important information that he/she should remember.

2. Present information verbally if the student has difficulty remembering written information.

3. Have the student outline, highlight, underline, or summarize information that should be remembered.

4. Use concrete examples and experiences in sharing information with the student.

5. Teach the student to recognize main points, important facts, etc.

6. Make sure the student has adequate opportunities for repetition of information through different experiences to facilitate memory.

7. Present information to the student in the most clear and concise manner possible.

8. Reduce distracting stimuli when the student is attempting to recall important information.

9. Teach the student to rely on resources in the environment to recall information (e.g., notes, textbooks, pictures, etc.).

10. Provide auditory cues to help the student recall information (e.g., key words, a brief verbal description to clue the student, etc.).

11. Have the student make notes, lists, etc., of important information to carry with him/her at all times.

12. When the student is required to recall information, remind him/her of the situation in which the material was originally presented (e.g., Remember yesterday when we talked about . . .?, Remember when we were outside and I told you about the . . .?).

13. Make the material meaningful to the student. Remembering is more likely to occur when the material is meaningful and the student can relate the material to real experiences.

14. Relate the information being presented to the student's previous experiences.

15. Have the student follow a regular routine of daily events to establish consistency in his/her behavior pattern.

16. Have the student quietly repeat to himself/herself information just heard to help him/her remember the important facts.

17. Do not require the student to learn more information than he/she is capable of remembering at any time.

18. Give the student a choice of answers (e.g., more than one possible answer, multiple-choice on a worksheet, etc.) to facilitate his/her ability to recognize the correct answer.

19. Provide reminders throughout the educational environment to help the student be more successful in remembering information (e.g., rules, lists, schedules, etc.).

20. Help the student use memory aids to recall words (e.g., link a name to another word such as, Mr. Green is a colorful person).

21. Provide the student with adequate opportunities for repetition of information through different experiences to facilitate his/her memory.

22. Review daily those skills, concepts, tasks, etc., which have been previously introduced to help the student remember information previously presented.

23. Have the student take notes when directions are being given following the *What, How, Materials*, and *When* format.

24. Use daily drill activities to help the student memorize math facts, vocabulary words, etc.

25. Identify the student's most effective learning mode. Use it consistently to facilitate the student's understanding (e.g., If the student does not understand directions or information given verbally, present it in written form. If the student has difficulty understanding written information or directions, present it verbally.).

26. Provide the student opportunities to apply new skills or information to other situations (e.g., when he/she learns to count by fives, have him/her practice adding nickels; vocabulary words learned should be pointed out in reading selections; etc.).

27. Present directions following the outline of *What, How, Materials*, and *When*.

28. Have the student listen and take notes for *Who, What, Where, When, How*, and *Why* while concepts are presented.

29. Present concepts following the outline of *Who, What, Where, When, How*, and *Why*.

30. Call on the student when he/she is most likely to be able to successfully respond.

Goal:

1. The student will improve his/her ability to understand concepts at a faster pace.

Objectives:

1. The student will use visual cues to aid his/her ability to understand concepts at a faster pace with _____% accuracy.
2. The student will use auditory cues to aid his/her ability to understand concepts at a faster pace with _____% accuracy.
3. The student will use visual and auditory cues to aid his/her ability to understand concepts at a faster pace with _____% accuracy.
4. The student will learn _____ new concepts per week.
5. The student will independently review concepts and pass a weekly review with the teacher with _____% accuracy.
6. The student will independently review concepts and pass a monthly review with the teacher with _____% accuracy.

Interventions:

1. Have the student practice a new concept independently, with an aide, teacher, or a peer before attempting it with the entire group or being graded on it.

2. Have the student be a peer tutor to teach concepts just learned to another student.

3. Reduce the emphasis on competition. Competitive activities may increase the student's anxiety and reduce the student's ability to remember information.

4. Initiate a *Learn a Concept a Day* program with the student and incorporate the concept into the assigned activities for the day.

5. Provide practice of new concepts with a computer software program or a hand-held educational device that gives immediate feedback to the student.

6. Give the student fewer concepts to learn at one time. Spend as much time as needed on each concept for the student to understand it.

7. Recognize quality work (e.g., display the student's work, congratulate the student, etc.).

8. Provide the student with new information in the most direct manner possible (e.g., a list of facts, a summary of important points, outline of important events, etc.).

9. Develop crossword puzzles which contain only the student's spelling words and have him/her complete them.

10. Underline, circle, or highlight important information from any material the student is to learn (e.g., science, math, geography, etc.).

11. Use wall charts to introduce new concepts with visual images/pictures for the student to associate with previously learned concepts.

12. Reinforce the student for learning new concepts: (a) give the student a tangible reward (e.g., classroom privileges, line leading, passing out materials, five minutes free time, etc.) or (b) give the student an intangible reward (e.g., praise, fist bump, smile, etc.).

13. Evaluate the appropriateness of the task to determine (a) if the task is too easy, (b) if the task is too difficult, or (c) if the length of time scheduled for the task is adequate.

14. Give the student a list of key words, phrases, or main points to learn for each new concept introduced.

15. Write sentences, passages, paragraphs, etc., for the student to read which reinforce new concepts.

16. Have the student review new concepts each day for a short period of time rather than two or three times per week for longer periods of time.

17. Provide the student with opportunities to use new concepts frequently throughout the day.

18. Have the student highlight or underline key words, phrases, and sentences from reading assignments, newspapers, magazines, etc.

19. Have the student quiz others over new concepts (e.g., teacher, aide, peers, etc.).

20. Choose a peer to participate in daily drill activities with the student.

21. Do not require the student to learn more information than he/she is capable of learning at any time.

22. Audio record important information. The student can replay the recording as often as necessary.

23. Allow the student to use resources to help him/her successfully perform tasks (e.g., calculator, multiplication tables, dictionary, a peer, etc.).

24. Have the student use physical or online information resources (e.g., encyclopedia, dictionary, etc.) to successfully perform tasks.

25. Provide the student with various times throughout the day when he/she can participate in drill activities with the teacher, aide, peer, etc.

26. Provide the student with opportunities for drill activities in the most interesting manner possible (e.g., computer, calculator, games, films, music, etc.).

10   Does not demonstrate the ability to maintain concentration on a particular activity for extended periods of time

Goals:

1. The student will set goals for himself/herself.
2. The student will develop a plan to achieve stated goals.
3. The student will learn to delay gratification when working diligently toward a goal.
4. The student will develop self-reliance by persistently striving toward a goal.

Objectives:

1. The student will write project goals for himself/herself on _____ out of _____ assignments.
2. The student will write out a plan for achieving stated goals on _____ out of _____ assignments.
3. The student will develop in writing a list of criteria for evaluating his/her progress on _____ out of _____ project assignments.
4. The student will become involved in sustained creative endeavors _____ times per week.
5. The student will engage in creative problem-solving activities _____ times per week.

Interventions:

1. Have the student write a goal or a set of goals to achieve before beginning a task.

2. Have the student plan and organize a project as part of an extended independent study:

- Write a description of the specific problem to be investigated and the objectives to be completed.
- Write a plan for achieving the goal or set of goals.
- Develop a time schedule for achieving each step of the plan.
- Prepare a list of steps for getting started (e.g., letters to write, people to interview, sites to be visited, maps to obtain, etc.).
- List resources to use in achieving the goal (e.g., persons, books, periodicals, equipment, etc.).
- Anticipate any problems that might arise in pursuing the goals.
- Use evaluative thinking in the development of a list of criteria for judging goal achievement.
- Have the student self-evaluate at length his/her independent study results (e.g., performance, product, etc.).

3. Make sure that the student's academic tasks are on his/her ability level.

4. Have the student participate in activities that require sequenced analytical thinking (e.g., puzzles, codes, ciphers, scientific research involving experiment documentation, etc.).

5. Have the student participate in games requiring concentration (e.g., checkers, chess, matching games, etc.).

6. Have the student be a peer tutor and work directly with another student who has trouble concentrating.

7. Reinforce the student for his/her ability to concentrate and complete projects and assignments.

8. Encourage the student to engage in a hobby that requires categorizing (e.g., stamps, baseball cards, rocks, etc.).

9. Have the student write creative anecdotes, stories, poetry, plays, etc., with or without a stimulus (e.g., open-ended sentences, photographs, etc.).

10. Ask the student to demonstrate the use of a computer program to another student.

11. Encourage the student to practice total concentration by designating a time limit in which to complete a competitive exercise.

12. Provide the student with an opportunity to work on his/her hobby during class time (e.g., gathering research information, using a laboratory, etc.).

13. Allow the student extended time to learn to use technology (e.g., independent hands-on time to explore new software, word processing programs, writing a program, etc.).

14. Ask the student to concentrate on directing an ad campaign and writing appropriate advertisements (e.g., promoting a school event, selling a club product, raising funds, etc.):

- Have the student compare and contrast ad campaigns of a specific category of products seen on TV commercials (e.g., cosmetics, laundry detergents, cars, etc.).
- Provide materials and space for the student to produce his/her own TV commercial.

15. Have the student spend time developing a survey for peers to answer (e.g., likes and dislikes, attitudes, wants and needs, etc.).

16. Ask the student to prepare an argument for a debate on a given subject.

17. Allow the student to present a lecture on a subject in which he/she has a particular interest and expertise.

18. Ask the student to develop interesting and educational learning experiences for a current unit of study:

- Provide materials for the student to develop a learning center.
- Have the student consider the best method of evaluating student progress in his/her learning center.

19. Allow the student to teach games involving concentration to other students (e.g., classmates, younger students, etc.).

11 Does not demonstrate an effective organizational system when completing homework assignments

Goal:

1. The student will improve his/her organizational skills.

Objectives:

1. The student will use available time to work on assignments, perform responsibilities, read, etc., with prompting, on _____ out of _____ occasions.
2. The student will independently use available time to work on assignments, perform responsibilities, read, etc., on _____ out of _____ occasions.
3. The student will prioritize and complete assignments, with verbal prompts, on _____ out of _____ occasions.
4. The student will independently prioritize and complete assignments on _____ out of _____ occasions.
5. The student will put materials where they belong, with reminders, on _____ out of _____ occasions.
6. The student will independently put materials where they belong on _____ out of _____ occasions.

Interventions:

1. Identify a specific area to study that is free of clutter (e.g., desk, table, etc.).

2. Identify and use a place to study that is quiet and free from movement or other distractions (e.g., no music or television, away from siblings, isolated from discussions or phone calls).

3. Choose a time for studying that allows for maximum concentration. This will be an individual preference (e.g., after school, after one hour of play and relaxation, after dinner, etc.).

4. Have the student study at the same time each day. In the event he/she does not have an assignment, he/she should use this time for reading or reviewing.

5. Provide the student with needed materials to be organized at his/her work area (e.g., paper, pencils, pens, ruler, eraser, pencil sharpener, tape, crayons, colored pencils, scissors, stapler, dictionary, thesaurus). This will reduce the need for the student to interrupt his/her own work to look for materials.

6. Keep the identified work area at a comfortable room temperature. A room kept too warm could make the student drowsy.

7. Have the student study graphics, pictures, and captions within chapters.

8. Have the student prioritize his/her assignments on the basis of due dates and divide study time according to assignments.

9. Encourage parents/guardians to be available to answer questions or check for completion and/or accuracy of homework. Being available does not require sitting with the student but being near by and available.

10. Have the student break lengthy projects into manageable steps and complete one step each night (e.g., information gathering, organizing information, writing introduction, etc.).

11. It is important the student be required to follow a routine of studying and preparing for school each day.

12. Have the student plan for short breaks while he/she is studying (e.g., drink of water, stretching break, restroom break, etc.).

13. Have extra reading material available at the study area to read when assignments are complete.

14. Have the student review nightly for two to three nights before a test.

15. After reading a chapter, have the student summarize the chapter using the *Outline Form*.

16. Have the student answer *Who, What, Where, When, How*, and *Why* using the *Outline Form* when reading for content.

17. Require that the student write deadlines for assignments on an assignment sheet with both teacher and parent signatures.

18. Have the student show a parent his/her progress on homework assignments at the end of each study period.

19. Make sure the student is aware of those specified times when he/she can watch television, visit with a friend, etc.

20. Have the student use the same structure for all academic activities (e.g., routine format for tasks, time, etc.).

21. Provide an organizer for materials inside the student's desk.

22. Have the student use the *Flash Card Study Aid* when preparing for tests.

23. Allow a set of school texts to be kept at the student's home for his/her use (e.g., spelling book, reading book, science book, etc.) if he/she regularly has difficulty remembering to take necessary materials home.

12 Does not demonstrate an understanding of directionality

Goals:

1. The student will improve his/her understanding of abstract concepts (e.g., spatial relationships, directionality, classifications, generalizations).
2. The student will improve his/her awareness and attention to information and activities in the environment.

Objectives:

1. The student will demonstrate directionality by imitating the placement of objects (e.g., left-right, forward-backward, east-west, etc.) with _____% accuracy.
2. The student will independently demonstrate directionality (e.g., left-right, forward-backward, east-west, etc.) with _____% accuracy.
3. The student will recognize directionality (e.g., left-right, forward-backward, east-west, etc.) with visual and verbal cues with _____% accuracy.
4. The student will independently recognize directionality (e.g., left-right, forward-backward, east-west, etc.) with _____ % accuracy.

Interventions:

1. Teach north, south, east, and west using the classroom, playground, school building, etc.

2. Use concrete examples when teaching concepts of up-down, high-low, above-below, etc. Use books, balls, regular classroom materials, etc., when trying to convey these concepts.

3. Make sure to use the terms right and left as part of the directions you give to the student (e.g., refer to the windows on the left side of the room, the wall-mounted board on the right side of the room, etc.).

4. Identify directions in the classroom with signs (e.g., label the ceiling up, label the floor down, etc.).

5. Have the student practice following directions on paper. Instruct the student to make a mark or picture on the right, left, middle, top, and bottom parts of the paper according to the directions given.

6. Avoid the problem of mirror images by standing next to the student when giving right and left directions.

7. Design an obstacle course using materials in the room. Students can step into the box, crawl over the desk, walk under the coat rack, stand on the table, etc.

8. Hang directional signs in the room (e.g., turn left, games under cabinet, etc.).

9. Play *Simon Says* for practice with directions (e.g., Raise your left hand., Walk behind the chair., etc.).

10. Conduct scavenger hunts. Have the student look for a pencil in the desk, a book under the table, a glass on the chair, etc.

11. Have the student sort left and right gloves, shoes, paper hand, and foot cutouts, etc.

12. Review daily the concepts of directionality.

13. Label strips of paper left and right and attach them around the student's wrists.

14. Have the student practice walking forward and backward, moving toy cars and trucks forward and backward, etc.

15. Point out doors which are labeled push and pull and activities which require pushing and pulling (e.g., opening drawers, opening doors, etc.).

16. Emphasize activities which require the action of off and on (e.g., we turn lights on for light and off when we do not need them, we turn the stove on to heat things and off when things are hot, we put clothes on to go to school, leaves fall off a tree in the fall, etc.).

17. Use concrete examples and experiences in teaching directionality (e.g., east-west signs on the wall, left-right armbands, etc.).

18. Teach the concept of above and below with examples in the classroom (e.g., the ceiling is above our heads and the floor below our feet, etc.).

19. Teach the concept of before and after with examples from the student's daily routine (e.g., we wake up before we eat breakfast, we go to school after we eat breakfast, we eat lunch after we have morning free time, etc.).

20. Have the student find things that represent the concept of in and out (e.g., we pour milk in a glass and pour it out, we walk in a room and walk out, etc.).

21. Have the student identify objects which move up and down (e.g., airplanes, teeter-totter, etc.).

22. Identify objects which represent over and under (e.g., a bridge is over water, people sleep under covers, birds fly over our heads, rugs are under our feet, etc.).

13 Fails to demonstrate logical thinking

Goal:

1. The student will improve his/her skills in logical thinking.

Objectives:

1. The student will make responsible decisions, with assistance, in _____ out of _____ situations.
2. The student will independently make responsible decisions in _____ out of _____ situations.
3. The student will solve problems, with assistance, in _____ out of _____ situations.
4. The student will independently solve problems in _____ out of _____ situations.
5. The student will make correct inferences, with assistance, in _____ out of _____ situations.
6. The student will independently make correct inferences in _____ out of _____ situations.

Interventions:

1. Give the student responsibilities that require logical thinking (e.g., assign the student to water plants and provide a watering can and a glass, telling the student to use the most appropriate container, etc.).

2. Each day provide the student with problem-solving situations which require logical thinking (e.g., What do you do if a stranger takes you by the arm in a department store? What do you do if you see smoke coming out of a neighbor's house?).

3. Make sure the student experiences the consequences of his/her behavior (e.g., appropriate behavior results in positive consequences while inappropriate behavior results in negative consequences).

4. Provide the student with a list of questions involving logic to answer verbally (e.g., Why do we post wet paint signs? Why do we have stop signs at intersections? Why do we wear seat belts?).

5. When something is broken, lost, etc., have the student identify what could have been done to prevent the situation. Discuss with the student the value of properly maintaining and organizing materials.

6. Have the student read stories involving a moral (e.g., *The Tortoise and the Hare*, *The Boy Who Cried Wolf*, etc.) and explain the reason for the outcome of the story.

7. Have the student read short stories without endings. Have the student develop logical endings for the stories.

8. Give the student situations/pictures and have him/her explain what variables are related (e.g., Snow is falling and the wind is blowing. Is the temperature hot or cold? What should you wear outdoors?).

9. Have the student sequence rearranged cartoon strips and explain the logic of the sequence he/she created.

10. Give the student fill-in-the-blank statements requiring an appropriate response from multiple-choice possibilities (e.g., The boy's dog was dirty so the boy decided to give his dog a _____ [dog biscuit, bath, toy].).

11. Show the student pictures of dangerous situations and have him/her explain why it is dangerous (e.g., a child running into the street from between parked cars, a child riding a bicycle without using his/her hands, etc.).

12. Use cause-and-effect relationships as they apply to nature and people. Discuss what led up to a specific situation in a story or a picture, what could happen next, etc.

13. Set aside time each day for a problem-solving game, analogies, decision-making activities, assigned responsibilities, etc.

14. Make sure that the student can verbalize the reason for real-life outcomes of behavior (e.g., why the student had to leave the class line on the way to free time, why he/she earned the privilege of being line leader, etc.).

15. Have the student develop rules and explain why each rule is necessary.

16. Reinforce those students in the classroom who demonstrate logical thinking (e.g., making responsible decisions, solving problems, making references, etc.).

17. Have the student answer questions such as, Why do we have rules? Why do you have to be a certain age before you can drive a car?, etc.

18. Have the student answer analogy situations (e.g., a garage is to a car as a house is to a _____).

19. Make sure the student is attending to the source of information (e.g., eye contact is being made, hands are free of materials, student is looking at the assignment, etc.).

20. Have the student question any directions, explanations, and instructions he/she does not understand.

21. Reinforce the student for appropriate decision making: (a) give the student a tangible reward (e.g., classroom privileges, line leading, passing out materials, five minutes free time, etc.) or (b) give the student an intangible reward (e.g., smile, fist bump, etc.).

22. Have the student identify appropriate consequences for rules (e.g., consequences for following rules and consequences for not following rules). Have the student explain the choice of consequences he/she identified.

Goals:

1. The student will improve his/her critical thinking skills.
2. The student will improve his/her generalization skills.

Objectives:

1. The student will demonstrate generalization of knowledge by correctly defining a newly learned word _____% of the time.
2. The student will demonstrate generalization of knowledge by illustrating the knowledge in at least three different modes with _____% accuracy.
3. The student will demonstrate generalization of knowledge by placing new knowledge into several different categories with _____% accuracy.
4. The student will generalize rote information learned to everyday situations (e.g., counting to 100 and counting pennies) in _____ out of _____ trials.
5. The student will generalize concrete information to abstract situations (e.g., labeling objects/pictures and telling a story or talking about the items without the objects/pictures present) in _____ out of _____ trials.
6. The student will demonstrate comprehension of multiple-meaning words in _____ out of _____ trials.
7. The student will utilize deductive and inductive thinking skills in _____ out of _____ trials.
8. The student will generalize information learned to problem-solving situations in _____ out of _____ trials.
9. The student will generalize information learned to quizzes, tests, etc., in _____ out of _____ trials.

Interventions:

1. Present concepts following the *Who, What, Where, When, How,* and *Why* outline.

2. If the context of a word which the student is having difficulty generalizing appears too difficult, introduce the word by using an alternate text written at a lower reading level.

3. Have the student choose a general category (e.g., plants) and make lists of subcategories (e.g., flowers, trees, and bushes).

4. Have the student be a peer tutor to teach a concept he/she has mastered to another student. This can serve as reinforcement for the student.

5. Identify concepts related to a topic and explain to the student how a person can generalize from one to another (e.g., numbers to money, fuel to energy, words to sentences, etc.).

6. Use pictures, diagrams, wall-mounted board, and gestures when presenting information.

7. Have the student keep a list of words that he/she is having difficulty generalizing. Provide opportunities for the student to use these words frequently to facilitate generalization.

8. Have the student develop a series of responses representing his/her ability to generalize information to common situations in the environment (e.g., Cars should not be driven more than 55 miles per hour on the highway because . . . Appropriate responses could include safety, conservation of fuel, care of vehicle, and fines for speeding.).

9. Have the student play analogy games involving multiple-choice possibilities (e.g., Food is to a person as gasoline is to a(n) _____ [skateboard, automobile, house].).

10. Have the student listen and take notes following the *Who, What, Where, When, How,* and *Why* format when concepts are presented.

11. Have the student's hearing checked if it has not been recently checked.

12. Make sure the student applies a newly learned skill to a real-life situation as soon as possible to facilitate generalization (e.g., when he/she learns to count by fives have him/her practice adding nickels).

13. Use multiple modalities (e.g., auditory, visual, tactile, etc.) when presenting instructional material that requires the student to generalize knowledge. Utilize the modality which is stronger for the student.

14. Give the student another copy of his/her text and have him/her underline important words. Attach definitions to the back of the page.

15. Teach the student to define words/concepts in his/her own words. This skill builds comprehension and aids in generalization.

16. Ask the parents to encourage the student to generalize concepts learned at school to everyday situations.

17. Deliver instructions by using examples of relationships (e.g., rely on what has already been learned, use examples from the student's environment, etc.).

18. Use concrete examples and experiences in teaching concepts and when sharing information with the student.

19. Have the student explain outcomes, consequences, etc., (e.g., when the student earns a reward or privilege, make sure he/she can explain that it was the result of hard work and accomplishment, etc.).

20. Have the student prepare for tests using the *Who, What, Where, When, How,* and *Why* format.

21. Develop tests and quizzes for the student using the *Who, What, Where, When, How,* and *Why* format.

22. Have the student look for shapes in the environment when teaching shapes (e.g., find all the circles in the room).

23. Reinforce the student for generalizing information from one situation to another: (a) give the student a tangible reward (e.g., classroom privileges, line leading, passing out materials, five minutes free time, etc.) or (b) give the student an intangible reward (e.g., praise, fist bump, smile, etc.).

24. Name a category or group and ask the student to identify as many things as possible which belong in the group. Begin with large categories (e.g., living things) and move to more specific categories (e.g., things which are green).

25. Relate what the student has learned in one setting or situation to other situations (e.g., vocabulary words learned should be pointed out in reading selections, math word problems, story writing, etc.).

26. Call attention to situations in the classroom which generalize to more global situations (e.g., being on time for class is the same as being on time for work; school work not done during work time has to be made up before school, after school, or during recreational time, just as responsibilities at places of employment would have to be completed at night or weekends if not completed on the job; etc.).

27. When presenting explanations and information, be sure to use vocabulary that is within the student's level of comprehension.

28. Use a variety of instructional approaches to help the student generalize knowledge gained to real-life situations (e.g., after studying the judicial system, organize a simulated courtroom trial for the students; etc.).

29. Determine if the student is distracted by the surrounding words when reading. If so, have him/her expose one line, phrase, or word at a time until he/she improves this skill.

30. Have the student write letters, fill out applications, etc., to see the generalization of handwriting, spelling, grammar, sentence structure, etc., to real-life situations.

31. Have the student practice new concepts/ words several times over a period of weeks.

32. Give the student pairs of objects and ask him/her to name the ways in which they are alike and the ways they are different. Progress from concrete objects which can be seen and touched to abstract ideas which cannot be seen or touched.

33. Provide the student with opportunities to apply a new skill to a real-life situation (e.g., when the student learns to count by fives, have him/her practice adding nickels; when the student learns to tell time using instructional materials, call upon him/her to tell time throughout the day; when the student learns to identify sight words in isolation, have him/her point out these words in text; when the student learns new spelling words, have him/her write a story using the words).

34. Determine if a word which the student is having difficulty generalizing looks different to the student when it is surrounded by other words. Print and highlight the word in a phrase on a card. Have the student tell you how he/she sees the word.

35. When the student is required to generalize knowledge from one situation to another, provide him/her with visual and/or auditory cues to help him/her remember information previously presented (e.g., repeat key words, expose part of a picture, etc.).

36. Make sure the student understands that all objects, people, ideas, actions, etc., can be grouped based on how they are alike. Provide the student with concrete examples (e.g., dogs, cats, cows, and horses are all mammals).

37. Provide the student with simulated situations in which he/she can generalize skills learned (e.g., generalize math skills to making change, financing a car, computing interest earned from savings, etc.).

38. Identify concepts that are related and explain the relationship to the student (e.g., numbers to money, fuel to energy, words to sentences, etc.).

39. Tell the student immediately when he/she is not understood; the student needs this immediate feedback.

40. Use multisensory methods to teach concepts so that recall and generalization can be facilitated by different kinds of memory. Use slides, charts, pictures, graphs, diagrams, films, manipulatives, etc.

41. Teach for comprehension by telling the student what he/she is going to learn. Check for understanding over several days.

42. Reinforce those students in the classroom who generalize information appropriately.

43. Evaluate the appropriateness of the task to determine (a) if the task is too easy, (b) if the task is too difficult, or (c) if the length of time scheduled to complete the task is adequate.

44. Use daily drill activities to help the student memorize flash cards with math facts, sight words, etc.

45. Have the student respond to what if questions (e.g., What if it rained for 40 days and 40 nights?, What if there were no rules and laws?, etc.).

46. Have the student unscramble words of a statement into correct grammatical order. This encourages conscious placement of words to create meaning and aids in generalization.

47. Make sure that the student is provided with an explanation of why he/she is learning particular information or skills (e.g., we learn to spell, read, and write to be able to communicate; we learn to solve math problems to be able to make purchases, use a checking account, measure, and cook; etc.).

48. Have the student role-play various real-life situations to facilitate generalization.

49. Have the student manipulate sentences from questions to statements and vice-versa. Check to make sure that the new form contains the appropriate information and makes sense.

15 Demonstrates difficulty with visual memory

Goals:

1. The student will improve his/her short-term memory.
2. The student will improve his/her long-term memory.
3. The student will improve his/her visual memory.
4. The student will improve his/her awareness and attention to information and activities in the environment.
5. The student will improve his/her skills in logical thinking.

Objectives:

1. The student will match visual images (e.g., pictures, letters, numbers, etc.) with _____% accuracy.
2. The student will recognize visual images (e.g., pictures, letters, numbers, etc.) presented, removed from sight, and presented again with _____% accuracy.
3. The student will recall visual images (e.g., pictures, letters, numbers, words, etc.) at short intervals (10 to 15 minutes) with _____% accuracy.
4. The student will recall visual images (e.g., pictures, letters, numbers, words, etc.) at intervals of several hours with _____% accuracy.
5. The student will recall visual images (e.g., pictures, letters, numbers, words, etc.) at intervals of days or weeks with _____% accuracy.

Interventions:

1. Have the student read and follow one-, two-, and three-step directions.

2. Have the student listen and take notes for *Who, What, Where, When, How,* and *Why* when concepts are presented.

3. Use multiple modalities (e.g., auditory, visual, tactile, etc.) when presenting directions, explanations, and instructional content.

4. Provide the student with auditory cues to help him/her remember the information previously presented (e.g., say key words, give a brief oral description to clue the student, etc.).

5. Cut pictures from a cartoon strip. Show the pictures to the student in the correct sequence. Shuffle the pictures and ask the student to place them in the correct sequence.

6. Have the student play games involving concentration (e.g., matching numbers, words, symbols, etc., by turning them over and remembering their location).

7. Present directions following the outline of *What, How, Materials,* and *When.*

8. Reduce visual distractions (e.g., cover other information on the page, expose only a portion of a picture at a time, etc.) by isolating the information that is presented to the student.

9. Identify the student's most effective learning mode. Use it consistently to facilitate the student's understanding (e.g., if the student has difficulty understanding written information or directions, present the information verbally).

10. Audio record stories, directions, etc., so the student may listen to the information while reading along.

11. Highlight or underline important information the student reads (e.g., directions, reading assignments, math word problems, etc.).

12. Reduce the amount of information on a page (e.g., less print to read, fewer problems, isolate information this is presented to the student, etc.) if it is causing visual distractions for the student.

13. Provide the student with more than one exposure to the visual information prior to requiring him/her to remember it.

14. Teach the student to learn sequences and lists of information in segments (e.g., phone numbers are learned as 123, then 874, then 1710, etc.).

15. Have the student take notes when directions are being given following the *What, How, Materials*, and *When* format.

16. Present concepts following the outline of *Who, What, Where, When, How*, and *Why*.

17. Make it pleasant and positive for the student to ask questions about things not understood. Reinforce the student by assisting, congratulating, praising, etc.

18. Teach the student to recognize common visual symbols (e.g., a red octagon means stop, a skull and crossed bones represents poison, etc.).

19. Provide the student with written directions, rules, lists, etc. Reinforce the student for being able to recall the information given in written form.

20. Reinforce the student for remembering information received visually: (a) give the student a tangible reward (e.g., classroom privileges, line leading, five minutes free time, etc.) or (b) give the student an intangible reward (e.g., praise, fist bump, smile, etc.).

21. Evaluate the appropriateness of the task to determine if (a) the task is too easy, (b) the task is too difficult (e.g., too much information to remember) or (c) the length of time required for the student to remember is adequate (e.g., the presentation of information was too brief, time lapse between presentation of material and request for recall was too long, etc.).

22. Remind the student of the situation in which the material was originally presented to help him/her remember information (e.g., Remember yesterday when we talked about . . .?, Remember when we were outside and we looked at the . . .?).

23. Draw the student's attention to key aspects of visual images (e.g., by highlighting, outlining, drawing arrows, etc.).

24. Provide auditory information (e.g., verbal directions or instructions, etc.) to support information the student receives visually.

25. Provide the student with visual cues to help him/her remember the information previously presented (e.g., using key words printed on the wall-mounted board, exposing part or all of a picture, etc.).

26. Have the student recall days of the week, months of the year, birth dates, addresses, phone numbers, etc., after seeing this information in written form.

16   Does not check completed work for accuracy

Goals:

1. The student will improve the accuracy of school assignments.
2. The student will improve the quality of school assignments.

Objectives:

1. The student will perform school assignments with _____% accuracy.
2. The student will check school assignments to correct errors on _____ out of _____ trials.
3. The student will turn in school assignments for the teacher to proofread and provide feedback for corrections and improvement on _____ out of _____ trials.
4. The student will redo corrected school assignments with _____% accuracy.
5. The student will have a peer check his/her school assignments and correct errors found on _____ out of _____ trials.

Interventions:

1. Establish classroom rules:
- Concentrate while working.
- Work quietly.
- Remain in your seat.
- Finish task.
- Meet task expectations.

Review rules often. Reinforce the student for following the rules.

2. Allow the student to perform school work in a quiet place (e.g., study carrel, library, resource room, etc.) to reduce distractions.

3. Recognize accuracy and quality (e.g., display the student's work, congratulate the student, etc.).

4. Have the student maintain a chart representing the number of tasks completed and the accuracy rate of each task.

5. Assess student performance in a variety of ways (e.g., have the student give verbal explanations, simulations, physical demonstrations, etc.).

6. Have the student maintain a record (e.g., chart or graph) of his/her performance in checking work for accuracy.

7. Reinforce the student for beginning, working on, completing, and checking assignments for accuracy.

8. Provide the student with a variety of assignments and have him/her choose a minimum number from the total to complete (e.g., present the student with 10 academic tasks from which 6 must be finished that day).

9. Reinforce conscientiousness in improving accuracy and quality of assignments (e.g., double checking spelling, proper positioning of letters, adequate spacing, etc.): (a) give the student a tangible reward (e.g., classroom privileges, line leading, passing out materials, five minutes free time, etc.) or (b) give the student an intangible reward (e.g., praise, fist bump, smile, etc.).

10. Provide the student with additional time to perform school work to facilitate quality.

11. Have the student practice an assignment with the teacher, an aide, or a peer before completing the assignment for a grade.

12. Deliver reinforcement for any and all measures of improvement in checking work for accuracy.

13. Maintain consistent assignment formats and expectations.

14. Have the student question any directions, explanations, and instructions he/she does not understand.

15. Require that work not checked for accuracy when the assignment was completed be checked at another time (e.g., break time, recreational time, after school, etc.).

16. Offer the student assistance checking his/her work for accuracy frequently throughout the day.

17. Reinforce the student for checking work for accuracy based on the number of times he/she can be successful. As the student demonstrates success, gradually increase the required number of times work is checked for accuracy for reinforcement.

18. Reinforce the student for checking his/her work for accuracy: (a) give the student a tangible reward (e.g., classroom privileges, line leading, passing out materials, five minutes free time, etc.) or (b) give the student an intangible reward (e.g., praise, fist bump, smile, etc.).

19. Assess the quality and clarity of directions, explanations, and instructions given to the student.

20. Maintain mobility throughout the classroom to monitor the student checking his/her work for accuracy.

21. Provide the student with clearly stated criteria for acceptable work.

22. Provide the student with clearly stated written directions for homework so that someone at home may be able to provide assistance in checking his/her work for accuracy.

23. Make sure that your comments take the form of constructive criticism rather than criticism that can be perceived as personal, threatening, etc., (e.g., instead of telling the student he/she always makes the same mistake, suggest another way to avoid making the mistake).

24. Make sure that all educators who work with the student maintain consistent expectations for accuracy and quality.

25. Reduce the emphasis on competition. Competitive activities may cause the student to rush through work. Students who compete academically and fail to succeed may cease to try to do well and do far less than they are able.

26. Build varying levels of difficulty into assignments to facilitate the student's self-confidence and at the same time provide a challenge (e.g., easier problems are intermingled with problems designed to measure knowledge gained).

27. Provide adequate repetition and drill to assure minimal accuracy of assignments (i.e., require mastery/minimal accuracy before moving to the next skill level).

28. Provide frequent interactions and encouragement to facilitate the student's confidence and optimism for success (e.g., make statements such as, You're doing great. Keep up the good work. I'm really proud of you.).

29. Provide the student with evaluative feedback for completed assignments (i.e., identify what the student did successfully, what errors were made, and what should be done to correct the errors).

30. Teach the student procedures for improving accuracy and quality of work (e.g., listen to directions, make sure directions are understood, work at an acceptable pace, check for errors, correct for neatness, copy the work over, etc.).

31. Establish levels of expectations for accuracy and quality of assignments and have the student to correct or repeat assignments until the expectations are met.

32. Provide time at school for the student to check homework for accuracy if it has not been checked. (The student's failure to check homework for accuracy may be the result of variables in the home over which he/she has no control.)

33. Modify academic tasks (e.g., format, requirements, length, etc.).

34. Provide instruction and task format in a variety of ways (e.g., verbal instructions, written instructions, demonstrations, simulations, manipulatives, drill activities with peers, etc.).

35. Give shorter assignments, but give them more frequently. As the student demonstrates success, increase the length of assignments and decrease the frequency.

36. Have the student read/review school work with the teacher to become aware of the quality of his/her work.

37. Provide the student with a number line and alphabet strip on his/her desk to use as a reference for the correct form of letters and numbers to reduce errors.

38. Supervise the student while he/she is performing school work to monitor accuracy and quality.

39. Identify resource personnel (e.g., librarian, special education teacher, etc.) from whom the student may receive additional assistance or other personnel with the expertise or time to help.

40. Give the student a list of specific strategies for checking the accuracy of completed work:
- Check math problems with the inverse operation.
- Check language assignments for capitalization, punctuation, and neatness.
- Use the dictionary to check spelling in written work.
- Check spelling quizzes for careless errors.
- Check written paragraphs using the *Who, What, Where, When, How*, and *Why* format.
- Check tests and quizzes for careless errors and omitted or incomplete answers.

41. Provide parents with information regarding appropriate ways in which to help their child with homework (e.g., read directions with the student, work a few problems together, answer questions, check the completed assignment, etc.).

42. Make sure the assignments measure knowledge of content and not related skills such as reading or writing.

43. Choose a peer to model checking his/her work for accuracy for the student.

44. Modify instructions to include more concrete examples to facilitate student learning.

45. Provide the student with the necessary materials to perform assignments (e.g., pencil with eraser, paper, dictionary, handwriting sample, etc.).

46. Communicate with parents (e.g., notes home, phone calls, etc.) to share information about the student's progress. The parents may reinforce the student at home for checking completed work at school.

47. Conduct a preliminary evaluation of the student's work. Require him/her to make necessary corrections before final grading.

48. Provide the student with opportunities for checking work for accuracy prior to grading assignments.

49. Monitor the first problem or part of the assignment to make sure the student knows what is expected.

50. Reduce distracting stimuli (e.g., place the student in the front row, provide a carrel or office space away from distractions, etc.). This is to be used as a means of reducing distracting stimuli and not as a form of punishment.

51. Teach the student to practice basic study skills (e.g., reading for the main idea, note taking, summarizing, highlighting, studying in a good environment, using time wisely, etc.).

52. Work the first few problems of an assignment with the student to make sure that he/she knows what to do, how to complete the assignment, etc.

53. Structure the environment to provide the student with increased opportunity for help or assistance checking his/her work for accuracy.

54. Have the student make corrections after assignments have been checked by the teacher.

55. Allow the student to put an assignment away and check it for accuracy at a later time.

56. Make sure that homework relates to concepts already taught rather than introducing a new concept.

57. Allow the student to respond to alternative assignment questions (e.g., more generalized questions that represent global understanding).

58. Structure the environment (e.g., seating arrangements, supervision, etc.) to provide the student with increased opportunity for help or assistance on academic or homework tasks.

59. Provide the student with self-checking materials to check his/her work for accuracy.

60. Provide the student with shorter tasks, but more of them throughout the day (e.g., 4 assignments of 5 problems each rather than one assignment of 20 problems).

61. Teach the student direction-following skills: (a) listen carefully, (b) ask questions, (c) use environmental cues, and (d) rely on examples provided, etc.

62. Teach the student note-taking skills.

63. Provide the student with step-by-step written directions for performing assignments. Make the last step checking work for accuracy.

64. Reinforce those students in the classroom who turn in assignments which are accurate and of high quality.

65. Interact frequently with the student to monitor his/her task performance.

66. Communicate clearly to the student when it is time to check his/her work for accuracy.

67. Make sure that the student is assigned tasks short enough that he/she can complete the assignment and check for accuracy within the given period of time. As the student demonstrates success, gradually increase the length of the assignments.

68. Assign the student shorter tasks while increasing accuracy and quality expectations.

69. Evaluate the appropriateness of tasks assigned if the student consistently fails to complete assignments with minimal accuracy.

70. Provide a time during the day when the student can receive assistance at school if he/she has difficulty completing homework assignments with minimal accuracy.

71. Arrange a time for the student to study with a peer tutor before completing a graded assignment.

72. Provide multiple opportunities for the student to learn information covered by assignments (e.g., films, visitors, community resources, etc.).

73. Reinforce those students in the classroom who check their work for accuracy.

74. Evaluate the appropriateness of the task to determine (a) if the task is too easy, (b) if the task is too difficult, or (c) if the length of time scheduled to complete the task is adequate.

75. Write a contract with the student specifying what behavior is expected (e.g., checking work for accuracy) and what reinforcement will be made available when the terms of the contract have been met.

76. Allow the student to make corrections after assignments have been checked the first time.

77. Monitor the student's performance to understand errors and determine where learning problems exist.

78. Work not completed according to teacher directions and expectations, must be completed during recreational or break time.

79. It is not necessary to grade every assignment completed by the student. Assignments may be used to evaluate student ability or knowledge and provide feedback. Grades may not need to be assigned until mastery/minimal accuracy has been attained.

80. Do not expect mastery too soon after introducing new information, skills, etc.

81. Speak with the student to explain (a) what he/she is doing wrong (e.g., not checking work for accuracy) and (b) what he/she should be doing (e.g., checking work for accuracy).

82. Check a few problems with the student to model checking work for accuracy.

83. Provide the student with work samples of acceptable levels of accuracy and quality. The student is to match the quality of the sample before turning in the assignment.

17   Does not demonstrate an understanding of spatial relationships

Goals:

1. The student will improve his/her understanding of abstract concepts (e.g., spatial relationships, directionality, classifications, generalizations).
2. The student will improve his/her auditory memory.
3. The student will improve his/her awareness and attention to information and activities in the environment.
4. The student will improve his/her skills in logical thinking.

Objectives:

1. The student will demonstrate spatial relationships by imitating the placement of objects (e.g., near-far, above-below, over-under, etc.) with _____% accuracy.
2. The student will independently demonstrate spatial relationships (e.g., near-far, above-below, over-under, etc.) with _____% accuracy.
3. The student will recognize spatial relationships (e.g., near-far, above-below, over-under, etc.) with visual and verbal cues with _____% accuracy.
4. The student will recognize spatial relationships (e.g., near-far, above-below, over-under, etc.) independently with _____% accuracy.

Interventions:

1. Call attention to spatial relationships which occur naturally in the environment (e.g., a bird flying over a tree, a squirrel running under a bush, etc.).

2. Attach paper bands labeled left and right around the student's wrists. Remove the paper bands when the student can successfully identify left and right.

3. Provide the student with a variety of pictures representing spatial concepts. Have the student match the pictures with the concepts.

4. Have the student question any directions, explanations, and instructions he/she does not understand.

5. Include spatial relationships in directions given to the student (e.g., Write your name on the dotted line. Keep your feet under your desk.).

6. Use concrete examples and experiences in teaching concepts and sharing information with the student.

7. Provide repeated physical demonstrations of spatial relationships.

8. Emphasize spatial relationships which have particular meaning to the student (e.g., students who live near school walk and students who live far from school ride the bus).

9. Identify areas and objects in the classroom with cards indicating spatial concepts (e.g., a light fixture labeled above; a rug labeled under; walls labeled north, south, east, west; etc.).

10. Introduce each spatial concept individually before pairing the concepts. Avoid introducing spatial relationships such as near-far at the same time.

11. Have the student physically perform spatial relationships (e.g., have the student stand near the teacher, far from the teacher, on a table, sit under a table, etc.).

12. Review daily those spatial relationships which have previously been introduced.

13. When introducing spatial concepts, rely on tangible objects rather than the spoken and printed word (e.g., use a concrete medium rather than abstract symbols).

14. Have the student follow simple map directions for abstract concepts such as left and right; north, south, east, and west. Begin with a map of the school and progress to maps of the community, state, nation, etc., with increasingly complex directions.

15. Have the student practice spatial relationship concepts with peers (e.g., *Simon Says*, *Follow the Leader*, following directions, etc.).

16. Give the student a series of spatial relationship directions to follow (e.g., crawl under the table, stand near the closet, put the marker below the clock, etc.).

17. Evaluate the appropriateness of the task to determine (a) if the task is too easy, (b) if the task is too difficult, or (c) if the length of time scheduled to complete the task is adequate.

18   Does not follow multi-step directions

Goal:

1. The student will follow multi-step verbal directions.

Objectives:

1. The student will follow one-step verbal directions on _____ out of _____ trials.
2. The student will follow two-step verbal directions on _____ out of _____ trials.
3. The student will follow multi-step verbal directions on _____ out of _____ trials.
4. The student will follow verbal directions in correct sequential order on _____ out of _____ trials.
5. The student will follow _____ out of _____ verbal directions on _____ out of _____ trials.
6. The student will demonstrate the ability to follow verbal directions by listening carefully and completing the task with _____% accuracy on _____ out of _____ trials.
7. The student will follow verbal directions with teacher assistance on _____ out of _____ trials.
8. The student will independently follow verbal directions on _____ out of _____ trials.
9. The student will listen to verbal directions on his/her ability level and follow them in correct sequential order on _____ out of _____ trials.
10. The student will complete one step of the verbal direction before going on to the next step on _____ out of _____ trials.

Interventions:

1. Establish classroom rules:
- Concentrate while working.
- Work quietly.
- Remain in your seat.
- Finish task.
- Meet task expectations.

Review rules often. Reinforce the student for following the rules.

2. Establish assignment rules:
- Listen to directions.
- Wait until all directions have been given.
- Ask questions about anything you do not understand.
- Begin assignments only when you are sure about what is required.
- Make sure you have all of the materials necessary to complete the assignment.

3. Have the student attempt a new assignment/ activity in a private place (e.g., carrel, office, quiet study area, etc.) to reduce the fear of public failure.

4. Provide the student with a predetermined signal (e.g., turning lights off and on, hand signals, etc.) when he/she begins a task before receiving directions or instructions.

5. Provide the student with a schedule of activities so he/she will know exactly what and how much there is to do in a day.

6. Provide the student with a variety of assignments. Require him/her to select a minimum number from the total (e.g., present the student with ten academic tasks from which he/she must finish six that day).

7. Provide the student with a sample of the assignment/activity which has been partially completed by a peer or teacher (e.g., book reports, projects).

8. Have the student practice a new skill (e.g., jumping rope, dribbling a basketball) alone or with a peer or a teacher before attempting it with the entire group.

9. Make sure the student achieves success when following directions.

10. Allow the student the opportunity to complete the assignment/activity in a variety of ways (e.g., video record, with a calculator, verbally, etc.).

11. Have the student question any directions, explanations, and instructions he/she does not understand.

12. Evaluate the appropriateness of assigned tasks to determine (a) if the task is too easy, (b) if the task is too difficult, or (c) if the length of time scheduled is adequate.

13. Deliver simple verbal directions.

14. Maintain mobility to provide assistance to the student.

15. Prevent the student from becoming overstimulated (e.g., frustrated, angry, etc.) by an activity.

16. Have the student begin each assignment within a specified period of time (e.g., three minutes, five minutes, etc.).

17. Reinforce the student for beginning assignments after receiving directions, instructions, etc.

18. Give a signal (e.g., clapping hands, turning lights off and on, etc.) before giving verbal directions.

19. Assess the quality and clarity of directions, explanations, and instructions given to the student.

20. Have the student practice direction-following skills on non-academic tasks.

21. Tell the student that directions will be given only once.

22. Reduce the number of directions given at one time (e.g., give the student the next step after he/she completes a step).

23. Deliver directions/instructions before handing out materials.

24. Make sure that the student has all the materials he/she needs to complete the assignment/activity.

25. Make sure the student has all the necessary materials before beginning the task.

26. Rewrite directions at a lower reading level.

27. Give the student a one-step direction. Add more steps to the direction over time.

28. Allow the student the option of performing the assignment at another time (e.g., earlier/later in the day, another day, etc.).

29. Structure the environment (e.g., peer tutoring, the need for homework directions, frequent interactions, etc.) to provide the student with the increased opportunity for help or assistance on academic tasks.

30. Allow the student to perform new assignments/activities in a variety of places around the building (e.g., resource room, library, learning center, etc.).

31. Reduce distracting stimuli (e.g., place the student in the front row, provide a carrel or office space away from distractions, etc.). This is used as a means of reducing distracting stimuli and not as a form of punishment.

32. Reinforce those students who receive directions before beginning a new task.

33. Provide the student with self-checking materials. He/she may check his/her work privately and reduce the fear of public failure.

34. Provide the student with shorter tasks given more frequently (e.g., give the student five math problems four times a day).

35. Teach the student direction-following skills (e.g., listen carefully, write down important points, ask for clarification, wait until all directions are received before beginning).

36. Communicate clearly to the student when it is time to begin.

37. Interact frequently with the student during an activity to help him/her follow directions.

38. Do not require the student to complete the assignment/activity in one sitting.

39. Follow a less desirable task with a highly desirable task. Make completion of the first task necessary to perform the second.

40. Help the student with the first few items of a task. Gradually reduce the amount of help.

41. Have the student repeat the oral directions to the teacher.

42. Write a contract with the student specifying what behavior is expected (e.g., beginning assignments after listening to directions) and what reinforcement will be made available when the terms of the contract have been met.

43. Specify exactly what is to be done for the completion of a task (e.g., definite starting and stopping points, minimum requirement, etc.).

44. Have the student wait to begin an activity after directions are given, until the teacher gives him/her a signal (e.g., hand signal, bell ringing, etc.).

45. Speak with the student to explain (a) what he/she is doing wrong (e.g., not following directions when performing academic tasks) and (b) what he/she should be doing (e.g., listening to directions, asking for clarification if directions are not understood, taking notes, following one step at a time, etc.).

46. Have the student explain to the teacher what he/she thinks should be done to complete an assignment/activity.

47. Provide alternatives to the traditional format for directions (e.g., audio record directions, summarize directions, directions given by peers, etc.).

48. Give directions in a variety of ways to facilitate the student's probability of understanding (e.g., if the student does not understand verbal directions, present them in written form).

49. Choose a peer or volunteer to help the student begin a task.

50. Have the student wait for other students to begin before he/she begins the task.

51. Provide clearly stated directions, written or verbal (e.g., make the directions as simple and concrete as possible).

19   Does not grasp basic concepts or information related to academic tasks

Goal:

1. The student will improve his/her ability to grasp basic concepts related to academic tasks.

Objectives:

1. The student will use visual cues to aid his/her ability to grasp concepts with _____% accuracy.
2. The student will use auditory cues to aid his/her ability to grasp concepts with _____% accuracy.
3. The student will use visual and auditory cues to aid his/her ability to grasp concepts with _____% accuracy.
4. The student will learn _____ new concepts per week.
5. The student will independently review concepts and pass a weekly review with the teacher with _____% accuracy.
6. The student will independently review concepts and pass a monthly review with the teacher with _____% accuracy.

Interventions:

1. Have the student practice a new concept alone, with an aide, the teacher, or a peer before attempting it with the entire group or being graded on it.

2. Have the student be a peer tutor and teach concepts he/she just learned to another student.

3. Give the student alternative assignments. As the student demonstrates success, gradually introduce more components of the regular assignments.

4. Reduce the emphasis on competition. Competitive activities may cause the student to hurry and make mistakes.

5. Initiate a *Learn a Concept a Day* program with the student and incorporate the new concept into the assigned activities for the day.

6. Give the student fewer concepts to learn at one time. Spend additional time on each concept until the student has mastered it.

7. Provide practice for new concepts by using a computer software program or a hand-held educational device that gives the student immediate feedback.

8. Choose a peer to spend time each day engaged in drill activities with the student.

9. Give the student a list of key words, phrases, or main points to learn for each new concept introduced.

10. Develop crossword puzzles which contain only the student's spelling words and have him/her complete them.

11. Audio record important information for the student to replay as often as necessary.

12. Make sure the student has mastery of concepts at each level before introducing a new skill.

13. Underline, circle, or highlight important information from any material the student is to learn (e.g., science, math, geography, etc.).

14. Have the student use new concepts frequently throughout the day.

15. Provide the student with the information he/she needs to learn in the most direct manner possible (e.g., a list of facts, a summary of important points, an outline of important events, etc.).

16. Have the student review new concepts each day for a short period of time rather than two or three times per week for longer periods of time.

17. Reinforce new concepts by writing sentences, passages, paragraphs, etc., for the student which highlights the concept.

18. Have the student highlight or underline key words, phrases, and sentences from reading assignments, newspapers, magazines, etc.

19. Have the student use resources (e.g., encyclopedia, dictionary, etc.) to provide information to help him/her be successful when performing tasks.

20. Allow the student to use resources to help him/her successfully perform tasks (e.g., calculator, multiplication tables, dictionary, etc.).

21. Provide the student with various times throughout the day when he/she can engage in drill activities with the teacher, an aide, a peer, etc.

22. Use wall charts with visual images to introduce new concepts. Teach the student to associate these images with previously learned concepts.

23. Provide the student with opportunities for drill activities in the most interesting manner possible (e.g., working with a computer, using a calculator, playing educational games, watching a film, listening to music, etc.).

20 Does not perform academically at his/her ability level

Goal:

1. The student will perform academically at his/her ability level.

Objectives:

1. The student will perform academic tasks with _____% accuracy.
2. The student will meet a _____% level of mastery on academic tasks.
3. The student will perform academic tasks on his/her ability level on _____ out of _____ trials.
4. The student will perform tasks designed to meet his/her level of ability with _____% accuracy.

Interventions:

1. Establish classroom rules:
- Concentrate while working.
- Work quietly.
- Remain in your seat.
- Finish task.
- Meet task expectations.

Review rules often. Reinforce students for following the rules.

2. Present concepts following the *Who, What, Where, When, How,* and *Why* outline.

3. Have the student be a peer tutor to teach a concept he/she has mastered to another student as reinforcement.

4. Provide the student with a variety of assignments. Require him/her to select a minimum number from the total amount to complete (e.g., present the student with ten academic tasks from which he/she must complete six that day).

5. Assess student performance in a variety of ways (e.g., have the student give verbal explanations, simulations, physical demonstrations, etc.).

6. Have the student develop a flow chart of the steps necessary to complete a task.

7. Have the student maintain a chart representing the number of tasks he/she has completed and the accuracy rate of each task.

8. Audio record assignments and allow the student to replay questions as often as necessary.

9. Have the student practice an assignment with the teacher, aide, or a peer before completing the assignment independently for a grade.

10. Audio record the assignments and allow the student to listen to directions/instructions as often as necessary.

11. Maintain a consistent format and expectation for assignments.

12. Have the student listen and take notes following the *Who, What, Where, When, How,* and *Why* format when concepts are presented.

13. Deliver reinforcement for any and all measures of improvement.

14. Have the student question any directions, explanations, and instructions he/she does not understand before beginning a task to reinforce comprehension.

15. Assess the appropriateness of assigning homework to the student.

16. Do not grade every assignment completed by the student. Assignments may be used to evaluate student ability or knowledge and provide feedback. Grades may not need to be assigned until mastery/minimal accuracy has been attained.

17. Provide frequent interactions and encouragement to build the student's confidence and optimism for success (e.g., tell the student he/she is doing great, to keep up the good work, etc.).

18. Make sure that homework assignments do not introduce new concepts but relate to concepts already taught.

19. Give the student alternative assignments. As the student demonstrates success, gradually introduce more components of the regular assignments.

20. Have reference materials readily available in the classroom (e.g., dictionary, thesaurus, list of frequently misspelled words, etc.).

21. Encourage the student to avoid ingesting any substance (e.g., drugs, alcohol, cold remedies, etc.) that might further alter his/her ability to perform up to his/her ability level.

22. Assess the quality and clarity of directions, explanations, and instructions given to the student.

23. Provide the student with clearly stated step-by-step directions for homework so that someone at home may be able to provide assistance.

24. Make sure that your comments take the form of constructive criticism rather than criticism that can be perceived as personal, threatening, etc., (e.g., instead of telling the student he/she always makes the same mistake, suggest another way to avoid making the mistake).

25. Reduce the emphasis on competition. Students who compete academically and fail to succeed may cease to try to do well and do far less than they are able.

26. Monitor student performance to understand errors and determine where learning problems exist.

27. Have the student perform difficult assignments in the resource room where the resource teacher can answer questions.

28. Build varying degrees of difficulty into assignments to build the student's self-confidence and provide a challenge (e.g., easier problems are intermingled with problems designed to measure knowledge gained).

29. Provide the student with evaluative feedback for assignments completed (i.e., identify what the student did successfully, what errors were made, and what should be done to correct the errors).

30. Have the student prepare for tests using the *Who, What, Where, When, How,* and *Why* format.

31. Develop tests and quizzes for the student using the *Who, What, Where, When, How,* and *Why* format.

32. Provide time at school for homework to be completed or redone if assigned homework has not been completed or has resulted in failure. (The student's failure to complete homework assignments may be the result of variables in the home over which he/she has no control.)

33. Modify academic tasks (e.g., format, requirements, length, etc.).

34. Provide instruction and task format in a variety of ways (e.g., verbal instructions, written instructions, demonstrations, simulations, manipulatives, drill activities with peers, etc.).

35. Provide a variety of formats for the student to learn information (e.g., videos, visitors, community resources, etc.).

36. Give shorter assignments more frequently. As the student demonstrates success, increase the length of the assignments and decrease the frequency.

37. Assess the appropriateness of giving the student assignments which require copying if the student's ability level makes it impossible for him/her to complete the assignment.

38. Make sure the student has mastery of the concepts at each level before introducing a new skill level.

39. Allow the student to highlight important information in written materials.

40. Have the student read his/her written work out loud when proofing.

41. Reinforce the student for improving academic task and homework performance: (a) give the student a tangible reward (e.g., classroom privileges, free homework pass, five minutes free time, etc.) or (b) give the student an intangible reward (e.g., praise, fist bump, smile, etc.).

42. Assess the student's performance in a variety of ways (e.g., have the student give verbal explanations, simulations, physical demonstrations, etc.).

43. Identify the student's preferred learning style (e.g., visual, auditory, etc.) and use it consistently to facilitate the student's understanding.

44. Identify resource personnel (e.g., librarian, special education teacher, other personnel with expertise or time to help, etc.) from whom the student may receive additional assistance.

45. Have the student make corrections after assignments have been checked by the teacher.

46. Make sure the assignments measure knowledge of content and not related skills such as reading or writing.

47. Modify instruction to include more concrete examples to facilitate student learning.

48. Communicate with parents (e.g., notes home, phone calls, etc.) to share information about the student's progress. The parents may reinforce the student at home for improving his/her academic task and homework performance.

49. Provide adequate repetition/drill of concepts/skills to help the student achieve minimal accuracy on assignments. Require mastery/minimal accuracy before moving to the next skill level.

50. Have the student redo assignments of poor quality if you are certain the task is within the student's ability level.

51. Establish a minimum level of accuracy which will be accepted as a level of mastery.

52. Monitor the student's performance of the first problem or part of the assignment to make sure the student knows what is expected.

53. Give directions on a one-to-one basis before assigning a task.

54. Choose different people (e.g., peer, paraprofessional, tutor, counselor, etc.) to help the student improve work performance.

55. Reduce distracting stimuli (e.g., place the student in the front row, provide a carrel or office space away from distractions, etc.). This is used as a means of reducing distracting stimuli and not as a form of punishment.

56. Teach the student to practice basic study skills (e.g., reading for the main idea, note taking, summarizing, highlighting, studying in a good environment, using time wisely, etc.).

57. Work the first few problems of an assignment with the student to make sure that he/she knows what to do, how to complete the assignment, etc.

58. Structure the environment (e.g., provide a peer tutor, seat the student near the teacher or aide, etc.) to provide the student with increased opportunity for help or assistance on academic or homework tasks.

59. Have the student repeat directions, explanations, and instructions after they have been given to reinforce retention.

60. Allow the student to put an assignment away and return to it at a later time when he/she might be more successful.

61. Provide parents with information regarding appropriate ways in which to help their child with homework (e.g., read directions with the student, work a few problems together, answer questions, check the completed assignment, etc.).

62. Modify homework assignments to provide practice/reinforcement of skills presented in class.

63. Have the student verbally respond to tasks.

64. Allow the student to respond to alternative assignment questions (e.g., general questions that represent global understanding).

65. Provide the student with sample letters, reports, forms, etc., as references for written communication.

66. Provide the student with self-checking materials. Have the student make corrections before turning in assignments.

67. Teach the student direction-following skills: (a) listen carefully, (b) ask questions, (c) use environmental cues, and (d) rely on examples provided, etc.

68. Teach the student direction-following skills (e.g., listen carefully, write down steps, etc.).

69. Teach the student test-taking skills (e.g., organization, test-taking skills, etc.).

70. Teach the student information-gathering skills (e.g., listen carefully, write down important points, ask for clarification, wait until all information is presented before beginning a task, etc.).

71. Teach the student note-taking skills. Emphasize noting main concepts rather than details and data.

72. Interact frequently with the student to monitor his/her task performance.

73. Do not require the student to learn more information than he/she is capable of remembering at any time.

74. Provide the student with supplemental activities which offer review and repetition of skills presented to the general class population.

75. Provide the student with the opportunity to review assignments prior to them being graded.

76. Allow the student to audio record information from lectures and seminars and make notes from those recordings.

77. Assess the degree of task difficulty to determine whether or not the student will require additional information, time, assistance, etc., before beginning a task.

78. Evaluate the appropriateness of tasks assigned if the student consistently fails to complete assignments with minimal accuracy.

79. Set aside time at the end of each class period for the student to complete unfinished assignments.

80. Evaluate the appropriateness of the task to determine (a) if the task is too easy, (b) if the task is too difficult, or (c) if the length of time scheduled to complete the task is adequate.

81. Present directions/instructions in the student's preferred learning style (e.g., visual, auditory, etc.).

82. Have assignments read to the student.

83. Arrange a time for the student to study with a peer tutor before completing an assignment to be graded.

84. Reinforce those students in the classroom who show improvement on academic task and homework performance.

85. Write a contract with the student specifying what behavior is expected (e.g., completing an assignment with _____% accuracy) and what reinforcement will be made available when the terms of the contract have been met.

86. Provide a time during the day when the student can receive assistance at school if he/she has difficulty completing homework assignments with minimal accuracy.

87. Seat the student close to the source of information to maintain his/her attention (e.g., in the front row or near the speaker during a lecture).

88. Monitor the student's performance to understand errors and determine where learning problems exist.

89. Organize assignments by dividing them into small segments. Assign a deadline for each segment and provide the student with a reward after completing each segment of the assignment.

90. Speak to the student to explain (a) what he/ she is doing wrong (e.g., performing below his/her ability level, failing assignments, etc.) and (b) what he/she should be doing (e.g., improving his/her academic task and homework performance).

91. Provide repetition and drill to ensure that the student achieves minimal accuracy on assignments (i.e., require mastery/minimal accuracy before moving to the next skill level).

92. Choose a peer to work a few problems with the student to serve as a model and help the student begin an assignment.

93. Do not expect mastery too soon after introducing new information, skills, etc.

94. Allow the student to use educational aids to assist in the completion of assignments (e.g., calculator, dictionary, models of tasks, etc.).

95. Give the student written/verbal repetition to aid retention of information.

96. Arrange for individual assignments when the group setting is overly distracting.

97. Have the student use word processing programs that check spelling, grammar, etc.

98. Provide the student with written reminders of task sequences.

99. Allow the student to correct assignments after they have been checked the first time.

21 Does not perform or complete classroom assignments during class time

Goal:

1. The student will complete assignments within a specified time period.

Objectives:

1. The student will begin assignments after receiving directions or instructions on _____ out of _____ trials.
2. The student will work on assignments within a specified time period (indicate length of time).
3. The student will complete assignments with assistance within a specified time period (indicate length of time).
4. The student will independently complete assignments within a specified time period (indicate length of time).
5. The student will ask for clarification of directions or instructions not understood within specified time period (indicate length of time) on _____ out of _____ trials.

Interventions:

1. Establish classroom rules:
   - Concentrate while working.
   - Work quietly.
   - Remain in your seat.
   - Finish task.
   - Meet task expectations.

   Review rules often. Reinforce students for following the rules.

2. Establish assignment rules:
   - Listen to directions.
   - Wait until all directions have been given.
   - Ask questions about anything you do not understand.
   - Begin the assignment only when you are sure about the requirements.
   - Make sure you have all the materials necessary.

3. Give directions in steps (e.g., give the student each additional step after completion of the previous step).

4. Have the student keep a chart or graph representing the number of class assignments he/she has completed.

5. Present one assignment at a time. As each assignment is completed, deliver reinforcement along with the presentation of the next assignment.

6. Have the student question any directions, explanations, and instructions he/she does not understand.

7. Provide the student with a variety of assignments, requiring him/her to choose a minimum number from the total (e.g., present the student with 10 academic tasks from which he/she must finish 6 in a given time period).

8. Provide the student with a variety of assignments. Require him/her to select a minimum number from the total amount to complete (e.g., present the student with ten academic tasks from which he/she must complete six that day).

9. Provide the student with a schedule of activities so that he/she knows exactly what and how much there is to do in a given period of time.

10. Have the student use a timer to complete tasks within a given period of time.

11. Reduce the emphasis on academic and social competition. Fear of failure may cause the student to not want to complete the required number of assignments in a given period of time.

12. Make sure the student achieves success when following directions.

13. Maintain visibility to and from the student to make sure the student is attending. The teacher should be able to see the student and the student should be able to see the teacher. Make eye contact possible at all times.

14. Teach the student organizational and assignment completion skills:
- Begin with a clean and organized desk.
- Read directions carefully.
- Collect all the materials necessary.
- Ask for assistance if needed.
- Look for the main idea.
- Follow examples provided.
- Answer questions you know first and leave those you are unsure of for last.

15. Encourage the student to ask for clarification of directions for classroom assignments.

16. Follow a less desirable assignment with a highly desirable assignment. Have the student complete the first before beginning the second.

17. Give the student alternative assignments. As the student demonstrates success, gradually introduce more components of the regular assignment.

18. Prevent the student from becoming over-stimulated by an activity (e.g., frustrated, angry, etc.).

19. Have the student begin each assignment within a specified period of time (e.g., three minutes, five minutes, etc.).

20. Reinforce the student for beginning, working on, and completing assignments.

21. Along with the student, chart those assignments that have been completed in a given period of time.

22. Assess the quality and clarity of directions, explanations, and instructions given to the student.

23. Supervise the student during class assignments to maintain on-task behavior.

24. Reinforce the student for completing the required number of assignments in a given time period: (a) give the student a tangible reward (e.g., classroom privileges, line leading, passing out materials, five minutes free time, etc.) or (b) give the student an intangible reward (e.g., praise, fist bump, smile, etc.).

25. Reinforce the student for completing assignments based on the amount of work he/she can successfully complete in a given period of time. As the student demonstrates success, gradually increase the number of assignments required in a given period of time.

26. Do not reward early completion of assignments. Hurrying to complete assignments may cause the student to fail to follow directions.

27. Teach the student direction-following skills (e.g., listen carefully, write down important points, ask for clarification, wait until all directions are received before beginning).

28. Reduce the emphasis on early completion. Hurrying to complete assignments may cause the student to fail to follow directions.

29. Deliver directions verbally to facilitate the student understanding class assignments.

30. Deliver directions/instructions before handing out materials.

31. Ask the student why he/she is not completing the required number of assignments in a given period of time. The student should have the most accurate perception as to why he/she is not completing the required number of assignments in a given period of time.

32. Provide clearly stated directions in written or verbal form (e.g., make the directions as simple and concrete as possible).

33. Have the student time his/her assignment and monitor his/her pace to complete the assignment within the time limit.

34. Have the student schedule his/her own time for assignments (e.g., 20 minutes for each of three assignments, 15 minutes for each of four assignments, etc.) to pace himself/herself.

35. Have the student complete his/her assignments in a private place (e.g., carrel, office, quiet study area, etc.) to reduce the anxiety of public failure.

36. Have the student practice direction-following skills on nonacademic tasks (e.g., recipes, games, etc.).

37. Tell the student exactly how long he/she has to work and when he/she must be finished.

38. Rewrite directions at a lower reading level.

39. Choose a peer to help the student with class assignments.

40. Provide the student with more than enough time to finish an activity. As the student demonstrates success, gradually decrease the amount of time provided to finish an activity.

41. Practice direction-following skills on nonacademic tasks.

42. Communicate with parents (e.g., notes home, phone calls, etc.) to share information about the student's progress. The parents may reinforce the student at home for completing the required number of assignments in a given period of time at school.

43. Be consistent in the number of assignments required to be completed in a given period of time.

44. Allow natural consequences to occur when the required number of assignments are not completed within a given period of time (e.g., students who do not complete the required number of assignments do not get to perform more desirable activities).

45. Maintain a consistent routine of daily activities.

46. Allow the student the option of performing the assignment at another time (e.g., earlier/later in the day, on another day, or take the assignment home).

47. Structure the environment (e.g., peer tutoring, directions for work sent home, frequent interactions, etc.) to provide the student with increased opportunity for help or assistance on assignments.

48. Reduce distracting stimuli (e.g., place the student on the front row, provide a carrel or office space away from distractions, etc.). This is used as a means of reducing distracting stimuli and not as a form of punishment.

49. Work the first few problems with the student to start the student on the assignment.

50. Provide the student with shorter tasks given more frequently (e.g., give the student five math problems four times a day).

51. Provide the student with step-by-step written directions for completing class assignments.

52. Interact frequently with the student to help him/her follow directions for the assignments.

53. Interact frequently with the student to maintain involvement with class assignments (e.g., ask the student questions; ask the student's opinion; stand close to the student; seat the student near the teacher's desk, etc.).

54. Communicate clearly to the student the date the assignment is to be completed.

55. Communicate clearly to the student the length of time he/she has to complete an assignment.

56. Make sure that the student has all the materials he/she needs to complete the assignments.

57. Make sure that the student is attending to the teacher when directions are given (e.g., making eye contact, hands free of writing materials, looking at assignment, etc.).

58. Assess the degree of task difficulty in comparison with the student's ability to perform the task.

59. Explain to the student that work not done during work time will have to be made up at other times (e.g., break time, before school, after school, lunchtime, etc.).

60. Assign the student shorter tasks (e.g., modify a 20-problem math activity to four activities of five problems each to be done at various times during the day). As the student demonstrates success, gradually increase the number of problems per activity and decrease the number of activities.

61. Have the student chart the assignments he/she has completed in a given period of time.

62. Modify assignments to prevent the student from becoming overstimulated by an assignment (e.g., frustrated, angry, etc.).

63. Provide the student with the opportunity to perform assignments/activities in a variety of ways (e.g., audio/video record, with a calculator, verbally, etc.).

64. Evaluate the appropriateness of the task to determine (a) if the task is too easy, (b) if the task is too difficult, or (c) if the length of time scheduled to complete the task is adequate.

65. Maintain consistent expectations within the ability level of the student.

66. Have the student record the time it took him/her to complete each assignment to accurately determine how much time is spent on each assignment.

67. Reinforce those students in the classroom who complete the required number of assignments in a given period of time.

68. Reinforce those students in the classroom who perform or complete assignments during class time.

69. Repeat directions to facilitate the student's understanding of them.

70. Write a contract with the student specifying what behavior is expected (e.g., performing/completing class assignments) and what reinforcement will be made available when the terms of the contract have been met.

71. Present the assignment in the most attractive, interesting manner possible.

72. Allow the student additional time to complete class assignments.

73. Have the student explain to the teacher what he/she should do to complete the assignments.

74. Allow the student access to pencils, pens, etc., only after directions have been given.

75. Speak to the student to explain (a) what he/she is doing wrong (e.g., not working during work time) and (b) what the student should be doing (e.g., working during work time).

76. Specify exactly what is to be done for the completion of a task (e.g., make definite starting and stopping points, establish a minimum requirement, etc.).

77. Provide alternatives for the traditional format of directions (e.g., audio record directions, summarize directions, directions given by peers, etc.).

78. Make sure the student understands the natural consequences of not completing assignments (e.g., students who do not finish their work will not get to participate in more desirable activities).

79. Give directions in a variety of ways to facilitate the student's understanding (e.g., if the student does not understand verbal directions, present them in written form).

80. Take steps to deal with the student's refusal to perform an assignment to avoid group contagion (e.g., refrain from arguing with the student, place the student in a carrel or other quiet place to work, remove the student from the group or classroom, etc.).

81. Have the student repeat the verbal directions to the teacher.

22 Does not prepare for assigned activities

Goals:

1. The student will be prepared for school assignments.
2. The student will be prepared for assigned activities.

Objectives:

1. The student will be prepared for assigned activities by reading the assigned material for _____ out of _____ activities.
2. The student will complete his/her assigned tasks such as book reports, projects, etc., by the due date on _____ out of _____ trials.
3. The student will complete his/her homework prior to coming to the assigned activity on _____ out of _____ trials.
4. The student will correctly answer questions covering the assigned reading material on _____ out of _____ trials.
5. The student will read necessary information prior to coming to the assigned activity on _____ out of _____ trials.
6. The student will study and perform classroom quizzes with _____% accuracy.
7. The student will study and perform classroom tests with _____% accuracy.
8. The student will study for _____ out of _____ quizzes/tests.

Interventions:

1. Chart completed homework assignments.

2. Establish school assignment rules:
   - Concentrate while working.
   - Work quietly.
   - Finish task.
   - Meet task expectations.
   - Turn in task.

   Review rules often. Reinforce students for following the rules.

3. Present directions following the *What, How, Materials*, and *When* outline.

4. Present concepts following the *Who, What, Where, When, How, Why*, and *Vocabulary* outline.

5. Have the student develop a checklist/chart to follow which will allow him/her to monitor all assignments.

6. Have the student establish a routine to follow before coming to class (e.g., check which activity is next, determine what materials are necessary, collect materials, etc.)

7. Provide the student with a written list of assignments to be completed each day. Have him/her cross each assignment out as it is completed.

8. Provide the student with a list of necessary materials for each activity of the day.

9. Have the student develop a method of organization that works best for him/her (e.g., daily list, weekly list, etc.) and use that method consistently. Delete accomplished tasks to keep an up-to-date list.

10. Find a tutor (e.g., a volunteer in the community, peer, etc.) to help the student complete his/her school assignments.

11. Have the student establish a routine and utilize a weekly schedule. Have the student develop a checklist/chart for daily school assignments to be completed.

12. Provide the student with a backpack, etc., to take homework assignments and materials to and from home.

13. Have the student keep a chart/graph of the number of assignments turned in to his/her teacher.

14. Consider carefully the student's ability level when expecting him/her to be able to study for a specific amount of time.

15. Choose a peer to accompany the student to specified activities to make sure the student has the necessary materials.

16. Deliver reinforcement for any and all measures of homework improvement in being prepared for assignments.

17. Have the student time activities to monitor personal behavior and accept time limits.

18. Provide the student with adequate time at school to prepare for assigned activities (e.g., supervised study time).

19. Have the student listen and take notes for *Who, What, Where, When, How,* and *Why* when concepts are presented.

20. Deliver reinforcement for any and all measures of improvement.

21. Have the student question any directions, explanations, and instructions he/she does not understand.

22. Do not use homework as a punishment (i.e., homework should not be assigned as a consequence for inappropriate behavior at school).

23. Model being prepared for assigned activities.

24. Assess the appropriateness of assigning the student homework if his/her ability level or circumstances at home make it impossible for him/her to complete and return the assignments.

25. Create a learning center at school, open at a specified time each school day, where professional educators are available to help with homework.

26. Develop a school/home assignment sheet to be reviewed and signed by the parents each evening. Communicate with the parents and student to establish clear expectations and positive consequences for completing and returning the assignment sheet.

27. Schedule the student's time at school so homework will not be absolutely necessary if he/she takes advantage of the time provided in school to complete assignments.

28. Review on a daily basis those skills, concepts, tasks, etc., which have been previously introduced.

29. Reinforce the student for being prepared for assigned activities: (a) give the student a tangible reward (e.g., classroom privileges, line leading, passing out materials, five minutes free time, etc.) or (b) give the student an intangible reward (e.g., praise, fist bump, smile, etc.).

30. Reinforce the student for being prepared for assigned activities based on the number of times he/she can be successful. As the student demonstrates success, gradually increase the number of times he/she must be prepared for assigned activities for reinforcement.

31. Assign short tasks that can be quickly and accurately completed. As the student demonstrates success, gradually increase the length of tasks.

32. Reinforce those students who complete their assignments at school during the time provided.

33. Assess the quality and clarity of directions, explanations, and instructions given to the student.

34. Send explanations home each day so the student's parents may help their child with his/her school assignments if necessary.

35. Give the student alternative homework assignments. As the assignments are routinely performed and returned to school, gradually introduce more components of the regular homework assignment.

36. Take proactive steps to deal with a student's refusal to perform a school assignment and prevent contagion in the classroom (e.g., refrain from arguing with the student, place the student in a carrel or other quiet place to work, remove the student from the group or classroom, etc.).

37. Have the student set a timer to complete assignments in a reasonable period of time.

38. Help the student develop an awareness of the consequences of his/her behavior by writing down or talking through problems which may occur due to his/her inability to complete assignments (e.g., if you do not return the assignment to school, you are in danger of failing the class and may not get the credit you need for graduation).

39. Minimize the materials needed for assigned activities.

40. Provide time each day for the student to organize his/her materials (e.g., before school, break time, at lunch, at the end of the day, etc.).

41. Provide time at school for homework completion when the student cannot be successful completing assignments at home.

42. Teach the student skills for taking notes.

43. Teach the student skills for taking tests.

44. Establish a timeline for completing a school assignment. Expect the student to meet each deadline to complete the project on time.

45. Have the student anticipate future tasks/assignments and develop plans for addressing them.

46. Make sure the student has mastered the concepts presented at school. All homework should be a form of practice for what has been learned at school.

47. Make sure the student has all the materials necessary to complete school assignments (e.g., pencils, paper, erasers, etc.).

48. Ask the student why he/she is unprepared for assigned activities. Help the student develop a plan for being prepared for assigned activities.

49. Choose a peer to help the student review information needed to successfully complete a school assignment.

50. Choose a peer to help the student with homework.

51. Have the student chart his/her completed assignments.

52. Send home one homework assignment at a time. As the student demonstrates success completing assignments at home, gradually increase the number of homework assignments sent home.

53. Deliver directions verbally and in written format to facilitate the probability of the student understanding school assignments.

54. Make sure that homework is designed to provide drill activities rather than introduce new information.

55. Have the student make it a habit to periodically review notes, daily calendar of events, or tasks that need to be completed.

56. Send homework assignments and materials home with someone other than the student (e.g., brother, sister, neighbor, etc.).

57. Choose a peer to model being prepared for assigned activities for the student.

58. Communicate with parents (e.g., notes home, phone calls, etc.) to share information about the student's progress. The parents may reinforce the student at home for being prepared for assigned activities at school.

59. Have the student leave necessary materials at specified activity areas.

60. Have the student take notes following the *What, How, Materials*, and *When* format when directions are being given.

61. Allow natural consequences to occur for failure to turn in homework assignments (e.g., students who do not finish their homework do not get to participate in more desirable activities).

62. Allow natural consequences to occur when the student is unprepared for assigned activities (e.g., the student may fail a test or quiz, work not done during work time must be completed during recreational time, etc.).

63. Reduce the number/length of assignments. As the student demonstrates success, gradually increase the number/length of assignments.

64. Work a few problems of the school assignment with the student to start the student on the assignment.

65. Communicate with the parents or guardians to inform them of the student's assignments and what they can do to help the student prepare for his/her assigned activities.

66. Arrange with the student's parents to pick up homework each day if the student has difficulty remembering to take it home.

67. Meet with the student's parents to discuss with them appropriate ways to help their child with school assignments.

68. Assist the student in performing his/her school assignments. As the student demonstrates success, gradually decrease the assistance and have the student assume more responsibility.

69. Encourage the parents to provide the student with a quiet, comfortable place and adequate time to study and prepare for school assignments.

70. Encourage the student to put completed homework assignments in a designated place to be taken to school (e.g., in front of the door, at the bottom of the stairs, etc.).

71. Have the student repeat the school assignment to reinforce the student's awareness of the assignment.

72. Encourage the parents to set aside quiet time each night when the family turns off the TV, music, etc.; to read, do homework, write letters, etc.

73. Teach the student time-management skills. Have the student make a daily plan and follow it. Encourage the student to avoid becoming distracted by events, impulses, and moods.

74. Provide the student with structure for all academic activities (e.g., specific directions, routine format for tasks, time limits, etc.).

75. Do not require the student to learn more information than he/she is capable of learning at any time.

76. Make sure that the student understands the relationship between inappropriate behavior and the consequences which follow (e.g., forgetting to complete his/her school assignments may result in a low grade).

77. Set up a homework system for the student (e.g., two days a week drill with flash cards, three days a week do assignments from a book, etc.). This will add some variety to homework.

78. Follow a less desirable task with a more desirable task. Make completion of the first necessary to perform the second.

79. Make positive comments about school and the importance of completing assignments.

80. Maintain a consistent number of homework assignments (i.e., assign the same amount of homework each day).

81. Assess the degree of task difficulty to determine whether or not the student will require additional information, time, assistance, etc., before beginning a task.

82. Reinforce those students in the classroom who are prepared for assigned activities.

83. Provide individual assistance to the student to help him/her prepare for assigned activities (e.g., set aside time during the day, study hall, or after school, etc.).

84. Repeat directions to facilitate the student's probability of understanding.

85. At the end of the day, remind the student what materials are required for specified activities for the next day (e.g., send a note home, verbal reminder, etc.).

86. Present assignments/tasks in the most attractive and interesting manner possible.

87. Evaluate the appropriateness of the assignment to determine (a) if the task is too easy, (b) if the task is too difficult, or (c) if the length of time scheduled to complete the task is adequate.

88. Identify resource personnel from whom the student may receive additional assistance (e.g., librarian, special education teacher, other personnel with expertise or time to help, etc.).

89. Write a contract with the student specifying what behavior is expected (e.g., studying for tests or quizzes) and what reinforcement will be made available when the terms of the contract have been met.

90. Make sure the student understands that assignments not completed and turned in on time must still be completed and turned in late.

91. Teach the student how to study for a test.

92. Set aside time at the end of the day for the student to complete unfinished assignments.

93. Speak to the student to explain (a) what he/she is doing wrong (e.g., not turning in assignments) and (b) what he/she should be doing (e.g., completing homework/school assignments and returning them to school).

94. Specify exactly what is to be done for the completion of an assignment (e.g., make definite starting and stopping points, a minimum requirement, etc.).

95. Make sure that failure to be prepared for assigned activities results in losing the opportunity to participate in activities or a failing grade for that day's activity.

96. Choose a peer tutor to help the student prepare for assigned activities.

97. Give directions in a variety of ways to facilitate the student's understanding (e.g., if the student does not understand verbal directions, present them in written form).

98. Provide the student with verbal reminders of materials required for each activity.

99. Provide the student with written directions to follow in preparing for all assigned activities.

100. Allow the student to perform a highly desirable task after turning in his/her assignments.

101. Maintain consistent expectations within the ability level of the student.

102. Develop a contract with the student and his/her parents requiring that homework be done before more desirable activities take place at home (e.g., playing, watching television, going out for the evening, etc.).

Goal:

1. The student will remain on task.

Objectives:

1. The student will remain on task until the task is completed on _____ out of _____ trials.
2. The student will remain on task for the required length of time with supervision on _____ out of _____ trials.
3. The student will remain on task without supervision for the required length of time on _____ out of _____ trials.
4. The student will rely on environmental cues (e.g., timers, clocks, bells, other students) to remain on task for the required length of time on _____ out of _____ trials.
5. The student will ask for clarification of directions or instructions not understood on _____ out of _____ trials.
6. The student will demonstrate on-task behavior by sitting quietly at his/her seat, looking at his/her materials, and performing the task for _____ minutes at a time.
7. The student will remain on task for _____ minutes at a time.
8. The student will remain on task long enough to complete the task on _____ out of _____ tasks.
9. The student will maintain eye contact with the teacher for _____ minutes at a time.

Interventions:

1. Establish classroom rules:
- Concentrate while working.
- Work quietly.
- Remain in your seat.
- Finish task.
- Meet task expectations.

Review rules often. Reinforce students for following the rules.

2. Assess the degree of task difficulty to determine whether or not the student will require additional information, time, assistance, etc., before beginning a task.

3. Provide the student with a quiet place in which to work where auditory and visual stimuli are reduced. This is used to reduce distracting stimuli and not as punishment.

4. Have the student maintain a chart representing the amount of time he/she has spent on task.

5. Reward the student for being productive in the presence of auditory and visual stimuli for short periods of time. As the student demonstrates success, gradually increase the length of time the student is required to be productive.

6. Schedule a fun educational activity (e.g., computer game) during the day to provide incentive for the student to stay on task and behave appropriately.

7. Provide the student with a carrel or divider at his/her desk to reduce auditory and visual stimuli.

8. Provide the student with a list of assignments for the day and have the student choose the order in which he/she will perform the tasks.

9. Provide the student with a variety of assignments and have him/her choose a minimum number from the total to complete (e.g., present the student with 10 academic tasks from which he/she must finish 6 that day).

10. Provide the student with a predetermined signal (e.g., hand signal, verbal cue, etc.) when he/she begins to display off-task behaviors.

11. Schedule highly desirable activities contingent upon staying on task a required amount of time (i.e., staying on task for a required amount of time earns the student the opportunity to participate in a desirable activity).

12. Provide the student with a timer to be used to facilitate the amount of time during which he/she maintains attention (e.g., have the student work on the activity until the timer goes off).

13. Have the student define a goal. Assist the student in developing specific strategies to achieve his/ her goal and following through on those strategies.

14. Use multiple modalities to accommodate more than one learning style (e.g., visual, auditory, tactile, etc.) when presenting directions/ instructions, explanations, and instructional content.

15. Have the student time activities to monitor personal behavior and time limits.

16. Provide the student with adequate transition time between activities to facilitate on-task behavior after activities have begun (e.g., after break time, lunch, special activities, etc.).

17. Have the student assemble all materials needed prior to beginning a task to reduce interruptions.

18. Provide an incentive statement along with a directive (e.g., When you complete this assignment, you may earn a pass to the water fountain.).

19. Remove the student from an activity until he/she can demonstrate appropriate on-task behavior.

20. Deliver reinforcement for any and all measures of improvement.

21. Have the student question any directions, explanations, and instructions he/she does not understand.

22. Model for the student appropriate behavior in the presence of auditory and visual stimuli in the classroom (e.g., continuing to work, asking for quiet, moving to a quieter part of the classroom, etc.).

23. Reduce the number of current assignments by adding new assignments after previous assignments have been completed.

24. Make participation in extracurricular activities dependent upon completion of class assignments.

25. Have the student organize assignments by dividing them into small segments. Set deadlines and provide the student with a reward after completing each segment of the assignment.

26. Reinforce the student for attending to a task based on the length of time he/she can be successful. As the student demonstrates success, gradually increase the length of time required for reinforcement.

27. Help the student develop attention-maintaining behaviors (e.g., maintain eye contact, take notes on the subject, ask questions related to the subject, etc.).

28. Allow the student to close the classroom door or windows to reduce auditory and visual distractions from outside of the classroom.

29. Reduce the emphasis on competition. Repeated failure may cause the student to remove himself/herself from competition by not remaining on task.

30. Assist the student in completing class assignments. As the student demonstrates success, gradually decrease assistance and have the student to independently remain on task.

31. Set time limits for completing assignments.

32. Reward the student for completing an assignment within the amount of time allotted.

33. Reduce distracting stimuli which could interfere with the student's ability to remain on task (e.g., provide enough room to move without physical contact, keep noise level to a minimum, keep movement in the environment to a minimum, etc.).

34. Seat the student away from those peers who create the most auditory and visual stimulation in the classroom.

35. Encourage the student to develop a 30 second definition of his/her goal to help himself/herself stay on task and focused (e.g., I will listen carefully. The better I listen the better I will perform.).

36. Help the student develop an awareness of himself/herself and the environment. Have the student periodically, step back and ask himself/herself: *Am I on task and paying attention? What should I be doing now?*

37. Provide the student with headphones to wear if auditory stimuli interfere with his/her ability to function. As the student functions more successfully in the presence of auditory stimuli, gradually reduce the amount of time the headphones are worn.

38. Identify the student's most effective learning mode. Use it consistently to facilitate the student's understanding and remaining on task for longer periods of time.

39. Choose a peer, paraprofessional, etc., to cue the student (e.g., the person can touch the student's arm as a signal that he/she is not remaining on task) when he/she is off task.

40. Have the student ask for help when he/she needs it.

41. Maintain visibility to and from the student. The teacher should be able to see the student, and the student should be able to see the teacher. Make eye contact possible at all times.

42. Make sure the student has all the materials necessary to perform assignments.

43. Make sure the student has enough work space to perform the task.

44. Have the student ask himself/herself questions (e.g., What's next?) to keep himself/herself focused on assignments/projects.

45. Have the student chart his/her own record of on-task behavior. Reinforce the student for increasing the amount of time spent on task.

46. Acknowledge the student when his/her hand is raised. Provide assistance as soon as possible.

47. Provide assignments that involve immediate, short-term tasks.

48. Create a quiet area in the classroom where absolute silence must be observed.

49. Monitor the student's performance in activities or tasks to make sure the student begins, works on, and completes an assignment and will be ready to move to the next activity in his/her routine.

50. Have the student participate in small-group activities (e.g., free time, math, reading, etc.) to reduce the level of auditory and visual stimuli in the group. As the student demonstrates success, gradually increase the size of the group.

51. Provide the student with increased opportunities for help or assistance on academic tasks (e.g., peer tutoring, directions for work, frequent interactions, etc.).

52. Make sure the student knows what to do when he/she cannot successfully perform assignments (e.g., raise hand, ask for assistance, go to the teacher, etc.).

53. Allow the student to leave the task and return to it at a later time when he/she should be more successful remaining on task.

54. Encourage the student to manage his/her class performance as if he/she were self-employed. This should increase his/her motivation to be organized and fulfill his/her responsibilities.

55. Make sure only those materials necessary for performing the task (e.g., pencil, textbook, paper, etc.) are on the student's desk. Additional materials may distract the student.

56. Choose a peer to model on-task behavior for the student.

57. Present tasks in the most attractive and interesting manner possible.

58. Allow the student some movement while performing tasks. Monitor and limit the amount of movement.

59. Communicate with parents (e.g., notes home, phone calls, etc.) to share information about the student's progress. The parents may reinforce the student at home for staying on task in the classroom.

60. Designate a specific period of time (e.g., each hour on the hour, last five minutes of class, after completing a task, etc.) when it is permissible for the student to talk with his/her peers.

61. Place the student with peers who will be appropriate role models and should facilitate his/her academic and behavioral success.

62. Structure the environment to reduce the opportunity for off-task behavior. Reduce lag time by providing the student with enough activities to maintain productivity.

63. Provide the student with shorter tasks which do not require extended periods of attention to be successful. As the student demonstrates success, gradually increase the length of the tasks.

64. Provide the student with shorter tasks which do not require extended attention to be successful. As the student demonstrates success, gradually increase the length of the tasks.

65. Provide flexibility in scheduling so the student may perform alternative activities which result in more successful on-task behavior.

66. Reinforce the student for staying on task in the classroom: (a) give the student a tangible reward (e.g., classroom privileges, line leading, passing out materials, five minutes free time, etc.) or (b) give the student an intangible reward (e.g., praise, fist bump, smile, etc.).

67. Assess the degree of task difficulty in relation to the student's ability to successfully perform the task.

68. Use more interesting or stimulating activities as a reward for completing less interesting activities (e.g., after completing a rough draft on paper, the student can choose graphics available on the computer).

69. Reduce auditory and visual stimuli to a level at which the student can successfully function. As the student demonstrates success, gradually increase the auditory and visual stimuli.

70. Reduce auditory and visual stimuli in the classroom as much as possible for all learners.

71. Interact frequently with the student to maintain involvement in the activity (e.g., ask the student questions, ask the student's opinion, stand close to the student, seat the student near the teacher's desk, etc.).

72. Provide assistance when the student has the most difficulty attending to an activity for the required amount of time.

73. Make sure that the student understands the relationship between inappropriate behavior and the consequences which follow (e.g., failure to remain on task will result in incomplete assignments).

74. Communicate clearly with the student the length of time he/she has to complete an assignment. The student may want to use a timer to facilitate completing the tasks within the given period of time.

75. Move objects used for tactile stimulation (e.g., pens, paper clips, loose change, etc.) away from the student's reach.

76. Reward the student (e.g., take a break, get a drink of water, talk briefly with a peer, etc.) for concentrating on an assignment for a specific length of time.

77. Allow the student to take a break while working on monotonous assignments to relieve restlessness and improve concentration.

78. Allow the student to take assignments/ tasks to other areas of the school (e.g., library, study hall, learning center, etc.) where he/she can remain on task.

79. Follow a less desirable task with a more desirable task. Make completion of the first task necessary to perform the second task.

80. Give the student one task to perform at a time. Introduce the next task when the student has successfully completed the current task.

81. Assign the student shorter tasks but more of them (e.g., modify a 20-problem math activity to 4 activities of 5 problems each, to be performed at various times during the day). As the student demonstrates success, gradually increase the number of problems for each activity and decrease the number of activities.

82. Develop a classroom environment that is quiet and uncluttered (e.g., clean, well-lighted, fresh-smelling, and at a comfortable temperature).

83. Seat the student so that he/she experiences the least amount of auditory and visual stimuli.

84. Provide the student with the opportunity to move to a quiet place in the classroom any time auditory and visual stimuli interfere with his/her ability to function successfully.

85. Consider individual needs of the student (e.g., hunger, need for rest, comfort level, etc.) which may be interfering with his/her on-task behavior. Intervene to correct the situation or change the expectations.

86. Set clear expectations for the completion of tasks. Consistently deliver reinforcement and consequences to all students.

87. Be proactive. Work with the school counselor to design a schedule to facilitate student's success (e.g., physical education scheduled the last period of the day, intersperse electives which allow greater freedom of movement with classes requiring extended periods of concentration, etc.).

88. Reinforce those students in the classroom who demonstrate on-task behavior.

89. Remove any peer from the immediate environment who may be interfering with the student's ability to remain on task.

90. Provide activities which increase the opportunities for active participation.

91. Make sure to recognize the student when his/her hand is raised to let him/her know assistance will be provided as soon as possible.

92. Set aside time at the end of each class period to complete assignments.

93. Write a contract with the student specifying what behavior is expected (e.g., establish a reasonable length of time to stay on task) and what reinforcement will be made available when the terms of the contract have been met.

94. Teach the student how to manage his/her time until assistance can be provided (e.g., try the problem again, go on to the next problem, wait quietly, etc.).

95. Specify exactly what is to be done for the completion of a task (e.g., indicate definite starting and stopping points, indicate the minimum requirements, etc.).

96. Speak to the student to explain (a) what he/she is doing wrong (e.g., not attending to the tasks) and (b) what he/she should be doing (e.g., attending to the tasks).

97. Help the student learn to be satisfied with his/her best effort rather than some arbitrary measure of success. Success is measured individually according to ability levels and progress of any kind is a measure of success.

98. Make sure the student understands that work not done during work time must be completed at other times (e.g., lunch, during assemblies, after school, etc.).

99. Make sure the student understands the instructions/directions for the task (e.g., present instructions in a variety of ways; have the student verbalize what he/she is to do to perform the activity; etc.).

100. Minimize stimulation which interferes with the student's ability to remain on task (e.g., maintain a routine schedule of events, schedule special activities for the end of the day, etc.).

101. Provide a routine that will minimize off-task behavior which may result in negative consequences.

102. Have the student work with a peer who manages time well.

103. Have the student work with a peer tutor to maintain his/her attention to tasks.

104. Have the student communicate with appropriate personnel (e.g., counselor, nurse, administrator, etc.) about concerns (e.g., home, peer, personal problems, etc.) which interfere with his/her ability to stay on task.

105. Assist the student in writing a contract for himself/herself designating a time to complete an assignment and avoid procrastination.

106. Have the student's cooperative work experience/vocational education teacher provide him/her with interventions to assist in remaining on task at his/her job.

107. Evaluate the auditory and visual stimuli in the classroom to determine what level of stimuli the student can respond to in an appropriate manner.

108. Teach the student appropriate ways to respond to visual and auditory stimuli in the classroom (e.g., moving to another part of the room, asking others to be quiet, leaving the group, etc.).

Goal:

1. The student will turn in homework assignments.

Objectives:

1. The student will complete a task before going on to the next task on _____ out of _____ trials.
2. The student will complete _____ out of _____ assigned tasks per day.
3. The student will attempt _____ out of _____ assigned tasks per day.
4. The student will remain on task for _____ out of _____ minutes per class period.
5. The student will use the time provided to work on assigned tasks to complete _____ tasks per day.
6. The student will complete _____ out of _____ homework assignments each day.
7. The student will complete _____ out of _____ homework assignments each week.
8. The student will bring _____ out of _____ of his/her completed homework assignments to school and turn them in each day.
9. The student will bring _____ out of _____ of his/her completed homework assignments to school and turn them in each week.
10. The student will carry his/her homework assignments to and from school in a backpack to prevent loss on _____ out of _____ trials.
11. The student will perform _____ out of _____ homework assignments at home and return them to school each day.
12. The student will perform _____ out of _____ homework assignments at home and return them to school each week.

Interventions:

1. Establish homework assignment rules:
- Concentrate while working.
- Finish task.
- Meet task expectations.
- Turn in task.

Review rules often. Reinforce students for following the rules.

2. Allow natural consequences to occur for failure to turn in homework assignments (e.g., students who do not finish their homework do not get to participate in more desirable activities).

3. Assess the appropriateness of assigning the student homework if his/her ability or circumstances at home make it impossible to complete and return the assignments.

4. Provide the student with a certain number of problems to do on an assignment. Have the student choose a minimum number from the total (e.g., present the student with ten math problems from which six must be completed).

5. Provide the student with a schedule of activities so he/she knows exactly what and how much there is to do in a day.

6. Provide the student with a variety of assignments. Have the student choose a minimum number from the total (e.g., present the student with ten academic tasks from which six must be finished).

7. Have the student maintain a record (e.g., chart or graph) of his/her performance in completing assignments.

8. Make directions as simple and concrete as possible.

9. Have the student question any directions, explanations, and instructions he/she does not understand.

10. Do not assign homework as a punishment (e.g., homework should not be assigned as a consequence for inappropriate behavior at school).

11. Have the student time assignments to monitor personal behavior and time limits.

12. Provide the student with a backpack, etc., to take homework assignments and materials to and from home.

13. Maintain mobility to provide assistance to the student when completing class assignments.

14. Schedule the student's time at school so that homework will not be necessary if he/she takes advantage of the time provided at school to complete assignments.

15. Create a learning center at school where professional educators are available to help with homework assignments before school begins, the last hour of each school day, etc.

16. Prevent the student from becoming over-stimulated by an activity (e.g., frustrated, angry, etc.).

17. Have the student begin each assignment within a specified period of time (e.g., three minutes, five minutes, etc.).

18. Assess the quality and clarity of directions, explanations, and instructions the student does not understand.

19. Reinforce those students who complete their assignments at school during the time provided.

20. Reinforce the student for completing classroom assignments/homework. As the student demonstrates success, gradually increase the number of times the student must complete assignments/homework for reinforcement.

21. Assign homework in a consistent manner (i.e., assign the same amount of homework each day).

22. Make sure the student has mastered the concepts presented at school. All homework should be a form of practice for what has been learned at school.

23. Take proactive steps to deal with a student's refusal to perform a class/homework assignment and prevent contagion (e.g., refrain from arguing with the student, place the student in a carrel or other quiet place to work, remove the student from the group or classroom, etc.).

24. Provide time at school for homework completion when the student cannot be successful in performing assignments at home.

25. Use a timer to help the student monitor how much time he/she has to finish an assignment.

26. Deliver directions verbally to help the student understand homework assignments.

27. Choose a peer to help the student with homework.

28. Assign small amounts of homework, (e.g., one or two problems to perform may be sufficient to begin the homework process). As the student demonstrates success, gradually increase the amount of homework assigned.

29. Give the student alternative homework assignments. As the assignments are routinely performed and returned to school, gradually introduce more components of the regular homework assignment.

30. Meet with parents to instruct them in appropriate ways to help their child with homework.

31. Rewrite directions at a lower reading level.

32. Send homework assignments and materials directly to the home with someone other than the student (e.g., sibling, neighbor, bus driver, etc.).

33. Choose a peer to model turning in homework assignments for the student.

34. Provide the student with more than enough time to finish an activity. As the student demonstrates success, gradually decrease the amount of time provided to finish an activity.

35. Provide a set of necessary materials for completing homework to be kept at home. Send directions for homework with the student.

36. Communicate with parents (e.g., notes home, phone calls, etc.) to share information about the student's progress. The parents may reinforce the student at home for turning in homework at school.

37. Maintain a consistent number of homework assignments (i.e., assign the same amount of homework each day).

38. Have the student chart or graph the number of homework assignments he/she turns in to the teacher.

39. Introduce the student to other resource persons who may be able to help him/her do homework (e.g., other teachers, librarian, etc.).

40. Arrange with the student's parents to have homework picked up each day if the student has difficulty remembering to take it home.

41. Find a tutor (e.g., peer, volunteer, etc.) to work with the student at home.

42. Allow the student to perform a highly desirable task when his/her homework has been turned in to the teacher.

43. Reduce distracting stimuli (e.g., place the student on the front row, provide a carrel or office space away from distractions, etc.). This is used as a means of reducing distracting stimuli and not as a form of punishment.

44. Encourage the parents to provide the student with a quiet, comfortable place and adequate time to do homework.

45. Along with a directive, provide an incentive statement (e.g., After your work is finished, you may play a game.).

46. Structure the environment to provide the student with increased opportunities for help or assistance.

47. Make sure that homework provides drill activities and does not introduce new information.

48. Provide the student with shorter tasks given more frequently.

49. Chart homework assignments the student has completed.

50. Communicate clearly to the student the length of time he/she has to complete an assignment.

51. Set up a homework system for the student (e.g., 2 days a week drill with flash cards, 3 days a week do assignments from a book, etc.). This will add some variety to homework.

52. Structure time limits so the student knows exactly how long he/she has to work and when the work must be finished.

53. Reinforce those students in the classroom who turn in their homework assignments.

54. Write a contract with the student specifying what behavior is expected (e.g., turning in homework) and what reinforcement will be made available when the terms of the contract have been met.

55. Repeat directions to facilitate the student's understanding of them.

56. Evaluate the appropriateness of the homework assignment to determine (a) if the task is too easy, (b) if the task is too difficult, or (c) if the length of time scheduled to complete the task is adequate.

57. Have the student repeat the directions verbally to the teacher.

58. Maintain consistent expectations within the ability level of the student.

59. Specify exactly what is to be done for the completion of a task (e.g., indicate definite starting and stopping points, indicate a minimum requirement, etc.).

60. Develop a contract with the student and his/her parents that requires homework to be done before more desirable activities (e.g., playing, watching television, going out for the evening, etc.) take place at home.

61. Present homework assignments in the most attractive and interesting manner possible.

62. Allow the student additional time to turn in homework assignments.

63. Speak to the student to explain (a) what he/she is doing wrong (e.g., not turning in homework assignments) and (b) what he/she should be doing (e.g., completing homework assignments and returning them to school).

64. Provide the student with written directions for doing homework assignments.

65. Reinforce the student for turning in homework assignments: (a) give the student a tangible reward (e.g., classroom privileges, line leading, passing out materials, five minutes free time, etc.) or (b) give the student an intangible reward (e.g., praise, fist bump, smile, etc.).

66. Reinforce the student for turning in his/her homework. As the student demonstrates success, gradually increase the required number of homework assignments to be turned in for reinforcement.

67. Give directions in a variety of ways to facilitate the student's understanding (e.g., if the student does not understand verbal directions, present them in written form).

68. Work a few problems with the student to help him/her begin an assignment.

Goal:

1. The student will independently perform assignments.

Objectives:

1. The student will attempt to perform a given assignment before asking for teacher assistance on _____ out of _____ trials.
2. The student will read necessary directions, instructions, explanations, etc., before asking for teacher assistance on _____ out of _____ trials.
3. The student will independently complete _____ out of _____ assignments per school day.
4. The student will ask for teacher assistance only when necessary when performing assignments on _____ out of _____ trials.
5. The student will work for _____ minutes without requiring assistance from the teacher on _____ out of _____ trials.

Interventions:

1. Establish classroom rules:
- Concentrate while working.
- Work quietly.
- Request assistance when needed.
- Remain in your seat.
- Finish task.
- Meet task expectations.

Review rules often. Reinforce students for following the rules.

2. Provide the student with a variety of assignments and have him/her choose a minimum number of assignments to perform independently (e.g., present the student with 10 academic tasks from which six must be completed that day).

3. Have the student use a daily calendar to write down assignments, projects, due dates, etc. Use the calendar to develop the student's time-management skills.

4. Have the student keep a chart/graph representing the number of assignments performed independently.

5. Have the student develop a checklist/chart to follow which will allow him/her to complete all assignments.

6. Engage the help of a peer, paraprofessional, parent, etc., to remind the student of assignments.

7. Have the student assemble all materials necessary to work on a project, assignment, etc., to reduce the need to search for materials.

8. Communicate to the student an interest in his/her success.

9. Have the student review and update his/her assignment calendar daily. Encourage the student to prepare in advance for assignments, due dates, etc.

10. Encourage parents to set aside and enforce a consistent time period at home for the student to complete homework. All family members should work on tasks (e.g., correspondence, balancing accounts, reading, etc.) during this time.

11. Encourage the student to ask for clarification of any directions, explanations, and instructions before beginning a task to facilitate comprehension.

12. Give the student alternative assignments. As those assignments are routinely performed, gradually introduce more components of the regular assignments.

13. Detail expectations at the beginning of each period so the student will know what is required.

14. Reinforce the student for beginning, working on, and completing assignments.

15. Maintain mobility throughout the classroom to determine the student's attention to task.

16. Set time limits for completing assignments.

17. Reinforce the student for completing assignments independently: (a) give the student a tangible reward (e.g., classroom privileges, free homework pass, five minutes free time, etc.) or (b) give the student an intangible reward (e.g., praise, fist bump, smile, etc.).

18. Reinforce the student for completing assignments independently based on the number of times he/she can be successful. As the student demonstrates success, gradually increase the number of times the student must independently complete assignments for reinforcement.

19. Allow the student more decision-making opportunities relative to class activities and assignments.

20. Have the student use electronic reminders to assist him/her in completion of assignments (e.g., programmable watch, computer programs, voicemail, etc.).

21. Choose a peer, friend, etc., who displays the ability to organize an assignment prior to beginning it. Have the student observe that person and model the behaviors which allow him/her to organize assignments.

22. Make sure that directions, explanations, and instructions are delivered on the student's ability level.

23. Encourage the student to follow a less desirable task with a more desirable task. Make completion of the first necessary to perform the second.

24. Make sure that assignments given to the student are appropriate for his/her level of development and ability.

25. Assess the appropriateness of giving the student assignments which require copying if the student's ability level makes it impossible for him/her to complete the assignment.

26. Have the student schedule independent working times when he/she is most likely to maintain attention (e.g., one hour after medication, 45 minutes after dinner, first thing in the morning, etc.).

27. Make sure the student is paying attention when he/she is given instruction. Have the student make eye contact and repeat the information to check for understanding.

28. Create an environment that is quiet and uncluttered (e.g., clean, well-lighted, fresh-smelling, and at a comfortable temperature).

29. Present assignments in the most interesting manner possible.

30. Provide a written list of directions for a long-term assignment.

31. Call on the student often to encourage communication.

32. Communicate with parents, agencies, or the appropriate parties to inform them of the problem, determine the cause of the problem, and consider possible solutions to the problem.

33. Communicate with the student's parents (e.g., notes home, phone calls, etc.) to share information about their child's progress. The parents may reinforce the student at home for completing assignments independently.

34. Reinforce the student for performing assignments independently.

35. Allow the student to set a timer to complete assignments within a given period of time.

36. Schedule recreational activities at the end of the day. Make participation in these activities dependent upon completion of assignments.

37. Provide the student with step-by-step written directions for assignments.

38. Reduce distracting stimuli (e.g., place the student in the front row, provide a carrel or quiet place away from distractions, etc.). This is to be used as a means of reducing stimuli and not as a form of punishment.

39. Encourage the student to reward himself/herself (e.g., take a ten minute break, speak briefly with a relative, phone a friend, etc.) for concentrating on an assignment for a specific length of time.

40. Provide the student with structure for all academic activities (e.g., specific directions, routine format for tasks, time limits, etc.).

41. Communicate clearly with the student the length of time he/she has to complete an assignment. The student may want to use a timer to complete the tasks within the given period of time.

42. Encourage the student to take a break while working on monotonous assignments to relieve restlessness and improve concentration. Set a definite time limit for breaks.

43. Assess the degree of task difficulty to determine whether or not the student will require additional information, time, assistance, etc., before beginning a task.

44. Have the student prioritize tasks by importance (e.g., task A must be done today, task B can be done today, and task C can wait until tomorrow).

45. Assign the student shorter tasks. As the student demonstrates success, gradually increase the length of the tasks.

46. Communicate to the student that he/she is a worthwhile individual.

47. Instruct the student in thinking through instructions/directions before beginning a task.

48. Explain to the student that work not done during work time will have to be done during other times (e.g., break time, recreational time, after school, etc.).

49. Be consistent in expecting the student to complete assignments. Do not allow the student to not complete assigned tasks one time and expect tasks to be completed the next time.

50. Maintain consistent expectations within the ability level of the student.

51. Reinforce those students in the classroom who complete assignments independently.

52. Communicate expectations to the student for the successful completion of assignments.

53. Organize assignments by dividing them into small segments. Set deadlines and provide the student with a reward after completing each segment of the assignment.

54. Allow the student additional time to complete assignments when working independently.

55. Speak to the student to explain (a) what he/she is doing wrong (e.g., off task, failing to complete assignments) and (b) what he/she should be doing (e.g., attending to the task, completing assignments sequentially, completing tasks).

56. Do not give directions to the student from across the room. Go to student, get his/her undivided attention, and explain the directions to him/her.

57. Create challenges in assignments to facilitate interest and motivation (e.g., stress problem solving and creative/critical thinking rather than drill/repetition, etc.).

58. Make sure the student understands the relationship between inappropriate behavior and the consequences which follow (e.g., not completing assignments independently results in lower grades, less responsibility, etc.).

59. Specify exactly what is to be done for the completion of an assignment (e.g., indicate definite starting and stopping points, indicate the minimum requirements, etc.).

60. Teach the student time-management skills. Have the student make a daily plan and follow it. Encourage the student to avoid becoming distracted by events, impulses, and moods.

61. Work a few problems of the assignment with the student to start the student on the assignment.

62. Assist the student in writing a contract for himself/herself designating a time to complete an assignment and avoid procrastination.

63. Structure the environment to facilitate task completion. Make sure the student's tasks are on his/her ability level, be sure that instructions are clear, and maintain frequent interactions with the student to facilitate success.

64. Write a contract with the student specifying what behavior is expected (e.g., complete assigned project by due date) and what reinforcement will be made available when the terms of the contract have been met.

65. Instruct the student on ways to reduce distracting activities which interfere with his/her responsibilities (e.g., turn off the TV when it is time to complete tasks, do not allow friends to come over when it is time to do homework, etc.).

Goals:

1. The student will improve his/her short-term memory.
2. The student will improve his/her long-term memory.
3. The student will improve his/her understanding of abstract concepts (e.g., spatial relationships, directionality, classifications, generalizations).
4. The student will improve his/her visual memory.
5. The student will improve his/her auditory memory.

Objectives:

1. The student will remember the events in a daily routine with _____% accuracy.
2. The student will remember the days of the week with _____% accuracy.
3. The student will remember the months of the year with _____% accuracy.
4. The student will remember the seasons with _____% accuracy.
5. The student will remember the alphabet with _____% accuracy.
6. The student will follow an established routine in performing assignments, preparing lunch, etc., with _____% accuracy.

Interventions:

1. Have the student maintain a notebook in which he/she keeps notes regarding necessary sequential information (e.g., lists of things to do, schedule of events, days of the week, months of the year, etc.).

2. Provide the student with a *Schedule of Daily Events* for each day's activities at school.

3. Use multiple modalities to accommodate more than one learning style (e.g., visual, auditory, tactile, etc.) when presenting directions/instructions, explanations, and instructional content.

4. Involve the student in activities in which he/she can be successful and will help him/her feel good about himself/herself. Repeated failures may result in frustration and impatience.

5. Assign the student additional activities which require the use of sequences to facilitate his/her ability to remember sequences.

6. Clarify instructions/directions/expectations before assigning a task.

7. Have the student question any directions, explanations, and instructions he/she does understand.

8. Consider carefully the student's age and experience before expecting him/her to remember lengthy sequences of activities.

9. Encourage the student to ask people to repeat parts of a conversation he/she was unable to follow.

10. Instruct the student to ask himself/herself questions (e.g., What's next?) to keep himself/herself focused on assignments/projects.

11. Encourage the student to avoid ingesting any substance (e.g., drugs, alcohol, cold remedies, etc.) that might further alter his/her ability to remember.

12. Have the student carry a notepad with him/her at all times to write information down to help him/her remember.

13. Make sure that your comments take the form of constructive criticism rather than criticism that can be perceived as personal, threatening, etc., (e.g., instead of telling the student he/she always makes the same mistake, suggest another way to avoid making the mistake).

14. Have the student ask for help when he/she needs it.

15. Reduce the emphasis on competition. Competitive activities may cause the student to omit necessary steps in a task.

16. Establish a timeline for completing a project. Expect the student to meet each deadline to complete the project on time.

17. Write down verbal directions. Cross each step off as it is completed.

18. Practice sequential memory activities daily. Practice those sequences which the student needs to memorize (e.g., important phone numbers, addresses, etc.).

19. Help the student develop an awareness of himself/herself and the environment. Instruct the student to periodically step back and ask himself/herself: *Am I on task and following the necessary steps? What should I be doing now?*

20. Assist the student in developing a flow chart of the steps necessary to complete a task.

21. Assist the student in developing a checklist/chart to follow which will allow him/her to complete all assignments.

22. Stop at various points during the presentation of information to check the student's comprehension.

23. Encourage the student to eat a balanced diet and get plenty of rest to facilitate his/her memory.

24. Have the student use electronic reminders to assist him/her in following a routine (e.g., a programmable watch, computer programs, voicemail, etc.).

25. Provide the student with environmental cues and prompts (e.g., lists of jobs to perform, schedule of daily events, bell, timer, etc.).

26. Maintain a consistent sequence of activities to facilitate the student's success (e.g, the student has math every day at one o'clock, recess at two o'clock, etc.).

27. Encourage the student to establish a routine for himself/herself by developing a weekly schedule and a weekend schedule. Assist the student in developing a checklist/chart for daily assignments to be completed.

28. Provide the student with frequent opportunities to recite sequences throughout the day to facilitate memory skills.

29. Allow the student to highlight sequential information in written materials.

30. Instruct the student to imagine the steps required to complete a task before beginning that task.

31. Make sure the activities in which the student engages are not too difficult for him/her.

32. Assign a task that involves immediate, short-term steps.

33. Teach the student to make reminders for himself/herself (e.g., notes, lists, etc.).

34. Help the student use memory aids.

35. Have the student maintain notes, written reminders, etc., to remember sequences.

36. Choose different people (e.g., peer, counselor, paraprofessional, etc.) to help the student improve his/her memory skills.

37. Make it pleasant and positive for the student to ask questions about things he/she does not understand. Reinforce the student by assisting, congratulating, praising, etc.

38. Instruct the student to post needed sequential information in a readily accessible location (e.g., folder, on desktop, in front of text book, etc.).

39. Encourage the student to practice patience and follow the necessary steps in tasks. If the student is impatient, he/she is more likely to omit necessary steps in a sequence.

40. Have the student practice remembering sequences by engaging in sequential activities which are purposeful to him/her (e.g., operating equipment, following recipes, opening a combination lock, etc.).

41. Reinforce the student for remembering sequences based on the number of times he/she can be successful. As the student demonstrates success, gradually increase the length of the sequence required for reinforcement.

42. Reinforce the student for remembering sequences: (a) give the student a tangible reward (e.g., classroom privileges, line leading, passing out materials, five minutes free time, etc.) or (b) give the student an intangible reward (e.g., praise, fist bump, smile, etc.).

43. Have the student repeat directions, explanations, and instructions after they have been given to reinforce retention.

44. Have the student be responsible for helping a peer remember sequences.

45. Maintain a consistent daily routine in the classroom.

46. Give the student short sequences (e.g., two components, three components, etc.) to remember. As the student demonstrates success, gradually increase the length of the sequence.

47. Prevent frustrating or anxiety-producing situations from occurring (e.g., do not place the student in a competitive situation which requires sequencing skills).

48. Teach and practice different strategies to remember steps in a task:
- repetition,
- mnemonic,
- acronym, and
- association.

49. Do not require the student to learn more information than he/she is capable of remembering at any time.

50. Teach and have the student practice listening for key information when he/she is being given directions or receiving information (e.g., write down main points, ideas, step-by-step instructions, etc.).

51. Deliver information to the student on a one-to-one basis or use a peer tutor.

52. Establish a rule (e.g., take your time and follow sequential directions). This rule should be consistent and followed by everyone in the classroom. Talk about the rule often and reward the student for following the rule.

53. Allow the student to audio record information from lectures and seminars and make notes from those recordings.

54. Provide written reminders of task sequences.

55. Assess the degree of task difficulty to determine whether or not the student will require additional information, sequencing models, time, assistance, etc., before beginning a task.

56. Have the student identify the main characters, sequence the events, and report the outcome of a short story he/she has just read.

57. Demonstrate new skills. Allow the student to practice hands-on learning of new skills.

58. Make instructions meaningful to the student by relating instructions to past experiences.

59. Have the student sequence the activities which occurred during a field trip or special event.

60. Reinforce those students in the classroom who remember sequences.

61. Reward other students in the classroom for following necessary steps in tasks.

62. Evaluate the appropriateness of the task to determine (a) if the task is too easy, (b) if the task is too difficult, or (c) if the length of time scheduled to complete the task is adequate.

63. Use written/verbal repetition to aid retention of information.

64. Tell the student what to listen for when being given directions or receiving information, etc.

65. Break a sequence into units and have the student learn one unit at a time.

66. Teach the student to use environmental resources to remember sequences (e.g., calendar, dictionary, etc.).

67. Teach the student to use associative cues or mnemonic devices to remember sequences.

68. Have the student quietly repeat to himself/herself information just heard to help him/her remember the important facts.

69. Encourage the student to use an electronic organizer for phone numbers, reminders, and messages.

70. Encourage the student to use visual reminders (e.g., attach a note to a backpack, place a self-adhesive note on the inside of his/her locker, etc.).

71. Have the student work with a peer who is able to successfully follow the necessary steps in tasks.

27   Has difficulty attending when directions are given

Goals:

1. The student will improve listening skills in academic settings.
2. The student will improve listening skills in nonacademic settings.
3. The student will attend more successfully to specific sounds in the environment.

Objectives:

1. The student will maintain eye contact when information is being communicated _____% of the time.
2. The student will quietly listen when verbal directions are given _____% of the time.
3. The student will repeat what is said with _____% accuracy.
4. The student will respond appropriately to what is said, with prompting, with _____% accuracy.
5. The student will independently respond appropriately to what is said to him/her with _____% accuracy.

Interventions:

1. Establish classroom rules:
   - Concentrate while working.
   - Work quietly.
   - Remain in your seat.
   - Finish task.
   - Meet task expectations.

   Review rules often. Reinforce students for following the rules.

2. Reinforce the student for attending to directions based on the length of time he/she can be successful. As the student demonstrates success, gradually increase the required length of time spent attending to directions for reinforcement.

3. Write a contract with the student specifying what behavior is expected (e.g., attending to directions) and what reinforcement will be made available when the terms of the contract have been met.

4. Assess the quality and clarity of directions, explanations, and instructions given to the student.

5. Structure the environment to reduce distracting stimuli (e.g., place the student on the front row, provide a carrel or quiet place away from distractions, etc.). This is used as a means of reducing distracting stimuli and not as a form of punishment.

6. Give directions in a variety of ways to facilitate the student's understanding (e.g., if the student does not understand verbal directions, present them in written form).

7. Follow a less desirable task with a more desirable task. Make the completion of the first necessary to perform the second.

8. Divide large tasks into smaller tasks (e.g., assign an outline for a book report, then the first rough draft, etc.).

9. Choose a peer tutor to work directly with the student as a model for attending to directions.

10. Provide clearly stated directions, written or verbal (e.g., make directions as simple and concrete as possible).

11. Make sure the student knows that directions will only be given once.

12. Give directions in steps (e.g., give the student one step at a time).

13. Try various groupings to determine the group in which the student attends most successfully.

14. Reinforce the student for beginning, working on, and completing assignments.

15. Assign the student shorter tasks. As the student demonstrates success, gradually increase the length of his/her tasks.

16. Make sure the student's academic tasks are on his/her ability level.

17. Present assignments in small amounts (e.g., assign 10 problems, use pages removed from workbooks, etc.).

18. Separate the student from peers who may be encouraging or stimulating the inappropriate behavior.

19. Maintain physical contact with the student while talking to him/her (e.g., touch the student's hand or shoulder).

20. Deliver one-, two-, and three-step directions to the student. As the student demonstrates success in concentrating, increase the number of steps.

21. Highlight or underline important information the student is to read (e.g., directions, reading assignments, math word problems, etc.).

22. Have the student participate in games which require varying degrees of attention (e.g., tic-tac-toe, checkers, chess, etc.).

23. Reduce distracting stimuli in and around the student's desk (e.g., materials in the desk, on the desk, etc.).

24. Seat the student close to the source of information.

25. Tell the student what to listen for when being given directions, receiving information, etc.

26. Have the student make eye contact while delivering information to him/her.

27. Use a variety of modalities to communicate with the student (e.g., auditory, visual, tactile, etc.).

Goals:

1. The student will improve his/her short-term memory.
2. The student will improve his/her long-term memory.
3. The student will improve his/her understanding of abstract concepts (e.g., spatial relationships, directionality, classifications, generalizations).
4. The student will improve his/her visual memory.
5. The student will improve his/her auditory memory.
6. The student will improve his/her awareness and attention to information and activities in the environment.

Objectives:

1. The student will recognize similarities between people, places, things, and concepts with _____% accuracy.
2. The student will recognize differences between people, places, things, and concepts with _____% accuracy.
3. The student will match similarities of people, places, things, and concepts with _____% accuracy.
4. The student will match differences of people, places, things, and concepts with _____% accuracy.
5. The student will verbally or in written form identify similarities of people, places, things, or concepts with _____% accuracy.
6. The student will verbally or in written form identify differences of people, places, things, and concepts with _____% accuracy.

Interventions:

1. Make sure the student understands that all objects, people, ideas, actions, etc., can be grouped based on how they are alike. Provide the student with concrete examples.

2. Give the student pairs of objects and have the student name all the ways in which they are alike and then the ways in which they are different. Proceed from simple things which can be seen and touched to more abstract ideas which cannot be seen or touched.

3. Name a category or group and ask the student to identify as many things as possible which belong in the group. Begin with large categories (e.g., living things) and move to smaller categories (e.g., living things which are green).

4. Explain that each new word which is learned is an example of some category. When defining a word, it should first be put into a category (e.g., a hammer is a tool, anger is an emotion, etc.).

5. Present a series of objects and have the student create a category into which they fit.

6. Present a series of objects or words and have the student tell which ones do not belong in the same category as the others.

7. Give the student a list of words or pictures and have him/her identify the categories to which they belong. (Love and hate are both emotions. Love fits into the specific category of good feelings, and hate fits into the specific category of negative or unhappy feelings.)

8. Explain that words can be categorized according to many different attributes, such as size, function, texture, etc.

9. Ask the student to help make lists of some categories which fit inside larger categories (e.g., flowers, trees, and bushes are all categories which can be included in the plant category).

10. Play the game *I'm Thinking of an Object.* Describe an object and have the student guess the object based on questions he/she has asked about it.

11. Suggest that parents ask for the student's help when grocery shopping by having him/her make a list of items needed in a particular food group (e.g., dairy products, meats, etc.).

12. Have the student cut out pictures for a notebook of favorite foods, television shows, or other categories. The student can then group the pictures in accurate categories.

13. Use pictures, diagrams, wall-mounted board, and gestures when delivering information verbally.

14. Give the student specific categories and have him/her name as many items as possible within the categories (e.g., objects, persons, places, etc.).

15. Give the student a word and ask the student to list as many words as possible which have similar meanings (i.e., synonyms).

16. Make the subject matter meaningful to the student (e.g., explain the purpose of an assignment, relate the subject matter to the student's environment, etc.).

17. Stop at various points during the presentation of information to check the student's comprehension.

29 Has difficulty describing objects or events across several dimensions including category, function, composition, similarities/differences, and other attributes

Goals:

1. The student will improve his/her vocabulary skills (descriptive language).
2. The student will describe objects/events across several dimensions.

Objectives:

1. The student will demonstrate the ability to name members of a given category with _____ % accuracy.
2. The student will demonstrate the ability to name members of a category which contains at least two attributes with _____ % accuracy.
3. The student will demonstrate the ability to describe an object by comparing similarities and differences with _____ % accuracy.
4. The student will demonstrate the ability to describe an unseen object by at least four attributes with _____ % accuracy.
5. The student will identify the most prominent characteristics of an object with _____ % accuracy.
6. The student will demonstrate binary classification skills (e.g., These items are round. These items are not round.) in _____ out of _____ trials.
7. The student will categorize objects, pictures, or events by function, composition, etc., in _____ out of _____ trials.
8. The student will describe objects, pictures, or events across several specified dimensions in _____ out of _____ trials.
9. The student will spontaneously describe objects, pictures, or events across several dimensions in _____ out of _____ trials.

Interventions:

1. Have the student's hearing checked if it has not been recently checked.

2. Reinforce the student for describing objects or events across several dimensions: (a) give the student a tangible reward (e.g., classroom privileges, line leading, passing out materials, five minutes free time, etc.), or (b) give the student an intangible reward (e.g., praise, fist bump, smile, etc.).

3. Determine whether or not the student has a limited expressive and/or receptive vocabulary which would influence his/her ability to describe objects or events across several dimensions.

4. Have the student draw or cut out pictures to illustrate attributes of a noun across several dimensions (e.g., car - color: red/black/beige; function: to transport/race; size: small/medium/large; etc.).

5. Determine whether or not the student can supply specific descriptive information (e.g., category, function, composition, etc.) when asked leading questions even though he/she may not utilize the information during spontaneous descriptions.

6. Have the student divide objects, pictures, or cards that label objects, persons, places, etc., in the environment into different categories based on similar attributes (e.g., function, color, size, use, composition, etc.). Point out the similarities and differences between items as they change categories (e.g., a ball and an apple may both be red, round, and smooth; but you can only eat the apple.).

7. Reinforce those students in the classroom who use a variety of information when describing an object or event.

8. Make sure the student understands that all objects, people, ideas, actions, etc., can be grouped based on how they are alike. Provide the student with concrete examples.

9. Explain to the student how to classify new words according to various characteristics (e.g., size, function, composition, similarities/ differences, etc.) so he/she will have a way of storing the words in his/her memory.

10. Give the student pairs of objects and ask him/her to name all the ways in which they are alike and then the ways in which they are different. Proceed from simple things which can be seen and touched to more abstract ideas which cannot be seen or touched.

11. Name a category or group and ask the student to identify as many things as possible which belong in the group. Begin with large categories (e.g., living things) and move to smaller categories (e.g., living things which are green).

12. Explain that each new word which is learned is an example of some category (e.g., a hammer is a tool, anger is an emotion, etc.).

13. Present a series of objects or words and have the student tell which one does not belong in the same category as the others and why.

14. Present the student with a series of objects and have the student create categories into which they will fit. Encourage the student to verbalize attributes that the objects have in common.

15. Have the student arrange books according to attributes he/she chooses (e.g., color, height, subject, thickness, etc.).

16. Give the student a list of words and have him/her identify the categories into which the words belong (e.g., Love and hate are both emotions. Love fits into the smaller category of good feelings, and hate fits into the smaller category of negative or unhappy feelings.).

17. Ask the student to help make lists of some categories which fit inside larger categories (e.g., flowers, trees, and bushes are all smaller categories which can be included in the plant category).

18. Choose a peer to work with the student to improve his/her ability to describe objects and events across several dimensions.

19. Provide the student with an object or event to describe. Audio record his/her description and play it back to help him/her identify the types of descriptors he/she uses spontaneously (e.g., function, size, composition, category, etc.).

20. Give the student a list of words and ask him/her to tell the opposite of each word or provide as many synonyms or word associations as possible for each word to facilitate his/her descriptive abilities.

21. Discuss with parents the ways in which they can help the student develop an expanded vocabulary (e.g., encourage the student to read the newspaper, novels, magazines, or other materials; use a variety of information sources to facilitate descriptive abilities, etc.).

22. Send home new vocabulary words and encourage parents to use them in activities and general conversation.

23. Suggest that the parents ask for the student's help when grocery shopping by having him/her make a list of items needed in a particular food group (e.g., dairy products, meats, etc.).

24. Provide the student with several attribute categories to be targeted during the description of an object or an event (e.g., function, classification, composition, size, color, etc.). Have the student place a check under the appropriate attribute category each time he/she uses a descriptor from that category during his/her presentation.

25. Formulate activities for your class which require the description of objects:

- Have the student make a catalog of Earth Stuff for aliens who have never seen anything on our planet.
- Have the student practice sorting a box of junk by different attributes (e.g., color, function, size, composition, similarities/differences, etc.).
- Have the student play *I Spy* with an emphasis on naming multiple attributes of the object (e.g., I spy something red that is used with my thumb, is made of metal and plastic, etc.).
- Have the student construct a caterpillar with each segment being an attribute of the main word listed on the head.
- Have the student describe one of a pair of similar pictures to another student by using enough attributes that his/her classmate can choose the correct picture.
- Have the student study advertisements on TV, in the newspaper, etc., and identify the attributes that are represented throughout the advertisement. Have the student make his/her own commercial using as many attributes as possible.

26. Have the student provide information based on his/her five senses, (e.g., taste: delicious, yummy, bitter; feel: rough, bumpy, smooth; sight: pretty, beautiful, ugly; sound: loud, noisy, quiet; smell: fragrant, sweet, pungent). Emphasize the use of each sense to facilitate use of a variety of descriptors.

27. Facilitate the student's ability to describe objects based on their component parts by having him/her name all the parts of a common object in his/her environment (e.g., desk - top, drawer, legs, handles, pencil well, etc.). When the student gains proficiency in describing objects he/she can see, have him/her describe familiar objects that are not in the immediate environment (e.g., a school bus).

28. Have the student choose a favorite object or event and keep a running list of ways to describe it. Have the student continue to add descriptors to the list as he/she becomes more proficient with different attribute classifications.

29. Give the student specific categories and have the student name as many items as possible within the category.

30 Has difficulty pretending, role-playing, and imagining

Goals:

1. The student will improve his/her abstract thinking skills.
2. The student will demonstrate the ability to pretend, role-play, and imagine.

Objectives:

1. The student will differentiate between reality and fantasy in stories, movies, everyday situations, etc., in _____ out of _____ trials.
2. The student will demonstrate the ability to pantomime a verb with _____% accuracy.
3. The student will demonstrate the ability to act out a series of narrated actions with _____% accuracy.
4. The student will demonstrate the ability to role-play a character in a familiar story _____% of the time.
5. The student will imitate an adult or peer in an imaginative role in _____ out of _____ trials.
6. The student will create an imaginative role to act out in _____ out of _____ trials.
7. The student will demonstrate the ability to provide appropriate answers to what if questions with _____% accuracy.

Interventions:

1. Have the student practice repeating what you or another student has said while imitating inflectional patterns and facial expressions. Video record this activity and have the student analyze his/her success at this activity.

2. Provide the student with a wordless picture book and have him/her narrate the story.

3. Have the student draw a picture of himself/herself and narrate a story in which he/she is the main character.

4. Pair the student with a peer and have them take turns interviewing and being interviewed. This may be done with the students being themselves or pretending to be another person or fictitious character.

5. Have the student watch a video or television program. Have him/her tell what he/she thinks might have happened before or after the story.

6. Ask the student to provide pictures of himself/herself at various ages. Help the student to explain what his/her reactions to certain situations might have been at those particular ages. Then ask the student to guess what his/her reaction might be in ten years.

7. Have the student pantomime a sequence which has been printed on a piece of paper (e.g., opening a piece of candy, placing it in his/her mouth, discovering that it is sour).

8. Use puppets to retell a story or act out an activity. Have the student do the same by following your model.

9. Narrate a series of actions and have the student act them out as you do so (e.g., riding a bike, walking a dog, etc.). You may also want to pantomime a series of actions and have the student guess what you are doing.

10. Have the student identify an animal or an object from sounds on a recording (e.g., cat, lion, train, etc.) and act out the animal or object.

11. Have the student give answers to what if questions (e.g., What if you were ten feet tall? What if dinosaurs still roamed the earth?).

12. Have the student role-play being someone else in specific situations (e.g., talking on the phone, being a cashier in a grocery store, etc.).

13. Create a group activity in which students are to create rules for a fictitious society.

14. Use pictures/cartoons with captions removed and have the student develop his/her own captions.

15. Have the student's hearing checked if it has not been recently checked.

16. Have the student participate in a pantomime in which he/she makes a peanut butter sandwich, rides a horse, etc.

17. Set up fictitious situations in the classroom (e.g., restaurant, gas station, grocery store, etc.) and have the student role-play working in each situation. Have him/her change roles often.

18. Reinforce the student for pretending, role-playing, and imagining in appropriate situations: (a) give the student a tangible reward (e.g., classroom privileges, line leading, passing out materials, five minutes free time, etc.), or (b) give the student an intangible reward (e.g., praise, fist bump, smile, etc.).

19. Have the student place sequence cards in the appropriate order and explain the sequence. Have the student tell what might have happened before or after the provided sequence.

20. Have the student act out verbs (e.g., balancing, stumbling, eating, etc.).

21. Have the student answer questions as if he/she were someone else, a particular animal, etc.

22. Have the student take written messages to different persons in the school setting (e.g., librarian, school counselor, principal, etc.). Later, have the student deliver messages verbally.

23. Utilize short plays in the classroom setting with all students switching roles often.

24. Have the student imitate the facial expressions/activities of you or a peer and then reverse roles.

25. Reinforce those students in the classroom who demonstrate appropriate pretending, role-playing or imagining.

26. Evaluate the appropriateness of the task to determine (a) if the task is too easy, (b) if the task is too difficult, or (c) if the length of time scheduled to complete the task is adequate.

27. Have the student pantomime the function of an object such as a hairbrush, a hammer, a paintbrush, etc.

28. Help the student create and perform a short skit which revolves around a topic that is interesting to him/her.

31 Has difficulty retrieving, recalling, or naming objects, persons, places, concepts, etc.

Goals:

1. The student will improve his/her short-term memory.
2. The student will improve his/her long-term memory.
3. The student will improve his/her understanding of abstract concepts (e.g., spatial relationships, directionality, classifications, generalizations).
4. The student will improve his/her visual memory.
5. The student will improve his/her auditory memory.
6. The student will improve his/her awareness and attention to information and activities in the environment.

Objectives:

1. The student will recall or name objects, persons, places, etc., after they are presented and then removed with _____% accuracy.
2. The student will recall or name objects, persons, places, etc., at short intervals (10 to 15 minutes) with _____% accuracy.
3. The student will recall or name objects, persons, places, etc., at intervals of several hours with _____% accuracy.
4. The student will recall or name objects, persons, places, etc., at intervals of days or weeks with _____% accuracy.
5. The student will recall or name objects, persons, places, etc., with visual or verbal cues _____% of the time.
6. The student will independently recall or name objects, persons, places, etc., _____% of the time.

Interventions:

1. Have the student complete fill-in-the-blank sentences with appropriate words (e.g., objects, persons, places, etc.).

2. Present concepts following the *Who, What, Where, When, How,* and *Why* outline.

3. Have the student use a *Schedule of Daily Events* to recall assignments to be reviewed.

4. Have the student be a classroom messenger. Give the student a verbal message to deliver to another teacher, secretary, administrator, etc. As the student demonstrates success, gradually increase the length of the messages.

5. Reduce distracting stimuli (noise and motion) around the student (e.g., place the student on the front row, provide a carrel or quiet place away from distractions, etc.). This is used as a means of reducing distracting stimuli and not as a form of punishment.

6. Have the student compete against himself/herself by timing how fast he/she can name a series of pictured objects. The student tries to increase his/her speed each time.

7. Have the student listen and take notes following the *Who, What, Where, When, How,* and *Why* format when concepts are presented.

8. Have the student recall, at the end of the school day, three activities in which he/she participated during the day. As he/she demonstrates success, gradually increase the number of activities the student is required to recall.

9. Use multiple modalities (e.g., auditory, visual, tactile, etc.) when presenting instructional content.

10. Give the student specific categories and have him/her name as many items as possible within that category (e.g., objects, persons, places, etc.).

11. Give the student a choice of answers on worksheets (e.g., fill-in-the-blank, multiple-choice, etc.). This increases the student's opportunity for recognizing the correct answer.

12. Review daily those skills, concepts, tasks, etc., which have been previously introduced.

13. Reinforce the student for demonstrating accurate memory skills: (a) give the student a tangible reward (e.g., classroom privileges, line leading, passing out materials, five minutes free time, etc.) or (b) give the student an intangible reward (e.g., praise, fist bump, smile, etc.).

14. Reinforce the student for demonstrating accurate memory skills based on the length of time the student can be successful. As the student demonstrates success, gradually increase the length of time required for reinforcement.

15. When the student has difficulty with recalling information, remind the student that this can happen to everyone and not to be upset. Everyone has areas where they are weak and areas of strength as well.

16. Stop at various points during the presentation of information to check the student's comprehension.

17. Identify the student's most effective learning mode. Use it consistently to facilitate the student's understanding (e.g., if the student does not understand information verbally, present it in written form; if the student has difficulty understanding written information, present it verbally.).

18. Describe objects, persons, places, etc., and have the student name the items described.

19. Label objects, persons, places, etc., in the environment to help the student recall their names.

20. Use concrete examples and experiences in sharing information with the student.

21. Make the material meaningful to the student. Remembering is more likely to occur when the material is meaningful and can be related to real-life experiences.

22. Have the student prepare for tests using the *Who, What, Where, When, How*, and *Why* format.

23. Make sure the student has repetition of information through different experiences to facilitate his/her memory.

24. Have the student outline, highlight, underline, or summarize information he/she needs to remember.

25. Make sure the student is attending to the source of information (e.g., eye contact is being made, hands are free of materials, student is looking at the assignment, etc.).

26. Teach concepts through associative learning (i.e., build new concepts based on previous learning).

27. Help the student use memory aids to recall words (e.g., link a name to another word such as, Mr. Green is a colorful person).

28. Have the student take notes from classes, presentations, lectures, etc., to help him/her facilitate recall.

29. Have the student make notes, lists, etc., of things he/she needs to be able to recall. The student should carry these reminders with him/her.

30. Show the student an object or a picture of an object for a few seconds and then remove it. Ask the student to recall specific attributes (e.g., color, size, shape, etc.) of the object.

31. After a field trip or special event, have the student recall the activities which occurred.

32. Choose a peer to participate in memory activities with the student (e.g., memory games, flash cards, math facts, etc.).

33. Make sure the student receives information from a variety of resources (e.g., texts, discussions, films, slide presentations, etc.) to facilitate his/her memory/recall.

34. Encourage the student to play word games such as Hangman®, Scrabble®, Password™, etc.

35. Develop tests and quizzes for the student using the *Who, What, Where, When, How,* and *Why* format.

36. Teach the student to recognize key words and phrases related to information to facilitate his/her memory skills.

37. Have the student practice repetition of information to facilitate memory skills (e.g., repeating names, phone numbers, dates of events, etc.).

38. When the student is required to recall information, remind him/her of the situation in which the material was originally presented (e.g., Remember yesterday when we talked about . . .?, Remember when we were outside and I told you about the . . .?).

39. Give the student a series of words describing objects, persons, places, etc., and have him/her identify the opposite of each word.

40. Give the student a series of words (e.g., objects, persons, places, etc.) and have the student list all the words he/she can think of with similar meanings (i.e., synonyms).

41. Give the student a series of words or pictures and have him/her name the category to which they belong (e.g., objects, persons, places, etc.).

42. After reading a short story, have the student recall the main characters, the sequence of events, and the outcome of the story.

43. Provide opportunities for the student to overlearn material presented to facilitate being able to recall the information.

44. Have the student memorize the first sentence or line of a poem, song, etc. As the student experiences success, require him/her to memorize more lines.

45. Evaluate the appropriateness of the information to be recalled to determine (a) if the task is too difficult and (b) if the length of time scheduled to complete the task is adequate.

46. Teach the student how to organize information into smaller units (e.g., break a number sequence into small units - 132563 into 13, 25, 63).

47. Encourage the student to use semantic mapping techniques to facilitate visual memory.

48. Provide the student with verbal cues to stimulate recall of material previously presented (e.g., key words, a brief oral description, etc.).

49. Call on the student when he/she is most likely to be able to successfully respond.

50. Have the student audio record important information he/she should remember.

32   Has difficulty understanding analogies

Goals:

1. The student will improve his/her vocabulary skills.
2. The student will improve his/her critical thinking skills.
3. The student will demonstrate understanding and use of analogies.

Objectives:

1. The student will point to objects/pictures or perform actions which represent target vocabulary in _____ out of _____ trials.
2. The student will label objects/pictures or perform actions with appropriate target vocabulary in _____ out of _____ trials.
3. The student will demonstrate comprehension of analogies by stating the relationship between the first pair with _____ % accuracy.
4. The student will provide synonyms, antonyms, and homonyms for target vocabulary in _____ out of _____ trials.
5. The student will complete given analogies in _____ out of _____ trials.
6. The student will explain the relationships within given analogies in _____ out of _____ trials.
7. The student will demonstrate comprehension of analogies by completing actor/action analogies with _____ % accuracy.
8. The student will use analogies in structured oral/written work in _____ out of _____ trials.
9. The student will use analogies in everyday speaking situations in _____ out of _____ trials.
10. The student will correctly identify analogies when they occur in social studies, English, and science textbooks _____ % of the time.

Interventions:

1. Have the student's hearing checked if it has not been recently checked.

2. Reinforce the student for demonstrating comprehension of analogies: (a) give the student a tangible reward (e.g., classroom privileges, line leading, passing out materials, five minutes free time, etc.) or (b) give the student an intangible reward (e.g., praise, fist bump, smile, etc.).

3. Determine whether or not the student has a limited expressive and/or receptive vocabulary which would influence his/her ability to comprehend analogies.

4. Determine whether or not the student has difficulty with synonymous and opposite relationships or with classification across several dimensions. Proficiency in these areas will facilitate comprehension of analogies.

5. Use visual aids whenever possible to illustrate the relationships in analogies.

6. Have the student physically demonstrate the uses of objects while you point out the analogous relationship (e.g., An egg beater goes with an egg like a rolling pin goes with cookie dough. A screwdriver goes with a screw like a hammer goes with a nail.).

7. Have the student match pairs of objects that go together in similar ways (e.g., a big jar and a big lid with a little jar and a little lid), then remove one item and have the student identify what is missing.

8. Replace the terminology used in analogies (e.g., Dessert is to last as salad is to first.) with a typical sentence format (e.g., The dessert comes last and the salad comes _____.) to assess if the student's comprehension improves. Teach the student how to reword analogies in this manner.

9. Have the student complete worksheets for which he/she chooses the missing element in an analogy (e.g., dog is to bark as cat is to _____ or apple is to red as _____ is to yellow, etc.).

10. Choose a peer who understands analogies to work with the student to improve his/her comprehension and use of analogies. Have the students work together to solve analogies and develop their own analogies.

11. Have the class apply analogies to their personal experiences in their written and oral work.

12. Have the student produce analogies based on his/her five senses (e.g., taste: sugar is sweet just like a lemon is sour; feel: sandpaper is rough just like wax paper is smooth; sight: a bunny is cute just like a monster is ugly; sound: cymbals are loud just like a flute is soft; smell: a rose is fragrant just like garbage is pungent).

13. Have the student identify the relationship between the first two items in an analogy and then determine whether or not the second two items possess the same type of relationship. Point out that this type of relationship is necessary to produce an analogy.

14. Have the student identify the relationship between the first items of each pair and the second items of each pair in an analogy (e.g., Hammer is to pound as screwdriver is to turn - hammer and screwdriver are both tools; pound and turn are both actions). Point out that these types of relationships are necessary to produce an analogy.

15. Teach the meanings of terminology used in analogies (e.g., *as* means *is like*, *equals*, etc.; and *is to* means *goes with*, etc.).

16. Use analogies throughout the day in all subject areas to facilitate generalization of comprehension and use of analogies (e.g., World War II is to Germany as the Vietnamese War is to North Vietnam. The sap of a tree is analogous to the blood in your body. Multiplication is to division as addition is to subtraction.).

17. Reinforce those students in the classroom who demonstrate appropriate comprehension and use of analogies.

33 Has difficulty understanding cause-and-effect relationships

Goal:

1. The student will improve his/her understanding of cause-and-effect relationships.

Objectives:

1. The student will demonstrate the ability to understand causal words (e.g., if, when, after, before, unless , provided, although, since, until, as, though, etc.) with _____ % accuracy.
2. The student will demonstrate the ability to use causal words (e.g., if, when, while, after, before, unless, provided, although, since, until, as, though, etc.) in sentences with _____ % accuracy.
3. The student will be able to state reasons why an event occurred (e.g., The cup fell on the floor because it was too close to the edge of the table.) in _____ out of _____ trials.
4. The student will differentiate between logical and illogical conclusions in _____ out of _____ trials.
5. The student will be able to explain why a conclusion is logical or illogical in _____ out of _____ trials.
6. The student will spontaneously determine possible outcomes for daily events in _____ out of _____ trials.

Interventions:

1. Have the student's hearing checked if it has not been check in the past year.

2. Evaluate the appropriateness of the task to determine (a) if the task is too easy, (b) if the task is too difficult, or (c) if the length of time scheduled to complete the task is adequate.

3. Reinforce the student for demonstrating understanding of cause-and-effect relationships: (a) give the student a tangible reward (e.g., classroom privileges, line leading, passing out materials, five minutes free time, etc.) or (b) give the student an intangible reward (e.g., praise, fist bump, smile, etc.).

4. Reinforce those students in the classroom who demonstrate logical thinking and understanding of cause-and-effect relationships.

5. Have the student ask questions about directions, explanations, instructions, procedures, and/or concepts he/she does not understand.

6. Give the student responsibilities that require logical thinking (e.g., assign the student to water plants and provide him/her with a watering can and a glass telling him/her to use the more appropriate container).

7. Have the student develop rules and explain why each rule is necessary.

8. Each day provide the student with problem-solving situations which require understanding of cause-and-effect (e.g., You walk on thin ice and it begins to crack. What do you do?, You see smoke coming out of a neighbor's house and no one is home. What do you do?, etc.).

9. Make sure that the student experiences the consequences of his/her behavior (e.g., appropriate behavior results in positive consequences while inappropriate behavior results in negative consequences).

10. Provide the student with a list of questions, involving logic and cause-and-effect, which he/she answers verbally (e.g., Why do we post wet paint signs? Why do we have stop signs at intersections? Why do we wear seat belts?).

11. Have the student discuss the value of having materials and equipment properly organized, maintained, and serviced.

12. When something is broken, lost, etc., have the student identify what could have been done to prevent the situation as well as steps to resolve it.

13. Have the student explain outcomes, consequences, etc., (e.g., when the student earns a reward or privilege, make sure he/she can explain that it was the result of hard work and accomplishment).

14. Have the student respond to what if questions (e.g., What if it rained for forty days and forty nights?, What if there were no rules and laws?, etc.).

15. Relate what the student has learned in one setting or situation to other situations (e.g., vocabulary words learned should be pointed out in reading selections, math word problems, story writing, etc.).

16. Call attention to situations in the classroom which will generalize to future real-life situations (e.g., being on time for class is the same as being on time for work; school work not done during work time has to be made up before school, after school, or during recreational time, just as responsibilities at places of employment would have to be completed at night or on weekends if not completed on the job; etc.).

17. Have the student read stories involving a moral (e.g., *The Tortoise and the Hare*, *The Boy Who Cried Wolf*, etc.) and explain the reason for the outcome of the story.

18. Give the student situations/pictures and have him/her explain what variables are related (e.g., Snow is falling and the wind is blowing. Is the temperature hot or cold? What should you wear outdoors?).

19. Have the student sequence cartoon strips, after they have been cut apart and rearranged. Explain the cause-and-effect of the sequence created.

20. Give the student fill-in-the-blank statements requiring an appropriate response from multiple-choice possibilities (e.g., The boy threw the rock against the window, so the window _____ [opened, shut, broke].).

21. Have the student work with peers to brainstorm several solutions to a problem.

22. Use a variety of instructional approaches to help the student generalize knowledge gained to real-life situations (e.g., after studying the judicial system, provide a simulated courtroom trial).

23. Teach the student to define words/concepts in his/her own words. This skill builds comprehension and aids in generalization of decision-making skills.

24. Show the student pictures of dangerous situations and have him/her explain why they are dangerous (e.g., a child running into the street between parked cars, a child riding a bicycle without using his/her hands, etc.).

25. Use cause-and-effect relationships as they apply to nature and people. Discuss what led up to a specific situation in a story or picture, what could happen next, etc.

26. Make sure that the student can verbalize the reason for real-life outcomes of behavior (e.g., why the student had to leave the class line on the way to recess, why he/she earned the privilege of being line leader, etc.).

27. Have the student identify appropriate consequences for rules (e.g., consequences for following rules and consequences for not following rules). Have the student explain the choice of consequences he/she identified.

28. Have the student answer such questions as Why do we have rules? Why do you have to be a certain age before you can drive a car?, etc.

29. Have the student complete analogies (e.g., a garage is to a car as a house is to a _____).

30. Have the student answer a series of *who, what, when, why, how, how many*, and *how much* questions which gradually increase in complexity. Use material from the student's workbooks, literature books, etc., as well as questions which reflect the student's interest.

31. Create a problem-solving unit for the whole classroom. Place the student in a small group that will allow him/her to have ample opportunity for participation.

32. Comprehension of cause-and-effect requires that the student be able to ask himself/herself questions. Have the student ask questions related to his/her daily work and/or the daily schedule.

33. Encourage and model thinking out loud while planning.

34. Set aside time each day for a problem-solving game, discussion of cause-and-effect, analogies, decision-making activities, assigned responsibilities, etc.

35. Have the student(s) approach problem solving scientifically: state the problem, form a hypothesis, test the hypothesis, evaluate, and draw conclusions.

Goals:

1. The student will complete assigned tasks.
2. The student will improve his/her ability to remain on task.
3. The student will improve his/her awareness and attention to information and activities in the environment.

Objectives:

1. The student will work on a task for _____ out of _____ minutes per day.
2. The student will work on a task until completed on _____ out of _____ trials.
3. The student will attend to an activity for _____ minutes.
4. The student will attend to an activity until it is completed on _____ out of _____ trials.
5. The student will complete a task before going on to the next task on _____ out of _____ trials.

Interventions:

1. Evaluate the appropriateness of the task to determine (a) if the task is too easy, (b) if the task is too difficult, or (c) if the length of time scheduled to complete the task is adequate.

2. Choose a peer to help the student with class assignments.

3. Assess the degree of task difficulty in comparison with the student's ability to perform the task.

4. Assign the student shorter tasks (e.g., modify a math activity with 20 problems to 4 activities of 5 problems each, to be done at various times during the day). As the student demonstrates success, gradually increase the number of problems per activity and decrease the number of activities.

5. Present tasks in the most interesting manner possible.

6. Reduce distracting stimuli (e.g., place the student in the front row, provide a carrel or quiet place away from distractions). This is used as a means of reducing stimuli and not as a form of punishment.

7. Interact frequently with the student to maintain his/her involvement with class assignments (e.g., ask the student questions, ask the student's opinions, stand close to the student, seat the student near the teacher's desk, etc.).

8. Allow the student additional time to complete class assignments.

9. Supervise the student during class assignments to maintain on-task behavior.

10. Deliver directions verbally to facilitate the student understanding class assignments.

11. Repeat directions to facilitate the student's understanding of them.

12. Encourage the student to ask for clarification of directions for classroom assignments.

13. Follow a less desirable task with a highly desirable task. Make completion of the first task necessary to perform the second.

14. Give directions in a variety of ways to facilitate the student's understanding (e.g., if the student does not understand verbal directions, present them in written form).

15. Provide the student with step-by-step written directions for class assignments.

16. Structure the environment (e.g., seat the student close to the teacher's desk, seat the student near a peer who can provide assistance, etc.) in a way that provides the student with the increased opportunity for help or assistance.

17. Give the student alternative assignments. As those assignments are routinely performed, gradually introduce more components of the regular assignments.

18. Maintain consistent expectations within the ability level of the student.

19. Allow the student the option of performing the assignment at another time (e.g., earlier in the day, later in the day, on another day, at home, etc.).

20. Provide the student with a variety of assignments. Require him/her to select a minimum number from the total amount to complete (e.g., present the student with ten academic tasks from which he/she must finish six that day).

21. Maintain mobility to be frequently near the student to provide cues and prompts to assist the student in performing classroom assignments.

22. Make sure the student understands the natural consequences of not completing assignments (e.g., students who do not finish their work will not get to participate in more desirable activities).

23. Communicate with parents (e.g., notes home, phone calls, etc.) to share information about the student's progress. The parents may reinforce the student at home for completing assignments at school.

24. Modify the task assignment so the student will be able to complete the assignment during class time (e.g., individualize spelling lists by matching lists to the student's ability level).

25. Teach the student basic study skills (e.g., finding key words and phrases, underlining or highlighting important facts, identifying *Who, What, Where, When, How*, and *Why*, etc.).

26. Teach direction-following skills (e.g., key words in directions, use of sequential words in directions to perform steps such as first, then, next, etc.).

27. Have the student use a timer to facilitate completing tasks within a given period of time.

28. Have the student take notes following the *What, How, Materials*, and *When* format when directions are being given.

29. Present assignments following the *What, How, Materials*, and *When* format.

30. Maintain a consistent routine of daily activities.

31. Work a few problems with the student to help him/her begin an assignment.

32. Reinforce the student for beginning, working on, and completing assignments.

33. Choose a peer to model completion of assignments for the student.

34. Have the student question any directions, explanations, and instructions he/she does not understand.

35. Assess the quality and clarity of directions, explanations, and instructions given to the student.

36. Communicate clearly to the student the length of time he/she has to complete an assignment.

37. Communicate clearly to the student the date the assignment is to be completed.

38. Have the student time his/her assignments and monitor his/her pace to complete the assignment within the time limit.

39. Require the student to verbally repeat directions, explanations, and instructions he/she has read.

40. Provide the student with more than enough time to finish a task. As the student demonstrates success, gradually decrease the amount of time provided to complete a task.

41. Have the student repeat the oral directions to the teacher.

42. Provide the student with a *Schedule of Daily Events* so that he/she knows exactly what and how much there is to do in a day.

43. Prevent the student from becoming overstimulated by an activity (e.g., frustrated, angry, etc.).

44. Specify exactly what is to be done for the completion of a task (e.g., indicate definite starting and stopping points, indicate a minimum requirement, etc.).

45. Require the student to begin each assignment within a specified period of time (e.g., three minutes, five minutes, etc.).

46. Provide the student with shorter tasks given more frequently (e.g., give the student five math problems four times a day).

47. Provide clearly stated directions in written or verbal form. Make the directions as simple and concrete as possible.

48. Interact frequently with the student during an activity to help him/her follow directions for the assignments.

49. Provide alternatives for written directions (e.g., audio record directions, summarize directions, directions given by peers, etc.).

50. Have the student practice direction-following skills on nonacademic tasks.

51. Give directions in steps (e.g., give the student the next step after he/she completes the previous step).

52. Make sure the student achieves success when following directions.

53. Do not reward early completion of tasks. Hurrying to complete tasks may cause the student to fail to focus on the task.

54. Read directions, explanations, and instructions to the student when necessary.

55. Establish assignment rules:
- Listen to directions.
- Wait until all directions have been given.
- Ask questions about anything you do not understand.
- Begin assignment only when you are sure about what you are supposed to do.
- Make sure you have all the materials necessary.

56. Allow the student access to pencils, pens, etc., only after the directions for a task have been given.

57. Make sure the student is attending to the teacher when directions are given (e.g., making eye contact, hands free of writing materials, looking at the assignment, etc.).

58. Maintain visibility to and from the student to make sure the student is attending. The teacher should be able to see the student, and the student should be able to see the teacher. Make eye contact possible at all times.

59. Present one assignment at a time. As each assignment is completed, deliver reinforcement along with the presentation of the next assignment.

60. Provide the student with the opportunity to complete assignments/activities in a variety of ways (e.g., audio/video record, with a calculator, verbally, etc.).

61. Have the student explain to the teacher what he/she needs to do to complete an assignment.

62. Make sure that the reading demands of the assignment are within the ability level of the student.

63. Teach the student key words and phrases to look for when reading directions and instructions (e.g., key words such as circle, underline, match, etc.).

64. Audio record directions, explanations, and instructions to facilitate the student's success.

65. Shorten the length of assignments so the student can complete his/her assignments in the same amount of time as other students.

66. Provide the student with additional time to complete assignments if necessary, for the student to be successful.

67. When testing, make sure the student's knowledge of content is being assessed rather than the student's ability to read directions, instructions, and information.

68. Maintain mobility to be frequently near the student to provide reading assistance.

69. Have the student practice timed drills consisting of reading directions, explanations, information, etc., to reduce reading time.

70. Keep written directions as concise and concrete as possible.

71. Provide the student with a copy of written directions at his/her desk in addition to those on the wall-mounted board, posted in the classroom, etc.

72. Make sure that the print is large enough for the student to read to facilitate successful completion of the task.

73. As the student becomes successful, gradually increase the level of difficulty/complexity of written directions, explanations, instructions, information, etc.

74. Modify or rewrite the material presented to the student at his/her reading level.

75. Reduce the emphasis on competition. Competitive activities may make it difficult for the student to finish assignments because of frustration with reading difficulties.

76. Reinforce the student for focusing on/completing tasks based on the amount of work he/she can successfully complete. As the student demonstrates success, gradually increase the amount of completed work required for reinforcement.

77. Provide the student a quiet place (e.g., carrel, study booth, etc.) where he/she may go to engage in reading activities.

78. Write a contract with the student specifying what behavior is expected (e.g., attempting/completing class assignments) and what reinforcement will be made available when the terms of the contract have been met.

79. Reinforce the student for finishing assignments within a reasonable length of time for him/her. As he/she demonstrates success, gradually reduce the length of time available.

80. Choose a peer to read directions, explanations, and instructions to the student to facilitate the student's success.

81. Seat the student close to the source of written information (e.g., wall-mounted board, projector, etc.).

Goals:

1. The student will improve his/her skills.
2. The student will demonstrate the ability to use information learned from his/her mistakes to improve performance.
3. The student will improve his/her independent behavior.

Objectives:

1. The student will independently review concepts and pass a review with the teacher with _____%
accuracy.
2. The student will correct errors in written work on _____ out of _____ occasions.
3. The student will generalize information given or learned to problem-solving situations with _____ %
accuracy.
4. The student will generalize information learned to quizzes, tests, homework, etc., with _____%
accuracy.
5. With assistance, the student will demonstrate his/her ability to progress based upon his/her
experience on _____ out of _____ occasions.
6. The student will independently demonstrate his/her ability to progress based upon his/her
experience on _____ out of _____ occasions.

Interventions:

1. Provide the student with more than enough time to finish an activity. As the student demonstrates success, gradually decrease the amount of time provided to finish an activity.

2. Assign the student shorter activities. As the student demonstrates success, gradually increase the length of the activities.

3. Maintain a consistent daily routine in the classroom.

4. Maintain consistent expectations within the ability level of the student.

5. Provide the student with clearly stated expectations for all situations.

6. Identify expectations of different environments and help the student develop the skills to be successful in those environments.

7. Reduce distracting stimuli around the student (e.g., place the student on the front row, provide a carrel or quiet place away from distractions, etc.). This is used as a means of reducing stimuli and not as a form of punishment.

8. Evaluate the appropriateness of the task to determine (a) if the task is too easy, (b) if the task is too difficult, or (c) if the length of time scheduled to complete the task is adequate.

9. Reinforce those students in the classroom who improve skills, learn from their mistakes, etc.

10. Establish classroom rules:
- Concentrate while working.
- Work quietly.
- Remain in your seat.
- Finish task.
- Meet task expectations.

Review rules often. Reinforce students for following the rules.

11. Make sure the student is provided with an explanation of why he/she is learning particular information or skills (e.g., we learn to spell, read, and write to be able to communicate; we learn to solve math problems to be able to make purchases, use a checking account, measure, cook, etc.).

12. Reduce abstractions by giving concrete examples and firsthand experiences. Use simple demonstrations.

13. Relate what the student has learned in one setting or situation to other situations (e.g., vocabulary words learned should be pointed out in reading selections, math word problems, story writing, etc.).

14. Make sure the student's vision and hearing have been recently checked.

15. Have the student write letters, fill out applications, etc., to see the generalization of handwriting, spelling, grammar, sentence structure, etc., to real-life situations.

16. Provide the student with situations in which he/she can generalize skills learned in mathematics to simulations of the use of money (e.g., making change, financing a car, computing interest earned from savings, etc.).

17. Have the student question any directions, explanations, or instructions he/she does not understand.

18. Deliver all directions, questions, explanations, and instructions in a clear, concise manner and at an appropriate rate for the student.

19. Teach the student direction-following skills (e.g., stop doing other things; listen to what is being said; do not begin until all information is delivered; question any directions, explanations, and instructions you do not understand).

20. Make sure the student knows how to ask questions, ask for directions, etc.

21. Have the student be a peer tutor to teach a concept he/she has mastered to another student. This can serve as a reinforcement for the student.

22. Make sure the student has mastery of concepts at each level before introducing a new skill level.

23. Review daily those skills, concepts, tasks, etc., which have been previously introduced.

24. Identify the student's most effective learning mode. Use it consistently to facilitate the student's understanding (e.g., if the student does not understand directions or information given verbally, present it in written form; if the student has difficulty understanding written information or directions, present it verbally).

25. Use demonstrations along with the presentation of information.

26. Refer to previously presented related information when presenting a new concept.

27. Explain to the student (a) what he/she is doing wrong (e.g., failing to consider previous mistakes when completing a task) and (b) what the student should be doing (e.g., applying information learned from previous mistakes to current tasks).

28. Reinforce the student for improving his/her skills: (a) give the student a tangible reward (e.g., classroom privileges, line leading, five minutes free time, passing out materials, etc.) or (b) give the student an intangible reward (e.g., praise, fist bump, smile, etc.).

29. Teach the student study skills.

30. Have the student maintain a chart representing the number of tasks completed and the accuracy rate of each task.

31. Teach the student note-taking skills.

32. Deliver reinforcement for any and all measures of improvement.

33. Evaluate the appropriateness of tasks assigned if the student consistently fails to improve skills, learn from mistakes, etc.

34. Teach the student to practice basic study skills (e.g., reading for the main idea, note taking, summarizing, highlighting, studying in a good environment, using time wisely, etc.).

35. Monitor student performance to understand errors and determine where learning problems exist.

36. Reduce the emphasis on competition. Students who compete academically and fail to succeed may cease to try to do well and do far less than they are able.

37. Allow/require the student to make corrections after assignments have been checked the first time.

38. Maintain a consistent assignment format and expectations to avoid confusing the student.

39. Provide the student with evaluative feedback for assignments completed (e.g., identify what the student did successfully, what errors were made, and what should be done to correct the errors).

40. Provide frequent interactions and encouragement to support the student's confidence and optimism for success (e.g., You're doing great., Keep up the good work., I'm really proud of you., etc.).

41. Build varying degrees of difficulty into assignments to facilitate the student's self-confidence and at the same time provide a challenge (e.g., easier problems are intermingled with problems designed to measure knowledge gained).

42. Do not require the student to learn more information than he/she is capable of remembering at any time.

43. Provide the student with self-checking materials so he/she may check work privately and reduce the fear of public failure.

44. As soon as the student learns a skill, make sure that he/she applies it to a real-life situation (e.g., when the student learns to count by fives, have him/her practice adding nickels).

45. Explain to the student that he/she should be satisfied with his/her best effort rather than perfection.

46. Use a variety of instructional approaches to help the student generalize knowledge gained to real-life situations (e.g., after studying the judicial system, provide a simulated courtroom trial; etc.).

47. Use concrete examples and experiences when teaching concepts and sharing information with the student.

48. When the student is required to generalize knowledge from one situation to another, provide him/her with visual and/or auditory cues to help in remembering the information previously presented (e.g., provide key words, expose part of a picture, etc.).

49. Use pictures, diagrams, wall-mounted board, and gestures when delivering information verbally.

50. Use vocabulary that is within the student's level of comprehension when delivering explanations and information.

51. Use daily drill activities to help the student memorize math facts, sight words, etc.

52. Reinforce the student for adjusting his/her behavior based on the length of time the student can be successful. As the student demonstrates success, gradually increase the length of time required for reinforcement.

53. Communicate with parents (e.g., notes home, phone calls, etc.) to share information about the student's progress. They may reinforce the student at home for adjusting his/her behavior based upon experience. Encourage parents to reinforce their child for learning from experience.

54. Write a contract with the student specifying what behavior is expected (e.g., stopping a behavior when it is no longer acceptable) and what reinforcement will be made available when the terms of the contract have been met.

55. Have the student question any directions, explanations, or instructions he/she does not understand.

56. Explain to the student the benefits of best efforts of behavior adjustment based upon his/her mistakes and other previous experiences.

57. Establish time limits and provide the student with this information before the activity begins.

58. Specify exactly what is to be done for the completion of a task (e.g., establish definite starting and stopping points, a minimum requirement, etc.).

59. Have the student explain what he/she thinks should be done to correctly perform the activity.

60. When mistakes are behavioral in nature, introduce the student to his/her own unique set of trouble signals or red flags. Help him/her develop ways of coping with problematic situations (e.g., locating a quiet area to regain composure, counting to five silently, etc.). Reinforce the student for using these skills.

61. Structure time limits so the student knows exactly how long he/she has to work and when he/she must be finished.

62. Provide a transition period between activities so the student has time to adjust behaviors to meet new expectations and reflect upon the preceding activity. During transition, provide the student opportunities to rehearse his/her upcoming expectations.

63. Assign the student shorter activities. As the student demonstrates success, gradually increase the length of activities.

64. Maintain consistent expectations for routine community-based activities.

65. Whenever possible, allow natural consequences for success and failure in the teaching setting (e.g., make highly reinforcing activities contingent upon completion of less desirable tasks).

66. Make sure the student has all the materials he/she needs to perform the activity.

67. Have the student repeat the instructions verbally to the teacher.

68. Help the student with the first few items on a task. Gradually reduce the amount of help over time.

69. Allow the student the option of performing the assignment at another time (e.g., such as on another day) to minimize frustration with failure.

70. Prevent the student from becoming so stimulated by any event or activity that he/she cannot control his/her behavior.

71. Make sure the student assigns practical value to his/her ability to learn from mistakes.

72. Observe the student's current skill levels in the process of developing strategies to teach tasks. This will help minimize frustration and may help in the development of strategies for progressive tasks.

73. Incidentally teach and reinforce the process of learning from experience throughout the student's day.

74. Introduce the student to using a diary so he/she may recount daily experiences, including his/her successes and failures. Help the student develop consequences for both success and failure.

75. Build low-risk social and educational activities within the student's day in which he/she may learn from his mistakes.

76. Privately address the student about failures to minimize fear of failure and to maximize communication with the student.

77. Develop subsequent tasks based on the student's current errors and success rate rather than demanding immediate correction of work done incorrectly.

78. Reduce the emphasis on academic and/or social failure.

79. Assist the student in responding appropriately to redirection in academic situations (e.g., help the student correct one or two items to get him/her started).

80. Remove the student from an activity if he/she fails to respond appropriately to redirection in academic and social situations.

81. Rehearse with the student the steps he/she has decided to take to promote more successful task completion.

Goals:

1. The student will improve his/her ability to grasp concepts at a faster pace.
2. The student will improve his/her ability to understand abstract concepts.

Objectives:

1. The student will use visual cues to aid his/her ability to grasp concepts at a faster pace with _____% accuracy.
2. The student will use auditory cues to aid his/her ability to grasp concepts at a faster pace with _____% accuracy.
3. The student will use visual and auditory cues to aid his/her ability to grasp concepts at a faster pace with _____% accuracy.
4. The student will learn _____ new concepts per week.
5. The student will independently review concepts and pass a weekly review with the teacher with _____% accuracy.
6. The student will independently review concepts and pass a monthly review with the teacher with _____% accuracy.
7. The student will match pictures of abstract concepts (e.g., dimensionality, size, space, shape, etc.) with tangible representations with _____% accuracy.
8. The student will identify abstract concepts (e.g., dimensionality, size, space, shape, etc.), with visual and verbal cues, with _____% accuracy.
9. The student will identify abstract concepts (e.g., dimensionality, size, space, shape, etc.) independently with _____% accuracy.

Interventions:

1. Give the student fewer concepts to learn at one time. Spend more time on each concept until the student learns it correctly.

2. Choose a peer to spend time each day engaged in drill activities with the student.

3. Have the student use new concepts frequently throughout the day.

4. Have the student highlight or underline key words, phrases, and sentences from reading assignments, newspapers, magazines, etc.

5. Develop crossword puzzles which contain only the student's spelling words and have him/her complete them.

6. Write sentences, passages, paragraphs, etc., for the student to read which reinforce new concepts.

7. Have the student be a peer tutor to teach concepts just learned to another student.

8. Have the student review new concepts each day for a short period of time rather than two or three times per week for longer periods of time.

9. Use wall charts to introduce new concepts with visual images, such as pictures for the student to associate with previously learned concepts.

10. Initiate a *Learn a Concept a Day* program with the student and incorporate the concept into the assigned activities for the day.

11. Have the student use resources (e.g., encyclopedia, dictionary, etc.) to provide information to help him/her be successful when performing tasks.

12. Allow the student to use devices to help him/her successfully perform tasks (e.g., calculator, multiplication tables, dictionary, etc.).

13. Encourage the student to review new concepts each evening for a short period of time.

14. Provide the student with times throughout the day when he/she can participate in drill activities with the teacher, an aide, a peer, etc.

15. Provide the student with opportunities for drill activities in the most interesting manner possible (e.g., working with the computer, using a calculator, playing educational games, watching a film, listening to music, etc.).

16. Give the student a list of key words, phrases, or main points to learn for each new concept introduced.

17. Underline, circle, or highlight important information from any material the student is to learn (e.g., science, math, geography, etc.).

18. Provide the student with the information he/she needs to learn in the most direct manner possible (e.g., a list of facts, a summary of important points, an outline of important events, etc.).

19. Audio record important information the student can listen to as often as necessary.

20. Use computer software which provides repeated drill of general concepts and facts.

21. Use computer software which has the capability of programming the student's individual spelling words, facts, etc., for repeated drill and practice.

22. Use concrete examples in teaching the student new information and concepts.

23. Divide the sequence into units and have the student learn one unit at a time.

24. Make sure the student has adequate opportunities for repetition of information through different experiences to facilitate his/her memory.

25. Make sure the student receives information from a variety of sources (e.g., texts, discussions, films, etc.) to facilitate the student's memory/recall.

26. When a student is required to recall information, remind him/her of the situation in which the material was originally presented (e.g., Remember when we talked about . . .?).

27. Have the student listen and take notes for the *Who, What, Where, When, How*, and *Why* while concepts are presented.

28. Present concepts following the outline of *Who, What, Where, When, How*, and *Why*.

29. Have the student prepare for tests using the *Who, What, Where, When, How*, and *Why* system.

30. Develop tests and quizzes for the student using the *Who, What, Where, When, How*, and *Why* approach.

31. Label tangible objects in the classroom with signs that convey abstract concepts (e.g., larger, smaller, square, triangle, etc.).

32. Use concrete examples when teaching abstract concepts (e.g., numbers of objects to convey more than or less than, rulers and yardsticks to convey concepts of height or width, etc.).

33. Play *Simon Says* to facilitate the understanding of abstract concepts (e.g., find the largest desk, touch something that is a rectangle, etc.).

34. Conduct a scavenger hunt. Have the student look for the smallest pencil, tallest boy, etc., in the classroom.

35. Teach shapes using common objects in the environment (e.g., round clocks, rectangular desks, square tiles on the floor, etc.).

36. Provide repeated physical demonstrations of abstract concepts (e.g., identify things far away and close to the student, small box in a large room, etc.).

37. Evaluate the appropriateness of having the student learn abstract concepts at this time.

38. Teach abstract concepts (e.g., dimensionality, size, shape, etc.) one at a time before pairing the concepts.

39. Review daily those abstract concepts which have been previously introduced. Introduce new abstract concepts only after the student has mastered those previously presented.

40. When introducing abstract concepts, rely on tangible objects (e.g., boxes for dimensionality, family members for size, distances in the classroom for space, cookie cutters for shape, etc.). Do not introduce abstract concepts by using their descriptive titles such as square, rectangle, triangle, etc., without a tangible object.

41. Have the student match the names of abstract concepts (e.g., triangle, square, circle, etc.) with objects (e.g., floor tile, clock, etc.).

42. Give the student direction-following assignments (e.g., Go to the swing that is the farthest away. Go to the nearest sandbox.).

43. Choose a peer to spend time each day with the student pointing out abstract concepts in the classroom (e.g., the rectangle-shaped light switch plate, the round light fixture, the tallest girl, etc.).

44. Have the student question any directions, explanations, and instructions, he/she does not understand.

45. Have the student physically perform spatial relationships (e.g., have the student stand near the teacher, far from the teacher, over a table, under a table, etc.).

46. Call attention to spatial relationships which occur naturally in the environment (e.g., a bird flying over a tree, a squirrel running under a bush, etc.).

47. Practice, drill, and review every day.

48. For more abstract concepts (e.g., left and right; north south, east, and west), have the student follow simple map directions. Begin with a map of the school and progress to a map of the community, state, nation, etc., with more complex directions to follow.

49. Attach paper bands labeled left and right around the student's wrists. Remove the paper bands when the student can successfully identify left and right.

50. Use real coins and dollar bills, clocks, etc., to teach abstract concepts of money, telling time, etc.

51. Use a scale, ruler, measuring cups, etc., to teach abstract concepts using measurement.

52. Make sure to use the terms right and left as part of the directions you give to the student (e.g., refer to the windows on the left side of the room, the wall-mounted board on the right side of the room, etc.).

53. Have the student practice following directions on paper. Instruct the student to make a mark or picture on the right, left, middle, top, and bottom parts of the paper according to the directions given.

54. Avoid the problem of mirror image by standing next to the student when giving right and left directions.

55. Have the student sort left and right gloves, shoes, hand and foot paper cutouts, etc.

56. Relate what the student has learned in one setting or situation to other situations (e.g., vocabulary words learned should be pointed out in reading selections, math problems, story writing, etc.).

57. Make sure the student is attending to the source of information (e.g., eye contact is being made, hands are free of materials, etc.) when delivering directions that involve abstract concepts.

58. Do not require the student to learn more information than he/she is capable of remembering at any time.

59. Label abstract concepts throughout the classroom (e.g., triangle shapes and names on the walls, left and right sides of a desk, compass directions on the wall, etc.) to help the student understand abstract concepts.

60. Present assignments in small amounts (e.g., assign 10 problems, use pages removed from workbooks, etc.).

61. Provide parents with necessary information to help the student with homework and study activities at home.

62. Communicate with parents or guardians so they may help the student study for tests and quizzes (e.g., send home directions, explanations, and instructions relating to content covered on tests, quizzes, material to review, etc.).

63. Make available for the student a learning center area where a variety of information is available in content areas (e.g., the library may have a section with films, slides, video, recorded lectures, etc., on such subjects as Pilgrims, the Civil War, the judicial system, etc.).

37   Performs assignments carelessly

Goals:
1. The student will improve the accuracy of school assignments.
2. The student will improve the quality of school assignments.

Objectives:
1. The student will perform school assignments with _____% accuracy.
2. The student will check school assignments to correct errors on _____ out of _____ trials.
3. The student will turn in school assignments for the teacher to proofread and provide feedback for corrections and improvement on _____ out of _____ trials.
4. The student will redo corrected school assignments with _____% accuracy.
5. The student will have a peer check his/her school assignments and correct errors found on _____ out of _____ trials.

Interventions:

1. Provide the student with clearly stated criteria for acceptable work.

2. Speak with the student to explain (a) what he/she is doing wrong (e.g., turning in work that is illegible, messy, etc.) and (b) what he/she should be doing (e.g., taking time to complete assignments with care, taking time to proofread).

3. Write a contract with the student specifying what behavior is expected (e.g., improving the quality of work) and what reinforcement will be made available when the terms of the contract have been met.

4. Communicate with parents (e.g., notes home, phone calls, etc.) to share information about the student's progress. The parents may reinforce the student at home for improving the quality of his/her work at school.

5. Evaluate the appropriateness of the task to determine (a) if the task is too easy, (b) if the task is too difficult, or (c) if the length of time scheduled to complete the task is adequate.

6. Choose a peer to work with the student to model completing assignments accurately.

7. Allow the student to perform schoolwork in a quiet place (e.g., study carrel, library, resource room, etc.) to reduce distractions.

8. Assign the student shorter tasks while increasing the expectations for quality.

9. Supervise the student while he/she is performing schoolwork to monitor quality.

10. Have the student read/review his/her schoolwork with the teacher to become more aware of the quality of his/her work.

11. Provide the student with samples of work as models for acceptable quality. The quality of the student's work is to match the quality of the sample before he/she turns in the assignment.

12. Provide the student with additional time to perform schoolwork to achieve quality.

13. Teach the student steps for doing quality work (e.g., listen to directions, make sure directions are understood, work at an acceptable pace, check for errors, correct for neatness, copy the work over, etc.).

14. Recognize quality schoolwork (e.g., display the student's work, congratulate the student, etc.).

15. Conduct a preliminary evaluation of the student's assignment. Require him/her to make necessary corrections before turning in the work for a final grade.

16. Provide the student with the materials necessary to complete the assignment (e.g., pencil with eraser, paper, dictionary, handwriting sample, etc.).

17. Make sure that all educators who work with the student maintain consistent expectations for the quality of his/her work.

Goals:

1. The student will improve listening skills in academic settings.
2. The student will improve listening skills in nonacademic settings.
3. The student will attend more successfully to specific sounds in the environment.
4. The student will improve his/her awareness and attention to information and activities in the environment.

Objectives:

1. The student will maintain eye contact, when information is being communicated, _____% of the time.
2. The student will listen quietly, when verbal directions are given, _____% of the time.
3. The student will be able to repeat what is said to him/her with _____% accuracy.
4. The student will respond appropriately to what is said, with reminders, _____% of the time.
5. The student will independently respond appropriately to what is said to him/her _____% of the time.

Interventions:

1. Have the student's hearing checked if it has not been recently checked.

2. Speak to the student to explain (a) what he/she is doing wrong (e.g., failing to follow directions, explanations, and instructions) and (b) what he/she should be doing (e.g., following directions, explanations, and instructions).

3. Reinforce those students in the classroom who follow directions, explanations, and instructions.

4. Reinforce the student for listening based on the length of time the student can be successful. As the student demonstrates success, gradually increase the length of time required for reinforcement.

5. Write a contract with the student specifying what behavior is expected (e.g., following directions, explanations, and instructions) and what reinforcement will be made available when the terms of the contract have been met.

6. Have the student question any directions, explanations, and instructions he/she does not understand.

7. Determine which stimuli in the environment interfere with the student's ability to listen successfully. Reduce or remove those stimuli from the environment.

8. Remove the distracting stimuli in the student's immediate environment (e.g., books, writing materials, personal property, etc.).

9. Reduce visual and auditory stimuli in and around the classroom which interfere with the student's ability to listen successfully and follow directions (e.g., close the classroom door and windows, draw the shades, etc.).

10. Deliver information loudly enough to be heard by the student.

11. Deliver information to the student on a one-to-one basis. As the student demonstrates the ability to listen successfully, gradually include students in the group with him/her.

12. Maintain eye contact with the student when delivering information. As the student demonstrates the ability to listen successfully, gradually decrease the amount of eye contact.

13. Deliver information in a clear and concise manner.

14. Deliver information in both verbal and written form.

15. Maintain visibility to and from the student at all times to ensure that he/she is attending.

16. Evaluate the difficulty level of information presented to the student to determine if the information is presented at a level the student can understand.

17. Deliver a predetermined signal to the student (e.g., hand signal, turn lights off and on, etc.) prior to delivering information.

18. Make sure the student is not engaged in activities that interfere with directions, explanations, and instructions (e.g., looking at other materials, putting away materials, talking to others, etc.).

19. Ask the student to repeat or paraphrase information heard to determine successful listening.

20. Teach the student listening skills (e.g., have hands free of writing materials, clear desk of nonessential materials, attend to the source of information, etc.) to facilitate his/her ability to listen successfully.

21. Call the student by name prior to delivering information.

22. Verbally present information to the student that is necessary for his/her successful performance.

23. Have the student take notes when information is verbally presented.

24. Maintain a consistent format in which information is verbally presented.

25. Make sure that the student is seated close enough to see and hear the teacher when information is being delivered.

26. Present directions following the *What, How, Materials,* and *When* outline.

27. Have the student take notes following the *What, How, Materials,* and *When* format when directions are being given.

28. Seat the student close to the source of information in the classroom. As the student demonstrates success, gradually move him/her farther away from the source of information.

39 Requires slow, sequential, substantially broken-down presentation of concepts

Goals:

1. The student will improve his/her short-term memory.
2. The student will improve his/her long-term memory.
3. The student will improve his/her understanding of abstract concepts (e.g., spatial relationships, directionality, classifications, generalizations).
4. The student will improve his/her visual memory.
5. The student will improve his/her auditory memory.
6. The student will improve his/her awareness and attention to information and activities in the environment.
7. The student will improve his/her skills in logical thinking.

Objectives:

1. The student will understand what is said or presented to him/her at a slowed pace with _____% accuracy.
2. The student will maintain eye contact when information is being communicated _____% of the time.
3. The student will quietly listen when verbal directions are given _____% of the time.
4. The student will be able to repeat what is said or presented to him/her with _____ % accuracy.
5. The student will respond appropriately to what is said or presented, with prompting, with _____ % accuracy.
6. The student will independently respond appropriately to what is said or presented to him/her with _____% accuracy.

Interventions:

1. Use multiple modalities (e.g., auditory, visual, tactile, etc.) when presenting directions, explanations, and instructional content. Determine which modality is stronger and utilize that modality.

2. Use concrete examples of experiences in teaching concepts and sharing information with the students.

3. Review daily those skills, concepts, tasks, etc., which have been previously introduced.

4. Use pictures, diagrams, wall-mounted board, and gestures when delivering information verbally.

5. Reinforce the student for listening to what is said: (a) give the student a tangible reward (e.g., classroom privileges, line leading, five minutes free time, passing out materials, etc.) or (b) give the student an intangible reward (e.g., praise, fist bump, smile, etc.).

6. Have the student repeat or paraphrase what is said to him/her to determine what he/she heard.

7. Reinforce the student for listening carefully based on the length of time the student can be successful. As the student demonstrates success, gradually increase the length of time required for reinforcement.

8. Speak to the student to explain (a) what he/she is doing wrong (e.g., not listening carefully) and (b) what the student should be doing (e.g., listening carefully).

9. Evaluate the difficulty level of information verbally delivered to the student (i.e., information should be communicated on the student's ability level).

10. Have the student question any directions, explanations, and instructions he/she does not understand.

11. Give the student short directions, explanations, or presentations of concepts. As the student demonstrates success, gradually increase the length of the directions, explanations, or presentations of concepts.

12. Maintain a consistent format for the delivery of verbal instructions.

13. Make sure the student is attending to the source of information (e.g., making eye contact, hands free of writing materials, looking at the assignment, etc.).

14. Provide the student with written directions and instructions to supplement verbal directions and instructions.

15. Emphasize or repeat word endings, key words, etc.

16. Speak clearly and concisely when delivering directions, explanations, and instructions.

17. Place the student near the source of information.

18. Reduce distracting stimuli (e.g., noise and motion in the classroom) to facilitate the student's ability to listen successfully.

19. Stop at key points when delivering directions, explanations, and instructions to determine the student's comprehension.

20. Deliver directions, explanations, and instructions at an appropriate rate.

21. Identify a list of word endings, key words, etc., that the student will practice listening for when someone is speaking.

22. Deliver oral questions and directions that involve only one concept or step. As the student demonstrates success, gradually increase the number of concepts or steps presented in oral questions and directions.

23. Move the student away from other students who may interfere with his/her ability to attend to directions, explanations, and instructions.

24. Teach the student listening skills (e.g., listen carefully, write down important points, ask for clarification, wait until all directions are received before beginning, etc.).

25. Use demonstrations along with the presentation of information.

26. Visually scan all materials for new words. Use simple terms when possible. Teach new vocabulary and provide practice through application.

27. Give concrete examples and hands-on experiences to reduce abstractions.

28. Present a new concept by relating it to previously presented information.

29. Prepare or obtain manuals with simple definitions of technical vocabulary, simple vocabulary and sentence structure, step-by-step instructions, and diagrams or pictures.

30. Sequence known concepts with skills or concepts not mastered to facilitate the recognition of relationships to new skills and concepts.

31. Highlight or underline the important facts in reading material.

32. Rewrite instructions at an appropriate reading level for the student.

33. Present concepts using the student's most effective learning mode.

34. Provide the student with a written copy of material presented verbally.

35. Provide the student with a verbal presentation of material if he/she has difficulty with the written presentation of concepts.

36. Audio record the presentation of new concepts. Allow the student to listen to it as often as necessary.

37. Choose a peer to repeat the presentation of concepts to the student when he/she does not understand.

38. Have the student be a peer tutor to teach units of information he/she has mastered to another student.

39. Develop tests and quizzes for the student using the *Who, What, Where, When, How*, and *Why* format.

40. Have the student listen and take notes for *Who, What, Where, When, How*, and *Why* when concepts are presented.

41. Have the student take notes using semantic mapping techniques.

42. Provide the student with the information he/she needs (e.g., list of facts, a summary of important points, outline of important events, etc.) to facilitate learning.

43. Present concepts following the *Who, What, Where, When, How*, and *Why* outline.

40   Turns in incomplete or inaccurately finished assignments

Goals:

1. The student will complete classroom assignments during class time.
2. The student will turn in homework assignments.
3. The student will improve his/her academic task-related behavior.
4. The student will improve his/her academic performance.
5. The student will complete assignments with at least minimal accuracy.

Objectives:

1. The student will complete a task before going on to the next task on _____ out of _____ trials.
2. The student will complete _____ out of _____ assigned tasks per day.
3. The student will attempt _____ out of _____ assigned tasks per day.
4. The student will remain on task for _____ out of _____ minutes per class period.
5. The student will use the time provided to work on assigned tasks to complete _____ tasks per day.
6. The student will complete _____ out of _____ homework assignments each day.
7. The student will complete _____ out of _____ homework assignments each week.
8. The student will bring _____ out of _____ of his/her completed homework assignments to school and turn them in each day.
9. The student will bring _____ out of _____ of his/her completed homework assignments to school and turn them in each week.
10. The student will carry his/her homework assignments to and from school in a backpack to prevent their loss on _____ out of _____ trials.
11. The student will perform _____ out of _____ homework assignments at home and return them to school each day.
12. The student will perform _____ out of _____ homework assignments at home and return them to school each week.

Interventions:

1. Speak with the student to explain (a) what he/she is doing wrong (e.g., turning in work which is incomplete) and (b) what he/she should be doing (e.g., taking time to check for completeness of assignments).

2. Assess the appropriateness of the assignment for the student.

3. Provide the student with structure for all academic activities (e.g., specific directions, routine format for tasks, time limits, etc.).

4. Interact frequently with the student to monitor his/her task performance.

5. Have the student question any directions, explanations, and instructions he/she does not understand.

6. Choose a peer to accompany the student to specified activities to make sure the student has the necessary materials.

7. Provide the student with a list of necessary materials for each activity of the day.

8. Provide the student with an organizational system for beginning assignments (e.g., name on paper, numbers listed on left column, etc.).

9. Make sure that all educators who work with the student maintain consistent expectations for the completion of assignments.

10. Provide the student with assignment forms to facilitate completing assignments (e.g., provide blank number equations for word problems which the student fills in, etc.).

11. Provide the student with verbal reminders of materials required for each activity.

12. Provide the student with evaluative feedback for completed assignments: identify what the student did successfully, what errors were made, and what should be done to correct the errors.

13. Minimize the steps needed to complete assignments accurately.

14. Maintain a consistent format and expectation for assignments.

15. Do not grade every assignment completed by the student. Assignments may be used to evaluate student ability or knowledge and provide feedback. Grades may not need to be assigned until mastery/minimal accuracy has been attained.

16. Have the student verbally respond to tasks.

17. Have the student perform assignments, in which he/she might experience difficulty, in the resource room where the resource teacher can answer questions.

18. Provide the student with opportunities for reviewing assignments prior to grading them.

19. Arrange a time for the student to study with a peer tutor before completing an assignment to be graded.

20. Evaluate the appropriateness of the task to determine (a) if the task is too easy, (b) if the task is too difficult, or (c) if the length of time scheduled to complete the task is adequate.

21. Assign the student shorter tasks while increasing the expectations for quality.

22. Provide the student with clearly stated criteria for acceptable work.

23. Choose a peer to help the student with assignments.

24. Work the first few problems of an assignment with the student to make sure that he/she understands what to do, how to complete the assignment, etc.

25. Modify academic tasks (e.g., format, requirements, length, etc.).

26. Provide the student with clearly stated step-by-step written directions for homework so that someone at home may be able to provide assistance.

27. Make sure that homework assignments do not introduce new concepts but relate to concepts already taught.

28. Work through the steps of written directions as they are delivered to facilitate the student accurately following the directions.

29. Choose a peer to model turning in completed homework assignments for the student.

30. Meet with the student's parents to instruct them in appropriate ways to help their child with homework.

31. Choose a peer to model following written directions for the student.

32. Teach the student the steps of following written directions (e.g., read carefully, write down important points, ask for clarification, etc.).

33. Give directions in a variety of ways to facilitate the student's understanding (e.g., if the student does not understand written directions, present them verbally).

34. Allow the student additional time to complete and turn in assignments.

35. Repeat directions to facilitate the student's understanding of them.

36. Provide the student with written directions for doing assignments.

37. Maintain consistent expectations within the ability level of the student.

38. Maintain a consistent format for assigning homework (i.e., assign the same amount of homework each day).

39. Teach the student how to prioritize assignments (e.g., according to importance, length, due date, etc.).

40. Provide adequate time for the completion of activities.

41. Establish a minimum level of accuracy which will be accepted as a level of mastery.

42. Deliver reinforcement for any and all measures of improvement.

43. Do not expect mastery too soon after introducing new information, skills, etc.

44. Recognize quality schoolwork (e.g., display the student's work, congratulate the student, etc.).

45. Evaluate the appropriateness of tasks assigned if the student consistently fails to complete assignments with minimal accuracy.

46. Provide a time during the day when the student can receive assistance at school if he/she has difficulty completing homework assignments with minimal accuracy.

47. Make sure the assignments measure knowledge of content and not related skills such as reading or writing.

48. Have assignments read to the student.

49. Have the student read/review his/her schoolwork with the teacher to become more aware of the quality of his/her work.

50. Provide the student with samples of work as models for acceptable quality. The quality of the student's work is to match the quality of the sample before he/she turns in the assignment.

51. Provide the student with additional time to perform schoolwork to achieve quality.

52. Teach the student steps for doing quality work (e.g., listen to directions, make sure directions are understood, work at an acceptable pace, check for errors, correct for neatness, copy the work over, etc.).

53. Conduct a preliminary evaluation of the student's assignment. Require him/her to make necessary corrections before turning it in for a grade.

54. Provide the student with the materials necessary to complete the assignment (e.g., pencil with eraser, paper, dictionary, handwriting sample, etc.).

55. Provide the student with shorter assignments given more frequently. As the student demonstrates success, increase the length of the assignments and decrease the frequency.

56. Structure the environment (e.g., peer tutors, seat the student near the teacher or aide, etc.) in a way that provides the student with the increased opportunity for help or assistance on academic or homework tasks.

57. Provide the student with self-checking materials and require the student to make corrections before turning in assignments.

41   Confuses operational signs when working math problems

Goals:

1. The student will demonstrate knowledge of basic number concepts.
2. The student will improve his/her ability to recognize an addition sign.
3. The student will improve his/her ability to recognize a subtraction sign.
4. The student will improve his/her ability to recognize a multiplication sign.
5. The student will improve his/her ability to recognize a division sign.
6. The student will demonstrate the ability to solve problems involving fractions or decimals.

Objectives:

1. The student will recognize operational signs (e.g., +, -, ÷, x) with _____% accuracy.
2. The student will change from one math operation to another, when two operations are involved, with _____% accuracy.
3. The student will change from one math operation to another, when three operations are involved, with _____% accuracy.
4. The student will change from one math operation to another, when four operations are involved, with _____% accuracy.

Interventions:

1. Evaluate the appropriateness of the task to determine (a) if the task is too easy, (b) if the task is too difficult, or (c) if the length of time scheduled for the task is adequate.

2. Have the student practice recognizing operational symbols (e.g., flash cards of x, +, -, ÷).

3. Use a written reminder beside math problems to indicate which math operation is to be used (e.g., addition, subtraction, multiplication, division). As the student demonstrates success, gradually reduce the use of reminders.

4. Enlarge the math operation symbols next to the problems so the student will be more likely to observe the symbol.

5. Color-code math operation symbols next to math problems so the student will be more likely to observe the symbol.

6. Require the student to go through the math problems on each daily assignment highlighting or otherwise marking the operation of each problem before he/she begins to solve them.

7. Work the first problem or two of the math assignment for the student so he/she knows what operation to use.

8. Use a separate piece of paper for each type of math problem. As the student demonstrates success, gradually introduce different types of math problems on the same page.

9. Place the math operation symbols randomly around the room and have the student practice identifying the operation involved as he/she points to the symbol.

10. Provide the student with a math operation symbol reference sheet to keep and use at his/her desk (e.g., + means add, - means subtract, x means multiply, ÷ means divide).

11. At the top of each sheet of math problems, provide a math operational symbol reminder for the student (e.g., + means add, - means subtract, x means multiply, ÷ means divide).

12. Have the student practice matching math operation symbols to the word identifying the operation using flash cards (e.g., +, -, x, ÷; add, subtract, multiply, divide).

13. Have the student solve his/her math problems using a calculator.

14. Choose a peer to work with the student to provide reminders as the student solves his/her math problems.

15. Make sure the student knows why he/she is learning a math concept. Provide the student with concrete examples and opportunities for him/her to apply those concepts in real-life situations.

16. Have the student check his/her math assignments using a calculator to reinforce the memorization of math facts.

17. Do not require the student to learn more information than he/she is capable of learning at any time.

18. Provide operational sign practice using a computer software program or a hand-held educational device that gives immediate feedback to the student.

19. Make sure the student has mastery of math concepts at each level before introducing a new skill level.

20. Highlight operational signs to draw the student's attention to the signs before beginning the operation.

42   Does not make use of columns when working math problems

Goals:
1. The student will demonstrate knowledge of basic number concepts.
2. The student will demonstrate his/her knowledge of place value.

Objectives:
1. The student will recognize the ones place value with _____% accuracy.
2. The student will recognize the tens place value with _____% accuracy.
3. The student will recognize the hundreds place value with _____% accuracy.
4. The student will recognize the thousands place value with _____% accuracy.
5. The student will solve math problems using the ones place column with _____% accuracy.
6. The student will solve math problems using the tens place column with _____% accuracy.
7. The student will solve math problems using the hundreds place column with _____% accuracy.
8. The student will solve math problems using the thousands place column with _____% accuracy.
9. The student will work math problems from right to left with _____% accuracy.

Interventions:

1. Choose a peer to model the use of columns when working math problems for the student.

2. Develop a marked column format (e.g., /thousands/hundreds/tens/ones/) which can be copied from an original for the student to use in solving all assigned math problems.

3. Have the student exchange 10 pennies for a dime and correlate that activity with grouping ten ones and placing a 1 in the tens column and a 0 in the ones column.

4. Have the student practice labeling columns to represent ones, tens, hundreds, etc.

5. Have the student practice regrouping a number in different positions and determining its value (e.g., 372, 723, 237).

6. Have the student practice using columns when solving math problems by using a computer program which automatically chooses the correct column at input.

7. Have the student talk through math problems as he/she is solving them to identify errors he/she is making.

8. Have the student use a calculator to solve math problems involving the use of columns.

9. Make sure the student has the prerequisite skills to learn place value (e.g., counting verbally, understanding sets, writing numbers to 100, etc.).

10. Teach the student the concepts and terminology necessary to learn place value (e.g., set, column, middle, left, digit, etc.).

11. Teach the student why he/she is learning a math concept. Provide the student with concrete examples and opportunities for him/her to apply the concept in real-life situations.

12. Teach the student that math problems of addition, subtraction, and multiplication move from right to left beginning with the ones column.

13. Teach the student that the collective value of ten *ones* is equal to one *ten* and that ten *tens* is equal to one *hundred*.

14. Teach the student the zero concept in place value (e.g., there are no tens in the number 207 so a zero is put in the tens column).

15. Use money concepts to help the student learn place value by association (e.g., $1.26 is the same as six pennies or six ones, two dimes or two tens, one dollar or one hundred).

16. Provide practice with a computer software program or a hand-held educational device that gives immediate feedback to the student.

17. Provide the student with a masked window to help the student use columns accurately.

18. Provide the student with learning experiences in grouping tangible objects into groups of ones, tens, hundreds, etc.

19. Use vertical lines on graph paper to help the student visualize columns and put a single digit in each column.

20. Teach the student to place a number in the ones column and move to the left to the next column from ones to tens, hundreds, thousands, etc.

21. Use manipulative objects (e.g., base ten blocks, connecting links, etc.) to provide a visual image when teaching the student place value.

22. Provide the student with color-coded columns to help the student use columns accurately.

23. Reinforce the student for accurately using columns when solving math problems: (a) give the student a tangible reward (e.g., classroom privileges, line leading, passing out materials, five minutes free time, etc.) or (b) give the student an intangible reward (e.g., praise, fist bump, smile, etc.).

24. Provide the student with many opportunities to indicate the value of columns in multiple-digit numbers (e.g., 56= ( ) tens and ( ) ones; 329= ( ) hundreds, ( ) tens, and ( ) ones; etc.).

25. Require the student to check all his/her math assignments for accuracy. Reinforce the student for each correction made in the use of columns.

26. Provide the student with self-checking materials to reinforce the use of columns.

43   Does not remember math facts

Goals:

1. The student will demonstrate knowledge of basic number concepts.
2. The student will demonstrate the ability to recall math facts.

Objectives:

1. The student will add two numbers with sums of nine or less with _____% accuracy.
2. The student will solve subtraction problems of one-digit numbers with _____% accuracy.
3. The student will use a number line to solve simple addition problems involving the basic math facts with _____% accuracy.
4. The student will use a number line to solve simple subtraction problems involving the basic math facts with _____% accuracy.
5. The student will add two one-digit numbers with _____% accuracy.
6. The student will solve subtraction problems involving the basic math facts with _____% accuracy.
7. The student will solve addition problems with more than one column, not requiring regrouping, with _____% accuracy.
8. The student will solve subtraction problems with more than one column, not requiring regrouping, with _____% accuracy.
9. The student will multiply two one-digit numbers with _____% accuracy.
10. The student will solve division problems involving one-digit divisors and one-digit quotients with _____% accuracy.

Interventions:

1. Be sure addition and subtraction facts have been mastered before introducing multiplication and division facts.

2. Separate the basic addition and subtraction facts into sets. Require the student to memorize each set in succession.

3. Build upon and reinforce math facts the student has mastered. As the student demonstrates success, add one new fact at a time.

4. Choose a peer to drill the student each day on math facts (e.g., flash cards).

5. Choose one fact the student has not mastered and make it the student's fact of the day. Review it several times throughout the day.

6. Develop a math facts reference sheet for addition, subtraction, multiplication, or division for the student to use at his/her desk when solving math problems.

7. Develop and post basic addition, subtraction, multiplication, and division charts which the student can use in solving math problems.

8. Provide opportunities for the student to apply math facts in real-life situations (e.g., getting change in the cafeteria, measuring the length of objects in industrial arts, etc.).

9. Have students complete a math facts quiz sheet as they arrive each morning.

10. Have the student complete a math facts worksheet and use a calculator to check and correct the answers.

11. Have the student independently solve half of his/her math problems each day. Allow him/her to use a calculator to solve the other half of the assignment as reinforcement.

12. Have the student perform timed drills to reinforce basic math facts. The student competes against his/her own best times.

13. Have the student play a math facts game with other students. Let each student take turns answering and checking facts.

14. Have the student practice skip counting to reinforce multiplication facts (e.g., 5s: 5, 10, 15, 20, 25, 30, etc.).

15. Have the student use a calculator for drill activities of basic math facts.

16. Have the student use a calculator to reinforce memorization of math facts. Have the student solve several problems each day using a calculator.

17. Have the student use a number line attached to his/her desk to add and subtract.

18. Have the student use technological devices for math facts drill activities.

19. Review daily those skills, concepts, tasks, etc., which have been previously introduced.

20. If a student has difficulty memorizing facts, allow him/her to keep a chart of facts at his/her desk to use as a reference.

21. Provide practice and reinforcement of math facts using computer software programs that provide game-like activities.

22. Provide practice of math facts using a computer software program or a hand-held educational device that gives immediate feedback to the student.

23. Provide the student with many concrete experiences to help learn and remember math facts. Use popsicle sticks, tongue depressors, paper clips, buttons, etc., to form groupings to teach math facts.

24. Using the tracking technique to help the student learn math facts, present a few facts at a time. As the student demonstrates success, gradually increase the number of facts the student must memorize.

25. Reinforce the student for improving retention of math facts: (a) give the student a tangible reward (e.g., classroom privileges, line leading, passing out materials, five minutes free time, etc.) or (b) give the student an intangible reward (e.g., praise, fist bump, smile, etc.).

26. Have the student practice facts at home with flash cards, computer programs, or hand-held games.

27. Reduce the emphasis on competition. Competitive activities may cause the student to hurry and make mistakes when solving math problems.

28. Teach the student that subtraction facts are the inverse of addition facts. The same concept holds true for multiplication and division.

29. Use daily drill activities to help the student memorize math facts (e.g., written problems, flash cards, etc.).

30. Play class games to reinforce math facts (e.g., bingo, teacher-made games, etc.).

31. Use fingers to teach the student to form addition and subtraction combinations. Have the student hold up fingers and add or subtract other fingers to find the correct answer.

32. Do not require the student to learn more information than he/she is capable of learning at any time.

33. Use manipulative objects (e.g., peg board, base ten blocks, etc.) to provide a visual image when teaching the student basic math facts.

44 Does not understand abstract math concepts without concrete examples

Goals:

1. The student will demonstrate knowledge of basic number concepts.
2. The student will demonstrate his/her knowledge of abstract math concepts.
3. The student will demonstrate the ability to solve math word problems.

Objectives:

1. The student will demonstrate knowledge of one-to-one relationships of numbers to objects with _____% accuracy.
2. The student will use manipulatives to solve math problems with _____% accuracy.
3. The student will solve math problems independently and then check his/her work using manipulatives with _____% accuracy.
4. The student will solve math problems with verbal assistance and without manipulatives with _____% accuracy.
5. The student will solve math problems independently with _____% accuracy.

Interventions:

1. Choose a peer to provide concrete examples associated with each math problem (e.g., 9 minus 7 becomes 9 apples minus 7 apples) and assist the student in solving the math problems.

2. Evaluate the appropriateness of having the student learn abstract concepts at this time (i.e., Is it too difficult for the student?).

3. Have the student be a peer tutor and teach a concept he/she has mastered to another student. This can serve as reinforcement for the student.

4. Have the student draw pictures to illustrate math problems.

5. Have the student play games with colored chips with values assigned to each color to learn the concept of one, tens, etc.

6. Have the student practice the concept of regrouping by borrowing and carrying from manipulatives arranged in columns set up like math problems.

7. Have the student use sets of objects from the environment to practice addition, subtraction, multiplication, and division problems.

8. Have the student use concrete manipulatives in real-life situations (e.g., use measuring cups to prepare a recipe, use money to purchase items from the store).

9. Introduce abstract math concepts with a concrete example (e.g., use a liquid and measuring cups with ounces indicated to introduce liquid measurement).

10. Make sure all of the student's math problems have concrete examples associated with them (e.g., 9 minus 7 becomes 9 apples minus 7 apples, etc.).

11. Make sure the student has mastery of math concepts at each level before introducing a new skill level.

12. Do not require the student to learn more information than he/she is capable of learning at any time.

13. Teach the student why he/she is learning a math concept. Provide the student with concrete examples and opportunities for him/her to apply those concepts in real-life situations.

14. Use abstract concepts to describe tangible objects in the environment (e.g., larger, smaller, square, triangle, etc.).

15. Make it pleasant and positive for the student to ask questions about things he/she does not understand. Reinforce the student by assisting the student, congratulating, praising, etc.

16. Teach the student concepts such as square and cube separately. It may be confusing to introduce both concepts at the same time.

17. Introduce abstract symbols and terms after the student has worked with concrete manipulatives and mastered the concept (e.g., ounce - oz.; cup - c.; pint - pt.).

18. Provide physical objects to teach math concepts (e.g., provide the student with a yardstick when referring to a yard, etc.).

19. Provide repeated physical demonstrations of abstract concepts (e.g., identify things far away and close to the student, a small box in a large room, etc.).

20. Provide the student with clock stamps that he/she completes when practicing the concept of telling time.

21. Provide the student with computer software which uses graphics associated with math problems.

22. Work the first problem or two with the student explaining how to associate concrete examples with each problem (e.g., 9 minus 7 becomes 9 apples minus 7 apples).

23. Review daily previously introduced abstract concepts. Introduce new abstract concepts only after the student has mastery of those concepts previously presented.

24. Teach shapes using common objects in the environment (e.g., round clocks, rectangular desks, square tiles on the floor, etc.).

25. Teach the student abstract concepts (e.g., dimensionality, size, space, shape, etc.) one at a time before pairing the concepts.

26. Use a scale, ruler, measuring cups, etc., to teach math concepts using measurement.

27. Use actual coins, dollar bills, clocks, etc., to teach concepts of money, telling time, etc.

28. Use concrete examples when teaching abstract concepts (e.g., objects to convey more than, less than; rulers and yardsticks to convey height, width, etc.).

29. Have the student follow a recipe to make a treat for the class using measuring cups, teaspoons, etc.

30. Use the following steps when introducing an abstract concept:
- concrete - cups and liquid,
- practice - use cups to solve problems,
- abstract - word problems with cups,
- practice - prepare a recipe,
- review,
- test.

31. Provide the student with money stamps to solve money problems (e.g., penny, nickel, dime, etc.)

Goals:

1. The student will demonstrate knowledge of basic number concepts.
2. The student will demonstrate his/her knowledge of place value.
3. The student will improve his/her ability to solve addition, subtraction, multiplication, or division problems (choose one or more operations for the goal).

Objectives:

1. The student will demonstrate skip counting by adding manipulatives by 2s, 3s, 4s, 5s, etc., with _____% accuracy.
2. The student will use skip counting to add by 2s, 3s, 4s, 5s, etc., with _____% accuracy.
3. The student will be able to supply missing numbers in a skip counting series (e.g., 2, 4, 6, _____, 10, 12) with _____% accuracy.

Interventions:

1. Have the student count the value of nickels, dimes, quarters, etc., by adding repeated, equal increments.

2. Choose a peer to work with the student to help him/her understand the concept of skip counting.

3. Have the student use a number line when counting by 2s, 5s, 10s, etc., so he/she can see that the increments are being added.

4. Have the student count by 2s, 5s, 10s, etc., and write the numbers as he/she counts. The student can then go back to the numbers he/she has written and see that the increment used (e.g., 2, 5, 10, etc.) is added to each number.

5. Have the student use tangible objects (pennies, paper clips, etc.) when counting by 2s, 5s, 10s, etc., to see that the total number is increasing in equal increments.

6. Have the student use a calculator to do skip counting, adding 2, 5, 10, etc., to each successive number to see that skip counting increases by the increment used in counting.

7. Have the student use a clock in the classroom to count by 2s, 5s, 10s, etc.

8. Teach the student number concepts and the relationship of number symbols to number of objects before requiring him/her to solve math problems involving addition.

9. Provide the student with a number line on his/her desk to use as a reference for skip counting.

10. Teach the student why he/she is learning the concept. Provide the student with concrete examples and opportunities for him/her to apply the concept in real-life situations.

11. Use manipulative objects (e.g., base ten blocks, etc.) to provide a visual image when teaching the student the concept of skip counting.

12. Do not require the student to learn more information than he/she is capable of learning at any time.

13. Have the student practice a new skill or assignment alone or with an aide, the teacher, or a peer before attempting it with the entire group or before being graded on it.

14. Have the student be a peer tutor and teach a concept he/she has mastered to another student. This can serve as reinforcement for the student.

15. Provide skip counting practice using a computer software program or a hand-held educational device that gives immediate feedback to the student.

16. Make sure the student has mastery of math concepts at each level before introducing a new skill level.

46 Does not understand the concept of time

Goals:

1. The student will demonstrate knowledge of basic number concepts.
2. The student will demonstrate his/her knowledge of time.

Objectives:

1. The student will be able to tell time to the hour with _____% accuracy.
2. The student will be able to tell time to the half-hour with _____% accuracy.
3. The student will be able to tell time to the quarter-hour with _____% accuracy.
4. The student will be able to tell time to the minute with _____% accuracy.
5. The student will be able to name the days of the week in order with _____% accuracy.
6. The student will be able to name the months of the year in order with _____% accuracy.
7. The student will be able to identify the day, number, month, and year (e.g., Monday, the 26th of January, 2002) on a calendar with _____% accuracy.

Interventions:

1. Call on the student to indicate the time when the clock is on the hour, the half-hour, the quarter-hour, etc.

2. Have the student solve word problems involving time concepts on his/her ability level (e.g., At 10 minutes after 9 o'clock, you will begin walking to school. It takes 10 minutes to walk to school. What time will it be when you arrive?).

3. Have the student indicate when the clock in the classroom is on the quarter-hour.

4. Have the student indicate when the clock in the classroom is on the hour.

5. Have the student indicate when the clock in the classroom is on the half-hour.

6. Have the student learn to recognize one specific important time (e.g., time for lunch) and let the teacher know when the clock has reached that specific time.

7. Have the student recognize when events occur in the environment (e.g., recess at 10:15, lunch at 11:45, dismissal at 3:20, etc.).

8. Have the student set the hands on a clock as the teacher/tutor indicates times of the day.

9. Have the student work with a peer each day practicing skills required for telling time.

10. Allow the student to borrow a watch to wear during the school day while he/she is learning to tell time.

11. Make sure the student can count by common divisors of time (e.g., 1 minute, 5 minutes, 10 minutes, 15 minutes, 30 minutes, an hour, etc.).

12. Teach the student to read a digital clock or watch.

13. Provide the student with a clock face with hands to manipulate when learning to tell time.

14. Make sure there is a standard clock in the classroom for the student to use as a visual reference.

15. Do not require the student to learn more information than he/she is capable of at any time.

16. Teach the student the number of hours in a day, days in a week, weeks in a year, etc.

17. Teach the student why he/she is learning the concept of time. Provide the student with concrete examples and opportunities for him/her to apply the concept in real-life situations.

18. Teach the student all concepts involved in telling time (e.g., counting by 15s, 10s, 5s; the big hand and the little hand; etc.).

19. Teach the student the concept of the length of a minute, 5 minutes, 10 minutes, 15 minutes, 1 hour, 90 minutes, 24 hours, etc.

20. Teach the student the concepts of morning, afternoon, evening, and night.

21. Teach the student the terms used in telling time (e.g., a quarter 'til, half-past, ten 'til, a quarter after, etc.).

22. Use a large clock face to set the hands and have the student indicate the time. Begin with the hours, half-hours, quarter-hours, etc.

23. Provide practice telling time using a computer software program or a hand-held educational device that gives immediate feedback to the student.

24. Reinforce the student for telling time correctly: (a) give the student a tangible reward (e.g., classroom privileges, line leading, five minutes free time, passing out materials, etc.) or (b) give the student an intangible reward (e.g., praise, fist bump, smile, etc.).

25. Teach the student which seasons come before and after other seasons (i.e, the order of the seasons).

47   Fails to change from one math operation to another

Goals:

1. The student will demonstrate knowledge of basic number concepts.
2. The student will demonstrate the ability to change math operations, when solving problems.

Objectives:

1. The student will recognize math operation symbols with _____% accuracy.
2. The student will describe or demonstrate the operation required of math operation symbols with _____% accuracy.
3. The student will change from one math operation to another, with assistance (e.g., written and verbal cues), with _____% accuracy.
4. The student will change from one math operation to another independently with _____% accuracy.

Interventions:

1. Assess the quality and clarity of directions, explanations, and instructions given to the student.

2. Develop a math reference sheet for the student to keep at his/her desk (e.g., steps used in doing subtraction, multiplication, addition, and division problems).

3. Evaluate the appropriateness of the task to determine (a) if the task is too easy, (b) if the task is too difficult, or (c) if the length of time scheduled for the task is adequate.

4. Have the student check his/her math assignments using a calculator to reinforce the learning of math facts.

5. Have the student estimate math solutions before solving a problem as a tool for self-checking.

6. Have the student verbally explain the problem to a teacher, assistant, or peer before solving the problem.

7. Have the student practice recognizing series of math symbols (e.g., +, -, ÷, x).

8. Have the student solve math problems using a calculator.

9. Do not require the student to learn more information than he/she is capable of learning at any time.

10. Teach the student why he/she is learning a math concept. Provide the student with concrete examples and opportunities for him/her to apply those concepts in real-life situations.

11. Have the student talk through math problems as he/she solves them to identify errors he/she is making.

12. Make sure the student recognizes all math operation symbols (e.g., +, -, ÷, x).

13. Enlarge the math operation symbols so the student will be more likely to observe the symbols.

14. Provide math practice using a computer software program or a hand-held educational device that gives immediate feedback to the student.

15. Choose a peer to help the student solve math problems.

16. Provide the student with computer software or a hand-held educational device that requires him/her to solve a variety of math problems.

17. Provide the student with self-checking materials to reinforce solving problems correctly.

18. Recognize quality work (e.g., display the student's work, congratulate the student, etc.).

19. Reduce the amount of information on a page (e.g., fewer problems, less print, etc.) if it is causing visual distractions for the student.

20. Reduce the number of problems on a page (e.g., five problems to a page with the student required to do four pages of problems throughout the day).

21. Reinforce the student for correctly changing from one math operation to another: (a) give the student a tangible reward (e.g., classroom privileges, line leading, passing out materials, five minutes free time, etc.) or (b) give the student an intangible reward (e.g., praise, fist bump, smile, etc.).

22. Require the student to go through math assignments and highlight or otherwise mark the operation of each problem before beginning to solve the math problems.

23. Speak to the student to explain (a) what he/she is doing wrong (e.g., adding instead of subtracting) and (b) what he/she should be doing (e.g., adding addition problems, subtracting subtraction problems, etc.).

24. Teach the student direction-following skills: (a) listen carefully, (b) ask questions, (c) use environmental cues, (d) rely on examples provided, and (e) wait until all directions have been given before beginning.

25. Use a separate piece of paper for each math operation (i.e., place problems with the same operation on the same piece of paper). As the student demonstrates success, gradually introduce problems with different operations on the same page.

26. Use a written reminder beside each math problem to indicate which operation is to be used (e.g., division, addition, subtraction, etc.). As the student demonstrates success, gradually reduce the use of reminders.

27. Color-code the operation symbol for each math problem (e.g., make addition signs green, subtraction signs red, etc.). As the student demonstrates success, gradually reduce the use of color-coding.

28. Use visual cues (e.g., stop signs or red dots) on the student's paper when he/she must change operations. Have the student raise his/her hand when reaching stop signs and provide the student with instructions for the next problem.

29. Work the first problem or two of a math assignment for the student so he/she knows which operation to use.

48 Fails to correctly solve math problems involving fractions or decimals

Goals:
1. The student will demonstrate knowledge of basic number concepts.
2. The student will demonstrate the ability to solve problems involving fractions.
3. The student will demonstrate the ability to solve problems involving decimals.

Objectives:
1. The student will be able to recognize fractional values with _____% accuracy.
2. The student will be able to recognize decimal values with _____% accuracy.
3. The student will be able to solve addition problems involving fractions, which do not require regrouping, with _____% accuracy.
4. The student will be able to solve addition problems involving decimals, which do not require regrouping, with _____% accuracy.
5. The student will be able to solve subtraction problems involving fractions, which do not require regrouping, with _____% accuracy.
6. The student will be able to solve subtraction problems involving decimals, which do not require regrouping, with _____% accuracy.
7. The student will be able to solve multiplication problems involving fractions, which do not require regrouping, with _____% accuracy.
8. The student will be able to solve multiplication problems involving decimals, which do not require regrouping, with _____% accuracy.
9. The student will be able to solve simple division problems involving fractions, which do not require regrouping, with _____% accuracy.
10. The student will be able to solve simple division problems involving decimals, which do not require regrouping, with _____% accuracy.
11. The student will be able to solve long division problems involving fractions, which do not require regrouping, with _____% accuracy.
12. The student will be able to solve long division problems involving decimals, which do not require regrouping, with _____% accuracy.
13. The student will be able to solve addition problems involving fractions, which require regrouping, with _____% accuracy.
14. The student will be able to solve addition problems involving decimals, which require regrouping, with _____ % accuracy.
15. The student will be able to solve subtraction problems involving fractions, which require regrouping, with _____% accuracy.
16. The student will be able to solve subtraction problems involving decimals, which require regrouping, with _____% accuracy.
17. The student will be able to solve multiplication problems involving fractions, which require regrouping, with _____% accuracy.
18. The student will be able to solve multiplication problems involving decimals, which require regrouping, with _____% accuracy.
19. The student will be able to solve simple division problems involving fractions, which require regrouping, with _____% accuracy.
20. The student will be able to solve simple division problems involving decimals, which require regrouping, with _____% accuracy.
21. The student will be able to solve long division problems involving fractions, which require regrouping, with _____% accuracy.
22. The student will be able to solve long division problems involving decimals, which require regrouping, with _____% accuracy.

Interventions:

1. Teach the student that 8/8 equals a whole, 10/10 equals a whole, etc.

2. Choose a peer to work with the student on problems involving fractions or decimals.

3. Provide a variety of restaurant menus for the student to select items from for a meal. Have him/ her compute the cost of the items (each involving a decimal point).

4. Cut pieces of paper into equal numbers (e.g., fourths, sixths, tenths, etc.). Have the student add fractions together, subtract fractions, etc.

5. Develop a reference sheet for fractions and decimals for the student to keep at his/her desk.

6. For math problems involving fractions with unlike denominators, have the student use a tangible object such as a ruler to help him/her solve the problem (e.g., compare 3/4 to 7/8).

7. Have the student do rote counting by decimals (e.g., .2, .4, .6, .8, etc.).

8. Have the student do rote counting by fractions (e.g., 2/8, 4/8, 6/8, etc.).

9. Have the student earn a hypothetical income and solve money-related math problems using decimals (e.g., taxes, social security, savings, rent, food, clothing, auto payments, recreation, etc.). Match the level of difficulty to the student's ability level.

10. Have the student practice solving problems involving fractions and decimals using computer software.

11. Have the student solve fraction problems using real-life measurement such as ounces, inches, pounds, etc., to determine weight, length, volume, etc.

12. Have the student solve math problems involving decimals using tangible objects (e.g., two dollar bills and one fifty cent piece equals $2.50, etc.).

13. Have the student solve math problems involving decimals using tangible objects (e.g., pennies which are one-tenth of a dime, inch cubes which are one-twelfth of a foot, etc.).

14. Have the student solve math problems involving fractions using tangible objects (e.g., pennies which are one-tenth of a dime, inch cubes which are one-twelfth of a foot, etc.).

15. Have the student solve money problems to practice decimal problems.

16. Have the student use a calculator when learning to solve problems involving decimals.

17. Provide the student with a newspaper or catalog. Have him/her make a list of things advertised which he/she would like to purchase and then determine the total cost of the items he/she selected.

18. Do not require the student to learn more information than he/she is capable of learning at any time.

19. Teach the student why he/she is learning the concepts of factions and decimals. Provide the student with concrete examples and opportunities for him/her to apply these concepts in real-life situations.

20. Teach the student number concepts and the relationships of number symbols to numbers of objects before requiring him/her to solve math problems involving fractions and decimals.

21. Teach the student the concept of regrouping (e.g., changing mixed numerals into improper fractions, etc.).

22. Provide practice with fractions and decimals using a computer software program or a hand-held educational device that gives immediate feedback to the student.

23. Provide the student daily with a shopping list of items and a corresponding list with the cost of each item (each involving a decimal point). Have the student determine the total cost of his/her purchase.

24. Provide the student with enjoyable math activities involving fractions and decimals which he/she can perform for drill and practice either alone or with a peer (e.g., computer games, math games, manipulatives, etc.).

25. Provide the student with manipulatives which represent the fractions involved in solving a problem.

26. Reinforce the student for correctly solving problems involving fractions or decimals: (a) give the student a tangible reward (e.g., classroom privileges, line leading, passing out materials, five minutes free time, etc.) or (b) give the student an intangible reward (e.g., praise, fist bump, smile, etc.).

27. Provide the student with many concrete experiences to help him/her learn to use fractions and decimals (e.g., exchanging money, cutting pie-shaped pieces, measuring, weighing, telling time, etc.).

28. Provide the student with paper which has blank boxes and decimal points to guide the student to proper placement of decimal numbers when solving problems involving decimals.

29. Work the first few problems of the math assignment with the student to make sure that he/she understands/follows the directions and the operations necessary to solve the problems.

49 Fails to correctly solve math problems requiring addition

Goals:

1. The student will demonstrate knowledge of basic number concepts.
2. The student will demonstrate his/her knowledge of place value.
3. The student will improve his/her ability to solve addition problems.

Objectives:

1. The student will demonstrate understanding of number values to 100 with _____% accuracy.
2. The student will demonstrate understanding of number values above 100 with _____% accuracy.
3. The student will demonstrate understanding of place value with _____% accuracy.
4. The student will solve addition problems which do not require regrouping with _____% accuracy.
5. The student will solve addition problems requiring regrouping with _____% accuracy.

Interventions:

1. Give the student alternative math assignments. As the student demonstrates success, gradually introduce more components of the regular assignments.

2. Call on the student when he/she is most likely to be able to successfully respond.

3. Choose a peer to model how to solve addition problems for the student.

4. Deliver information to the student on a one-to-one basis or use a peer tutor.

5. Develop a math facts reference sheet for addition for the student to use at his/her desk when solving math problems.

6. Discuss and provide the student with a list of words and phrases which indicate an addition operation in word problems (e.g., together, altogether, sum, in all, both, gained, received, total, saved, etc.).

7. Evaluate the appropriateness of the task to determine (a) if the task is too easy, (b) if the task is too difficult, or (c) if the length of time scheduled for the task is adequate.

8. Provide opportunities for the student to apply addition facts in real-life situations (e.g., getting change in the cafeteria, measuring the length of objects in industrial arts, etc.).

9. Have the student be a peer tutor and teach a concept he/she has mastered to another student. This can serve as reinforcement for the student.

10. Have the student add numbers of objects. Have him/her then pair number symbols with the correct number of objects while he/she solves simple addition problems. As the student demonstrates success in solving simple addition problems, gradually remove the objects.

11. Have the student check all math work. Reinforce the student for each error he/she corrects.

12. Have the student independently solve half of his/her addition facts/problems each day. Allow him/her to use a calculator to solve the rest of the problems as reinforcement.

13. Have the student group objects into sets and then add the sets together to obtain a sum.

14. Have the student perform timed drills with addition math facts. The student competes against his/her own best time.

15. Have the student solve addition problems by manipulating objects and stating the process(es) involved.

16. Have the student talk through the math problems as he/she solves them to identify errors he/she is making.

17. Have the student use a calculator for drill of basic addition facts.

18. Have the student use a calculator to reinforce the process of addition. Have the student solve several addition problems each day using a calculator.

19. Provide the student with a number line attached to his/her desk to help solve addition problems.

20. Deliver all directions, questions, explanations, and instructions in a clear, concise manner and at an appropriate rate for the student.

21. Make sure that the language used to communicate with the student about addition is consistent (e.g., Add the numbers., What is the total?, or Find the sum., etc.).

22. Make sure the student has mastery of math concepts at each level before introducing a new skill level.

23. Do not require the student to learn more information than he/she is capable of learning at any time.

24. Teach the student the concepts of more than, less than, equal, and zero. The use of tangible objects should facilitate the learning process.

25. Teach the student why he/she is learning the concept of addition. Provide the student with concrete examples and opportunities for him/her to apply the concept in real-life situations.

26. Teach the student number concepts and the relationship of number symbols to numbers of objects before requiring him/her to solve math problems involving addition.

27. Provide practice of addition facts using a computer software program or a hand-held educational device that gives immediate feedback to the student.

28. Provide the student with a quiet place to work (e.g., office, study carrel, etc.). This is used as a means of reducing distracting stimuli and not as a form of punishment.

29. Provide the student with enjoyable math activities during free time in the classroom (e.g., computer games, math games, manipulatives, etc.).

30. Provide the student with increased opportunity for help or assistance on academic tasks (e.g., peer tutoring, directions for assignments sent home, frequent interactions, etc.).

31. Provide the student with many concrete experiences to help him/her learn and remember math facts. Use popsicle sticks, tongue depressors, paper clips, buttons, fingers, etc., to form groupings to teach addition facts.

32. Provide the student with opportunities for tutoring by peers or teachers. Allow the student to tutor others when he/she has mastered a concept.

33. Provide the student with self-checking materials. Require corrections to be made before turning in assignments.

34. Provide the student with shorter math tasks, but give more of them throughout the day (e.g., four assignments of five problems each rather than one assignment of twenty problems).

35. Reduce the emphasis on competition. Competitive activities may cause the student to hurry and solve addition problems incorrectly.

36. Reinforce the student for attempting and completing work. Emphasize the number or problems correctly solved. Encourage the student to see how many more he/she can correctly solve without help. Have the student maintain a private chart of his/her math performance.

37. Reinforce the student for correctly solving addition problems: (a) give the student a tangible reward (e.g., classroom privileges, line leading, passing out materials, five minutes free time, etc.) or (b) give the student an intangible reward (e.g., praise, fist bump, smile, etc.).

38. Have the student use graph paper to line up the numbers correctly in columns.

39. Teach the student to use resources in the environment to help him/her solve math problems (e.g., counting figures, counting numbers of objects, using a calculator, etc.).

40. Use daily drill activities to help the student memorize addition facts (e.g., written problems, flash cards, etc.).

41. Work the first problem or two of the math assignment with the student to make sure that he/she understands the directions and the operation necessary to solve the problems.

50 Fails to correctly solve math problems requiring division

Goals:

1. The student will demonstrate knowledge of basic number concepts.
2. The student will demonstrate his/her knowledge of place value.
3. The student will improve his/her ability to solve division problems.

Objectives:

1. The student will demonstrate understanding of number values to 100 with _____% accuracy.
2. The student will demonstrate understanding of number values above 100 with _____% accuracy.
3. The student will demonstrate understanding of place value with _____% accuracy.
4. The student will solve division problems which do not require regrouping with _____% accuracy.
5. The student will solve division problems requiring regrouping with _____% accuracy.

Interventions:

1. Give the student alternative math assignments. As the student demonstrates success, gradually introduce more components of the regular assignments.

2. Call on the student when he/she is most likely to be able to successfully respond.

3. Choose a peer to model how to solve division problems for the student.

4. Deliver information to the student on a one-to-one basis or use a peer tutor.

5. Develop a math fact reference sheet for division for the student to use at his/her desk when solving math problems.

6. Discuss and provide the student with a list of words and phrases which usually indicate a division operation in word problems (e.g., into, share, each, average, quotient, half as many, etc.).

7. Evaluate the appropriateness of the task to determine (a) if the task is too easy, (b) if the task is too difficult, or (c) if the length of time scheduled for the task is adequate.

8. Provide opportunities for the student to apply division facts in real-life situations (e.g., money, average length of time it takes to do a job, etc.).

9. Give the student several objects (e.g., one inch cubes, plastic links, etc.) and have him/her divide them into groups.

10. Have the student be a peer tutor and teach a concept he/she has mastered to another student. This can serve as reinforcement for the student.

11. Have the student check all math work. Reinforce the student for each error he/she corrects.

12. Have the student independently solve half of his/her math problems each day. Allow him/her to use a calculator to solve the other half of the assignment as reinforcement.

13. Teach the student to divide numbers of objects. Have the student pair number symbols with the number of objects while solving the division problem. In the last step, the student divides without using objects.

14. Have the student list all the skills necessary to work a division problem (e.g., subtraction, multiplication, etc.).

15. Have the student perform timed drills with division facts as reinforcement. The student competes against his/her own best time.

16. Have the student practice the division tables each day with a peer using flash cards.

17. Have the student solve math problems by manipulating objects and stating the process(es) involved.

18. Have the student talk through math problems as he/she solves them to identify errors he/she is making.

19. Have the student use a calculator for drill of basic division facts.

20. Have the student use a calculator to reinforce the process of division. Have the student solve several division problems each day using a calculator.

21. Identify specific division problems the student fails to correctly solve. Target those problems for additional instruction, tutoring, and drill activities.

22. Deliver all directions, questions, explanations, and instructions in a clear, concise manner and at an appropriate rate for the student.

23. Make sure that the language used to communicate with the student about division is consistent (e.g., Divide the numbers., What is the divisor?, What is the dividend?, etc.).

24. Make sure the student has mastery of math concepts at each level before introducing a new skill level.

25. Teach the student the concept of sets. Have the student practice dividing sets into two subsets, etc., to reinforce the concept of division.

26. Do not require the student to learn more information than he/she is capable of learning at any time.

27. Teach the student the concepts of more than, less than, equal, and zero. The use of tangible objects should facilitate the learning process.

28. Teach the student why he/she is learning the concept of division. Provide the student with concrete examples and opportunities for him/her to apply the concept in real-life situations.

29. Teach the student number concepts and the relationship of number symbols to numbers of objects before requiring him/her to solve math problems involving division.

30. Provide practice of division facts using a computer software program or a hand-held educational device that gives immediate feedback to the student.

31. Provide the student with a quiet place to work (e.g., office, study carrel, etc.). This is used as a means of reducing distracting stimuli and not as a form of punishment.

32. Provide the student with enjoyable math activities during free time in the classroom (e.g., computer games, math games, manipulatives, etc.).

33. Provide the student with increased opportunity for help or assistance on academic tasks (e.g., peer tutoring, directions for assignments sent home, frequent interactions, etc.).

34. Provide the student with many concrete experiences to help him/her learn and remember math facts. Use popsicle sticks, tongue depressors, paper clips, buttons, fingers, etc., to form groupings to teach division facts.

35. Provide the student with opportunities for tutoring by peers or teachers. Allow the student to tutor others when he/she has mastered a concept.

36. Provide the student with self-checking materials. Require corrections to be made before turning in assignments.

37. Provide the student with shorter math tasks, but give more of them throughout the day (e.g., four assignments of five problems each rather than one assignment of twenty problems).

38. Reduce the emphasis on competition. Competitive activities may cause the student to hurry and solve division problems incorrectly.

39. Reinforce the student for attempting and completing work. Emphasize the number of problems correctly solved. Encourage the student to see how many more he/she can correctly solve without help. Have the student maintain a private chart of his/her math performance.

40. Reinforce the student for correctly solving division problems: (a) give the student a tangible reward (e.g., classroom privileges, line leading, passing out materials, five minutes free time, etc.) or (b) give the student an intangible reward (e.g., praise, fist bump, smile, etc.).

41. Use practical applications of division. Have each student bring something that must be divided among the whole class.

42. Teach the student to use resources in the environment to help him/her solve math problems (e.g., counting figures, counting numbers of objects, using a calculator, etc.).

43. Use daily drill activities to help the student memorize division facts (e.g., written problems, flash cards, etc.).

44. Teach the student that any number divided by one remains that number.

45. Use task analysis on each problem to determine the point at which the student is unable to complete the calculations correctly.

46. Work the first problem or two of the assignment with the student to make sure that he/she understands the directions and the operation necessary to solve the problems.

51 Fails to correctly solve math problems requiring multiplication

Goals:

1. The student will demonstrate knowledge of basic number concepts.
2. The student will demonstrate his/her knowledge of place value.
3. The student will improve his/her ability to solve multiplication problems.

Objectives:

1. The student will demonstrate understanding of number values to 100 with _____% accuracy.
2. The student will demonstrate understanding of number values above 100 with _____% accuracy.
3. The student will demonstrate understanding of place value with _____% accuracy.
4. The student will solve multiplication problems which do not require regrouping with _____% accuracy.
5. The student will solve multiplication problems which require regrouping with _____% accuracy.

Interventions:

1. Give the student alternative math assignments. As the student demonstrates success, gradually introduce more components of the regular assignments.

2. Choose a peer to model how to solve multiplication problems for the student.

3. Call on the student when he/she is most likely to be able to successfully respond.

4. Deliver information to the student on a one-to-one basis or use a peer tutor.

5. Develop a math facts reference sheet for multiplication for the student to use at his/her desk when solving math problems.

6. Discuss and provide the student with a list of words and phrases which usually indicate a multiplication operation (e.g., area, each, times, product, double, triple, twice, etc.).

7. Evaluate the appropriateness of the task to determine (a) if the task is too easy, (b) if the task is too difficult, or (c) if the length of time scheduled for the task is adequate.

8. Have the student use a calculator for drill of basic multiplication facts.

9. Have the student check all math work. Reinforce the student for each error he/she corrects.

10. Have the student practice the multiplication tables each day with a peer using flash cards.

11. Have the student be a peer tutor and teach a concept he/she has mastered to another student. This can serve as reinforcement for the student.

12. Have the student count by equal distances on a number line. Demonstrate that the equal distances represent skip counting, which is the concept of multiplication.

13. Have the student independently solve half of his/her multiplication problems each day. Allow him/her to use a calculator to solve the other half of the assignment as reinforcement.

14. Have the student perform timed drills with multiplication facts as reinforcement. The student competes against his/her own best time.

15. Have the student solve multiplication problems by manipulating objects and stating the process(es) involved.

16. Have the student talk through math problems as he/she solves them to identify errors he/she is making.

17. Have the student use a calculator to reinforce the process of multiplication. Have the student solve several multiplication problems each day using a calculator.

18. Identify specific multiplication problems the student fails to correctly solve. Target those problems for additional instruction, tutoring, and drill activities.

19. Deliver all directions, questions, explanations, and instructions in a clear, concise manner and at an appropriate rate for the student.

20. Make sure the student has mastery of math concepts at each level before introducing a new skill level.

21. Do not require the student to learn more information than he/she is capable of learning at any time.

22. Teach the student why he/she is learning the concept of multiplication. Provide the student with concrete examples and opportunities for him/her to apply those concepts in real-life situations.

23. Teach the student number concepts and the relationship of number symbols to numbers of objects before requiring him/her to solve math problems involving multiplication.

24. Teach the student that multiplication is a way of adding that takes less time. Give examples of how much longer it takes to add than to multiply.

25. Practice skip counting by 2s, 3s, and 5s.

26. Provide practice of multiplication facts using a computer software program or a hand-held educational device that gives immediate feedback to the student.

27. Provide the student with a quiet place to work (e.g., office, study carrel, etc.). This is used as a means of reducing distracting stimuli and not as a form of punishment.

28. Provide the student with enjoyable math activities during free time in the classroom (e.g., computer games, math games, manipulatives, etc.).

29. Provide the student with increased opportunity for help or assistance on academic tasks (e.g., peer tutoring, directions for assignments sent home, frequent interactions, etc.).

30. Provide the student with many concrete experiences to help him/her learn and remember math facts. Use popsicle sticks, tongue depressors, paper clips, buttons, fingers, etc., to form groupings to teach multiplication facts.

31. Provide the student with opportunities for tutoring by peers or teachers. Allow the student to tutor others when he/she has mastered a concept.

32. Provide the student with self-checking materials. Require corrections to be made before turning in assignments.

33. Provide the student with shorter math tasks, but give more of them throughout the day (e.g., four assignments of five problems each rather than one assignment of twenty problems).

34. Reduce the emphasis on competition. Competitive activities may cause the student to hurry and solve multiplication problems incorrectly.

35. Reinforce the student for attempting and completing work. Emphasize the number of problems correctly solved. Encourage the student to see how many more he/she can correctly solve without help. Have the student maintain a private chart of his/her math performance.

36. Reinforce the student for correctly solving multiplication problems: (a) give the student a tangible reward (e.g., classroom privileges, line leading, passing out materials, five minutes free time, etc.) or (b) give the student an intangible reward (e.g., praise, fist bump, smile, etc.).

37. Have the student use graph paper to line up the numbers correctly in columns.

38. Teach the student that any number times one remains that number.

39. Teach the student that any number times zero will be zero.

40. Teach the student to use resources in the environment to help him/her solve math problems (e.g., counting figures, counting numbers of objects, using a calculator, etc.).

41. Use daily drill activities to help the student memorize multiplication facts (e.g., written problems, flash cards, etc.).

42. Work the first problem or two of the math assignment with the student to make sure that he/she understands the directions and the operation necessary to solve the problems.

52 Fails to correctly solve math problems requiring regrouping (i.e., borrowing and carrying)

Goals:

1. The student will demonstrate knowledge of basic number concepts.
2. The student will demonstrate his/her knowledge of place value.
3. The student will demonstrate the ability to solve math problems requiring regrouping.

Objectives:

1. The student will solve addition math problems which do not require regrouping with _____% accuracy.
2. The student will solve subtraction math problems which do not require regrouping with _____% accuracy.
3. The student will solve multiplication math problems which do not require regrouping with _____% accuracy.
4. The student will solve addition math problems requiring regrouping with _____% accuracy.
5. The student will solve subtraction math problems requiring regrouping with _____% accuracy.
6. The student will solve multiplication math problems requiring regrouping with _____% accuracy.

Interventions:

1. Choose a peer to model how to correctly solve math problems that require regrouping for the student.

2. Develop a math reference sheet for the student to keep at his/her desk (e.g., steps used in solving subtraction problems, addition problems, etc.).

3. Develop a regrouping reference sheet for the student to use at his/her desk when solving math problems which require regrouping.

4. Evaluate the appropriateness of the task to determine if the student has mastered the skills needed for regrouping.

5. Provide opportunities for the student to apply regrouping in real-life situations (e.g., getting change in the cafeteria, figuring how much items cost when added together while shopping, etc.).

6. Have the student check his/her math assignments using a calculator to reinforce the learning of math facts.

7. Have the student independently solve half of his/her math problems each day. Allow him/her to use a calculator to solve the other half of the assignment as reinforcement.

8. Have the student perform timed drills to reinforce regrouping. The student competes against his/her own best time and score.

9. Have the student play games using colored chips. Assign a value to each color to teach that a ten chip is equal to ten chips with a value of one.

10. Have the student practice the concepts of borrowing and carrying from graphic representations of sets.

11. Have the student practice the concept of regrouping by borrowing and carrying objects set up in columns like math problems.

12. Have the student raise his/her hand after completing several problems so the teacher can check his/her work before continuing.

13. Have the student solve math problems by manipulating objects to practice regrouping.

14. Have the student solve money math problems using pennies and dimes to practice regrouping.

15. Have the student talk through math problems as he/she solves them to identify errors he/she is making.

16. Have the student use Cuisenaire® rods when solving borrowing and carrying math problems.

17. Make sure that the language used to communicate with the student about regrouping is consistent (e.g., borrow, carry, etc.).

18. Provide the student with a number line on his/her desk to use as a reference.

19. Make sure the student has mastery of math concepts at each level before introducing a new skill level.

20. Do not require the student to learn more information than he/she is capable of learning at any time.

21. Teach the student the concepts of more than, less than, equal, and zero. The use of tangible objects should facilitate the learning process.

22. Teach the student number concepts and the relationship of number symbols to numbers of objects before requiring him/her to solve math problems involving regrouping.

23. Make sure the student understands the concept of place value and that problems are solved beginning with the ones column on the right and moving to the left.

24. Provide regrouping practice using a computer software program or a hand-held educational device that gives immediate feedback to the student.

25. Provide the student with learning experiences in grouping tangible objects into groups of ones, tens, hundreds, etc.

26. Provide the student with many concrete experiences to help him/her learn and remember regrouping skills. Use popsicle sticks, tongue depressors, paper clips, buttons, base ten blocks, etc., to form groupings to teach regrouping.

27. Provide the student with opportunities for tutoring by peers or teachers. Allow the student to tutor others when he/she has mastered a concept.

28. Provide the student with shorter math assignments, but give more of them throughout the day (e.g., four assignments of five problems each rather than one assignment of twenty problems).

29. Reduce the emphasis on competition. Competitive activities may cause the student to hurry and make mistakes when regrouping.

30. Reinforce the student for attempting and completing work. Emphasize the number of problems correctly solved. Encourage the student to see how many more he/she can correctly solve without help. Have the student maintain a private chart of his/her math performance.

31. Reinforce the student for correctly solving math problems that require regrouping: (a) give the student a tangible reward (e.g., classroom privileges, line leading, five minutes free time, etc.) or (b) give the student an intangible reward (e.g., praise, fist bump, smile, etc.).

32. Require the student to check addition problems using subtraction.

33. Require the student to check subtraction problems using addition (e.g., difference plus the subtrahend equals the minuend). Reinforce the student for each error he/she corrects.

34. Use daily drill activities to help the student with regrouping (e.g., written problems, flash cards, etc.).

35. Use manipulative objects (e.g., base ten blocks) to teach the student regrouping.

36. Work the first problem or two of the math assignment with the student to make sure that he/she understands directions and the operation necessary to solve the problems.

53 Fails to correctly solve math problems requiring subtraction

Goals:

1. The student will demonstrate knowledge of basic number concepts.
2. The student will demonstrate his/her knowledge of place value.
3. The student will improve his/her ability in subtraction.

Objectives:

1. The student will demonstrate understanding of number values to 100 with _____% accuracy.
2. The student will demonstrate understanding of number values above 100 with _____% accuracy.
3. The student will demonstrate understanding of place value with _____% accuracy.
4. The student will solve subtraction problems which do not require regrouping with _____% accuracy.
5. The student will solve subtraction problems requiring regrouping with _____% accuracy.

Interventions:

1. Give the student alternative math assignments. As the student demonstrates success, gradually introduce more components of the regular assignments.

2. Choose a peer to model how to solve subtraction problems for the student.

3. Call on the student when he/she is most likely to be able to successfully respond.

4. Deliver information to the student on a one-to-one basis or use a peer tutor.

5. Develop a math facts reference sheet for subtraction for the student to use at his/her desk when solving math problems.

6. Discuss and provide the student with a list of words and phrases which usually indicate subtraction operations (e.g., difference between, from, left, how many less, how much taller, how much farther, etc.).

7. Evaluate the appropriateness of the task to determine (a) if the task is too easy, (b) if the task is too difficult, or (c) if the length of time scheduled for the task is adequate.

8. Provide opportunities for the student to apply subtraction facts in real-life situations (e.g., getting change in the cafeteria, measuring the length of objects in industrial arts, etc.).

9. Have the student be a peer tutor and teach a concept he/she has mastered to another student. This can serve as reinforcement for the student.

10. Have the student check all math work. Reinforce the student for each error he/she corrects.

11. Have the student independently solve half of his/her subtraction problems each day. Allow him/her to use a calculator to solve the other half of the assignment as reinforcement.

12. Have the student subtract a certain number of objects from a group, then pair number symbols with the objects while the student solves the subtraction problem. In the last step, the student subtracts the number symbols without using objects.

13. Have the student perform timed drills with subtraction facts as reinforcement. The student competes against his/her own best times.

14. Have the student solve subtraction problems by manipulating objects and stating the process(es) involved.

15. Have the student talk through math problems as he/she solves them to identify errors he/she is making.

16. Have the student use a calculator for drill of basic subtraction facts.

17. Have the student use a calculator to reinforce the process of subtraction. Have the student solve several problems each day using a calculator.

18. Provide the student with a number line attached to his/her desk to help solve subtraction problems.

19. Deliver all directions, questions, explanations, and instructions in a clear, concise manner and at an appropriate rate for the student.

20. Make sure that the language used to communicate with the student about subtraction is consistent (e.g., Subtract the numbers., What is the difference?, etc.).

21. Make sure the student has mastery of math concepts at each level before introducing a new skill level.

22. Teach the student the concepts of more than, less than, equal, and zero. The use of tangible objects should facilitate the learning process.

23. Teach the student why he/she is learning a math concept. Provide the student with concrete examples and opportunities for him/her to apply those concepts in real-life situations.

24. Teach the student the concept of subtraction (e.g., You have three toys and I take away two of them. How many do you have left?).

25. Teach the student number concepts and the relationship of number symbols to numbers of objects before requiring him/her to solve math problems involving subtraction.

26. Provide subtraction practice using a computer software program or a hand-held educational device that gives immediate feedback to the student.

27. Provide the student with a quiet place to work (e.g., office, study carrel, etc.). This is used as a means of reducing distracting stimuli and not as a form of punishment.

28. Provide the student with enjoyable math activities during free time in the classroom (e.g., computer games, math games, manipulatives, etc.).

29. Provide the student with increased opportunity for help or assistance on academic tasks (e.g., peer tutoring, directions for assignments sent home, frequent interactions, etc.).

30. Provide the student with many concrete experiences to help him/her learn and remember subtraction facts. Use popsicle sticks, paper clips, fingers, etc., to form groupings to teach subtraction facts.

31. Provide the student with opportunities for tutoring by peers and teachers. Allow the student to tutor others when he/she has mastered a concept.

32. Provide the student with self-checking materials. Require corrections to be made before turning in assignments.

33. Provide the student with shorter math tasks, but give more of them throughout the day (e.g., four assignments of five problems each rather than one assignment of twenty problems).

34. Reduce the emphasis on competition. Competitive activities may cause the student to hurry and solve subtraction problems incorrectly.

35. Reinforce the student for attempting and completing work. Emphasize the number or problems correctly solved. Encourage the student to see how many more he/she can correctly solve without help. Have the student maintain a private chart of his/her math performance.

36. Reinforce the student for correctly solving subtraction problems: (a) give the student a tangible reward (e.g., class privileges, line leading, passing out materials, five minutes free time, etc.) or (b) give the student an intangible reward (e.g., praise, fist bump, smile, etc.).

37. Require the student to check subtraction problems using addition (i.e., the difference plus the subtrahend equals the minuend). Reinforce the student for each error he/she corrects.

38. Have the student use graph paper to line up the numbers correctly in columns.

39. Teach the student to use resources in the environment to help him/her solve math problems (e.g., counting figures, counting numbers of objects, using a calculator, etc.).

40. Use daily drill activities to help the student memorize subtraction facts (e.g., written problems, flash cards, etc.).

41. Do not require the student to learn more information than he/she is capable of learning at any time.

42. Work the first problem or two of the math assignment with the student to make sure that he/she understands the directions and the operation necessary to solve the problems.

Goals:
1. The student will demonstrate knowledge of basic number concepts.
2. The student will demonstrate his/her knowledge of place value.
3. The student will demonstrate the ability to solve math word problems.
4. The student will demonstrate the ability to apply math skills to the use of money.

Objectives:
1. The student will solve money problems involving coins, which do not require regrouping, with _____% accuracy.
2. The student will solve money problems involving coins, which require regrouping, with _____% accuracy.
3. The student will solve money problems involving dollars, which do not require regrouping, with _____ % accuracy.
4. The student will solve money problems involving dollars, which require regrouping, with _____ % accuracy.
5. The student will solve money problems involving dollars and coins, which do not require regrouping, with _____% accuracy.
6. The student will solve money problems involving dollars and coins, which require regrouping, with _____% accuracy.

Interventions:

1. Separate the basic addition and subtraction facts into sets to be memorized by the student.

2. Provide a variety of restaurant menus for the student to select items from for a meal. Have him/her compute the cost of the items.

3. Choose a peer to work with the student every day practicing coin values, paper money values, money combinations, etc.

4. Have the student use a calculator to reinforce solving problems involving money. Have the student solve several money problems each day using the calculator.

5. Have the student earn a hypothetical income and solve money-related math problems. The difficulty level of the problems should match the student's ability level (e.g., taxes, social security, savings, rent, food, clothing, auto payments, recreation, etc.).

6. Have the student match equal values of bills (e.g., five one-dollar bills to a five-dollar bill, two five-dollar bills to a ten-dollar bill, etc.).

7. Have the student match equal values of coins (e.g., two nickels to a dime, two dimes and a nickel to a quarter, five nickels to a quarter, etc.).

8. Have the student talk through money math problems as he/she solves them to identify errors he/she is making.

9. Provide the student with a newspaper or a catalog. Have him/her make a list of items advertised which he/she would like to purchase and then determine the total cost of the items he/she selected.

10. Provide the student with real money to simulate transactions in the classroom (e.g., purchasing lunch, groceries, snacks, clothing, etc.). Have the student practice acting as both a customer and a clerk.

11. Teach the student to count by ones, fives, tens, twenties.

12. Teach the student to count by pennies, nickels, dimes, quarters, half-dollars.

13. Teach the student to recognize all of the coins (e.g., penny, nickel, dime, quarter, half-dollar).

14. Make sure the student knows all the processes necessary to solve problems involving the use of money (e.g., the student can solve math problems of the same difficulty as those involving money).

15. Do not require the student to learn more information than he/she is capable of learning at any time.

16. Teach the student why he/she is learning the concept of money. Provide the student with concrete examples and opportunities for him/her to apply the concept in real-life situations.

17. Teach the student to recognize common denominations of paper money (e.g., one dollar bill, five dollar bill, ten dollar bill, twenty dollar bill, etc.).

18. Make sure the student understands all math operations involved in using money (e.g., addition, subtraction, multiplication, division, decimals, etc.).

19. Provide practice solving money problems using a computer software program or a hand-held educational device that gives immediate feedback to the student.

20. Review daily those skills, concepts, tasks, etc., which have been previously introduced.

21. Provide the student with math word problems involving the use of money. make sure the appropriate operation is clearly stated.

22. Reduce the emphasis on competition. Competitive activities may cause the student to hurry and make mistakes solving problems involving money.

23. Reinforce the student for correctly solving problems involving money: (a) give the student a tangible reward (e.g., classroom privileges, line leading, passing out materials, five minutes free time, etc.) or (b) give the student an intangible reward (e.g., praise, fist bump, smile, etc.).

24. Provide the student with a daily shopping list of items and a corresponding list of the cost of each item. Have the student determine the total cost of his/her purchase.

25. Use real coins when teaching the student coin recognition and values (e.g., count by ones, fives, tens, etc.; matching combinations of coins; etc.).

26. Provide real-life situations for the student to practice using money (e.g., paying for lunch in the cafeteria line, making purchases from book order clubs, purchasing a soft drink, etc.).

55   Fails to correctly solve problems using measurement

Goal:

1. The student will demonstrate the ability to apply math skills to solve problems involving measurement.

Objectives:

1. The student will solve math problems involving length (e.g., inches, feet, yards, or miles) with _____% accuracy.
2. The student will solve math problems involving liquid measurement (e.g., ounces, cups, pints, quarts, gallons, etc.) with _____% accuracy.
3. The student will solve math problems involving dry weight (e.g., ounces, pounds, or tons) with _____% accuracy.

Interventions:

1. Choose a peer to model solving measurement problems for the student.

2. Assign the student measurement activities that he/she will want to perform successfully (e.g., following a cooking recipe, building a model, etc.).

3. Call on the student when he/she is most likely to be able to successfully respond.

4. Develop a measurement reference sheet for the student to use at his/her desk when solving math problems involving measurement.

5. Discuss and provide the student with a list of words and phrases which usually indicate a measurement problem (e.g., pound, inches, millimeter, kilogram, etc.).

6. Evaluate the appropriateness of the task to determine (a) if the task is too easy, (b) if the task is too difficult, or (c) if the length of time scheduled for the task is adequate.

7. Provide opportunities for the student to apply measurement skills in real-life situations (e.g., cooking, measuring the length of objects, etc.).

8. Have the student begin solving problems using same and whole units of measurement (e.g., 10 pounds minus 8 pounds, 24 inches plus 12 inches, etc.). Introduce fractions and mixed units (e.g., pounds and ounces, etc.) only after the student has demonstrated success with same and whole units.

9. Have the student participate in a hands-on experience by following a simple recipe (e.g., gelatin, peanut butter cookies, etc.).

10. Have the student practice basic measurement skills (e.g., pound, ounce, inch, foot, etc.) using everyday measurement devices in the environment (e.g., scale, measuring cup, ruler, etc.).

11. Have the student practice measurement skills in the environment to find an item's length, weight, etc.

12. Have the student practice using smaller units of measurement to create larger units of measurement (e.g., twelve inches to make one foot, three feet to make one yard, eight ounces to make one cup, four cups to make one quart, etc.).

13. Have the student solve simple measurement problems using measurement devices before solving the problems on paper (e.g., five inches plus four inches using a ruler; three liquid ounces plus five liquid ounces using a measuring cup, etc.).

14. Have the student use a calculator to solve measurement problems, check the accuracy of problems worked, etc.

15. Let students use dry ingredients such as macaroni, beans, rice, etc., to measure fractions of a cup.

16. Make sure the language used to communicate with the student about measurement is consistent (e.g., meters, grams, etc.).

17. Make sure the student has mastery of math concepts at each level before introducing a new skill.

18. Do not require the student to learn more information than he/she is capable of learning at any time.

19. Make sure the student knows the basic concepts of fractions before requiring him/her to solve problems involving fractional measurement (e.g., ¼ inch, 1½ feet, etc.).

20. Teach the student why he/she is learning measuring concepts. Provide the student with concrete examples and opportunities for him/her to apply the concepts in real-life situations.

21. Provide practice solving measurement problems using a computer software program or a hand-held educational device that gives immediate feedback to the student.

22. Provide the student with enjoyable measurement activities during free time in the classroom (e.g., computer games, math games, etc.).

23. Reduce the emphasis on competition. Competitive activities may cause the student to hurry and make mistakes solving measurement problems.

24. Reinforce the student for correctly solving problems involving measurement: (a) give the student a tangible reward (e.g., classroom privileges, line leading, passing out materials, five minutes free time, etc.) or (b) give the student an intangible reward (e.g., praise, fist bump, smile, etc.).

25. Review daily those skills, concepts, tasks, etc., which have been previously introduced.

26. Work the first problem or two of the math assignment with the student to make sure that he/she understands directions and the operation necessary to solve the problem.

Goals:

1. The student will demonstrate knowledge of basic number concepts.
2. The student will demonstrate his/her knowledge of place value.

Objectives:

1. The student will recognize the ones place value with _____% accuracy.
2. The student will recognize the tens place value with _____% accuracy.
3. The student will recognize the hundreds place value with _____% accuracy.
4. The student will recognize the thousands place value with _____% accuracy.

Interventions:

1. Develop a math reference sheet for the student to keep at his/her desk (e.g., steps used in doing subtraction, multiplication, addition, and division problems).

2. Have the student check his/her math assignments using a calculator to reinforce learning math facts.

3. Have the student practice regrouping a number in different positions and determining its value (e.g., 372, 627, 721).

4. Have the student talk through math problems as he/she is solving them to identify place value errors the student is making.

5. Have the student use a calculator to reinforce learning math facts. Have the student solve several problems each day using a calculator.

6. Make sure the student has mastery of math concepts at each level before introducing a new skill level.

7. Make sure the student has the prerequisite skills to learn place value (e.g., counting, writing numbers to 100, etc.).

8. Do not require the student to learn more information than he/she is capable of learning at any time.

9. Teach the student the concepts and terminology necessary to learn place value (e.g., set, column, middle, left, digit, etc.).

10. Use manipulative objects (e.g., base ten blocks, connecting links, etc.) to teach the student place value and to provide a visual image.

11. Use vertical lines or graph paper to help the student visualize columns and put a single digit in a column.

12. Teach the student that addition, subtraction, and multiplication problems are worked from right to left beginning with the ones column.

13. Teach the student that the collective value of ten *ones* is equal to one *ten* and that ten *tens* is equal to one *hundred*.

14. Teach the student the zero concept in place value (e.g., there are no tens in the number 207 so a zero is put in the tens column).

15. Money concepts will help the student learn place value association (e.g., $1.26 is the same as six pennies or six ones; two dimes or two tens; one dollar or one hundred).

16. Provide practice with place value using a computer software program or a hand-held educational device that gives immediate feedback to the student.

17. Provide the student with concrete experiences to help him/her learn and remember math facts.

18. Provide the student with learning experiences in grouping tangible objects into groups of *tens, hundreds*, etc., (e.g., popsicle sticks, tongue depressors, paper clips, buttons, etc.).

19. Reduce the emphasis on competition. Competitive activities may cause the student to hurry and make mistakes solving math problems.

20. Have the student practice labeling columns to represent ones, tens, hundreds, etc.

21. Choose a peer to work with the student each day on place value activities (e.g., flash cards).

22. Teach the student why he/she is learning a math concept. Provide the student with concrete examples and opportunities for him/her to apply those concepts in real-life situations.

57   Fails to follow necessary steps in math problems

Goals:

1. The student will demonstrate his/her knowledge of place value.
2. The student will demonstrate knowledge of basic number concepts.
3. The student will improve his/her ability to follow the necessary steps in solving math problems.

Objectives:

1. The student will follow the necessary steps to solve addition problems not requiring regrouping with _____% accuracy.
2. The student will follow the necessary steps to solve addition problems requiring regrouping with _____% accuracy.
3. The student will follow the necessary steps to solve subtraction problems not requiring regrouping with _____% accuracy.
4. The student will follow the necessary steps to solve subtraction problems requiring regrouping with _____% accuracy.
5. The student will follow the necessary steps to solve multiplication problems not requiring regrouping with _____% accuracy.
6. The student will follow the necessary steps to solve multiplication problems requiring regrouping with _____% accuracy.
7. The student will follow the necessary steps to solve simple division problems with _____% accuracy.
8. The student will follow the necessary steps to solve long division problems with _____% accuracy.
9. The student will follow the necessary steps to solve math word problems with _____% accuracy.
10. The student will follow the necessary steps to solve math problems involving fractions with _____% accuracy.
11. The student will follow the necessary steps to solve math problems involving decimals with _____% accuracy.
12. The student will follow the necessary steps to solve math problems involving time with _____% accuracy.
13. The student will follow the necessary steps to solve math problems involving measurement with _____% accuracy.

Interventions:

1. Allow the student to use a calculator for math computation and emphasize the math process.

2. Assess the degree of task difficulty to determine whether or not the student will require additional information, time, assistance, etc., before beginning a math assignment.

3. Assign the student math problems which require the same operation to make it easier for the student to follow steps in solving the problems. As the student demonstrates success, introduce problems with a different operation.

4. Have the student circle each math problem's operation symbol before he/she solves any math problems.

5. Have the student ask for help when needed.

6. Use demonstration and hands-on learning when teaching new math skills.

7. Have the student write the name of the operation beside each word problem before he/she solves any math word problems. Check the student's choice of operations before he/she begins to solve the problems.

8. Color-code math operation symbols next to math problems so the student will be more likely to observe the symbol.

9. Develop a math reference sheet for the student to keep at his/her desk (e.g., steps used in doing subtraction, multiplication, addition, and division problems).

10. Have the student check his/her answers to math problems on a calculator.

11. Have the student be a peer tutor for another student who is learning new math concepts. Explaining the steps in basic math problems will help the student reinforce his/her own skills.

12. Have the student ask himself/herself questions (e.g., What is next?) to keep himself/herself focused on solving a problem.

13. Have the student repeat directions, explanations, and instructions after they have been given to reinforce retention.

14. Have the student question any directions, explanations, and instructions he/she does not understand before beginning a task to reinforce comprehension.

15. Have the student raise his/her hand after completing several problems so the teacher can check his/her work before continuing.

16. Have the student relate math problems to real-life situations so that he/she will better understand the steps involved in solving the problem (e.g., If I work 6 hours at $4.35 an hour, will I earn enough to buy 2 shirts which cost $12.99 each?).

17. Have the student talk through math problems as he/she is solving them to identify errors he/she is making.

18. Have the student verbally explain steps to the teacher for solving a math problem to check proper sequence of steps.

19. Have the student verbally state the steps required to complete a specific math operation (e.g., the steps in long division are ÷, x, -, bring down, etc.).

20. Have the student work math problems at the board so the teacher can see the steps being performed.

21. Have the student write down directions, explanations, and instructions after they have been given to reinforce retention.

22. Highlight the math symbol for each math problem using a highlight marker.

23. Have the student ask for help when needed. List the steps in solving math problems on the wall-mounted board, bulletin board, etc.

24. Provide sample problems, formulas, formats, etc., as references for solving math problems.

25. Make sure that your comments take the form of constructive criticism rather than criticism that can be perceived as personal, threatening, etc., (e.g., instead of telling the student he/she always makes the same mistake, suggest another way to avoid making the mistake).

26. Provide the student with a number line on his/her desk to use as a reference.

27. Make sure the student has mastery of math concepts at each level before introducing a new skill level.

28. Do not require the student to learn more information than he/she is capable of learning at any time.

29. Make sure the student recognizes all math operation symbols (e.g., x, -, +, ÷).

30. Teach the student the definitions of specific math vocabulary (e.g., sum, difference, quotient, product, etc.).

31. Enlarge the math operation symbols next to the problems so the student will be more likely to observe the symbol.

32. Use an overhead projector or wall-mounted board to model all steps required when solving a math problem.

33. Model the proper sequence of steps when solving math problems on the wall-mounted board or overhead projector before the student begins a new assignment.

34. Observe the student as he/she solves a math problem to identify and correct error patterns.

35. Pair the student with another student to solve math problems on the wall-mounted board and reinforce the proper sequence of steps.

36. Post necessary sequential information in a readily accessible location (e.g., bulletin board, desktop, inside the student's math folder, etc.).

37. Provide math activities that require active learning rather than memorization.

38. Provide math practice using a computer software program or a hand-held educational device that gives immediate feedback to the student.

39. Provide the student with a list to keep at his/her desk of the steps necessary for the problems he/she is attempting to solve.

40. Provide the student with a computer software program or a hand-held educational device that reinforces the correct sequence of steps in solving math problems.

41. Provide the student with written reminders of task sequences.

42. Place all math problems involving the same steps together on a single line, on a separate sheet of paper, etc.

43. Reduce the emphasis on competition. Competitive activities may cause the student to hurry and not follow the necessary steps in math problems.

44. Work the first problem or two of a math assignment with the student so he/she will know which steps to use.

45. Choose a peer to work with the student while he/she learns to follow the steps in solving math problems.

46. Teach and provide practice with different strategies to remember steps in a task:
- repetition,
- mnemonic,
- acronym, and
- association.

47. Use a separate piece of paper for each type (e.g., addition, subtraction, etc.) of math problem. As the student demonstrates success, gradually introduce different types of problems on the same page.

48. Use large colored arrows to indicate where the student should begin to work problems.

49. Have the student use vertical lines or graph paper to help him/her keep math problems in the correct columns.

50. Use visual cues (e.g., stop signs, red dots, etc.) to signal when the student must change operations while solving a multi-step math problem.

51. Use written reminders next to math problems to indicate which step is to be done. As the student demonstrates success, gradually reduce the use of reminders.

52. Use written/verbal repetition to aid the retention of information.

53. Evaluate the appropriateness of the task to determine (a) if the task is too easy, (b) if the task is too difficult, or (c) if the length of time scheduled for the task is adequate.

54. Reinforce the student for following the necessary steps in math problems: (a) give the student a tangible reward (e.g., classroom privileges, free homework pass, passing out materials, five minutes free time, etc.) or (b) give the student an intangible reward (e.g., fist bump, praise, smile, etc.).

58 Has difficulty grasping concepts involving time, space, quantity, quality, and directionality

Goal:

1. The student will improve his/her understanding of concepts.

Objectives:

1. The student will differentiate between appropriate and inappropriate concept words in statements involving time, space, quantity, quality, and/or directionality in _____ out of _____ trials.
2. The student will select the appropriate concept word in response to questions involving time, space, quantity, quality, and/or directionality in _____ out of _____ trials.
3. The student will identify and correct inappropriate concept words in sentences in _____ out of _____ trials.
4. The student will utilize appropriate concept words during structural language activities in _____ out of _____ trials.
5. The student will spontaneously utilize appropriate concept words in sentences in _____ out of _____ trials.
6. The student will utilize appropriate concept words during conversational speech in _____ out of _____ trials.

Interventions:

1. Have the student's hearing checked if it has not been recently checked.

2. Evaluate the appropriateness of the task to determine (a) if the task is too easy, (b) if the task is too difficult, or (c) if the length of time scheduled for the task is adequate.

3. Explain that it is important to understand concepts involving time, space, quantity, quality, and directionality because they are necessary for learning and communication.

4. Reinforce the student for demonstrating appropriate comprehension and use of concepts: (a) give the student a tangible reward (e.g., classroom privileges, line leading, passing out materials, five minutes free time, etc.) or (b) give the student an intangible reward (e.g., praise, fist bump, smile, etc.).

5. Have the student question any directions, explanations, and instructions he/she does not understand.

6. Have the student explain each step of directions in his/her own words. Repeating your directions exactly may not necessarily indicate the student's comprehension.

7. Review daily those spatial relationships which have been previously introduced.

8. Reinforce those students in the classroom who demonstrate appropriate comprehension and use of concepts.

9. Choose a peer to model appropriate comprehension and use of concepts for the student.

10. Choose a peer to practice concepts with the student through activities such as *Simon Says* or *Follow the Leader*.

11. Introduce spatial concepts individually before pairing the concepts.

12. Provide repeated physical demonstrations of spatial relationships.

13. Give the student a series of spatial relationship directions to follow (e.g., crawl under the table, stand near the closet, put the marker below the clock, etc.).

14. Provide the student with a variety of pictures representing spatial concepts. Have the student match the concepts which have similar and opposing relationships.

15. Emphasize spatial relationships which have particular meaning to the student (e.g., students who live near school walk and students who live far from school ride the bus).

16. Include spatial relationships in directions given to the student (e.g., Write your name on the dotted line., Keep your feet under your desk., etc.).

17. Introduce spatial concepts using concrete objects rather than actions.

18. Have the student follow simple map directions to practice more abstract concepts such as left and right; north, south, east and west, etc. Begin with a map of the school and progress to a map of the community, state, nation, etc., with more complex directions to follow.

19. Label areas and objects in the classroom with cards indicating spatial concepts (e.g., a light fixture labeled above; a rug labeled under; walls labeled north, south, east, west; etc.).

20. Teach the student relationships of left and right by placing paper bands labeled left and right around his/her wrists. Discontinue the paper bands when the student can successfully identify left and right.

21. Provide the student with a statement which includes an inaccurate spatial relationship. Have him/her identify the error and correct it.

22. Develop the concept of time by showing the student pictures of different seasonal events (e.g., holidays, swimming, ice skating, etc.) and have him/her match the appropriate season with the activity.

23. Have the student match pictures of clothing with the appropriate season.

24. Ask the parents to help facilitate the student's comprehension and use of concepts at home. The parents may praise the student when comprehension and/or use of concepts is demonstrated.

25. Provide drill work for series such as days of the week, seasons, and months of the year until the student's responses are automatic.

26. Teach the student that some concepts have multiple meanings (e.g., before can be a concept of time in before lunch or a concept of space in standing before the class).

27. Have the student play barrier games. Place a screen between two students so they cannot see each other's paper, objects, etc. Have one student give the other student directions (e.g., Mark an **x** below an **o**.). Check to see how accurately the instructions were followed.

28. Use the calendar every day to discuss with the student what he/she did yesterday, is doing today, or will do tomorrow.

29. Have the student identify a concept to master as a goal. As the student masters the correct use of the concept, put it on a list with a star and identify another concept to master.

30. Print the day's schedule on the board and refer to it frequently using words like before, after, etc.

31. Video the student and his/her classmates performing various actions. Play the recording without sound and have the student narrate the action using appropriate concept words (e.g., before, after, under, over, etc.). A prerecorded video could also be used for this activity.

32. Observe the class engaged in various activities and describe your observations using appropriate concept words. Have students also use concept words to describe various classroom activities.

33. Use groups of food to teach the concepts of few, some, most, least, etc. Let the student eat the food group which he/she describes accurately.

34. Teach the student the concepts of morning, afternoon, evening, etc.

35. Teach the student which season comes before and after other seasons.

36. Teach the student the progression of time from second to minute to hour, etc., and from day to week to month to year.

37. Use the terms right and left as part of the directions you give to the student (e.g., refer to the windows on the left side of the room, the wall-mounted board on the right side of the room, etc.).

38. Identify directions in the classroom with signs (e.g., label the ceiling up, label the floor down, etc.).

39. Have the student practice following directions on paper. Instruct the student to make a mark or picture on the right, left, middle, top, and bottom parts of the paper according to the directions given.

40. Avoid the problem of mirror image by standing next to the student when giving right and left directions.

41. Design an obstacle course using materials in the room. Students can step into the box, crawl over the desk, walk under the coat rack, stand on the table, etc.

42. Use concrete examples when teaching the concepts of up-down, high-low, above-below, etc. Use books, balls, regular classroom materials, etc., when trying to convey these concepts.

43. Hang directional signs in the room (e.g., turn left, games under cabinet, etc.).

44. Conduct scavenger hunts. Have the student look for a pencil in the desk, a book under the table, a glass on the chair, etc.

45. Have the student sort left and right gloves, shoes, hand and foot paper cutouts, etc.

46. Teach north, south, east, and west using the classroom, playground, school building, etc.

47. Have the student practice walking forward and backward, moving toy cars and trucks forward and backward, etc.

48. Have the student identify objects which move up and down (e.g., airplane, teeter-totter, etc.).

49. Point out doors which are labeled push and pull and activities which require pushing and pulling(e.g., opening drawers, opening doors, etc.).

50. Have the student find things that represent the concept of in and out (e.g., we pour milk in a glass and pour it out, we walk in a room and walk out, etc.).

51. Identify objects which represent over and under (e.g., a bridge is over water, people sleep under covers, birds fly over our heads, rugs are under our feet, etc.).

52. Teach the concept of above and below with examples in the classroom (e.g., the ceiling is above our heads and the floor is below our feet, etc.).

53. Teach the concept of before and after with examples from the student's daily routine (e.g., we wake up before we eat breakfast, we go to school after we eat breakfast, we eat lunch after we have morning recess, etc.).

54. Emphasize activities which require the action of off and on (e.g., We turn lights on for light and off when we do not need them. We turn the stove on to heat things and off when the food is hot. We put clothes on to go to school, leaves fall off a tree in the fall, etc.).

55. Call attention to spatial relationships which occur naturally in the environment (e.g., a bird flying over a tree, a squirrel running under a bush, etc.).

Goal:

1. The student will improve his/her ability to solve math word problems.

Objectives:

1. The student will demonstrate comprehension of key math vocabulary in _____ out of _____ trials.
2. The student will identify the key vocabulary and relevant information in word problems in _____ out of _____ trials.
3. The student will match math vocabulary with the process indicated in _____ out of _____ trials.
4. The student will restate word problems in his/her own words in _____ out of _____ trials.
5. The student will solve addition word problems not requiring regrouping with _____% accuracy.
6. The student will solve addition word problems requiring regrouping with _____% accuracy.
7. The student will solve word problems involving decimals with _____% accuracy.
8. The student will solve word problems involving fractions with _____% accuracy.
9. The student will solve word problems involving long division with _____% accuracy.
10. The student will solve word problems involving measurement with _____% accuracy.
11. The student will solve word problems involving more than one operation with _____% accuracy.
12. The student will solve word problems involving multiplication requiring regrouping with _____% accuracy.
13. The student will solve word problems involving simple multiplication with _____% accuracy.
14. The student will solve word problems involving simple division with _____% accuracy.
15. The student will solve word problems involving time with _____% accuracy.
16. The student will solve subtraction word problems not requiring regrouping with _____% accuracy.
17. The student will solve subtraction word problems requiring regrouping with _____% accuracy.

Interventions:

1. Make sure that it is not an inability to read that is the cause of the student's difficulty solving math word problems.

2. Have the student read the word problem silently and then aloud. Have him/her identify the mathematical operation required.

3. Provide short and concise word problems that require a one-step process.

4. Teach the student clue or key words to look for in word problems that indicate mathematical operations.

5. Have the student verbally analyze the steps that are required to solve word problems (e.g., What is given?, What is asked?, What operation(s) is used?, etc.).

6. Represent the numerical amounts presented in the word problems in concrete forms (e.g., problems involving money can be represented by providing the student with the appropriate amount of real or play money).

7. Have the student write a number sentence after reading a math word problem. (This process will help the student see the numerical relationship prior to finding the answer.)

8. Have the student create word problems for number sentences. Place the number sentences on the wall-mounted board and have the student tell or write word problems that could be solved by the number sentence.

9. Have the student restate math word problems in his/her own words.

10. Ask the student to identify the primary question that must be answered to solve a given word problem. Continue this activity using more difficult word problems containing two or more questions. Make sure the student understands that questions are often implied rather than directly asked.

11. Have the student write word problems involving specific operations. Have other students in the classroom solve these problems.

12. Supplement textbook problems with teacher-made problems that deal with classroom experiences and include students' names to make them more realistic and meaningful to the student.

13. Use word problems that are related to the student's experiences and are of interest to him/her.

14. Make sure the student reads through the entire word problem before attempting to solve it.

15. Teach the student to break down each word problem into specific steps.

16. Have the student make notes to set the word problem up in written form as he/she reads it.

17. Have the student simulate situations which relate to math word problems (e.g., trading, selling, buying, etc.).

18. Have the student solve word problems by manipulating objects and by stating the process(es) used.

19. Help the student recognize common patterns in word problems (e.g., how many, add or subtract, etc.).

20. Discuss words and phrases which usually indicate an addition operation (e.g., together, altogether, sum, in all, both, gained, received, total, won, saved, etc.). Provide the student with a list of those words and phrases.

21. Discuss words and phrases which usually indicate a subtraction operation (e.g., difference between, from, left, how many [more, less], how much [taller, farther, heavier], withdrawal, spend, lost, remain, more, etc.). Provide the student with a list of those words and phrases.

22. Discuss words and phrases which usually indicate a multiplication operation (e.g., area, each, times, product, double, triple, twice, etc.). Provide the student with a list of those words and phrases.

23. Discuss words and phrases which usually indicate a division operation (e.g., into, share, each, average, monthly, daily, weekly, yearly, quotient, half as many, etc.). Provide the student with a list of those words and phrases.

24. Teach the student to convert words into their numerical equivalents to solve word problems (e.g., two weeks = 14 days, one-third = 1/3, one year = 12 months, one quarter = 25 cents, one yard = 36 inches, etc.).

25. Teach the student math vocabulary often found in word problems (e.g., dozen, amount, triple, twice, etc.).

26. Allow the student to use a calculator when solving word problems.

27. Require the student to read math word problems at least twice before beginning to solve the problem.

28. Have the student begin solving simple word problems which combine a single operation with words such as:

$$\begin{array}{r} 7 \text{ apples} \\ \underline{\text{and} \quad 3 \text{ apples}} \\ \text{equals } 10 \text{ apples} \end{array}$$

As the student demonstrates success, gradually change the problems to a math word problem.

29. Present the student with phrases to be translated into number sentences (e.g., six less than ten equals or 10 - 6 =) before introducing word problems.

30. Choose a peer to model solving math word problems for the student.

31. Reduce the number of problems assigned to the student at one time (e.g., 5 problems instead of 10).

32. Demonstrate for the student how to solve math word problems by reading the problem and solving the problem on paper step-by-step.

33. Speak with the student to explain (a) what he/she is doing wrong (e.g., using the wrong operation, failing to read the problem carefully, etc.) and (b) what the student should be doing (e.g., using the appropriate operation, reading the problem carefully, etc.).

34. Evaluate the appropriateness of the tasks to determine (a) if the task is too easy, (b) if the task is too difficult, or (c) if the length of time scheduled to complete the task is adequate.

35. Correlate word problems with computation procedures just learned in the classroom (e.g., multiplication, operations with multiplication word problems, etc.).

36. Teach the student the meaning of mathematical terms (e.g., sum, dividend, etc.). Frequently review terms and their meanings.

37. Highlight or underline key words in math problems (i.e., reference to the operation involved, etc.).

38. Provide the student with a checklist to follow in solving math word problems (e.g., what information is given, what question is asked, what operation(s) is used).

39. Provide the student with a number line on his/her desk to use as a reference.

40. Teach the student why he/she is learning to solve math word problems. Provide the student with concrete examples and opportunities to apply these concepts in real-life situations.

41. Have the student talk through math word problems as he/she is solving them to identify errors the student is making.

42. Provide the student with a math reference sheet to keep at his/her desk (e.g., steps used in doing subtraction, multiplication, addition, and division problems).

43. Have the student check his/her word problems using a calculator to reinforce the learning of math facts.

44. Teach the student the concepts of more than, less than, equal to, and zero. The use of tangible objects should facilitate the learning process.

45. Do not require the student to learn more information than he/she is capable of learning at any time.

46. Have the student be a peer tutor and teach a concept that he/she has mastered to another student. This can serve as reinforcement for the student.

47. Provide practice solving math word problems using a computer software program or a hand-held educational device that gives immediate feedback to the student.

48. Make sure the student has mastery of math concepts at each level before introducing a new skill level.

49. Have the student manipulate objects (e.g., apples, oranges, toy cars, toy airplanes, etc.) as the operation is described.

50. Reduce the emphasis on competition. Competitive activities may cause the student to hurry and solve math word problems incorrectly.

51. Provide the student with a quiet place to work (e.g., office or study carrel, etc.). This is used as a means of reducing distracting stimuli and not as a form of punishment.

52. Have the student question any directions, explanations, and instructions he/she does not understand.

53. Reinforce the student for correctly solving math word problems: (a) give the student a tangible reward (e.g., classroom privileges, line leading, passing out materials, five minutes free time, etc.) or (b) give the student an intangible reward (e.g., praise, fist bump, smile, etc.).

54. Recognize quality work (e.g., display the student's work, congratulate the student, etc.).

60   Has difficulty understanding abstract concepts

Goals:

1. The student will develop an understanding of abstract concepts.
2. The student will improve his/her abstract reasoning skills.

Objectives:

1. The student will demonstrate an understanding of spatial relationships such as near-far, above-below, over-under, etc., on _____ out of _____ trials.
2. The student will use manipulatives to further develop his/her abstract reasoning skills on _____ out of _____ trials.
3. The student will match pictures of abstract concepts such as dimensionality, size, shape, space, etc., with tangible representations on _____ out of _____ trials.
4. The student will identify abstract concepts such as dimensionality, size, shape, space, etc., with visual and verbal cues on _____ out of _____ trials.
5. The student will independently identify abstract concepts such as dimensionality, size, shape, space, etc., on _____ out of _____ trials.

Interventions:

1. Use abstract concepts to describe tangible objects in the environment (e.g., larger, smaller, square, triangle, etc.).

2. Label tangible objects in the classroom with signs that convey abstract concepts (e.g., larger, smaller, square, triangle, etc.).

3. Use concrete examples when teaching abstract concepts (e.g., numbers of objects to convey more than or less than, rulers and yardsticks to convey concepts of height or width, etc.).

4. Play *Simon Says* to facilitate the understanding of abstract concepts (e.g., Find the largest desk., Touch something that is a rectangle., etc.).

5. Conduct a scavenger hunt. Have the student look for the smallest pencil, tallest boy, etc., in the classroom.

6. Teach shapes using common objects in the environment (e.g., round clocks, rectangular desks, square tiles on the floor, etc.).

7. Evaluate the appropriateness of having the student learn abstract concepts at this time.

8. Teach abstract concepts (e.g., dimensionality, size, shape, etc.) one at a time before pairing the concepts.

9. Provide repeated physical demonstrations of abstract concepts (e.g., identify things far away and close to the student, identify a small box in a large room, etc.).

10. Review daily abstract concepts which have been previously introduced. Introduce new abstract concepts only after the student has mastery of those previously presented.

11. Choose a peer to spend time each day with the student pointing out abstract concepts in the classroom (e.g., the rectangular light switch plate, the round light fixture, the tallest girl, etc.).

12. Rely on tangible objects (e.g., boxes for dimensionality, family members for size, distances in the classroom for space, cookie cutters for shape, etc.) when introducing abstract concepts. Do not introduce abstract concepts by using their descriptive titles such as square, rectangle, triangle, etc., without a tangible object.

13. Have the student match the names of abstract concepts (e.g., square, circle, etc.) with objects (e.g., floor tile, clock, etc.).

14. Give the student direction-following assignments (e.g., Go to the swing which is the farthest away., Go to the nearest sandbox., etc.).

15. Have the student sort left and right gloves, shoes, hand and foot paper cutouts, etc.

16. Have the student physically perform spatial relationships (e.g., have the student stand near the teacher, far from the teacher, on a table, under a table, etc.).

17. Have the student question any directions, explanations, and instructions he/she does not understand.

18. Call attention to spatial relationships which occur naturally in the environment (e.g., a bird flying over a tree, a squirrel running under a bush, etc.).

19. Have the student follow simple map directions to practice more abstract concepts such as left and right; north, south, east, and west. Begin with a map of the school and progress to a map of the community, state, nation, etc., with more complex directions to follow.

20. Teach the student relationships of left and right by placing paper bands labeled left and right around his/her wrists. Discontinue the paper bands when the student can successfully identify left and right.

21. Use a scale, ruler, measuring cups, etc., to teach abstract measurement concepts.

22. Avoid the problem of mirror image by standing next to the student when giving right and left directions.

23. Do not require the student to learn more information than he/she is capable of learning at any time.

24. Use real coins and dollar bills, clocks, etc., to teach abstract concepts of money, telling time, etc.

25. Use the terms right and left as part of the directions you give to the student (e.g., refer to the windows on the left side of the room, the wall-mounted board on the right side of the room, etc.).

26. Have the student practice following directions on paper. Instruct the student to make marks or pictures on the right, left, middle, top, and bottom parts of the paper according to the directions given.

27. Relate what the student has learned in one setting or situation to other situations (e.g., vocabulary words learned should be pointed out in reading selections, math problems, story writing, etc.).

28. Make sure the student is attending to the source of information (e.g., eye contact is being made, hands are free of materials, etc.) when delivering directions that involve abstract concepts.

29. Label abstract concepts throughout the classroom (e.g., triangle shapes on the walls, left and right sides of a desk, compass directions on the walls, etc.) to help the student understand abstract concepts.

61 Works math problems from left to right instead of right to left

Goals:

1. The student will demonstrate knowledge of basic number concepts.
2. The student will demonstrate his/her knowledge of place value.
3. The student will demonstrate the ability to work math problems from right to left.

Objectives:

1. The student will use the ones column first when working math problems with _____% accuracy.
2. The student will use the ones column, then the tens column, when working math problems with _____% accuracy.
3. The student will use the ones column, then the tens column, then the hundreds column, when working math problems with _____% accuracy.
4. The student will work math problems from right to left with _____% accuracy.

Interventions:

1. Choose a peer to model working math problems from right to left for the student.

2. Develop a math reference sheet for the student to keep at his/her desk (e.g., steps used in doing addition, subtraction, multiplication, and division problems).

3. Display a large poster-board sign or use the wall-mounted board to create a message that indicates reading begins to the left and math problems begin to the right (e.g., READING BEGINS ON THE LEFT. MATH BEGINS ON THE RIGHT.).

4. Have the student check his/her math assignments using a calculator.

5. Have the student talk through math problems as he/she is solving them to identify errors the student is making.

6. Have the student use a calculator to solve math problems.

7. Have the student verbally explain steps to the teacher for solving a math problem to check the student's thinking processes.

8. Provide the student with a number line on his/her desk to use as a reference.

9. Teach the student why he/she is learning a math concept. Provide the student with concrete examples and opportunities for him/her to apply those concepts in real-life situations.

10. Make sure the student has mastered place value concepts and understands that columns to the left are higher values than those to the right.

11. Make sure the student has mastery of math concepts at each level before introducing a new skill level.

12. Make sure the student understands place value and can explain the concept of the ones column, the tens column, etc.

13. Model proper right-to-left solving of math problems on the wall-mounted board or overhead projector before the student begins a new assignment.

14. Pair the student with another student to solve math problems on the wall-mounted board.

15. Provide math practice using a computer software program or a hand-held educational device that gives immediate feedback to the student.

16. Provide the student practice solving math problems on the computer, which will automatically solve problems right to left.

17. Put the student's math problems on graph paper or vertically lined paper to align columns. Include a reminder to begin each problem at the right.

18. Recognize quality work (e.g., display the student's work, congratulate the student, etc.).

19. Reduce the amount of information on a page (e.g., fewer math problems, less print, etc.) if it is visually distracting for the student.

20. Reduce the emphasis on competition. Competitive activities may cause the student to hurry and make mistakes in math problems.

21. Reinforce proper right-to-left problem solving through the use of math games.

22. Reinforce the student for doing math problems from right to left: (a) give the student a tangible reward (e.g., classroom privileges, line leading, passing out materials, five minutes free time, etc.) or (b) give the student an intangible reward (e.g., praise, fist bump, smile, etc.).

23. Require the student to solve math problems by place value (e.g., begin with the ones column, then the tens column, hundreds column, etc.).

24. Write the place value above each math problem to remind the student to begin with the ones column to solve the problems.

25. Speak to the student to explain (a) what he/she is doing wrong (e.g., working math problems from left to right) and (b) what he/she should be doing (e.g., working math problems from right to left).

26. Use a marker to highlight the ones column to show the student where to begin to work math problems.

27. Use large colored arrows to indicate where the student begins to work math problems (e.g., right to left).

28. Work the first problems for the student as he/she watches to provide a demonstration and an example.

29. Require the student to work each math problem using a bookmark/strip of paper to cover all columns except the one on the right. Move the marker to the left as he/she moves from the ones column to the tens columns to the hundreds column, etc.

62   Does not comprehend written communication

Goals:

1. The student will improve his/her comprehension of written communication.
2. The student will improve his/her ability to comprehend written communication in academic settings.
3. The student will improve his/her ability to comprehend written communication in nonacademic settings.

Objectives:

1. The student will read all directions before beginning tasks and activities on _____ out of _____ occasions.
2. The student will verbally state written directions with _____% accuracy.
3. The student will follow one-step written directions on _____ out of _____ occasions.
4. The student will follow two-step written directions on _____ out of _____ occasions.
5. The student will follow multi-step written directions on _____ out of _____ occasions.
6. The student will demonstrate an understanding of signs on _____ out of _____ occasions.
7. The student will demonstrate an understanding of symbols on _____ out of _____ occasions.
8. The student will demonstrate an understanding of warnings on _____ out of _____ occasions.

Interventions:

1. Reinforce the student for demonstrating comprehension of written communication: (a) give the student a tangible reward (e.g., classroom privileges, line leading, passing out materials, five minutes free time, etc.) or (b) give the student an intangible reward (e.g., praise, fist bump, smile, etc.).

2. Speak to the student to explain (a) what he/she is doing wrong (e.g., ignoring written communication) and (b) what the student should be doing (e.g., paying attention to written communication).

3. Provide alternatives to the traditional format of presenting written communication (e.g., audio record, summarize written communication and information presented by peers, etc.).

4. Write a contract with the student specifying what behavior is expected (e.g., demonstrating comprehension and paying close attention to written communication) and what reinforcement will be made available when the terms of the contract have been met.

5. Communicate with parents (e.g., notes home, phone calls, etc.) to share information about the student's progress. The parents may reinforce the student at home for demonstrating comprehension of written communication at school.

6. Evaluate the appropriateness of the task to determine (a) if the task is too easy, (b) if the task is too difficult, or (c) if the length of time scheduled to complete the task is adequate.

7. Choose a peer to model how to comprehend written communication for the student.

8. Have the student ask questions about directions, explanations, instructions, signs, symbols, warnings, etc., he/she does not understand.

9. Give information in a variety of ways to facilitate the student's understanding (e.g., if the student does not understand written communication, present the information verbally).

10. Provide clearly stated written communication (e.g., make the written communication as simple and concrete as possible).

11. Reduce distracting stimuli in the environment to facilitate the student's ability to comprehend written communication (e.g., place the student on the front row, provide a carrel or office space away from distractions, etc.). This is used as a means of reducing distracting stimuli and not as a form of punishment.

12. Interact frequently with the student to help him/her comprehend written communication.

13. Structure the environment (e.g., peer tutoring, directions for work sent home, frequent interactions, etc.) to provide the student with increased opportunity for help or assistance when comprehension of written communication is necessary.

14. Reinforce those students in the classroom who demonstrate comprehension of written communication.

15. Assess the quality and clarity of written directions, explanations, and instructions given to the student.

16. Have the student practice following written directions on nonacademic tasks (e.g., following a recipe, putting together a model, scavenger hunt, etc.).

17. Have the student practice observing and comprehending written communication on nonacademic tasks, (e.g., symbols for male and female, exit signs, warning labels on poisonous substances, etc.).

18. Have the student verbally interpret written communication to his/her teacher.

19. Reduce the amount of written communication that the student must comprehend, (e.g., give written directions one step at a time, audio record text material, choose a peer to interpret signs and symbols, etc.).

20. Give a signal (e.g., clapping hands, turning lights off and on, etc.) before presenting written communication.

21. Provide written directions before handing out materials.

22. Make sure the student achieves success when demonstrating comprehension of written communication.

23. Prevent the student from becoming overstimulated (e.g., frustrated, angry, etc.) by an activity that involves the comprehension of written material.

24. Make sure the student is attending to the teacher (e.g., making eye contact, hands free of writing materials, looking at assignment, etc.) before presenting written communication.

25. Maintain visibility to and from the student. The teacher should be able to see the student and the student should be able to see the teacher. Make eye contact possible at all times to make sure the student is comprehending written communication.

26. Teach the student skills for comprehending written communication, (e.g., read all information, identify key words, ask for an explanation of any information not understood).

27. Make sure that written communications are written on the student's reading level.

28. Reduce the emphasis on competition. Competitive activities may cause the student to begin the task without understanding important written communication.

29. Provide the student with a copy of written communication (e.g., directions, information, rules, etc.) at his/her desk in addition to on the wall-mounted board, posted in the classroom, etc.

30. Audio record information (e.g., directions, textbook information, etc.) for the student to listen to individually and replay as necessary.

31. Develop direction-following assignments/ activities (e.g., informal activities designed to have the student carry out directions in steps with increasing degrees of difficulty, etc.).

32. Maintain a consistent format of written directions.

33. Choose a peer to help the student with any written communications he/she does not understand.

34. Seat the student close to the source of the written communication (e.g., wall-mounted board, projector, bulletin board, etc.).

35. Seat the student far enough away from peers to facilitate increased opportunities for attending to written communication.

36. Make sure that the print is large and dark enough to facilitate the student's success in reading and comprehending written communication.

37. Transfer written information from texts and workbooks when pictures or other stimuli make it difficult for the student to attend to written communication.

38. Work the first problem or problems with the student to make sure that he/she demonstrates comprehension of the written directions.

39. Have the student carry out written directions one step at a time and check with the teacher to make sure that each step is successfully completed before attempting the next.

40. As the student demonstrates success, gradually increase the level of difficulty or complexity of written communications.

41. Make sure that written communication is presented at a level at which the student can be successful (i.e., two-step or three-step directions should not be given to students who can only successfully follow one-step directions).

42. Work through the steps of written directions as they are delivered to make sure the student accurately follows the directions.

43. Choose a peer to demonstrate the necessary steps in following written directions.

44. Maintain mobility within the school building and the classroom to be frequently near the student to provide assistance with the comprehension of written communication (e.g., directions, signs, symbols, warnings, etc.).

45. Use a sight word approach to teach the student key words (e.g., circle, underline, match, etc.) and phrases when reading written communication.

46. Have the student maintain a vocabulary notebook with definitions of words whose meanings he/she did not know.

47. Make sure the student learns dictionary skills to independently find the meanings of words.

48. Write notes and letters to the student to provide reading material which he/she will want to read for comprehension. Students may be encouraged to write notes and letters to classmates at a time set aside each day, once a week, etc.

49. Give the student time to read a selection more than once. Emphasize accuracy not speed.

50. Have the student supply missing words in sentences provided by classmates and/or the teacher to facilitate comprehension skills.

51. Reduce the amount of material the student reads at one time (e.g., reduce reading material to single sentences on a page, a single paragraph, etc.). As the student demonstrates success, gradually increase the amount of material he/she reads at one time.

52. Avoid placing the student in uncomfortable reading situations (e.g., reading aloud in a group, reading with time limits, etc.).

53. Stop the student at various points throughout a reading selection to check for comprehension.

54. Audio record the student's reading material and have him/her listen to the recording while simultaneously reading the material.

55. Have the student read ahead on a subject to be discussed in class or read directions ahead so that he/she is familiar with new vocabulary and concepts that will be used during instructional periods.

56. Outline reading material for the student using words and phrases on his/her ability level.

57. Choose a peer who demonstrates good comprehension skills to assist the student with comprehension of directions, signs, symbols, and warnings not understood.

58. Teach the student to identify main points in written communication to facilitate his/her comprehension.

59. Have the student outline, underline, or highlight important points in written material.

60. Have the student read high-interest signs, advertisements, notices, etc., from newspapers, magazines, movie promotions, etc., placing an emphasis on comprehension skills.

61. Reduce the amount of information on a page (e.g., less print to read, fewer pictures, etc.) if it is visually distracting for the student.

62. Highlight or underline important information the student should pay close attention to when reading.

63. Provide the student with opportunities to read and demonstrate comprehension of signs within the school and surrounding community (e.g., sign identifying office, cafeteria, library; exit signs, etc.).

64. Teach the student to use context clues to assist in the comprehension of written communication.

65. Have the student maintain a notebook of signs, symbols, and warnings and their meanings to refer to when he/she is unsure of their meanings.

63 Does not comprehend what he/she reads

Goal:

1. The student will improve his/her reading comprehension skills.

Objectives:

1. The student will read and correctly answer _____ out of _____ comprehension questions about sight words on his/her level of ability.
2. The student will read and correctly answer _____ out of _____ comprehension questions covering individual phrases on his/her level of ability.
3. The student will read and correctly answer _____ out of _____ comprehension questions covering individual sentences on his/her level of ability.
4. The student will read and correctly answer _____ out of _____ comprehension questions covering individual paragraphs on his/her level of ability.
5. After reading a short passage on his/her level of ability, the student will correctly answer _____ out of _____ comprehension questions covering the material.
6. After reading a short passage on his/her level of ability to the teacher, the student will be able to correctly answer _____ out of _____ comprehension questions.
7. After independently reading a 3-page passage on his/her level of ability, the student will correctly answer _____ out of _____ comprehension questions.

Interventions:

1. Have the student prepare test questions based on information that has been read to facilitate the ability to focus on key elements of the reading material.

2. Have the student read a story. Provide statements out of sequence which reflect the main points of the story. Have the student arrange the statements in the correct order to demonstrate comprehension.

3. Have the student read a short paragraph which contains one or more errors which make comprehension difficult. If the student does not recognize the errors, encourage the student to stop frequently while reading to ask himself/ herself: *Does this make sense?*

4. When the student encounters a new word or one whose meaning is not understood, have the student construct sentences in which the word is used in the correct context.

5. Have the student maintain a vocabulary notebook with definitions of words whose meanings he/she did not know.

6. Pair the student with a peer to summarize material to answer the questions *Who, What, Where, When, How,* and *Why.*

7. Have the student use a highlighter pen to highlight the facts requested by the teacher.

8. Provide the student with a quiet place (e.g., carrel, study booth, etc.) where he/she may go to engage in reading activities.

9. Have the student read ahead on a subject to be discussed in class so that he/she is familiar with new vocabulary and concepts that will be used during instructional periods.

10. Have the student write and answer the questions *Who, What, Where, When, How,* and *Why* using the *Flash Card Study Aid.*

11. Have the student's hearing checked if it has not been recently checked.

12. Maintain mobility in the classroom to be frequently near the student to provide reading assistance.

13. Reduce the emphasis on competition. Competitive activities may increase the student's anxiety and reduce the student's ability to comprehend information.

14. Choose a peer who demonstrates good comprehension skills to read with the student and help him/her with the meanings of words not understood.

15. Reinforce the student for demonstrating comprehension of reading material: (a) give the student a tangible reward (e.g., classroom privileges, line leading, passing out materials, five minutes free time, etc.) or (b) give the student an intangible reward (e.g., praise, fist bump, smile, etc.).

16. Teach the student to draw from personal learning experiences to facilitate comprehension of reading material. Provide a variety of learning experiences at school to expand the student's background of knowledge.

17. Have the student look for story elements when reading a selection (e.g., setting, characters, plot, ending).

18. Have the student look for key words (e.g., Christopher Columbus, Spain, New World, etc.).

19. Have the student look for direction words (e.g., circle, underline, choose, list, etc.).

20. Have the student look for action words (e.g., sailed, discovered, founded).

21. Have the student look for the key words and main ideas when reading that will answer *Who, What, Where, When, How*, and *Why* (e.g., Christopher Columbus sailed from Spain to discover the New World during the year 1492.).

22. After reading a selection, have the student complete a semantic map answering the questions *Who, What, Where, When, How*, and *Why*.

23. Have the student read high-interest signs, advertisements, notices, etc., from newspapers, magazines, movie promotions, etc., placing an emphasis on comprehension skills.

24. Teach the student to identify main points in material to facilitate his/her comprehension.

25. Avoid placing the student in uncomfortable reading situations (e.g., reading aloud in a group, reading with time limits, etc.).

26. Have the student read independently each day to practice reading skills.

27. Highlight or underline important information the student should pay close attention to when reading.

28. Reduce the amount of information on a page (e.g., less print to read, fewer pictures, etc.) if it is visually distracting for the student.

29. Make sure the student is practicing comprehension skills which are directly related to high-interest reading activities (e.g., adventure, romance, mystery, sports, etc.).

30. Make sure the student is reading material on his/her ability level. If not, modify or adjust reading material to the student's ability level.

31. Make sure the student learns the meanings of all commonly used prefixes and suffixes.

32. Make sure the student learns dictionary skills to independently find the meaning of words.

33. Cut out pictures from magazines and newspapers and have the student match captions to them. This activity could be varied by having one student write the caption while another student determines if it is appropriate.

34. Make a list of main points from the student's reading material, written on the student's reading level.

35. Reduce the amount of material the student reads at one time (e.g., reduce reading material to single sentences on a page, a single paragraph, etc.). As the student demonstrates success, gradually increase the amount of material to be read at one time.

36. Have the student supply missing words in sentences provided by classmates and/or the teacher to facilitate comprehension skills.

37. Have the student list new or difficult words in categories such as people, food, animals, things that are hot, etc.

38. Have the student take notes while reading to facilitate comprehension.

39. Teach the student meanings of abbreviations to assist in comprehending material read.

40. Include frequent written assignments on topics which are of interest to the student to reinforce the correlation between writing and reading ability.

41. Have the student identify one word each day that he/she does not understand. Have the student define the word and then require him/her to use that word throughout the day in various situations.

42. Find the central word or phrase around which the story is constructed. Check for pinpoint words that relate back to the central word/phrase and determine the number of times they are used and how this helps to develop the story.

43. Have the student verbally paraphrase material just read to assess his/her comprehension.

44. Underline or highlight important points before the student reads the material silently.

45. Make it pleasant and positive for the student to ask questions about things not understood.

46. Teach new vocabulary words prior to having the student read the material.

47. Have the student read progressively longer segments of reading material to build comprehension skills (e.g., begin with a single paragraph and progress to several paragraphs, chapters, short stories, etc.).

48. Audio record lectures to provide an additional source of information for the student.

49. Audio record the student's reading material and have him/her listen to the recording while simultaneously reading the material.

50. Have the student outline reading material using the *Outline Form.*

51. Give the student high-interest reading material on his/her ability level (e.g., comic books, adventure stories, etc.) requiring him/her to answer the questions *Who, What, Where, When, How*, and *Why.*

52. Have the student audio record what he/she reads to facilitate comprehension by replaying and listening to the material read.

53. Prior to reading a selection, familiarize the student with the general content of the story (e.g., when reading a selection about birds, have the students brainstorm and discuss birds to develop a point of reference).

54. Have the student dictate stories which are then put in print for him/her to read, placing an emphasis on comprehension skills.

55. Write paragraphs and short stories requiring skills the student is currently developing. These passages should be of high interest to the student using his/her name, family members, friends, pets, and interesting experiences.

56. Make available for the student a learning center area where a variety of information is available for him/her in content areas (e.g., the library may have a section with films, slides, videos, and recorded lectures on such subjects as pilgrims, the Civil War, the judicial system, etc.).

57. Use lower grade-level texts as alternative reading material in subject areas.

58. Reduce distracting stimuli in the environment to facilitate the student's ability to concentrate on what he/she is reading (e.g., place the student on the front row, provide a carrel or office space away from distractions, etc.). This should be used as a means of reducing distracting stimuli and not as punishment.

59. Outline reading material for the student using words and phrases on his/her ability level.

60. Determine whether or not the student can make inferences, predictions, determine cause-effect, etc., in everyday experiences. Teach these skills in contexts that are meaningful to the student to facilitate the ability to use these concepts when reading.

61. Introduce new words and their meanings to the student before reading new material.

62. Teach the student to think about the reading selection and predict what will happen prior to reading the selection.

63. Choose a peer tutor to study with the student for quizzes, tests, etc.

64. Give the student time to read a selection more than once. Emphasize accuracy not speed.

65. Write notes and letters to the student to provide reading material which he/she will want to read for comprehension. Students may be encouraged to write notes and letters to classmates at a time set aside each day, once a week, etc.

66. Have the student outline, underline, or highlight important points in written material.

67. Teach the student to use context clues to identify the meanings of words and phrases not known.

68. Teach the student to use related learning experiences in his/her classes (e.g., filmstrips, movies, audio recordings, demonstrations, discussions, lectures, videos, etc.). Encourage teachers to provide alternative learning experiences for the student.

69. Stop the student at various points throughout a reading selection to check for comprehension.

70. Use a sight word approach to teach the student key words (e.g., circle, underline, match, etc.) and phrases when reading directions and instructions.

71. Have the student match vocabulary words with pictures representing the words.

72. Use reading series material with high interest, low vocabulary for the older student.

73. Have the student identify words he/she does not comprehend. Have him/her find the definitions of these words in the dictionary.

74. Have the student work with a peer and teacher. The first student will dictate a short paragraph to be typed by the teacher and will also compose a comprehension question. The second student, after listening to the process, will read the story verbally and point out the answer. Then student roles can be reversed.

75. Provide the student with written direction-following activities that target concrete experiences (e.g., following a recipe, following directions to put a model together, etc.) to facilitate comprehension.

76. Provide the student with written one-step, two-step, and three-step direction-following activities (e.g., sharpen your pencil, open your text to page 121, etc.).

64 Does not discriminate between similar letters and words

Goals:

1. The student will improve his/her word attack skills.
2. The student will improve his/her sight-word vocabulary.
3. The student will improve his/her phonics skills.

Objectives:

1. The student will recognize the letters of the alphabet with _____% accuracy.
2. The student will recognize similar letters of the alphabet (e.g., m and n, b and d), when presented individually, with _____% accuracy.
3. The student will recognize similar letters of the alphabet (e.g., m and n, b and d), when presented together, with _____% accuracy.
4. The student will recognize similar letters of the alphabet (e.g., m and n, b and d), when they appear in words, with _____% accuracy.
5. The student will recognize a sight-word vocabulary, when the words are presented individually, with _____% accuracy.
6. The student will recognize a sight-word vocabulary, when the words are presented together, with _____% accuracy.
7. The student will recognize a sight-word vocabulary, when the word appears in reading material, with _____% accuracy.

Interventions:

1. Have the student's hearing checked if it has not been recently checked.

2. Each day have the student practice those letters and words he/she cannot discriminate.

3. Take every opportunity throughout the day to emphasize a designated letter or word the student cannot discriminate (e.g., identify the sound when speaking, writing, reading, etc.).

4. Use highlight markers (e.g., pink and yellow) to have the student mark the letters and words in a passage he/she does not discriminate (e.g., all m's marked with the pink marker and all n's marked with the yellow marker).

5. Make a list of words the student cannot discriminate. Have the student and a peer work together with flash cards to develop the student's ability to recognize the differences in the letters and words.

6. Audio record stories and paragraphs the student can listen to while reading along.

7. Have the student read aloud to the teacher each day to provide evaluative feedback relative to his/her ability to discriminate letters and words.

8. Verbally correct the student as often as possible when he/she does not discriminate between letters and words so he/she hears the correct pronunciation of the reading material.

9. Have the student write those letters and words he/she has trouble discriminating to facilitate correctly identifying them.

10. Teach the student to use context clues in reading. These skills will be particularly helpful when he/she is unable to discriminate between letters and words.

11. Make sure the student looks closely at word endings and beginnings to discriminate similar words (e.g., cap and cat).

12. Identify a letter or word each day which the student has difficulty discriminating. Have the student underline or highlight that letter or word each time he/she reads it that day.

13. Provide the student with an alphabet strip at his/her desk to use as a reference when reading or performing assignments.

14. Reduce the emphasis on competition. Competitive activities may cause the student to hurry and not discriminate between similar letters and words.

15. Have the student cut letters out of magazines or newspapers and glue the letters in sequence to make words, sentences, etc.

16. Make sure that the student's knowledge of a particular skill is being assessed rather than the student's ability to read directions, instructions, etc.

17. Make sure that the reading demands of all subjects and assignments are within the ability level of the student. If they are not, modify or adjust the reading material to the student's ability level.

65   Does not know all the letters of the alphabet

Goal:

1. The student will learn all the letters of the alphabet.

Objectives:

1. The student will recognize five lower-case letters of the alphabet at a time until all letters are learned with _____% accuracy.
2. The student will recognize five upper-case letters of the alphabet at a time until all letters are learned with _____% accuracy.

Interventions:

1. Set up a system of reinforcers, either tangible (e.g., computer time, helper for the day, etc.) or intangible (e.g., praise, fist bump, smile, etc.), to encourage the student to learn the letters of the alphabet.

2. Provide the student with an alphabet strip at his/her desk to use as a reference when reading or performing assignments.

3. Each day have the student print those letters of the alphabet he/she does not know.

4. Choose a peer to work with the student on one letter of the alphabet each day (e.g., tracing the letter, printing the letter, recognizing the letter in words in a paragraph, etc.).

5. Have the student read and write friends' first names which include letters the student does not recognize.

6. Introduce letters to the student as partners (e.g., Aa, Bb, Cc, Dd, etc.).

7. Have the student say the letters of the alphabet in sequence. Repeat by rote several times a day.

8. Present the alphabet to the student on flash cards. This is an appropriate activity for a peer tutor to conduct with the student each day.

9. Identify a letter the student does not know. Have the student find the letter in all the words in a paragraph or on a page of a book.

10. Put each letter of the alphabet on an individual card. Have the student collect and keep the letters he/she knows with the goal to collect all the letters of the alphabet.

11. Start by teaching the names of letters in the student's first name only. When the student has mastered the letters in his/her first name, go on to the last name, parents' names, etc.

12. Give the student a word which begins with each letter of the alphabet (e.g., apple, bad, cat, etc.). Go over several of the words each day, stressing the alphabet letters being learned.

13. Take every opportunity throughout the day to emphasize a designated letter for that day (e.g., identify the letter when speaking, writing, reading, etc.).

14. Use daily drills to help the student memorize the alphabet.

15. Avoid placing the student in uncomfortable reading situations (e.g., reading aloud in a group, identifying that the student's reading group is the lowest level, etc.).

Goals:

1. The student will improve his/her word attack skills.
2. The student will improve his/her sight-word vocabulary.
3. The student will improve his/her phonics skills.
4. The student will improve his/her verbal reading skills.
5. The student will improve his/her reading comprehension.

Objectives:

1. The student will independently read brief information in the environment (e.g., labels, signs, names of persons, etc.) on _____ out of _____ trials.
2. The student will independently read short selections of reading material (e.g., cartoons, comic books, sentences, etc.) on _____ out of _____ trials.
3. The student will independently read short stories on _____ out of _____ trials.
4. The student will independently read library books, books of interest in the classroom, magazine stories, etc., on _____ out of _____ trials.

Interventions:

1. Have the student be a peer tutor to teach younger students reading or to read verbally to younger students.

2. Pair the class with a class at a lower grade level on a weekly basis. Let each student read to a younger child.

3. Make reading materials easily accessible to the student in the classroom.

4. Make visiting the library an enjoyable weekly experience.

5. Incorporate listening skills/techniques as part of the daily routine in reading class (e.g., listening center where the student reads along as a recording plays, teacher reads to the student, students read to each other, etc.).

6. Make memberships in paperback book clubs available to the student.

7. Encourage interest in reading by having students share interesting things they have read. This should be informal sharing in a group and not necessarily a book report.

8. Find a book series by an author that the student finds enjoyable. Make these books available for the student to read.

9. To encourage reading, make sure that the student knows he/she is not reading for assessment purposes but for enjoyment.

10. Read excerpts of your favorite children's books to entice the student to read the same book.

11. Encourage the student to find books about different subjects being taught or discussed (e.g., when studying electricity, encourage the student to read a book about Thomas Edison, etc.).

12. Assist the student in finding reading material which fits his/her interests and reading level. The student may not be comfortable or able to find books by himself/herself in the library.

13. Audio record reading material for the student to listen to as he/she reads along.

14. Provide the student with high-interest reading material that is also short in length so the student can finish reading the material without difficulty.

15. Have the student read high-interest signs, advertisements, notices, etc., from newspapers, magazines, movie promotions, etc.

16. Encourage interesting reading by highlighting an author a month. The teacher should share information about an author, read books by the author, and have additional titles by the author available for independent reading.

17. Develop a reading area in the classroom that is appealing to the student (e.g., tent, bean bag chair, carpeted area, etc.).

18. While teaching a unit in a content area, bring in related fiction or nonfiction books to share with your students to spark interest in reading.

19. Avoid placing the student in uncomfortable reading situations (e.g., reading aloud in a group, identifying that the student's reading group is the lowest level, etc.).

20. Include predictable reading books in the class library. Predictability can make books more appealing to beginning readers and build confidence.

21. Make sure the student is reading material on his/her ability level.

22. Have the student read lower grade-level stories to younger children to build his/her feelings of confidence relative to reading.

23. Provide the student with many high-interest reading materials (e.g., comic books, magazines relating to sports, fashion, etc.).

24. Expose the student to materials with large print. Large print can appear less intimidating to the student who does not choose to read.

25. Modify or adjust reading materials to the student's ability level.

26. Write periodic letters or notes to the student to encourage him/her to write back.

27. Set up a system of reinforcers, either tangible (e.g., extra computer time, helper for the day, etc.) or intangible (e.g., smile, fist bump, praise, etc.), to encourage the student and facilitate his/her success in reading.

28. Set aside a fixed or random time (e.g., a half-hour daily, an hour a week, etc.) for reading. Everyone, teacher included, chooses a book that he/she likes and reads it for pleasure.

29. Provide the student a quiet place (e.g., carrel, study booth, office, etc.) where he/she may go to participate in reading activities.

30. Read, or have someone read, high-interest material to the student to promote his/her interest in reading.

31. Encourage the student to read material with many illustrations and a limited amount of print. As the student demonstrates success, gradually decrease the number of pictures and increase the amount of print.

32. Encourage parents to make reading material on the student's interest and reading level available to the student at home.

33. Teach the student necessary reading skills before expecting him/her to read independently.

34. Write paragraphs and short stories for the student. These passages should be of high interest to the student using his/her name, family members, friends, pets, and interesting experiences.

35. Have the student dictate stories which are then put in print for him/her to read.

36. Conduct a survey of the student's interests to provide reading material in those interest areas.

37. Encourage parents to read to their child at home and to have their child read to them. Encourage parents to read for their own enjoyment to serve as a model for their child.

38. Have the student write to the author of books he/she reads to encourage an interest in reading more by the same author.

39. Provide reading material in various settings (e.g., art books in the art center, science books in the science center, weather books in the weather center, etc.).

67   Does not read or follow written directions

Goal:

1. The student will follow written directions.

Objectives:

1. The student will read all directions before beginning tasks and activities on _____ out of _____ trials.
2. The student will verbally state written directions on _____ out of _____ trials.
3. The student will follow one-step directions on _____ out of _____ trials.
4. The student will follow two-step directions on _____ out of _____ trials.
5. The student will follow multi-step directions on _____ out of _____ trials.
6. The student will ask for clarification of written directions not understood on _____ out of _____ trials.
7. The student will follow written directions with assistance on _____ out of _____ trials.
8. The student will independently follow written directions on _____ out of _____ trials.

Interventions:

1. Establish classroom rules:
- Concentrate while working.
- Work quietly.
- Remain in your seat.
- Finish task.
- Meet task expectations.

Review rules often. Reinforce students for following the rules.

2. Deliver a predetermined signal (e.g., clapping hands, turning lights off and on, etc.) before giving written directions.

3. Have the student maintain a record (e.g., chart or graph) of his/her performance in following written directions.

4. Provide the student with a copy of written directions at his/her desk in addition to on the wall-mounted board, posted in the classroom, etc.

5. Provide the student with an audio recorded copy of written directions.

6. Make sure the student achieves success when following written directions.

7. Transfer directions from texts and workbooks when pictures or other stimuli make it difficult to attend to or follow written directions.

8. Have the student question any written directions, explanations, or instructions he/she does not understand.

9. Make sure that directions are given at a level at which the student can be successful (e.g., two-step or three-step directions should not be given to students who can only successfully follow one-step directions).

10. Prevent the student from becoming overstimulated (e.g., frustrated, angry, etc.) by an activity.

11. Assess the quality and clarity of written directions, explanations, and instructions given to the student.

12. Reduce the emphasis on competition. Competitive activities may cause the student to hurry to begin the task without following written directions.

13. Teach the student written direction-following skills (e.g., read carefully, write down important points, ask for clarification, wait until all directions are received before beginning, etc.).

14. Make sure that written directions are presented on the student's reading level.

15. Provide clearly stated written directions (i.e., make the directions as simple and concrete as possible).

16. Seat the student far enough away from peers to facilitate attending to written directions.

17. Deliver all directions, questions, explanations, and instructions in a clear and concise manner and at an appropriate rate for the student.

18. Reinforce the student for following written directions based on the length of time the student can be successful. As the student demonstrates success, gradually increase the length of time required for reinforcement.

19. Reinforce the student for following written directions: (a) give the student a tangible reward (e.g., classroom privileges, line leading, passing out materials, five minutes free time, etc.) or (b) give the student an intangible reward (e.g., praise, fist bump, smile, etc.).

20. Have the student practice following written directions on nonacademic tasks (e.g., recipes, games, etc.).

21. Maintain a consistent format for written directions.

22. Maintain visibility to and from the student. The teacher should be able to see the student and the student should be able to see the teacher. Make eye contact possible at all times.

23. Deliver written directions before handing out materials.

24. Make sure the student has all the materials needed to complete the assignment or activity.

25. Choose a peer to help the student with any written directions not understood.

26. Require that assignments done incorrectly, for any reason, be redone.

27. Reduce written directions to individual steps (e.g., give the student each additional step after completion of the previous step).

28. Highlight, circle, or underline key words (e.g., match, circle, underline, etc.) in written directions.

29. Choose a peer to model how to appropriately follow written directions for the student.

30. As the student becomes more successful in following directions, gradually increase the level of difficulty or complexity of written directions.

31. Communicate with parents (e.g., notes home, phone calls, etc.) to share information about the student's progress. The parents may reinforce the student at home for following written directions at school.

32. Practice following written directions on nonacademic tasks (e.g., recipes, games, etc.).

33. Have the student carry out written directions one step at a time and check with the teacher to make sure that each step is successfully completed before attempting the next.

34. Structure the environment (e.g., peer tutoring, directions for work sent home, frequent interactions, etc.) to provide the student with increased opportunities for help or assistance on academic tasks.

35. Make sure that the print is bold and large enough to facilitate the student's success in following written directions.

36. Work the first few problems of an assignment with the student to make sure that he/she accurately follows the written directions

37. Provide the student a quiet place (e.g., carrel, study booth, etc.) where he/she may go to participate in activities which require following written directions.

38. Interact frequently with the student to help him/her follow written directions.

39. Make sure that the student is attending to the teacher (e.g., eye contact, hands free of writing materials, looking at assignment, etc.) before giving written directions.

40. Give the student one task to complete at a time. Introduce the next task when the student has successfully completed the previous task.

41. Follow a less desirable task with a highly desirable task. Make completion of the first task necessary to complete the second task.

42. Reduce distracting stimuli in the environment to facilitate the student's ability to follow written directions (e.g., place the student on the front row, provide a carrel or office space away from distractions, etc.). This is used as a means of reducing distracting stimuli and not as a form of punishment.

43. Reinforce those students in the classroom who follow written directions.

44. Develop assignments/activities for the following of written directions (e.g., informal activities designed to have the student carry out directions in steps, increasing the level of difficulty).

45. Audio record directions for the student to listen to individually and replay as necessary.

46. Evaluate the appropriateness of the task to determine (a) if the task is too easy, (b) if the task is too difficult, or (c) if the length of time scheduled to complete the task is adequate.

47. Write a contract with the student specifying what behavior is expected (e.g., following written directions) and what reinforcement will be made available when the terms of the contract have been met.

48. Have the student quietly repeat to himself/herself information just read to help remember the important facts.

49. Speak to the student to explain (a) what he/she is doing wrong (e.g., not following written directions) and (b) what he/she should be doing (e.g., following written directions).

50. Seat the student close to the source of the written directions (e.g., teacher, aide, peer, wall-mounted board, projector, etc.).

51. Give directions in a variety of ways to facilitate the student's understanding (e.g., if the student does not understand written directions, present them verbally).

52. Require the student to wait until the teacher gives him/her a signal to begin the task (e.g., hand signal, ring bell, etc.).

53. Use vocabulary that is within the student's level of comprehension when delivering directions, explanations, and information.

54. Use visual cues in written directions (e.g., green dot to start, red dot to stop, arrows, etc.).

55. Present directions in both written and verbal form.

56. Have the student read written directions to his/her teacher.

68 Does not summarize/retell important concepts after reading a selection

Goal:

1. The student will improve his/her reading comprehension skills.

Objectives:

1. The student will demonstrate comprehension of selected reading vocabulary in _____ out of _____ trials.
2. The student will restate a sentence/paragraph/story in his/her own words in _____ out of _____ trials.
3. The student will identify the main idea of a sentence/paragraph/story in _____ out of _____ trials.
4. The student will demonstrate the ability to break down a complex sentence into its component parts by giving two shorter sentences which convey the same information as the longer sentence with _____% accuracy.
5. The student will predict an outcome based on given information in _____ out of _____ trials.
6. The student will identify cause and effect from given information in _____ out of _____ trials.
7. The student will demonstrate comprehension of words which denote causality by completing dependent clauses beginning with because, when, and therefore (e.g., John liked red licorice because . . .) with _____% accuracy.
8. The student will identify inferred meaning based on given information in _____ out of _____ trials.
9. The student will demonstrate comprehension of newspaper paragraphs by matching the correct headlines to the paragraphs with _____% accuracy.

Interventions:

1. Teach the student to recognize main points, important facts, etc., by answering *Who, What, Where, When, How*, and *Why*.

2. Have the student look for key words and main ideas that answer *Who, What, Where, When, How*, and *Why* when reading a selection.

3. Have the student answer in writing the questions *Who, What, Where, When, How*, and *Why* using a *Flash Card Study Aid*.

4. After reading a selection, have the student complete a semantic map answering the questions *Who, What, Where, When, How*, and *Why*.

5. Make sure the student is reading material on his/her ability level.

6. Modify or adjust reading material to the student's ability level.

7. Read shorter selections with the student, discussing the story in a one-to-one situation. As the student demonstrates success, gradually increase the length of selections.

8. Audio record reading material for the student to listen to as he/she reads along. Have the student stop at various points to retell/summarize the selection.

9. After reading a short story, have the student identify the main characters, sequence the events, and report the outcome of the story.

10. Relate the information being read to the student's experiences.

11. Be sure the material is meaningful to the student. Comprehension is more likely to occur when the material is meaningful and the student can relate to real experiences.

12. Have the student verbally paraphrase material he/she has read to assess his/her comprehension.

13. Prior to reading a selection, prepare an outline for the student to reference and add details to while reading the selection.

14. Make a list of main points from the student's reading material. Have the student discuss each main point after reading the selection.

15. Teach the student how to identify main points in reading material to facilitate his/her comprehension.

16. Have the student outline, underline, or highlight important points in reading material.

17. Have the student take notes while he/she is reading to facilitate comprehension.

18. Underline or highlight important points before the student reads the selection.

19. Have the student's vision checked if it has not been recently checked.

20. Have the student think about the selection and predict what will happen, prior to completing the selection.

21. Have the student look for key concepts when reading a selection.

22. Have the student read independently each day to practice reading skills.

23. Teach new vocabulary words prior to having the student read the material.

24. Choose a peer tutor to read with the student to develop comprehension skills.

25. Prior to reading a selection, familiarize the student with the general content of the story (e.g., if the selection is about elephants, brainstorm and discuss elephants to develop a point of reference).

26. When reading verbally with the student, pause at various points to discuss material read up to that point. Have the student predict what will happen next before continuing.

27. Have the student complete a Fiction Frame after reading a selection.

28. Give the student time to read a selection more than once. Emphasize comprehension rather than speed.

29. Have the student look for story elements when reading a selection (e.g., setting, characters, plot, ending).

69 Fails to correctly answer comprehension questions from reading activities

Goals:

1. The student will improve his/her word attack skills.
2. The student will improve his/her sight-word vocabulary.
3. The student will improve his/her phonics skills.
4. The student will improve his/her verbal reading skills.
5. The student will improve his/her reading comprehension.

Objectives:

1. The student will read and answer comprehension questions about individual words with _____% accuracy.
2. The student will read and answer comprehension questions about individual phrases with _____% accuracy.
3. The student will read and answer comprehension questions about individual sentences with _____% accuracy.
4. The student will read and answer comprehension questions about individual paragraphs with _____% accuracy.
5. The student will read and answer comprehension questions about short stories or chapters with _____% accuracy.
6. The student will answer comprehension questions from reading activities with _____% accuracy.

Interventions:

1. Have the student's vision checked if it has not been recently checked.

2. Make sure the student is reading material on his/her ability level. If not, modify or adjust reading material to the student's ability level.

3. Reinforce the student for demonstrating comprehension of reading material: (a) give the student a tangible reward (e.g., classroom privileges, line leading, passing out materials, five minutes free time, etc.) or (b) give the student an intangible reward (e.g., praise, fist bump, smile, etc.).

4. Reduce distracting stimuli in the environment to facilitate the student's ability to concentrate on what he/she is reading (e.g., place the student on the front row; provide a carrel or office space away from distractions; etc.). This should be used as a means of reducing distracting stimuli and not as a form of punishment.

5. Teach the student to use context clues to identify the meanings of words and phrases not known.

6. Audio record the student's reading material and have him/her listen to the recording while simultaneously reading the material.

7. Have the student read ahead on a subject to be discussed in class so that he/she is familiar with new vocabulary and concepts that will be used during instructional periods.

8. Outline reading material for the student using words and phrases on his/her ability level.

9. Choose a peer who demonstrates good comprehension skills to read with the student and help him/her with the meanings of words not understood.

10. Have the student take notes while reading to facilitate comprehension.

11. Teach the student to draw from personal learning experiences to facilitate comprehension of reading material. Provide a variety of learning experiences at school to expand the student's background of knowledge.

12. Maintain mobility in the classroom to frequently be near the student to provide reading assistance.

13. Have the student verbally paraphrase material just read to assess his/her comprehension.

14. Teach the student to identify main points in material to facilitate his/her comprehension.

15. Underline or highlight important points before the student reads the material silently.

16. Have the student outline, underline, or highlight important points in reading material.

17. Provide the student with written direction-following activities that target concrete experiences (e.g., following a recipe, following directions to put a model together, etc.) to facilitate comprehension.

18. Provide the student with written one-step, two-step, and three-step direction-following activities (e.g., sharpen your pencil, open your text to page 121, etc.).

19. Have the student read progressively longer segments of reading material to build comprehension skills (e.g., begin with a single paragraph and progress to several paragraphs, chapters, short stories, etc.).

20. Have the student read high-interest signs, advertisements, notices, etc., from newspapers, magazines, movie promotions, etc., placing an emphasis on comprehension skills.

21. Reduce the emphasis on competition. Competitive activities may make it difficult for the student to comprehend what he/she reads.

22. Use a sight word approach to teach the student key words (e.g., circle, underline, match, etc.) and phrases when reading directions and instructions.

23. Have the student list new or difficult words in categories such as people, food, animals, things that are hot, etc.

24. Have the student maintain a vocabulary notebook with definitions of words whose meanings he/she did not know.

25. When the student encounters a new word or one whose meaning is not understood, have the student construct sentences in which the word is used in the correct context.

26. Make sure the student learns dictionary skills to independently find the meanings of words.

27. Have the student identify words he/she does not comprehend. Have him/her find the definitions of these words in the dictionary.

28. Have the student identify one word each day that he/she does not understand. Have the student define the word and then require him/her to use that word throughout the day in various situations.

29. Have the student match vocabulary words with pictures representing the words.

30. Introduce new words and their meanings to the student before reading new material.

31. Make sure the student learns the meanings of all commonly used prefixes and suffixes.

32. Write notes and letters to the student to provide reading material which he/she will want to read for comprehension. Students may be encouraged to write notes and letters to classmates at a time set aside each day, once a week, etc.

33. Give the student time to read a selection more than once. Emphasize accuracy not speed.

34. Have the student supply missing words in sentences provided by classmates and/or the teacher to facilitate comprehension skills.

35. Cut out pictures from magazines and newspapers and have the student match captions to them. This activity could be varied by having one student write a caption while another student determines if it is appropriate.

36. Have the student read a short paragraph which contains one or more errors which make comprehension difficult. If the student does not recognize the errors, encourage the student to stop frequently while reading to ask himself/herself: *Does this make sense?*

37. Determine whether or not the student can make inferences, predictions, determine cause-effect, etc., in everyday experiences. Teach these skills in contexts that are meaningful to the student to facilitate the ability to use these concepts when reading.

38. Have the student read a story. Provide statements out of sequence which reflect the main points of the story. Have the student arrange the statements in the correct order to demonstrate comprehension.

39. Have the student prepare test questions based on information that has been read to facilitate the ability to focus on key elements of the reading material.

40. Include frequent written assignments on topics which are of interest to the student to reinforce the correlation between writing and reading ability.

41. Reduce the amount of material the student reads at one time (e.g., reduce reading material to single sentences on a page, a single paragraph, etc.). As the student demonstrates success, gradually increase the amount of material to be read at one time.

42. Avoid placing the student in uncomfortable reading situations (e.g., reading aloud in a group, reading with time limits, etc.).

43. Stop the student at various points throughout a reading selection to check for comprehension.

44. Reduce the amount of information on a page (e.g., less print to read, fewer pictures, etc.) if it is visually distracting for the student.

45. Highlight or underline important information the student should pay close attention to when reading.

46. Make it pleasant and positive for the student to ask questions about things not understood.

47. Have the student use a highlighter pen to highlight the facts requested by the teacher.

48. Have the student work with a peer and teacher. The first student would dictate a short paragraph to be typed by the teacher and would also compose a comprehension question. The second student, after listening to the process, would read the story verbally and point out the answer. Then student roles could be reversed.

49. Present directions following the outline of *What, How, Materials*, and *When*.

50. Have the student take notes when directions are being given following *What, How, Materials*, and *When* format.

51. When concepts are presented, have the student listen and take notes for *Who, What, Where, When, How*, and *Why*.

52. Present concepts following the outline of *Who, What, Where, When, How*, and *Why*.

Goals:

1.   The student will improve his/her word attack skills.
2.   The student will improve his/her phonics skills.

Objectives:

1.   The student will use picture clues to identify words in a story with _____% accuracy.
2.   The student will use context clues to identify words in a story with _____% accuracy.
3.   The student will use phonics clues to identify words with _____% accuracy.
4.   The student will use word attack skills to identify words with _____% accuracy.

Interventions:

1.   Prepare a list of words and phrases from the student's reading material which he/she does not recognize. Have the student practice using phonics skills, context clues, picture clues, etc., to decode these words.

2.   Have the student identify words and phrases that he/she does not recognize. Make these words the student's word list to be learned.

3.   Teach the student word attack skills using root words to which various prefixes and suffixes may be added.

4.   Reinforce the student each time he/she makes an attempt to sound out a word. As the student demonstrates success, gradually increase the number of attempts required for reinforcement.

5.   Use a peer tutor to review word attack skills previously learned utilizing games and activities.

6.   Make sure the student uses a sight vocabulary to support weaknesses in phonics skills.

7.   Make sure the student develops an awareness of hearing word sounds (e.g., have the student listen to words beginning with a /bl/ sound: *blue, black, block, blast*).

8.   Make sure the student develops an awareness of seeing letter combinations that make the sounds (e.g., have the student circle all of the words in a reading passage that begin with the /bl/ blend).

9.   Provide practice with reading /bl/ words, /pl/ words, /pr/ words, etc., by presenting a high-interest paragraph or story that contains these words.

10.   Demonstrate skills for decoding words (e.g., using contractions from conversation, write the abbreviated form of the word and the two complete words to show how to recognize the contraction).

11.   Encourage the student to try several sounds to arrive at the correct answer (e.g., omit letters from a word used in context and give several choices to be filled in).

12.   Write paragraphs and short stories requiring word attack skills the student is currently learning. These passages should be of high interest to the student using his/her name, family members, friends, pets, and interesting experiences.

13.   Have the student dictate stories which are then put in print for him/her to read. Require the student to place an emphasis on word attack skills.

14.   Have the student read high-interest signs, advertisements, notices, etc., from newspapers, magazines, movie promotions, etc., placing emphasis on word attack skills.

15.   Make sure the student is practicing word attack skills which are directly related to high-interest reading activities (e.g., adventure, romance, mystery, sports, etc.).

16. Encourage the student to scan the newspapers, magazines, etc., and underline words he/she can decode using word attack skills (e.g., phonics, context clues, picture clues, etc.).

17. Require the student to verbally explain context clues in sentences to identify words not known.

18. Have the student use related pictures to help identify words in sentences not known.

19. Teach the student the most common prefixes and suffixes to add to root words he/she can identify.

20. When the student has difficulty with word attack skills, encourage him/her to continue working on developing word attack skills. Everyone has areas of weakness that require extra work.

21. Have the student be a peer tutor to teach a concept he/she has mastered to another student. This can serve as a reinforcement for the student.

22. Avoid placing the student in uncomfortable reading situations (e.g., reading aloud in a group, identifying that the student's reading group is the lowest level, etc.).

23. Audio record difficult reading material for the student to listen to as he/she reads along.

24. Use reading material with pictures and predictable reading to help the student master word attack skills.

25. Have the student read aloud to the teacher each day to provide evaluative feedback.

26. Introduce new words and their meanings to the student before he/she reads new materials. These may be entered in a vocabulary notebook kept by the student as a reference for new vocabulary words.

27. Teach the foundation for reading and writing in a sequential, systematic method with much positive reinforcement.

28. Teach the student individual consonant and vowel sounds.

29. Allow the student to use the wall-mounted board so that teaching and learning become active. The student hears, writes, and sees the sounds in isolation and then joins them together to make words.

30. The student should practice vocabulary words from required reading material by writing them while saying the sounds.

31. Teach the student pronunciation rules (e.g., vowel sounds, blends, etc.). Start with simple words and sounds where the student achieves 95%-100% accuracy. Do not move on to more difficult words until practice, drill, and review of preceding lessons produces accuracy.

32. Use D'Nealian® handwriting when teaching sounds by hearing, writing, and saying. This eliminates many potential reversal problems.

33. Have the student memorize word meanings and practice spotting the most common prefixes and suffixes. Using a sheet of paper with a window cut in it, target the base word.

34. Play alphabet bingo with the student using phonics instead of letter names.

Goals:

1. The student will improve his/her sight-word vocabulary.
2. The student will improve his/her reading comprehension.

Objectives:

1. The student will use picture cues to comprehend words with _____% accuracy.
2. The student will use visual or verbal cues to comprehend words with _____% accuracy.
3. The student will use a dictionary to comprehend words with _____% accuracy.
4. The student will independently read complete sentences with _____% accuracy.

Interventions:

1. Have the student make a list of new words he/she has learned. The student can add words to the list at his/her own rate.

2. Provide the student with a quiet place (e.g., carrel, study booth, etc.) where he/she may go to engage in reading activities.

3. When the student encounters a new word or one whose meaning he/she does not know, have the student construct sentences in which the word is used in the correct context.

4. Provide the student with a variety of visual teaching materials to support word comprehension (e.g., filmstrips, pictures, charts, etc.).

5. Have the student identify a word a day that he/she does not understand. Have the student define the word and require him/her to use that word throughout the day in various situations.

6. Have the student maintain a vocabulary notebook with definitions of words whose meanings he/she does not know.

7. Have the student develop a picture dictionary representing those words which are difficult for him/her to recognize.

8. Anticipate new vocabulary words and teach them in advance of reading a selection.

9. Teach the student synonyms and antonyms of familiar words to strengthen his/her vocabulary.

10. Teach new vocabulary words and concepts prior to reading a selection.

11. Reinforce the student for asking the meanings of words he/she does not understand.

12. Reduce the emphasis on competition. Competitive activities may make it difficult for the student to comprehend what he/she reads.

13. Have the student look for vocabulary definitions within the material read (e.g., The long house, an Indian dwelling, was used by Eastern Indians.).

14. Have the student look for vocabulary words in italics, boldface, headings, and captions.

15. Choose a peer to help the student, when needed, with the meanings of words not understood.

16. Have the student read high-interest signs, advertisements, notices, etc., from newspapers, magazines, movie promotions, etc.; placing an emphasis on vocabulary skills

17. Avoid placing the student in uncomfortable reading situations (e.g., reading aloud in a group, identifying that the student's reading group is the lowest level, etc.).

18. Label objects and activities in the classroom to help the student associate words with tangible aspects of the environment.

19. Reduce the amount of information on a page (e.g., less print to read, fewer pictures, etc.) if it is visually distracting for the student.

20. Make sure the student is developing a sight-word vocabulary of the most commonly used words in his/her reading material.

21. Make sure the student is reading material on his/her ability level.

22. Design classroom games (e.g., *Jeopardy, Pictionary,* etc.) to review vocabulary words periodically.

23. Make sure the student learns dictionary skills to independently find meanings of words.

24. Make sure the student learns the meaning of all commonly used prefixes and suffixes.

25. Reinforce the student for looking up the definitions of words he/she does not understand.

26. Make a list of main points from the student's reading material, written on the student's reading level.

27. Modify or adjust reading material to the student's ability level.

28. Have the student list new or difficult words in categories such as people, food, animals, etc.

29. Have the student teach new vocabulary to his/her peers (e.g., require the student to be creative by showing, acting out, drawing or making an example of the word).

30. Have the student match objects or pictures with sounds produced by that object (e.g., phone ring, vacuum cleaner, etc.).

31. Set up a system of reinforcers either tangible (e.g., extra computer time, helper for the day, etc.) or intangible (e.g., smile, fist bump, praise, etc.) to encourage the student and facilitate his/her success in reading.

32. Prepare a written list of vocabulary words. Verbally present a sentence with a word missing and have the student determine which vocabulary word should be used.

33. Have the student verbally paraphrase material that has just been read to assess comprehension.

34. Review new vocabulary words periodically with the student (e.g., weekly or bi-weekly).

35. Make it pleasant and positive for the student to ask the meanings or look up words he/she does not understand. Reinforce the student by assisting him/her, congratulating, praising, etc.

36. Teach the student to predict what will happen in the story based on new vocabulary words and the title page.

37. Teach the student to read for the main point in sentences, paragraphs, etc.

38. Make sure that the reading demands of all subjects and assignments are within the ability level of the student. If they are not, modify or adjust the reading material to the student's ability level.

39. Have the student audio record what he/she reads to facilitate comprehension by replaying and listening to the material.

40. Prior to reading a selection, familiarize the student with the general content of the story to develop a point of reference. Through this approach, introduce new vocabulary words.

41. Have the student dictate stories which are put in print for him/her to read, placing an emphasis on comprehension skills.

42. Write paragraphs and short stories requiring skills the student is currently developing. These paragraphs should be of high interest to the student using his/her name, family members, friends, pets, and interesting experiences.

43. Before reading, tell the student what he/she is to find in the story (e.g., who are the main characters, what are the main events, etc.).

44. Do not require the student to learn more information than he/she is capable of learning at any time.

45. Make sure that the student's knowledge of a particular skill is being assessed rather than the student's ability to read directions, instructions, etc. Reading directions, instructions, etc., to the student can facilitate success.

46. Use a lower grade-level text as alternative reading material in subject areas.

47. Reduce distracting stimuli in the environment to facilitate the student's ability to concentrate on what he/she is reading (e.g., place the student on the front row, provide a carrel or office space away from distractions). This is used as a means of reducing distracting stimuli and not as a form of punishment.

48. Outline reading material for the student using words and phrases on his/her reading level.

49. Introduce new words and their meanings to the student before he/she reads new material.

50. Give the student time to read a selection more than once. Emphasize comprehension rather than speed.

51. Write notes and letters to the student to provide reading material which he/she will want to read for comprehension. Students may be encouraged to write each other notes and letters at a time set aside each day, week, etc.

52. Have the student outline, underline, or highlight important vocabulary in reading material.

53. Make sure the student underlines or circles words not understood. These words will become the student's vocabulary assignment for the week.

54. Have the student use new vocabulary words in follow-up assignments (e.g., have the student use these words on written assignments, crossword puzzles, etc.).

55. Teach the student to use context clues to identify words not understood.

56. Use a sight word approach to teach the student key words (e.g., circle, underline, match, etc.) and phrases when reading directions and instructions.

57. Have the student match vocabulary words with pictures representing the words.

58. Have the student review vocabulary words by providing related clues. The student then identifies the vocabulary word.

59. Use reading series material with high interest (e.g., adventure, romance, mystery, sports, etc.) and low vocabulary.

60. Use the current vocabulary words being studied by the student in daily classroom conversation.

61. Have the student identify words he/she does not comprehend. Have him/her find the definitions of these words in the dictionary.

72   Fails to finish assignments because of reading difficulties

Goals:

1. The student will improve his/her word attack skills.
2. The student will improve his/her sight-word vocabulary.
3. The student will improve his/her phonics skills.
4. The student will improve his/her verbal reading skills.
5. The student will improve his/her reading comprehension.

Objectives:

1. The student will increase his/her rate of reading to _____ sentences per _____ minute time period.
2. The student will increase his/her rate of reading to _____ paragraphs per _____ minute time period.
3. The student will finish reading assignments within a given time period _____% of the time.

Interventions:

1. Make sure that the reading demands of the assignment are within the ability level of the student.

2. Audio record directions, explanations, and instructions to facilitate the student's success.

3. Choose a peer to read directions, explanations, and instructions to the student to facilitate success.

4. Require the student to verbally repeat directions, explanations, and instructions.

5. Read directions, explanations, and instructions to the student when necessary.

6. Use a sight word approach to teach the student key words (e.g., circle, underline, match, etc.) and phrases when reading directions and instructions.

7. Deliver all directions, explanations, and instructions verbally.

8. Reduce all directions, explanations, and instructions to a minimum.

9. Shorten the length of assignments that require reading so the student can complete assignments in the same length of time as the other students.

10. Provide the student with additional time to complete the assignment.

11. Deliver directions, explanations, and instructions prior to handing out materials.

12. Make sure that the student's knowledge of a particular skill is being assessed rather than the student's ability to read directions, instructions, and content.

13. Maintain mobility to provide assistance to the student.

14. Maintain a consistent format in which written directions, explanations, and instructions are delivered.

15. Have the student practice timed drills consisting of reading directions, explanations, content, etc., to reduce reading time.

16. Provide more than enough time for the student to complete an assignment.

17. Assess the quality and clarity of written directions, explanations, instructions, content, etc.

18. Keep written directions as simple and concrete as possible.

19. Reduce distracting stimuli in the environment to facilitate the student's ability to follow written directions (e.g., place the student on the front row; provide a carrel or office space away from distractions; etc.). This is used as a means of reducing distracting stimuli and not as a form of punishment.

20. Reduce written directions to individual steps. Give the student an additional step after completion of the previous step.

21. Make sure the student achieves success when following written directions.

22. Prevent the student from becoming overstimulated (e.g., frustrated, angry, etc.) by an activity.

23. Provide the student with a copy of written directions at his/her desk in addition to on the wall-mounted board, posted in the classroom, etc.

24. Seat the student close to the source of the written information (e.g., wall-mounted board, projector, etc.).

25. Make sure the print is bold and large enough to facilitate the student's success in following written directions.

26. Transfer directions from texts and workbooks when pictures or other stimuli make it difficult to attend to or follow written directions.

27. Provide the student a quiet place (e.g., carrel, study booth, etc.) where he/she may go to participate in activities which require following written directions.

28. Work the first problem or problems with the student to make sure that he/she follows written directions.

29. Have the student carry out written directions one step at a time and then check with the teacher to make sure that each step is successfully completed before attempting the next.

30. As the student demonstrates success, gradually increase the level of difficulty or complexity of written directions, explanations, instructions, content, etc.

31. Modify or adjust the reading level of material presented to the student to facilitate success.

32. Reduce the emphasis on competition. Competitive activities may make it difficult for the student to finish assignments because of frustration with reading difficulties.

33. Introduce new words and their meanings to the student before he/she reads new materials. These may be entered in a vocabulary notebook kept by the student as a reference for new vocabulary words.

34. Avoid placing the student in uncomfortable reading situations (e.g., reading aloud in a group, identifying that the student's reading group is the lowest level, etc.).

35. Audio record difficult reading material for the student to listen to as he/she reads along.

36. Give the student time to read a selection more than once. Emphasize comprehension rather than speed.

37. Use reading series material with high interest (e.g., adventure, romance, mystery, sports, etc.) and low vocabulary.

38. Reduce the amount of material the student reads at one time (e.g., reduce reading material to single sentences on a page, a single paragraph, etc.). As the student demonstrates success, gradually increase the amount of material to be read at one time.

39. Make the subject matter meaningful to the student (e.g., explain the purpose of an assignment, relate the subject matter to the student's environment, etc.).

40. Give the student one task to complete at a time. Introduce the next task when the student has successfully completed the previous task.

41. Reduce the amount of information on a page (e.g., less print to read, fewer pictures on the page, isolate information that is presented to the student) if it is visually distracting for the student.

42. Have the student read material to the teacher to determine if it is on his/her reading level.

43. Have the student use his/her finger to point to words that are being read. The teacher should observe as the student points to the words while reading. This would help to determine the causes of slow reading.

44. Reduce the student's anxiety level by not requiring the student to finish a reading assignment within a specified time period.

45. Teach the student that work not done during work time must be completed at other times such as free time, recess, after school, etc.

46. Have the student question any directions, explanations, and instructions he/she does not understand.

47. Choose a peer to model how to complete assignments for the student.

48. Evaluate the appropriateness of the task to determine (a) if the task is too easy, (b) if the task is too difficult, or (c) if the length of time scheduled to complete the task is adequate.

49. Communicate with parents (e.g., notes home, phone calls, etc.) to share information about the student's progress. The parents may reinforce the student at home for finishing assignments at school.

50. Write a contract with the student specifying what behavior is expected (e.g., finishing assignments) and what reinforcement will be made available when the terms of the contract have been met.

51. Reinforce the student for finishing assignments based on the number of times he/she can be successful. As the student demonstrates success, gradually increase the number of times required for reinforcement.

52. Reinforce those students in the classroom who finish assignments.

53. Establish classroom rules:
- Concentrate while working.
- Work quietly.
- Remain in your seat.
- Finish task.
- Meet task expectations.

Review rules often. Reinforce students for following the rules.

54. Speak to the student to explain (a) what he/she is doing wrong (e.g., failing to finish assignments) and (b) what he/she should be doing (e.g., finishing assignments).

55. Reinforce the student for finishing assignments: (a) give the student a tangible reward (e.g., classroom privileges, line leading, passing out materials, five minutes free time, etc.) or (b) give the student an intangible reward (e.g., praise, fist bump, smile, etc.).

Goals:

1. The student will improve his/her sight-word vocabulary.
2. The student will improve his/her verbal reading skills.

Objectives:

1. The student will recognize words on grade level, with assistance (e.g., verbal cues, picture cues, context cues, etc.), with _____% accuracy.
2. The student will independently recognize words on grade level with _____% accuracy.

Interventions:

1. Provide the student with a computer software program or a hand-held educational device to practice sight words he/she is learning. Drill and repetition is often necessary to commit words to memory.

2. Provide the student with a quiet area (e.g., carrel, study booth, etc.) where he/she may go to practice sight words.

3. Have the student read aloud to the teacher each day to provide evaluative feedback.

4. Start with simple words and sounds where the student achieves 95%-100% accuracy. Do not move on to more difficult words until practice, drill, and review of preceding lessons produces accuracy.

5. Teach the student word attack skills using root words to which various prefixes and suffixes may be added.

6. Reduce the emphasis on competition. Competitive activities may cause the student to hurry and make errors.

7. Teach the student individual consonant and vowel sounds.

8. When the student has difficulty with reading words on grade level, encourage him/her to continue working. Everyone has areas of weakness that require extra work.

9. Maintain mobility to be frequently near the student to provide reading assistance.

10. Have the student read high-interest signs, advertisements, notices, etc., from newspapers, movie promotions, magazines, etc.; placing an emphasis on reading skills.

11. Encourage classroom teachers to include more alternative learning experiences in their classrooms (e.g., lectures, demonstrations, guest speakers, field trips, discussions, films, film-strips, slides, videos, etc.).

12. Provide the student with increased opportunity for help or assistance on academic tasks (e.g., peer tutoring, directions for work sent home, frequent interactions, etc.).

13. Make sure the student is practicing reading skills which are directly related to high-interest reading activities (e.g., adventure, romance, mystery, sports, etc.).

14. Make a list of main points from the student's reading material, written on the student's reading level.

15. Provide the student with many high-interest reading materials (e.g., comic books, magazines, etc.) to practice sight words.

16. Reduce the amount of material the student reads at one time (e.g., reduce reading material to single sentences on a page, a single paragraph, etc.). As the student demonstrates success, gradually increase the amount of material to be read at one time.

17. Audio record difficult reading material for the student to listen to as he/she reads along.

18. Modify or adjust reading materials to the student's ability level.

19. Set up a system of reinforcers, either tangible (e.g., computer time, helper for the day, etc.) or intangible (e.g., smile, praise, fist bump, etc.) to encourage the student and facilitate his/her success in reading.

20. Audio record lectures to provide an additional source of information for the student.

21. Encourage the student to read material with many illustrations and context clues to support learning new sight words.

22. Make sure that the reading demands of all subjects and assignments are within the ability level of the student. If they are not, modify or adjust the reading material to the student's ability level. A lower grade-level text may be an alternative.

23. Have the student dictate stories which are then put in print for him/her to read, placing an emphasis on reading skills.

24. Write paragraphs and short stories requiring skills the student is currently developing. These passages should be of high interest to the student using his/her name, family members, friends, pets, and interesting experiences.

25. Make available for the student a learning center area where a variety of information is available in content areas (e.g., the library may have a section with films, slides, videos, or recorded lectures on such subjects as Pilgrims, the Civil War, the judicial system, etc.).

26. Make sure that the student's knowledge of a particular skill is being assessed rather than the student's ability to read directions, instructions, etc. Reading the directions to the student may facilitate success.

27. Use D'Nealian® handwriting when teaching sounds by hearing, writing, and saying. This eliminates many potential reversal problems.

28. Use lower grade-level texts as alternative reading material in subject areas.

29. Outline reading material for the student using words and phrases on his/her reading level.

30. Allow students to use the wall-mounted board so that teaching and learning become active. The student hears, writes, and sees the sounds in isolation.

31. Choose a peer tutor to study with the student for quizzes, tests, etc.

32. Use a highlight marker to identify key words and phrases for the student. These words and phrases become the student's sight words.

33. Choose a peer tutor to practice sight words with the student to reinforce words learned.

34. Teach the student to use related learning experiences in his/her classes (e.g., filmstrips, movies, audio recordings, demonstrations, discussions, videos, lectures, etc.). Encourage teachers to provide a variety of learning experiences for the student to facilitate learning grade level sight words.

35. Teach the student to use context clues to identify words and phrases he/she does not know.

36. Teach the student to use context clues to identify sight words the student is learning.

37. Use a sight word approach to teach the student key words (e.g., circle, underline, match, etc.) and phrases when reading directions and instructions.

38. Have the student practice vocabulary words from required reading material by writing the words while saying the sounds.

39. Use reading series material with high interest (e.g., adventure, romance, mystery, sports, etc.) and low vocabulary.

40. Have the student identify words and phrases that he/she does not recognize. Make these words the student's list of words to be learned.

41. Create a list of words and phrases from the student's reading material which he/she will not recognize (e.g., have the science teacher identify the words the student will not recognize in the following week's assignment). These words and phrases will become the student's list of reading words for the following week.

Goals:

1. The student will improve his/her decoding skills.
2. The student will improve his/her sight-word vocabulary.
3. The student will improve his/her phonics skills.
4. The student will improve his/her verbal reading skills.
5. The student will improve his/her reading comprehension.

Objectives:

1. The student will use picture clues to identify words in a story with _____% accuracy.
2. The student will use context clues to identify words in a story with _____% accuracy.
3. The student will use phonics clues to identify words with _____% accuracy.
4. The student will use decoding skills to identify words with _____% accuracy.

Interventions:

1. Teach the student word attack skills using root words to which various prefixes and suffixes may be added.

2. Obtain a list of words and phrases from the student's reading material which he/she does not recognize. Have the student practice phonics skills, context clues, structural analysis, etc., using these words.

3. Use a peer tutor to review word attack skills by utilizing games and activities.

4. Write paragraphs and short stories which require the use of decoding skills the student is currently learning. These passages should be of high interest to the student using his/her name, family members, friends, pets and interesting activities.

5. Have the student dictate stories which are then put in print for him/her to read, placing an emphasis on decoding skills.

6. Encourage the student to scan newspapers, magazines, etc., and underline words he/she can identify using decoding skills.

7. Teach the student the most common prefixes and suffixes to add to root words he/she can identify.

8. Teach the student to use context clues to identify words and phrases he/she does not know.

9. Develop a list of phonics sounds the student needs to master. Remove sounds from the list as the student demonstrates mastery of phonics skills.

10. Reinforce the student for using decoding skills when attempting to decode a word.

11. Have the student read high-interest signs, advertisements, notices, etc., from newspapers, magazines, movie promotions, etc.; placing an emphasis on decoding skills.

12. Make sure the student develops an awareness of seeing letter combinations that stand for a sound, prefix, or suffix (e.g., have the student highlight all words in a reading passage that contain the suffix or prefix).

13. Encourage the student to look for known sight words within a word to be decoded (e.g., for the word *interesting*, have the student identify the sight word *interest* to help decode the word).

14. Teach the student to be aware of word sounds and parts (e.g., read words with the /bl/ blend: blue, black, block, etc.).

15. Provide practice with reading a targeted group of words (e.g., words ending with -ing, etc.) by presenting a high-interest paragraph or story that contains these words.

16. Demonstrate skills for decoding words by modeling decoding words on the wall-mounted board or overhead projector (e.g., for the word *unassuming*, model decoding the word parts: un-, -ing, plus the root, to correctly read the word).

17. Encourage the student to try several sounds to arrive at the correct answer.

18. Have the student make a list of phonics skills he/she has mastered. The student continues to add to the list as he/she masters more and more skills.

19. Have the student identify syllables as he/she reads them to help him/her recognize word parts.

20. Encourage the student to learn additional basic sight words to assist him/her in reading.

21. Reduce the emphasis on competition. Competitive activities may cause the student to rush and not apply decoding skills accurately.

22. Provide the student with a list of common prefixes and suffixes to be posted on his/her desk to use as a reference when decoding words.

Goal:

1. The student will follow written instructions.

Objectives:

1. The student will read all instructions before beginning tasks and activities on _____ out of _____ trials.
2. The student will verbally state written instructions on _____ out of _____ trials.
3. The student will follow one-step instructions on _____ out of _____ trials.
4. The student will follow two-step instructions on _____ out of _____ trials.
5. The student will follow multi-step instructions on _____ out of _____ trials.
6. The student will ask for clarification of written instructions not understood on _____ out of _____ trials.
7. The student will follow written instructions with assistance on _____ out of _____ trials.
8. The student will independently follow written instructions on _____ out of _____ trials.

Interventions:

1. Provide written instructions on the student's reading level.

2. Maintain a consistent format for written instructions.

3. Transfer instructions from texts and workbooks to a piece of paper when pictures or other stimuli make it difficult for the student to attend to or follow written instructions.

4. Highlight, circle, or underline key words (e.g., circle, underline, match, etc.) in written instructions.

5. Evaluate the appropriateness of the task to determine (a) if the task is too easy, (b) if the task is too difficult, or (c) if the length of time scheduled to complete the task is adequate.

6. Choose a peer to model how to follow written instructions for the student.

7. Have the student question any written directions, explanations, instructions, etc., he/she does not understand.

8. Choose a peer to work with the student to help him/her follow written instructions.

9. Teach the student the steps of following written instructions (e.g., read carefully, write down important points, ask for clarification, etc.).

10. Give instructions in a variety of ways to facilitate the student's probability of understanding (e.g., if the student does not understand written instructions, present them verbally).

11. Provide clearly stated written instructions. Make the instructions as simple and concrete as possible.

12. Interact frequently with the student during an activity to help him/her follow written instructions.

13. Reduce distracting stimuli in the environment to facilitate the student's ability to follow written instructions (e.g., place the student on the front row, provide a carrel or office space away from distractions, etc.). This is used as a means of reducing distracting stimuli and not as a form of punishment.

14. Structure the environment (e.g., peer tutoring, directions for work sent home, frequent interactions, etc.) in a way that provides the student with the increased opportunity for help or assistance on academic tasks.

15. Provide alternatives for presenting written instructions (e.g., audio record instructions, summarize instructions, instructions given by peers, etc.).

16. Assess the quality and clarity of written directions, explanations, and instructions given to the student.

17. Practice following written instructions on nonacademic tasks (e.g., recipes, games, etc.).

18. Have the student read written instructions to the teacher.

19. Reduce written instructions to individual steps (e.g., give the student the next step after he/she completes a step).

20. Deliver a predetermined signal (e.g., clapping hands, turning lights off and on, etc.) before giving written instructions.

21. Deliver written instructions before handing out materials.

22. Make sure the student achieves success when following written instructions.

23. Reduce the emphasis on competition. Competitive activities may cause the student to hurry to begin a task and not follow written instructions.

24. Require the student to wait to begin an activity after receiving written instructions until the teacher gives him/her a signal (e.g., hand signal, bell ringing, etc.).

25. Make sure that the student is attending to the teacher (e.g., eye contact, hands free of writing materials, looking at the assignment, etc.) before giving written instructions.

26. Maintain visibility to and from the student. The teacher should be able to see the student, and the student should be able to see the teacher. Make eye contact possible at all times to make sure the student is attending to written instructions.

27. Present instructions in both written and verbal form.

28. Provide the student with a copy of written instructions at his/her desk in addition to those on the wall-mounted board, posted in the classroom, etc.

29. Audio record instructions for the student to replay as necessary.

30. Develop assignments/activities which require following written instructions (e.g., informal activities designed to have the student carry out instructions in steps).

31. Choose a peer to help the student with any written instructions he/she does not understand.

32. Seat the student close to the written instructions (e.g., wall-mounted board, etc.).

33. Make sure that the print is large enough for the student to read to facilitate following the written instructions.

34. Work the first few problems of an assignment with the student to make sure that he/she accurately follows the written instructions.

35. Work through the steps of written instructions as they are delivered to facilitate the student accurately following the instructions.

36. Have the student carry out written instructions one step at a time and check with the teacher after completing each step. If the student has successfully completed the step, he/she may attempt the next step.

37. Make sure that instructions are given at the level at which the student can be successful (e.g., two-step or three-step instructions should not be given to students who can only successfully follow one-step instructions).

38. Use visual cues in written instructions (e.g., green dot to start, red dot to stop, arrows, etc.).

39. Provide the beginning reader with written instructions supplemented with picture clues. As the student demonstrates success, gradually phase out the picture clues.

40. Teach instruction words to be sight words (e.g., circle, fill-in, match).

41. Keep written instructions as concise and concrete as possible.

42. As the student becomes successful, gradually increase the level of difficulty/complexity of written instructions, explanations, information, etc.

43. Have the student take notes when directions are being given following *What, How, Materials*, and *When* format.

44. Present instructions following the *What, How, Materials*, and *When* outline.

76 Has difficulty understanding what he/she reads even though he/she has adequate word attack skills

Goal:

1. The student will improve his/her reading comprehension skills.

Objectives:

1. The student will demonstrate comprehension of selected reading vocabulary in _____ out of _____ trials.
2. The student will restate a sentence/paragraph/story in his/her own words in _____ out of _____ trials.
3. The student will identify the main idea of a sentence/paragraph/story in _____ out of _____ trials.
4. The student will demonstrate the ability to break down a complex sentence into its component parts by giving two shorter sentences which convey the same information as the longer sentence with _____% accuracy.
5. The student will predict an outcome based on given information in _____ out of _____ trials.
6. The student will identify cause and effect from given information in _____ out of _____ trials.
7. The student will demonstrate comprehension of words which denote causality by completing dependent clauses beginning with because, when, and therefore (e.g., John liked red licorice because . . .) with _____% accuracy.
8. The student will identify inferred meaning based on given information in _____ out of _____ trials.
9. The student will demonstrate comprehension of newspaper paragraphs by matching the correct headline to each paragraph with _____% accuracy.

Interventions:

1. Have the student's hearing checked if it has not been recently checked.

2. Make sure the student is reading material on his/her ability level. If not, modify or adjust reading material to the student's ability level.

3. Reinforce the student for demonstrating comprehension of reading material: (a) give the student a tangible reward (e.g., classroom privileges, line leading, passing out materials, five minutes free time, etc.) or (b) give the student an intangible reward (e.g., praise, fist bump, smile, etc.).

4. Reduce distracting stimuli in the environment to facilitate the student's ability to concentrate on what he/she is reading (e.g., place the student on the front row, provide a carrel or office space away from distractions, etc.). This should be used as a means of reducing distracting stimuli and not as a form of punishment.

5. Teach the student to use context clues to identify the meanings of words and phrases he/she does not know.

6. Audio record the student's reading material and have him/her listen to the recording while simultaneously reading the material.

7. Have the student read ahead on a subject to be discussed in class so that he/she is familiar with new vocabulary and concepts that will be used during instructional periods.

8. Outline reading material for the student using words and phrases on his/her ability level.

9. Choose a peer who demonstrates good comprehension skills to read with the student and help him/her with the meanings of words not understood.

10. Teach the student to draw from personal learning experiences to facilitate comprehension of reading material. Provide a variety of learning experiences at school to expand the student's background of knowledge.

11. Maintain mobility in the classroom to frequently be near the student to provide reading assistance.

12. Have the student verbally paraphrase material he/she has just read to assess his/her comprehension.

13. Teach the student to identify main points in material he/she has read to facilitate his/her comprehension.

14. Underline or highlight important points before the student reads the material silently.

15. Have the student outline, underline, or highlight important points in reading material.

16. Have the student take notes while he/she is reading to facilitate comprehension.

17. Provide the student with written direction-following activities that target concrete experiences (e.g., following a recipe, following directions to put a model together, etc.) to facilitate comprehension.

18. Provide the student with written one-step, two-step, and three-step direction-following activities (e.g., sharpen your pencil, open your text to page 121, etc.).

19. Have the student read progressively longer segments of reading material to build comprehension skills (e.g., begin with a single paragraph and progress to several paragraphs, chapters, short stories, etc.).

20. Have the student read high-interest signs, advertisements, notices, etc., from newspapers, magazines, movie promotions, etc., placing an emphasis on comprehension skills.

21. Reduce the emphasis on competition. Competitive activities may make it difficult for the student to comprehend what he/she reads.

22. Use a sight word approach to teach the student key words (e.g., circle, underline, match, etc.) and phrases when reading directions and instructions.

23. Have the student list new or difficult words in categories such as people, food, animals, things that are hot, etc.

24. Have the student maintain a vocabulary notebook with definitions of words whose meanings he/she does not know.

25. When the student encounters a new word or one whose meaning he/she does not understand, have the student construct sentences in which the word is used in the correct context.

26. Make sure the student learns dictionary skills to independently find the meaning of words.

27. Have the student identify words he/she does not comprehend. Finding the definitions of these words can then become the dictionary assignment.

28. Have the student identify one word each day which he/she does not understand. Have the student define the word and then require him/her to use that word throughout the day in various situations.

29. Have the student match vocabulary words with pictures representing the words.

30. Introduce new words and their meanings to the student before he/she reads new material.

31. Make sure the student learns the meaning of all commonly used prefixes and suffixes.

32. Write notes and letters to the student to provide reading material which he/she will want to read for comprehension. Students may be encouraged to write notes and letters to classmates at a time set aside each day, once a week, etc.

33. Give the student time to read a selection more than once. Emphasize accuracy not speed.

34. Have the student supply missing words in sentences provided by classmates and/or the teacher to facilitate comprehension skills.

35. Cut out pictures from magazines and newspapers and have the student match captions to them. This activity could be varied by having one student write the caption while another student determines if it is appropriate.

36. Have the student read a short paragraph which contains one or more errors which make comprehension difficult. If the student does not recognize the errors, encourage him/her to stop frequently while reading to ask himself/herself if it makes sense.

37. Determine whether or not the student can make inferences, predictions, determine cause-effect, etc., in everyday experiences. Teach these skills in contexts that are meaningful to the student to facilitate his/her ability to use these concepts when reading.

38. Have the student read a story. Provide statements out of sequence which reflect the main points of the story. Have the student arrange the statements in the correct order to demonstrate comprehension.

39. Have the student prepare test questions based on information he/she has read to facilitate his/her ability to focus on key elements of the reading material.

40. Include frequent written assignments on topics which are of interest to the student to reinforce the correlation between writing and reading ability.

Goals:
1. The student will improve his/her word attack skills.
2. The student will improve his/her phonics skills.

Objectives:
1. The student will verbally produce short vowel sounds with _____% accuracy.
2. The student will recognize short vowel sounds in words with _____% accuracy.
3. The student will decode single syllable words with short vowel sounds with _____% accuracy.
4. The student will verbally produce long vowel sounds with _____% accuracy.
5. The student will recognize long vowel sounds in words with _____% accuracy.
6. The student will demonstrate the vowel-consonant-silent e rule with _____% accuracy.
7. The student will decode words following the vowel-consonant-silent e pattern with _____% accuracy.
8. The student will use phonics skills to sound out words when reading with _____% accuracy.

Interventions:

1. Set up a system of motivators, either tangible (e.g., extra computer time, free time, etc.) or intangible (e.g., smile, fist bump, praise, etc.), to encourage the student and facilitate his/her success in reading.

2. Prepare a list of words and phrases from the student's reading material which he/she does not recognize. Have the student practice phonics skills using these words.

3. Have the student identify words and phrases that he/she does not recognize. Make these words the student's word list to be learned.

4. Teach the student word attack skills using root words to which various prefixes and suffixes may be added.

5. Reinforce the student each time he/she makes an attempt to sound out a word. As the student demonstrates success, gradually increase the number of attempts required for reinforcement.

6. Use a peer tutor to review previously instructed phonics concepts by utilizing games and activities.

7. Teach the student to use context clues to identify words and phrases he/she does not know.

8. Make sure the student uses a sight vocabulary to support weaknesses in phonics skills.

9. Make sure the student develops an awareness of hearing word sounds (e.g., have the student listen to words beginning with a /bl/ sound: *blue, black, block, blast*).

10. Make sure the student develops an awareness of seeing letter combinations that produce sounds (e.g., have the student circle all of the words in a reading passage that begin with the /bl/ blend).

11. Provide practice with reading /bl/ words, /pl/ words, /pr/ words, etc., by presenting a high-interest paragraph or story that contains these words.

12. Demonstrate skills for decoding words (e.g., using contractions from conversation, write the abbreviated form of the word and the two complete words to show how to recognize the contraction, etc.).

13. Encourage the student to try several sounds to arrive at a correct answer (e.g., omit letters from a word used in context and give several choices to be filled in).

14. Encourage the student to scan newspapers, magazines, etc., and underline learned phonics elements.

15. Develop a list of phonics sounds the student needs to master. Remove sounds from the list as the student demonstrates mastery of phonics skills.

16. Write paragraphs and short stories requiring phonics skills the student is currently learning. These passages should be of high interest to the student using his/her name, family members, friends, pets, and interesting experiences.

17. Have the student dictate stories which are then put in print for him/her to read, placing an emphasis on reading skills.

18. Have the student read high-interest signs, advertisements, notices, etc., from newspapers, magazines, movie promotions, etc., placing an emphasis on phonics skills.

19. Make sure the student is practicing phonics skills which are directly related to high-interest reading activities (e.g., adventure, romance, mystery, sports, etc.).

20. Have the student make a list of phonics skills that have been mastered (e.g., words he/she can identify by sounding out). The student continues to add to the list as he/she identifies more and more words.

21. Teach the student all beginning sounds before expecting him/her to blend sounds into words.

22. Audio record difficult reading material for the student to listen to as he/she reads along.

23. Make sure that the reading demands of all subjects and assignments are within the ability level of the student. If they are not, modify or adjust the reading material to the student's ability level.

24. Make sure that the student's knowledge of a particular skill is being assessed rather than the student's ability to read directions, instructions, etc. Reading the directions to the student may facilitate success.

25. Provide the student with verbal reminders or prompts when he/she is unsure of sounds that letters make when blended together.

26. Reduce the amount of information on a page (e.g., less print to read, fewer pictures to look at, etc.) if it is visually distracting for the student.

27. Avoid placing the student in uncomfortable reading situations (e.g., reading aloud in a group, identifying that the student's reading group is the lowest level, etc.).

28. Determine if the student has instant recall of all consonant and vowel sounds and combinations.

29. Practice active learning at the wall-mounted board by having students hear, write, and read words.

30. Practice, drill, and review every day.

31. Have students say sounds as they write them.

32. Allow students to write a story, paragraph, or sentence using phonetic shorthand. This narrowing of sounds helps the student to identify the sounds with letters used to construct words.

Goals:

1. The student will improve his/her word attack skills.
2. The student will improve his/her phonics skills.

Objectives:

1. The student will recognize letters of the alphabet with _____% accuracy.
2. The student, when presented a letter, will be able to recognize the sound that it makes with _____% accuracy.
3. The student, when presented a sound, will be able to recognize the letter of the alphabet that represents the sound with _____% accuracy.
4. The student will recognize sound-symbol relationships with _____% accuracy.

Interventions:

1. Have the student's hearing checked if it has not been recently checked.

2. Have the student practice daily those sound-symbol relationships he/she does not know.

3. Have the student read and write friends' first names which include the sound-symbol relationships that he/she does not recognize.

4. Have the student say the sounds that consonants make as he/she points to them (e.g., d makes the /d/ sound, etc.).

5. Present the alphabet to the student on flash cards and have him/her make the sounds as the letters are flashed (e.g., d makes the /d/ sound, etc.). This is an appropriate activity for a peer tutor to conduct with the student each day.

6. Identify a sound the student does not know. Have the student circle all the words containing that sound in a paragraph or a page of a book.

7. Put each letter of the alphabet on an individual card. Have the student collect all the letters for which he/she knows the sound. The goal is to collect all the letters of the alphabet.

8. Provide the student with sounds (e.g., /d/, /b/, /p/, etc.) and have him/her write or otherwise identify the letters that make the sounds.

9. Start by teaching the student sounds in the student's first name only. When the student has mastered the sounds in his/her first name, go on to the last name, parents' names, etc.

10. Take every opportunity throughout the day to emphasize a designated sound for that day (e.g., identify the sound when speaking, writing, reading, etc.).

11. Identify a letter for the day. Have the student listen for the sound made by that letter and identify the sound-symbol relationship each time the sound is heard.

12. Assign the student a sound-symbol relationship. Have the student use a highlight marker to identify each word in a passage in which the sound-symbol relationship appears.

13. Use an audio card reader to pair the sounds of letters with the symbols of letters.

14. Do not require the student to learn more information than he/she is capable of learning at any time.

15. Have the student be a peer tutor to teach a concept he/she has mastered to another student. This can serve as reinforcement for the student.

16. Review daily those skills previously introduced.

17. Use both auditory and visual cues to help the student master sound-symbol relationships (e.g., use a picture of an apple for the letter *a* and the sound it makes).

18. Practice, drill, and review every day.

19. Have the student make the sounds of letters as he/she writes words containing the letters (e.g., /d/ /a/ /d/).

20. Provide the student with a desktop chart of sounds. Instruct the student to point to and say the sound the teacher says.

21. Have the student make sentences with words that begin with only one target letter sound (e.g., Tongue twisters tease Tootsie's tonsils.).

22. Teach intensive phonics as a foundation for reading, spelling, and handwriting.

Goals:

1. The student will improve his/her ability to concentrate.
2. The student will improve his/her attention to reading activities.

Objectives:

1. The student will read lines of words without losing his/her place with _____% accuracy.
2. The student will read lists of words without losing his/her place with _____% accuracy.
3. The student will read paragraphs without losing his/her place with _____% accuracy.
4. The student will read sentences without losing his/her place with _____% accuracy.

Interventions:

1. Have the student use his/her finger to move down the page as he/she reads each line.

2. Have all students in a small-group setting point to all words being read verbally. Proceed by having each student read just one sentence, then move automatically to the next student without a break for discussion.

3. Have the student place a ruler or paper strip under each line as he/she reads it. The student then moves the ruler or paper strip under the next line and so on.

4. Consider carefully the student's ability level and experience when expecting him/her to read large amounts of written information independently.

5. Have the student read aloud to maintain his/her place.

6. Have the student read aloud to the teacher each day. Provide evaluative feedback relative to maintaining his/her place while reading.

7. Have the student read aloud to the teacher each day to provide evaluative feedback relative to omissions.

8. Give written directions that are specific and simple to understand.

9. Choose a peer to assist the student in maintaining his/her place during reading activities.

10. Encourage the student to avoid ingesting any substance (e.g., drugs, alcohol, cold remedies, etc.) that might further alter his/her ability to track when reading.

11. Have the student's vision checked if it has not been recently checked.

12. Reduce the emphasis on competition. Competitive activities may cause the student to hurry and omit words or lose his/her place when reading.

13. Do not criticize when correcting the student; be honest yet supportive. Never cause the student to feel negatively about himself/herself.

14. Have the student read directions aloud to aid comprehension.

15. Help the student read directions and review what to do when he/she has difficulty following written directions.

16. Establish an environmental setting for the classroom that promotes optimal individual performance (e.g., quiet room, background music, fresh air, etc.).

17. Make a reading window for each textbook the student uses. The student moves the reading window down and across the page as he/she reads.

18. Provide a quiet place for the student to work (e.g., office space, a study carrel, etc.).

19. Avoid placing the student in uncomfortable reading situations (e.g., reading aloud in a group, identifying that the student's reading group is the lowest level, etc.).

20. Reduce the amount of information on a page (e.g., less print to read, fewer problems, isolate information that is presented to the student, etc.) if it is visually distracting for the student.

21. Make sure the student is paying attention when he/she is reading directions. Have him/her repeat the directions to check for understanding.

22. Reduce the amount of material the student reads at one time (e.g., reduce reading material to single sentences on a page, a single paragraph, etc.).

23. Modify or adjust reading materials to the student's ability level.

24. Verbally correct the student's omissions as often as possible so he/she correctly reads the reading material.

25. Have the student highlight or underline the material as he/she reads.

26. Have the student read verbally and strive for 95%-100% accuracy in maintaining is/her place.

27. Have the student read verbally, working for 95%-100% accuracy with no omissions.

28. Audio record the student reading so he/she can hear omissions.

29. Audio record the student reading aloud. Play it back so that he/she can hear how successfully he/she maintained his/her place when reading.

30. Make sure that the reading demands of all subjects and assignments are within the ability level of the student. If they are not, modify or adjust the reading material to the student's ability level.

31. Assist the student in reading directions. As the student demonstrates success, gradually reduce the assistance and require the student to independently assume more responsibility.

32. In a small-group setting, have the students point to all words as they are read verbally. Have a student read just one sentence, then move automatically to the next student without a break for discussion.

33. Enlarge the print the student is reading.

34. Make sure that the student's knowledge of a particular skill is being assessed rather than the student's ability to read directions, etc.

35. Provide extra time for the student to read directions.

36. Make a list of those words in which the student makes omissions. Have the student practice reading these words.

37. Give the student extra time to read a selection more than once. Emphasize comprehension rather than speed.

38. Have the student point to every word read to hold his/her place.

39. Have the student point to syllables, words, etc., while reading to recognize omissions.

40. Have the student point to syllables, words, etc., as he/she reads them to maintain his/her place.

41. Use a highlight marker to identify key syllables, words, etc., for the student. These words and phrases become the student's sight words.

42. Have the student outline, underline, or highlight important information in printed materials.

43. Correct the student's omissions verbally as often as possible so that he/she hears the correct pronunciation of the reading material.

44. Explain to the student when he/she does not maintain his/her place when reading exactly what he/she did wrong, what should have been done, and why.

80 Omits, adds, substitutes, or reverses letters, words, or sounds when reading

Goals:

1. The student will improve his/her ability to concentrate.
2. The student will improve his/her phonics skills.
3. The student will improve his/her word attack skills.

Objectives:

1. The student will independently read complete phrases with _____% accuracy.
2. The student will independently read complete sentences with _____% accuracy.
3. The student will read complete phrases after he/she has been corrected by the teacher with _____% accuracy.
4. The student will read complete sentences after he/she has been corrected by the teacher with _____% accuracy.

Interventions:

1. Require all students in a small group to point, look, and listen when other group members read verbally.

2. Have the student develop a sight word list of root words to be able to decode words with prefixes and suffixes and increase his/her word attack skills.

3. Have the student place a ruler or paper strip under each line as he/she reads it. The student then moves the ruler or paper strip under the next line and so on.

4. Correct the student's omissions, additions, substitutions, and reversals verbally as often as possible so that he/she correctly reads the reading material.

5. Have the student read aloud to the teacher each day. Provide evaluative feedback relative to his/her omissions, additions, substitutions, and reversals while reading.

6. Provide the student with an alphabet strip on his/her desk to use as a reference for correct letter formation to reduce reversal-related errors when reading.

7. Have the student use an electronic speaking dictionary to find word definitions and pronunciations.

8. Use a sight word approach to teach the student key words (e.g., circle, underline, match, etc.) and phrases when reading directions and instructions.

9. Instruct the student to ask for clarification if he/she does not understand written directions.

10. Teach the student word attack skills using root words to which various prefixes and suffixes may be added.

11. Encourage the student to avoid ingesting any substance (e.g., drugs, alcohol, cold remedies, etc.) that might further alter his/her ability to read material accurately.

12. Use a kinesthetic approach by having the child point to each word as he/she reads verbally. Stop the student for immediate correction if necessary, while continuing with ample praise for hard work and success.

13. Have the student's vision checked if it has not been recently checked.

14. Reduce the emphasis on competition. Competitive activities may cause the student to omit, add, substitute, or reverse letters, words, or sounds when reading.

15. Do not criticize when correcting the student; be honest yet supportive. Never cause the student to feel negatively about himself/herself.

16. Have the student ask for help when he/she needs it.

17. Establish an environmental setting for the classroom that promotes optimal individual performance (e.g., quiet room, background music, fresh air, etc.).

18. Teach reading, spelling, and handwriting simultaneously.

19. Reduce the amount of information on a page (e.g., less print to read, fewer problems, isolate information that is presented to the student, etc.) if it is visually distracting for the student.

20. Make sure the student is learning basic sight word lists to assist in reading.

21. Audio record difficult reading material for the student to listen to while he/she reads along.

22. Reduce the amount of material the student reads at one time (e.g., reduce reading material to single sentences on a page, a single paragraph, etc.). As the student demonstrates success, gradually increase the amount of material to be read at one time.

23. Modify or adjust reading materials to the student's ability level.

24. Set up a system of reinforcers, either tangible (e.g., extra computer time, helper for the day, etc.) or intangible (e.g., smile, fist bump, praise, etc.), to encourage the student and facilitate his/her success in reading.

25. Keep a phonics chart with simple pictures available at all times for the student to use when decoding words.

26. Audio record the student reading aloud. Play it back so that he/she can hear omissions, additions, substitutions, or reversals.

27. Assist the student in reading written information. As the student demonstrates success, gradually decrease the assistance and require the student to independently assume more responsibility.

28. Make sure that the reading demands of all subjects and assignments are within the ability level of the student. If they are not, modify or adjust the reading material to the student's ability level.

29. Make sure that the student's knowledge of a particular skill is being assessed rather than the student's ability to read directions, instructions, etc. Reading directions, instructions, etc., to the student can facilitate success.

30. Provide extra time for the student to read directions.

31. Have the student write those words in which he/she omits, adds, substitutes, or reverses letters or sounds. Have the student practice reading those words.

32. Make a list of those words which the student has made omission, addition, substitution, or reversal errors when reading. Have the student practice reading those words.

33. Use a highlight marker to identify key syllables, words, etc., for the student. These words and phrases become the student's sight words.

34. Use a cardboard window to focus attention on a single line as it is read.

35. Have the student point to syllables, words, etc., as he/she reads them to help him/her recognize omissions, additions, substitutions, or reversals.

36. Teach the student to use context clues when reading to aid word recognition and meaning. These skills will be particularly helpful when he/she is experiencing difficulty with reversals.

37. Teach the student basic sight word lists (e.g., Dolch) to assist in reading.

38. Make a list of words and phrases from the student's reading material which he/she will not recognize (e.g., have the science teacher identify the words and phrases the student will not recognize in the following week's assignment). These words and phrases will become the student's list for reading activities for the following week.

39. Have the student identify words and phrases that he/she does not recognize. Make these words part of the student's sight word list to be learned.

40. Audio record pronunciations of words which the student commonly mispronounces so that he/she can hear the correct pronunciation. Have the student practice pronouncing the words.

41. Have the student read written information more than once. Emphasize accuracy not speed.

81 Reads words correctly in one context but not in another

Goals:

1. The student will improve his/her sight-word vocabulary.
2. The student will improve his/her verbal reading skills.

Objectives:

1. The student will recognize a sight word from a series of words with _____% accuracy.
2. The student will recognize sight words in phrases with _____% accuracy.
3. The student will recognize sight words in sentences with _____% accuracy.
4. The student will recognize words from one context to another, with assistance, with _____% accuracy.
5. The student will independently recognize words from one context to another with _____% accuracy.

Interventions:

1. Provide the student with a dictionary and require him/her to find the definitions of those words he/she did not recognize.

2. Have the student maintain a list with definitions of those words he/she most frequently fails to recognize in different contexts.

3. Provide the student with a quiet place (e.g., carrel, study booth, etc.) where he/she may go to participate in reading activities.

4. Have the student read aloud to the teacher each day to provide evaluative feedback.

5. Reduce the emphasis on competition. Competitive activities may cause the student to hurry and not recognize words in a particular context.

6. Identify words the student does not recognize in different contexts and put these words on flash cards. Have the student match these words to the same words in sentences, paragraphs, short stories, etc.

7. Make a reading window for the student. The student moves the reading window down and across the page as he/she reads.

8. Avoid placing the student in uncomfortable reading situations (e.g., reading aloud in a group, identifying that the student's reading group is the lowest level, etc.).

9. Reduce the amount of information on a page (e.g., less print to read, fewer pictures to look at, etc.) if it is causing visual distractions for the student.

10. Make sure the student is reading material on his/her ability level.

11. Provide the student with large-print reading material to facilitate the student's success in recognizing words in different contexts.

12. Audio record difficult reading material for the student to listen to as he/she reads along.

13. Require the student to read a selection each day which includes the vocabulary currently being studied.

14. Have the student read short sentences to make it easier to recognize words in different contexts. As the student demonstrates success, present longer sentences for him/her to read.

15. Write paragraphs and short stories using those words the student most frequently fails to recognize in different contexts. These paragraphs should be of high interest to the student using his/her name, family members, friends, pets, and interesting experiences.

16. Use a lower grade-level text as alternative reading material in subject areas.

17. Reduce distracting stimuli in the environment to facilitate the student's ability to concentrate on what he/she is reading (e.g., place the student on the front row, provide a carrel or office space away from distractions). This is used as a means of reducing distracting stimuli and not as a form of punishment.

18. Have the student list those words he/she most frequently fails to recognize into categories such as people, food, animals, etc., to help the student recognize those words in different contexts.

19. Write notes and letters to the student to provide reading material which includes words that frequently give the student difficulty.

20. Use daily drill activities to help the student memorize vocabulary words.

21. Teach the student to use context clues to identify words not understood.

22. Highlight or underline those words the student most frequently fails to recognize in different contexts.

23. Highlight or underline those words in reading material the student is unable to recognize. Have the student identify those words as he/she encounters them while reading.

82 Understands what is read to him/her but not what he/she reads silently

Goals:

1. The student will improve his/her oral reading skills.
2. The student will improve his/her reading comprehension.

Objectives:

1. The student will demonstrate comprehension of individual words he/she reads with _____% accuracy.
2. The student will demonstrate comprehension of individual phrases he/she reads with _____% accuracy.
3. The student will demonstrate comprehension of individual sentences he/she reads with _____% accuracy.
4. The student will demonstrate comprehension of individual paragraphs he/she reads with _____% accuracy.
5. The student will demonstrate comprehension of short stories, chapters, etc., he/she reads with _____% accuracy.
6. The student will comprehend reading material with _____% accuracy.

Interventions:

1. Pair the student with a peer to summarize material read to answer the questions *Who, What, Where, When, How,* and *Why.*

2. Have the student quietly read aloud when reading to himself/herself.

3. Use a sight word approach to teach the student key words (e.g., circle, underline, match, etc.) and phrases when reading directions and instructions.

4. Use lower grade-level texts as alternative reading material in subject areas.

5. Have the student practice comprehension skills which are directly related to high-interest reading activities (e.g., adventure, romance, mystery, sports, etc.).

6. Have the student look for action words (e.g., sailed, discovered, founded, etc.).

7. Have the student look for direction words (e.g., circle, underline, choose, list, etc.).

8. Have the student look for key words (e.g., Christopher Columbus, Spain, New World, etc.).

9. After reading a selection, have the student complete a semantic map answering the questions *Who, What, Where, When, How,* and *Why.*

10. Have the student read high-interest signs, advertisements, notices, etc., from newspapers, magazines, movie promotions, etc., placing emphasis on comprehension skills.

11. Teach the student to identify main points in material he/she has read to assess comprehension.

12. Have the student answer in writing the questions *Who, What, Where, When, How,* and *Why* using the *Flash Card Study Aid.*

13. Have the student read independently each day to practice reading skills.

14. Reduce the amount of information on a page (e.g., less print to read, fewer pictures to look at, etc.) if it is causing visual distractions for the student.

15. Make sure the student is reading material on his/her ability level.

16. Make sure the student is practicing comprehension skills which are directly related to high-interest reading activities (e.g., adventure, romance, mystery, sports, etc.).

17. Make a list of main points from the student's reading material, written on the student's reading level.

18. Modify or adjust reading material to the student's ability level.

19. Audio record difficult reading material for the student to listen to as he/she reads along.

20. Have the student take notes while reading to facilitate comprehension.

21. Teach the student meanings of abbreviations to assist in comprehending material read.

22. Have the student underline or highlight important points in reading material.

23. Have the student verbally paraphrase material he/she has just read to assess his/her comprehension.

24. Underline or highlight important points before the student reads the assigned material silently.

25. Teach new vocabulary words prior to having the student read the material.

26. Have the student read progressively longer segments of reading material to build comprehension skills (e.g., begin with a single paragraph and progress to several paragraphs, short stories, chapters, etc.).

27. Provide the student a quiet place (e.g., carrel, study booth, etc.) where he/she may go to engage in reading activities.

28. Make sure that the reading demands of all subjects and assignments are within the ability level of the student. If they are not, modify or adjust the reading material to the student's ability level.

29. Teach the student when reading to look for key words and main ideas that answer *Who, What, Where, When, How,* and *Why* (e.g., Christopher Columbus sailed from Spain to discover the New World during the year 1492.).

30. Give the student high-interest reading material on his/her ability level (e.g., comic books, adventure stories, etc.) requiring him/her to answer the questions *Who, What, Where, When, How,* and *Why*.

31. Have the student outline reading material using the *Outline Form*.

32. Have the student practice reading and following written directions to facilitate comprehension (e.g., following a recipe, following directions to put together a model, etc.).

33. Have the student audio record what he/she reads to facilitate comprehension by replaying and listening to the material read.

34. Prior to reading a selection, familiarize the student with the general content of the story (e.g., if the selection is about elephants, brainstorm and discuss elephants to develop a point of reference).

35. Have the student dictate stories which are then put in print for him/her to read, placing emphasis on comprehension skills.

36. Write paragraphs and short stories requiring reading skills the student is currently developing. These passages should be of high interest to the student using his/her name, family members, friends, pets, and interesting experiences.

37. Do not require the student to learn more information than he/she is capable of learning at any time.

38. Outline reading material the student reads silently using words and phrases on his/her reading level.

39. Make available for the student a learning center where a variety of information is available in content areas (e.g., the library may have a selection of films, slides, videos, recorded lectures, etc.).

40. Make sure that the student's knowledge of a particular skill is being assessed rather than the student's ability to read directions, instructions, etc. Reading directions, instructions, etc., to the student may facilitate his/her success.

41. Reduce distracting stimuli in the environment to facilitate the student's ability to concentrate on what he/she is reading (e.g., place the student in the front row, provide a carrel or office space away from distractions, etc.). This is used as a means of reducing distracting stimuli and not as a form of punishment.

42. When reading verbally with the student, pause at various points to discuss material read up to that point. Have the student predict what will happen next before continuing.

43. Write notes and letters to the student to provide reading material which he/she will want to read for comprehension. Students may be encouraged to write each other notes and letters at a time set aside each day, once a week, etc.

44. Give the student time to read a selection more than once. Emphasize comprehension rather than speed.

45. Teach the student to think about the reading selection and predict what will happen next, prior to completing the selection.

46. Have the student outline, underline, or highlight important points in reading material.

47. Teach the student to use context clues to identify words and phrases he/she does not know.

48. Stop at various points while the student is reading silently to check for comprehension.

49. Use reading series materials with high interest (e.g., adventure, romance, mystery, sports, etc.) and low vocabulary.

83 Can only write simple, short, noncomplex sentences

Goal:

1. The student will expand sentence length and complexity in written work.

Objectives:

1. The student will use a complex subject in a written sentence with _____% accuracy.
2. The student will combine two short sentences into one longer sentence with _____% accuracy.
3. The student will use a compound verb in a written sentence with _____% accuracy.
4. The student will use embedded clauses in written sentences with _____% accuracy.
5. The student will include a dependent clause in a written sentence with _____% accuracy.
6. The student will expand, in writing, the length and complexity of a given sentence in _____ out of _____ trials.
7. The student will edit his/her written work for length and complexity of sentences in _____ out of _____ trials.

Interventions:

1. Have the student's hearing checked if it has not been recently checked.

2. Determine the type of verbal model the student has at home. Without placing negative connotations on his/her parents' language skills, explain the purpose of using elaborate sentences.

3. Assess whether or not the student uses complex sentences when speaking. Proficiency in spoken language typically precedes and influences the type of language used in written work.

4. Reinforce the student for increasing his/her use of complex sentences: (a) give the student a tangible reward (e.g., classroom privileges, line leading, passing out materials, five minutes free time, etc.) or (b) give the student an intangible reward (e.g., praise, fist bump, smile, etc.).

5. Teach the student that sentences express thoughts about a subject and what that subject is or does. Explain that complex thoughts require complex sentences which include descriptive words and connecting words.

6. Teach the student more complex sentences by asking questions to assess his/her comprehension (e.g., Before you get a drink of water, finish your social studies. What should you do first? or Everyone except Mark went to lunch. Did Mark go to lunch?).

7. Reinforce those students in the classroom who use complex sentences.

8. When the student uses short, simple sentences which lack complexity in his/her written work, provide him/her with models of expansion and conjoining using his/her sentences as a framework.

9. Provide the student with an elaborated sentence and have him/her identify the descriptive vocabulary used. If necessary, ask the student questions to elicit the appropriate information.

10. Provide evaluative prompts to remind the student to expand his/her written sentences (e.g., write Tell me more about _____. or insert marks to indicate the appropriate placement for more descriptive vocabulary, etc.).

11. Provide worksheets with sentences which begin with compound subjects and have the student complete the thought (e.g., The bear and the frog _____.). This activity can be expanded by providing verb phrases without subjects or short sentences without objects or prepositional phrases.

12. Have the student use conjunctions to expand sentences containing opposites (e.g., A man is big, but a boy is little.).

13. Provide the student with conjunctions to be used in sentence expansion, including sentence combining, compound subjects and verbs, etc.

14. During the day, write down some of the student's simple sentences. Read the sentences to the student and ask him/her questions requiring additional descriptive vocabulary to expand the sentences (e.g., Student: My dog can run. Teacher: What color is your dog? How big is your dog? How fast can your dog run? Encourage the student to use these words to make his/her original sentence longer. Student: My big, black dog can run fast. Accept any additional expansions the student incorporates into his/her sentences without expecting all the descriptors to be used initially.).

15. Have the student write sentences about a specific topic, object, activity, etc. Encourage the use of descriptive words and phrases where appropriate.

16. Provide the student with a topic sentence, opinion statement, or statement of fact. Have him/her expand upon the original idea using as much detail as possible.

17. Have the student assist in adding descriptive words and phrases to other students' simple sentences.

18. Ask the parents to encourage the student's use of more complex sentences at home by praising him/her when longer sentences are used.

19. Video the student and his/her classmates performing various actions. Play the recording without sound and have the student write a story about what is happening. Encourage the use of descriptive words and phrases where appropriate. A prerecorded video could also be used for this activity.

20. Give the student several short sentences and have him/her combine them to make one longer sentence. (e.g., The dog is big. The dog is brown. The dog is mine. - The big, brown dog is mine.).

21. Give the student a list of transition words (e.g., therefore, although, because, etc.) and have him/her write sentences using each word.

22. Give the student a group of related words (e.g., author, read, love, best-seller, etc.) and have him/her write sentences that include all the words.

23. Make groups of cards containing subjects, verbs, adjectives, etc. Have the student combine cards in various ways to construct sentences which are appropriate in complexity. Have him/her write the sentences.

24. Build lists by providing nouns that go with a specific adjective (e.g., red could be followed by apple, car, book, etc.). Have the student select one of the nouns and build a list of appropriate adjectives (e.g., car could have the adjectives big, metal, expensive, etc.). Have the student write sentences using the phrases he/she has developed.

25. Using a wordless picture book, have the student write a story. Encourage the use of longer, more complex sentences.

26. If the student's noncomplex sentences reflect the lack of a language-enriching home environment, explain to the student that language can be fun and that you will help him/her discover this.

27. Encourage verbal output. Generally, students who use very short sentences also talk less than most students. If a student does not speak in complex sentences, he/she will probably not use complex sentences in written work.

28. Encourage written output with an emphasis on content and complexity rather than spelling and punctuation.

29. Teach the student the difference between communicating verbally and in written form. When speaking, less complex sentences may be more acceptable because of the availability of nonverbal cues to facilitate the message. Such cues are not available in written work.

30. Provide the student with a sentence and three choices of conjunctions. Have the student write three different sentences using each conjunction to expand upon the original sentence (e.g., The truck crashed (and, when, but) _____.). Point out the differences in the sentences based on the choice of conjunction.

31. Have several students build a sentence while someone writes it down (e.g., The first student starts with a word (e.g., I). The next student adds the second word (e.g., like.) This process continues as long as possible to create one long, complex sentence.).

32. Pair the student with a peer. Have them take turns writing descriptions of classroom objects or activities. Have the students combine all or parts of their short sentences into longer, more complex sentences.

33. Have the student write process statements to sequence an activity (e.g., how to make a peanut butter and jelly sandwich). Have him/her focus on using as much detail as possible.

34. Have the student write sentences about a scene from a busy picture or poster with emphasis on using as much detail as possible.

84 Composes incomplete sentences or expresses incomplete thoughts when writing

Goals:

1. The student will improve his/her ability in written expression.
2. The student will improve his/her grammatical skills when writing.
3. The student will improve his/her skills in written expression by way of complete sentences.
4. The student will improve his/her skills in written expression by way of complete thoughts.
5. The student will use complete thoughts in complete sentences.

Objectives:

1. The student will change an incomplete written sentence to a complete one with _____% accuracy.
2. The student will choose between complete and incomplete written sentences in _____ out of _____ trials.
3. The student will verbally imitate a complete sentence in _____ out of _____ trials.
4. The student will write complete sentences which express thoughts with _____% accuracy and legible handwriting.
5. The student will write complete sentences which express thoughts with _____% accuracy.
6. The student will write phrases which express thoughts with _____% accuracy.
7. The student will write single words which express thoughts with _____% accuracy.

Interventions:

1. Model writing in complete sentences or thoughts in legible handwriting for the student to imitate.

2. After the student proofreads his/her written work, have him/her explain why specific sentences do or do not express complete thoughts.

3. Assess whether or not the student uses complete sentences or expresses complete thoughts when speaking. Proficiency in spoken language typically precedes and influences the type of language used in written work.

4. Ask questions which stimulate language. Avoid those which can be answered by yes/no or a nod of the head (e.g., ask the student what he/she did at recess instead of asking if he/she played on the slide, ask the student what he/she did on vacation instead of asking if he/she stayed home over the holidays, etc.).

5. Assign the student shorter tasks while increasing the quality of expectations.

6. Check the student's written work at various points throughout the assignment to make sure the student is using complete sentences and thoughts in legible handwriting.

7. Give the student a group of related words (e.g., author, read, love, best-seller, etc.) and have him/her make up a paragraph including all the words. Emphasize the use of complete sentences or thoughts in legible handwriting.

8. Choose a topic for a paragraph or story and alternate writing sentences with the student to provide a regular model of the components of a complete sentence.

9. Ask the parents to encourage the student's use of complete sentences and thoughts, both verbal and written, by praising him/her when these are used at home.

10. Encourage the student to read written work aloud to help identify incomplete sentences and thoughts.

11. Establish levels of expectations for quality handwriting performance. Require the student to correct or repeat assignments until the expectations are met.

12. Give the student a factual statement (e.g., some animals are dangerous) and have him/her compose several complete sentences relating to that fact.

13. Make sure the student is aware of the types of errors made when writing (e.g., not completing sentences or thoughts, writing too big or small, etc.).

14. Provide exercises for making sentences out of groups of words.

15. Give the student a note card to keep at his/her desk as a reminder that all sentences must have a subject and a verb.

16. Give the student scrambled words and have him/her put them in the correct order to form a complete sentence.

17. Provide the student with clearly stated criteria for acceptable work (e.g., neatness, complete sentences, legible handwriting, etc.).

18. Give the student several short sentences and have him/her combine them to make one longer complete sentence (e.g., The dog is big. The dog is brown. The dog is mine. - The big, brown dog is mine.).

19. Have a number of students build a sentence while someone writes it down (e.g., The first one starts with a word (e.g., I). The next student adds the second word (e.g., like.) This process continues as long as possible to create one long, complete sentence.).

20. Choose a peer to model writing in complete sentences or thoughts for the student. Have the students work together, perform assignments together, etc.

21. Provide older students with functional writing opportunities (e.g., job application forms, reinforcer surveys, order forms, checks to write, customer surveys, etc.).

22. Choose a peer to read the student's written work aloud to help him/her identify incomplete sentences.

23. Have the student assist in grading or proofreading other students' written work to make him/her more aware of incomplete sentences or thoughts.

24. Have the student give verbal or written process statements to sequence an activity (e.g., how to make a peanut butter and jelly sandwich). Have him/her focus on making each statement a complete thought.

25. Have the student identify who he/she thinks is a good writer and why.

26. Give the student a list of conjunction words (e.g., therefore, although, because, etc.) and have him/her make sentences using each word.

27. Have the student read/go over schoolwork with the teacher to become aware of the quality of his/her work.

28. Have the student read/go over written communication to become aware of the quality of his/her work.

29. Have the student write a daily log, expressing his/her thoughts in complete sentences.

30. Choose a peer to model writing and speaking in complete sentences or thoughts for the student.

31. Identify the qualities a good writer possesses (e.g., writing in complete sentences or thoughts, using appropriate vocabulary, etc.) and have the student evaluate himself/herself on each characteristic. Set a goal for improvement in only one or two areas at a time.

32. If the student's errors reflect the lack of a language-enriching home environment, explain to the student that language can be fun and that you and he/she will work together to help him/her discover this.

33. Make sure that parents and all educators who work with the student maintain consistent expectations of writing quality.

34. Give the student a series of written phrases and have him/her indicate which ones express a complete thought.

35. Make sure the student has the necessary materials to write with legible handwriting (e.g., pen with ink, sharpened pencil, lined paper, etc.).

36. Reduce the emphasis on competition. Competitive activities may cause the student to hurry and not write in complete sentences or thoughts.

37. Teach the concept of verb and noun phrases as soon as possible so the student has a means of checking to see if a sentence is complete.

38. Have the student's hearing checked if it has not been recently checked.

39. Have the student use a pencil grip (e.g., three-sided, foam, rubber, etc.) to help him/her appropriately grip the pencil or pen.

40. Make groups of cards containing subjects, verbs, adjectives, etc. Have the student combine the cards in various ways to construct complete sentences.

41. Teach the student the construction of a complete sentence. Point out the subject/verb/object components through the use of objects, pictures, and/or written sentences (depending on the student's abilities).

42. Give the student a series of complete and incomplete sentences, both written and oral. Ask him/her to identify which are correct and incorrect and make appropriate modifications.

43. Teach the student that a complete sentence has to express a complete thought about a subject and what that subject is or does.

44. Play a game by providing students with a box labeled *Trash*. Provide sentence strips with complete and incomplete sentences. Instruct students to throw incomplete sentences in the trash.

45. Have the student write letters to friends, relatives, etc., to create additional ways he/she can practice writing complete sentences and thoughts in legible handwriting.

46. Provide a multitude of writing opportunities for the student to practice expressing complete sentences and thoughts in legible handwriting (e.g., writing letters to sports and entertainment figures, relatives, or friends; writing for free information on a topic in which the student is interested).

47. Provide the student with a topic (e.g., rules to follow when riding your bike) and have him/her write complete sentences about it.

48. Provide the student with additional time to complete schoolwork to achieve quality.

49. When correcting/grading the student's writing, provide specific evaluative feedback which will assist the student in constructing complete sentences (e.g., Student writes: Going to the show. Teacher comments: Who is going? or Subject is missing.). After checking the student's written work, make sure he/she makes all necessary corrections.

50. Provide the student with ample opportunity to master handwriting skills (e.g., instruction in letter positioning, directions, spacing, etc.).

51. Provide the student with examples of subjects and verbs on a classroom chart.

52. Read verbally to the student to stimulate the student's thought and writing processes.

53. Give the student a subject and have him/her write as many complete sentences in legible handwriting as possible about the subject.

54. Recognize quality work (e.g., display the student's work, congratulate the student, etc.).

55. Reinforce the student for using complete sentences or thoughts when writing: (a) give the student a tangible reward (e.g., classroom privileges, line leading, passing out materials, five minutes free time, etc.) or (b) give the student an intangible reward (e.g., praise, fist bump, smile, etc.).

56. Reinforce the students in the classroom who use complete sentences or thoughts when writing.

57. Require the student to proofread all written work. Reinforce him/her for completing sentences or thoughts in legible handwriting.

58. Speak to the student and explain that he/she is using incomplete sentences or thoughts when writing. Explain the importance of expressing complete thoughts in written work.

59. Teach the student the difference between communicating verbally and in written form. When speaking, using incomplete or run-on sentences, pronouns without referents, etc., is more acceptable because nonverbal cues can be used to clarify the message. However, such cues are not available in written work.

60. When correcting the student's written work, be sure to provide written and verbal evaluative feedback which is designed to be instructional (e.g., help the student rewrite for better completion of sentence or thoughts, rewrite legibly for student, etc.).

61. Provide the student, both verbally and in written form, with sentence starters (e.g., Go _____, Run _____, Today I _____, Anyone can _____, etc.) and have him/her write complete sentences.

62. Have the student use a different size pencil or pencil grip to assist him/her with fine motor skills to produce acceptable writing.

63. Have the student correct a series of phrases by making each a complete sentence.

64. Teach the student to proofread each sentence in isolation to check for a complete thought.

65. Use adhesive material (e.g., tape, non-slip material, etc.) to keep paper positioned appropriately for handwriting.

66. Teach the student to use a typewriter or computer if inadequate fine motor skills make handwriting skills difficult for him/her.

67. Provide the student with appropriate time limits for the completion of written assignments.

85 Does not use appropriate subject-verb agreement when writing

Goals:

1. The student will improve his/her grammatical skills when writing.
2. The student will improve his/her ability in written expression.

Objectives:

1. The student will verbally conjugate common verbs with _____% accuracy.
2. The student will conjugate common verbs in written form with _____% accuracy.
3. The student will write sentences requiring subject-verb agreement with _____% accuracy.
4. The student will use subject-verb agreement when writing with _____% accuracy.

Interventions:

1. After checking the student's written work, make sure he/she makes all necessary corrections in subject-verb agreement.

2. Assess the type of grammatical model to which the student is exposed at home. Without placing negative connotations on his/her parents' grammatical style, explain the difference between standard and nonstandard grammar.

3. Correct the student each time he/she uses subject-verb agreement incorrectly when speaking.

4. Have the student make up sentences with verbs and subjects given to him/her to use.

5. Explain that certain forms of verbs go with certain subjects and that correct subject-verb agreement requires the appropriate match of subject and verb. Teach the student the various possibilities of subject-verb agreement and how to select the correct one.

6. Give the student a choice of answers (e.g., more than one possible answer, multiple-choice on a worksheet, etc.) to facility his/her ability to recognize the correct answer.

7. Have the student pick out the correct verb when given choices on fill-in-the-blank worksheets (e.g., They _____ (have, has) a new dog.).

8. Provide the student with a computer software program or a hand-held educational device that gives practice and reinforcement in subject-verb agreement.

9. Give the student a series of sentences with both incorrect and correct usage of verbs and ask the student to identify which are correct and incorrect.

10. Have the student find examples of correct subject-verb agreement in his/her favorite books or magazines.

11. Give the student a series of sentences, both written and oral, and have him/her identify which are grammatically correct and incorrect.

12. Have the student practice correct subject-verb agreement by providing the student with several sentences with errors on the wall-mounted board or overhead projector. The student is to correct the subject-verb errors and discuss them with the teacher.

13. Speak to the student to explain that he/she is using inappropriate subject-verb agreement. Emphasize the importance of writing grammatically correct sentences.

14. Have the student read the written work of peers in which subject-verb agreement is used correctly.

15. Highlight or underline subject-verb agreements in the student's reading to call attention to the appropriate combinations.

16. Have the student's hearing checked if it has not been recently checked.

17. Play *Concentration* to match subject-verb agreement.

18. Have the student help correct other students' written work by checking subject-verb agreement and correcting the assignment.

19. Identify the most common errors the student makes in subject-verb agreement. Have the student spend time each day writing one or more of these subject-verb combinations in correct form.

20. Make a list of the correct forms of subject-verbs the student has difficulty writing correctly. Have the student keep the list at his/her desk for a reference when writing.

21. Make a list of those verbs the student most commonly uses incorrectly. This list will become the guide for learning activities in subject-verb agreement.

22. Have the student complete worksheets on which he/she must supply the correct verb forms to go with specific subjects (e.g., He _____ the dishes.).

23. Teach the student that different forms of verbs go with different subjects and that correct subject-verb agreement requires the appropriate verb form. Have the student practice matching verb forms to lists of subjects.

24. Make sure the student receives instruction in subject-verb agreement for those subject-verb combinations he/she commonly has difficulty writing correctly.

25. Review daily those skills, concepts, tasks, etc., which have been previously introduced.

26. Teach the student the meaning of subject and verb by demonstrating through the use of objects, pictures, and/or written sentences (depending on the student's abilities).

27. Teach the student plural forms of words (e.g., have the student point to a picture of a cat and point to a picture of cats).

28. Model appropriate subject-verb agreement when speaking so the student learns appropriate subject-verb agreement through verbal exposure.

29. Have the student be a peer tutor to teach a concept he/she has mastered to another student as reinforcement.

30. Provide a review of standard subject-verb agreement rules through a chart posted in the classroom (e.g., cows run, a cow runs, etc.).

31. Provide the student with increased opportunity for help or assistance on academic tasks (e.g., peer tutoring, directions for work sent home, frequent interactions, etc.).

32. Recognize quality work (e.g., display the student's work, congratulate the student, etc.).

33. Reduce the emphasis on competition. Competitive activities may cause the student to hurry and make errors in subject-verb agreement.

34. Do not require the student to learn more information than he/she is capable of learning at any time.

35. Reinforce the student for using appropriate subject-verb agreement when writing: (a) give the student a tangible reward (e.g., classroom privileges, line leading, passing out materials, five minutes free time, etc.) or (b) give the student an intangible reward (e.g., praise, fist bump, smile, etc.).

36. Require the student to proofread his/her written work for subject-verb agreement. Reinforce the student for correcting all errors.

37. Teach the student that sentences express thoughts about a subject and what that subject is or does.

38. Give the student specific verb forms and have him/her supply appropriate subjects to go with each (e.g., _____ runs.).

39. Show the student pictures of people, places, or things. Ask him/her to make a statement about each picture. Have the student identify the subject and verb of the verbal sentence and tell whether or not they agree.

86 Fails to copy letters, words, sentences, and numbers from a model at a close proximity

Goals:

1. The student will improve his/her ability to copy from the wall-mounted board, textbook, etc.
2. The student will improve his/her handwriting skills (e.g., copying from a model, letter formation, letter size, and spacing).

Objectives:

1. The student will be able to form letters and numbers with _____% accuracy.
2. The student will copy letters and numbers from a model at a close proximity replicating formation, size, and spacing with _____% accuracy.
3. The student will copy sentences and numbers from a model at a close proximity replicating formation, size, shape, and spacing with _____% accuracy.
4. The student will copy words and sentences from a model at a close proximity replicating formation, size, and spacing with _____% accuracy.
5. The student will trace letters and numbers from a model at a close proximity replicating formation, size, and spacing with _____% accuracy.

Interventions:

1. Allow the student periods of rest to avoid eye fatigue.

2. Assess the appropriateness of giving the student assignments which require copying at a close proximity if the student's ability makes it impossible to complete the assignments.

3. Assign short-term tasks that can be quickly and accurately copied. As the student demonstrates success, gradually increase the length of tasks.

4. Assist the student in copying information. As the student demonstrates success, gradually decrease the assistance and require the student to assume more responsibility.

5. Explain to the student exactly what he/she is doing wrong (e.g., not carefully completing work), and what he/she should be doing (e.g., working slowly and carefully).

6. Have the student copy small amounts of material (e.g., a sentence or line) at a time.

7. Change the format of the materials from which the student copies (e.g., have less material on a page, remove or cover pictures on pages, enlarge the print, etc.).

8. Check what the student has copied from the wall-mounted board, textbook, etc., for accuracy. Working quickly is acceptable if the student performs the task accurately.

9. Consider carefully the student's ability level and experience before expecting him/her to complete copying tasks on his/her own.

10. Encourage the student to develop a 30 second definition of his/her goal to help him/her stay on task and focus (e.g., I will copy this sentence perfectly. The better I focus and stay on task, the better I will perform.).

11. Encourage the student to monitor his/her neatness. Awareness should reduce production of poor quality work.

12. Make sure that the student has only those materials necessary for copying (e.g., pencil, pen, paper, etc.) on his/her desk.

13. Establish a timeline for completing a project. Expect the student to meet each deadline to complete the project on time.

14. Establish rules for completing tasks (e.g., have the student take his/her time, ask for help when necessary, proofread material copied from the board, textbook, etc.). These rules should be consistent and followed by everyone in the classroom. Talk about the rules often.

15. Assess the level of task difficulty to determine whether or not the student will require additional time, assistance, etc., to copy written information.

16. Evaluate the appropriateness of the task to determine (a) if the task is too easy, (b) if the task is too difficult, or (c) if the length of time scheduled to complete the task is adequate.

17. Evaluate the visual and auditory stimuli in the classroom. Remove or reduce the extraneous environmental stimuli.

18. Give recognition for quality work (e.g., display the student's work, congratulate the student, etc.).

19. Provide a variety of ways for the student to obtain information without him/her copying it (e.g., teacher made material, commercially produced material, photocopy of the material, etc.).

20. Give the student a short break while he/she is working on monotonous assignments to relieve restlessness and improve concentration.

21. Choose a peer to assist the student in copying material (e.g., read the material aloud as the student copies it, copy the material for the student, etc.).

22. Have the student ask for help when he/she needs it.

23. Provide the student with the necessary materials to complete assignments (e.g., pencil with eraser, paper, dictionary, handwriting sample, etc.). Be sure that the student has only the necessary materials on the desk.

24. Maintain a consistent format from which the student copies.

25. Have the student read his/her written work out loud when proofing.

26. Establish an environmental setting for the classroom that promotes optimal individual performance (e.g., quiet room, background music, fresh air, etc.).

27. Have the student question any directions, explanations, and instructions he/she does not understand.

28. Place the material from which the student is to copy at a distance. As the student demonstrates success, gradually move the material closer to the student.

29. Have the student work on the assignment at another time (e.g., later in the day, during lunch, etc.) when he/she should be able to concentrate better.

30. Reinforce the student for copying letters, words, sentences, and numbers from a model at a close proximity: (a) give the student a tangible reward (e.g., classroom privileges, line leading, passing out materials, five minutes free time, etc.) or (b) give the student an intangible reward (e.g., praise, fist bump, smile, etc.).

31. Help the student complete writing tasks so he/she will not have to hurry.

32. Highlight or underline the material the student is to copy.

33. Enlarge the print the student is to copy.

34. Choose a peer to proofread all of the student's work before it is submitted.

35. Identify any particular letters or numbers the student has difficulty copying and have him/her practice copying those letters or numbers.

36. Have the student's vision checked if it has not been recently checked.

37. Increase supervision (e.g., by teacher, peer, paraprofessional, etc.) of the student while he/she is performing assignments which require copying.

38. Instruct the student to list five qualities of a peer who produces neat work. Have him/her choose one of those qualities to work on each week for five weeks until all five have been completed.

39. Have the student practice writing letters, words, and sentences by tracing over a series of dots.

40. Maintain consistent expectations for the student to complete a task neatly and accurately.

41. Make sure that the material to be copied has a sharp contrast with the background/foreground to maximize visibility (e.g., black on white projections, white marker on green wall-mounted board, etc.).

42. Use an overhead projector to enlarge the material to be copied.

43. Have the student proofread all of his/her work before submitting it.

44. If the student wears glasses, encourage him/her to wear them if needed while working.

45. Provide the student with a number line and alphabet strip on his/her desk to use as a reference for correct form of letters and numbers to reduce errors.

46. Make sure there is no glare on the material to be copied from a distance.

47. Teach the student that work not done accurately will be redone, corrected, etc., during his/her recreation time.

48. Make sure the student's desk is free of all material except that from which he/she is copying.

49. Make sure the student has all the materials necessary prior to beginning an assignment to reduce unnecessary distractions while copying.

50. Match the student's assignments with his/her activity level. When the student is feeling highly active, assign tasks which require a great level of movement. When the student is most likely to maintain attention, assign more sedentary tasks (e.g., copying from textbook, wall-mounted board, etc.).

51. Provide an incentive statement along with a directive (e.g., When you have copied the work correctly, you can work on the computer.).

52. Provide more hands-on activities instead of copying materials from books.

53. Modify the material from which the student is to copy (e.g., reduce the amount of material to be copied, enlarge the print, etc.).

54. Provide the student with a private place to work (e.g., study carrel, private office, etc.). This is used to reduce distracting stimuli and not as a form of punishment.

55. Provide the student with the material to be copied at his/her desk if he/she is unable to copy it from a distance.

56. Teach the student the relationship between inappropriate behavior and the consequences which follow (e.g., failing to copy the directions will result in homework assignments being done incorrectly).

57. Recognize quality work (e.g., display student's work, congratulate the student, etc.).

58. Reduce distracting stimuli (e.g., noise and motion in the classroom) to facilitate the student's ability to copy letters, words, sentences, and numbers from a model.

59. Reduce the emphasis on competition. Competitive activities may cause the student to hurry and be careless when copying.

60. Have the student use word processing on the computer as an alternative to using pencil and paper.

61. Use the computer keyboard and monitor as an alternative writing tool.

62. Require the student to proofread all written work. Reinforce the student for each correction made.

63. Seat the student farther from the material being copied.

64. Require the student to complete a task again if it has been done incorrectly due to his/her hurrying just to get it completed.

65. Set aside time at the end of each class period for the student to complete unfinished assignments.

66. Use a frame or window to cover all material except that which the student is to copy.

87   Fails to copy letters, words, sentences, and numbers from a model at a distance

Goal:

1. The student will improve his/her handwriting skills (e.g., copying from a model, letter formation, letter size, and spacing).

Objectives:

1. The student will be able to correctly form letters and numbers with _____% accuracy.
2. The student will copy letters, words, sentences, and numbers from a model at a close proximity replicating formation, size, and spacing with _____% accuracy.
3. The student will copy letters, words, sentences, and numbers from a model at a distance with the assistance of cues and prompts (e.g., lined paper, verbal cues, alphabet strips, number lines, etc.) with _____% accuracy.
4. The student will copy letters, words, sentences, and numbers from a model at a distance replicating formation, size, and spacing with _____% accuracy.

Interventions:

1. Have the student's vision checked if it has not been recently checked.

2. Enlarge the print the student is to copy.

3. Change the format of the material the student is to copy (e.g., less material to be copied, enlarge the print, etc.).

4. Seat the student closer to the material being copied.

5. Highlight or underline the material the student is copying.

6. Have the student copy small amounts of material (e.g., a sentence or line) at a time.

7. Make sure that the student has only those materials necessary for copying (e.g., pencil, pen, paper, etc.) on his/her desk.

8. Provide the student with a private place to work (e.g., study carrel, office, etc.). This is used to reduce distracting stimuli and not as a form of punishment.

9. Use a variety of ways for the student to obtain information without him/her copying it (e.g., teacher-made material, commercially produced material, photocopy of the material, etc.).

10. Choose a peer to assist the student in copying the material (e.g., read the material aloud as the student copies it, copy the material for the student, etc.).

11. Maintain a consistent format from which the student copies.

12. Make sure that the material to be copied has a sharp contrast with the background/foreground to maximize visibility (e.g., black on white projections, white marker on green wall-mounted board, etc.).

13. Make sure there is no glare on the material to be copied from a distance.

14. Place the material from which the student is to copy close to him/her. As the student demonstrates success, gradually move the material away from him/her.

15. Provide the student with material to copy at his/her desk if he/she is unable to copy it from a distance.

16. Identify any particular letters or numbers the student has difficulty copying and have him/her practice copying those letters and numbers.

17. Have the student practice writing letters, words, and sentences by tracing over a series of dots.

18. Provide the student with a number line and alphabet strip on his/her desk to use as a reference for the correct form of letters and numbers to reduce errors.

19. Require the student to proofread all written work. Reinforce the student for each correction made.

20. Recognize quality work (e.g., display student's work, congratulate the student, etc.).

21. Provide the student with the necessary materials to complete assignments (e.g., pencil with eraser, paper, dictionary, handwriting sample, etc.). Be sure that the student has only the necessary materials on the desk.

22. Assess the appropriateness of giving the student assignments which require copying at a distance if the student's ability makes it impossible to complete the assignment.

23. Reduce the emphasis on competition. Competitive activities may cause the student to hurry and commit errors.

24. If the student wears glasses, encourage him/her to wear them for board work.

25. Reduce distracting stimuli (e.g., noise and motion in the classroom) to facilitate the student's ability to copy letters, words, sentences, and numbers from a model at a distance.

26. Have the student question any directions, explanations, and instructions he/she does not understand.

27. Evaluate the appropriateness of the task to determine (a) if the task is too easy, (b) if the task is too difficult, or (c) if the length of time scheduled to complete the task is adequate.

28. Use the computer keyboard and monitor as an alternative writing tool.

29. Reinforce the student for copying letters, words, sentences, and numbers from a model at a distance: (a) give the student a tangible reward (e.g., classroom privileges, line leading, passing out materials, five minutes free time, etc.) or (b) give the student an intangible reward (e.g., praise, fist bump, smile, etc.).

88   Fails to correctly organize writing activities

Goals:

1. The student will improve his/her ability to organize writing activities.
2. The student will improve his/her ability in written expression.

Objectives:

1. The student will write in sequence (e.g., numbers, letters, days, months, etc.), after he/she has been corrected by the teacher, with _____% accuracy.
2. The student will independently sequence (e.g., numbers, letters, days, months, etc.) when writing with _____% accuracy.
3. The student will write a complete sentence with subject-verb agreement on _____ out of _____ trials.
4. The student will write complete sentences with correct word order on _____ out of _____ trials.
5. The student will write two related complete sentences describing a single subject (e.g., event, personal experience, etc.) on _____ out of _____ trials.
6. The student will write three related complete sentences describing a single subject (e.g., event, personal experience, etc.) on _____ out of _____ trials.
7. The student will write a series of three or more sentences which correctly sequence a series of events on _____ out of _____ trials.
8. The student will write a paragraph of three or more related sentences with introduction and closing sentences on _____ out of _____ trials.

Interventions:

1. At the top of a piece of paper, write five or six sentences out of sequence about a story the student has read. Have the student cut the sentences apart and paste them in the proper order on the bottom of the paper.

2. Check the student's work frequently to make sure that the student is organizing the writing activity appropriately.

3. Give the student a group of related words (e.g., *author, read, love, bestseller*, etc.) and have him/her write an appropriately organized paragraph that includes each word.

4. Give the student several short sentences and have him/her combine them to make one longer complete sentence (e.g., The dog is big. The dog is brown. The dog is mine. - The big, brown dog is mine.).

5. Have the student arrange a series of statements on a topic in an appropriate order so that they make sense in a paragraph.

6. Have the student begin to practice organizational writing skills by writing simple sentences with subjects and verbs. Have the student then expand the sentences by adding adjectives, adverbs and prepositional phrases.

7. Have the student create stories about topics which are of interest. The student is more likely to try to be successful if he/she is writing about something of interest.

8. Have the student develop an outline or skeleton of what he/she is going to write. From the outline, the student can then practice organizational skills in writing.

9. Have the student develop organizational skills in writing simple sentences. As the student demonstrates success, gradually increase the complexity of sentence structure required and move on to paragraphs, short stories, etc.

10. Have the student read a short story and then list the events of the story. From that list, have the student construct a paragraph using the correct sequence of events.

11. Reduce distracting stimuli by placing the student in a study carrel or office when engaged in writing activities. This is used as a means of reducing distracting stimuli and not as a form of punishment.

12. Have the student read his/her own written work aloud to help him/her identify errors in organization.

13. Provide practice organizing writing activities using a computer software program or a hand-held educational device that gives the student immediate feedback.

14. Have the student write a paragraph describing the events of a daily comic strip.

15. Using a written essay that the student has not seen, cut the paragraphs apart and ask him/her to reconstruct the essay by putting the paragraphs in an appropriate order.

16. Have the student write step-by-step directions (e.g., steps in making a cake) so he/she can practice sequencing events.

17. Help the student brainstorm ideas about a topic and then show him/her how to put these ideas into outline form by combining some ideas and discarding others.

18. Teach the student writing concepts at each level before introducing a new skill level.

19. Have the student practice writing paragraphs according to *Who, What, Where, When, How,* and *Why.*

20. Make sure the student is not interrupted or hurried when engaging in writing activities.

21. Have the student write a daily log, expressing his/her thoughts in complete sentences.

22. Do not require the student to learn more information than he/she is capable of learning at any time.

23. Teach the student that paragraphs, essays, etc., need an introduction, a middle section where information is contained, and a conclusion or ending.

24. Have the student read sentences, paragraphs, stories, etc., written by peers who demonstrate good organizational skills in writing.

25. Provide the student with a paragraph in which a statement does not belong. Have the student find the irrelevant statement.

26. Provide the student with appropriate time limits for the completion of assignments.

27. Recognize quality work (e.g., display student's work, congratulate the student, etc.).

28. Have the student practice organizational skills in writing activities. Have him/her participate in writing activities designed to promote success (e.g., writing a letter to a friend, rock star, famous athlete, etc.).

29. Reduce the emphasis on competition. Competitive activities may cause the student to hurry and not correctly organize his/her writing activities.

30. Reinforce the student for correctly organizing writing activities: (a) give the student a tangible reward (e.g., classroom privileges, line leading, passing out materials, etc.) or (b) give the student an intangible reward (e.g., praise, fist bump, smile, etc.).

31. Require the student to proofread all written work. Reinforce all corrections in organization.

32. Teach outlining principles to the student so he/she understands the difference between main ideas and supporting details.

33. Have the student write a weekly account of the previous week, past weekend, etc., with primary attention given to organization (e.g., sequencing events, developing a paragraph, using correct word order, etc.).

34. When correcting the student's organizational skills in writing, be sure to provide evaluative feedback which is designed to be instructional (e.g., help the student rewrite for better organization, rewrite passages for the student, etc.).

89   Fails to form letters correctly when printing or writing

Goal:

1. The student will improve his/her handwriting skills (e.g., copying from a model, letter formation, letter size, and spacing).

Objectives:

1. The student will trace lowercase letters of the alphabet in manuscript, replicating formation with _____% accuracy.
2. The student will trace uppercase letters of the alphabet in manuscript, replicating formation with _____% accuracy.
3. The student will copy lowercase letters of the alphabet in manuscript at close range, replicating formation with _____% accuracy.
4. The student will copy uppercase letters of the alphabet in manuscript at close range, replicating formation with _____% accuracy.
5. The student will trace lowercase letters of the alphabet in cursive, replicating formation with _____% accuracy.
6. The student will trace uppercase letters of the alphabet in cursive, replicating formation with _____% accuracy.
7. The student will copy lowercase letters of the alphabet in cursive at close range, replicating formation with _____% accuracy.
8. The student will copy uppercase letters of the alphabet in cursive at close range, replicating formation with _____% accuracy.
9. The student will print lowercase letters of the alphabet, replicating formation with _____% accuracy.
10. The student will print uppercase letters of the alphabet, replicating formation with _____% accuracy.
11. The student will write lowercase letters of the alphabet, replicating formation with _____% accuracy.
12. The student will write uppercase letters of the alphabet, replicating formation with _____% accuracy.

Interventions:

1. Make sure the student is instructed in each letter formation. Give the student verbal and physical descriptions and demonstrations.

2. Provide the student with physical prompts by moving the student's hand, giving him/her a feeling of directionality.

3. Use arrows to show the student directionality when tracing or using dot-to-dot to form letters.

4. Check the student's writing position. A right-handed person writing in cursive should tilt the paper to the left so the lower left-hand corner points toward the person's midsection. As writing progresses, the paper should shift, not the writing arm.

5. Use color cues for lines (e.g., red for the top line, yellow for the middle line, green for the bottom line) to indicate where letters are to be made.

6. Draw simple shapes and lines for the student to practice forming on lined paper.

7. Highlight the base line or top line on the paper to help the student stay within the given spaces.

8. Make sure the student sits in an appropriate size chair with feet touching the floor, his/her back pressed against the back of the chair, shoulders slightly inclined, arms resting on the desk, and elbows just off the lower edge of the desk.

9. Have the student practice tracing letters at his/her desk.

10. Have the student practice tracing letters on the wall-mounted board.

11. Have the student practice forming letters correctly by tracing over a series of dots.

12. Check the student's pencil grip. The pencil should be held between the thumb and the index and middle fingers, one inch from its tip, with the top pointing toward the right shoulder (if right-handed).

13. Have the student practice tracing with reduced cues. Write the complete letter and have the student trace it. As the student demonstrates success, gradually provide less of the letter for him/her to trace (e.g., dashes, then dots).

14. Identify those letters the student does not form correctly. Have him/her practice the correct form of one or more of the letters each day.

15. To facilitate appropriate holding of a pencil, put colored tape on parts of the pencil to correspond to finger positions. Then put colored tape on the student's fingernails and have the student match colors.

16. Provide the student with an alphabet strip attached to his/her desk in either printed or written form as a model for correct letter formations.

17. Reinforce the student for making correct letters: (a) give the student a tangible reward (e.g., classroom privileges, line leading, passing out materials, five minutes free time, etc.) or (b) give the student an intangible reward (e.g., praise, fist bump, smile, etc.).

18. Have the student practice forming letters correctly by using writing activities to facilitate the student wanting to be successful (e.g., writing a letter to a friend, rock star, famous athlete; filling out a job application, contest form, etc.).

19. Recognize quality work (e.g., display the student's work, congratulate the student, etc.).

20. Provide the student with the necessary materials to complete the assignment (e.g., pencil with eraser, paper, handwriting sample, etc.). Be sure that the student has only those necessary materials on the desk.

21. Do not require the student to learn more information than he/she is capable of learning at any time.

22. Teach the student handwriting skills at each level before introducing a new skill level.

23. Check the student's handwritten work at various points throughout a handwriting activity to make sure that the student is forming letters correctly.

24. Require the student to proofread all written work. Reinforce the student for each correction made.

25. Reduce the emphasis on competition. Competitive activities may cause the student to hurry and not form letters correctly.

26. Provide tactile stimulation for the child (e.g., sand, fur, clay, wood, etc.).

27. Use specific manipulatives (strings, toothpicks, etc.) to form letters for visual models.

28. Choose a peer to model working daily on drills involving letter formation, ending and connecting strokes, spacing, and slant for the student.

Goal:

1. The student will improve his/her use of formal rules of writing (e.g., capitalization and punctuation).

Objectives:

1. The student will use periods when writing with _____% accuracy.
2. The student will use question marks when writing with _____% accuracy.
3. The student will use exclamation marks when writing with _____% accuracy.
4. The student will use commas when writing with _____% accuracy.
5. The student will use quotation marks when writing with _____% accuracy.
6. The student will use colons when writing with _____% accuracy.
7. The student will use semicolons when writing with _____% accuracy.

Interventions:

1. After checking the student's work, require him/her to make all necessary corrections in punctuation.

2. Check the student's work at various points throughout an assignment to make sure the student is using punctuation when appropriate.

3. Display a chart of punctuation rules in the front of the classroom.

4. Give the student a list of sentences in which the punctuation has been omitted. Have the student supply the correct punctuation with colored pencils.

5. Review with the student common punctuation rules before starting a creative writing activity.

6. Give the student a series of sentences representing all the punctuation rules. Have the student identify the rules for each punctuation. Remove each sentence from the assignment when the student can explain the rules for punctuation in the sentence.

7. Provide the student with computer software which provides practice and reinforcement in punctuating sentences and other creative writing assignments (e.g., addresses, letters, etc.).

8. Give the student sentences requiring him/her to fill in specific punctuation he/she is learning to use (e.g., periods, commas, question marks, etc.).

9. Have the student participate in writing activities which facilitate him/her doing well on punctuation and other writing skills (e.g., writing letters to a friend, rock star, famous athlete, etc.).

10. Teach the student what all punctuation marks look like and their uses.

11. Have the student keep a list of basic rules of punctuation at his/her desk to use as a reference when writing (e.g., use a period at the end of a sentence, etc.).

12. Give the student a set of three cards; one with a period, one with a question mark, and one with an exclamation point. As you read a sentence to the student, have him/her hold up the appropriate punctuation card.

13. Have the student practice correct punctuation by providing the student with several sentences with errors on the wall-mounted board. The student is to correct the punctuation errors and discuss them with the teacher.

14. Write a contract with the student specifying what behavior is expected (e.g., using punctuation correctly) and what reinforcement will be made available when the terms of the contract have been met.

15. Have the student practice using one form of punctuation at a time before going on to another (e.g., period, question mark, etc.).

16. Highlight or underline punctuation in passages from the student's reading assignment. Have the student explain why each form of punctuation is used.

17. Do not require the student to learn more information than he/she is capable of learning at any time.

18. Use a newspaper to locate different types of punctuation. Have the student circle periods in red, commas in blue, etc.

19. Make sure the student receives instruction in the rules of punctuation (e.g., periods belong at the end of sentences, question marks are used when a question is asked, etc.).

20. Require the student to proofread all written work for correct punctuation. Reinforce the student for each punctuation correction he/she makes.

21. Model appropriate punctuation through charts and overheads for student reference during all creative writing activities.

22. Provide practice with punctuation using a computer program or hand-held educational device that gives the student immediate feedback.

23. Provide the student with the necessary materials to complete the assignment (e.g., pencil with eraser, paper, dictionary, handwriting sample, etc.). Be sure that the student has only the necessary materials on the desk.

24. Make a notebook for punctuation rules to be used to help with proofreading work.

25. Recognize quality work (e.g., display student's work, congratulate the student, etc.).

26. Reduce the emphasis on competition. Competitive activities may cause the student to hurry and make errors in punctuation.

27. Provide the student with a list of examples of the forms of punctuation he/she is expected to use (e.g., periods, commas, question marks, exclamation points, etc.). The student keeps the examples at his/her desk and refers to them when writing.

28. Teach the student punctuation at each level before introducing a new skill level.

29. Reinforce the student for using correct punctuation when writing: (a) give the student a tangible reward (e.g., classroom privileges, line leading, five minutes free time, etc.) or (b) give the student an intangible reward (e.g., praise, fist bump, smile, etc.).

Goal:

1. The student will improve his/her use of formal rules of writing (e.g., capitalization and punctuation).

Objectives:

1. The student will write capital letters with _____% accuracy.
2. The student will use capitalization in drills of capitalization rules (e.g., personal pronoun I, first letter of first word in a sentence, etc.) with _____% accuracy.
3. The student will write capital letters at the beginning of words requiring capitalization from lists given verbally (e.g., names of persons, rivers, cities, states, etc.) with _____% accuracy.
4. The student will use capitalization when writing with _____% accuracy.

Interventions:

1. After checking the student's work, require him/her to make all necessary corrections in capitalization.

2. Check the student's work at various points throughout an assignment to make sure the student is using capitalization where needed.

3. Display a capitalization rules chart in the front of the classroom.

4. Emphasize one rule of capitalization until the student masters that rule, then move on to another rule (e.g., proper names, cities, states, streets, etc.).

5. Find names, cities, states, etc., on a news information page and underline them.

6. Give the student a series of sentences representing all the capitalization rules. Have the student identify the rules for each capitalization. Remove each sentence from the assignment when the student can explain the rules for the capitalization in the sentence.

7. Have the student participate in writing activities which facilitate him/her doing well in capitalization and other writing skills (e.g., writing letters to a friend, rock star, famous athlete, etc.).

8. Have the student practice writing words which are always capitalized (e.g., countries, bodies of water, nationalities, languages, days of the week, months of the year, etc.).

9. Highlight or underline all the capitalized letters in a passage or paragraph and have the student explain why each is capitalized.

10. Make a notebook of rules for capitalization to be used to proofread work.

11. Provide the student with a list of rules for capitalization at his/her desk to use as a reference.

12. Teach the student one capitalization rule before introducing a new rule.

13. Have the student practice correct capitalization by providing the student with several sentences with errors on the wall-mounted board or overhead projector. The student is to correct the capitalization errors and discuss them with the teacher.

14. Do not require the student to learn more information than he/she is capable of learning at any time.

15. Teach the student how to form all the capital letters of the alphabet.

16. Make sure the student proofreads his/her work for correct capitalization. Reinforce the student for each correction made in capitalization.

17. Review with the student common capitalization rules before starting a creative writing activity.

18. Make sure the student receives instruction in the rules of capitalization (e.g., first word of a sentence, the pronoun I, proper names, cities, states, streets, months, days of the week, dates, holidays, titles of movies, books, newspapers, magazines, etc.).

19. Model appropriate capitalization of sentences when assigning creative writing activities. This could be done on the wall-mounted board, an overhead projector, or in chart form.

20. Reinforce the student for capitalizing correctly: (a) give the student a tangible reward (e.g., classroom privileges, line leading, five minutes free time, etc.) or (b) give the student an intangible reward (e.g., praise, fist bump, smile, etc.).

21. Write a contract with the student specifying what behavior is expected (e.g., using capitalization correctly) and what reinforcement will be made available when the terms of the contract have been met.

22. Provide the student with lists of words and have him/her indicate which should be capitalized (e.g., water, new york, mississippi, etc.).

23. Provide the student with the necessary materials to complete the assignment (e.g., pencil with eraser, paper, dictionary, handwriting sample, etc.). Be sure that the student has only the necessary materials on the desk.

24. Recognize quality work (e.g., display student's work, congratulate the student, etc.).

25. Provide the student with a list of examples of capitalization (e.g., proper names, cities, streets, holidays, etc.) that the student keeps at his/her desk to refer to when writing.

26. Reduce the emphasis on competition. Competitive activities may cause the student to hurry and make capitalization mistakes.

27. Provide the student with computer software that provides practice and reinforcement in capitalizing words.

28. Provide practice with capitalization using a computer software program or a hand-held educational device that gives the student immediate feedback.

92   Fails to use verb tenses correctly when writing

Goals:
1. The student will improve his/her grammatical skills when writing.
2. The student will improve his/her ability in written expression.

Objectives:
1. The student will use the present verb tense when writing with _____% accuracy.
2. The student will use the past verb tense when writing with _____% accuracy.
3. The student will use the future verb tense when writing with _____% accuracy.

Interventions:

1. Provide the student with examples of verb tenses for those verbs most commonly used incorrectly and have the student keep the examples for reference.

2. Make a list of those verbs the student most commonly uses incorrectly. This list will become the guide for learning activities in verb tenses.

3. Write a contract with the student specifying what behavior is expected (e.g., using correct verb tenses) and what reinforcement will be made available when the terms of the contract have been met.

4. Choose a peer to model the correct use of verb tenses for the student.

5. Teach the student that changes must be made to a verb to indicate when an event happened (e.g., past, present, future).

6. Have the student complete worksheets in which he/she must supply the correct verb tense to go in the sentence (e.g., Yesterday I _____ to my house.).

7. Have the student pick out the correct verb tense on multiple-choice worksheets (e.g., Tomorrow she _____ [ate, eat, will eat] her supper.).

8. Give the student a verb and have him/her supply appropriate sentences to go with each (e.g., played: John played at my house last night.).

9. Have the student write sentences with a verb in past, present, and future tenses.

10. Have the student listen to examples of incorrect verb tenses, identify each error, and correct it.

11. Present a series of sentences and ask the student to change the tense from past to present, present to future, etc.

12. Give the student a series of sentences (both verbal and written) and ask him/her to indicate if each is grammatically correct.

13. Ask the parents to encourage the student's correct use of verb tenses by praising him/her when his/her grammar is correct.

14. Explain the importance of correct written communication and what would happen if the verb tenses were used incorrectly (e.g., confusion as to when an event took place).

15. Make sure the student proofreads all written work and makes corrections in verb tenses. Reinforce the student for each correction.

16. Allow the student to assist in proofreading or grading other students' papers to facilitate awareness of correct verb tense usage.

17. Encourage the student to read written work aloud to find errors in verb tenses.

18. Read a series of sentences to the student and have him/her identify if each one is in the past, present, or future tense.

19. Provide the student with a list of all tenses of verbs most commonly used. Have him/her keep this list at his/her desk.

20. Choose a peer to practice verb tenses with the student. Each tense is used in a sentence rather than only conjugating verbs.

21. Make conjugating of verb tenses a daily activity.

22. Recognize quality work (e.g., display the student's work, congratulate the student, etc.).

23. Provide the student with the necessary materials to complete the assignment (e.g., pencil with eraser, paper, dictionary, handwriting sample, etc.). Be sure the student has only those necessary materials on the desk.

24. Do not require the student to learn more information than he/she is capable of learning at any time.

25. Teach the student writing concepts at each level before introducing a new skill level.

26. Give the student a choice of answers (e.g., more than one possible answer, multiple-choice on a worksheet, etc.) to facility his/her ability to recognize the correct answer.

27. Check the student's work at various points throughout the assignment to make sure the student is using appropriate verb tenses.

28. Have the student participate in writing activities designed to facilitate him/her wanting to be successful in writing (e.g., writing a letter to a friend, rock star, famous athlete, etc.).

29. Reinforce those students in the classroom who use correct verb tenses when writing.

30. Reinforce the student for using appropriate verb tenses when writing: (a) give the student a tangible reward (e.g., classroom privileges, line leading, passing out materials, five minutes free time, etc.) or (b) give the student an intangible reward (e.g., praise, fist bump, smile, etc.).

93 Fails to write within a given space

Goal:

1. The student will improve his/her handwriting skills (e.g., copying from a model, letter formation, letter size, and spacing).

Objectives:

1. The student will write within horizontal lines drawn on paper with _____% accuracy.
2. The student will write within vertical lines drawn on paper with _____% accuracy.
3. The student will write within horizontal lines drawn on primary paper with _____% accuracy.
4. The student will write within vertical margins on paper with _____% accuracy.
5. The student will write within a given space on standard lined paper with _____% accuracy.

Interventions:

1. Have the student's vision checked if it has not been recently checked.

2. Evaluate the appropriateness of the task to determine (a) if the task is too easy, (b) if the task is too difficult, or (c) if the length of time scheduled to complete the task is adequate.

3. Check the student's paper position. A right-handed person writing in cursive should tilt the paper to the left so the lower left-hand corner points toward the person's midsection and as writing progresses, the paper should shift, not the writing arm.

4. Check the student's pencil grip. The pencil should be held between the thumb and the index and middle fingers, holding the instrument one inch from its tip.

5. Make sure the student is shifting his/her paper as writing progresses.

6. Draw a margin on the right side of the student's paper as a reminder for him/her to write within a given space.

7. Place a ruler or construction paper on the baseline, making certain the student touches the line for each letter.

8. Use ruled paper with a midline. Explain to the student that the shoulder of lowercase letters (a, b, c, d, e, g, h, etc.) touch the midline.

9. Highlight lines on the paper for the student to use as a prompt.

10. Reinforce the student for each word or letter correctly spaced.

11. Have the student look at correctly written material to serve as a model for him/her to imitate.

12. Darken the lines on the paper so the student can more easily use them to write within the given space.

13. Allow the student to draw his/her own lines on paper for writing activities.

14. Allow the student to use a ruler as a guide or bottom line.

15. Provide the student with a physical prompt by guiding his/her hand as he/she writes.

16. Have the student correct his/her own writing errors.

17. Have the student complete a practice page before completing the actual assignment.

18. Have the student practice writing letters, words, and sentences by tracing over a series of dots.

19. Provide the student with extra large sheets of paper on which to write. As the student demonstrates success, gradually reduce the size of the paper to standard size.

20. Recognize quality work (e.g., display student's work, congratulate the student, etc.).

21. Provide the student with the necessary materials to complete the assignment (e.g., pencil with eraser, paper, dictionary, handwriting sample, etc.). Be sure that the student has only the necessary materials on the desk.

22. Use vertical lines or graph paper to help the student space letters correctly.

23. Make a border so the student knows when he/she has written to the edge of the writing space.

24. Check the student's work at various points throughout the assignment to make sure that the student is writing within a given space.

25. Assign the student shorter writing assignments. As the student demonstrates success, gradually increase the number of writing assignments over time.

26. Give the student one handwriting task to complete at a time. Introduce the next task when the student has successfully completed the previous task.

27. Have the student participate in writing activities designed to facilitate the student wanting to be successful in writing (e.g., writing a letter to a friend, rock star, famous athlete, etc.).

94 Has difficulty understanding and using synonyms, antonyms, and homonyms

Goals:

1. The student will improve his/her vocabulary skills.
2. The student will demonstrate understanding and use of antonyms.
3. The student will demonstrate understanding and use of synonyms.
4. The student will demonstrate understanding and use of homonyms.

Objectives:

1. The student will point to objects/pictures or perform actions which represent target vocabulary in _____ out of _____ trials.
2. The student will label objects/pictures or perform actions with appropriate target vocabulary in _____ out of _____ trials.
3. The student will provide synonyms/antonyms/homonyms for target vocabulary in _____ out of _____ trials.
4. The student will restate a given sentence using synonyms/antonyms for target vocabulary in _____ out of _____ trials.
5. The student will use target vocabulary (including synonyms, antonyms, and homonyms) in oral/written sentences in _____ out of _____ trials.
6. The student will use target vocabulary (including synonyms, antonyms, and homonyms) in everyday speaking situations in _____ out of _____ trials.
7. The student will give the correct antonym of a word which begins with the prefix un-, im-, in-, ig-, dis-, or ir- with _____% accuracy.
8. The student will choose the correct homonym to complete a given sentence (e.g., The wind (blue/blew) the curtains.) in _____ out of _____ trials.

Interventions:

1. Have the student's hearing checked if it has not been recently checked.

2. Determine the type of language model the student has at home. Without placing negative connotations on the language model in the student's home, explain the difference between language which is rich in vocabulary and that which does not include a variety of vocabulary.

3. Give the student a list of words and ask him/her to provide an antonym, synonym, or homonym where appropriate.

4. Have the class apply new synonyms, antonyms, and homonyms to their personal experiences in written and verbal work.

5. Reinforce the student for using synonyms, antonyms, and homonyms accurately: (a) give the student a tangible reward (e.g., classroom privileges, line leading, passing out materials, five minutes free time, etc.) or (b) give the student an intangible reward (e.g., praise, fist bump, smile, etc.).

6. Determine whether or not the student has a limited expressive and/or receptive vocabulary which would influence his/her ability to understand and/or use synonyms, antonyms, and homonyms.

7. Teach the student the meanings of same and different as they relate to synonyms and antonyms. Emphasize similarities and differences between concrete objects, pictures, actions, etc., to facilitate the understanding of these word relationships before targeting new vocabulary.

8. Use visual aids whenever possible when introducing new synonyms, antonyms, or homonyms.

9. Explain to the student how to classify new words as to antonym and synonym (e.g., pretty, beautiful, and attractive are all similar in meaning and the opposite of ugly) so he/she will have a way of storing the words in his/her memory.

10. Have the student divide objects, pictures, or cards that label objects, persons, places, etc., in the environment (depending on his/her ability level) into different categories based on similar attributes (e.g., function, color, size, use, composition, etc.). Point out the similarities and differences between items as they change categories (e.g., a ball and an apple may both be red, round, and smooth; but you can only eat the apple; etc.).

11. Have the student physically demonstrate (himself/herself or with an object) antonym pairs (e.g., walk/run, up high/down low, quickly/slowly, etc.), synonyms for a given word (e.g., walk - saunter, stroll, meander, etc.), and homonym pairs (e.g., ate/eight, won/on, etc.).

12. Have the student illustrate or cut out pictures of antonym and homonym pairs that are difficult to act out (e.g., the word rough could be written with letters that are jagged and irregular or cut out of sandpaper and smooth could be written with fluid lines or cut out of wax paper; boy/buoy could be illustrated or cut out; etc.).

13. Give the student three words and have him/her choose the synonyms or antonyms (e.g., nice, kind, mean).

14. Have the student draw or cut out pictures to illustrate opposite attributes of a noun (e.g., tall/short tree, happy/sad person, etc.).

15. Reinforce those students in the classroom who use antonyms, synonyms, and homonyms correctly.

16. Choose a peer who demonstrates proficiency with antonyms, synonyms, and homonyms to work with the student to improve his/her comprehension of antonyms, synonyms, and homonyms.

17. Explain to the student how to use context clues to determine the meaning of synonyms, antonyms, and homonyms he/she hears or sees (i.e., listening to or looking at the surrounding words and determining what type of word would be appropriate).

18. Explain to the student where he/she can go to find word meanings in the classroom library (e.g., dictionary, thesaurus, encyclopedia, etc.).

19. Have the student maintain a vocabulary notebook with definitions of words whose meanings he/she does not know. Have him/her use synonyms along with the dictionary definitions. He/she can place antonyms and/or homonyms in close proximity to each other in his/her notebook.

20. Prepare a list of new words which the student will encounter reading an assignment. Help him/her (or choose a peer to help) look up each word and practice saying them and using them in sentences. Use synonyms, antonyms, and homonyms that are already a part of the student's vocabulary to facilitate understanding and word meanings.

21. Audio record the student's spontaneous speech, noting specific words he/she uses. Have the student make a list of other words (synonyms) which could be substituted for these words.

22. Discuss with parents the ways in which they can help the student develop an expanded vocabulary (e.g., encourage the student to read news articles, novels, magazines, or other materials; use a variety of information sources to look for synonyms, antonyms, homonyms, etc.).

23. Send home new vocabulary words and encourage parents to use them in activities and general conversation.

24. Have the student provide synonyms or antonyms based on his/her five senses (e.g., taste: delicious, yummy vs. bitter; feel: rough, bumpy vs. smooth; sight: pretty, beautiful vs. ugly; sound: loud, noisy vs. quiet; smell: fragrant, sweet vs. pungent). Emphasize the use of each sense to facilitate recall of the vocabulary.

25. Point out the relative nature of some antonyms by providing a variety of examples (e.g., younger/older, short/tall, right/left, etc.).

26. Post an *Overused Word for the Day* (e.g., awesome) and have the class list synonyms and/or antonyms under it during the day. Have the student separate the synonyms and antonyms at the end of the day.

27. Have the student construct a caterpillar with each segment being a synonym of the main word listed on the head.

28. Have the student underline or highlight examples of synonyms in news articles or magazines.

29. Use carrier phrases to elicit antonyms (e.g., If it isn't _____, then it's _____. or If it's _____, then it's not _____.).

30. Highlight or underline specific words in a sentence and have the student change the sentence meaning by replacing the words with their antonyms (e.g., The <u>short</u>, <u>ugly</u> man looked <u>mean</u>. becomes The <u>tall</u>, <u>handsome</u> man looked <u>friendly</u>.) or keep the meaning of the sentence the same by using synonyms (e.g., The <u>short</u>, <u>ugly</u> man looked <u>mean</u>. would become either The <u>small</u>, <u>disgusting</u> man looked <u>dangerous</u>. or The man wasn't <u>tall</u> or <u>friendly-looking</u>.).

31. Have the student identify pairs of words as either antonyms or synonyms (e.g., polish/shine = synonyms; happy/sad = antonyms; etc.).

32. Have the student make a list of antonyms that are formed by adding a prefix to the original word (e.g., <u>un</u>happy, <u>im</u>mature, <u>in</u>audible, <u>dis</u>like, etc.).

33. Play a variation of *Simon Says* where the students perform the opposite action that *Simon Says*. Have the students work with partners if this activity seems too difficult.

34. Divide the class into antonym and synonym teams and have them provide as many antonyms or synonyms as possible for designated words (e.g., big - antonyms = little, tiny, minuscule, etc., and synonyms = large, huge, gigantic, etc.).

35. Provide the student with a word. Have him/her make a chain with alternating links of antonyms and synonyms for the word (e.g., male-female-boy-girl-man-woman, etc.).

36. Have the student provide an association for a given noun and then state its opposite (e.g., chair: sit/stand; lunch: full/hungry; desk: work/play; etc.).

37. Have the student list verbs to go with a specific noun, adjectives to go with a specific noun, or adverbs to go with a specific verb. Have the student identify the words on his/her list that are synonyms and/or antonyms.

38. Display a different pair of homonyms each day and have the students use them in their written and verbal class work throughout the day.

39. Have the student complete worksheets for which he/she chooses the correct homonym to fill in a blank (e.g., The prisoner wanted to _____ (cell, sell) the picture he had hanging in his _____ (cell, sell).

40. Have the student use pairs of homonyms in the same illustration (e.g., The colonels were selling kernels of corn.).

41. Provide the student with a choice of homonyms from which to choose the correct synonym or antonym for given words (e.g., inexpensive (synonym) = cheep/cheap; or girl (antonym) = boy/buoy).

42. Have the student match lists of homonyms with their definitions (e.g., Definitions - inexpensive, a sound a little bird makes; Homonyms - cheap, cheep).

43. Specifically identify synonyms, antonyms, and homonyms throughout the day as they are used in various classes:
- Let's find the Mediterranean Sea on the map. That sea is spelled s-e-a. When we see with our eyes, that see is spelled s-e-e.
- When I said the South had less manufacturing capability than the North which had more, I used two sets of antonyms: North and South; more and less.
- The larger or bigger of the numbers is called the dividend. Larger and bigger are synonyms.

Ask music, art, P.E., etc., teachers to point out this information during their classes as well.

Goals:

1. The student will improve his/her ability in written expression.
2. The student will improve his/her attention to writing assignments.
3. The student will improve his/her concentration.
4. The student will improve his/her grammatical skills when writing.
5. The student will improve his/her writing skills.

Objectives:

1. The student will write in complete phrases, after he/she has been corrected by the teacher, with _____% accuracy.
2. The student will independently use complete phrases when writing with _____% accuracy.
3. The student will complete sentences when writing, after he/she has been corrected by the teacher, with _____% accuracy.
4. The student will independently use complete sentences when writing with _____% accuracy.

Interventions:

1. Assess the level of task difficulty to determine whether or not the student will require additional information, time, assistance, etc., before assigning a task.

2. Assist the student in writing information. As the student demonstrates success, gradually decrease the assistance and require the student to assume more responsibility

3. Check the student's performance for accuracy when writing. Working quickly is acceptable if the student performs the task accurately.

4. Check the student's work at various points throughout a writing assignment for any omissions, additions, or substitutions.

5. Consider carefully the student's ability level and experience before expecting the student to complete tasks independently.

6. Dictate sentences to the student so he/she can practice writing simple sentences accurately.

7. Encourage the student to create stories about topics which interest him/her to provide more experiences in writing.

8. Have the student practice writing simple sentences successfully without omissions, additions, or substitutions.

9. Give the student a group of related words (e.g., baseball, fans, glove, strikeout, etc.) and have him/her write a paragraph that includes each word.

10. Establish an environmental setting for the classroom that promotes optimal individual performance (e.g., quiet room, background music, fresh air, etc.).

11. Give the student a list of transition words (e.g., therefore, although, because, etc.) and have him/her make sentences using each word.

12. Require the student to proofread all written work. Reinforce the student for each correction made.

13. Evaluate the visual and auditory stimuli in the environment and remove or reduce the extraneous environmental stimuli.

14. Explain to the student exactly what he/she is doing wrong (hurrying to get things completed) and, what he/she should be doing (working slowly and carefully).

15. Make sure the student is not interrupted or hurried when engaged in writing activities.

16. Have the student assist in grading or proofreading other students' written work to become more aware of omissions, additions, or substitutions.

17. Give dictation sentences to the student to encourage successful writing of simple sentences.

18. Encourage the student to read all written work aloud to understand omissions, additions, or substitutions.

19. Give the student scrambled words from a sentence and have him/her put them in the correct order to form the sentence.

20. Have the student ask for help when he/she needs it.

21. Have the student write a daily log or diary expressing thoughts in complete sentences.

22. Increase supervision (e.g., by a paraprofessional, peer, etc.) of the student while he/she is writing.

23. Maintain consistent expectations for the student to write information without omitting, adding, or substituting words.

24. Make a list of the student's most common omissions, additions, and substitutions and have him/her refer to the list when engaged in writing activities to check for errors.

25. Teach the student the relationship between writing errors and the consequences which follow (e.g., omitting, adding, or substituting words when writing directions down may result in homework assignments being done incorrectly).

26. Make sure that the writing assignments given to the student are appropriate for his/her level of development and ability.

27. Teach the student to use context clues when reading to aid word recognition and meaning.

28. Make sure the student has written work proofread by someone (e.g., aide, peer, etc.) for omissions, additions, or substitutions before turning in the completed assignment.

29. Have the student engage in writing activities designed to facilitate him/her wanting to be successful in writing (e.g., writing a letter to a friend, rock star, famous athlete, etc.).

30. Recognize quality work (e.g., display the student's work, congratulate the student, etc.).

31. Make sure you are not requiring too much of the student at one time and causing him/her to hurry to get things done.

32. Reduce distracting stimuli when the student is engaged in writing activities by placing the student in a carrel or office space. This is used as a means of reducing the distracting stimuli and not as a form of punishment.

33. Have the student read simple passages and audio record them. Have the student underline passages that were omitted.

34. Reduce the emphasis on competition. Competitive activities may cause the student to hurry and omit, add, or substitute words when writing.

35. Require the student to rewrite an assignment if it has been done incorrectly due to his/her hurrying just to get it completed.

36. Have the student complete fill-in-the-blank stories and sentences and then read them aloud.

37. Speak to the student to explain what he/she is doing wrong (e.g., substituting words, leaving words out, etc.) and what he/she should be doing (e.g., writing each word carefully, rereading written work, etc.).

38. Make sure the student is aware of the types of errors made (e.g., omits words, substitutes words, etc.) to be more conscious of them when writing.

39. Have the student proofread all written work for omissions, additions, or substitutions. Reinforce the student for correcting omissions, additions, or substitutions.

40. When correcting the student's written work, provide evaluative feedback which is constructive (e.g., point out omissions, additions, and substitutions; explain to the student the effect these mistakes have on content and meaning; have the student rewrite his/her work to correct the omissions, additions, and substitutions; etc.).

41. Have the student's vision checked if it has not been recently checked.

Goal:

1. The student will improve his/her handwriting skills (e.g., copying from a model, letter formation, letter size, and spacing).

Objectives:

1. The student will recognize letters and numbers with _____% accuracy.
2. The student will be able to copy letters and numbers with _____% accuracy.
3. The student will form letters and numbers correctly when writing with _____% accuracy.

Interventions:

1. Have the student's vision checked if it has not been recently checked.

2. Use board activities (e.g., drawing lines, circles, etc.) to teach the student the correct direction for forming each letter or number.

3. Physically guide the student's hand, providing the feeling of the correct direction.

4. Place letters on transparencies and project them on the wall-mounted board or paper. Have the student trace the letters.

5. Have the student trace letters and numbers in magazines, newspapers, etc., which he/she typically reverses when writing.

6. When correcting papers with reversed letters, use direction arrows to remind the student of the correct direction.

7. Identify the letters and numbers the student reverses and have him/her practice forming one or more of the letters correctly each day.

8. Teach the student to recognize the correct form of letters and numbers when he/she sees them (e.g., *b, d, 2, 5*, etc.).

9. Teach the student to check all work for those letters and numbers he/she typically reverses. Reinforce the student for correcting any reversed letters and numbers.

10. Provide the student with visual cues to aid in making letters and numbers (e.g., arrows indicating strokes).

11. Provide the student with large letters and numbers to trace which he/she typically reverses.

12. Give the student letters and numbers on separate cards and have him/her match the letters and numbers that are the same.

13. Have the student keep a card with the word *bed* at his/her desk to help remember the correct form of *b* and *d* in a word he/she knows.

14. Have the student keep a list of the most commonly used words which contain letters he/she reverses. This list can be used as a reference when the student is writing.

15. After identifying those letters and numbers the student reverses, have him/her highlight or underline those letters and numbers found in a magazine, news article, etc.

16. Point out the subtle differences between letters and numbers that the student reverses. Have the student scan five typewritten lines containing only the letters or numbers that are confusing (e.g., *nnhnhhnn*). Have the student circle the n's and the h's with different colors.

17. Cursive handwriting may prevent reversals and may be used by some students as an alternative to manuscript.

18. Recognize quality work (e.g., display the student's work, congratulate the student, etc.).

19. Provide the student with a number line and alphabet strip on his/her desk to use as a reference to correctly form letters and numbers.

20. Reduce the emphasis on competition. Competitive activities may cause the student to hurry and reverse numbers and letters when writing.

21. Make sure that the student's formation of letters is consistently correct.

22. Reinforce the student for making letters and numbers correctly when writing: (a) give the student a tangible reward (e.g., classroom privileges, line leading, passing out materials, five minutes free time, etc.) or (b) give the student an intangible reward (e.g., smile, fist bump, praise, etc.).

23. Have the student participate in writing activities designed to facilitate the student wanting to be successful in writing (e.g., writing a letter to a friend, rock star, famous athlete, etc.).

24. Have the student practice writing letters, words, and sentences by tracing over a series of dots.

25. Require the student to proofread all written work. Reinforce the student for each correction made.

Goal:

1. The student will improve his/her handwriting skills (e.g., copying from a model, letter formation, letter size, and spacing).

Objectives:

1. The student will trace lowercase letters of the alphabet, replicating size with_____% accuracy.
2. The student will trace uppercase letters of the alphabet, replicating size with _____% accuracy.
3. The student will copy lowercase letters of the alphabet at close range, replicating size with _____% accuracy.
4. The student will copy uppercase letters of the alphabet at close range, replicating size with _____% accuracy.
5. The student will print lowercase letters of the alphabet, replicating size with _____% accuracy.
6. The student will print uppercase letters of the alphabet, replicating size with _____% accuracy.
7. The student will write lowercase letters of the alphabet in cursive, replicating size with _____% accuracy.
8. The student will write uppercase letters of the alphabet in cursive, replicating size with _____% accuracy.

Interventions:

1. Check the student's writing posture. Have the student sit in an appropriately sized chair with feet touching the floor, his/her back pressed against the back of the chair, shoulders slightly inclined, arms resting comfortably on the desk, and elbows just off the edge of the desk.

2. Check the student's paper position. A right-handed person writing in cursive should tilt the paper to the left so the lower left-hand corner points toward the person's midsection. As writing progresses, the paper should shift not the writing arm.

3. Check the student's pencil grip. The pencil should be held between the thumb and the index and middle fingers, holding the instrument one inch from its tip.

4. Use paper that has a midline and a descender space.

5. Have the student identify ascending (*b, d, f, h, i, k, l,* t), x-height (*a, c, e, m, n, o, r, s, u, v, w, x, z),* and descending (*g, j, p, q, y*) letters to help him/her locate the correct placement of each group.

6. Make sure the student is shifting his/her paper as writing progresses.

7. Evaluate writing alignment by drawing a horizontal line across the tops of the letters that are to be of the same size.

8. Highlight lines on the paper as a reminder for the student to make correct letter size.

9. Choose a peer to model making letters the appropriate size when writing for the student.

10. Provide the student with samples of letters of the appropriate size for activities that require writing.

11. Provide the student with an alphabet strip at his/her desk with letters the size he/she is to form.

12. Write letters on the student's paper and have him/her trace them.

13. Write letters on the student's paper in a broken line and have the student connect the lines.

14. Using examples written on grid paper, have the student copy the examples beneath them.

15. Darken the lines on the student's paper which are used for correct letter size.

16. Have the student correct his/her mistakes in letter size.

17. Draw boxes to indicate the size of specific letters in relationship to the lines on the paper.

18. Using tracing paper, have the student trace over specific letters or words.

19. Provide the student with clearly stated criteria for acceptable work (e.g., neatness, etc.).

20. Recognize quality work (e.g., display the student's work, congratulate the student, etc.).

21. Provide the student with the necessary materials to complete the assignment (e.g., pencil with eraser, paper, dictionary, handwriting sample, etc.). Be sure that the student has only those necessary materials on the desk.

22. Teach the student handwriting skills at each level before introducing a new skill level.

23. Check the student's work at various points throughout the assignment to make sure that the student is making letters the appropriate size.

24. Using a series of dots, have the student trace words or sentences.

25. Provide the student with a number line and alphabet strip on the desk to use as a reference for the correct formation of the letters and numbers to reduce errors.

26. Use vertical lines or graph paper to help the student space letters correctly.

27. Provide the student with a different size pencil or pencil grip.

28. Evaluate the appropriateness of the task to determine (a) if the task is too easy, (b) if the task is too difficult, or (c) if the length of time scheduled to complete the task is adequate.

29. Using an original story written by the student, prepare a transparency to use on an overhead projector. Project the story onto a paper on the wall that the student will trace. This is particularly appropriate for those students who tend to write too small.

30. Reinforce the student for using appropriate letter size when writing: (a) give the student a tangible reward (e.g., classroom privileges, line leading, passing out materials, five minutes free time, etc.) or (b) give the student an intangible reward (e.g., praise, fist bump, smile, etc.).

31. Have the student's vision checked if it has not been recently checked

98 Uses inappropriate spacing between words or sentences when writing

Goal:

1. The student will improve his/her handwriting skills (e.g., copying from a model, letter formation, letter size, and spacing).

Objectives:

1. The student will space correctly between letters and numbers with _____% accuracy.
2. The student will space correctly between words when writing with _____% accuracy.
3. The student will space correctly between sentences when writing with _____% accuracy.

Interventions:

1. Have the student's vision checked if it has not been recently checked.

2. Have the student sit in an appropriately sized chair with feet touching the floor, his/her back pressed against the back of the chair, shoulders slightly inclined, arms resting on the desk, and elbows just off the lower edge of the desk.

3. Check the student's paper position. A right-handed person writing in cursive should tilt the paper to the left so the lower left-hand corner points toward the person's midsection and as writing progresses, the paper should shift, not the writing arm.

4. Place dots between letters and have the student use fingers as a spacer between words.

5. Make sure the student is shifting his/her paper when writing.

6. Using appropriate spacing, print or write words or sentences. Have the student trace what was written.

7. Reduce the emphasis on competition. Competitive activities may cause the student to hurry and not use correct spacing when writing words and sentences.

8. Provide the student with samples of handwritten words and sentences he/she can use as a reference for correct spacing.

9. Have the student leave a finger space between each word he/she writes.

10. Draw vertical lines for the student to use to space letters and words (e.g., | | | |).

11. Teach the student to always look at the next word to determine if there is enough space before the margin.

12. Provide the student with graph paper. Have him/her write letters in each block, while skipping a block between words and sentences.

13. Recognize quality work (e.g., display student's work, congratulate the student, etc.).

14. Provide the student with the necessary materials to complete the assignment (e.g., pencil with eraser, paper, dictionary, handwriting sample, etc.). Be sure that the student has only necessary materials on his/her desk.

15. Check the student's work at various points throughout an assignment to make sure the student is using appropriate spacing.

16. Give the student one handwriting task to complete at a time. Introduce the next task when the student has successfully completed the previous task.

17. Assign the student fewer tasks. As the student demonstrates success, gradually increase the number of tasks over time.

18. Have the student practice writing letters, words, and sentences by tracing over a series of dots.

19. Use vertical lines or graph paper to help the student space letters correctly.

20. Have the student participate in writing activities designed to facilitate the student wanting to be successful in writing (e.g., writing a letter to a friend, rock star, famous athlete, etc.).

21. Have the student look at correctly spaced written material as a model for correct spacing.

22. Reinforce the student for each word and/ or sentence that is appropriately spaced: (a) give the student a tangible reward (e.g., classroom privileges, line leading, five minutes free time, etc.) or (b) give the student an intangible reward (e.g., praise, fist bump, smile, etc.).

23. Have the student complete a practice page before completing the actual assignment.

Goal:

1. The student will use correct grammatical forms in written work.

Objectives:

1. The student will choose between correct and incorrect grammatical forms in written sentences in _____ out of _____ trials.
2. The student will use correct grammar in simple, written sentences with _____% accuracy.

Interventions:

1. Have the student's hearing checked if it has not been recently checked.

2. Speak to the student to explain that he/she is using incorrect grammar when writing. Explain the importance of writing in grammatically correct sentences.

3. Determine the type of grammatical model to which the student is exposed at home. Without placing negative connotations on the parents' grammatical style, explain the difference between standard and nonstandard grammar.

4. Assess whether or not the student uses appropriate grammar when speaking. Proficiency in spoken language typically precedes and influences the type of language used in written work.

5. Choose a peer to model the correct use of grammar in verbal and written work for the student.

6. Evaluate the appropriateness of requiring the student to write with correct grammar (e.g., developmentally, a child may not utilize appropriate grammar when writing until the age of 6 or 7).

7. Reinforce the student for writing in grammatically correct sentences: (a) give the student a tangible reward (e.g., classroom privileges, line leading, passing out materials, five minutes free time, etc.) or (b) give the student an intangible reward (e.g., praise, fist bump, smile, etc.).

8. Have the student complete worksheets in which he/she must supply the correct grammatical forms (e.g., They _____ to the show yesterday.).

9. Require the student to proofread his/her written work for correct grammatical usage.

10. Have the student help correct other students' written work by checking grammatical usage and correcting the errors.

11. Explain that certain verbs go with certain subjects and that correct subject-verb agreement requires the appropriate match of subject and verb. Teach the student verb tenses and how to select the correct tense to go with a subject. Have the student practice matching verb tenses to a list of subjects.

12. Provide the student with examples of correct subject-verb agreement for those combinations he/she most commonly uses incorrectly.

13. Give the student a series of sentences with both correct and incorrect grammar. Ask the student to identify which are correct and incorrect. Have the student correct the incorrect sentences.

14. Identify the most common grammatical errors the student makes. Have the student spend time each day practicing the correct grammatical forms.

15. Have the student complete worksheets in which he/she must choose the correct grammatical form (e.g., I (seen, have seen) that show before.).

16. During the day, write down specific grammatical errors produced by the student. Read the sentences to the student and have him/her verbally make appropriate corrections.

17. Write down specific grammatical errors made by the student during the day. Give the written sentences to the student and have him/her make appropriate corrections. At first, mark the errors for him/her to correct. As the student becomes more proficient with this task, have him/her find and correct the errors independently.

18. Have the student listen to examples of incorrect grammar, identify each error, and then provide the correct form in writing.

19. When speaking privately with the student, restate his/her grammatical error with a rising inflection (e.g., He done it?) to see if the student recognizes errors and spontaneously makes appropriate corrections.

20. Give the student a series of sentences, both written and oral, and have him/her identify which are grammatically correct and incorrect.

21. Ask the parents to encourage the student's correct use of grammar at home by praising him/her when correct grammar is used.

22. Identify the grammatical forms the student has difficulty writing correctly. Provide a list of the correct forms which the student can keep at his/her desk for a reference when writing.

23. Reduce the emphasis on competition. Competitive activities may cause the student to hurry and make grammatical errors.

24. Have the student identify a verb to master using correctly. As the student masters the correct use of the verb, he/she puts it on a list with a star and identifies another verb to master.

25. Highlight or underline correct grammatical forms in the student's written work to reinforce the appropriate usage.

26. Highlight or underline correct grammatical forms in the student's reading material to call attention to the appropriate usage.

27. After checking the student's written work, make sure he/she makes all necessary grammatical corrections.

100 Has limited note-taking skills

Goals:

1. The student will improve his/her academic task-related behavior.
2. The student will improve his/her note-taking skills.

Objectives:

1. The student will write key words presented in lessons on _____ out of _____ trials.
2. The student will write key phrases presented in lessons on _____ out of _____ trials.
3. The student will audio record information presented in class and write notes from taped information on _____ out of _____ trials.
4. The student will take notes from information presented visually (e.g., wall-mounted board, overhead projector, etc.) on _____ out of _____ trials.
5. The student will take notes from information presented auditorily (e.g., audio recorder, lecture, etc.) on _____ out of _____ trials.
6. The student will take notes during class when necessary with verbal prompts on _____ out of _____ occasions.
7. The student will independently take notes during class when necessary on _____ out of _____ occasions.
8. The student will rely on environmental cues (e.g., other students, visual aids) to take notes during class when necessary on _____ out of _____ occasions.
9. The student will take notes related to the presentation on _____ out of _____ occasions.

Interventions:

1. Evaluate the appropriateness of the task to determine (a) if the task is too easy, (b) if the task is too difficult, or (c) if the length of time scheduled to complete the task is adequate.

2. Have the student question any directions, explanations, and instructions he/she does not understand.

3. Make sure the student uses any necessary aids (e.g., eyeglasses, hearing aid, etc.) to facilitate note taking.

4. Teach the student to use the outline format (e.g., *Who, What, Where, When, How,* and *Why*). The student should practice this technique with attention given to note-taking skill development.

5. Teach the student to use the mapping format (e.g., *Who, What, Where, When, How,* and *Why*). The student should practice this technique with attention given to note-taking skill development.

6. Teach the student to listen and look for direction words (e.g., circle, underline, choose, list, etc.).

7. Provide a standard format for taking lecture notes (e.g., have paper and pencil or pen ready, listen for main ideas or important information, write a shortened form of main ideas or important information, ask to have any main ideas or important information repeated when necessary, etc.).

8. The teacher should pause periodically during a lecture to allow students to fill in gaps in their notes and think about the information presented.

9. Require the student to review the previous day's notes for a short period of time before a new lecture.

10. Teach the student to write the key words and main ideas that answer *Who, What, Where, When, How,* and *Why* when taking notes. Students should then be given time periodically to go back to fill in connecting details (e.g., The student writes, Christopher Columbus - Spain - New World - 1492, and is given time to go back to fill in sailed from - to discover the - during the year, resulting in a complete statement: Christopher Columbus sailed from Spain to discover the New World during the year 1492.).

11. Teach the student to learn and use abbreviations for words frequently used to take notes more efficiently. Give the student the list of *Selected Abbreviations and Symbols* as a resource.

12. The teacher should give students several minutes at the end of a lecture to individually review their notes and ask questions to clarify points.

13. Choose a peer for the student to review notes with at the end of each lecture. The review helps the student clarify information and facilitates retention of the material.

14. Teach the student to listen and look for key words (e.g., Christopher Columbus, Spain, New World, etc.).

15. Require the student to review lecture notes the first five minutes of each homework session (e.g., read notes silently, read notes verbally, cover notes with a cover sheet and review from memory, etc.).

16. Have the student keep his/her notes organized in a folder for each subject or activity.

17. Teach the student to associate a familiar word or symbol with new information. This association will facilitate the student's memory.

18. Use multiple modalities (e.g., auditory, visual, etc.) when delivering a lecture.

19. Teach the student that it is acceptable to write notes in incomplete sentences.

20. Point out to the student that instructions, directions, lectures, etc., should be written in the form of notes when they are presented.

21. Check the student's notes before he/she begins an assignment to determine if they contain adequate information for the assignment.

22. Provide the student with an outline or questions to be completed during the presentation of instructions, directions, lectures, etc.

23. Teach the student to listen and look for action words (e.g., sailed, discovered, founded, etc.).

24. Provide the student with samples of students' notes of classroom instructions, directions, lectures, etc., that have been given so that he/she may learn what information is necessary when taking notes.

25. Make sure the student is in the best location in the classroom (e.g., near the board, teacher, or other source of information) to receive information for note taking.

26. Provide supervision of the student's note taking.

27. Teach the student to use the double-column format (e.g., *Who, What, Where, When, How*, and *Why*). The student should practice this technique with attention given to note-taking skill development.

28. Present instructions, directions, lectures, etc., clearly and loudly enough for the student to hear.

29. Summarize for the student the main points of instructions, directions, lectures, etc.

30. Maintain visibility to and from the student when delivering instructions, directions, lectures, etc., to facilitate successful note taking.

31. Match the rate of delivery of the instructions, directions, lectures, etc., to the student's ability to take notes.

32. Provide instructions, directions, lectures, etc., in sequential steps to facilitate student note taking.

33. Teach the student to divide his/her paper in the middle when taking notes. Have him/her write main ideas and key words on the left side of the paper and fill in details and connecting points on the right side of the paper. The details and connecting points may be filled in after the lecture or during a pause.

34. Present information in short segments for the student to take notes. As the student experiences success, gradually increase the length of the segments that are presented.

35. Make sure that the vocabulary used in presenting instructions, directions, lectures, etc., is appropriate for the student's ability level.

36. Place the student next to a peer so the student can copy the notes taken by the peer.

37. Make sure the student has adequate surface space on which to write when taking notes (e.g., uncluttered desk top).

38. Reduce distracting stimuli (e.g., other students talking, outdoor activities, movement in the classroom, hallway noise, etc.) that interferes with the student's note taking.

39. Present the information in the most interesting manner possible.

40. Make sure the student has all the materials necessary for note taking (e.g., paper, pencil with eraser, pen, etc.).

41. Have the student audio record instructions, directions, lectures, etc., as an alternative to written note taking.

101 Does not use word endings correctly when spelling or omits them

Goal:

1. The student will improve his/her spelling skills.

Objectives:

1. The student will recognize word endings with _____% accuracy.
2. The student will demonstrate the ability to write word endings with _____% accuracy.
3. The student will use word endings which do not require changes in spelling of the root word with _____% accuracy.
4. The student will use word endings which require changes in spelling of the root word with _____% accuracy.

Interventions:

1. Attach a list of suffixes (e.g., *-ed, -ing, -ly, -er, etc.*) and sample words to the student's desk for him/her to use as a reference when writing.

2. Choose a peer to participate in daily practice activities using suffixes with the student.

3. Teach the student spelling skills at each level before introducing a new skill level.

4. Do not require the student to learn more information than he/she is capable of learning at any time.

5. Give the student a few words to learn to spell at a time. Spend extra time on each word until the student can spell it correctly.

6. Have the student keep a copy of the rules for word endings at his/her desk.

7. Recognize quality work (e.g., display the student's work, congratulate the student, etc.).

8. Have the student keep a dictionary of most misspelled words. Require the student to check the spelling of all words he/she is not sure are spelled correctly.

9. Highlight or underline word endings (e.g., *-ed, -ing, -ly, -er,* etc.) in the student's reading assignments to call attention to the appropriate use of word endings.

10. Identify a list of words the student has difficulty spelling correctly. Use this list as ongoing spelling words for the student.

11. Have the student practice a new skill or assignment alone, with an aide, the teacher, or a peer before attempting it with the entire group or before being graded on it.

12. Make sure the student correctly hears the misspelled sounds. Have the student say the words aloud to determine if the student is aware of the letters or sound units in the words

13. Have the student spend time each day practicing the use of a single word ending (e.g., -ing). When the student demonstrates mastery of the word ending, introduce a new one.

14. Have the student use the dictionary to find the correct spelling of any words he/she does not spell correctly. Emphasize spelling accurately.

15. Reduce the emphasis on competition. Competitive activities may cause the student to hurry and make mistakes using word endings.

16. Have the student use his/her current spelling words in a meaningful manner (e.g., writing a letter to a friend, rock star, famous athlete, etc.) to facilitate his/her spelling improvement.

17. Make sure the student has received instruction in using word endings (e.g., *-ed, -ing, -ly, -er*, etc.).

18. Provide practice with word endings using a computer software program or a hand-held educational device that gives the student immediate feedback.

19. Require the student to proofread all written work for spelling errors. Reinforce the student for correcting each spelling error.

20. Use wall charts showing word endings (e.g., *-ed, -ing, -ly, -er,* etc.) and sample words for the student to use as a reference when writing.

21. Reinforce the student for using word endings correctly when spelling: (a) give the student a tangible reward (e.g., classroom privileges, line leading, passing out materials, five minutes free time, etc.) or (b) give the student an intangible reward (e.g., praise, fist bump, smile, etc.).

22. Have the student be a peer tutor to teach spelling words he/she has mastered to another student. This can serve as reinforcement for the student.

Goal:

1. The student will improve his/her spelling skills.

Objectives:

1. The student will use the spelling rule *i* before *e* except after *c* with _____% accuracy.
2. The student will use the spelling rule words which end with a vowel plus y, add s to make plural with _____% accuracy.
3. The student will use the spelling rule words which end with a consonant plus y, change the y to i and add es to make plural with _____% accuracy.
4. The student will use the spelling rule words with one syllable, one vowel, and one consonant at the end, double the final consonant when adding an ending with _____% accuracy.

Interventions:

1. Attach a list of suffixes (e.g., *-ed, -ing, -ly, -er,* etc.) and sample words to the student's desk for use as a reference when writing.

2. Do not require the student to learn more information than he/she is capable of learning at any time.

3. Choose a peer to practice the use of spelling rules when writing words, sentences, etc., each day with the student.

4. Cut a spelling word apart letter by letter to make a puzzle. Have the student unscramble the letters and then arrange them to spell the word.

5. Do not require the student to learn too many spelling words at one time.

6. Give the student a magazine or news article. Have him/her highlight words which follow the spelling rule he/she is learning.

7. Have the student identify a list of words (e.g., 5, 10, or 15 words) each week which he/she wants to learn to spell. Teach the student to spell these words using the spelling rules.

8. Post a chart in the classroom with a list of words which represent the spelling rules. The student can refer to the list when completing written assignments (e.g., words that drop the silent *e* when adding *ing*, words that double the final consonant when adding *ing*, etc.).

9. Have the student keep a copy of the rules for word endings at his/her desk.

10. Make sure the student has had adequate practice using the spelling rules in writing words, sentences, etc.

11. Integrate spelling rules with the total language arts program (e.g., activities, methods, and materials related to the teaching of spelling, reading, and language as a whole rather than separately).

12. Have the student practice a new spelling skill alone, with an aide, the teacher, or a peer before attempting it with the entire group or before being graded on it.

13. Provide a computer software program or a hand-held educational device which gives practice and reinforcement for correctly spelling words.

14. Have the student practice a spelling rule until that rule is mastered (e.g., *i* before *e* except after *c*, etc.). When one rule is mastered, a new one is introduced.

15. Reduce the emphasis on competition. Competitive activities may cause the student to hurry and make mistakes.

16. Have the student spend time each day practicing the use of a single word ending (e.g., *-ed*). When the student demonstrates mastery of a word ending, introduce a new one.

17. Teach the student spelling skills at each level before introducing a new skill level.

18. Have the student type his/her list of spelling words.

19. Have the student use his/her current spelling words in a meaningful manner (e.g., writing a letter to a friend, rock star, famous athlete, etc.) to facilitate his/her spelling improvement.

20. Highlight or underline word endings (e.g., -ed, -ing, -ly, -er, etc.) in the student's reading assignments to call attention to the appropriate use of word endings.

21. Provide a salt (or sand) box in which the student can trace spelling words.

22. Have the student be a peer tutor to teach spelling words he/she has mastered to another student. This can serve as reinforcement for the student.

23. Make sure the student has adequate time to complete written assignments to facilitate the student's improvement in using spelling rules.

24. Have the student write current spelling words in different locations (e.g., wall-mounted board, transparencies, on a posted list at his/her desk, etc.) throughout the classroom as he/she is learning them.

25. Use daily drills to help the student memorize spelling rules.

26. Provide the student with adequate opportunities for repetition of information through different experiences to facilitate his/her memory.

27. Have the student keep a dictionary of frequently misspelled words. Require the student to check the spelling of all words he/she is not sure are spelled correctly.

28. Make up a rap song using the spelling rule.

29. Pair the student with a peer to proofread each other's work.

30. Have the student start a personal dictionary of misspelled words at his/her desk. Require him/her to check the spelling of all words he/she is not sure are spelled correctly.

31. Post a chart with a list of spelling rules so the student can refer to it when completing written assignments.

32. Provide the student with a list of words which represent the spelling rules to keep at his/her desk for reference (e.g., words that drop the silent e when adding -ing, words that double the final consonant when adding -ing, etc.).

33. Have the student practice basic spelling rules daily.

34. Provide the student with self-checking materials. Require corrections to be made before turning in assignments.

35. Recognize quality work (e.g., display the student's work, congratulate the student, etc.).

36. Reduce distracting stimuli in the classroom when the student is working on spelling and related activities (e.g., place the student in a carrel or office space).

37. Have the student practice using spelling rules in words, sentences, etc., which are written every day.

38. Provide the student with commercial or teacher-made games which provide practice using spelling rules.

39. Require the student to proofread his/her written assignments using spelling rules. Reinforce the student for each correction he/she makes when using spelling rules.

40. Review daily those spelling skills which have been previously introduced.

41. Teach the student to use spelling rules to spell words correctly rather than simply memorizing the spelling of words for testing purposes (e.g., dropping the silent e when adding ing, etc.).

42. Have the student use the dictionary to find the correct spelling of any words he/she does not spell correctly. Emphasize spelling accurately.

43. Review daily those spelling skills which have been previously introduced.

44. Teach the student why he/she is learning spelling rules (e.g., provide the student with a concrete example of how each word can be used in his/her life).

45. Provide the student with a list of spelling rules to keep at his/her desk. Require the student to refer to the rules when writing words, sentences, etc.

46. Have the student's hearing checked if it has not been recently checked.

47. Use wall charts showing word endings (e.g., *-ed, -ing, -ly, -er,* etc.) and sample words for the student to use as a reference when writing.

48. Require the student to verbally explain how he/she spells words using spelling rules (e.g., *i* before *e* except after *c*, etc.).

103 Has difficulty spelling words that do not follow the spelling rules

Goal:

1. The student will improve his/her spelling skills.

Objectives:

1. The student will spell an identified sight-word vocabulary with _____% accuracy.
2. The student will spell words that do not follow spelling rules with _____% accuracy.

Interventions:

1. Choose a peer to spend time each day having the student practice spelling words which do not follow spelling rules.

2. Cut a spelling word apart letter by letter to make a puzzle. Have the student unscramble the letters and then arrange them to spell the word.

3. Do not require the student to learn more information than he/she is capable of learning at any time.

4. Give the student fewer words to learn to spell at a time. Spend extra time on each word until the student can spell it correctly.

5. Have the student be a peer tutor to teach spelling words he/she has mastered to another student. This can serve as reinforcement for the student.

6. Have the student keep a dictionary of most misspelled words. Require the student to check the spelling of all words he/she is not sure are spelled correctly.

7. Make a list of the words the student most commonly misspells. Keep a copy of the list of correctly spelled words at his/her desk to use as a reference when writing.

8. Have the student make a song or chant of the word (e.g., L-A-UGH, L-A-UGH).

9. Require the student to proofread his/her written assignments for spelling errors. Reinforce the student for each correction he/she makes.

10. Provide opportunities for the student to read often so he/she sees in print those words he/she needs to learn to spell.

11. Have the student practice a new skill or assignment alone, with an aide, the teacher, or a peer before attempting it with the entire group or before being graded on it.

12. Teach the student spelling skills at each level before introducing a new skill level.

13. Have the student type his/her list of spelling words.

14. Use various activities to help strengthen and reinforce the phonetic spelling of words (e.g., writing a story, sentences, etc.).

15. Have the student use his/her current spelling words in a meaningful manner (e.g., writing a letter to a friend, rock star, famous athlete, etc.) to facilitate his/her spelling improvement.

16. Reduce distracting stimuli in the classroom when the student is working on spelling and related activities (e.g., place the student in a carrel or office space).

17. Have the student write current spelling words in different locations (e.g., wall-mounted board, transparencies, on a posted list at his/her desk, etc.) throughout the classroom as he/she is learning them.

18. Identify the most common words the student uses which do not follow spelling rules. Teach the student to spell these words.

19. Have the student write sentences, paragraphs, or a story each day about a favorite subject. Encourage the student to use available references (e.g., dictionary, lists of words, etc.) to facilitate correct spelling.

20. Integrate spelling with the total language arts program (e.g., activities, methods, and materials are related to the teaching of reading and language as a whole rather than separately).

21. Provide computer software that provides practice and reinforcement in spelling words correctly.

22. Make a list of frequently seen words which do not follow spelling rules for the student to keep at his/her desk.

23. Have the student identify a list of words (e.g., 5, 10, or 15 words) each week which he/she wants to learn to spell. These words become the student's spelling words for the week.

24. Make sure the student has adequate time to complete written assignments so that he/she will be more likely to spell words correctly.

25. Teach the student the sounds that letters and letter combinations make. Have the student practice making letter sounds as he/she sees the letters on flash cards.

26. Provide commercial or teacher-made games which provide practice spelling words which do not follow the spelling rules.

27. Provide the student with a spelling list of words he/she uses which do not follow the spelling rules. Add new words to the list as the student demonstrates mastery of any of the words.

28. Recognize quality work (e.g., display the student's work, congratulate the student, etc.).

29. Reinforce the student for spelling words that do not follow spelling rules: (a) give the student a tangible reward (e.g., classroom privileges, line leading, passing out materials, five minutes free time, etc.) or (b) give the student an intangible reward (e.g., praise, fist bump, smile, etc.).

30. Have the student use the dictionary to find the correct spelling of any words he/she does not spell correctly. Emphasize spelling accurately.

31. Make sure the student hears the sounds in the words misspelled. Have the student say the words aloud to determine if the student is aware of the letters or sound units in the words.

32. Use daily drills to help the student memorize spelling words (e.g., flash cards, writing the spelling words three times, etc.).

33. Make sure the student does not have too many words to learn to spell at one time.

34. Review daily those spelling words which have been previously introduced.

104 Has difficulty with phonetic approaches to spelling

Goal:

1. The student will improve his/her spelling skills.

Objectives:

1. The student will state the letters of the alphabet with _____% accuracy.
2. The student will recognize sounds made by letters of the alphabet with _____% accuracy.
3. The student will recognize letters of the alphabet which represent sounds with _____% accuracy.
4. The student will use phonetic approaches to spelling, with assistance, with _____% accuracy.
5. The student will independently use phonetic approaches to spelling with _____% accuracy.

Interventions:

1. Choose a peer to model spelling words phonetically. Have the student read what a peer writes phonetically.

2. Cut a word apart letter by letter to make a puzzle. Have the student unscramble the letters and then arrange them to spell the word.

3. Dictate one sound at a time for the student to write.

4. Do not require the student to learn more information than he/she is capable of learning at any time.

5. Have the student identify a list of words each week which he/she wants to learn to use in writing activities. Teach the student phonetic approaches to spelling these words.

6. Provide spelling practice using a computer software program or a hand-held educational device that gives the student immediate feedback.

7. Do not require the student to learn too many spelling words at one time.

8. Give the student fewer words to learn to spell at a time. Spend extra time on each word until he/she can spell it correctly.

9. Let the student dictate sounds for you to write.

10. Choose a peer to participate in daily drills spelling words phonetically with the student.

11. Have the student be a peer tutor to teach spelling words he/she has mastered to another student. This can serve as reinforcement for the student.

12. Reduce distracting stimuli in the classroom when the student is working on spelling and related activities (e.g., place the student in a carrel or office space).

13. Have the student practice a new spelling lesson or assignment alone, with an aide, the teacher, or a peer before attempting it with the entire group or before being graded on it.

14. Use flash cards to teach the words. Have students look at the word, say the word, then spell the word aloud as they are looking at the word.

15. Use various activities to help strengthen and reinforce the phonetic spelling of words (e.g., writing a story, sentences, etc.).

16. Have the student practice spelling phonetically the words most commonly used in everyday speech and writing.

17. Provide the student with a list of words he/she is required to spell phonetically. Provide the student with evaluative feedback indicating how the words can be spelled phonetically.

18. Have the student use a phonetic approach to spelling words in sentences written each day.

19. Teach the student spelling skills at each level before introducing a new skill level.

20. Help the student separate his/her spelling list into those words which are spelled phonetically and those which are not.

21. Integrate spelling with the total language arts program (e.g., activities, methods, and materials are related to the teaching of reading and language as a whole rather than separately).

22. Make sure the student correctly hears the sounds in the words he/she misspells. Have the student say the words aloud to determine if he/she is aware of the letters or sound units in the words.

23. Give the student short drills in spelling each day which require a selected phonetic sound. As the student demonstrates success, increase the number of phonetic sounds.

24. Provide the student with an example of phonetic spelling for those words he/she fails to attempt to spell phonetically.

25. Recognize quality work (e.g., display the student's work, congratulate the student, etc.).

26. Have the student keep a dictionary of most misspelled words. Require the student to check the spelling of all words he/she is not sure are spelled correctly.

27. Reinforce the student for spelling words phonetically: (a) give the student a tangible reward (e.g., classroom privileges, line leading, passing out materials, five minutes free time, etc.) or (b) give the student an intangible reward (e.g., praise, fist bump, smile, etc.).

28. Have the student use a phonetic approach to spelling any word he/she does not know how to spell.

29. Have the student write sentences, paragraphs, or a story each day about a favorite subject. Encourage the student to use a phonetic approach to spelling the words he/she does not know how to spell.

30. Teach the student the sound each letter makes. Have the student practice making letter sounds as he/she sees the letters on flash cards.

105 Omits, substitutes, adds, or rearranges letters or sound units when spelling words

Goal:

1. The student will improve his/her spelling skills.

Objectives:

1. The student will spell words or sound units with _____% accuracy.
2. The student will include all letters or sound units when spelling with _____% accuracy.
3. The student will include only those letters or sound units necessary when spelling, with _____% accuracy.
4. The student will arrange letters or sound units when spelling with _____% accuracy.
5. The student will sequence letters or sound units with _____% accuracy when spelling.

Interventions:

1. Choose a peer to participate in daily spelling word drills with the student.

2. Have the student type his/her list of spelling words.

3. Cut a word apart letter by letter to make a puzzle. Have the student unscramble the letters and then arrange them to spell the word.

4. Have the student keep a dictionary of most misspelled words. Require the student to check the spelling of all words he/she is not sure are spelled correctly.

5. Do not require the student to learn too many words at one time.

6. Give the student fewer words to learn to spell at a time. Spend extra time on each word until the student can spell it correctly.

7. Have the student be a peer tutor to teach spelling words he/she has mastered to another student. This can serve as reinforcement for the student.

8. Teach the student why he/she needs to spell words correctly (e.g., provide the student with a concrete example of how each word can be used in his/her life).

9. Have the student proofread all written work for omissions, substitutions, additions, or rearranged letters or sound units. Reinforce the student for each correction made.

10. Provide opportunities for the student to read often so he/she sees in print those words he/she needs to learn to spell.

11. Make sure that the student's spelling words are those which he/she sees frequently to facilitate correct spelling and use of the words.

12. Recognize quality work (e.g., display the student's work, congratulate the student, etc.).

13. Highlight or underline in the student's reading assignments those letters or sound units the student omits, substitutes, adds, or rearranges to direct the student's attention to the correct spelling of words.

14. Identify those words the student misspells by omitting, substituting, adding, or rearranging letters or sound units. Have the student practice spelling the words correctly in sentences written each day.

15. Provide magnetic or felt letters for the student to correctly sequence into spelling words.

16. Teach the student spelling skills at each level before introducing a new skill level.

17. Make a list of the words the student misspells by omitting, substituting, adding, or rearranging letters or sound units. Have the student practice spelling the words correctly. Remove each word from the list as the student demonstrates mastery.

18. Provide commercial or teacher-made games which provide practice spelling. The student should have a personalized list of words for this practice.

19. Have the student use the dictionary to find the correct spelling of any words he/she does not spell correctly. Emphasize spelling accurately.

20. Have the student identify a list of words (e.g., 5, 10, or 15 words) each week to learn to spell (e.g., if the student is interested in cars, identify words from automotive magazines, advertisements, etc.).

21. Use daily drills to help the student memorize spelling words.

22. Identify those words the student misspells by omitting, substituting, adding, or rearranging letters or sound units. Have the student start and frequently update a personalized dictionary with the words he/she misspells to use as a reference.

23. Provide personalized computer software which will allow the student to practice his/her personal word list.

24. Make sure the student correctly hears those letters or sound units omitted, substituted, added, or rearranged, when spelling words. Have the student say the words aloud to determine if the student is aware of the letters or sound units in the words.

25. Have the student use his/her current spelling words in a meaningful manner (e.g., writing a letter to a friend, rock star, famous athlete, etc.) to facilitate his/her spelling improvement.

26. Reinforce the student for spelling words correctly: (a) give the student a tangible reward (e.g., classroom privileges, line leading, five minutes free time, etc.) or (b) give the student an intangible reward (e.g., praise, fist bump, smile, etc.).

27. Provide spelling practice using a computer software program or a hand-held educational device that gives the student immediate feedback.

28. Reduce the emphasis on competition. Competitive activities may cause the student to hurry and misspell words.

Goal:

1. The student will improve his/her spelling skills.

Objective:

1. The student will increase the number of spelling words learned in a given time period (indicate one week, two weeks, a month, etc.).

Interventions:

1. Choose a peer to participate in daily spelling word drills with the student.

2. Develop crossword puzzles which contain only the student's spelling words and have him/her complete them.

3. Have the student indicate when he/she has learned one of his/her spelling words. When the student demonstrates he/she can spell the word, remove it from his/her current spelling list.

4. Give the student fewer words to learn to spell at a time. Spend extra time on each word until the student can spell it correctly.

5. Do not require the student to learn more information than he/she is capable of learning at any time.

6. Evaluate the appropriateness of the task to determine (a) if the task is too easy, (b) if the task is too difficult, or (c) if the length of time scheduled to complete the task is adequate.

7. Have the student highlight or underline spelling words in passages from reading assignments, newspapers, magazines, etc.

8. Provide spelling practice using a computer software program or a hand-held educational device that gives the student immediate feedback.

9. Have the student identify a list of words (e.g., 5, 10, or 15 words) each week to learn to spell (e.g., if the student is interested in cars, identify words from automotive magazines, advertisements, etc.).

10. Reduce the emphasis on competition. Competitive activities may cause the student to hurry and make spelling errors.

11. Have the student quiz others over spelling words (e.g., teacher, aide, peers, etc.).

12. Write sentences, passages, paragraphs, etc., for the student to read which repeat the student's spelling words throughout the written material.

13. Have the student use his/her current spelling words in sentences written each day.

14. Make sure that the student's spelling instruction is on a level where success can be met. As the student demonstrates success, gradually increase the level of difficulty.

15. Teach the student why he/she is learning each spelling word (e.g., provide the student with a concrete example of how each word can be used in his/her life).

16. Have the student write current spelling words in different locations (e.g., wall-mounted board, transparencies, on a posted list at his/her desk, etc.) throughout the classroom as he/she is learning them.

17. Initiate a *Learn to Spell a Word a Day* program with the student.

18. Have the student be a peer tutor to teach spelling words to another student.

19. Recognize quality work (e.g., display the student's work, congratulate the student, etc.).

20. Have the student use his/her current spelling words in a meaningful manner (e.g., writing a letter to a friend, rock star, famous athlete, etc.) to facilitate his/her spelling improvement.

21. Have the student review spelling words each day for a short period of time rather than two or three times per week for longer periods of time.

22. Have the student practice a list of new spelling words alone, with an aide, the teacher, or a peer before attempting it with the entire group or before being graded on it.

23. Reinforce the student for practicing the writing of the spelling words.

24. Have the student's current spelling words listed on the wall-mounted board at all times.

25. Integrate spelling with the total language arts program (e.g., activities, methods, and materials are related to the teaching of reading and language as a whole rather than separately).

26. Have the student use the dictionary to find the correct spelling of any words he/she does not spell correctly. Emphasize spelling accurately.

27. Tape a list of the student's current spelling words on his/her desk. Have the student practice them frequently.

28. Reinforce the student for learning to spell words correctly: (a) give the student a tangible reward (e.g., classroom privileges, line leading, passing out materials, five minutes free time, etc.) or (b) give the student an intangible reward (e.g., praise, fist bump, smile, etc.).

29. Use words for the student's spelling list which are commonly found in his/her daily surroundings (e.g., commercials, hazard signs, directions, lunch menu, etc.).

30. Require the student to proofread all written work for spelling errors. Reinforce the student for correcting each spelling error.

107 Spells words correctly in one context but not in another

Goal:

1. The student will improve his/her spelling skills.

Objectives:

1. The student will spell words in more than one context, with assistance, with _____%
   accuracy.
2. The student will independently spell words in more than one context with _____% accuracy.

Interventions:

1. Choose a peer to participate in daily spelling word drills with the student.

2. Have the student write his/her spelling words frequently over a period of time to facilitate the his/her visual memory of the spelling words.

3. Have the student identify a list of words (e.g., 5, 10, or 15) each week from an area of interest to learn to spell. If the student is interested in cars, he/she can identify words from automotive magazines, advertisements, etc.

4. Do not require the student to learn too many spelling words at one time.

5. Reinforce the student for practicing the writing of the spelling words within sentences and paragraphs.

6. Teach the student why he/she is learning each spelling word (e.g., provide the student with a concrete example of how each word can be used in his/her life).

7. Give tests and quizzes when the student is certain to succeed (e.g., after he/she has had adequate time to learn the information).

8. Have the student keep a dictionary of most misspelled words. Require the student to check the spelling of all words he/she is not sure are spelled correctly.

9. Require the student to proofread his/her written work, circling any words which he/she thinks are misspelled. The student then checks with the teacher or the dictionary to correct those misspellings.

10. Give the student fewer words to learn to spell at a time. Spend extra time on each word until the student can spell it correctly.

11. Make sure the student has adequate time to complete written assignments.

12. Have the student use his/her current spelling words in a meaningful manner (e.g., writing a letter to a friend, rock star, famous athlete, etc.) to facilitate his/her spelling improvement.

13. Provide opportunities for the student to read often so he/she sees in print those words he/she needs to learn to spell.

14. Integrate spelling with the total language arts program (e.g., activities, methods, and materials are related to the teaching of reading and language as a whole rather than separately).

15. Tape a list of the student's current spelling words on his/her desk. Have the student practice them frequently.

16. Require the student to proofread all of his/her written work for spelling errors. Reinforce him/her for correcting each spelling error.

17. Have the student write current spelling words in different locations (e.g., wall-mounted board, transparencies, on a posted list at his/her desk, etc.) throughout the classroom as he/she is learning them.

18. Write sentences, paragraphs, etc., for the student to read which repeat the student's spelling words throughout the written material.

19. Make sure that the student's spelling words are those which he/she sees frequently to facilitate correct spelling and use of the words.

20. Reduce the emphasis on competition. Competitive activities may cause the student to hurry and make spelling mistakes.

21. Provide the student with self-checking materials. Require corrections to be made before turning in assignments.

22. Have the student maintain a folder of all of his/her spelling words. Encourage the student to refer to the list when he/she is engaged in writing activities to check spelling.

23. Make sure the student has had adequate practice writing the spelling words (e.g., drills, sentence activities, etc.).

24. Recognize quality work (e.g., display the student's work, congratulate the student, etc.).

25. Provide opportunities for the student to use computer software to write stories. He/she should check the spelling of words using the computer's spell check.

26. Have the student write a sentence daily for each spelling word.

27. Reduce distracting stimuli in the classroom when the student is working on spelling and related activities (e.g., place the student in a carrel or office space).

28. Have the student use the dictionary to find the correct spelling of any words he/she does not spell correctly. Emphasize spelling accurately.

29. Teach the student to use spelling words rather than simply memorizing the spelling of the words for testing purposes (e.g., have the student use the words in writing activities each day).

30. Reinforce the student for spelling the word correctly in all contexts: (a) give the student a tangible reward (e.g., classroom privileges, line leading, passing out materials, five minutes free time, etc.) or (b) give the student an intangible reward (e.g., praise, fist bump, smile, etc.).

31. Use various activities to help strengthen and reinforce the visual memory of the spelling words (e.g., flash cards, word lists on the wall-mounted board, a list on the student's desk, etc.).

108 Does not express thoughts in verbal and written form

Goals:

1. The student will express thoughts clearly and thoroughly in a variety of writing activities.
2. The student will express thoughts clearly and thoroughly in a variety of speaking activities.
3. The student will develop leadership skills.

Objectives:

1. The student will show effective planning skills on _____ occasions per week.
2. The student will participate in activities requiring analysis (i.e., to take apart, identify a problem, etc.) in _____ assignments per week.
3. The student will participate in activities requiring synthesis (i.e., to create something new, unique, or original) in _____ assignments per week.
4. The student will participate in activities requiring evaluation (i.e., to judge, decide, or choose) in _____ assignments per week.
5. The student will complete _____ activities involving leadership training.

Interventions:

1. Have the student write eyewitness news articles about past events.

2. Facilitate an internship or mentorship with a professional who would be a role model for the student.

3. Give the student an opportunity to question a person who is an expert in a particular field (e.g., an anthropologist, mathematician, etc.).

4. Provide the student with opportunities to write for the school newspaper or a classroom newsletter.

5. Offer an opportunity for the student to interview professional speakers and writers who are role models in the daily work force (e.g., authors, journalists, city management leaders, business leaders, etc.).

6. Provide an opportunity for the student to role-play various situations in which persuasion is necessary (e.g., a commercial advertisement specialist trying to sell his/her campaign to a corporate president, a candidate running for public office, etc.).

7. Encourage the student to verbally acknowledge the feelings and expressions of others.

8. Ask the student to predict possible outcomes if a significant historical event could have been altered (e.g., the bombing of Pearl Harbor, etc.).

9. Encourage the student to voluntarily spend time and talk with others who have a special need (e.g., handicapped, nursing home residents, etc.).

10. Encourage the student to describe verbally and/or in writing his/her feelings (e.g., about events, prepared topics, impromptu class situations, etc.).

11. Invite guest speakers of various occupations (e.g., a dentist, social worker, etc.) to visit the classroom. Encourage the student to interview the speakers.

12. Have the student prepare a list of interview questions about a specific event (e.g., January 1, 2000; anniversary of the bombing of Pearl Harbor, etc.)

13. Encourage the student to become involved (e.g., individually, as a member of a team, etc.) in speaking and/or writing competitions.

14. Encourage the student to participate in debates of specific, controversial topics (e.g., evolution, nuclear arms race, etc.).

15. Encourage the student to write in a journal and/or diary on a daily basis.

16. Have the student prepare a written plan for objectives to meet in a composition or speech. Talk with the student about any anticipated problems he/she may encounter in meeting those objectives.

17. Have the student analyze commercial advertising:

- Ask the student to debate the merits of one product over another based on a TV commercial.
- Have the student write and illustrate an advertisement campaign for a new product of his/her design.

18. Have the student write an editorial about a controversial topic (e.g., environmental controls, economic development, school improvements, etc.).

19. Ask the student to design a bulletin board to celebrate a specific event (e.g., Black History Month, Columbus Day, etc.).

20. Have the student write a comparison of leaders who lived during the same time period (e.g., Martin Luther King Jr. and President John F. Kennedy, etc.):

- Have the student lead a group discussion about problems faced by those leaders.
- Encourage the student to hypothesize possible causes of those problems.

Goal:

1. The student will increase his/her use of complex sentences.

Objectives:

1. The student will imitate sentences which expand the length and complexity of his/her typical sentences in _____ out of _____ trials.
2. The student will expand the length and complexity of a given sentence in _____ out of _____ trials.
3. The student will spontaneously expand the length and complexity of his/her sentences during conversational speech in _____ out of _____ trials.

Interventions:

1. Encourage verbal output. Generally, students who use very short sentences also talk less than most students. Increasing their opportunities to communicate verbally will provide them with necessary practice.

2. Be sure that the student understands more complex sentences by asking questions to assess his/her comprehension (e.g., Before you get a drink of water, finish your social studies. What should you do first?).

3. Provide the student with conjunctions to be used in sentence expansion, including sentence combining, compound subjects and verbs, etc.

4. Have the student use conjunctions to expand sentences containing opposites (e.g., A man is big, but a boy is little.).

5. Using books without words, have the student tell the story. Encourage the use of longer, more complex sentences.

6. Ask the parents to encourage the student's use of more complex sentences at home by praising him/her when longer sentences are used.

7. Build lists by providing nouns that go with a specific adjective (e.g., red could be followed by apple, car, book, etc.). Have the student select one of the nouns and build a list of appropriate adjectives (e.g., car could be followed by big, metal, expensive, etc.). Have the student use this information to formulate complex sentences.

8. Make groups of cards containing subjects, verbs, adjectives, etc. Have the student combine the cards in various ways to construct sentences which are appropriate in complexity.

9. During the day, write down some of the student's simple sentences. Read the sentences to the student and ask him/her questions requiring additional descriptive vocabulary to expand the sentences (e.g., Student: My dog can run. Teacher: What color is your dog? What size is your dog? How fast can your dog run? Encourage the student to use these words to make his/her original sentence longer. Student: My big, black dog can run fast. Accept any expansions the student incorporates into his/her sentences without expecting all the descriptors to be used initially.).

10. When the student uses short, simple sentences which lack complexity, provide him/her with models of expansion and conjoining using his/her sentences as a foundation.

11. Make sure the student understands that sentences express thoughts about a subject and what that subject is or does. Explain that complex thoughts require complex sentences which include descriptive words and connecting words.

12. Ask questions which stimulate language. Avoid those which can be answered by yes/no or a nod of the head (e.g., ask the student what he/she did at recess instead of asking if he/she played on the slide, ask the student what he/she did on vacation instead of asking if he/she stayed home over the holidays).

13. Use gestural and/or verbal prompts to remind the student to expand his/her sentences (e.g., use a gesture to indicate you want the student to tell you more or point to specific parts of a picture or object he/she is describing to elicit specific descriptive vocabulary).

14. Give the student several short sentences and have him/her combine them to make one longer sentence (e.g., The dog is big. The dog is brown. The dog is mine. - The big, brown dog is mine.).

15. Give the student a list of transition words (e.g., therefore, although, because, etc.) and have him/her make sentences using each word.

16. Give the student a group of related words (e.g., author, read, love, best-seller, etc.) and have him/her make up sentences that include all the words.

17. Reinforce those students in the classroom who use complex sentences.

18. Have the student's hearing checked if it has not been recently checked.

19. Begin sentences with compound subjects and have the student complete the thought (e.g., The bear and the frog _____.). This activity can be expanded by providing verb phrases without subjects.

20. Determine the type of verbal model to which the student is exposed at home. Without placing negative connotations on his/her parents' language skills, explain the purpose of using complex sentences.

21. Reinforce the student for increasing his/her use of complex sentences: (a) give the student a tangible reward (e.g., classroom privileges, line leading, passing out materials, five minutes free time, etc.) or (b) give the student an intangible reward (e.g., praise, fist bump, smile, etc.).

22. Video the student and his/her classmates performing various actions. Play the recording without sound and have the student describe what is happening. Encourage the use of descriptive words and phrases where appropriate. A prerecorded video could also be used for this activity.

23. Provide the student with a sentence containing adjectives and adverbs. Have him/her identify the descriptive vocabulary used. If necessary, ask the student questions to elicit the appropriate information.

24. Have the student assist in adding descriptive words and phrases to other students' simple sentences.

25. Have the student make up sentences. Encourage the use of descriptive words and phrases where appropriate.

110 Does not communicate name, address, and phone number

Goals:

1. The student will improve the ability to communicate his/her name, address, and phone number.
2. The student will communicate his/her name, address, and phone number.

Objectives:

1. The student will be able to communicate his/her name, address, and phone number verbally with assistance on _____ out of _____ trials.
2. The student will be able to communicate his/her name, address, and phone number verbally without assistance on _____ out of _____ trials.
3. The student will be able to communicate his/her name, address, and phone number in writing with assistance on _____ out of _____ trials.
4. The student will be able to communicate his/her name, address, and phone number in writing without assistance on _____ out of _____ trials.
5. The student will be able to communicate his/her name, address, and phone number through sign language with assistance on _____ out of _____ trials.
6. The student will be able to communicate his/her name, address, and phone number through sign language without assistance on _____ out of _____ trials.

Interventions:

1. Provide cues for the student to follow when learning to write his/her name, address, and phone number. Reduce the cues as he/she demonstrates success at each level (e.g., write the information in highlight marker to trace over, reduce to dotted lines to follow, then dots marking beginning and endings of each letter or number, etc.).

2. Provide opportunities for the student to communicate his/her name, address, and phone number in a meaningful way (e.g., pen pals with whom to correspond, trade phone numbers with classmates to share information about class projects, etc.).

3. Do not require the student to learn more information than he/she is capable of learning at any time.

4. Role-play various situations which require the student to communicate his/her name, address, and phone number.

5. Make sure the student understands the importance of being able to communicate his/her name, address, and phone number.

6. Keep a written cue at the student's desk or work area to refer to if he/she has difficulty recalling his/her name, address, or phone number.

7. Have a discarded phone available in the classroom for the student to practice calling his/her phone number to reinforce the information kinesthetically.

8. Evaluate the appropriateness of the task to determine (a) if the task is too easy, (b) if the task is too difficult, or (c) if the length of time scheduled to complete the task is adequate.

9. Create games which require the student to communicate his/her name, address, and phone number.

10. Verbally or in sign language state the student's name, address, and phone number, then have him/her repeat the information verbally or in sign language.

11. Have the student write information in a notebook or on an index card to be referred to when needed.

12. Communicate with parents (e.g., notes home, phone calls, etc.) to share information about the student's progress. The parents may reinforce the student at home for communicating his/her name, address, and phone number at school.

13. Reinforce the student for communicating his/her name, address, and/or phone number based on the amount of information he/she can communicate successfully. As the student demonstrates success, gradually increase the amount of information required for reinforcement.

14. Have the student practice communicating his/her name, address, and/or phone number each day for a short period of time rather than only two or three days each week for longer periods of time.

15. Reinforce the student for communicating his/her name, address, and phone number: (a) give the student a tangible reward (e.g., classroom privileges, line leading, passing out materials, five minutes free time, etc.) or (b) give the student an intangible reward (e.g., praise, fist bump, smile, etc.).

16. Break information into units and have the student learn one unit at a time (e.g., divide a phone number into three groups: 573, 874, and 1710).

17. Provide letter and number tiles for the student to use to communicate his/her name, address, and phone number.

18. Choose a peer to model communicating personal information in community and classroom settings for the student.

19. Reinforce those students who can communicate their name, address, and phone number.

20. Reduce distracting stimuli (e.g., noise and movement in the classroom) when the student is trying to communicate his/her name, address, and phone number.

21. Audio record the student's name, address, and phone number so he/she can replay and listen to the information as often as necessary to facilitate memorization.

111 Does not comprehend graphic symbols, sign language, etc.

Goals:

1. The student will be able to comprehend graphic symbols.
2. The student will be able to comprehend sign language.

Objectives:

1. The student will demonstrate comprehension of graphic symbols on _____ out of _____ occasions.
2. The student will demonstrate comprehension of sign language on _____ out of _____ occasions.
3. Given assistance, the student will demonstrate his/her understanding of graphic symbols, sign language, etc., that are typically used in community life on _____ out of _____ occasions.
4. The student will independently demonstrate functional understanding of graphic symbols, sign language, etc., that are typically used in community life on _____ out of _____ occasions.

Interventions:

1. If appropriate, provide the student with a written copy of graphic symbols, sign language, etc., (e.g., directions, questions, announcements, etc.).

2. Communicate clearly to the student when it is time to concentrate on graphic symbols, sign language, etc.

3. Reduce the emphasis on competition. Competitive activities may cause the student to have difficulty concentrating on graphic symbols, sign language, etc.

4. Communicate in a variety of ways to facilitate the student's understanding (e.g., if the student does not understand graphic symbols or sign language, present information in written form or verbally).

5. Give the students multiple opportunities to demonstrate signs and symbols they are learning.

6. Give the student one task to perform at a time. Introduce the next task when the student has successfully completed the current task.

7. Reinforce the student for attending to graphic symbols, sign language, etc., based on the length of time the student can be successful. As the student demonstrates success, gradually increase the length of time the student must attend for reinforcement.

8. Have the student verbally paraphrase the meaning of graphic symbols or sign back sign language just observed to check for understanding.

9. Seat the student close to the sign language provider (e.g., teacher, aide, peer, etc.).

10. Reduce distracting stimuli to facilitate the student's ability to attend to graphic symbols, sign language, etc., (e.g., place the student in the front row, provide a carrel or office space away from distractions). This is used as a means of reducing distracting stimuli and not as a form of punishment.

11. Maintain visibility to and from the student. The teacher should be able to see the student and the student should be able to see the teacher. Make eye contact before engaging in sign language with the student.

12. Provide clear communication through graphic symbols, sign language, etc., (e.g., make communication as simple and concrete as possible).

13. When delivering information through graphic symbols, sign language, etc., be sure that it is within the student's level of comprehension.

14. Maintain consistent expectations within the ability of the student.

15. Teach the student a new symbol, sign, etc., each day. Review previously learned symbols, signs, etc., daily.

16. Interact frequently with the student when using graphic symbols, sign language, etc., to verify that he/she is comprehending.

17. Have a peer help the student with any graphic symbol, sign language, etc., he/she does not understand.

18. Encourage parents to reinforce and rehearse signs and graphic symbols used to communicate public information.

19. Designate a person as the primary individual to deliver communication through graphic symbols, sign language, etc.

20. Stop at various points when presenting information through graphic symbols, sign language, etc., to ensure the student is attending.

21. Have the student question any part of the graphic symbol, sign language, etc., that he/she does not understand.

22. Prevent the student from becoming overstimulated (e.g., frustrated, angry, etc.) by an activity involving communication through graphic symbols, sign language, etc.

23. Assess the quality and clarity of the graphic symbols, sign language, etc., presented to the student.

24. When a student is essentially nonverbal, provide him/her time and understanding to develop the rapport needed to facilitate communication.

25. Introduce the students to community members who frequently use or promote the use of signs/symbols in daily community life (e.g., traffic police) to help the students appreciate the importance of this communication.

26. Maintain a consistent format of graphic symbols, sign language, etc., used with the student.

27. Evaluate the appropriateness of presenting information through graphic symbols, sign language, etc., to determine (a) if the task is too easy, (b) if the task is too difficult, or (c) if the length of time scheduled to complete the task is adequate.

28. Communicate with parents (e.g., notes home, phone calls, etc.) to share information about the student's progress. The parents may reinforce the student at home for attending to and comprehending graphic symbols, sign language, etc.

29. Teach the student to communicate his/her needs in an appropriate manner (e.g., raise hand, touching another in a socially acceptable manner, etc.).

30. Have the student question any graphic symbol, sign language, etc., that he/she does not understand.

31. Choose a peer to model comprehension of graphic symbols, sign language, etc., for the student.

32. Deliver a predetermined signal (e.g., clapping hands, turning lights off and on, touching his/her shoulder, etc.) before engaging in communication using graphic symbols, sign language, etc.

33. Provide the student with a chart of meanings, letters, words, etc., indicated by graphic symbols, sign language, etc., (e.g., a picture of the symbol for the letter *a*, a graphic symbol of a playground with the word playground, etc.).

34. Seat the student far enough away from peers to facilitate increased opportunities for attending to graphic symbols, sign language, etc.

35. Make sure the student is attending to the necessary information (e.g., making eye contact, hands free of distracting materials, etc.) before presenting information through graphic symbols, sign language, etc.

112 Does not comprehend typical verbal communications

Goal:

1. The student will comprehend typical verbal communications.

Objectives:

1. The student will follow verbal directions in correct sequential order on _____ out of _____ trials.
2. The student will comprehend _____ out of _____ verbal communications.
3. The student will demonstrate the ability to comprehend verbal communication by listening carefully and summarizing the information with _____% accuracy.
4. The student will follow verbal directions with teacher assistance on _____ out of _____ trials.
5. The student will independently follow verbal directions on _____ out of _____ trials.
6. The student will follow one-step verbal directions on _____ out of _____ trials.
7. The student will demonstrate the ability to comprehend a conversation by listening carefully and responding appropriately on _____ out of _____ trials.
8. The student will demonstrate the ability to comprehend a question stated verbally by listening carefully and making an appropriate response on _____ out of _____ trials.
9. The student will repeat what is said with _____% accuracy.

Interventions:

1. Provide the student with a written copy of verbal communications (e.g., directions, questions, announcements, etc.).

2. When the student is required to recall information, remind him/her of the situation in which the material was originally presented (e.g., Remember yesterday when we talked about . . .?).

3. Allow the student to speak without being interrupted or hurried.

4. Follow a less desirable task with a more desirable task, making the completion of the first task necessary to perform the second.

5. Communicate clearly to the student when it is time to listen to verbal communications.

6. Use pictures, diagrams, and gestures when delivering information verbally.

7. Communicate in a variety of ways to facilitate the student's understanding (e.g., if the student does not understand verbal directions, present them in written form).

8. Use multiple modalities (e.g., auditory, visual, tactile, etc.) when presenting verbal communications to the student.

9. Work through steps of the verbal directions as they are delivered to make sure the student follows the directions accurately.

10. Maintain a consistent format of verbal communications with the student.

11. Have the student question any verbal communications he/she does not understand.

12. Reinforce the student for attending to verbal communications based on the length of time the student can be successful. As the student demonstrates success, gradually increase the length of time required for reinforcement.

13. Teach the student context cues to determine the meaning of words he/she hears.

14. State directions, questions, comments, etc., to the student individually.

15. Audio record information for the student to replay and repeat as necessary.

16. Interact frequently with the student to verify that he/she is comprehending verbal communications.

17. Give the student one task to perform at a time. Introduce the next task when the student has successfully completed the current task.

18. Present one concept at a time. Make sure the student understands each concept before presenting the next.

19. Reduce distracting stimuli to facilitate the student's ability to attend to verbal communications (e.g., place the student in the front row, provide a carrel or office space away from distractions, etc.). This is used as a means of reducing distracting stimuli and not as a form of punishment.

20. Use vocabulary that is within the student's level of comprehension when delivering directions, explanations, and information.

21. Seat the student close to the source of the verbal communication (e.g., teacher, aide, peer, etc.).

22. Stand directly in front of the student when delivering verbal communications (e.g., directions, explanations, questions, conversations, etc.).

23. Structure the environment to provide the student with increased opportunity for help or assistance on academic tasks (e.g., peer tutoring, directions for work sent home, frequent interactions, etc.).

24. Maintain visibility to and from the student. The teacher should be able to see the student and the student should be able to see the teacher. Make eye contact possible at all times when engaging in verbal communications with the student.

25. Have a peer help the student with any verbal communications he/she does not understand (e.g., directions, assignments, announcements, etc.).

26. Make sure the student achieves success when following verbal directions.

27. Spend time talking with the student on an individual basis and include topics that are of interest to the student.

28. Assess the appropriateness of the social situation in relation to the student's ability to function successfully.

29. Have the student maintain a record (e.g., chart or graph) of his/her responses to verbal communications (e.g., answering verbal questions, following verbal directions, etc.).

30. Before the student answers a question, have him/her rephrase the original question in his/her own words to check for comprehension.

31. Work the first problem or problems with the student to make sure that he/she accurately follows the verbal directions.

32. Call the student by name prior to bells ringing, announcements being made, directions being given, questions being asked, etc.

33. Designate a person as the primary individual to deliver verbal communications to the student.

34. Provide the student with a predetermined signal (e.g., lights turned off and on, hand signals, etc.) when he/she is not attending to verbal communications.

35. Have the student participate in practice activities designed to develop his/her listening skills (e.g., following one-, two-, or three-step directions; listening for the main point; listening games; etc.).

36. Prevent the student from becoming overstimulated by an activity (e.g., frustrated, angry, etc.) involving verbal communication.

37. Give verbal directions before handing out materials.

38. Have the student repeat or paraphrase information heard.

39. Have the student carry out one step of the verbal directions at a time. After each step, have him/her check with the teacher to make sure that each step is successfully followed before attempting the next.

40. Assess the quality and clarity of verbal communication presented to the student.

41. Have the student practice group listening skills (e.g., Everyone take out a piece of paper, write your name on the paper, and number your paper from 1 to 20.).

42. Rephrase directions, explanations, questions, comments, instructions, etc., to facilitate the student understanding what is being presented.

43. Have the student's hearing checked if it has not been recently checked.

44. Communicate with parents (e.g., notes home, phone calls, etc.) to share information about the student's progress. The parents may reinforce the student at home for attending to and comprehending verbal communications.

45. Have the student quietly repeat to himself/herself information just heard to help remember and comprehend the information.

46. Call on the student when he/she is most likely to be successful.

47. Provide alternatives for the traditional format of presenting verbal communications (e.g., audio record directions, summarize information, communication presented by peers, etc.).

48. Stop at various points when engaging in verbal communications to ensure that the student is attending.

49. Reduce the emphasis on competition. Competitive activities may cause the student to have difficulty concentrating on and comprehending verbal communications.

50. Make sure that all verbal communications with the student are delivered in the most clear and concise manner, at an appropriate rate for the student, and loudly enough to be heard.

51. Deliver a predetermined signal (e.g., clapping hands, turning lights off and on, touching his/her shoulder, etc.) before engaging in verbal communication.

52. Seat the student far enough away from peers to facilitate increased opportunities for attending to verbal communication.

53. Ask questions which stimulate language. Avoid those which can be answered by yes/no or a nod of the head (e.g., ask the student what he/she did at recess instead of asking if he/she played on the slide, ask the student what he/she did on vacation instead of asking if he/she stayed home over the holidays, etc.).

54. Make sure the student is attending to the speaker (e.g., making eye contact, hands free of distracting materials, looking at assignment, etc.) before communicating verbally with him/her.

55. Demonstrate directions, explanations, and instructions as they are presented verbally (e.g., use the wall-mounted board to work a problem for the student, begin playing a game with the student, etc.).

56. Make sure that verbal communications are expressed in a supportive rather than a threatening manner (e.g., Will you please . . . or You need . . . rather than You better . . . or If you don't . . .).

57. Make sure that verbal communications are presented on a level at which the student can be successful (e.g., two-step or three-step directions are not given to students who can only successfully follow one-step directions).

58. Make sure that verbal communications are delivered in a nonthreatening manner (e.g., positive voice, facial expression, language, etc.).

59. Make sure the student has all the materials needed to complete the assignment/activity when given verbal directions.

60. Present directions, explanations, and instructions as simply and clearly as possible (e.g., Get your book, turn to page 29, do problems 1 through 5.).

61. Make sure that competing sounds (e.g., talking, movement, noises, etc.) are silenced when directions are being given, public address announcements are being made, a conversation is being conducted, etc.

62. Teach the student direction-following skills (e.g., stop doing other things, listen carefully, write down important points, wait until all directions are given, question directions not understood, etc.).

63. After receiving verbal directions, require the student to wait until the teacher gives him/her a signal to begin a task (e.g., give a hand signal, ring a bell, etc.).

64. Establish classroom rules:
- Concentrate while working.
- Work quietly.
- Remain in your seat.
- Finish task.
- Meet task expectations.

Review rules often. Reinforce students for following the rules.

65. Provide clearly stated verbal communications (e.g., make verbal communication as simple and concrete as possible).

113 Demonstrates difficulty understanding the meaning of words indicating a question

Goals:

1. The student will improve his/her comprehension skills.
2. The student will demonstrate understanding and use of WH (*Who, What, Where, When, How,* and *Why*) interrogatives.

Objectives:

1. The student will demonstrate the ability to answer a question beginning with *who* with _____% accuracy.
2. The student will provide a person in response to *who* questions in _____ out of _____ trials.
3. The student will demonstrate the ability to answer a question beginning with *what* with _____% accuracy.
4. The student will provide a noun or verb in response to *what* questions (e.g., What is it? What are you doing?) in _____ out of _____ trials.
5. The student will demonstrate the ability to answer a question beginning with *where* with _____% accuracy.
6. The student will provide a place in response to *where* questions in _____ out of _____ trials.
7. The student will demonstrate the ability to answer a question beginning with *when* with _____% accuracy.
8. The student will provide a time in response to *when* questions in _____ out of _____ trials.
9. The student will demonstrate the ability to answer a question beginning with *why* with _____% accuracy.
10. The student will provide a reason in response to *why* questions in _____ out of _____ trials.
11. The student will demonstrate the ability to answer a question beginning with *how* with _____% accuracy.
12. The student will respond to a question immediately following a given statement (e.g., Teacher: We will eat lunch at noon. When will we eat lunch? Student: At noon.) in _____ out of _____ trials.
13. The student will provide appropriate responses to a variety of WH questions in everyday speaking situations in _____ out of _____ trials.

Interventions:

1. Ask the student a question which can be tied to information he/she has just heard or read (e.g., John Kennedy was the 35th president of the United States. - Who was the 35th president of the United States?). Gradually expand the amount of time which elapses between obtaining the information needed to answer a question and the actual question.

2. Use visual aids or demonstrations whenever possible to facilitate comprehension of questions.

3. Have the student restate/paraphrase information from an explanation, class discussion, a story read, etc., to assess comprehension before asking questions.

4. Determine whether the student knows the difference between telling and asking. Young students frequently confuse these concepts and launch into a lengthy narrative about some personal experience when asked if they have any questions.

5. A statement made by the student may be used to generate questions (e.g., if the student says he/she likes to watch TV, questions might include what is your favorite show, when is it on, how long is it on, and who are some of the characters in the show, etc.).

6. After audio recording the student's responses, have him/her identify the incorrect responses to questions and make the appropriate modifications.

7. Routinely audio record the student's speech and point out errors in his/her responses to questions. With each taping, reinforce the student as his/her responses become more appropriate.

8. Provide a written model for the student to see how statements can be changed into yes/no questions. Circle the word(s) that can move in a statement and draw arrows to show where they can move to make a question (e.g., Spot is a dog. - Is Spot a dog?). Point out that the answer to the question is contained in the original statement.

9. Post a schedule of daily routines for reference in conjunction with when questions during the day.

10. Point out the difference between rhetorical questions (e.g., Why would anybody order liver?) and questions which are meant to elicit a definite response (e.g., Who needs some paper?).

11. Choose a peer to model responding appropriately to questions for the student.

12. Allow the student to process one question at a time rather than a series of questions. Help the student break down questions which require processing multiple pieces of information into simpler components.

13. Have the student's hearing checked if it has not been recently checked.

14. Provide the student with question headings under which he/she can place responses to help him/her focus on appropriate types of responses (e.g., book belongs under *what*, the park belongs under *where*, tomorrow belongs under *when*, because belongs under *why*, etc.).

15. Restate questions in a simpler form when necessary to facilitate comprehension (e.g., When do you go to bed? could be restated as What time do you go to bed? or Why are you crying? could be simplified with What happened?).

16. Formulate activities for your class which require the comprehension of question forms:

- Have classmates interview the student as himself/herself when he/she was 3, in the future, as a famous character, as a character in a story read to or by the class, etc.
- Play guessing games involving pictures from catalogs, objects in the room, etc., which require appropriate responses to questions to gain information.
- Have the student perform actions or pantomime activities and ask *what* questions (e.g., What is he/she doing? What does he/she have?).
- Have the student use music, a chant, etc., to help increase automatic recall of months of the year, days of the week, etc., to facilitate responses to *when* questions.
- Use pictures which depict cause/effect information in conjunction with *why* questions (e.g., a picture of a broken cookie jar and a little boy crying, paired with the question, Why is the boy crying?).
- Have the student help plan a bulletin board by eliciting responses to various questions (e.g., Where should we put the board? When should we do the project? What theme should we use? Who will cut out the border? etc.). Ask the student to take notes so that he/she can provide the necessary information at a later time as needed.
- Have the student role-play working in a store, restaurant, etc., and have him/her answer questions from customers.
- Have the student feel an object he/she cannot see and answer questions about the object in the process of guessing its identity.
- Use maps of the school, neighborhood, city, country, etc., in conjunction with a *Where would you find . . .?* game.
- Have the student compose a paragraph which focuses on one question form at a time (e.g., Tell all about what you would see at the zoo; tell all about where you could find a fishing worm; tell all about why you like to go to the park; etc.).

17. Determine whether the student is experiencing memory problems vs. comprehension of the question by having him/her restate the question in his/her own words.

18. Ask the student to determine what he/she knows and what he/she needs to know before advancing to more complex types of questions (e.g., how much, how many, how often, why, etc.). This process may facilitate comprehension of math word problems, as well as processing information in other classes.

19. Determine whether the student comprehends dependent clauses in statements before requiring him/her to respond appropriately to questions which involve this type of information (e.g., We can go to the show if your mother is on time. Can we go to the show if your mother is late?).

20. Point out questions at the end of a chapter before presenting the material. Outline the information the student will need to obtain when reading by writing key words on the board under the appropriate WH headings (e.g., Who: opposing forces; When: date of the Battle of Lexington; etc.). Review the information the end of the lesson.

21. Reinforce the student for demonstrating comprehension of questions: (a) give the student a tangible reward (e.g., classroom privileges, line leading, passing out materials, five minutes free time, etc.) or (b) give the student an intangible reward (e.g., praise, fist bump, smile, etc.).

22. Place WH headings on the board and touch the appropriate one(s) as you give directions (e.g., The yellow reading group (touch *Who*) will have reading after gym (touch *When*). Please bring your workbooks (touch *What*) with you.).

114 Does not carry on conversations with peers or adults

Goals:

1. The student will improve his/her production of speech sounds.
2. The student will improve his/her conversational speech.
3. The student will improve the fluency of his/her speech.
4. The student will improve the ability to express himself/herself verbally.
5. The student will improve his/her grammatical speech.

Objectives:

1. The student will respond to conversational questions from peers _____% of the time.
2. The student will respond to conversational questions from adults _____% of the time.
3. The student will participate in conversation with peers _____% of the time he/she is spoken to by a peer.
4. The student will participate in conversation with adults _____% of the time he/she is spoken to by an adult.
5. The student will initiate conversations with peers (identify some criteria such as once a day, three times a day, etc.).
6. The student will initiate conversations with adults (identify some criteria such as once a day, three times a day, etc.).

Interventions:

1. Choose a peer to sit/work with the student (e.g., in different settings or activities such as art, music, P.E.; on the bus; tutoring; group projects; running errands in the building; free time; etc.) to facilitate the student's opportunity to participate in conversation.

2. Reinforce the student for carrying on conversations with peers and adults: (a) give the student a tangible reward (e.g., classroom privileges, line leading, passing out materials, five minutes free time, etc.) or (b) give the student an intangible reward (e.g., praise, fist bump, smile, etc.).

3. Spend time each day talking with the student on an individual basis about his/her friends.

4. Reinforce the student for carrying on a conversation with peers and adults based on the length of time he/she can be successful. As the student demonstrates success, gradually increase the length of time required for reinforcement.

5. Have the student run errands which will require interactions with teachers, administrators, staff, etc., (e.g., delivering attendance reports to the office, taking messages to other teachers, etc.).

6. Have the student play games which require carrying on conversations with others.

7. Have the student show visitors and new students around the school.

8. Choose a peer to spend time each day with the student.

9. Ask the student to be the leader of a small-group activity if he/she possesses mastery of skills or has an interest in that area.

10. Try various groupings to determine the group in which the student is most comfortable carrying on a conversation with peers and adults.

11. Evaluate the appropriateness of expecting the student to carry on a conversation with peers and adults.

12. Write a contract with the student specifying what behavior is expected (e.g., carrying on a conversation with peers and adults) and what reinforcement will be made available when the terms of the contract have been met.

13. Spend some time each day talking with the student on an individual basis about his/her interests.

14. Provide the student with many social and academic successes.

15. Have the student participate in simulated conversational activities with feedback designed to teach conversational skills (e.g., greetings, questions, topics of conversation, etc.).

16. Determine an individual(s) in the school environment with whom the student would most want to engage in a conversation (e.g., custodian, librarian, resource teacher, principal, older student, etc.). Allow the student to spend time with the individual(s) each day.

17. Greet or acknowledge the student as often as possible (e.g., hallways, cafeteria, welcome to class, acknowledge a job well done, etc.).

18. Pair the student with an outgoing student who participates in conversation with peers and adults on a frequent basis.

19. Give the student the responsibility of tutoring another student.

20. Have the student work with a peer who is nonthreatening (e.g., younger or smaller).

21. Encourage or reward others for initiating interactions with the student.

22. Communicate with parents (e.g., notes home, phone calls, etc.) to share information about the student's progress. The parents may reinforce the student at home for carrying on a conversation with peers and adults at school.

23. Provide the student with positive feedback which indicates he/she is successful, important, respected, etc.

24. Speak to the student to explain (a) what he/she is doing wrong (e.g., not carrying on a conversation with peers and adults) and (b) what he/she should be doing (e.g., carrying on a conversation with peers and adults).

25. Have sharing time at school. Encourage the student to talk about anything that interests him/her.

26. Choose a peer to model carrying on conversations with peers and adults for the student.

27. Acknowledge the student's attempts to communicate his/her needs (e.g., facial expressions, gestures, inactivity, self-deprecating comments, etc.).

28. Reinforce those students in the classroom who carrying on conversations with peers and adults.

29. Plan for one-to-one teacher-student interactions at various times throughout the school day.

30. Ask the student to choose another student to work with on a specific assignment. (If the student has difficulty choosing someone, determine the student's preference by other means, such as a class survey.)

31. Allow the student to be a member of a group without requiring active participation.

32. Interact with the student from a distance. Gradually decrease the distance until a close proximity is achieved.

33. Teach the student conversational questions (e.g., How are you?, What have you been up to?, How is it going?, etc.) to use when speaking to peers and adults.

34. Have the student deliver verbal messages to other staff members to facilitate his/her opportunity to carry on conversations.

115 Does not complete statements or thoughts when speaking

Goals:

1. The student will improve his/her production of speech sounds.
2. The student will improve his/her conversational speech.
3. The student will improve the fluency of his/her speech.
4. The student will improve the ability to express himself/herself verbally.
5. The student will improve his/her grammatical speech.

Objectives:

1. The student will speak in single words which express thoughts with _____% accuracy.
2. The student will speak in complete phrases which express thoughts with _____% accuracy.
3. The student will speak in complete sentences which express thoughts with _____% accuracy.
4. The student will adequately express thoughts (e.g., using correct words to express himself/herself) with _____% accuracy.

Interventions:

1. Allow the student to speak without being interrupted or hurried.

2. Use a private signal (e.g., touching earlobe, raising index finger, etc.) to remind the student to speak in complete sentences and use specific terminology.

3. Provide the student with a topic (e.g., rules to follow when riding your bike) and have him/her write complete sentences about it.

4. When the student is required to recall information, remind him/her of the situation in which the material was originally presented (e.g., Remember yesterday when we talked about . . .?, Remember when we were outside and I told you about the . . .?).

5. When the student is required to recall information, provide visual and/or auditory cues to help him/her remember the information (e.g., mention key words, expose part of a picture, etc.).

6. Ask the student leading questions to facilitate the process of speaking in complete sentences and using specific vocabulary.

7. Ask the parents to encourage the student's use of complete sentences and thoughts at home by praising him/her when these are used.

8. Provide frequent interactions and encouragement to support the student's confidence (e.g., tell the student he/she is doing great, to keep up the good work, and you're proud of him/her).

9. Increase the student's awareness of the problem by audio recording the student while he/she is speaking with another student who uses complete sentences. Replay the recording for the student to see if he/she can identify incomplete sentences and nondescript terminology. Have the student make appropriate modifications.

10. Teach the student the components of a complete sentence (i.e., subject, verb, and an object). Point out the components using objects, pictures, sentences, etc., depending on the student's abilities.

11. Make sure the student understands that a complete sentence has to express a complete thought about a subject and what that subject is or does, and that use of specific vs. nondescriptive vocabulary is important to clarify the message.

12. Make a list of the student's most common incomplete statements and uses of nondescriptive terminology. Spend time with the student practicing how to make these statements or thoughts complete and making appropriate replacements for nondescriptive vocabulary.

13. List the qualities a good speaker possesses (e.g., rate, diction, volume, vocabulary, etc.) and have the student evaluate himself/herself on each characteristic. Set a goal for improvement in only one or two areas at a time.

14. Make groups of cards containing subjects, verbs, adjectives, etc. Have the student combine the cards in various ways to construct complete sentences.

15. Encourage verbal output. Increase the student's opportunities to communicate verbally to provide him/her with necessary practice.

16. Focus on completeness of the student's thought and not the grammatical accuracy of the statement. Reinforce complete thoughts that include specific vocabulary.

17. When speaking privately with the student, restate his/her incomplete sentences and/or nondescriptive vocabulary with a rising inflection to indicate the need for more information (e.g., You saw the <u>stuff</u> in the sky? Your brown dog . . .?) to see if the student recognizes the problem and spontaneously makes appropriate corrections.

18. Have the student give process statements to sequence an activity (e.g., how to make a peanut butter and jelly sandwich). Have the student focus on making each statement a complete thought with specific vs. nondescriptive vocabulary.

19. Give the student a factual statement (e.g., Some animals are dangerous.) and have him/her provide several complete sentences relating to that topic.

20. Provide the student with sentence starters (e.g., Go _____. Run _____. Today I ___ Anyone can _____.) and have him/her write complete sentences.

21. Routinely audio record the student when he/she speaks and point out incomplete statements and nondescript terminology. With each taping, reinforce the student as his/her use of complete sentences and specific vocabulary improves.

22. After a field trip or special event, have the student retell the activities which occurred with an emphasis on using descriptive vocabulary and complete sentences.

23. Choose a peer to model speaking in complete sentences for the student. Assign the students to work together, perform assignments together, etc.

24. Have the student role-play various situations in which speaking well is important (e.g., during a job interview).

25. Have the student correct a series of phrases by making each a complete sentence.

26. Give the student several short sentences and have him/her combine them to produce one longer sentence (e.g., The dog is big. The dog is brown. The dog is mine. - The big, brown dog is mine.).

27. When the student uses incomplete sentences or nondescriptive terminology, provide the student with models of expansion and specific vocabulary using his/her statements as a foundation.

28. Have the student complete fill-in-the-blank sentences with appropriate words (e.g., objects, persons, places, etc.).

29. Video the student and classmates performing various actions. Play the recording without sound and have the student narrate observations in complete sentences with descriptive vocabulary. A prerecorded video could also be used for this activity.

30. Choose a topic for a paragraph or story and alternate making up sentences with the student to provide a model of the components of a complete sentence.

31. Ask questions which stimulate language. Avoid those which can be answered by yes/no or a nod of the head (e.g., ask the student what he/she did at recess instead of asking if he/she played on the slide, ask the student what he/she did on vacation instead of asking if he/she stayed home over the holidays, etc.).

32. Show the student an object or a picture of an object for a few seconds and remove it. Ask the student to recall specific attributes of the object (e.g., color, size, shape, etc.).

33. Give the student a series of words (e.g., objects, persons, places, etc.) and have the student list all the words he/she can think of with similar meanings (i.e., synonyms).

34. Give the student a series of words or pictures and have him/her name as many items as possible within that category (e.g., objects, persons, places, things that are hot, etc.).

35. Give the student a series of words describing objects, persons, places, etc., and have him/her identify the opposite of each word.

36. Give the student a series of complete and incomplete sentences, both written and oral. Ask him/her to identify which are correct and incorrect and make appropriate modifications.

37. Give the student a group of related words (e.g., *baseball, fans, glove, strikeout,* etc.) and have him/her write a paragraph that includes each word.

38. Give the student a list of transition words (e.g., *therefore, although, because,* etc.) and have him/her write sentences using each word.

39. Have the student make notes, lists, etc., of vocabulary that is needed to be recalled and have the student carry these reminders for reference.

40. Have the student keep a list of times and/or situations in which he/she is nervous, anxious, etc., and has more trouble than usual with speech. Help the student identify ways to feel more successful in those situations.

41. Teach the student to recognize key words and phrases related to information to facilitate his/her recall.

42. Have the student identify a good speaker and give the reasons he/she thinks that person is a good speaker.

43. Make sure the student receives information from a variety of sources (e.g., textbooks, presentations, discussions, etc.) to facilitate memory/recall.

44. Have the student complete worksheets in which he/she must replace nondescriptive or inaccurate vocabulary with specific and appropriate terminology (e.g., The thing tastes good. could be changed to The cake [meal, soda, etc.] tastes good., He used the digger to make the hole. could be changed to He used the shovel [backhoe, spade, etc.] to make the hole, etc.).

45. Label objects, persons, places, etc., in the environment to help the student be able to recall names.

46. Have the student's hearing checked if it has not been recently checked.

47. Have the student compete against himself/herself by timing how fast he/she can name a series of pictured objects. Each time, the student tries to improve his/her speed.

48. Have the student describe himself/herself and/or classmates in complete sentences with emphasis on specific vocabulary to differentiate one student from another.

49. Call on the student when he/she is most likely to be able to successfully respond.

50. Using a wordless picture book, audio record the student telling the story using descriptive vocabulary and complete sentences. Replay it for the student. Have the student listen for complete/incomplete sentences and specific/nondescriptive terminology and make appropriate corrections.

51. After reading a short story, have the student recall the main characters, sequence the events, and retell the outcome of the story.

52. Encourage the student to use gestures when necessary to clarify his/her message. Gestures may also facilitate recall of vocabulary the student is having difficulty retrieving.

53. Provide the student with the first sound of a word he/she is having difficulty retrieving to facilitate recall.

54. Speak to the student to explain that he/she is using incomplete sentences or thoughts when speaking. Explain the importance of speaking in complete sentences and choosing specific words to express ideas.

55. When the student has difficulty during a conversation, remind him/her that this occasionally happens to everyone.

56. Reinforce the student for using complete sentences or thoughts when speaking: (a) give the student a tangible reward (e.g., classroom privileges, line leading, passing out materials, five minutes free time, etc.) or (b) give the student an intangible reward (e.g., praise, fist bump, smile, etc.).

57. Reinforce the students in the classroom who use complete sentences or thoughts when speaking.

58. Have a number of students build a sentence together (e.g., The first one starts with a word (e.g., I). The next student adds the second word (e.g., like.) This process continues as long as possible to create one long, complete sentence. Do not accept nondescriptive terminology.

59. Make a list of the attributes which are likely to help a person become a good speaker (e.g., takes his/her time, thinks of what to say before starting, etc.).

60. Provide the student with an appropriate model to imitate speaking in complete sentences or thoughts (e.g., speak clearly, slowly, concisely, and in complete sentences, statements, and thoughts).

61. Describe objects, persons, places, etc., and have the student name the items described.

62. Give the student specific categories and have him/her name as many items as possible within that category (e.g., things that are cold, objects, persons, places, etc.).

63. Give the student a subject and have him/her write as many complete sentences about it as possible, emphasizing the use of specific vocabulary.

64. Give the student scrambled words and have him/her put them in the correct order to form a complete sentence.

65. Teach the concept of verb and noun phrases as soon as possible so the student has a means of checking to see if a sentence is complete.

66. Encourage the student to use an appropriate synonym when experiencing difficulty retrieving the exact word he/she wants to say.

67. Help the student use memory aids to recall words, such as linking a name to another word (e.g., Mr. Green is a very colorful person).

68. Demonstrate acceptable and unacceptable speech including incomplete thoughts and nondescriptive terminology, such as thing or stuff, etc. Have the student critique each example making suggestions for improvement.

69. Have the student complete associations (e.g., knife, fork, and _____; men, women, and _____; etc.).

70. Reduce the emphasis on competition. Competitive activities may cause the student to hurry and not speak in complete sentences.

Goal:

1. The student will improve his/her conversational skills.

Objectives:

1. The student will provide an appropriate word for an incomplete phrase in _____ out of _____ trials (e.g., knife, fork, and _____).
2. The student will identify an object/action when presented with a description in _____ out of _____ trials.
3. The student will differentiate between complete and incomplete statements in _____ out of _____ trials.
4. The student will verbally repeat a complete sentence in _____ out of _____ trials.
5. The student will use complete sentences during structured language activities in _____ out of _____ trials.
6. The student will use complete sentences during everyday speaking situations in _____ out of _____ trials.
7. The student will demonstrate word-finding ability by listing items which fall into a given category (e.g., fruit) with _____ % accuracy.
8. The student will demonstrate the ability to complete a previously incomplete thought by adding the appropriate information to it _____ % of the time.

Interventions:

1. Allow the student to speak without being interrupted or hurried.

2. Use a private signal (e.g., touching earlobe, raising index finger, etc.) to remind the student to speak in complete sentences and use specific terminology.

3. Provide the student with a topic (e.g., rules to follow when riding your bike) and have him/her make up complete sentences about it.

4. Ask the student leading questions to facilitate the process of speaking in complete sentences and using specific vocabulary.

5. When the student is required to recall information, remind him/her of the situation in which the material was originally presented (e.g., Remember yesterday when we talked about . . .?, Remember when we were outside and I told you about the . . .?).

6. Ask the parents to encourage the student's use of complete sentences and thoughts at home by praising him/her when these are used.

7. Focus on the completeness of the student's thought and not the grammatical accuracy of the statement. Reinforce complete thoughts that include specific vocabulary.

8. Teach the student the components of a complete sentence (i.e., subject, verb, and an object). Point out the components using objects, pictures, sentences, etc., depending on the student's abilities.

9. Make sure the student understands that a complete sentence has to express a complete thought about a subject and what that subject is or does, and that use of specific vs. nondescript vocabulary is important to clarify the message.

10. Make groups of cards containing subjects, verbs, adjectives, etc. Have the student combine the cards in various ways to construct complete sentences.

11. When the student uses incomplete sentences or nondescriptive terminology, provide him/her with models of expansion and specific vocabulary using his/her statements as a foundation.

12. Encourage verbal output. Increase the student's opportunities to communicate verbally to provide him/her with necessary practice.

13. Increase the student's awareness of the problem by audio recording the student while he/she is speaking with another student who uses complete sentences. Replay the recording for the student. Have him/her identify incomplete sentences and nondescript terminology and make appropriate modifications.

14. Make a list of the student's most common incomplete statements and uses of nondescriptive terminology. Spend time with him/her practicing how to make these statements or thoughts complete and making appropriate replacements for nondescriptive vocabulary.

15. When speaking privately with the student, restate his/her incomplete sentence and/or nondescriptive vocabulary with a rising inflection to indicate the need for more information (e.g., You saw the stuff in the sky? Your brown dog . . . ?) and to assess if the student recognizes the problem and spontaneously makes appropriate corrections.

16. Have the student give process statements to sequence an activity (e.g., how to make a peanut butter and jelly sandwich). Have him/her focus on making each statement a complete thought with specific vs. nondescriptive vocabulary.

17. Give the student a factual statement (e.g., some animals are dangerous) and have him/her provide several complete sentences relating to that topic.

18. Provide the student with sentence starters (e.g., Go _____. Run _____. Today I _____. Anyone can _____.) and have him/her make up complete sentences.

19. Routinely audio record the student when he/she speaks and point out incomplete statements and nondescript terminology. With each taping, reinforce the student as his/her use of complete sentences and specific vocabulary improves.

20. After a field trip or special event, have the student retell the activities which occurred with an emphasis on using descriptive vocabulary and complete sentences.

21. List the qualities a good speaker possesses (e.g., rate, diction, volume, vocabulary, etc.) and have the student evaluate himself/herself on each characteristic. Set a goal for improvement in only one or two areas at a time.

22. Have the student role-play various situations in which speaking well is important (e.g., during a job interview).

23. Have the student correct a series of phrases, making each a complete sentence.

24. Give the student several short sentences and have him/her combine them to produce one longer sentence (e.g., The dog is big. The dog is brown. The dog is mine. - The big, brown dog is mine.).

25. Have the student complete fill-in-the-blank sentences with appropriate words (e.g., objects, persons, places, etc.).

26. Have several students build a sentence together (e.g., The first one starts with a word (e.g., I). The next student adds the second word (e.g., like.) This process continues as long as possible to create one long, complete sentence. Do not accept nondescriptive terminology.

27. Choose a topic for a paragraph or story and alternate making up sentences with the student to provide a model of the components of a complete sentence.

28. Show the student an object or a picture of an object for a few seconds and remove it. Ask the student to recall specific attributes of the object (e.g., color, size, shape, etc.).

29. Give the student a series of words or pictures and have him/her name the category to which they belong (e.g., objects, persons, places, things that are hot, etc.).

30. Give the student a group of related words (e.g., *baseball, fans, glove, strikeout*, etc.) and have him/her write a paragraph that includes each word.

31. Give the student a series of words (e.g., objects, persons, places, etc.) and have him/her list all the words he/she can think of with similar meanings (synonyms).

32. Give the student a list of transition words (e.g., *therefore, although, because*, etc.) and have him/her make up sentences using each word.

33. Give the student a series of complete and incomplete sentences, both written and oral. Ask him/her to identify which are correct and incorrect and make appropriate modifications.

34. Give the student a series of words describing objects, persons, places, etc., and have him/her identify the opposite of each word.

35. Have the student make notes, lists, etc., of vocabulary he/she needs to be able to recall and carry these reminders with him/her for reference.

36. Have the student keep a list of times and/or situations in which he/she is nervous, anxious, etc., and has more trouble than usual with speech. Help the student identify ways to feel more successful in those situations.

37. Teach the student to recognize key words and phrases related to information to facilitate his/her recall.

38. Make sure the student receives information from a variety of sources (e.g., textbooks, presentations, discussions, etc.) to facilitate his/her memory/recall.

39. Have the student complete worksheets in which he/she must replace nondescriptive or inaccurate vocabulary with specific and appropriate terminology (e.g., The thing tastes good. could be changed to The cake [meal, soda, etc.] tastes good. or He used the digger to make the hole. could be changed to He used the shovel [backhoe, spade, etc.] to make the hole.).

40. Label objects, persons, places, etc., in the environment to help the student be able to recall names.

41. Choose a peer who speaks in complete sentences to model for the student. Assign the students to work together, perform assignments together, etc.

42. Have the student's hearing checked if it has not been recently checked.

43. Have the student compete against himself/herself by timing how fast he/she can name a series of pictured objects. He/she tries to improve his/her speed.

44. Have the student describe himself/herself and/or his/her classmates in complete sentences with emphasis on specific vocabulary to differentiate one student from another.

45. Video the student and his/her classmates performing various actions. Play the recording without sound and have the student narrate his/her observations in complete sentences with descriptive vocabulary. A prerecorded video could also be used for this activity.

46. After reading a short story, have the student recall the main characters, sequence the events, and retell the outcome of the story.

47. Using a wordless picture book, audio record the student telling the story using descriptive vocabulary and complete sentences. Replay it for the student. Have the student listen for complete/incomplete sentences and specific/ nondescriptive terminology and make appropriate corrections.

48. Have the student identify a good speaker and give the reasons why that person is a good speaker.

49. Encourage the student to use gestures when necessary to clarify his/her message. Gestures may also facilitate recall of vocabulary the student is having difficulty retrieving.

50. Provide the student with the first sound of a word he/she is having difficulty retrieving to facilitate recall.

51. Speak to the student to explain that he/she is using incomplete sentences or thoughts when speaking. Explain the importance of speaking in complete sentences and choosing specific words to express ideas.

52. When the student has difficulty during a conversation, remind him/her that this occasionally happens to everyone.

53. Reinforce the student for using complete sentences or thoughts when speaking: (a) give the student a tangible reward (e.g., classroom privileges, line leading, passing out materials, five minutes free time, etc.) or (b) give the student an intangible reward (e.g., praise, fist bump, smile, etc.).

54. Reduce the emphasis on competition. Competitive activities may cause the student to hurry and not speak in complete sentences.

55. Reinforce the students in the classroom who use complete sentences or thoughts when speaking.

56. Describe objects, persons, places, etc., and have the student name the items described.

57. Make a list of the attributes which are likely to help a person become a good speaker (e.g., takes his/her time, thinks of what to say before starting, etc.).

58. Provide the student with an appropriate model to imitate speaking in complete sentences or thoughts (e.g., speak clearly, slowly, concisely, and in complete sentences, statements and thoughts).

59. Teach the concept of verb and noun phrases as soon as possible so the student has a means of checking to see if a sentence is complete.

60. Give the student specific categories and have him/her name as many items as possible within that category (e.g., things that are cold, objects, persons, places, etc.).

61. Give the student a subject and have him/her make up as many complete sentences about it as possible, emphasizing the use of specific vocabulary.

62. Give the student scrambled words and have him/her put them in the correct order to form a complete sentence.

63. Encourage the student to use an appropriate synonym when he/she experiences difficulty retrieving the exact word he/she wants to say.

64. Help the student use memory aids to recall words (e.g., link a name to another word such as, Mr. Green is a colorful person).

65. Demonstrate acceptable and unacceptable speech including incomplete thoughts and nondescriptive terminology, such as thing or stuff, etc. Have the student critique each example making suggestions for improvement.

66. Have the student complete associations (e.g., knife, fork, and _____; men, women and _____; etc.).

67. Ask questions which stimulate language. Avoid those which can be answered by yes/no or a nod of the head (e.g., ask the student what he/she did at recess instead of asking if he/she played on the slide, ask the student what he/she did on vacation instead of asking if he/she stayed home over the holidays, etc.).

Goal:

1. The student will use appropriate ritualistic greetings/closings.

Objectives:

1. The student will maintain appropriate eye contact during greetings/closings _____ % of the time.
2. The student will use an appropriate greeting/closing during a mock situation in _____ out of ___ trials.
3. The student will use an appropriate greeting/closing during everyday activities with peers in _____ out of _____ trials.
4. The student will use an appropriate greeting/closing during everyday activities with authority figures in _____ out of _____ trials.
5. The student will demonstrate appropriate physical contact during greetings/closings _____ % of the time.
6. The student will demonstrate appropriate body language during greetings/closings _____ % of the time.
7. The student will demonstrate the ability to say farewell appropriately to both peers and adults in a variety of situations _____ % of the time.

Interventions:

1. Have the student run errands which will require verbal and/or nonverbal interactions with other students, teachers, administrators, etc.

2. Have the student practice repeating what you or another student has said while imitating inflectional patterns and facial expressions. Video record this activity and have the student analyze his/her success at this activity.

3. Have the student show visitors and new students around the school.

4. Choose a peer to model the use of ritualistic greetings and closings for the student.

5. Set up fictitious situations in the classroom (e.g., restaurant, gas station, grocery store, etc.) and have the students in the class role-play working in each situation. Have them change roles often and emphasize the use of ritualistic greetings and closings in the role-play situation.

6. Teach a communication unit to the entire classroom which includes the basic rules of conversation.

7. Assess the appropriateness of the social situation in relation to the student's ability to be successful.

8. Teach the student social interaction skills (e.g., ways in which to appropriately respond to others when first seeing them or when leaving them, etc.). Be specific about appropriate phrases to use and situations in which they would be used.

9. Have the student participate in simulated conversational activities with feedback designed to facilitate conversational skills (e.g., greetings, closings, questions, topics of conversations, etc.).

10. Teach the student that he/she should respond differently depending on the person to whom he/she is talking. Discuss how age, position, and/or familiarity can change the form of the greeting/closing used (e.g., What's happening? How are you doing?).

11. Audio record the student. Have him/her listen to the recording to decide if he/she is using appropriate/inappropriate greetings/closings in different settings.

12. Determine an individual(s) in the school environment with whom the student would most want to engage in a conversation (e.g., custodian, librarian, resource teacher, principal, older student, etc.). Allow the student to spend time talking with the individual(s) each day. Make sure these people model appropriate use of greetings/closings.

13. Reinforce the student for using ritualistic greetings/closings when appropriate: (a) give the student a tangible reward (e.g., classroom privileges, line leading, passing out materials, five minutes free time, etc.) or (b) give the student an intangible reward (e.g., praise, fist bump, smile, etc.).

14. Provide opportunities for appropriate interactions within the classroom.

15. Greet or acknowledge the student as often as possible (e.g., hallways, cafeteria, welcome to class, acknowledge a job well done, etc.). Encourage him/her to acknowledge you in return.

16. Have the student use a discarded phone to practice greetings/closings.

17. Pair the student with a peer and have them take turns being interviewed and interviewing. This may be done with the students being themselves or pretending to be fictitious characters. Emphasize the appropriate use of ritualistic greetings/closings.

18. Pair the student with an outgoing student who engages in appropriate verbal interactions on a frequent basis.

19. Have the student practice taking messages to different persons in the school setting (e.g., librarian, school counselor, principal, etc.). Include ritualistic greetings/closings in the practice. When the student is ready, have him/her deliver messages.

20. Help the student develop social awareness (e.g., people may be embarrassed by what you say, feelings can be hurt by comments, tact is the best policy, remember interactions which have made you feel good and treat others in the same manner, etc.).

21. Point out examples of appropriate verbal and nonverbal language involving ritualistic greetings and closings as they occur during the day.

22. Teach the student appropriate body language and explain the effect it can have on communication.

23. Have the student's hearing checked if it has not been recently checked.

24. Use a private signal (e.g., holding up a finger, etc.) to remind the student to use appropriate greetings/closings.

25. Prompt the student to help him/her use greetings/closings appropriately (e.g., Teacher: How are you? Student does not respond. Teacher: I'm fine today. How are you?).

26. Model appropriate use of ritualistic greetings and/or closings.

27. Speak with the student to explain that he/she is not using ritualistic greetings/closings when appropriate. Be specific about the situation(s) in which they are not being used.

28. Teach a unit which is centered around finding examples of language which are appropriate for use in ritualistic greetings and closings.

29. Experiment with various groupings to determine the situation in which the student is most comfortable carrying on conversations with peers and adults.

30. Reinforce other students in the classroom for appropriate use of ritualistic greetings and closings.

31. Teach the student to be aware of listener response to determine if the meaning of his/her greeting/closing has been received accurately.

32. Teach the student appropriate verbal and nonverbal responses to common everyday situations.

33. Encourage appropriate eye contact in all communicative interactions.

34. Provide the student with many academic and social successes.

35. Teach the student conversational rules (e.g., explain that it is appropriate to greet a person when you're seeing him/her for the first time of the day but not when it's been only five minutes since the last encounter).

36. Communicate to the student that he/she is a worthwhile individual.

37. Rephrase the student's words to assist the student in using more appropriate greetings/ closings.

38. Teach the student conversational phrases (e.g., How are you? I'm fine. How's it going? See you later.) to use when greetings/ closings are appropriate.

39. Teach the student communication skills (e.g., hand raising, expressing needs in written and/or verbal form, etc.).

Goals:

1. The student will improve his/her response time.
2. The student will give logical and relevant responses.

Objectives:

1. The student will demonstrate the ability to tell the speaker, in his/her own words, what the speaker said with _____% accuracy.
2. The student will maintain appropriate eye contact during verbal interactions in _____ out of _____ trials.
3. The student will respond appropriately to questions which can be answered yes or no _____% of the time.
4. The student will respond appropriately to questions which begin with the words *what, who, when, where, how much, how many, how* and *why* with _____% accuracy.
5. The student will differentiate between logical and absurd statements in _____ out of _____ trials.
6. The student will correctly relate what is silly in a sentence containing a verbal absurdity _____% of the time.

Interventions:

1. Have the student take written messages to different persons in the school setting (e.g., librarian, school counselor, principal, etc.). Later, have the student deliver messages verbally.

2. Provide the student with a wordless picture book and have him/her narrate the story.

3. Have the student practice repeating what you or another student has said while imitating inflectional patterns and facial expressions. Video record this activity and have the student analyze his/her success at this activity.

4. Encourage the whole class to wait quietly for any student to respond to a question.

5. Have the student watch a video or television program and then tell you what he/she thinks might have happened before or after the story.

6. Have the student practice appropriate verbal interactions with peers and teacher(s).

7. Pair the student with an outgoing peer who engages in relevant verbal interactions on a frequent basis.

8. When the student is slow to respond or makes an irrelevant response, have him/her rephrase the original question in his/her own words to check for comprehension.

9. Have the student give answers to what if questions (e.g., What if you were ten feet tall? What if dinosaurs still roamed the earth?).

10. Pause often when you speak to the student to encourage participation in the communication act.

11. Alternating with a peer, have the student take turns adding words to a sentence to create one long sentence. The sentence should be as long as possible without becoming a run-on sentence. Check to ensure that all additions to the sentence are relevant.

12. Set up fictitious situations in the classroom (e.g., restaurant, gas station, grocery store, etc.). Have the student role-play working in each situation. Have him/her change roles often.

13. Evaluate the appropriateness of the task to determine (a) if the task is too easy, (b) if the task is too difficult, or (c) if the length of time scheduled to complete the task is adequate.

14. Have the student place sequence cards in the appropriate order and explain the sequence. Have the student tell what he/she thinks might have happened before or after the provided sequence.

15. Make sure the rate of speech being used is appropriate for the situation.

16. Make a recording of environmental sounds and have the student identify them. Ask leading questions if necessary.

17. Have the student role-play being someone else in specific situations (e.g., talking on the phone, being a cashier in a grocery store, etc.). Make sure all responses are relevant to the situation.

18. Have the student make up sentences or stories using new words he/she has learned.

19. Determine an individual(s) in the school environment with whom the student would most want to engage in a conversation (e.g., custodian, librarian, resource teacher, principal, older student, etc.). Allow the student to spend time carrying on a conversation with the individual(s) each day.

20. Choose a peer to model relevant responses for the student.

21. Reinforce the student for responding quickly and with relevant responses: (a) give the student a tangible reward (e.g., classroom privileges, line leading, passing out materials, five minutes free time, etc.) or (b) give the student an intangible reward (e.g., praise, fist bump, smile, etc.).

22. Ask the student to provide pictures of himself/herself at various ages. Help the student to explain what his/her reactions to certain situations might have been at those particular ages. Then ask the student to guess what his/her reaction might be in ten years.

23. Pair the student with a peer and have them take turns being interviewed and interviewing. This may be done with the students being themselves or pretending to be another person or a fictitious character.

24. Place interesting pictures or objects on a table. Have the student choose one and quickly describe it in detail.

25. Use pictures/cartoons with captions removed and have the student develop his/her own captions.

26. Communicate with the student as often as possible to understand the student's needs and to provide an opportunity for relevant verbal interaction. Be sure to spend some time talking with the student about topics which are of interest to him/her.

27. Give the student a list of words and have him/her provide antonyms, synonyms, and/or associated words.

28. Discuss with the student what is expected (e.g., responding more quickly and with relevant responses).

29. When the student makes an irrelevant response, immediately rephrase his/her response to make it relevant.

30. Have the student's hearing checked if it has not been recently checked.

31. Use a private signal (e.g., holding up a finger, etc.) to remind the student to respond quickly and/or with a relevant response.

32. Have the student compete against himself/herself by timing how fast he/she can name a series of pictured objects. Have the student try to improve his/her speed as proficiency increases.

33. Prompt the student to help him/her respond more quickly and with relevant verbal responses (e.g., Student: That thing. Teacher: What thing, what is it doing?).

34. Communicate to the student that he/she is a worthwhile individual.

35. Model appropriate responses for the student to imitate.

36. Explain to the student where he/she can go to find word meanings in the classroom library (e.g., dictionary, thesaurus, encyclopedia, etc.).

37. Audio record the student. Him/her listen to the recording to facilitate his/her awareness of times when he/she responds slowly and/or makes an irrelevant response.

38. Obtain the student's attention before giving instructions or asking a question.

39. Always allow the student to finish responding before you begin talking. Reinforce other students in the classroom for allowing the student to finish responding before they begin talking.

40. Play word games such as *Twenty Questions*, in which you provide cues to clarify questions (e.g., Is it edible? Is it alive?) and then gradually fade the cues.

41. Reinforce other students in the classroom who respond quickly and in a relevant manner.

42. Create a *Feeling Box* and place an unseen item in the box. Have the student describe what it feels like while another student tries to guess what it is.

43. Provide the student with many academic and social successes.

44. Make a list of emotions (e.g., sad, scared, happy, etc.) and have the student express them in a sentence.

45. Teach the student communication skills (e.g., hand raising, expressing needs in written and/or verbal form, etc.).

46. Point out examples of relevant verbal responses as they occur during the day.

47. Reduce the emphasis on competition. Failure may cause the student to be reluctant to respond.

48. Provide the student with direct eye contact and communicate to him/her that you expect him/her to do the same with you.

119 Lacks spontaneity, originality, and/or variety in verbal interactions

Goals:

1. The student will expand his/her verbal interactions.
2. The student will improve his/her abstract thinking skills.
3. The student will demonstrate spontaneous, original speech.

Objectives:

1. The student will demonstrate the ability to say one statement several times, each time stressing a different word to change the meaning of the sentence, with _____ % accuracy.
2. The student will reduce his/her use of overused words/phrases _____ % of the time.
3. The student will increase his/her use of interesting adjectives _____ % of the time.
4. The student will provide synonyms and antonyms for target vocabulary in _____ out of _____ trials.
5. The student will provide associations for target vocabulary in _____ out of _____ trials.
6. The student will provide multiple meanings for target vocabulary in _____ out of _____ trials.
7. The student will describe objects/pictures and events across several dimensions (including category, function, composition, etc.) in _____ out of _____ trials.
8. The student will identify and utilize similes and metaphors in _____ out of _____ trials.

Interventions:

1. Have the student take written messages to different persons in the school setting (e.g., librarian, school counselor, principal, etc.). Later, have the student deliver messages verbally.

2. Provide the student with a wordless picture book and have him/her narrate the story.

3. Create a group activity in which students are to create rules for a fictitious society.

4. Have the student practice repeating what you or another student has said while imitating inflectional patterns and facial expressions. Video record this activity and have the student analyze his/her success at this activity.

5. Encourage the whole class to wait quietly for any student to respond to a question.

6. Have the student watch a video or television program and then tell you what he/she thinks might have happened before or after the story.

7. Choose a peer to model verbal interactions which are spontaneous and include originality and variety for the student.

8. Expand upon the student's limited vocabulary to facilitate his/her using more variety in verbal interactions (e.g., Student: That's ugly. Teacher: That's the most unattractive animal I've ever seen.).

9. Have the student give answers to what if questions (e.g., What if you were ten feet tall? What if dinosaurs still roamed the earth?).

10. Set up fictitious situations in the classroom (e.g., restaurant, gas station, grocery store, etc.). Have the student role-play working in each situation. Have him/her change roles often.

11. Alternating with a peer, have the student take turns adding words to a sentence to create one long sentence. The sentence should be as long as possible without becoming a run-on sentence.

12. Evaluate the appropriateness of the task to determine (a) if the task is too easy, (b) if the task is too difficult, or (c) if the length of time scheduled to complete the task is adequate.

13. Prompt the student to help him/her create more interesting verbal interactions (e.g., Student: That thing. Teacher: What thing, what is it doing?).

14. Use puppets to retell a story or act out an activity. Have the student do the same by following your model.

15. Have the student place sequence cards in the appropriate order and explain the sequence. Have the student tell what he/she thinks might have happened before or after the provided sequence.

16. Spend time talking with the student on an individual basis about his/her interests.

17. Model the inclusion of spontaneous statements which contain originality and variety in your verbal interactions.

18. Make a recording of environmental sounds and ask the student to identify them. Ask leading questions if necessary.

19. Have the student role-play being someone else in specific situations (e.g., talking on the phone, being a cashier in a grocery store, etc.).

20. Have the student make up sentences or stories using new words he/she has learned.

21. Determine an individual(s) in the school environment with whom the student would most want to engage in a conversation (e.g., custodian, librarian, resource teacher, principal, older student, etc.). Allow the student to spend time carrying on a conversation with the individual(s) each day.

22. Use pictures/cartoons with captions removed and have the student develop his/her own captions.

23. Ask the student to provide pictures of himself/herself at various ages. Help the student to explain what his/her reactions to certain situations might have been at those particular ages. Then ask the student to guess what his/her reaction might be in ten years

24. Play word games such as *Twenty Questions* in which you provide cues to clarify questions (e.g., Is it edible? Is it alive?). Gradually fade the cues.

25. Pair the student with a peer. Have them take turns being interviewed and interviewing. This may be done with the students being themselves or pretending to be another person or fictitious character.

26. Explain to the student that overused words/phrases limit the meaning of what he/she is trying to say and that together you will work on reducing the number of times these words/phrases are used. Teach the student appropriate alternatives for the overused words/phrases.

27. Brainstorm words/phrases that are overused in your school to facilitate the student's awareness of them.

28. Brainstorm different ways to replace overused words/phrases.

29. Place interesting pictures or objects on a table and have the student choose one and describe it in detail. Provide assistance in utilizing originality and variety in the descriptions.

30. Communicate with the student as often as possible to understand the student's needs and to provide an opportunity for spontaneous verbal interaction.

31. Give the student a list of words and have him/her provide antonyms, synonyms, and/or associated words as appropriate.

32. Reinforce the student for using new or more difficult words when speaking.

33. Point out examples of descriptive language as they occur during the day.

34. Help the student create and perform a short skit which revolves around a topic that is interesting to him/her.

35. Reinforce the student for verbal interactions which are spontaneous, original, or contain variety: (a) give the student a tangible reward (e.g., classroom privileges, line leading, passing out materials, five minutes free time, etc.) or (b) give the student an intangible reward (e.g., praise, fist bump, smile, etc.).

36. Have the student draw a picture of himself/herself and then narrate a story in which he/she is the main character.

37. Have the student's hearing checked if it has not been recently checked.

38. Use a private signal (e.g., holding up a finger, etc.) to remind the student to limit the number of overused words/phrases.

39. Communicate to the student that he/she is a worthwhile individual.

40. Audio record the student. Have him/her listen to the recording to become aware of those words/phrases he/she is overusing.

41. Pair the student on a frequent basis with an outgoing student who engages in appropriate verbal interactions.

42. Teach a unit centered around finding examples of language which are spontaneous and which include originality and variety.

43. Reinforce other students in the classroom for spontaneous verbal interactions which are original and contain variety.

44. Create a *Feeling Box* and place an unseen item in the box. Have the student describe what it feels like while another student tries to guess what it is.

45. Provide the student with many academic and social successes.

46. Make a list of emotions (e.g., sad, scared, happy, etc.) and have the student express each of them in a sentence.

47. Teach the student communication skills (e.g., hand raising, expressing needs in written and/or verbal form, etc.).

48. Acknowledge the student's attempts to communicate his/her needs (e.g., facial expressions, gestures, inactivity, self-deprecating comments, etc.).

49. Explain to the student where he/she can go to find word meanings in the classroom library (e.g., dictionary, thesaurus, encyclopedia, etc.).

120 Omits, adds, substitutes, or rearranges sounds or words when speaking

Goals:

1. The student will improve his/her production of speech sounds.
2. The student will improve his/her conversational speech.
3. The student will improve the fluency of his/her speech.
4. The student will improve the ability to express himself/herself verbally.
5. The student will improve his/her grammatical speech.

Objectives:

1. The student will use complete phrases, with assistance, when speaking with _____% accuracy.
2. The student will independently use complete phrases when speaking with _____% accuracy.
3. The student will complete sentences, with assistance, when speaking with _____% accuracy.
4. The student will independently use complete sentences when speaking with _____% accuracy.
5. The student will verbally sequence (e.g., numbers, letters, days, months, etc.), with assistance, with _____% accuracy.
6. The student will independently verbally sequence (e.g., numbers, letters, days, months, etc.) with _____% accuracy.

Interventions:

1. Using pictures of similar sounding words, say each word and have the student point to the appropriate picture (e.g., *run* and *one*, or *bat* and *back*).

2. Provide the student with a word list containing the target words. Have the student practice the words daily. As the student masters the word list, add more words. Using words from the student's everyday vocabulary, reading lists, spelling lists, etc., will facilitate transfer of correct production of the target word into everyday speech.

3. Have the student write sentences using the target sound or words.

4. Show the student a picture and name it. Have the student show thumbs up each time the target sound is produced accurately and thumbs down if the target sound is produced inaccurately.

5. Involve parents by asking them to rate their child's speech for a specific length of time (e.g., during dinner count no errors, a few errors, or many errors).

6. Play a game, such as *Simon Says* in which the student tries to reproduce the target sound or words when produced by the teacher or peers.

7. Evaluate the appropriateness of requiring the student to accurately produce certain sounds (e.g., developmentally, certain sounds may not be produced accurately until the age of 8 or 9).

8. During oral reading, underline targeted sounds or words and reinforce the student for correct production.

9. Make cards with the target sound and cards with vowels. Have the student combine a target sound card with a vowel card to make a syllable that he/she can produce (e.g., *ra, re, ro,* and *ar, er, or*).

10. Play a board game that requires the student to name pictures containing the target sound or words. The student has to produce the target sound or words correctly before he/she can move on the game board. (This activity can be simplified or expanded based on the level of success of the student.)

11. Reinforce the student for correct productions of the target sound: (a) give the student a tangible reward (e.g., classroom privileges, line leading, passing out materials, five minutes free time, etc.) or (b) give the student an intangible reward (e.g., praise, fist bump, smile, etc.).

12. Use a puppet to produce targeted words correctly and incorrectly. The student earns a sticker for correctly distinguishing a set number of correct/incorrect productions the puppet makes.

13. Have the student cut out pictures of items containing the target sound or word. Display them where they can be practiced each day.

14. Audio record the student reading simple passages. Have him/her listen to the recording and mark error and/or correct productions.

15. Have the student tally the number of correct productions of the target sound when the teacher or a peer reads a list of words.

16. Have the student keep a notebook of difficult words encountered each day. These can be practiced by the student with teacher or peer assistance.

17. Provide the student with a list of words containing the target sound. (The student will probably be able to produce the target sound more easily at the beginning or end of a word than in the middle.) Have the student practice the words daily. As the student masters the word list, add more words. (Using words from the student's everyday vocabulary, reading lists, spelling lists, etc., will facilitate transfer of correct production of the target sound into everyday speech.)

18. Have the student keep a list of all the words he/she can think of which contain sounds that are difficult for him/her to produce accurately.

19. Have the student read a list of words and rate his/her production of the target sound or target word after each production.

20. Present the student with a list of topics. Have the student select a topic and then give a spontaneous speech for a specific length of time. Count errors and suggest ways for him/her to improve.

21. Have the student use a carrier phrase combined with a word containing the target sound (e.g., I like_____. I see_____.).

22. Have the student's hearing checked if it has not been recently checked.

23. Have the student raise a hand or clap hands when he/she hears the target sound produced during a series of isolated sound productions (e.g., /s/, /sh/, /r/, /m/, /r/, /t/, /k/, /r/, /z/, /w/, /n/, /r/, etc.).

24. Audio record a spontaneous monologue given by the student. Listen to the recording with him/her and tally error and/or correct productions. The teacher and the student should compare their analyses of the productions.

25. Speak to the student to explain what he/she needs to do differently (e.g., use the /r/ sound instead of the /w/ sound). The teacher should be careful to use the sound that is being targeted and not the letter name (e.g., /r/ not r).

26. Have the student stand up each time he/she hears the target sound produced accurately in contrast to the error sound (e.g., /w/, /r/, /r/, /w/, /w/, /w/, /r/, /r/, etc.).

27. Have the student stand up each time he/she hears targeted words produced accurately when contrasted with inaccurate productions (e.g., *play, pay, pay, play,* etc.).

28. Be sure that the student can hear the difference between words as they should be pronounced and the way the words sound when incorrectly produced (e.g., sounds added or omitted).

29. Be sure that the student can hear the difference between the sound as it should be pronounced (target sound) and the way he/she is producing it incorrectly (error sound).

30. Choose a peer who correctly produces the target sound or word to model for the student.

31. Use a drawing as a visual aid to show the student how the mouth looks during production of the target sound.

32. Have the student use phonics fun sheets to verbally practice his/her sound. These are also good for home practice.

121 Uses incorrect grammar when speaking

Goal:

1. The student will improve his/her oral sentence structure.

Objectives:

1. The student will differentiate between grammatically correct and incorrect sentences in _____ out of _____ trials.
2. The student will imitate grammatically correct sentences in _____ out of _____ trials.
3. The student will use grammatically correct sentences during structured language activities in _____ out of _____ trials.
4. The student will spontaneously use grammatically correct sentences in _____ out of _____ trials.
5. The student will use grammatically correct sentences in conversational speech in _____ out of _____ trials

Interventions:

1. Have the student complete worksheets in which he/she must choose the correct grammatical form.

2. After checking the student's written work, have him/her correct all grammatical errors.

3. Allow the student to speak without being interrupted or hurried.

4. Explain that certain forms of verbs go with certain subjects and that correct subject-verb agreement requires the appropriate match of subject and verb. Be sure that the student knows the various possibilities of subject-verb agreement and how to select the correct one. Have the student practice matching verb forms to lists of subjects.

5. Have the student identify a verb to master using correctly. As the student masters the correct use of the verb, he/she puts it on a list with a star and identifies another verb to master.

6. Use a private signal (e.g., touching earlobe, raising index finger, etc.) to remind the student to use correct grammatical forms when speaking.

7. Evaluate the appropriateness of requiring the student to speak in grammatically correct sentences (e.g., developmentally, a child may not utilize appropriate subject-verb agreement or irregular verb/plural forms until the age of 6 or 7).

8. Ask the parents to encourage the student's correct use of grammar at home by praising him/her when correct grammar is used.

9. When speaking privately with the student, restate his/her grammatical error with a rising inflection (e.g., He done it?) to assess if the student recognizes errors and spontaneously makes appropriate corrections.

10. Use plastic figures or cartoon stick figures to practice using targeted grammatical forms. Give the student points toward a favorite activity for each phrase or sentence he/she produces with the correct grammatical form.

11. Routinely audio record the student's speech and point out errors in grammatical usage. With each recording, reinforce the student as his/her use of grammar improves.

12. During the day, write down specific grammatical errors produced by the student. Read the sentences to the student and have him/her verbally make appropriate corrections.

13. Give the student a series of sentences with correct and incorrect grammar and ask the student to identify which are correct and incorrect and make appropriate modifications.

14. Have the student's hearing checked if it has not been recently checked.

15. Determine the type of grammatical model the student has at home. Without placing negative connotations on his/her parents' grammatical style, explain the difference between standard and nonstandard grammar.

16. Write down specific grammatical errors made by the student during the day. Give the written sentences to the student and have him/her make appropriate corrections. At first, mark the errors for the student to correct. As the student becomes more proficient with this task, have him/her find and correct the errors independently.

17. Reinforce the student for speaking in grammatically correct sentences: (a) give the student a tangible reward (e.g., classroom privileges, line leading, passing out materials, five minutes free time, etc.) or (b) give the student an intangible reward (e.g., praise, fist bump, smile, etc.).

18. Choose a peer to model correct grammar when speaking for the student.

19. Highlight or underline correct grammatical forms in the student's written work to reinforce the appropriate usage.

20. Reinforce those students in the classroom who speak in grammatically correct sentences.

21. Have the student retell a familiar story with emphasis on correct use of targeted grammatical forms.

22. Speak to the student to explain that he/she is using incorrect grammar when speaking. Explain the importance of using grammatically correct sentences when speaking.

23. Provide the student with examples of correct subject-verb agreement for those combinations he/she most commonly uses incorrectly.

24. Identify the most common grammatical errors the student makes. Have the student spend time each day practicing the correct grammatical forms.

25. Reduce the emphasis on competition. Competitive activities may cause the student to hurry and make grammatical errors.

26. Use simple comic strips with captions deleted. Have the student describe what is happening while focusing on correct use of targeted grammatical forms.

27. Highlight or underline correct grammatical forms in the student's reading material to call attention to the appropriate usage.

Goals:
1. The student will improve his/her voice quality.
2. The student will correctly discriminate vocal quality in himself/herself and others.
3. The student will demonstrate appropriate pitch.
4. The student will demonstrate appropriate voice volume.
5. The student will demonstrate appropriate nasality.
6. The student will demonstrate appropriate vocal quality.

Objectives:
1. The student will identify appropriate and inappropriate vocal qualities in _____ out of _____ trials.
2. The student will identify personal situations and vocal behaviors that might cause harsh, breathy, or hoarse vocal quality in _____ out of _____ trials.
3. The student will demonstrate proper breathing technique for phonation in _____ out of _____ trials.
4. The student will maintain proper breathing during conversation _____% of the time.
5. The student will demonstrate the difference between a hard glottal attack and easy onset of phonation during therapy _____% of the time.
6. The student will maintain easy onset of phonation during conversation _____% of the time.
7. The student will reduce instances of vocal abuse by _____% as measured against a baseline number of instances at the beginning of therapy.

Interventions:

1. Discuss how a person's voice changes when they are nervous, tired, angry, etc.

2. Have the student list occasions when he/she abuses his/her voice. Discuss alternate ways to communicate in these situations (e.g., walk over to a person instead of shouting across the room, blow a whistle outside to get someone's attention instead of yelling, etc.).

3. Have the student identify occasions when he/she uses good vocal habits vs. vocal abuse. Discuss ways to improve vocal habits during abusive situations.

4. Reinforce the student for appropriate voice quality: (a) give the student a tangible reward (e.g., classroom privileges, line leading, passing out materials, five minutes free time, etc.) or (b) give the student an intangible reward (e.g., praise, fist bump, smile, etc.).

5. Choose relaxation exercises to be used by the student (e.g., tensing and relaxing specific muscle groups, head rotation exercises, imagery, etc.).

6. Use puppets to demonstrate appropriate voice quality and voice quality that is intermittent or lost.

7. Have the student describe the vocal quality of famous people, cartoon characters, people at school or home, etc. Have him/her differentiate between vocal qualities that sound pleasant and those that sound intermittent or lost.

8. Involve parents by asking them to rate their child's voice quality (e.g., appropriate, too loud, harsh, breathy, etc.) for a specific length of time and/or in a specific situation (e.g., during playtime; at dinner; at bedtime; inside or outside; in the presence of family members, peers, or authority figures; etc.).

9. If the student uses shouting to gain attention, have him/her practice alternative methods of gaining attention (e.g., stressing a specific word in a sentence, using pitch variations, pausing before an important word, using gestures, etc.).

10. Have the student's hearing checked if it has not been recently checked.

11. When the student is about to engage in an activity that facilitates vocal abuse, have him/her wear a string bracelet, sticker, etc., to remind him/her to use alternate strategies and/or good vocal habits.

12. Help the student determine the times and circumstances when his/her voice quality is better/worse (e.g., after gym, early in the morning, late in the day, on Mondays, etc.).

13. Establish a quiet time during the day when no one speaks except in an emergency. Soft music could be played in the background.

14. Demonstrate laryngeal tension by having the student vocalize (e.g., say eee or ah) while trying to lift himself/herself up from a sitting position in a hard chair.

15. Have the student list all the different sound effects that he/she and his/her friends make while playing (e.g., motor noises, monster noises, etc.). Discuss the effect of those sounds on their voices. Suggest alternatives to throat noises (e.g., sounds made at the front of the mouth with tongue and lips).

16. Have the student rank, hierarchically, the situations in which his/her voice is not appropriate. Discuss these situations to facilitate the student's awareness of when he/she is using inappropriate vocal habits.

17. Have the student list reasons that might cause people to yell or talk very loudly (e.g., when angry, in a crowd, at a football game, etc.).

18. Have the student identify words that have a soft or loud connotation in stories that he/she reads (e.g., soft = shiver, warm, gentle, luminous; loud = bang, hate, stop, gang).

19. Have the student read a list of words and rate his/her productions as appropriate or harsh, breathy, hoarse, intermittent, lost, etc. If it is too difficult for the student to rate his/her own live voice, audio record the reading and replay it for him/her to rate.

20. Have the student differentiate between tension and relaxation by first tensing his/her body and then relaxing. (Feel the student's neck and shoulders to assess the presence or absence of tension.)

21. Encourage good posture while sitting, standing, walking, etc. Poor posture can obstruct good breath support which facilitates vocal quality.

22. Remind the student to use proper breathing techniques and a relaxed voice during music class, which can be a period of vocal stress.

23. Show a model or diagram of the location of the larynx to the student and discuss how it works.

24. Have the student tally the number of times he/she abuses his/her voice during a designated time (e.g., during recess). Encourage him/her to decrease the number from one occasion to the next.

25. Have the student describe reactions listeners have to a voice that is too loud, harsh, hoarse, or breathy (e.g., annoyance at someone who appears to be yelling, asking to have something repeated, etc.).

26. Discuss how clearing the throat irritates the throat. Encourage the student to get a drink instead.

27. Have the student demonstrate his/her best vocal quality.

28. Be sure the student can hear the difference between appropriate voice quality and voice quality that is intermittent or lost.

29. Help the student determine if he/she is participating in any activities during which his/her voice might be strained (e.g., gym, recess, cheerleading, drama, vocal music, baseball, soccer, etc.). Discuss ways that the student could avoid misusing his/her voice in these situations (e.g., clapping hands vs. yelling, walking over to a person vs. shouting at the person, performing actions vs. yelling, etc.).

30. Develop a short unit on vocal habits to be taught to the class to facilitate understanding of a voice problem caused by vocal abuse.

31. Audio record the student while he/she is speaking with another student who exhibits appropriate voice quality. Play the recording to see if the student can hear the difference between voice qualities.

32. When the student has a cold, sore throat, laryngitis, etc.; discuss how the throat might look and encourage the student to talk as little as possible. Do not encourage whispering as an alternative as it may also irritate his/her voice.

33. Establish a method that you can use to remind the student to use good vocal habits when he/she is abusing his/her voice (e.g., pointing to your throat, index finger to lips as for the quiet sign, etc.).

34. Demonstrate the larynx under tension by having the student push against your chin while you resist. Push against the student's chin while he/she resists. Vocalize while doing this activity (e.g., say eee or count).

35. Have the student demonstrate proper breath support for speaking using his/her diaphragm.

36. Provide the student with an appropriate voice model.

37. Have the student describe animal voices that sound abusive (e.g., lion - roar; mouse - squeaky) and compare them with his/her own voice quality.

38. Speak to the student to explain what he/she needs to do differently (e.g., use a quiet voice vs. a loud voice, whistle or clap vs. yelling, talk less, etc.).

123 Attends more successfully when close to the source of sound

Goals:

1. The student will attend more successfully to specific sounds in the environment.
2. The student will improve his/her awareness and attention to information and activities in the environment.
3. The student will improve listening skills in academic settings.
4. The student will improve listening skills in nonacademic settings.

Objectives:

1. The student will follow one-step verbal directions with _____% accuracy.
2. The student will follow two-step verbal directions with _____% accuracy.
3. The student will follow multi-step verbal directions with _____% accuracy.
4. The student will independently respond appropriately to what is said to him/her with _____% accuracy.
5. The student will independently respond appropriately to what is said to him/her _____% of the time.
6. The student will listen quietly when verbal directions are given _____% of the time.
7. The student will maintain eye contact when information is being communicated _____% of the time.
8. The student will repeat what is said with _____% accuracy.
9. The student will respond appropriately to what is said, with prompting, with _____% accuracy.

Interventions:

1. Maintain a consistent manner in which verbal questions are asked and directions are given.

2. Have the student take notes when directions are being given following *What, How, Materials*, and *When* format.

3. Interact frequently with the student to help him/her attend to a source of sound.

4. Interact frequently with the student to help him/her follow directions for an activity.

5. Reinforce the student for attending to information presented from any location in the classroom: (a) give the student a tangible reward (e.g., classroom privileges, line leading, passing out materials, five minutes free time, etc.) or (b) give the student an intangible reward (e.g., praise, fist bump, smile, etc.).

6. Provide directions on a one-to-one basis before assigning a task.

7. Call the student by name to gain his/her attention prior to delivering directions, explanations, or instructions.

8. Reinforce those students who attend to information from any location in the classroom.

9. Maintain mobility to provide assistance to the student, frequently be near the student, etc.

10. Deliver all directions, questions, explanations, and instructions at an appropriate rate for the student.

11. Give simple, specific directions as to what the student is to do.

12. Maintain visibility to and from the student to keep his/her attention when verbal questions/directions are being delivered. The teacher should be able to see the student and the student should be able to see the teacher. Make eye contact possible at all times.

13. Do not criticize when correcting the student; be honest yet supportive. Never cause the student to feel negatively about himself/herself.

14. Do not give directions to the student from across the classroom. Go to the student, get his/her undivided attention, and explain the directions to him/her.

15. Stop at various points during the presentation of directions, explanations, or instructions to check the student's comprehension of the information presented.

16. Give a signal to gain the student's attention before delivering directions, explanations, or instructions (e.g., clap hands, turn lights off and on, etc.).

17. Seat the student close to the source of information in the classroom. As the student demonstrates success, gradually move him/her away from the source of information.

18. Present directions following the outline of *What, How, Materials*, and *When*.

19. Have the student listen and takes notes for *Who, What, Where, When, How*, and *Why* while concepts are presented

20. Deliver verbal questions and directions that involve only one step. As the student demonstrates success, gradually increase the number of concepts or steps.

21. Make sure you have the student's undivided attention when you are talking to him/her. Stand close to the student, maintain eye contact, and have him/her repeat the information.

22. Be consistent in expecting the student to listen to and follow directions. Do not allow the student to not follow directions one time and expect directions to be followed the next time.

23. Write a contract with the student specifying what behavior is expected (e.g., attending to information presented from any location in the classroom) and what reinforcement will be made available when the terms of the contract have been met.

24. Avoid placing the student in situations that require listening for an extended period of time, such as lectures, seminars, etc. Provide the information for the student through an audio recording or lecture notes.

25. Move objects used for tactile stimulation (e.g., pens, paper clips, loose change, etc.) away from the student's reach.

26. Teach and practice effective communication skills. These skills include: listening, maintaining eye contact, and positive body language.

27. Remove the student from the situation until he/she can demonstrate self-control and follow directions when he/she has difficulty attending to and following directions in the presence of others (e.g., at an assembly, on a field trip, playing a game with peers, etc.).

28. Choose a peer to model responding to information from any location in the classroom for the student.

29. Allow the student to audio record information from lectures and seminars and make notes from those recordings.

30. Create an environment that is quiet and uncluttered (e.g., clean, well-lighted, fresh-smelling, and at a comfortable temperature).

31. Avoid seating the student near people with whom he/she may be tempted to talk with during lectures, assemblies, seminars, projects, etc.

32. Choose different people (e.g., peer, paraprofessional, counselor, etc.) to help the student improve his/her listening skills.

33. Move the student away from other students who may interfere with his/her ability to attend to directions, explanations, or instructions.

34. Provide the student with adequate opportunities for repetition of information through different experiences.

35. Deliver directions, explanations, or instructions loudly enough to be heard by the student.

36. Be sure the student has heard what was said by having him/her give acknowledgment (e.g., Okay! Will do!).

37. Establish rules for listening (e.g., listen to directions, ask questions about directions if they are not understood, follow the directions, etc.). These rules should be consistent and followed by everyone in the classroom. Talk about the rules often.

38. Present concepts following the outline of *Who, What, Where, When, How,* and *Why*.

39. Identify the student's most effective learning mode. Use it consistently to facilitate the student's understanding and remaining on task for longer periods of time.

40. Encourage the student to avoid ingesting any substance (e.g., drugs, alcohol, cold remedies, etc.) that might further alter his/her ability to direct or maintain attention.

41. Stand close to or directly in front of the student when delivering verbal questions and directions.

42. Present verbal questions and directions in a clear and concise manner.

43. Have the student's hearing checked if it has not been recently checked.

44. Instruct the student to ask people to repeat parts of a conversation he/she was unable to follow.

45. Instruct the student to listen for key information when being given directions or receiving information from a distance (e.g., write down main points, ideas, step-by-step instructions, etc.).

46. Instruct the student to ask for clarification if he/she does not understand information presented verbally.

47. Encourage the student to ask for clarification of any directions, explanations, and instructions before beginning a task to facilitate comprehension.

48. Instruct the student to write down verbal directions and mark each one off as it is completed.

49. Choose a peer, paraprofessional, friend, etc., to cue the student when he/she needs to maintain attention (e.g., the person can touch the student on the arm when it is time to listen).

50. Allow natural consequences to occur due to the student's failure to follow verbal directions or attend to information presented in public places.

51. Have the student repeat directions, explanations, and instructions after they have been given to facilitate retention.

52. Let the student know that directions will only be given once and that he/she will not be reminded to follow the directions.

53. Reduce distracting stimuli in the environment (e.g., make sure the classroom is quiet, reduce movement in the classroom, etc.).

54. Establish assignment rules (e.g., listen carefully, wait until all verbal directions have been given, ask questions about anything you do not understand, begin the assignment only when you are sure about what you are to do, make sure you have all the materials necessary, etc.).

55. Instruct the student to maintain attention to the source of information by maintaining eye contact, keeping hands free from other materials, and reducing other distractions.

56. Make sure the student is attending before delivering directions, explanations, or instructions (e.g., maintaining eye contact, hands free of writing materials, looking at the assignment, etc.).

57. Schedule important activities/assignments/ meetings at times when the student is most likely to maintain attention (e.g., one hour after medication, 45 minutes after lunch, first thing in the morning, etc.).

58. Present directions, explanations, and instructions as simply and clearly as possible (e.g., Get your book, turn to page 29, do problems 1 through 5.).

59. Consider carefully the student's age and experience before expecting him/her to be successful in activities that require listening.

60. Help the student develop an awareness of the consequences of his/her behavior by writing down or talking through problems which may occur due to his/her inability to maintain attention (e.g., not focusing on directions may cause misunderstanding of an assignment which could lead to a lower grade and losing a place on the soccer team).

61. Encourage the parents to take advantage of dinner and other family-gathering times for their child to talk and practice maintaining attention.

62. Have the student carry a notepad with him/her at all times and write information down he/she needs to remember.

63. Teach and practice active listening skills. Encourage the student to listen to what another person is saying and respond based on information received.

64. Reward the student (e.g., take a break, visit briefly with a peer, etc.) for maintaining eye contact and listening for a specific length of time.

65. Teach and practice information-gathering skills (e.g., listen carefully, write down important points, ask for clarification, wait until all information is presented before beginning a task, etc.).

66. Teach the student direction-following skills (e.g., listen carefully, write down important points, etc.).

67. Teach the student listening skills:
- Stop working.
- Clear desk of nonessential materials.
- Attend to the source of information.
- Write down important points.
- Ask for clarification.
- Wait until all directions are received before beginning.

68. Determine if the student heard a direction by having him/her repeat it.

124 Demonstrates difficulty with auditory memory

Goals:

1. The student will improve his/her short-term memory.
2. The student will improve his/her long-term memory.
3. The student will improve his/her auditory memory.
4. The student will improve his/her awareness and attention to information and activities in the environment.

Objectives:

1. The student will recognize information received auditorily (e.g., sounds, words, phrases, sentences, etc.) when presented, removed, and presented again with _____% accuracy.
2. The student will recall information received auditorily (e.g., sounds, words, phrases, sentences, etc.) at short intervals (10 to 15 minutes) with _____% accuracy.
3. The student will recall information received auditorily (e.g., sounds, words, phrases, sentences, etc.) at intervals of several hours with _____% accuracy.
4. The student will recall information received auditorily (e.g., sounds, words, phrases, sentences, etc.) at intervals of days or weeks with _____% accuracy.

Interventions:

1. Have the student's hearing checked if it has not been recently checked.

2. Draw the student's attention to key aspects of auditory communications as they occur (e.g., repeat important points, call the student by name, tell the student which information is particularly important, etc.).

3. Evaluate the appropriateness of the task to determine (a) if the task is too difficult (e.g., too much information to remember) or (b) if the length of time required for the student to remember the information is too long (e.g., time between presentation of material and request for recall is too long).

4. Provide the student with more than one source of directions, explanations, instructions, etc., before requiring him/her to remember information.

5. Provide the student with auditory cues when he/she is required to recall information to help him/her remember the information previously presented (e.g., Remember yesterday when I said . . ..).

6. Provide information visually to support information the student receives auditorily.

7. Teach the student to learn sequences and lists of information in segments (e.g., phone numbers are learned as 874, then 1710).

8. Provide the student with verbal directions, rules, lists, etc. Reinforce the student for being able to recall information which is presented in verbal form.

9. Provide stories, directions, etc., in a printed format so the student may read along as he/she listens.

10. Tell the student what to listen for before delivering auditory information.

11. Send the student to deliver verbal messages to other teachers in the building.

12. Present auditory information slowly enough for the student to comprehend the information being presented.

13. Have the student follow verbal one-, two-, and three-step directions.

14. While reading a story to the student, stop on occasion to ask questions about the plot, main characters, events in the story, etc.

15. Have the student pretend he/she is a waiter/waitress, take an order, and then repeat it.

16. Have the student paraphrase directions, explanations, and instructions soon after they have been given.

17. Use as much visual information as possible when teaching (e.g., wall-mounted board, overhead projections, pictures, etc.).

18. Have the student audio record directions, explanations, and instructions to replay as needed.

19. Use simple, concise sentences to convey information to the student.

20. Have the student recall names of friends, days of the week, months of the year, addresses, phone numbers, etc.

21. After listening to a story on a recording, CD, etc., have the student recall characters, main events, sequence of events, etc.

22. Have the student read along while listening to a recorded story or book.

23. Present directions following the *What, How, Materials*, and *When* outline.

24. Have the student take notes when directions are being given following *What, How, Materials*, and *When* format.

25. Reinforce the student for remembering information received auditorily: (a) give the student a tangible reward (e.g., special privileges, line leading, passing out materials, five minutes free time, etc.) or (b) give the student an intangible reward (e.g., praise, fist bump, smile, etc.).

26. Use pictures, diagrams, wall-mounted board, and gestures when presenting information.

27. Present concepts following the *Who, What, Where, When, How*, and *Why* outline.

28. Have the student prepare for tests using the *Who, What, Where, When, How*, and *Why* format.

29. Reduce distracting stimuli (e.g., noise and motion) around the student (e.g., place the student on the front row, provide a carrel or quiet place away from distractions, etc.). This is to be used as a means of reducing distracting stimuli and not as a form of punishment.

30. Use multiple modalities (e.g., auditory, visual, tactile, etc.) when presenting directions, explanations, and instructional content. Determine which modality is stronger and utilize that modality.

31. Make sure the student is attending to the source of information (e.g., eye contact is being made, hands are free of materials, student is looking at the assignment, etc.).

32. Stop at various points during a presentation of information to check the student's comprehension.

33. Provide the student with adequate opportunities for repetition of information through different experiences, to facilitate memory.

34. Provide information visually (e.g., written directions or instructions, etc.) to support information the student receives auditorily.

35. Deliver all directions, questions, explanations, and instructions in a clear, concise manner and at an appropriate rate for the student.

36. Use vocabulary that is on the student's level of comprehension when delivering directions, explanations, and information.

37. Have the student listen and take notes for *Who, What, Where, When, How*, and *Why* when concepts are presented.

125 Does not direct attention or fails to maintain attention to important sounds in the immediate environment

Goals:

1. The student will improve listening skills in academic settings.
2. The student will improve listening skills in nonacademic settings.
3. The student will attend more successfully to specific sounds in the environment.

Objectives:

1. The student will independently respond appropriately to environmental cues (e.g., bells, signs, etc.) _____% of the time.
2. The student will independently respond appropriately to what is said to him/her with _____% accuracy.
3. The student will listen quietly when verbal directions are given _____% of the time.
4. The student will maintain eye contact when information is being communicated _____% of the time.
5. The student will repeat what is said to him/her with _____% accuracy.
6. The student will respond appropriately to environmental cues (e.g., bells, signs, etc.), when given verbal reminders, _____% of the time.
7. The student will respond appropriately to what is said, with prompting, with _____% accuracy.

Interventions:

1. Maintain a consistent format in which auditory information in the immediate environment is delivered (e.g., morning announcements, recess bell, delivering directions, etc.).

2. Have the student take notes when directions are being given following *What, How, Materials*, and *When* format.

3. Do not allow the student to attend school activities unsupervised if the student does not maintain or direct attention to important sounds in the environment.

4. Stand directly in front of the student when delivering information.

5. Use vocabulary that is within the student's level of comprehension when delivering directions, explanations, and information.

6. Maintain visibility to and from the student at all times to ensure that he/she is attending.

7. Have the student listen and takes notes for *Who, What, Where, When, How*, and *Why* while concepts are presented.

8. Do not criticize when correcting the student; be honest yet supportive. Never cause the student to feel negatively about himself/herself.

9. Seat the student close to the source of important sounds (e.g., public address system, intercom, etc.).

10. Stop at various points during the presentation of information to check the student's comprehension.

11. Familiarize the student with all the sounds in the immediate environment (e.g., bells indicating change in class; microwave sounds; fire, earthquake, tornado alarms; etc.).

12. Write a contract with the student. It should be written within his/her ability level and focus on only one behavior at a time. Specify what behavior is expected and what reinforcement will be made available when the terms of the contract have been met.

13. Have a peer provide the student with a cue to remind him/her of important environmental sounds (e.g., tardy bell, intercom, etc.).

14. Have the student verbally explain the appropriate response to an environmental sound.

15. Be consistent in expecting the student to direct his/her attention to environmental sounds. Do not allow the student to be excused for failure to respond to environmental cues.

16. Evaluate the visual and auditory stimuli in the classroom. Remove or reduce the extraneous environmental stimuli.

17. Have a peer provide the student with the information he/she did not hear.

18. Deliver cues in a supportive rather than a threatening manner (e.g., The bell will ring in two minutes rather than hurry or you will be late!).

19. Have the student participate in activities to facilitate awareness of environmental sounds.

20. Have the student participate in activities designed to develop listening skills (e.g., following one-, two-, or three-step directions; listening for the main point; etc.).

21. Present concepts following the outline of *Who, What, Where, When, How*, and *Why*.

22. Give directions in a variety of ways to facilitate the student's ability to attend.

23. Present directions following the outline of *What, How, Materials*, and *When*.

24. Intervene when the student has not responded to an environmental sound. Explain exactly what he/she did not do, what he/she was supposed to do, and why.

25. Tell the student what to listen for when being given directions, receiving information, etc.

26. Have the student repeat information heard.

27. Consider the student's ability level when expecting him/her to maintain attention to important sounds in the environment.

28. Encourage the student to avoid ingesting any substance (e.g., drugs, alcohol, cold remedies, etc.) that might further alter his/her ability to direct or maintain attention to important sounds in the immediate environment.

29. Increase the volume of auditory indicators (e.g., bells, timers, intercom, etc.).

30. Reduce distracting stimuli in the immediate environment (e.g., place the student on the front row, provide the student with a carrel or office space away from distractions, etc.). This is used as a form of reducing distracting stimuli and not as a form of punishment.

31. Have the student's hearing checked if it has not been recently checked.

32. Deliver a predetermined signal (e.g., hand signal, turning lights off and on, etc.) prior to bells ringing, announcements being made, directions being given, etc.

33. Choose a peer, paraprofessional, counselor, etc., to cue the student when he/she has not attended to an important sound in the immediate environment.

34. Give a verbal cue (e.g., call the student by name) to gain the student's attention prior to bells ringing, announcements being made, directions being delivered, etc.

35. Choose a peer to model directing and maintaining his/her attention to sounds in the immediate environment for the student.

36. Demonstrate the appropriate way to direct attention to important sounds (e.g., pay attention to intercom announcements, bulletins, etc.).

37. Deliver directions one step at a time. As the student demonstrates the ability to direct and maintain attention, gradually increase the number of steps.

38. Stop at various points when delivering directions, announcements, etc., to ensure that the student is attending.

39. Have the student question any directions, explanations, and instructions he/she does not understand.

40. Reinforce those students in the classroom who direct and maintain their attention to important sounds in the immediate environment.

41. Seat the student far enough away from peers to facilitate his/her ability to successfully attend to sounds in the immediate environment.

42. Use auxiliary signals to gain attention (e.g., fire alarm with flashing light, flash class lights for announcements, etc.).

43. Instruct the student to maintain attention to important sounds by keeping hands free from other materials and reducing other distractions.

44. Make sure you direct your attention to environmental sounds when they occur to demonstrate to the student how to respond.

45. Make sure the student is attending (e.g., making eye contact, hands free of materials, etc.) before delivering directions, explanations, and instructions.

46. Make sure that competing sounds (e.g., talking, movement, noises, etc.) are silenced when directions are being given, public address announcements are being made, etc.

47. Make sure that directions, announcements, etc., are delivered in a clear and concise manner (e.g., keep phrases and sentences short).

48. Reinforce the student for directing and maintaining attention to important sounds in the environment: (a) give the student a tangible reward (e.g., classroom privileges, line leading, passing out materials, five minutes free time, etc.) or (b) give the student an intangible reward (e.g., praise, fist bump, smile, etc.).

49. Have the student question any sounds in the environment to which he/she does not know how to respond.

50. Deliver all directions, questions, explanations, and instructions in a clear, concise manner and at an appropriate rate for the student.

51. Use pictures, diagrams, wall-mounted board, and gestures when presenting information.

52. Reinforce the student for directing and maintaining his/her attention to important sounds in the immediate environment based on the length of time he/she can be successful. As the student demonstrates success, gradually increase the length of time required for reinforcement.

53. Help the student develop an awareness of the consequences of his/her behavior by writing down or talking through problems which may occur due to his/her inability to maintain attention (e.g., may be last in the lunch line if he/she does not hear the bell).

54. Determine if the student heard an environmental stimuli by asking the student to identify the sound.

55. Seat the student next to a peer who directs and maintains attention to sounds in the immediate environment.

56. Provide the student with public announcements, directions, and instructions in written form.

57. Allow natural consequences to occur (e.g., arriving late to class because he/she did not hear tardy bell, etc.) due to the student's inability to direct his/her attention to immediate sounds in the environment.

58. Teach the student listening skills:
- Stop working.
- Clear desk of nonessential materials.
- Attend to the source of information.
- Write down important points.
- Ask for clarification.
- Wait until all directions are received before beginning.

Goals:

1. The student will improve listening skills in academic settings.
2. The student will improve listening skills in nonacademic settings.

Objectives:

1. The student will maintain eye contact when information is being communicated _____% of the time.
2. The student will listen quietly when verbal directions are given _____% of the time.
3. The student will repeat what is said with _____% accuracy.
4. The student will respond appropriately to what is said, with reminders, _____% of the time.
5. The student will independently respond appropriately to what is said _____% of the time.

Interventions:

1. Play games that teach listening skills.

2. Deliver directives in a supportive rather than a threatening manner (e.g., telling the student to please listen to the directions rather than he/she had better listen).

3. Talk to the student before going into an assembly or group activity and remind him/her of the importance of listening to and following directions.

4. Have the student question any directions, explanations, and instructions he/she does not understand.

5. Deliver all directions, questions, explanations, and instructions in a clear, concise manner and at an appropriate rate for the student.

6. Demonstrate the appropriate way to listen to and follow directions.

7. Encourage parents to take advantage of dinner and other family-gathering times to talk with each other and practice maintaining attention.

8. Remove the student from the situation (e.g., at an assembly, when a guest speaker is present, etc.) until he/she can demonstrate self-control and follow directions.

9. Have the student carry a notepad with him/her at all times. Encourage him/her to write information down to help him/her maintain attention.

10. Make sure you have the student's undivided attention when you are talking to him/her. Stand close to the student, maintain eye contact, and have the student repeat the information.

11. Do not reinforce the student's inappropriate behavior by laughing when he/she has not listened to directions.

12. Determine if the student heard a direction by having the student repeat it.

13. Teach and practice information-gathering skills (e.g., listen carefully, write down important points, ask for clarification, wait until all information is presented before beginning a task, etc.).

14. Reduce the emphasis on competition in the classroom. Competition may cause the student to begin an activity before hearing all of what is said.

15. Establish rules for listening to and following directions (e.g., listen when someone is giving directions, ask questions about directions if they are not understood, etc.). These rules should be consistent and followed by everyone in the classroom. Talk about the rules often.

16. Help the student listen to and follow directions by reducing distractions.

17. Reduce distracting stimuli (e.g., noise and motion in the classroom) to facilitate the student's ability to listen successfully.

18. Encourage the student to write down verbal directions.

19. Emphasize or repeat key words, due dates, quantity, etc.

20. Use multiple modalities to accommodate more than one learning style (e.g., visual, auditory, tactile, etc.) when presenting directions/instructions, explanations, and instructional content.

21. Make sure the student knows that you expect him/her to listen to you (e.g., tell the student it is important that he/she listen carefully to what is said because his/her rough draft is due on Wednesday).

22. Encourage the student to ask for clarification of any directions, explanations, and instructions before beginning a task to ensure all needed information was heard.

23. Choose different people (e.g., peers, paraprofessionals, counselors, family members, etc.) to help the student improve his/her listening skills.

24. Reward the student's peers in the classroom for listening to and following directions.

25. Do not give directions to the student from across the room. Go to the student, get his/her undivided attention, and explain the directions to him/her.

26. Have the student's hearing checked if it has not been recently checked.

27. Have the student rehearse in his/her head information just heard to help him/her remember the important facts.

28. When correcting the student, be honest yet supportive. Never cause the student to feel negatively about himself/herself.

29. Maintain a consistent format in the verbal delivery of information.

30. Encourage the student to ask for clarification if he/she does not understand directions that are given verbally or in writing.

31. Give the student short directions, explanations, and instructions to follow. As the student demonstrates success, gradually increase the length of the directions, explanations, and instructions.

32. Allow natural consequences to occur (e.g., miss instructions for assignment, miss information on school activities, etc.) due to the student not listening to and following directions.

33. Have the student repeat or paraphrase what is said to him/her to determine what he/she heard.

34. Reinforce the student for listening (e.g., making eye contact, hands free of writing materials, looking at assignment, etc.) to what is said: (a) give the student a tangible reward (e.g., classroom privileges, five minutes free time, etc.) or (b) give the student an intangible reward (e.g., praise, fist bump, smile, etc.).

35. Be consistent in expecting the student to listen to and follow directions. Do not allow the student to not listen without accepting natural consequences.

36. Give the student directions with no more than two or three steps (e.g., open your text and turn to page 28). Directions that involve several steps can be confusing and cause the student to have difficulty following them.

37. Place the student near the source of information.

38. Stop at key points when delivering directions, explanations, and instructions to check the student's comprehension.

39. Help the student develop an awareness of himself/herself and those around him/her. Instruct the student to periodically step back and ask himself/herself: *Am I listening and paying attention? What should I be doing now?*

40. Help the student develop an awareness of the consequences of not listening by writing down or talking through problems which may occur due to his/her need to have verbal directions and questions frequently repeated (e.g., if he/she does not focus on the directions, he/she may miss information and produce poor quality work).

41. Reinforce the student for listening carefully based on the length of time the student can be successful. As the student demonstrates success, gradually increase the length of time the student is required to listen.

42. Provide the student with directions on a one-to-one basis before he/she begins a task.

43. Have the student ask for help when he/she needs it.

44. Teach the student the relationship between inappropriate behavior and the consequences which follow (e.g., not listening to and following directions may result in reduced grades, etc.).

45. Instruct the student to ask people to repeat parts of a conversation he/she was unable to follow.

46. Avoid placing the student in situations that require listening for an extended period of time, such as lectures, seminars, etc. Provide the information for the student through an audio recording or lecture notes.

47. Encourage the student to develop a 30 second definition of his/her goal to help stay on task and focus (e.g., I will listen carefully. The better I focus and stay on task, the better I will hear what is said.).

48. Write a contract with the student. It should be written within his/her ability level and focus on only one behavior at a time. Specify what behavior is expected and what reinforcement will be made available when the terms of the contract have been met.

49. Deliver directions, explanations, and instructions at an appropriate rate.

50. Teach and practice effective communication skills. These skills include: listening, maintaining eye contact, and positive body language.

51. Choose a classmate who has good communication skills. Encourage the student to observe that classmate and model his/her behaviors which promote good communication.

52. Instruct the student to maintain attention to the source of information by maintaining eye contact, keeping hands free from other materials, and reducing other distractions.

53. Choose a peer, paraprofessional, etc., to cue the student when he/she needs to maintain attention (e.g., the person can touch the student on the arm when it is time to listen).

54. Encourage the student to avoid ingesting any substance (e.g., drugs, alcohol, cold remedies, etc.) that might further alter his/her ability to direct or maintain attention.

55. Make sure the student is attending to the source of information (e.g., making eye contact, hands free of writing materials, looking at the assignment, etc.).

56. Allow natural consequences to occur (e.g., schoolwork not done on time, homework done incorrectly, etc.) due to the student's failure to follow verbal directions.

57. Evaluate the difficulty level of information verbally delivered to the student (e.g., information should be communicated on the student's ability level).

58. Encourage the student to recite a mantra to himself/herself when entering a situation where he/she will receive directions/instructions (e.g., listen carefully, listen carefully, listen carefully).

59. Teach active listening skills. Encourage the student to listen to what another person is saying and respond based on information received.

60. Have a peer provide the information the student does not hear.

61. Teach and have the student practice how to listen for key information when he/she is being given directions or receiving information (e.g., write down main points, ideas, step-by-step instructions, etc.).

62. Provide the student with written directions and instructions to supplement verbal directions and instructions.

63. Provide opportunities for the student to talk to others on a one-to-one basis. As the student becomes more successful at listening and maintaining attention, gradually include more people in conversations.

64. Give simple, specific directions to the student.

65. Speak to the student to explain (a) what he/she is doing wrong (e.g., not listening for key words, etc.) and (b) what he/she should be doing (e.g., listening for key words, etc.).

66. Consider carefully the student's age and experience when expecting him/her to listen to and follow directions.

67. Tell the student what to listen for when being given directions or receiving information, etc.

68. Identify a list of word endings, key words, etc., that the student will practice listening for when someone is speaking.

69. Present directions following the *What, How, Materials,* and *When* outline.

70. Teach the student listening skills:
- Stop working.
- Clear desk of nonessential materials.
- Attend to the source of information.
- Write down important points.
- Ask for clarification.
- Wait until all directions are received before beginning.

71. Be sure the student has heard what was said by having him/her give acknowledgment (e.g., Okay! Will do!).

72. Evaluate the visual and auditory stimuli in the classroom. Remove or reduce the extraneous environmental stimuli.

73. Speak clearly and concisely when delivering directions, explanations, and instructions.

74. Have the student take notes when directions are being given following *What, How, Materials,* and *When* format.

75. Have the student listen and take notes for *Who, What, Where, When, How,* and *Why* when concepts are presented.

76. Present concepts following the *Who, What, Where, When, How,* and *Why* outline.

77. Have the student prepare for tests using the *Who, What, Where, When, How,* and *Why* format.

Goal:

1. The student will follow verbal directions.

Objectives:

1. The student will complete one step of the verbal direction before going on to the next step on _____ out of _____ trials.
2. The student will demonstrate the ability to follow verbal directions by listening carefully and completing the task with _____% accuracy.
3. The student will follow _____ out of _____ verbal directions.
4. The student will follow one-step verbal directions on _____ out of _____ trials.
5. The student will follow verbal directions with teacher assistance on _____ out of _____ trials.
6. The student will independently follow verbal directions on _____ out of _____ trials.
7. The student will listen to verbal directions on his/her ability level and follow them in correct sequential order on _____ out of _____ trials.

Interventions:

1. Be sure the student has heard what was said by having him/her give acknowledgment (e.g., Okay! Will do!).

2. The teacher should be able to see the student, and the student should be able to see the teacher. Make eye contact possible at all times when giving verbal directions.

3. Assess the quality and clarity of verbal directions, explanations, and instructions given to the student.

4. Choose a peer to work with the student to help him/her follow verbal directions.

5. Deliver directions, explanations, and information using vocabulary that is within the student's level of comprehension.

6. Avoid placing the student in situations that require listening for an extended period of time, such as lectures, seminars, etc. Provide the information for the student through an audio recording or lecture notes.

7. Be consistent in expecting the student to listen to and follow directions. Do not allow the student to not follow directions one time and expect directions to be followed the next time.

8. Communicate clearly to the student when it is time to listen to verbal directions.

9. Maintain visibility to and from the student.

10. Clarify for the student that it is his/her behavior which determines whether consequences are positive or negative.

11. Assist the student in performing his/her responsibilities. As the student demonstrates success following verbal directions, gradually decrease the assistance and require the student to independently assume more responsibility.

12. Deliver a predetermined signal (e.g., clapping hands, turning lights off and on, etc.) before giving verbal directions.

13. Communicate with parents (e.g., notes home, phone calls, etc.) to share information about the student's progress. The parents may reinforce the student at home for following verbal directions at school.

14. Establish rules for listening to and following directions (e.g., listen when someone is giving directions, ask questions about directions if they are not understood, etc.). These rules should be consistent and followed by everyone in the class. Talk about the rules often.

15. Demonstrate directions, explanations, and instructions as they are presented verbally (e.g., use the wall-mounted board to work a problem for the student, begin playing a game with the student, etc.).

16. Demonstrate the steps of verbal directions as they are delivered to facilitate the student's success in accurately following the directions.

17. Develop direction-following assignments/activities (e.g., informal activities designed to have the student carry out verbal directions in steps with increasing degrees of difficulty).

18. Evaluate the visual and auditory stimuli in the classroom. Remove or reduce the extraneous environmental stimuli.

19. Do not criticize when correcting the student; be honest yet supportive. Never cause the student to feel negatively about himself/herself.

20. Do not give directions to the student from across the classroom. Go to the student, get his/her undivided attention, and explain the directions to him/her. As the student's ability to follow verbal directions increases, gradually increase the distance of communication.

21. Give verbal directions before handing out materials.

22. Give the student short directions, explanations, and instructions to follow. As the student demonstrates success, gradually increase the length of the directions, explanations, and instructions.

23. Help the student develop an awareness of the consequences of his/her behavior by writing down or talking through problems which may occur due to his/her need to have verbal directions and questions frequently repeated (e.g., may not complete assignments correctly, may not pass the class, and may not earn the credit needed for graduation).

24. Designate a person to deliver verbal directions to the student.

25. Encourage the student to recite a mantra to himself/herself when entering a situation where he/she will receive directions/instructions (e.g., listen carefully, listen carefully, listen carefully).

26. Establish classroom rules:
- Concentrate while working.
- Work quietly.
- Remain in your seat.
- Finish task.
- Meet task expectations.

Review rules often. Reinforce students for following the rules.

27. Evaluate the appropriateness of the task to determine (a) if the task is too easy, (b) if the task is too difficult, or (c) if the length of time scheduled to complete the task is adequate.

28. Facilitate the student's ability to follow verbal directions by communicating with the student's cooperative work experience/vocational education teacher to provide appropriate strategies and interventions at the student's job site.

29. Follow a less desirable task with a highly desirable task. Make the following of verbal directions and completion of the first task necessary to perform the second task.

30. Give directions in a variety of ways to facilitate the student's probability of understanding (e.g., if the student does not understand verbal directions, present them in written form).

31. Give the student one task to perform at a time. Introduce the next task when the student has successfully completed the current task.

32. Encourage the student to avoid ingesting any substance (e.g., drugs, alcohol, cold remedies, etc.) that might further alter his/her ability to listen to or follow verbal directions.

33. Encourage the student to ask for clarification of any directions, explanations, and instructions before beginning a task to facilitate comprehension.

34. Have a peer help the student with any verbal directions he/she does not understand.

35. Instruct the student to periodically step back and ask himself/herself: *Am I on task and paying attention? What should I be doing now?*

36. Have the student attend to the source of information by maintaining eye contact, keeping hands free from other materials, and reducing other distractions.

37. Require that assignments done incorrectly, for any reason, be redone.

38. Have the student maintain a record (e.g., chart or graph) of his/her performance in following verbal directions.

39. Reduce verbal directions to steps (e.g., give the student each additional step after completion of the previous step).

40. Have the student practice group listening skills (e.g., Everyone take out a piece of paper, write your name on the paper, and number your paper from 1 to 20.).

41. Make sure the student is attending (e.g., making eye contact, hands free of writing materials, looking at assignment, etc.) before verbal directions are given.

42. Have the student question any verbal directions, explanations, and instructions he/she does not understand.

43. Provide consistent, positive reinforcement for appropriate behavior. Ignore as many inappropriate behaviors as possible.

44. Have the student audio record directions, explanations, and instructions. Allow him/her to replay information as often as needed.

45. Have the student's hearing checked if it has not been recently checked.

46. Have the student practice verbal direction-following on nonacademic tasks (e.g., recipes, games, etc.).

47. Teach the student the relationship between inappropriate behavior and the consequences which follow (e.g., not listening to and following directions during football practice may result in being benched for a game).

48. Have the student repeat directions, explanations, and instructions after they have been given to facilitate retention.

49. Let the student know that directions will only be given once and that he/she will not be reminded to follow the directions.

50. Maintain a consistent format of verbal directions.

51. Allow natural consequences to occur (e.g., school or class detention, missed assignment, etc.) due to the student's failure to listen to and follow directions.

52. Deliver all directions, questions, explanations, and instructions in a clear, concise manner and at an appropriate rate for the student.

53. Present directions in both written and verbal form.

54. Make sure that verbal directions are delivered in a supportive rather than threatening manner (e.g., Will you please . . . or You need . . . rather than You better . . . or If you don't . . .).

55. Make sure the student achieves success when following verbal directions.

56. Make sure the student has all the materials needed to complete the assignment/activity.

57. Provide alternatives for the traditional format of presenting verbal directions (e.g., audio record directions, summarize directions, directions given by peers, etc.).

58. Have the student repeat directions or give an interpretation after receiving verbal directions.

59. Make sure the student knows that you expect him/her to listen to you (e.g., William, it is important that you listen carefully to what I have to say. The book report is due on Monday.).

60. Interact frequently with the student to help him/her follow verbal directions for the activity.

61. Make instructions meaningful to the student by relating instructions to past experiences.

62. Choose a peer to model appropriate listening to and following of verbal directions for the student.

63. Gain the student's attention before telling him/her to do something. Have the student make eye contact and repeat the information to check for understanding.

64. Prevent the student from becoming overstimulated (e.g., frustrated, angry, etc.) by an activity.

65. Provide clearly stated verbal directions (e.g., make the directions as simple and concrete as possible).

66. Make sure that verbal directions are given at the level at which the student can be successful (e.g., two-step or three-step directions are not given to students who can only successfully follow one-step directions).

67. Provide directions on a one-to-one basis before assigning a task.

68. Provide supplemental directions/ instructions in the student's preferred learning style (e.g., visual, auditory, etc.).

69. Work the first problem or problems with the student to make sure that he/she follows the verbal directions accurately.

70. Reduce the emphasis on competition. Competitive activities may cause the student to hurry to begin the task without verbal directions.

71. Provide the student with a written copy of verbal directions.

72. Speak to the student to explain (a) what he/she is doing wrong (e.g., ignoring verbal directions) and (b) what he/she should be doing (e.g., listening to and following through when given verbal directions).

73. Reduce distracting stimuli in the environment to facilitate the student's ability to follow verbal directions (e.g., place the student on the front row, provide a carrel or office space away from distractions, etc.). This is used as a means of reducing distracting stimuli and not as a form of punishment.

74. Make sure that verbal directions are delivered in a nonthreatening manner (e.g., positive voice, facial expression, language used, etc.).

75. Reduce the emphasis on early completion. Hurrying to complete assignments may cause the student to fail to follow directions.

76. Reinforce the student for following verbal directions: (a) give the student a tangible reward (e.g., classroom privileges, line leading, passing out materials, five minutes free time, etc.) or (b) give the student an intangible reward (e.g., praise, fist bump, smile, etc.).

77. Have the student carry out one step of the verbal directions at a time, checking with the teacher to make sure that each step is successfully followed before beginning the next.

78. Reinforce the student for following verbal directions based on the length of time he/she can be successful. As the student demonstrates success, gradually increase the length of time required for reinforcement.

79. Teach the student skills for following verbal directions (e.g., listen carefully, write down important points, use environmental cues, wait until all directions are received before beginning, etc.).

80. Reinforce those students in the classroom who follow verbal directions.

81. Require the student to wait until the teacher gives him/her a signal to begin a task (e.g., give a hand signal, ring a bell, etc.).

82. Reward the student (e.g., take a break, visit briefly with a peer, etc.) for maintaining eye contact and listening for a specific length of time.

83. Structure the environment to provide the student with increased opportunities for help or assistance on academic tasks (e.g., peer tutoring, directions for work sent home, frequent interactions, etc.).

84. Provide the student with a predetermined signal (e.g., lights turned off and on, hand signals, etc.) when he/she is not following verbal directions.

85. Audio record directions for the student to listen to and replay as necessary.

86. Teach and have the student practice listening for key information when he/she is being given directions or receiving information (e.g., write down main points, ideas, step-by-step instructions, etc.).

87. Teach and practice effective communication skills. These skills include: listening, maintaining eye contact, and positive body language.

88. Work through the steps of the verbal directions as they are delivered to make sure the student follows the directions accurately.

89. Teach and provide practice in information-gathering skills (e.g., listen carefully, write down important points, ask for clarification, wait until all information is presented before beginning a task, etc.).

90. Teach the student listening skills:
- Stop working.
- Clear desk of nonessential materials.
- Attend to the source of information.
- Write down important points.
- Ask for clarification.
- Wait until all directions are received before beginning.

91. Seat the student close to the source of the verbal directions (e.g., teacher, aide, peer, etc.).

92. Seat the student far enough away from peers to facilitate attending to verbal directions.

93. Use vocabulary that is within the student's level of comprehension when delivering directions, explanations, and information.

94. Write a contract with the student specifying what behavior is expected (e.g., following verbal directions) and what reinforcement will be made available when the terms of the contract have been met.

95. Teach and provide practice in active listening skills. Have the student listen to what another person is saying and respond based on information received.

96. Write down verbal directions. Instruct the student to mark each step off as it is completed.

97. Provide the student with a clearly understood list of consequences for inappropriate behavior.

98. Stand next to the student when giving verbal directions.

128 Does not listen to what other students are saying

Goals:

1. The student will attend to what other students say.
2. The student will improve listening skills in nonacademic settings.

Objectives:

1. The student will listen quietly when other students are speaking on _____ out of _____ occasions.
2. The student will maintain eye contact when other students are speaking on _____ out of _____ occasions.
3. The student will repeat what other students have said with _____% accuracy.
4. The student will respond appropriately to what other students say on _____ out of _____ occasions.

Interventions:

1. Instruct the student to maintain attention to the source of information by maintaining eye contact, keeping hands free from other materials, and reducing other distractions.

2. Do not force the student to interact with someone when he/she is not completely comfortable.

3. Have the student work with a peer and the teacher. The first student will dictate a short paragraph to be typed by the teacher and will also compose a comprehension question. The second student, after listening to the process, will read the story verbally and point out the answer. Then student roles can be reversed.

4. Be consistent in expecting the student to listen to what others are saying. Do not provide missed information if the student fails to listen.

5. Consider carefully the student's ability level and experience when expecting him/her to be a good listener.

6. Have the student's hearing checked if it has not been recently checked.

7. Model the appropriate way to listen by listening to the student when he/she talks.

8. Allow the student some movement while listening to other students. Monitor and limit the amount of movement.

9. Encourage the student to develop a 30 second definition of his/her goal to help stay on task and focus on the speaker (e.g., I will listen carefully. The better I focus and stay on task, the better I will listen.).

10. Determine if the student heard what was said by having him/her repeat it.

11. Develop the student's awareness of the consequences of his/her behavior by writing down or talking through problems which may occur due to his/her inability to maintain attention (e.g., not focusing on directions may cause misunderstanding of an assignment which could lead to a lower grade and losing a place on the soccer team).

12. Do not criticize when correcting the student; be honest yet supportive. Never cause the student to feel negatively about himself/herself.

13. Do not ignore the student when he/she wants to tell you something. When you ignore the student, he/she may think that it is acceptable to ignore others when they speak to him/her.

14. Encourage parents to take advantage of dinner and other family-gathering times to talk with each other and practice maintaining attention.

15. Choose a classmate who has good communication skills. Encourage the student to observe that classmate and model his/her behaviors which promote good communication.

16. Help the student develop an awareness of himself/herself and those around him/her. Instruct the student to periodically step back and ask himself/herself: *Am I on task and paying attention? What should I be doing now?*

17. Encourage the student to interact with others.

18. Make sure the student is near the students who are speaking.

19. Establish rules for listening (e.g., listen when others are talking, ask questions if you do not understand, etc.). These rules should be consistent and followed by everyone in the class. Talk about the rules often.

20. Evaluate the visual and auditory stimuli in the classroom. Remove or reduce the extraneous environmental stimuli.

21. Teach and have the student practice listening for key information when he/she is being given directions or receiving information (e.g., write down main points, ideas, step-by-step instructions, etc.).

22. Choose a peer, paraprofessional, student, etc., to cue the student when he/she needs to maintain attention (e.g., the person can touch the student on the arm when it is time to listen).

23. Write a contract with the student. It should be written within his/her ability level and focus on only one behavior at a time. Specify what behavior is expected and what reinforcement will be made available when the terms of the contract have been met.

24. Have other students stand directly in front of the student when speaking to him/her so the student will be more likely to listen to what others are saying.

25. Provide opportunities for the student to talk to others on a one-to-one basis. As the student becomes more successful at listening and maintaining attention, gradually include more people in conversations.

26. Reduce the emphasis on competition in the classroom. Competition may cause the student to become excited or distracted and not listen to what other students are saying.

27. Have the student rehearse in his/her head information just heard from other students to facilitate remembering important information.

28. Instruct the student to ask for clarification if he/she does not understand information presented verbally.

29. Instruct the student to ask people to repeat parts of a conversation he/she was unable to follow.

30. Allow natural consequences to occur (e.g., miss information, miss a school activity, etc.) due to the student not listening to others.

31. Instruct the student's peers to preface statements with the student's name to gain his/her attention before speaking.

32. Make sure that competing sounds (e.g., talking, noises, motion in the classroom, etc.) are silenced when other students are talking to facilitate the student's ability to listen to what others are saying.

33. Encourage the student to recite a mantra to himself/herself when entering a situation where he/she will receive directions/instructions (e.g., listen carefully, listen carefully, listen carefully).

34. Make sure that other students speak clearly and concisely when speaking to the student.

35. Have the student repeat or paraphrase what other students have said to him/her to determine what the student heard.

36. Choose different people (e.g., peers, paraprofessionals, counselors, etc.) to help the student maintain attention to conversations.

37. Provide group settings that are quiet, well-lighted, and at a comfortable temperature.

38. Talk to the student before beginning an activity and remind him/her of the importance of listening to others.

39. Have the student practice listening to what other students are saying (e.g., following simple instructions, sharing information, etc.).

40. Reduce the number of visual distractions in the classroom when listening is required (e.g., move the student's work area away from windows, doors, etc.).

41. Teach and practice information-gathering skills (e.g., listen carefully, write down important points, ask for clarification, wait until all information is presented before beginning a task, etc.).

42. Reduce the occurrence of situations that may contribute to difficulty maintaining attention (e.g., timed activities, competition, long meetings, etc.).

43. Provide the student with frequent opportunities to meet new people.

44. Reinforce the students in the classroom who listen to what other students are saying.

45. Remove the student from the situation (e.g., school assembly, school play, guest speaker, etc.) when he/she has difficulty listening until he/she can demonstrate self-control.

46. Schedule opportunities for peer interaction at times when the student is most likely to maintain attention (e.g., one hour after medication, 45 minutes after lunch, first thing in the morning, etc.).

47. Model respecting others and what they are saying.

48. Reinforce the student for listening to what other students are saying based on the length of time the student can be successful. As the student demonstrates success, gradually increase the number of times or length of time required to listen.

49. Instruct the student to sit close to the source of information to facilitate his/her ability to maintain attention.

50. Make sure the student is attending to what other students are saying (e.g., making eye contact, stopping other activities, responding appropriately, etc.).

51. Talk to the student before going to an activity (e.g., assembly, school play, field trip, etc.) and remind him/her of the importance of listening when others are speaking.

52. Teach active listening skills. Provide opportunities for the student to listen to what another person is saying and respond based on information received.

53. Teach and practice effective communication skills. These skills include: listening, maintaining eye contact, and positive body language.

54. Reinforce the student for listening (e.g., making eye contact, putting aside materials, etc.) to what is said to him/her by other students: (a) give the student a tangible reward (e.g., classroom privileges, passing out materials, five minutes free time, etc.) or (b) give the student an intangible reward (e.g., praise, fist bump, smile, etc.).

55. Teach the student listening skills:
- Stop working.
- Clear desk of nonessential materials.
- Attend to the source of information.
- Write down important points.
- Ask for clarification.
- Wait until all directions are received before beginning.

56. Treat the student with respect. Talk in an objective manner at all times.

57. Speak to the student to explain (a) what he/she is doing wrong (e.g., not listening to what other students are saying) and (b) what he/she should be doing (e.g., listening to other students when they speak to him/her, listening to other students when they speak to a group, etc.).

129 Does not take notes during class when necessary

Goals:

1. The student will improve his/her academic task-related behavior.
2. The student will take notes during class.

Objectives:

1. The student will take notes during class when necessary with verbal prompts on _____ out of _____ occasions.
2. The student will independently take notes during class when necessary on _____ out of _____ occasions.
3. The student will rely on environmental cues (e.g., other students, visual aids) to take notes during class when necessary on _____ out of _____ occasions.
4. The student will take notes related to the presentation on _____ out of _____ occasions.

Interventions:

1. Reinforce the student for taking notes during class when necessary: (a) give the student a tangible reward (e.g., classroom privileges, line leading, passing out materials, five minutes free time, etc.) or (b) give the student an intangible reward (e.g., praise, fist bump, smile, etc.).

2. Speak to the student to explain (a) what he/she is doing wrong (e.g., not taking notes) and (b) what he/she should be doing (e.g., taking notes).

3. Establish classroom rules:
- Concentrate while working.
- Work quietly.
- Remain in your seat.
- Finish task.
- Meet task expectations.

Review rules often. Reinforce the student for following the rules.

4. Reinforce those students in the classroom who take notes during class when necessary.

5. Reinforce the student for taking notes during class based on the length of time he/she can be successful. As the student demonstrates success, gradually increase the required length of time for taking notes for reinforcement.

6. Choose a peer to model taking notes during class for the student.

7. Write a contract with the student specifying what behavior is expected (e.g., taking notes) and what reinforcement will be made available when the terms of the contract have been met.

8. Communicate with parents (e.g., notes home, phone calls, etc.) to share information about the student's progress. The parents may reinforce the student at home for taking notes during class when necessary.

9. Have the student ask questions about directions, explanations, instructions he/she does not understand.

10. Teach the student note-taking skills (e.g., copy main ideas from the board, identify main ideas from lectures, condense statements into a few key words, etc.).

11. Provide a standard format for writing down directions or explanations (e.g., have paper and pencil or pen ready, listen for the steps in directions or explanations, write a shortened form of directions or explanations, ask to have any steps repeated when necessary, etc.).

12. Provide a standard format for taking lecture notes (e.g., have paper and pencil or pen ready, listen for main ideas or important information, write a shortened form of main ideas or important information, ask to have any main ideas or important information repeated when necessary, etc.).

13. Evaluate the appropriateness of note taking to determine (a) if the task is too easy, (b) if the task is too difficult, and (c) if the length of time scheduled to complete the task is adequate.

14. Point out to the student that instructions, directions, lectures, etc., should be written in the form of notes when they are presented.

15. Have the student practice legible manuscript or cursive handwriting during simulated and actual note-taking activities.

16. Have the student keep his/her notes organized in a folder for each subject or activity.

17. Check the student's notes before he/she begins an assignment to determine if they contain adequate information for the assignment.

18. Provide the student with an outline or questions to be completed during the presentation of instructions, directions, lectures, etc.

19. Provide the student with samples of students' notes of classroom instructions, directions, lectures, etc., that have been given so that he/she may learn what information is necessary when taking notes.

20. Make sure the student is in the best location in the classroom to receive information for note taking (e.g., near the board, teacher, or other source of information).

21. Make sure that supervision of the student's note taking can easily be provided.

22. Have the student prepare for tests using the *Who, What, Where, When, How*, and *Why* method. The teacher should then test this same information.

23. Present instructions, directions, lectures, etc., clearly and loudly enough for the student to hear.

24. Provide the student with both verbal and written instructions.

25. Match the rate of delivery of the instructions, directions, lectures, etc., to the student's ability to take notes.

26. Provide instructions, directions, lectures, etc., in sequential steps to facilitate student note taking.

27. Present information in short segments for the student to take notes. As the student experiences success, gradually increase the length of the segments that are presented.

28. Make sure the vocabulary used in presenting instructions, directions, lectures, etc., is appropriate for the student's ability level.

29. Make sure the student has all the materials necessary for note taking (e.g., paper, pencil, pen, etc.).

30. Make sure the student uses any necessary aids to facilitate note taking (e.g., eyeglasses, hearing aid, etc.).

31. Place the student next to a peer so the student can copy the notes taken by the peer.

32. Make sure the student has adequate surface space on which to write when taking notes (e.g., uncluttered desk top).

33. Reduce distracting stimuli that interferes with the student's note taking (e.g., other students talking, outdoor activities, movement in the classroom, hallway noise, etc.).

34. Present the information in the most interesting manner possible.

35. Have the student audio record instructions, directions, lectures, etc., as an alternative to written note taking.

36. Summarize the main points of instructions, directions, lectures, etc., for the student.

37. Present directions following the *What, How, Materials*, and *When* outline.

38. Maintain visibility to and from the student when delivering instructions, directions, lectures, etc., to facilitate the student's success in note taking.

39. Have the student take notes when directions are being given following *What, How, Materials*, and *When* format.

40. Have the student listen and take notes for *Who, What, Where, When, How*, and *Why* when concepts are presented.

41. Present concepts following the *Who, What, Where, When, How*, and *Why* outline.

130 Has difficulty differentiating speech sounds heard

Goals:

1. The student will improve listening skills in academic settings.
2. The student will improve listening skills in nonacademic settings.
3. The student will attend more successfully to specific sounds in the environment.

Objectives:

1. The student will produce different speech sounds (e.g., /ch/ and /sh/ blends) with _____ % accuracy.
2. The student will produce different speech sounds (e.g., /ch/ and /sh/ blends, vowel sounds, consonant sounds, rhyming words, etc.) with _____% accuracy.
3. The student will recognize similar speech sounds (e.g., /ch/ and /sh/ blends, vowel sounds, consonant sounds, rhyming words, etc.) with _____% accuracy.
4. The student will differentiate speech sounds heard (e.g., /ch/ and /sh/ blends, similar vowel sounds, similar consonant sounds, rhyming words, etc.) with _____% accuracy.

Interventions:

1. Have the student's hearing checked if it has not been recently checked.

2. Evaluate the level of difficulty of the information to which the student is expected to listen (e.g., /ch/ and /sh/ blends, similar consonant sounds, rhyming words, etc.).

3. Have the student repeat or paraphrase what is said to him/her to determine what was heard.

4. Make sure the student is attending to the source of information (e.g., making eye contact, hands free of writing materials, looking at assignments, etc.).

5. Emphasize or repeat /ch/ or /sh/ blends, similar vowel sounds, similar consonant sounds, rhyming words, etc.

6. Speak clearly and concisely when communicating with the student.

7. Place the student in the location most appropriate for him/her to hear what is being said.

8. Reduce distracting stimuli (e.g., noise and motion in the classroom) to facilitate the student's ability to listen successfully.

9. Have the student keep a notebook with pictures of words that rhyme.

10. Stop at key points when delivering directions, explanations, and instructions to determine student comprehension.

11. Identify a list of words with /ch/ and /sh/ blends, similar vowel sounds, similar consonant sounds, rhyming words, etc., that the student will practice listening for when someone else is speaking.

12. Stand directly in front of the student when delivering information.

13. Play a game in which the student tries to imitate the sounds made by the teacher or other students (e.g., *Simon Says*).

14. Use pictures of similar words to help the student recognize their differences (e.g., if the student has trouble differentiating /ch/ and /sh/ blends, use pictures of /ch/ and /sh/ words such as chips and ships).

15. Give the student simple words and ask him/her to rhyme them verbally with as many other words as possible.

16. Use fill-in-the-blank sentences and have the student pick the correct word from a group of similar words (e.g., I _____ (wonder, wander) what's in the box?).

17. Have the student make up poems and tongue twisters using /ch/ and /sh/ blends, similar vowel sounds, similar consonant sounds, and rhyming words.

18. Present pairs of words and have the student tell if the words rhyme.

19. Explain and demonstrate how similar sounds are made (e.g., where the tongue is placed, how the mouth is shaped, etc.).

20. Have the student listen to a series of directions and act out the ones that make sense (e.g., bake your head, rake your bread, shake your head).

21. Identify the speech sounds the student has difficulty differentiating. Spend time each day having the student listen to sounds and have the student use the sounds in conversation.

22. Teach the student listening skills:
- Stop working.
- Clear desk of nonessential materials.
- Attend to the source of information.
- Write down important points.
- Ask for clarification.
- Wait until all directions are received before beginning.

23. Encourage the student to watch the lips of the person speaking to him/her.

131 Has difficulty taking class notes

Goals:

1. The student will improve his/her academic task-related behavior.
2. The student will improve his/her academic performance.
3. The student will improve his/her ability to take class notes.

Objectives:

1. The student will write key words presented in lessons on _____ out of _____ trials.
2. The student will write key phrases presented in lessons on _____ out of _____ trials.
3. The student will take notes from an audio recording of information presented in class on _____ out of _____ trials.
4. The student will take notes from information presented visually (e.g., wall-mounted board, over-head projector, etc.) on _____ out of _____ trials.
5. The student will take notes from information presented auditorily (e.g., audio recording, lecture, etc.) on _____ out of _____ trials.
6. The student will take notes during class when necessary with verbal prompts on _____ out of _____ occasions.
7. The student will independently take notes during class when necessary on _____ out of _____ occasions.
8. The student will rely on environmental cues (e.g., other students, visual aids) to take notes during class when necessary on _____ out of _____ occasions.
9. The student will take notes related to the presentation on _____ out of _____ occasions.

Interventions:

1. Evaluate the appropriateness of note taking to determine (a) if the task is too easy, (b) if the task is too difficult, or (c) if the length of time scheduled to take notes is adequate.

2. Teach the student note-taking skills (e.g., copy main ideas from the board, identify main ideas from lectures, condense statements into a few key words, etc.).

3. Provide a standard format for writing down directions and explanations (e.g., have paper and pencil or pen ready, listen for the steps in directions or explanations, write a shortened form of directions or explanations, ask to have any steps repeated when necessary, etc.).

4. Have the student practice legible manuscript or cursive handwriting during simulated and actual note-taking activities.

5. Have the student question any directions, explanations, and instructions he/she does not understand.

6. Establish classroom rules:
- Concentrate while working.
- Work quietly.
- Remain in your seat.
- Finish task.
- Meet task expectations.

Review rules often. Reinforce students for following the rules.

7. Reinforce the student for taking notes during class based on the length of time he/she can be successful. As the student demonstrates success, gradually increase the required length of time for taking notes for reinforcement.

8. Write a contract with the student specifying what behavior is expected (e.g., taking notes) and what reinforcement will be made available when the terms of the contract have been met.

9. Present information in short segments for the student to take notes. As the student experiences success, gradually increase the length of the segments that are presented.

10. Have the student prepare for tests using the *Who, What, Where, When, How,* and *Why* format.

11. Provide instructions, directions, lectures, etc., in sequential steps to facilitate student note taking.

12. Provide a standard format for taking lecture notes (e.g., have paper and pencil or pen ready, listen for main ideas of important information, write a shortened form of main ideas or important information, ask to have any main ideas or important information repeated when necessary, etc.).

13. Choose a peer to model taking notes during class for the student.

14. Point out to the student that instructions, directions, lectures, etc., should be written in the form of notes when they are presented.

15. Have the student keep his/her notes organized in a folder for each subject or activity.

16. Check the student's notes before he/she begins an assignment to determine if they contain adequate information for the assignment.

17. Provide the student with an outline or questions to be completed during the presentation of instructions, directions, lectures, etc.

18. Provide the student with samples of students' notes of classroom instructions, directions, lectures, etc., that have been given so that he/she may learn what information is necessary when taking notes.

19. Make sure the student is in the best location in the classroom to receive information for note taking (e.g., near the board, teacher, or other source of information).

20. Provide supervision of the student's note taking.

21. Provide the student with both verbal and written instructions.

22. Maintain visibility to and from the student when delivering instructions, directions, lectures, etc., to facilitate the student's success in note taking.

23. Place the student next to a peer so the student can copy the notes taken by the peer.

24. Make sure that the instructions, directions, lectures, etc., are presented clearly and loudly enough for the student to hear.

25. Match the rate of delivery of the instructions, directions, lectures, etc., to the student's ability to take notes.

26. Make sure that the vocabulary used in presenting instructions, directions, lectures, etc., is appropriate for the student's ability level.

27. Make sure the student has all the materials necessary for note taking (e.g., paper, pencil, pen, etc.).

28. Make sure the student uses any necessary aids to facilitate note taking (e.g., eyeglasses, hearing aid, etc.).

29. Make sure the student has adequate surface space on which to write when taking notes (e.g., uncluttered desk top).

30. Reduce distracting stimuli that interferes with the student's note taking (e.g., other students talking, outdoor activities, movement in the classroom, hallway noise, etc.).

31. Summarize the main points of instructions, directions, concepts, etc., for the student.

32. Provide the student with a limited outline of notes. Have the student add to the outline during the class lecture.

33. Identify the most successful note-taking method for the student. Encourage use of this method for all note-taking activities. This will be more successful if all of the student's teachers allow him/her to use his/her preferred method.

34. Present the information in the most interesting manner possible.

35. Have the student listen and take notes for *Who, What, Where, When, How*, and *Why* when concepts are presented.

36. Present concepts following the *Who, What, Where, When, How*, and *Why* outline.

Goals:

1. The student will attend more successfully to specific sounds in the environment.
2. The student will improve listening skills in academic settings.
3. The student will improve listening skills in nonacademic settings.

Objectives:

1. The student will follow one-step verbal directions with _____% accuracy.
2. The student will follow two-step verbal directions with _____% accuracy.
3. The student will follow multi-step verbal directions with _____% accuracy.
4. The student will independently respond appropriately to what is said with _____% accuracy.
5. The student will listen quietly when verbal directions are given _____% of the time.
6. The student will maintain eye contact when information is being communicated _____% of the time.
7. The student will quietly listen when verbal directions are given _____% of the time.
8. The student will repeat what is said with _____% accuracy.
9. The student will respond appropriately to what is said, with prompting, with _____% accuracy.

Interventions:

1. Have the student audio record directions, explanations, and instructions so that he/she may replay information as often as needed.

2. Allow the student to audio record information from lectures and seminars and make notes from thse recordings.

3. Deliver a predetermined signal (e.g., hand signal, turning off and on lights, etc.) prior to bells ringing, announcements being made, etc.

4. ·Consider carefully the student's ability level and experience before expecting the student to be successful in activities that require listening.

5. Avoid placing the student in situations which require listening for an extended period of time, such as lectures, seminars, etc. Provide supplemental information through an audio recording or lecture notes.

6. Avoid seating the student near people with whom he/she may be tempted to talk with during lectures, guest speakers, group projects, etc.

7. Be consistent in expecting the student to listen. Hold the student accountable for not listening to important information.

8. Call the student by name prior to bells ringing, announcements being made, directions being given, etc.

9. Ask the student for immediate repetition of directions.

10. Reduce the number of visual distractions around the student (e.g., move the student's work area away from windows, doors, computer area, etc.).

11. Arrange for individual assignments when the group setting is overly distracting.

12. Deliver directions to the student individually.

13. Make sure that competing sounds (e.g., talking, movement, noises, etc.) are silenced when directions are being given, public address announcements are being made, etc.

14. Deliver directives in a supportive rather than a threatening manner (e.g., ask the student to please repeat the directions given rather than demanding he/she tell you what was just said).

15. Deliver verbal directions prior to handing out materials.

16. Deliver information slowly to the student.

17. Demonstrate appropriate listening behavior (e.g., sit up straight, eyes on speaker, etc.).

18. Demonstrate directions, explanations, and instructions as they are presented verbally (e.g., use the wall-mounted board to work a problem for the student, begin playing a game with the student, etc.).

19. Allow natural consequences to occur (e.g., miss assignments, miss information regarding a school event, etc.) due to the student's failure to follow directions.

20. Provide activities designed to teach listening skills.

21. Create an environment that is quiet and uncluttered (e.g., clean, well-lighted, fresh-smelling, and at a comfortable temperature).

22. Talk to the student before beginning an activity and remind him/her of the importance of listening to others.

23. Give the student directions to follow with no more than two or three steps (e.g., Please open your text and turn to page 28.). Directions that involve several steps can be confusing and cause the student to have difficulty following them.

24. Do not criticize when correcting the student; be honest yet supportive. Never cause the student to feel negatively about himself/herself.

25. Deliver information in a variety of ways (e.g., pictures, diagrams, gestures, etc.) to facilitate the student's ability to attend.

26. Do not give directions to the student from across the room. Go to the student, get his/her undivided attention, and explain the directions to him/her.

27. Encourage the student to ask for clarification of any directions, explanations, and instructions before beginning a task to facilitate comprehension.

28. Have the student ask for help when he/she needs it.

29. Help the student develop an awareness of himself/herself and the environment. Instruct the student to periodically step back and ask himself/herself: *Am I listening and paying attention? What should I be doing now?*

30. Help the student develop an awareness of the consequences of his/her behavior by writing down or talking through problems which may occur due to his/her inability to listen for sustained periods of time (e.g., not focusing on directions may cause misunderstanding of an assignment which could lead to a lower grade and losing a place on the soccer team).

31. Encourage the student to recite a mantra to himself/herself when entering a situation where he/she will receive directions/instructions (e.g., listen carefully, listen carefully, listen carefully).

32. Establish rules for listening (e.g., listen to directions, ask questions about directions if they are not understood, follow the directions, etc.). These rules should be consistent and followed by everyone in the class. Talk about the rules often.

33. Teach the student listening skills:
- Stop working.
- Clear desk of nonessential materials.
- Attend to the source of information.
- Write down important points.
- Ask for clarification.
- Wait until all directions are received before beginning.

34. Evaluate the difficulty level of information to which the student is expected to listen (e.g., information communicated on the student's ability level).

35. Give directions in a variety of ways to facilitate the student's ability to attend.

36. Allow the student to occasionally take assignments home when the school setting is overly distracting.

37. Choose a peer, paraprofessional, etc., to cue the student when he/she is not listening (e.g., the person can touch the student's arm as a signal that he/she is not focused on the speaker).

38. Evaluate the visual and auditory stimuli in the classroom. Remove or reduce the extraneous environmental stimuli.

39. Have a peer provide the information the student does not hear.

40. Have the student participate in practice activities designed to develop his/her listening skills (e.g., following one-, two-, or three-step directions; listening for the main point; etc.).

41. Choose a peer to model good listening skills for the student.

42. Have the student practice group listening skills (e.g., Everyone take out a piece of paper, write your name on the paper, and number your paper from 1 to 20.).

43. Make sure that your comments take the form of constructive criticism rather than perceived as personal, threatening, etc., (e.g., instead of telling the student he/she always makes the same mistake, suggest another way to avoid making the mistake).

44. Have the student practice listening to what other students are saying (e.g., following simple instructions, sharing information, etc.).

45. Ask the student to repeat parts of a conversation as the discussion is taking place.

46. Have the student question any directions, explanations, and instructions he/she does not understand.

47. Provide the student with public announcements, directions, and instructions in written form while presenting them verbally.

48. Have the student rehearse in his/her head information just heard to help him/her remember the important facts.

49. Have the student take notes when directions are being given following *What, How, Materials*, and *When* format.

50. Have the student's hearing checked if it has not been recently checked.

51. Have the student repeat directions, explanations, and instructions after they have been given to facilitate retention.

52. Identify the student's most effective learning mode. Use it consistently to facilitate the student's understanding (e.g., if the student does not understand directions or information given verbally, present it in written form).

53. Instruct the student to maintain attention to the source of information by maintaining eye contact, keeping hands free from other materials, and reducing other distractions.

54. Interact frequently with the student. Make sure that eye contact is being made to ensure that the student is attending.

55. Let the student know that directions will only be given once and that he/she will not be reminded to follow the directions.

56. Maintain visibility to and from the student at all times to ensure he/she is attending.

57. Write a contract with the student specifying what behavior is expected (e.g., listening to directions, explanations, and instructions) and what reinforcement will be made available when the terms of the contract have been met.

58. Make sure the student is attending (e.g., making eye contact, hands free of writing materials, etc.) before delivering directions, explanations, and instructions.

59. Make sure the student understands that if he/she does not listen to and follow directions when working in a group, participating in activities, etc., others may not want to work with him/her.

60. Gain the student's attention before giving him/her directions. Have the student make eye contact and repeat the information to check for understanding.

61. Play games designed to teach listening skills (e.g., *Simon Says, Red Light-Green Light, Mother May I?*, etc.).

62. Have the student carry a notepad with him/her at all times and write information down he/she needs to remember.

63. Have the student participate in practice activities designed to develop his/her listening skills (e.g., following one-, two-, or three-step directions; listening for the main point; etc.).

64. Present directions following the outline of *What, How, Materials*, and *When*.

65. Present one concept at a time. Make sure the student understands each concept before presenting the next.

66. Provide directions on a one-to-one basis.

67. Speak to the student when he/she does not listen to explain (a) what he/she is doing wrong (e.g., not listening to directions, explanations, and instructions) and (b) what he/she should be doing (e.g., listening to directions, explanations, and instructions) and why.

68. Have the student practice listening skills by taking notes when directions, explanations, and instructions are presented.

69. Reduce visual and auditory stimuli in and around the classroom which interfere with the student's ability to listen successfully (e.g., close the classroom door and windows, draw the shades, etc.).

70. Present directions, explanations, and instructions as simply and clearly as possible (e.g., Get your book, turn to page 29, do problems 1 through 5.).

71. Provide the student with public announcements, directions, and instructions in written form.

72. Reduce distracting stimuli in the immediate environment (e.g., place the student on or near the front row, provide the student with a carrel or office space away from distractions, etc.). This is used as a form of reducing distracting stimuli and not as a form of punishment.

73. Reinforce the student for listening: (a) give the student a tangible reward (e.g., classroom privileges, five minutes free time, etc.) or (b) give the student an intangible reward (e.g., praise, fist bump, smile, etc.).

74. Reinforce those students in the classroom who listen to directions, explanations, and instructions.

75. Teach information-gathering skills (e.g., listen carefully, write down important points, ask for clarification, wait until all information is presented before beginning a task, etc.).

76. Rephrase directions, explanations, and instructions to facilitate the student's understanding of what is being presented.

77. Reward the student for listening. Possible rewards include verbal praise (e.g., You did a great job listening to every step of the directions! You were able to tell me five details.).

78. Schedule important activities/assignments/lectures at times when the student is most likely to maintain attention (e.g., one hour after medication, 45 minutes after lunch, first thing in the morning, etc.).

79. Teach the student direction-following skills (e.g., stop doing other things, listen carefully, write down important points, wait until all directions are given, question any directions not understood, etc.).

80. Present concepts following the outline of *Who, What, Where, When, How,* and *Why.*

81. Stand directly in front of the student when delivering directions, explanations, and instructions.

82. Stop at various points when delivering directions, announcements, etc., to ensure that the student is attending.

83. Teach and have the student practice how to listen for key information when he/she is being given directions or receiving information (e.g., write down main points, ideas, step-by-step instructions, etc.).

84. Evaluate the difficulty level of information presented to the student to determine if the information is at a level the student can understand.

85. Remove the student from the situation when he/she has difficulty listening and following directions in the presence of others (e.g., at an assembly, when a guest speaker is present, etc.) until he/she can demonstrate self-control and follow directions.

86. Use multiple modalities (e.g., auditory, visual, tactile, etc.) when presenting directions, explanations, and instructional content. Utilize the modality which is stronger for the student.

87. When concepts are presented, have the student listen and takes notes for *Who, What, Where, When, How*, and *Why.*

88. Teach the student when to ask questions, how to ask questions, and what types of questions obtain what types of information.

89. Deliver directions, explanations, and information using vocabulary that is within the student's level of comprehension.

90. Have the student repeat or paraphrase information presented to determine if the student correctly heard what was said.

91. Seat the student close to the source of directions, explanations, and instructions to facilitate his/her ability to maintain attention.

92. Use pictures, diagrams, wall-mounted board, and gestures when presenting information.

133 Needs oral questions and directions frequently repeated

Goals:

1. The student will attend more successfully to specific sounds in the environment.
2. The student will follow directions without requiring repetition, explanations, etc.
3. The student will improve listening skills in academic settings.
4. The student will improve listening skills in nonacademic settings.

Objectives:

1. The student will independently respond appropriately to what is said to him/her with _____% accuracy.
2. The student will listen quietly when verbal directions are given _____% of the time.
3. The student will maintain eye contact when information is being communicated _____% of the time.
4. The student will repeat what is said to him/her with _____% accuracy.
5. The student will respond appropriately to what is said, with prompting, with _____% accuracy.

Interventions:

1. Have the student's hearing checked if it has not been recently checked.

2. Have the student carry a notepad with him/her at all times and write information down he/she needs to remember.

3. Assess the level of task difficulty to determine if the student will require additional information, time, assistance, etc., before assigning a task.

4. Deliver verbal questions and directions that involve only one concept or step. As the student demonstrates success, gradually increase the number of concepts or steps.

5. Call the student by name to gain his/her attention prior to delivering verbal questions and directions.

6. Communicate with parents (e.g., notes home, phone calls, etc.) to share information about the student's progress. The parents may reinforce the student at home for responding to verbal questions and directions without requiring repetition at school.

7. Demonstrate directions, explanations, and instructions as they are presented verbally (e.g., use the wall-mounted board to work a problem for the student, begin playing a game with the student, etc.).

8. Demonstrate the appropriate way to listen to verbal questions and directions (e.g., look at the person who is talking, ask questions, etc.).

9. Deliver information to the student on a one-to-one basis or use a peer tutor.

10. Deliver directions and requests in a supportive rather than a threatening manner (e.g., ask the student to please repeat the directions rather than demanding to tell what was just said).

11. Deliver directions, explanations, and information using vocabulary that is within the student's level of comprehension.

12. Deliver verbal directions prior to handing out materials.

13. Avoid placing the student in situations that require listening for an extended period of time, such as lectures, seminars, etc. Provide the information for the student through an audio recording or lecture notes.

14. Deliver questions and directions in written form.

15. Consider the student's ability level when expecting him/her to respond to verbal questions and directions.

16. Determine if the student correctly heard what was said by having him/her repeat it.

17. Discuss with the student the consequences of his/her behavior (e.g., if you begin a work assignment before all directions are understood, you may do things incorrectly).

18. Do not accept forgetting to listen as an excuse. Make the student accountable for missed information.

19. Encourage the student's parents to take advantage of dinner and other family-gathering times to talk with each other and practice maintaining attention.

20. Do not punish the student for asking questions.

21. Write down important information for the student (e.g., the assembly begins today at 1:40, math test tomorrow, early dismissal on Friday, etc.).

22. Do not talk to the student from across the classroom. Go to the student, get his/her undivided attention, and then speak to him/her.

23. Encourage teachers, coaches, paraprofessionals, school officials, etc., to give the student written directions along with verbal directions.

24. Encourage the student to ask for clarification of any directions, explanations, and instructions before beginning a task to facilitate comprehension.

25. Encourage the student to avoid ingesting any substance (e.g., drugs, alcohol, cold remedies, etc.) that might further alter his/her ability to direct or maintain attention.

26. Provide audio-recorded information from lectures and seminars. Develop questions from these recordings for the student.

27. Encourage the student to develop a 30 second definition of his/her goal to help him/her stay on task and focus (e.g., I will listen carefully. The better I listen the better I will perform.).

28. Give a signal to gain attention prior to delivering directions verbally to the student.

29. Help the student develop an awareness of the consequences of his/her behavior by writing down or talking through problems which may occur due to his/her need to have verbal directions and questions frequently repeated (e.g., not focusing on directions may cause misunderstanding of an assignment which could lead to a lower grade and losing a place on the soccer team).

30. Choose a peer to model good communication skills for the student.

31. Encourage the student to recite a mantra to himself/herself when entering a situation where he/she will receive directions/instructions (e.g., listen carefully, listen carefully, listen carefully).

32. Do not criticize when correcting the student; be honest yet supportive. Never cause the student to feel negatively about himself/herself.

33. Establish classroom rules:
- Concentrate while working.
- Work quietly.
- Remain in your seat.
- Finish task.
- Meet task expectations.

Review rules often. Reinforce students for following the rules.

34. Establish rules for listening (e.g., listen to directions, ask questions about directions if they are not understood, follow the directions, etc.). These rules should be consistent and followed by everyone in the classroom. Talk about the rules often.

35. Evaluate the appropriateness of requiring the student to respond to verbal questions and directions without needing repetition.

36. Evaluate the visual and auditory stimuli in the classroom. Remove or reduce the extraneous environmental stimuli.

37. Give the student one task to perform at a time. Introduce the next task after the student has followed directions and successfully completed the previous task.

38. Give directions in a very simple, direct manner.

39. Give the student directions to follow with no more than two or three steps (e.g., Please open your text and turn to page 28.). Directions that involve several steps can be confusing and cause the student to have difficulty following them.

40. Have the student practice listening skills by taking notes when directions, explanations, and instructions are presented.

41. Instruct the student to ask for clarification if he/she does not understand verbal or written directions.

42. Stand close to or directly in front of the student when delivering verbal questions and directions.

43. Encourage the student to maintain written reminders of task sequences.

44. Have the student ask for help when he/she needs it.

45. Teach the student listening skills:
- Stop working.
- Clear desk of nonessential materials.
- Attend to the source of information.
- Write down important points.
- Ask for clarification.
- Wait until all directions are received before beginning.

46. Have the student repeat or paraphrase the directions to the teacher.

47. Have the student practice group listening skills (e.g., Everyone take out a piece of paper, write your name on the paper, and number your paper from 1 to 20.).

48. Seat the student close to the source of information to facilitate his/her ability to maintain attention.

49. Have the student question any directions, explanations, and instructions he/she does not understand.

50. Have the student take notes relative to verbal questions and directions.

51. Help the student develop an awareness of himself/herself and the environment. Instruct the student to periodically step back and ask himself/herself: *Am I listening and paying attention? What is the question?*

52. Choose a peer to help the student follow verbal questions and directions.

53. Have the student take notes when directions are being given following *What, How, Materials*, and *When* format.

54. Choose a peer to model responding to verbal questions and directions without requiring repetition for the student.

55. Instruct the student to ask people to repeat the parts of a conversation he/she was unable to follow.

56. Instruct the student to maintain attention to the source of information by maintaining eye contact, keeping hands free from other materials, and reducing other distractions.

57. Have the student do those things that need to be done when it is discussed instead of later (e.g., organize needed materials for an assignment to be completed later).

58. Interact frequently with the student to help the student follow directions for an activity.

59. Maintain a consistent manner in which verbal questions and directions are delivered.

60. Maintain mobility to provide assistance to the student.

61. Deliver all directions, questions, explanations, and instructions in a clear, concise manner and at an appropriate rate for the student.

62. Maintain visibility to and from the student to keep his/her attention when verbal questions/ directions are being delivered. The teacher should be able to see the student and the student should be able to see the teacher. Make eye contact possible at all times.

63. Make sure that eye contact is being made between you and the student when delivering verbal questions and directions.

64. Provide questions and directions in written form.

65. Provide opportunities for the student to talk to others on a one-to-one basis. As the student becomes more successful at listening and maintaining attention, gradually include more people in conversations.

66. Make sure that your comments take the form of constructive criticism rather than perceived as personal, threatening, etc., (e.g., instead of telling the student he/she always makes the same mistake, suggest another way to avoid making the mistake).

67. Reduce the number of auditory distractions around the student (e.g., seat the student away from doors, windows, pencil sharpener; move the student to a quiet area, etc.).

68. Make sure the student is attending when you deliver verbal questions and directions (e.g., making eye contact, hands free of writing materials, looking at assignment, etc.).

69. Choose a peer, paraprofessional, etc., to cue the student when he/she needs to maintain attention (e.g., the person can touch the student on the arm when it is time to listen).

70. Gain the student's attention before telling him/her to do something. Have the student make eye contact and repeat the information to check for understanding.

71. Have the student's hearing checked if it has not been recently checked.

72. Present concepts following the outline of *Who, What, Where, When, How*, and *Why*.

73. Present verbal questions and directions in a variety of ways to facilitate the student's understanding (e.g., if the student does not understand verbal directions, present them in written form).

74. Provide information visually (e.g., written directions, instructions, etc.) to support the information the student receives auditorily.

75. Make sure that the expectations required of the student are appropriate for his/her level of development and ability.

76. Establish assignment rules (e.g., listen to directions, wait until all verbal directions have been given, ask questions about anything not understood, make sure you have all of the necessary materials, and begin the assignment when you are sure about what you are supposed to do, etc.).

77. Provide practice in listening for key information when directions are being given or information is being received (e.g., write down main points, ideas, step-by-step instructions, etc.).

78. Have the student repeat directions, explanations, and instructions after they have been given to facilitate retention.

79. Choose a peer to deliver and/or repeat verbal questions and directions.

80. Provide information visually (e.g., written directions, instructions, etc.) to support the information the student receives auditorily.

81. Reduce distracting stimuli (e.g., place the student on or near the front row, provide a carrel or office space away from distractions, etc.). This is used as a form of reducing distracting stimuli and not as a form of punishment.

82. Tell the student what to listen for when being given directions, receiving information, etc.

83. Make it pleasant and positive for the student to ask questions about things not understood. Reinforce the student by assisting, congratulating, praising, etc.

84. Reduce distractions to facilitate the student's ability to listen and follow directions.

85. Make instructions meaningful to the student by relating instructions to past experiences.

86. Reinforce the student for responding to verbal questions and directions without requiring frequent repetition: (a) give the student a tangible reward (e.g., classroom privileges, line leading, passing out materials, five minutes free time, etc.) or (b) give the student an intangible reward (e.g., praise, fist bump, smile, etc.).

87. Reinforce those students in the classroom who respond to verbal questions and directions without requiring repetition.

88. Write down verbal directions. Instruct the student to mark each step off as it is completed.

89. Reward other students for listening, following directions, and answering verbal questions.

90. Provide directions/instructions that will accommodate different learning styles (e.g., visual, auditory, etc.).

91. Make a written list of procedures the student is to follow (e.g., how to label papers, format for mathematic assignments, etc.).

92. Reward the student (e.g., take a break, visit briefly with a peer, etc.) for maintaining eye contact and listening for a specific length of time.

93. Schedule important activities/assignments/ lectures at times when the student is most likely to maintain attention (e.g., one hour after medication, 45 minutes after lunch, first thing in the morning, etc.).

94. Audio record the assignments and allow the student to replay directions/instructions as often as necessary.

95. Use pictures, diagrams, wall-mounted board, and gestures when presenting information.

96. Speak to the student to explain (a) what he/she is doing wrong (e.g., needing verbal questions and directions repeated) and (b) what he/she should be doing (e.g., responding to verbal questions and directions without requiring repetition).

97. Teach and practice active listening skills. Instruct the student to listen to what another person is saying and respond based on information received.

98. Teach and practice effective communication skills. These skills include: listening, maintaining eye contact, and positive body language.

99. Tell the student that verbal questions and directions will be given only once.

100. Provide directions/instructions on a one-to-one basis before assigning a task.

101. Reinforce the student for responding to verbal questions and directions without requiring repetition based on the number of times the student can be successful. As the student demonstrates success, gradually increase the number of times required for reinforcement.

102. Teach the student direction-following skills (e.g., listen carefully, write down steps, etc.).

103. Stop at various points during the presentation of directions, explanations, or instructions to check the student's comprehension of the information presented.

104. Use a timer to help the student monitor how much time he/she has to follow through with directions.

105. Have the student listen and takes notes for *Who, What, Where, When, How,* and *Why* while concepts are presented.

106. Write a contract with the student specifying what behavior is expected (e.g., following directions with one cue) and what reinforcement will be made available when the terms of the contract have been met.

Goals:

1. The student will attend more successfully to specific sounds in the environment.
2. The student will improve his/her awareness and attention to information and activities in the environment.
3. The student will improve listening skills in academic settings.
4. The student will improve listening skills in nonacademic settings.

Objectives:

1. The student will be able to repeat what is said to him/her with _____% accuracy.
2. The student will independently respond appropriately to what is said to him/her with _____% accuracy.
3. The student will listen quietly, when verbal directions are given, _____% of the time.
4. The student will maintain eye contact, when information is being communicated, _____% of the time.
5. The student will respond appropriately to what is said, with prompting, with _____% accuracy.
6. The student will respond appropriately to what is said, with prompting, _____% of the time.

Interventions:

1. Make sure that the student is seated close enough to make eye contact with and hear the teacher when information is being delivered.

2. Encourage the student to ask for clarification of any directions, explanations, and instructions before beginning a task to facilitate comprehension.

3. Avoid placing the student in situations that require listening for an extended period of time, such as lectures, seminars, assemblies, etc. Provide the information for the student through an audio recording or lecture notes.

4. Encourage the parents to take advantage of dinner and other family-gathering times to talk with each other and practice maintaining eye contact.

5. Deliver information in a clear, concise manner.

6. Make sure information is delivered loudly enough to be heard by the student.

7. Deliver information to the student on a one-to-one basis. As the student demonstrates the ability to listen successfully, gradually include more students in the group with him/her.

8. Determine which stimuli in the environment interfere with the student's ability to listen successfully. Reduce or remove those stimuli from the environment.

9. Teach the student listening skills:
- Stop working.
- Clear desk of nonessential materials.
- Attend to the source of information.
- Write down important points.
- Ask for clarification.
- Wait until all directions are received before beginning.

10. Encourage the student to ask people to repeat parts of a conversation he/she was unable to follow.

11. Deliver a predetermined signal (e.g., hand signal, turn lights off and on, etc.) to the student prior to delivering information.

12. Make sure the student is not engaged in activities that interfere with directions, explanations, and instructions (e.g., looking at other materials, putting away materials, talking to others, etc.).

13. Choose a peer to model good attending skills for the student.

14. Call the student by name to gain his/her attention prior to delivering information.

15. Reinforce the student for listening based on the length of time the student can be successful. As the student demonstrates success, gradually increase the length of time required for reinforcement.

16. Encourage the student to recite a mantra to himself/herself when entering a situation where he/she will receive directions/instructions (e.g., maintain eye contact, maintain eye contact, maintain eye contact).

17. Choose different people (e.g., peer, paraprofessional, counselor, friend, etc.) to help the student maintain eye contact.

18. Evaluate the difficulty level of information presented to the student. Determine if the information is presented at a level the student can understand.

19. Deliver information in both verbal and written form.

20. Choose a peer, paraprofessional, friend, etc., to cue the student when he/she needs to maintain eye contact (e.g., the person can touch the student on the arm when it is time to attend to a speaker).

21. Reinforce the student for listening based on the length of time the student can be successful. As the student demonstrates success, gradually increase the length of time required for reinforcement.

22. Have the student repeat directions, explanations, and instructions after they have been given to facilitate retention.

23. Have the student take notes when directions are being given following *What, How, Materials,* and *When* format.

24. Have the student take notes when information is verbally presented.

25. Have the student listen and takes notes for *Who, What, Where, When, How,* and *Why* while concepts are presented.

26. Have the student's hearing checked if it has not been recently checked.

27. Present directions following the outline of *What, How, Materials,* and *When.*

28. Instruct the student to maintain attention to the source of information by maintaining eye contact, keeping hands free from other materials, and reducing other distractions.

29. Maintain a consistent format in which information is verbally presented.

30. Maintain visibility to and from the student at all times to ensure that the student is attending.

31. Allow natural consequences to occur as a result of the student not listening (e.g., responding incorrectly, receiving a failing grade, etc.).

32. Evaluate the visual and auditory stimuli in the classroom. Remove or reduce the extraneous environmental stimuli.

33. Make the subject matter meaningful to the student (e.g., explain the purpose of an assignment, relate the subject matter to the student's environment, etc.).

34. Move objects used for tactile stimulation (e.g., pens, paper clips, loose change, etc.) away from the student's reach.

35. Have the student question any directions, explanations, and instructions he/she does not understand.

36. Help the student develop an awareness of himself/herself and the environment. Instruct the student to periodically step back and ask himself/herself: *Am I maintaining eye contact? What should I be doing now?*

37. Schedule important activities/assignments/ lectures at times when the student is most likely to maintain attention (e.g., one hour after medication, 45 minutes after lunch, first thing in the morning, etc.). Tell the student what to listen for when being given directions or receiving information, etc.

38. Present concepts following the outline of *Who, What, Where, When, How,* and *Why.*

39. Provide opportunities for the student to talk to others on a one-to-one basis. As the student becomes more successful at maintaining attention and eye contact, gradually include more people in conversations.

40. Reduce visual and auditory stimuli in and around the classroom which interfere with the student's ability to listen successfully (e.g., close the classroom door and windows, draw the shades, etc.).

41. Stop at various points during the presentation of information to check the student's comprehension.

42. Reinforce the student for attending to the source of information. Continuous eye contact is not necessary for reinforcement.

43. Teach and practice information-gathering skills (e.g., listen carefully, write down important points, ask for clarification, wait until all information is presented before beginning a task, etc.).

44. Reinforce the student for maintaining eye contact: (a) give the student a tangible reward (e.g., classroom privileges, five minutes free time, etc.) or (b) give the student an intangible reward (e.g., praise, fist bump, smile, etc.).

45. Provide directions on a one-to-one basis before assigning a task.

46. Teach and practice effective communication skills. These skills include: listening, maintaining eye contact, and positive body language.

47. Use multiple modalities (e.g., auditory, visual, tactile, etc.) when presenting directions, explanations, and instructional content. Utilize the modality which is stronger for the student.

48. Reinforce those students in the classroom who focus visual attention on the speaker.

49. Remove distracting stimuli in the student's immediate environment (e.g., books, writing materials, personal property, etc.).

50. Ask the student to repeat or paraphrase information heard to determine successful listening.

51. Seat the student close to the source of information in the classroom. As the student demonstrates success, gradually move him/her farther away from the source of information.

52. Speak to the student to explain (a) what he/she is doing wrong (e.g., not listening to directions, explanations, and instructions) and (b) what he/she should be doing (e.g., listening to directions, explanations, and instructions).

53. Teach and practice active listening skills. Instruct the student to listen to what another person is saying and respond based on information received.

54. Reinforce the student for listening: (a) give the student a tangible reward (e.g., classroom privileges, line leading, passing out materials, five minutes free time, etc.) or (b) give the student an intangible reward (e.g., praise, fist bump, smile, etc.).

55. Tell the student what to listen for when being given directions, receiving information, etc.

56. Verbally present information that is necessary for the student to know to perform a task successfully.

57. Maintain eye contact when delivering information to the student. As the student demonstrates the ability to listen successfully, gradually decrease the amount of eye contact.

58. Write a contract with the student specifying what behavior is expected (e.g., listening to directions, maintaining eye contact) and what reinforcement will be made available when the terms of the contract have been met.

59. Stop at various points during the presentation of information to ensure the student is attending and maintaining eye contact.

60. Help the student develop an awareness of the consequences of his/her behavior by writing down or talking through problems which may occur due to his/her inability to maintain attention (e.g., not focusing on directions may cause misunderstanding of an assignment which could lead to a lower grade and losing a place on the soccer team).

135 Omits a sound in a word

Goals:

1. The student will improve his/her articulation skills.
2. The student will improve his/her discrimination of speech sounds.
3. The student will improve his/her production of speech sounds in isolation.
4. The student will improve his/her production of speech sounds in syllables.
5. The student will improve his/her production of speech sounds in words.
6. The student will improve his/her production of speech sounds in sentences.
7. The student will improve his/her production of speech sounds in spontaneous speech.

Objectives:

1. The student will differentiate between correct and incorrect productions of words in _____ out of _____ trials.
2. The student will imitate the target sound in words of one syllable in _____ out of _____ trials.
3. The student will imitate the target sound in the ending position of words with two syllables in _____ out of _____ trials.
4. The student will imitate the target sound in the medial position in words of three syllables in _____ out of _____ trials.
5. The student will spontaneously produce age-appropriate speech sounds in words in _____ out of _____ trials.
6. The student will spontaneously produce age-appropriate speech sounds in sentences in _____ out of _____ trials.
7. The student will spontaneously produce age-appropriate speech sounds in conversational speech in _____ out of _____ trials.

Interventions:

1. Have the student's hearing checked if it has not been recently checked.

2. Evaluate the appropriateness of requiring the student to accurately produce certain sounds (i.e., developmentally, certain sounds may not be produced accurately until the age of 8 or 9).

3. Speak to the student to explain what he/she needs to do differently (e.g., include all the sounds in words instead of omitting sounds in words). The teacher should be careful to use the sound that is being targeted and not the letter name (e.g., /l/ not *el*).

4. Reinforce the student for correct productions of the target sound: (a) give the student a tangible reward (e.g., classroom privileges, line leading, passing out materials, five minutes free time, etc.) or (b) give the student an intangible reward (e.g., praise, fist bump, smile, etc.). Initially, each correct production may need reinforcement. As the student progresses, random reinforcement may be adequate.

5. Be sure that the student can hear the difference between words as they should be pronounced (all sounds included) and the way the words sound when incorrectly produced (sounds omitted).

6. Have the student raise a hand or clap hands when he/she hears the target sound produced during a series of isolated sound productions (e.g., /s/, /sh/, /l/, /m/, /t/, /k/, /z/, /w/, /n/, etc.).

7. Have the student stand up each time he/she hears targeted words produced accurately as contrasted with inaccurate productions (e.g., *play, pay, pay, play, pay,* etc.).

8. Show the student a picture and name it. Have the student show thumbs up each time the target sound is produced accurately and thumbs down if the target sound is produced inaccurately.

9. Using pictures of similar sounding words, say each word and have the student point to the appropriate picture (e.g., pay and play, or key and ski).

10. Have the student tally the number of correct productions of targeted words he/she hears when the teacher or a peer reads a list of words.

11. Audio record a spontaneous monologue given by the student. Listen to the recording with him/her and tally error and/or correct productions. The teacher and the student should compare their analyses of the productions.

12. Have the student read simple passages while audio recording them, listen to the recording, and mark errors and/or correct productions.

13. Have the student read a list of words and rate his/her production after each word.

14. Choose a peer to model correctly producing targeted words for the student.

15. Play a game, such as *Simon Says* in which the student tries to reproduce the targeted words when produced by the teacher or a peer.

16. Use a drawing as a visual aid to show the student how the mouth looks during production of the target sound.

17. Make cards with the target sound and cards with vowels. Have the student combine a target sound card with a vowel card to make a syllable that he/she can produce (e.g., *la, le, lo,* and *al, el, ol*).

18. Play a board game that requires the student to name pictures of the targeted words. The student has to produce the targeted words correctly before he/she can move on the game board. (This activity can be simplified or expanded based on the level of success of the student.)

19. Have the student cut out pictures of items that include the targeted words and display them where they can be practiced each day.

20. Provide the student with a list of the targeted words. Have him/her practice the words daily. As the student masters the word list, add more words. (Using words from the student's everyday vocabulary, reading lists, spelling lists, etc., will facilitate transfer of correct production of the target sound into everyday speech.)

21. Have the student use fun phonics sheets to practice pronouncing his/her target sounds. These are also good for home practice.

22. Have the student keep a notebook of difficult words encountered each day. These can be practiced by the student with teacher or peer assistance.

23. Have the student use a carrier phrase combined with a target word (e.g., I like _____. I see a _____.).

24. Have the student keep a list of all the words he/she can think of which contain sounds he/she has difficulty producing accurately.

25. Have the student make up sentences using targeted words.

26. During oral reading, underline targeted words and reinforce the student for correct productions.

27. Involve parents by asking them to rate their child's speech for a specific length of time (e.g., during dinner count no errors, a few errors, or many errors).

28. Present the student with a list of topics. Have the student select a topic and then give a spontaneous speech for a specific length of time. Count errors and suggest ways for him/her to improve.

136 Inserts an extra sound in a word

Goals:

1. The student will improve his/her articulation skills.
2. The student will improve his/her discrimination of speech sounds.
3. The student will improve his/her production of speech sounds in isolation.
4. The student will improve his/her production of speech sounds in syllables.
5. The student will improve his/her production of speech sounds in words.
6. The student will improve his/her production of speech sounds in sentences.
7. The student will improve his/her production of speech sounds in spontaneous speech.

Objectives:

1. The student will differentiate between correct and incorrect productions of words in _____ out of _____ trials.
2. The student will imitate the target sound in words with one syllable in _____ out of _____ trials.
3. The student will imitate the target sound in the ending position in words with two syllables in _____ out of _____ trials.
4. The student will imitate the target sound in the medial position in words with three syllables in _____ out of _____ trials.
5. The student will spontaneously produce age-appropriate speech sounds in words in _____ out of _____ trials.
6. The student will spontaneously produce age-appropriate speech sounds in sentences in _____ out of _____ trials.
7. The student will spontaneously produce age-appropriate speech sounds in conversational speech in _____ out of _____ trials.

Interventions:

1. Have the student's hearing checked if it has not been recently checked.

2. Evaluate the appropriateness of requiring the student to accurately produce certain sounds (i.e., developmentally, certain sounds may not be produced accurately until the age of 8 or 9).

3. Speak to the student to explain what he/she needs to do differently (e.g., not include extra sounds in words). The teacher should be careful to use the sound that is being targeted and not the letter name (e.g., /s/ not *es*).

4. Be sure that the student can hear the difference between words as they should be pronounced and the way the words sound when incorrectly produced (e.g., sounds added or omitted).

5. Reinforce the student for correct productions of target words: (a) give the student a tangible reward (e.g., classroom privileges, line leading, passing out materials, five minutes free time, etc.) or (b) give the student an intangible reward (e.g., praise, fist bump, smile, etc.). Initially, each correct production may need reinforcement. As the student progresses, random reinforcement may be adequate.

6. Have the student raise a hand or clap hands when he/she hears the target sound produced during a series of isolated sound productions (e.g., /s/, /sh/,/r/, /m/, /r/, /t/, /k/, /r/, /z/, /w/, /n/, /r/, etc.).

7. Use a puppet to produce targeted words correctly and incorrectly. The student earns a sticker for correctly distinguishing a set number of correct/incorrect productions the puppet makes.

8. Have the student stand up each time he/she hears targeted words produced accurately as contrasted with inaccurate productions (e.g., stit, sit, sit, stit, sit, etc.).

9. Show the student a picture and name it. Have the student show thumbs up each time the target sound is produced accurately and thumbs down if the target sound is produced inaccurately.

10. Using pictures of similar sounding words, say each word and have the student point to the appropriate picture (e.g., stick and sick, or ski and key).

11. Have the student tally the number of correct productions of targeted words when the teacher or a peer reads a list of words.

12. Audio record a spontaneous monologue given by the student. Listen to the recording with him/her and tally error and/or correct productions. The teacher and the student should compare their analyses of the productions.

13. Have the student read a list of words and rate his/her production after each word.

14. Have the student read simple passages while audio recording them, listen to the recording, and mark errors and/or correct productions.

15. Choose a peer to model correctly producing targeted words for the student.

16. Play a game, such as *Simon Says* in which the student tries to reproduce the targeted words when produced by the teacher or a peer.

17. Use a drawing as a visual aid to show the student how the mouth looks during production of the target sound.

18. Make cards with the target sound and cards with vowels. Have the student combine a target sound card with a vowel card to make a syllable that he/she can produce (e.g., *ra, re, ro,* and *ar, er, or*).

19. During oral reading, underline targeted words and reinforce the student for correct productions.

20. Play a board game that requires the student to name pictures of the targeted words. The student has to produce the targeted words correctly before he/she can move on the game board. (This activity can be simplified or expanded based on the level of success of the student.)

21. Have the student cut out pictures of items that include the targeted words and display them where they can be practiced each day.

22. Provide the student with a list of the targeted words. Have him/her practice the words daily. As the student masters the word list, add more words. (Using words from the student's everyday vocabulary, reading lists, spelling lists, etc., will facilitate transfer of correct production of the target sound into everyday speech.)

23. Have the student use fun phonics sheets to practice pronouncing his/her target sounds. These are also good for home practice.

24. Have the student keep a notebook of difficult words encountered each day. These can be practiced by the student with teacher or peer assistance.

25. Have the student use a carrier phrase combined with a word containing the target sound (e.g., I like _____. I see a _____.).

26. Have the student make up sentences using targeted words.

27. Have the student keep a list of all the words he/she can think of which contain sounds he/she has difficulty producing accurately.

28. Involve parents by asking them to rate their child's speech for a specific length of time (e.g., during dinner count no errors, a few errors, or many errors).

29. Present the student with a list of topics. Have the student select a topic and then give a spontaneous speech for a specific length of time. Count errors and suggest ways for him/her to improve.

Goals:
1. The student will improve his/her articulation skills.
2. The student will improve his/her discrimination of speech sounds.
3. The student will improve his/her production of speech sounds in isolation.
4. The student will improve his/her production of speech sounds in syllables.
5. The student will improve his/her production of speech sounds in words.
6. The student will improve his/her production of speech sounds in sentences.
7. The student will improve his/her production of speech sounds in spontaneous speech.

Objectives:
1. The student will identify listener behaviors that indicate an unfavorable reaction to his/her message in _____ out of _____ trials.
2. The student will restate an unintelligible statement in _____ out of _____ trials.
3. The student will differentiate between correct and incorrect productions of words in _____ out of _____ trials.
4. The student will spontaneously produce age-appropriate speech sounds in words in _____ out of _____ trials.
5. The student will spontaneously produce age-appropriate speech sounds in sentences in _____ out of _____ sentences.
6. The student will spontaneously produce age-appropriate speech sounds in conversational speech in _____ out of _____ trials.

Interventions:

1. Have the student's hearing checked if it has not been recently checked.

2. Provide the student with an appropriate model for targeted speech sounds.

3. Evaluate the appropriateness of requiring the student to accurately produce certain sounds (e.g., developmentally, certain sounds may not be produced accurately until the age of 8 or 9). This may naturally interfere with daily communication in some instances.

4. Speak to the student to explain what he/she needs to do differently (e.g., accurately produce sounds in words during everyday conversation). The teacher should be careful to use the <u>sound</u> that is being targeted and not the letter name (e.g., /r/ not *ar*).

5. Have the student stand up each time he/she hears targeted words accurately produced in conversation contrasted with inaccurate productions.

6. Reinforce the student for correct sound production during everyday conversation: (a) give the student a tangible reward (e.g., classroom privileges, line leading, passing out materials, five minutes free time, etc.) or (b) give the student an intangible reward (e.g., praise, fist bump, smile, etc.). Initially, each correct production may need reinforcement. As the student progresses, random reinforcement may be adequate.

7. Be sure that the student can hear the difference between target words when the sounds are accurately produced and when the sounds are inaccurately produced during conversational speech.

8. Use a puppet to accurately produce some words during a conversation and inaccurately produce others. The student earns a sticker for correctly distinguishing a set number of correct/incorrect productions.

9. Have the student tally the number of correct productions of targeted words when the teacher or a peer reads a paragraph or story.

10. Have the student read simple passages while audio recording them, listen to the recording, and mark errors and/or correct productions.

11. Audio record a spontaneous monologue given by the student. Listen to the recording with him/her and tally error and/or correct productions. The teacher and the student should compare their analyses of the productions.

12. Have the student read a paragraph or story and rate his/her production after each word.

13. Help the student correctly pronounce a word by slowing down his/her speech. Have him/her repeat each syllable after you and then put the first two syllables together. Add the third syllable (and fourth, etc.) when the previous ones are correct.

14. Use pictures of similar sounding words and have the student name each picture as the teacher points to it (e.g., run and one, or bat and back).

15. Play a board game that requires the student to describe pictures with correct articulation. The student needs to use accurate speech production before he/she can move on the game board. (This activity can be simplified or expanded based on the level of success of the student.)

16. Have the student cut out pictures of items containing the target sound or word. Display them where they can be practiced each day.

17. Provide the student with a word list containing the targeted words. Have him/her practice the words daily. As the student masters the word list, add more words. (Using words from the student's everyday vocabulary, reading lists, spelling lists, etc., will facilitate transfer of correct production of the targeted words into everyday speech.)

18. Have the student keep a notebook of words encountered each day which are difficult for him/her to accurately produce. These can be practiced by the student with teacher or peer assistance.

19. Have the student keep a list of all the words he/she can think of which are difficult for him/her to produce accurately.

20. Have the student use a carrier phrase combined with targeted words (e.g., I like _____. I see a _____.).

21. Have the student make up sentences using targeted words.

22. During oral reading, underline targeted words and reinforce the student for correct productions.

23. Involve parents by asking them to rate their child's speech for a specific length of time (e.g., during dinner count no errors, a few errors, or many errors).

24. Present the student with a list of topics. Have the student select a topic and then give a spontaneous speech for a specific length of time. Count errors and suggest ways for him/her to improve.

25. Teach the student ways to restate or rephrase a misunderstood message rather than continuing to repeat the original message with the same error pattern.

26. Make a short list of words in the student's regular curriculum which contain the target sounds and which he/she can articulate intelligibly. Ask the student questions which will require one or more of these words as an answer.

27. If the student has little or no intelligible speech, provide an augmentative communication board which contains pictures representing daily needs. This can be used to communicate toileting needs, hunger, etc., and can be expanded or changed as appropriate.

138 Demonstrates difficulty with topic initiation, maintenance, and/or closure including irrelevant, tangential, or associative responses; and/or tends to circumlocute - talking around instead of on the topic

Goal:

1. The student will improve his/her conversational skills.

Objectives:

1. The student will choose an appropriate response to use in situations, when given options, in _____ out of _____ trials.
2. The student will explain the parts of the conversational dyad with _____ % accuracy.
3. The student will choose appropriate statements to begin, maintain, or finish a conversation in structured language activities in _____ out of _____ trials.
4. The student will make an appropriate shift from one topic to another in structured language activities in _____ out of _____ trials.
5. The student will utilize appropriate statements to begin, maintain, or finish a conversation during everyday speaking activities in _____ out of _____ trials.
6. The student will make an appropriate shift from one topic to another in everyday speaking activities in _____ out of _____ trials.
7. The student will demonstrate the ability to stay on topic during a five minute conversation in _____ out of _____ trials.

Interventions:

1. Have the student's hearing checked if it has not been recently checked.

2. Reinforce the student for appropriate topic initiation, maintenance, and/or closure: (a) give the student a tangible reward (e.g., classroom privileges, line leading, passing out materials, five minutes free time, etc.) or (b) give the student an intangible reward (e.g., praise, fist bump, smile, etc.). Reinforce other students in the classroom when they demonstrate appropriate topic initiation, maintenance, and/or closure.

3. Model appropriate topic initiation, maintenance, and/or closure.

4. Speak with the student to explain that he/she is not demonstrating appropriate topic initiation, maintenance, and/or closure.

5. Choose a peer to model appropriate topic initiation, maintenance, and closure for the student.

6. Communicate to the student that he/she is a worthwhile individual.

7. Encourage appropriate eye contact in all communicative situations.

8. Teach the student communication skills (e.g., hand raising, expressing needs in written and/or verbal form, etc.).

9. Provide the student with many academic and social successes.

10. Determine an individual(s) in the school environment with whom the student would most want to engage in a conversation (e.g., custodian, librarian, resource teacher, principal, older student, etc.). Allow the student to spend time carrying on a conversation with the individual(s) each day. Make sure these people model appropriate topic initiation, maintenance, and/or closure.

11. Pair the student with an outgoing student who engages in appropriate verbal interactions on a frequent basis.

12. Provide opportunities for appropriate interactions within the classroom (e.g., peers engaged in appropriate interactions).

13. Assess the appropriateness of the social situation in relation to the student's ability to be successful.

14. Have the student show visitors and new students around the school.

15. Be sure to greet or acknowledge the student as often as possible (e.g., in the hallways or cafeteria, welcome to class, acknowledge a job well done, etc.). Encourage him/her to acknowledge you in return.

16. Have the student run errands which will require verbal and/or nonverbal interactions with other students, teachers, administrators, etc.

17. Experiment with various groupings to determine the group in which the student is most comfortable initiating and maintaining conversations with peers and adults.

18. Teach the student social interaction skills (e.g., ways in which to appropriately respond to others when first seeing them or when leaving them, etc.). Be specific about phrases which are appropriate to use and situations in which they would be used.

19. Teach the student conversational phrases (e.g., How are you? How's it going? See you later.) to use when initiating, maintaining or closing a conversation.

20. Teach the student conversational rules (e.g., explain that it is appropriate to greet a person when you're seeing him/her for the first time of the day but not when it's been only five minutes since the last encounter).

21. Teach the student appropriate verbal and nonverbal responses to common everyday situations.

22. Teach the student appropriate body language and explain the effect it can have on communication.

23. Teach the student that he/she should respond differently depending on the person to whom he/she is talking. Discuss how age, position, and/or familiarity can change the form of the greeting/closing used (e.g., What's happening? How are you doing?).

24. Have the student engage in simulated conversational activities with feedback designed to teach conversational skills (e.g., greetings, closings, questions, topics of conversation, topic maintenance, etc.).

25. Help the student develop social awareness (e.g., people may be embarrassed by what you say, feelings can be hurt by comments, tact is the best policy, remember interactions which have made you feel good and treat others in the same manner, etc.).

26. Teach a communication unit to the entire classroom which includes the basic rules of conversation.

27. Use a private signal (e.g., holding up a finger, etc.) to remind the student to use appropriate greetings, closings, and/or to continue speaking on the original topic.

28. Audio record the student. Have him/her listen to the recording to determine instances in which he/she is using inappropriate greetings or closings or switching topics at an inappropriate time.

29. Rephrase the student's words to assist the student in using more appropriate greetings/closings.

30. Rephrase the student's words to assist the student in topic maintenance (e.g., when the student switches topics, the teacher should rephrase his/her statement to redirect the conversation in the appropriate direction).

31. Allow the student to speak without being interrupted or hurried.

32. Prompt the student to help him/her utilize greetings/closings more appropriately (e.g., Teacher: How are you? Student does not respond. Teacher: I'm fine today. How are you?).

33. Pair the student with a peer. Have them take turns being interviewed and interviewing. This may be done with the students being themselves or pretending to be fictitious characters. Emphasize appropriate topic initiation, maintenance, and closure.

34. Point out examples of appropriate language usage (both verbal and nonverbal) involving topic initiation, maintenance, and/or closure which occur during the day.

35. Provide the student with a discarded phone to practice topic initiation, maintenance, and/or closure.

36. Provide opportunities for the student to play games which require taking turns with other students. The turn-taking skills developed in games are very important to conversation.

37. Have the student practice writing down messages to different persons in the school setting (e.g., librarian, school counselor, principal, etc.) and later delivering the messages.

38. Have the student practice saying what you or another student has said. Teach the student to imitate inflectional patterns and facial expressions as well as to repeat the words. Video record this activity and have the student analyze his/her success at this activity.

39. Teach the student to be aware of listener response to determine if the meaning of his/her greeting/closing has been received accurately or if the intended topic of conversation is being appropriately maintained.

40. Set up fictitious situations in the classroom (e.g., restaurant, gas station, grocery store, etc.) and have the students role-play working in each situation. Have them change roles often and emphasize appropriate topic initiation, maintenance, and closure.

41. Teach a unit centered around finding examples of language which would be appropriate for topic initiation, maintenance, and/or closure.

42. Have a sharing time at school. Encourage the student to talk about anything of interest to him/her while emphasizing appropriate topic initiation, maintenance, and closure.

43. Have the student work with a peer who is younger (e.g., choose a peer who is nonthreatening).

44. When the student has difficulty during a conversation, remind him/her that this occasionally happens to everyone and he/she should not become upset.

45. Reduce the emphasis on competition. Competitive activities may cause the student to hurry and not initiate, maintain, or close a topic appropriately.

46. Have the student practice descriptive statements or thoughts he/she can use when speaking.

47. Pair the student with a peer. Have them take turns asking questions which are conversation starters (e.g., What grade are you in? Do you have any brothers or sisters? Do you have any pets?). Have the student make a list of conversational starters he/she would feel comfortable using.

Goal:

1. The student will improve his/her sequencing skills.

Objectives:

1. The student will correctly answer questions involving time, degree, size, value, etc., in _____ out of _____ trials.
2. The student will correctly sequence pictures by time, degree, size, value, etc., in _____ out of _____ trials.
3. The student will correctly sequence verbal/written information by time, degree, size, value, etc., in _____ out of _____ trials.
4. The student will utilize appropriate sequential vocabulary during structured language activities in _____ out of _____ trials.
5. The student will utilize appropriate sequential vocabulary during everyday situations in _____ out of _____ trials.
6. The student will demonstrate the ability to sequence by describing classroom events in correct order at the close of the school day with _____% accuracy.
7. The student will demonstrate the ability to sequence by retelling the plot of a movie, television program, or book in correct order with _____% accuracy.
8. The student will demonstrate the ability to sequence by planning a logical series of steps which will result in a successful class field trip with _____% accuracy.

Interventions:

1. Have the student's hearing checked if it has not been recently checked.

2. Evaluate the appropriateness of the task to determine (a) if the task is too easy, (b) if the task is too difficult, or (c) if the length of time scheduled to complete the task is adequate.

3. Explain the importance of relating information in the correct order.

4. Discuss with the student the behavior that is expected (e.g., relating information in the correct order).

5. Reinforce the student for relating information in the correct order: (a) give the student a tangible reward (e.g., classroom privileges, line leading, passing out materials, five minutes free time, etc.) or (b) give the student an intangible reward (e.g., praise, fist bump, smile, etc.).

6. Informally assess the student's auditory and visual short-term memory skills to determine which is stronger. Use his/her stronger skills to facilitate retention of sequential information.

7. Draw the student's attention to key aspects of auditory communications as they occur to facilitate his/her ability to sequence the information accurately (e.g., repeat important points, tell the student which information is particularly important, etc.).

8. Teach the student to visualize information as if it were a movie, then play it back mentally when he/she needs to verbalize it.

9. Have the student carry out directions as soon as they are given to minimize the effect of irrelevant and distracting information on his/her ability to follow the instructions in the appropriate sequence.

10. Teach the student how to organize information into smaller units or segments (e.g., divide the number sequence 132563 into units of 13, 25, 63; and point out that phone numbers are learned as 573, then 581, then 0000).

11. Decrease the steps and/or stages involved in a sequence until the student meets with success. As the student demonstrates success, gradually increase the steps/stages.

12. Give the student one task to complete at a time. Introduce the next task when the student has successfully completed the previous task.

13. Have the student question any directions, explanations, and instructions he/she does not understand.

14. Reinforce those students in the classroom who demonstrate appropriate sequencing skills when speaking and/or following directions.

15. Choose a peer to model accurate sequencing of skills for the student. Have the peer assist the student in sequencing information to be presented verbally.

16. Review the morning and afternoon activities schedule with the student and have him/her repeat the sequence. As the student demonstrates success, gradually increase the length of the sequence.

17. Have the student practice following directions by engaging in sequential activities which are purposeful to him/her (e.g., operating equipment, following recipes, opening a combination lock, etc.).

18. At the end of the school day, have the student recall three activities in which he/she was engaged during the day in the correct order. As the student demonstrates success, gradually increase the number of activities the student is expected to recall.

19. Have the student sequence the activities which occurred on a field trip or special event.

20. Use the calendar every day to discuss with the student what he/she did yesterday, is doing today, or will do tomorrow.

21. Provide the student with environmental cues and prompts to facilitate his/her success in the classroom (e.g., posted rules, schedule of daily events, steps for completing tasks, etc.).

22. Teach the student to make reminders for himself/herself (e.g., notes, lists, etc.).

23. Provide the student with written lists of things to do, materials he/she will need, etc.

24. Have the student practice making notes for specific information and directions he/she wants and/or needs to remember. Encourage him/her to use these notes as a checklist to make sure that he/she has completed all the steps.

25. Teach the student information-gathering skills (e.g., listen carefully, write down important points, ask for clarification, wait until all information is received before beginning, etc.).

26. Teach the student to use associative cues or mnemonic strategies to remember sequences.

27. Have the student practice repetition of information to facilitate short-term memory skills (e.g., repeating names, phone numbers, dates of events, etc.).

28. Have the student repeat/paraphrase directions, explanations, and instructions after receiving them.

29. Maintain a consistent sequence of activities to facilitate the likelihood of student success (e.g., the student has math every day at one o'clock, recess at two o'clock, etc.).

30. Have the student keep a daily journal of activities to help him/her remember sequences.

31. Teach the student to use resources to remember sequences (e.g., calendar, dictionary, etc.).

32. Have the student maintain a notebook in which he/she keeps notes regarding necessary sequential information (e.g., lists of things to do, schedule of events, days of the week, months of the year, etc.).

33. Provide the student with frequent opportunities to recite sequences throughout the day to facilitate memory skills.

34. Assign activities to the student which require the use of sequences to facilitate his/her ability to remember and verbalize sequences.

35. Practice sequential memory activities each day for those sequences which the student needs to memorize (e.g., important phone numbers, addresses, etc.).

36. Present the student with a series of scrambled sentences and have him/her sequence them appropriately.

37. Teach the student to identify the main idea of a story and causal relationships within the story to facilitate recall of information in the correct sequence.

38. Use a flannel board and felt pieces to practice sequencing a familiar story or a familiar action.

39. Have the student observe peers playing a board game. Explain the rules of the game focusing on a start to finish sequence.

40. As the student sequentially describes how to do something, act out his/her instructions (using props at first). Perform only those parts of the task he/she specifically verbalizes to emphasize the importance of detail and sequence (e.g., if the student does not accurately give all the steps to make a peanut butter and jelly sandwich, the sandwich may not be edible.) Encourage the student to sequence the activity without the visual aids once he/she has demonstrated proficiency in sequencing the information with the visual prompts.

41. Have the student teach a peer how to complete a task (instruct the peer to perform only those directions which are specifically verbalized).

42. Have the student work with peers to write a skit and act it out to facilitate retention of sequential information from a story, historical event, etc.

43. Have the student retell his/her favorite TV show, movie, etc., in sequence.

44. Have the student separate objects from large to small, light to heavy, etc.

45. Use rhythm, music, etc., to teach automatic series (e.g., alphabet, days of the week, months of the year, etc.).

46. Teach the student to use sequencing words (e.g., first, second, third, next, then/now, before/after, soon/later, etc.).

47. Have the student identify sequential activities in art, music, P.E., etc.

48. Have the student act out routines in his/her day as he/she relates the information verbally (e.g., steps in feeding his/her pet, daily routine before coming to school, etc.).

49. Give the student the beginning of a story and have him/her complete the story with an emphasis on a logical sequence and conclusion.

50. Plan an imaginary trip to a different part of the world or a different time in history. Have the student sequence the necessary preparations.

51. Have the student be the class reporter and present the news of the preceding day according to the sequence of events.

52. As the class is involved in an activity, take a series of pictures. Have the student accurately sequence the pictures and verbalize the events in the correct order.

140 Distorts or mispronounces words or sounds when speaking (not attributed to dialect or accent)

Goals:

1. The student will improve his/her production of speech sounds.
2. The student will improve his/her conversational speech.
3. The student will improve the fluency of his/her speech.
4. The student will improve the ability to express himself/herself verbally.
5. The student will improve his/her grammatical speech.

Objectives:

1. The student will recognize words or sounds heard with _____% accuracy.
2. The student will pronounce words or sounds made in isolation with _____% accuracy.
3. The student will pronounce words or sounds when speaking with _____% accuracy.

Interventions:

1. Have the student's hearing checked if it has not been recently checked.

2. Be sure that the student can hear the difference between words as they should be pronounced and the way the words sound when incorrectly produced (sounds distorted).

3. Have the student raise a hand or clap hands when he/she hears the target sound produced during a series of isolated sound productions (e.g., /s/, /sh/,/r/, /m/, /r/, /t/, /k/, /r/, /z/, /w/, /n/, /r/, etc.).

4. Use a puppet to produce targeted words correctly and incorrectly. The student earns a sticker for correctly distinguishing a set number of correct/incorrect productions the puppet makes.

5. Have the student stand up each time he/she hears targeted words produced accurately as contrasted with inaccurate productions (e.g., *shoup, soup, soup, shoup, soup,* etc.).

6. Show the student a picture and name it. Have the student show thumbs up each time the target sound is produced accurately and thumbs down if the target sound is produced inaccurately.

7. Using pictures of similar sounding words, say each word and have the student point to the appropriate picture (e.g., *run* and *one*, *bat* and *back*).

8. Have the student tally the number of correct productions of targeted words when the teacher or a peer reads a list of words.

9. Audio record the student reading simple passages, listen to the recording and mark error and/or correct productions.

10. Audio record a spontaneous monologue given by the student. Listen to the recording with him/her and tally error and/or correct productions. The teacher and the student should compare their analyses of the productions.

11. Have the student read a list of words and rate his/her production after each word.

12. Choose a peer to model correctly producing targeted words for the student.

13. Play a game, such as *Simon Says* in which the student tries to reproduce the targeted words when produced by the teacher or peers.

14. Using pictures of similar sounding words, have the student say each word as the teacher points to a picture (e.g., *run* and *one*, *bat* and *back*).

15. Use a drawing as a visual aid to show the student how the mouth looks during production of the target sound.

16. Make cards with the target sound and cards with vowels. Have the student combine a target sound card with a vowel card to make a syllable that he/she can produce (e.g., *ra, re, ro,* and *ar, er, or*).

17. Play a board game that requires the student to name pictures of the targeted words. The student has to produce the targeted words correctly before he/she can move on the game board. (This activity can be simplified or expanded based on the level of success of the student.)

18. Have the student cut out pictures of items that include the targeted words and display them where they can be practiced each day.

19. Provide the student with a list of the targeted words. Have the student practice the words daily. As the student masters the word list, add more words. (Using words from the student's everyday vocabulary, reading lists, spelling lists, etc., will facilitate transfer of correct production of the target sound into everyday speech.)

20. Have the student use fun phonics sheets to practice pronouncing his/her target sounds. These are also good for home practice.

21. Have the student keep a notebook of difficult words encountered each day. These can be practiced by the student with teacher or peer assistance.

22. Have the student use a carrier phrase combined with a word containing the target sound (e.g., I like _____. I see a _____.).

23. Have the student keep a list of all the words he/she can think of which contain sounds the student can produce accurately.

24. Have the student write sentences using targeted words.

25. During oral reading, underline targeted words and reinforce the student for correct productions.

26. Involve parents by asking them to rate their child's speech for a specific length of time (e.g., during dinner count no errors, a few errors, or many errors).

27. Present the student with a list of topics. Have the student select a topic and then give a spontaneous speech for a specific length of time. Count errors and suggest ways for him/her to improve.

28. Reinforce the student for correct production of the target sound or words: (a) give the student a tangible reward (e.g., classroom privileges, line leading, passing out materials, five minutes free time, etc.) or (b) give the student an intangible reward (e.g., praise, fist bump, smile, etc.).

29. Speak to the student to explain what he/she needs to do differently (e.g., pronounce sounds accurately). The teacher should be careful to use the sound that is being targeted and not the letter name (e.g., /s/ not *s*).

30. Evaluate the appropriateness of requiring the student to accurately produce certain sounds (e.g., developmentally, certain sounds may not be produced accurately until the age of 8 or 9).

141   Does not form questions appropriately when speaking

Goal:

1.   The student will improve his/her question usage form.

Objectives:

1.   The student will imitate WH (*who, what, where, when, why*) questions in _____ out of _____ trials.
2.   The student will formulate WH (*who, what, where, when, why*) questions during structured language activities in _____ out of _____ trials.
3.   The student will formulate WH (*who, what, where, when, why*) questions in conversational speech in _____ out of _____ trials.
4.   The student will imitate yes/no questions in _____ out of _____ trials.
5.   The student will formulate yes/no questions during structured language activities in _____ out of _____ trials.
6.   The student will formulate yes/no questions in conversational speech in _____ out of _____ trials.

Interventions:

1.   Have the student's hearing checked if it has not been recently checked.

2.   Speak to the student to explain that he/she is using inappropriate question forms. Explain the importance of asking questions in the appropriate forms.

3.   Determine the type of grammatical model to which the student is exposed at home. Without placing negative connotations on the parents' grammatical style, explain the difference between standard and nonstandard grammar.

4.   Determine whether the student knows the difference between telling and asking. Young students frequently confuse these concepts and launch into a lengthy narrative about some personal experience when asked if they have any questions. (This may not be developmentally appropriate for a kindergarten or first-grade student.)

5.   Provide a written model for the student to demonstrate how statements can be changed into questions. Circle the word(s) that move in a statement and draw arrows to show where they move to make a question (e.g., Spot is a dog. - Is Spot a dog?).

6.   Reinforce the student for forming questions appropriately: (a) give the student a tangible reward (e.g., classroom privileges, line leading, passing out materials, five minutes free time, etc.) or (b) give the student an intangible reward (e.g., praise, fist bump, smile, etc.).

7.   Determine whether the student understands the concepts of time, quantity, space, etc., which underlie the comprehension of WH questions. Language comprehension typically precedes and influences expressive language skills.

8.   Determine whether the student understands the meaning of words indicating a question (e.g., *who, what, when, why*, etc.).

9.   Identify specific types of information provided in statements (e.g., The ball is red. - tells what color; I eat lunch at noon. - tells what time/when; Sue is my friend. - tells who) to help the student formulate appropriate WH questions, such as What color is the ball? What time do I eat lunch? Who is my friend?

10.   Choose a peer to model appropriate question forms for the student.

11. Increase the student's awareness of the problem by recording the student while he/she is speaking with another student who exhibits an appropriate questioning style. Play the audio recording for the student to see if he/she can identify correct/incorrect forms. Have him/her make appropriate corrections.

12. Use a private signal (e.g., touching earlobe, raising index finger, etc.) to remind the student to use appropriate question forms.

13. Routinely audio record the student's speech and point out errors in his/her question form. With each recording, reinforce the student as his/her questioning skills improve.

14. After audio recording the student's speech, have him/her identify the incorrect questioning skills and make the appropriate modifications.

15. Have the student complete worksheets in which he/she must change statements to questions.

16. When speaking privately with the student, restate his/her inappropriate question form with a rising inflection (e.g., Billy not here today?) to assess if the student recognizes errors and spontaneously makes appropriate corrections.

17. Ask the parents to encourage the student's correct use of question forms at home by praising him/her when appropriate question forms are used.

18. Formulate activities for your class which require the use of appropriate questioning techniques: (a) Plan a mystery activity and have the students ask: Where are we going? What will we do? When will we go? Who will we see? (b) Play *Twenty Questions* with emphasis on yes/no question forms, and (c) Have the student ask questions to obtain comparative information (e.g., How is a boot different from a shoe? How are a boot and a shoe the same? Which one is bigger?).

19. Have the student formulate a WH question after being presented with a one-word answer (e.g., Teacher says books. Student responds What do we read?).

20. Have the student identify the type of question that would be asked when given various answers (e.g., Teacher says quickly. Student responds with how question. Teacher says in the cabinet. Student responds with where question).

21. Have the student verbally change statements to questions.

142 Does not use appropriate subject-verb agreement when speaking

Goals:

1. The student will improve his/her conversational speech.
2. The student will improve his/her grammatical speech.
3. The student will improve his/her production of speech sounds.
4. The student will improve his/her verbal sentence structure.
5. The student will improve the ability to express himself/herself verbally.
6. The student will improve the fluency of his/her speech.
7. The student will use correct subject-verb agreement.

Objectives:

1. The student will differentiate between grammatically correct and incorrect sentences in _____ out of _____ trials.
2. The student will imitate appropriate subject-verb agreement during structured language activities in _____ out of _____ trials.
3. The student will imitate appropriate subject-verb agreement in sentences in _____ out of _____ trials.
4. The student will recognize correct subject-verb agreement with _____% accuracy.
5. The student will spontaneously use appropriate subject-verb agreement in sentences in _____ out of _____ trials.
6. The student will use appropriate subject-verb agreement in conversational speech in _____ out of _____ trials.
7. The student will use correct subject-verb agreement when speaking with _____% accuracy.
8. The student will use plural subjects with plural verbs with _____% accuracy.
9. The student will use single subjects with single verbs with _____% accuracy.

Interventions:

1. After audio recording the student's speech, have him/her identify incorrect subject-verb agreement and make appropriate corrections.

2. Determine the type of grammatical model to which the student is exposed at home. Without placing negative connotations on his/her parents' grammatical style, explain the difference between standard and nonstandard grammar.

3. Ask the parents to encourage the student's correct use of grammar at home by praising him/her when correct subject-verb agreement is used.

4. Choose a peer to model appropriate subject-verb agreement for the student.

5. Determine if the student's errors are the result of dialectical differences (the pattern of subject-verb agreement may not be atypical within his/her social group).

6. During the day, write down specific subject-verb errors produced by the student. Read the sentences to the student and have him/her make appropriate corrections verbally.

7. Evaluate the appropriateness of requiring the student to speak with subject-verb agreement (e.g., developmentally, a child may not utilize appropriate subject-verb agreement until the age of 6 or 7).

8. Explain that certain forms of verbs go with certain subjects and that correct subject-verb agreement requires the appropriate match of subject and verb. Be sure that the student knows the various possibilities of subject-verb agreement and how to select the correct one.

9. Give the student a series of written and verbal sentences and have him/her identify which are grammatically correct and incorrect.

10. Have the student complete worksheets in which he/she must choose the correct verb to go with a specific subject (e.g., I [saw, seen] a new car.).

11. Have the student complete worksheets in which he/she must choose the correct subject to go with a specific verb (e.g., [I, She] eats.).

12. Have the student select a verb to master using correctly as a goal. As the student masters the correct use of the verb, he/she puts it on a list with a star and selects another verb to master.

13. Have the student verbally construct sentences with specific verb forms and subjects.

14. Increase the student's awareness of the problem by audio recording the student when speaking with another student who exhibits appropriate subject-verb agreement. Play the recording for the student to analyze and see if he/she can identify correct/incorrect subject-verb forms.

15. Make a list of those verbs the student most commonly uses incorrectly. This list will become the guide for learning activities in subject-verb agreement.

16. Have the student's hearing checked if it has not been recently checked.

17. Make sure the student understands that sentences express thoughts about a subject and what that subject is or does.

18. Make sure the student understands the concept of subject and verb by demonstrating through the use of objects, pictures, and/or written sentences (depending on the student's abilities).

19. Make sure the student understands the concept of plurality (e.g., have the student point to a picture of a cat and point to a picture of cats).

20. Provide the student with examples of correct subject-verb agreement for those combinations he/she most commonly uses incorrectly.

21. Reinforce the student for appropriate use of subject-verb agreement: (a) give the student a tangible reward (e.g., classroom privileges, line leading, passing out materials, five minutes free time, etc.) or (b) give the student an intangible reward (e.g., praise, fist bump, smile, etc.).

22. Routinely audio record the student's speech and point out errors in subject-verb agreement. With each recording, reinforce the student as his/her use of grammar improves.

23. Speak to the student to explain that he/she is using inappropriate subject-verb agreement. Emphasize the importance of speaking in grammatically correct sentences.

24. Use a private signal (e.g., touching earlobe, raising index finger, etc.) to remind the student to use correct subject-verb agreement.

25. When speaking privately with the student, restate his/her subject-verb error with a rising inflection (e.g., He done it?) to assess if the student recognizes errors and spontaneously makes appropriate corrections.

26. Write down specific subject-verb errors made by the student during the day. Give the written sentences to the student and have him/her make appropriate corrections. At first, mark the errors for the student to correct. As the student becomes more proficient with this task, have him/her find and correct the errors independently.

Goals:

1. The student will decrease his/her dysfluent behavior.
2. The student will decrease his/her secondary dysfluency characteristics.

Objectives:

1. The student's dysfluent behavior will decrease by _____%.
2. The student will use slow, easy speech in a controlled one-to-one environment in _____ out of _____ trials.
3. The student will use slow, easy speech in the presence of peers in _____ out of _____ trials.
4. The student will use slow, easy speech in the presence of authority figures in _____ out of _____ trials.
5. The student will imitate echo speech correctly _____% of the time.
6. The student will demonstrate control by pseudo stuttering of various types (prolongations, part word repetitions, etc.) with _____% accuracy.
7. The student will monitor his/her speech _____% of the time.
8. The student will identify listener behaviors that indicate that his/her message was not fully understood in _____ out of _____ trials.

Interventions:

1. Have the student's hearing checked if it has not been recently checked.

2. Reinforce the student for speaking fluently: (a) give the student a tangible reward (e.g., classroom privileges, line leading, passing out materials, five minutes free time, etc.) or (b) give the student an intangible reward (e.g., praise, fist bump, smile, etc.).

3. Familiarize yourself and the student with the terms fluency, dysfluency, stuttering, easy speech, etc. Keep these words as neutral as possible, without negative connotations.

4. Evaluate the appropriateness of requiring the student to speak without dysfluency (i.e., developmentally, young children experience normal dysfluency in their speech and all persons are occasionally dysfluent).

5. Provide the student with an appropriate model of slow, easy speech. Lengthen the pauses between words, phrases, and sentences.

6. Choose a peer to model appropriate speech for the student. Pair the students to sit together, perform assignments together, etc.

7. During conversations, calmly delay your verbal responses by one or two seconds.

8. Audio record the student so he/she may listen to and evaluate his/her own speech.

9. Have the student identify a good speaker and give the reasons he/she thinks that person is a good speaker.

10. Develop a list of the attributes which are likely to help a person become a good speaker. Have the student practice each attribute.

11. During oral reading, underline or highlight words which are difficult for the student to say and provide reinforcement when he/she says them fluently.

12. Have the student keep a list of times and/or situations in which he/she has particular difficulty with speech (e.g., times when he/she is nervous, embarrassed, etc.). Discuss the reasons for this and seek solutions to the difficulty experienced.

13. Have the student practice techniques for relaxing (e.g., deep breathing, tensing and relaxing muscles, etc.) which he/she can employ when he/she starts to become dysfluent.

14. Have the student speak in unison with you while you are modeling slow, easy speech.

15. Have the student identify the specific words or phrases on which he/she becomes dysfluent and practice those particular words or phrases.

16. Encourage the student to maintain eye contact during all speaking situations. If the student is noticeably more fluent when eye contact is averted, attempt to facilitate eye contact on a gradual basis.

17. Reinforce the student's moments of relative fluency. Emphasize that these occurred during moments when he/she was speaking slowly and easily.

18. Empathize with the student and explain that he/she is not less valuable as a person because of dysfluency. Emphasize the student's positive attributes.

19. Empathize with feelings of anger which the student may be experiencing.

20. When the student is speaking fluently, try to extend the positive experience by allowing him/her to continue speaking.

21. Reinforce the student each time he/she answers a question or makes a spontaneous comment in class.

22. If the student is speaking too rapidly, remind him/her to slow down and take his/her time. Develop a private signal (e.g., raising one finger, touching earlobe, etc.) to avoid calling too much attention to his/her speech in front of the whole class.

23. Give the student your undivided attention when he/she is speaking to you so he/she will not feel a need to hurry or compete with others for attention.

24. If the student is more dysfluent when he/she is involved in another activity at the same time he/she is talking, encourage him/her to stop the other activity.

25. If the student is highly excited, wait until he/she is calmer before requiring any verbal explanations or interactions. A high level of excitement often interferes with fluency.

26. During moments of dysfluency, use non-verbal activities to relax the student.

27. Do not interrupt or finish the student's sentences even if you think you can anticipate what the student is going to say. This can be extremely frustrating and may decrease the student's willingness to engage in future communicative interactions.

28. Help the student learn to identify periods of dysfluency and periods of slow, easy speech.

29. Help the student identify situations in which he/she is more fluent or less fluent. Determine the features of the fluent situations that seem to facilitate fluency and transfer those features to the less fluent situations.

30. When the student is dysfluent during conversation, explain to him/her that this happens to everyone at times.

31. Have the student make a list of his/her strong points or the things he/she does well to facilitate his/her overall level of confidence.

32. Point out to the student that he/she is capable of fluent speech and is in control of his/her speech in many situations.

33. Model slow, easy speech for the student and encourage him/her to speak at a similar rate. Practice with the student for a short time each day until he/she is able to match the rate.

34. Provide the student with a list of sentences and encourage him/her to read these at a slow rate.

35. Prepare simple verbal reading passages in written form in which phrases are separated by large spaces (indicating a pause). Have the student practice reading the passages aloud.

36. Use a private cue (e.g., raise a finger, touch earlobe, etc.) to encourage the student to answer questions at a slow rate of speech.

37. Use a private cue (e.g., raise a finger, touch earlobe, etc.) to encourage the student to use a slow speaking rate during classroom activities.

38. Reduce the emphasis on competition. Competitive activities may increase the student's anxiety and cause him/her to be more dysfluent.

39. Provide the student with as many social and academic successes as possible.

40. Do not require the student to speak in front of other students if he/she is uncomfortable doing so. Have the student speak to the teacher or another student privately if he/she would be more comfortable.

41. As the student is able to speak fluently in more situations (e.g., delivering messages to the office, speaking with the counselor, etc.), gradually increase those experiences as long as the student continues to be successful.

42. Teach the student ways to restate or rephrase a misunderstood message rather than continuing to repeat the original message with the same error patterns.

43. When the student experiences a severe episode of dysfluency, respond by paraphrasing/ repeating the content of his/her message to communicate that the message has been understood.

44. Meet with the student's parents to determine his/her level of dysfluency at home, parental reactions to the dysfluency, and successful strategies the parents have employed when dealing with the dysfluent behavior.

45. Determine whether or not the student avoids certain situations because of his/her perception of increased dysfluency. Discuss with the student the aspects of those situations that seem to cause increased anxiety. Examine possible modifications that could be implemented in the classroom to facilitate frustration tolerance (e.g., if speaking in front of the whole class causes stress, reduce the number of listeners and gradually increase the size of the group as the student's frustration tolerance increases).

144 Dysfluent speech causes unfavorable listener reaction

Goals:

1. The student will decrease his/her dysfluent speech.
2. The student will decrease his/her secondary dysfluency characteristics.

Objectives:

1. The student's dysfluent speech will decrease by _____%.
2. The student will use slow, easy speech in a controlled one-to-one environment in _____ out of _____ trials.
3. The student will use slow, easy speech in the presence of peers in _____ out of _____ trials.
4. The student will use slow, easy speech in the presence of authority figures in _____ out of _____ trials.
5. The student will imitate echo speech correctly _____% of the time.
6. The student will demonstrate control by pseudo stuttering of various types with _____% accuracy.
7. The student will monitor his/her speech _____% of the time.
8. The student will identify listener behaviors that indicate that his/her message was not fully understood in _____ out of _____ trials.

Interventions:

1. Have the student's hearing checked if it has not been recently checked.

2. Reinforce the student for speaking fluently: (a) give the student a tangible reward (e.g., classroom privileges, line leading, passing out materials, five minutes free time, etc.) or (b) give the student an intangible reward (e.g., praise, fist bump, smile, etc.).

3. Familiarize yourself and the student with the terms fluency, dysfluency, stuttering, easy speech, etc. Keep these words as neutral as possible, without negative connotations.

4. Evaluate the appropriateness of requiring the student to speak without dysfluency (e.g., developmentally, young children experience normal dysfluency in their speech and all persons are occasionally dysfluent).

5. Provide the student with an appropriate model of slow, easy speech. Lengthen the pauses between words, phrases, and sentences.

6. Choose a peer to model appropriate speech for the student. Pair the students to sit together, complete assignments together, etc.

7. During conversations, calmly delay your verbal responses by one or two seconds.

8. Audio record the student so he/she may listen to and evaluate his/her own speech.

9. Have the student identify a good speaker and give the reasons he/she thinks that person is a good speaker.

10. Develop a list of the attributes which are likely to help a person become a good speaker. Have the student practice each attribute.

11. During oral reading, underline or highlight words which are difficult for the student to say and provide reinforcement when he/she says them fluently.

12. Have the student keep a list of times and/or situations in which he/she has particular difficulty with speech (e.g., times when he/she is nervous, embarrassed, etc.). Discuss the reasons for this and seek solutions to the difficulty experienced.

13. Have the student practice techniques for relaxing (e.g., deep breathing, tensing and relaxing muscles, etc.) which he/she can employ when he/she starts to become dysfluent.

14. Have the student identify the specific words or phrases on which he/she becomes dysfluent and practice those particular words or phrases.

15. Encourage the student to maintain eye contact during all speaking situations. If the student is noticeably more fluent when eye contact is averted, attempt to facilitate eye contact on a gradual basis.

16. Have the student speak in unison with you while you are modeling slow, easy speech.

17. Reinforce the student's moments of relative fluency. Emphasize that these occurred during moments when he/she was speaking slowly and easily.

18. Empathize with the student and explain that he/she is not less valuable as a person because of dysfluency. Emphasize the student's positive attributes.

19. Empathize with feelings of anger which the student may be experiencing.

20. When the student is speaking fluently, try to extend the positive experience by allowing him/her to continue speaking.

21. Reinforce the student each time he/she answers a question or makes a spontaneous comment in class.

22. If the student is speaking too rapidly, remind him/her to slow down and take his/her time. Develop a private signal (e.g., raising one finger, touching earlobe, etc.) to avoid calling too much attention to his/her speech in front of the whole class.

23. Give the student your undivided attention when he/she is speaking to you so he/she will not feel a need to hurry or compete with others for attention.

24. If the student is more dysfluent when he/she is involved in another activity at the same time he/she is talking, encourage him/her to stop the other activity.

25. If the student is highly excited, wait until he/she is calmer before requiring any verbal explanations or interactions. A high level of excitement often interferes with fluency.

26. During moments of dysfluency, use non-verbal activities to relax the student.

27. Do not interrupt or finish the student's sentences even if you think you can anticipate what the student is going to say. This can be extremely frustrating and may decrease the student's willingness to engage in future communicative interactions.

28. Help the student learn to identify situations in which he/she is more fluent or less fluent. Determine the aspects of the fluent situations that seem to facilitate fluency and try to transfer those features to the less fluent situations.

29. Help the student learn to identify periods of dysfluency and periods of slow, easy speech.

30. When the student is dysfluent during conversation, explain to him/her that this happens to everyone at times.

31. Have the student make a list of his/her strong points or the things he/she does well to facilitate his/her overall level of confidence.

32. Point out to the student that he/she is capable of fluent speech and is in control of his/her speech in many situations.

33. Model slow, easy speech for the student and encourage him/her to speak at a similar rate. Practice with the student for a short time each day until he/she is able to match the rate.

34. Provide the student with a list of sentences and encourage him/her to read these at a slow rate.

35. Prepare simple verbal reading passages in written form in which phrases are separated by large spaces (indicating a pause). Have the student practice reading the passages aloud.

36. Use a private cue (e.g., raise a finger, touch earlobe, etc.) to encourage the student to answer questions at a slow rate of speech.

37. Use a private cue (e.g., raise a finger, touch earlobe, etc.) to encourage the student to use a slow speaking rate during classroom activities.

38. Reduce the emphasis on competition. Competitive activities may increase the student's anxiety and cause him/her to be more dysfluent.

39. Provide the student with as many social and academic successes as possible.

40. Do not require the student to speak in front of other students if he/she is uncomfortable doing so. Have the student speak to the teacher or another student privately if he/she would be more comfortable.

41. As the student is able to speak fluently in more situations (e.g., delivering messages to the office, speaking with the counselor, etc.), gradually increase those experiences as long as the student continues to be successful.

42. Teach the student ways to restate or rephrase a misunderstood message rather than continuing to repeat the original message with the same error patterns.

43. When the student experiences a severe episode of dysfluency, respond by paraphrasing/repeating the content of his/her message to communicate that the message has been understood.

44. Meet with the student's parents to determine his/her level of dysfluency at home, parental reactions to the dysfluency, and successful strategies the parents have employed when dealing with the dysfluent behavior.

45. Determine whether or not the student avoids certain situations because of his/her perception of increased dysfluency. Discuss with the student the aspects of those situations that seem to cause increased anxiety. Examine possible modifications that could be implemented in the classroom to facilitate frustration tolerance (e.g., if speaking in front of the whole class causes stress, reduce the number of listeners and gradually increase the size of the group as the student's frustration tolerance increases).

46. Discuss and role-play with the entire class different disabilities and the accompanying frustrations they might feel if they were experiencing similar difficulties. Include speech problems in this discussion.

Goal:

1. The student will improve his/her conversational skills.

Objectives:

1. The student will choose an appropriate response to use in situations, when given options, in _____ out of _____ trials.
2. The student will explain the parts of the conversational dyad with _____% accuracy.
3. The student will choose appropriate statements to begin, maintain, or finish a conversation in structured language activities in _____ out of _____ trials.
4. The student will make an appropriate shift from one topic to another in structured language activities in _____ out of _____ trials.
5. The student will utilize appropriate statements to begin, maintain, or finish a conversation during everyday speaking activities in _____ out of _____ trials.
6. The student will make an appropriate shift from one topic to another in everyday speaking activities in _____ out of _____ trials.
7. The student will demonstrate the ability to stay on topic during a five minute conversation in _____ out of _____ trials.

Interventions:

1. Have the student's hearing checked if it has not been recently checked.

2. Evaluate the appropriateness of the task to determine (a) if the task is too easy, (b) if the task is too difficult, or (c) if the length of time scheduled to complete the task is adequate.

3. Reinforce the student when he/she uses language effectively and is able to obtain the desired results: (a) give the student a tangible reward (e.g., classroom privileges, line leading, passing out materials, five minutes free time, etc.) or (b) give the student an intangible reward (e.g., praise, fist bump, smile, etc.).

4. Reinforce students in the classroom who appropriately use verbal language as a tool to obtain desired results.

5. Be an appropriate model for the student by expressing yourself concisely and demonstrating that verbal language can be used as a tool to obtain desired results.

6. Have the student read short stories without endings and assist the student in expressing opinions, feelings, and/or emotions about the endings to the stories.

7. Each day provide the student with situations in which the student must use verbal language as a tool to obtain desired results (e.g., The student wants to get a drink. Indicate that he should tell you when he wants a drink rather than waiting for you to provide the break.).

8. Provide the student with a list of statements/questions which could be used to obtain specific results and assist him/her in using the statements at appropriate times (e.g., Would you help me move this? I would like to get a drink now.).

9. Ask the student to explain outcomes, consequences, etc., (e.g., explain that it was the result of hard work and accomplishment that he/she earned a privilege).

10. Use cause-and-effect relationships as they apply to nature and people. Discuss what led up to a specific situation in a story or picture, what could happen next, etc.

11. Have the student develop rules and explain why each is necessary.

12. Make sure that the student can verbalize the reason for real-life outcomes of behavior (e.g., why the student had to leave the class line on the way to recess, why he/she earned the privilege of being line leader, etc.).

13. Have the student identify appropriate consequences for rules (e.g., consequences for following rules and consequences for not following rules). Have the student explain the choice of consequences he/she identified.

14. Pair the student with a peer who is effective in using verbal language as a tool to obtain desired results.

15. Encourage verbal expression in your classroom and listen carefully when the student is using language as a tool. Set up situations where the student can see that his/her attempts at language usage have been successful.

146 Has limited expressive and/or receptive vocabulary

Goals:

1. The student will improve the ability to express himself/herself verbally.
2. The student will show an increase in receptive and expressive vocabulary.

Objectives:

1. The student will add _____ new adjectives to his/her vocabulary each week.
2. The student will add _____ new adverbs to his/her vocabulary each week.
3. The student will add _____ new nouns to his/her vocabulary each week.
4. The student will add _____ new opposites to his/her vocabulary each week.
5. The student will add _____ new prepositions to his/her vocabulary each week.
6. The student will add _____ new verbs to his/her vocabulary each week.
7. The student will add _____ new words to his/her vocabulary each week.
8. The student will be able to express his/her needs with _____% accuracy.
9. The student will be able to relate experiences with _____% accuracy.
10. The student will engage in conversation (identify some criteria such as once a day, three times a day, etc.).
11. The student will respond appropriately to conversational questions on _____out of _____ occasions.

Interventions:

1. Have the student sequence the activities which occurred on a field trip or special event with an emphasis on vocabulary.

2. During conversation, rephrase what the student has said using synonyms to expand his/her vocabulary (e.g., Students: The TV show was good. Teacher: I'm glad the TV show was entertaining.).

3. Have the student write sentences or stories using new words he/she has learned.

4. Allow the student to speak without being interrupted or hurried.

5. Determine the type of language model the student has at home. Without placing negative connotations on the language model in his/her home, explain the difference between language which is rich in meaning and that which includes a limited repertoire of vocabulary.

6. Encourage the student to use gestures when necessary to clarify his/her message. Gestures may also facilitate recall of vocabulary the student is having difficulty retrieving.

7. Ask questions which stimulate language. Avoid those which can be answered by yes/no or a nod of the head (e.g., ask the student what he/she did at recess instead of asking if he/she played on the slide, ask the student what he/she did on vacation instead of asking if he/she stayed home over the holidays, etc.).

8. Describe objects, persons, places, etc., to the student and have him/her name the items described.

9. Select relevant and appropriate reading material and have the student underline each unfamiliar word. Make a list of these words and review their meanings with the student until he/she can use them when speaking.

10. Have the student paste a picture from a magazine on one side of a piece of paper and list all of the vocabulary that could be associated with it on the other side (including verbs). Have the student dictate or write a story about the picture using the vocabulary.

11. Explain the importance of expanding one's vocabulary (i.e., comprehension and communication are based on the knowledge and use of appropriate/accurate vocabulary).

12. Discuss with the student's parents the ways in which they can help their child develop an expanded speaking vocabulary (e.g., encouraging the student to read the news, novels, magazines, or other materials for enjoyment). Emphasize to parents that they can set a good example by reading with the student.

13. Explain to the student where he/she can go to find word meanings in the classroom library (e.g., dictionary, thesaurus, encyclopedia, etc.).

14. Give the student a list of words and ask him/her to tell the opposite of each word.

15. Have the student list all the vocabulary he/she can think of that goes with a specific word (e.g., space - astronaut, lunar rover, rocket, shuttle, launch, etc.).

16. Refer to previously presented information that is related to the topic when presenting new vocabulary.

17. Explain to the student how to classify new words as to category, function, antonym, synonym, etc., to facilitate remembering the words.

18. Give the student or let the student choose a *Word of the Day* which is to be incorporated into conversations. Reinforce the student each time he/she uses the word.

19. Have the student act out verbs and label actions performed by classmates.

20. Encourage the student to apply new vocabulary to personal experiences in written and verbal work (e.g., Can you think of another word to use for sleep?).

21. Have the student demonstrate and identify different verbs of the same category (e.g., walk, creep, slither, saunter, march, etc.).

22. Audio record the student's spontaneous speech, noting specific words. Have the student list other words (synonyms) which could be substituted for the identified words.

23. Place interesting pictures or objects on a table and have the student describe them in detail. Provide assistance in formulating appropriate vocabulary to use when describing the object.

24. Have the student make up sentences or stories using new words he/she has learned.

25. Review daily new vocabulary words and their meanings. Have the student use the words daily.

26. Have the student provide as many adjectives as possible to go with a given noun (e.g., lady - pretty, tall, nice, etc.).

27. Give the student a picture of a specific location (e.g., grocery store) and have the student name as many objects, actions, persons, etc., as he/she can think of that can be found there.

28. Have the student provide associations for given words (e.g., circus - clown, elephant, trapeze, tent, lion tamer, etc.).

29. Use a multisensory approach to facilitate retention of new vocabulary words (e.g., the scent of fragrant flowers or freshly baked spice cake will facilitate retention of the vocabulary word aroma).

30. Encourage verbal output. Increase the student's opportunities to communicate verbally to provide him/her with necessary practice in using vocabulary.

31. Have the student role-play various situations in which good vocabulary skills are important (e.g., during a job interview, talking to a group of people, etc.).

32. Choose a peer to model comprehension and use of an expanded vocabulary for the student to facilitate his/her speaking vocabulary.

33. Use new words in a sentence completion activity. Have the student explain how the use of different words changes the meaning of the sentence (e.g., I like Jerry because he is _____ [sincere, humorous, competitive], etc.).

34. In addition to identifying objects, persons, actions, etc., have the student provide places where each could be seen (e.g., actor - TV, theater, stage, etc.).

35. Include new vocabulary in daily conversation as often as possible.

36. Attach labels to items in the student's environment (e.g., wall-mounted board, window, desk, doorway, etc.) for the student to make visual associations with the vocabulary words.

37. Make sure the student has mastery of vocabulary words at each level before introducing new words.

38. Do not require the student to learn more vocabulary words and meanings than he/she is capable of comprehending.

39. In addition to labeling objects, persons, places, etc., have the student provide verbs that could be used with each (e.g., book - read, browse through, skim, etc.).

40. Make sure the student's hearing has been recently checked.

41. Use pictures to help the student understand the meanings of new vocabulary words.

42. Explain to the student how to use context clues to determine the meanings of words he/she hears or sees (e.g., listening to or looking at the surrounding words and determining what type of word would be appropriate).

43. Make up or use games to teach comprehension and expression of new vocabulary. (Novel situations may help students learn new information.).

44. When the student is asked to recall new vocabulary, give him/her clues about the word (e.g., Remember when we talked about the animal that walks on all fours, barks, and people keep as pets?).

45. Teach new vocabulary within the context of known information (e.g., category, associations, etc.).

46. Have the student divide cards that are labeled with objects, persons, places, etc., in the environment into difference categories (e.g., function, color, size, use, composition, etc.). Point out the similarities and differences between items as they change categories (e.g., a ball and an apple may be red, round, and smooth; but you can only eat the apple, etc.).

47. Name a category and have the student identify things within the category. Introduce new words which belong in the same group.

48. Point out words that have a variety of meanings and use them appropriately in different contexts.

49. Have the student maintain a vocabulary notebook (picture or word) with definitions of words whose meanings he/she did not know.

50. Prepare a list of new words which the student will encounter while reading a given assignment. Help the student (or choose a peer to help the student) look up each word, practice saying it, and use it in a sentence before reading the given assignment.

51. Provide the student with fewer weekly vocabulary words. As the student demonstrates success, gradually increase the number of vocabulary words from week to week.

52. Have the student provide as many adverbs as possible to go with a given verb (e.g., run - slow, fast, crooked, etc.).

53. Reinforce the student for using an expanded speaking vocabulary: (a) give the student a tangible reward (e.g., classroom privileges, line leading, passing out materials, five minutes free time, etc.) or (b) give the student an intangible reward (e.g., praise, fist bump, smile, etc.).

54. Have the student participate in role-play to facilitate use of new vocabulary (e.g., set up an imaginary restaurant and have the student and peers play the various roles of customers, waiter/waitress, cook, etc., varying the time of day and the occasion).

55. Send home new vocabulary words and encourage parents to use them in activities and general conversation.

56. Take advantage of unusual or unique situations to teach new vocabulary. Typically, a student will retain information learned in a novel situation better than information learned during a regular routine. The uniqueness of the situation will also facilitate the student's memory skills when you provide a reminder to help the student recall the vocabulary (e.g., Remember yesterday during the fire drill when we talked about _____?).

57. Prompt the student to help him/her respond with adequate vocabulary (e.g., Student: That thing. Teacher: What thing, what is it doing?).

58. Review daily previously learned vocabulary words and their meanings. Have the student incorporate previously learned vocabulary words into daily conversation and activities.

59. To reinforce new vocabulary, write the new word on an envelope and put pictures inside that do and do not go with it (e.g., arctic - polar bears, snow, parrots, palm trees, etc.). Have the student remove the unrelated picture and explain why it doesn't belong.

60. Place objects inside a large purse, box, bag, etc., (e.g., different shaped blocks, pieces of fruit, school supplies, etc.). Have the student reach into the container for an item. Without looking, have the student describe the item as he/she feels it and then guess the item.

61. Have the student maintain a notebook of new vocabulary words to call upon for daily conversation and activities.

62. Use hands-on activities and manipulatives to teach vocabulary (e.g., under the heading *fruit* place pieces of fruit, under the heading *school supplies* provide school materials, etc.).

63. When teaching new vocabulary and engaging in conversation, be sure to use vocabulary that is within the student's level of comprehension.

64. Have the student name all the objects, persons, places, etc., in the environment that he/she can. Have the student point to items in the environment he/she was unable to name. The items the student was unable to name will become new vocabulary to be learned. Activities to facilitate increasing expressive vocabulary should focus on the items the student pointed to but could not name.

65. Give the student a series of words or pictures and have him/her name the category in which they belong (e.g., objects, persons, places, etc.).

66. Use visual aids whenever possible when introducing new vocabulary.

67. Reinforce those students in the classroom who use an expanded speaking vocabulary.

147 Has difficulty comprehending passive sentence form

Goals:

1. The student will improve his/her comprehension skills.
2. The student will demonstrate comprehension of nonliteral forms of speech.

Objectives:

1. The student will respond appropriately to questions/directions about passive sentences (e.g., The boy was being followed by his sister. Who was in front?) in _____ out of _____ trials.
2. The student will demonstrate comprehension of passive sentence form by acting out the passive sentence _____% of the time.
3. The student will demonstrate comprehension of passive sentence form by changing an active sentence into a passive one with _____% accuracy.
4. The student will restate a passive sentence in active form in _____ out of _____ trials.
5. The student will demonstrate comprehension of passive sentence form by stating whether or not a passive sentence and an active one have the same or different meanings with _____% accuracy.
6. The student will demonstrate comprehension of passive sentence form by identifying passive sentences in a textbook with _____% accuracy.

Interventions:

1. Have the student's hearing checked if it has not been recently checked.

2. Evaluate the appropriateness of the task to determine whether or not it is too difficult for the student (the comprehension of passive voice sentences may not be fully developed until approximately 7 years of age).

3. Determine whether or not the student understands the roles of the subject and object in a sentence by providing the student with active voice sentences (e.g., Ryan chased Matt.) and asking questions to determine his/her comprehension (e.g., Was Ryan chased?).

4. Explain passive voice sentences to the student by providing him/her with passive voice sentences (e.g., Matt was chased by Ryan.) and explaining that the subject and object have switched places in the sentence. Ask questions to determine his/her comprehension (e.g., Was Ryan chased?).

5. Demonstrate sentences in which the subject and object can exchange places and continue to make sense, through the use of manipulatives, pictures, etc., (e.g., Erin hugged Kelli. - Kelli hugged Erin.).

6. Reinforce the student for demonstrating appropriate comprehension and use of passive voice sentences: (a) give the student a tangible reward (e.g., classroom privileges, line leading, passing out materials, five minutes free time, etc.) or (b) give the student an intangible reward (e.g., praise, fist bump, smile, etc.).

7. Reinforce those students in the classroom who demonstrate appropriate comprehension and use of passive voice sentences.

8. Demonstrate sentences in which the subject and object cannot exchange places and continue to make sense, through the use of manipulatives, pictures, etc., (e.g., The boy threw the ball. The ball threw the boy.).

9. Have the student demonstrate the meaning of active/passive voice sentences by acting them out or illustrating them.

10. Provide the student with two sentences (e.g., The man kicked the football. The football kicked the man.) and have him/her identify the one that make sense. (If the student demonstrates difficulty with this task, he/she may be experiencing difficulty comprehending picture and/or verbal absurdities.)

11. Have students role-play sentences presented in active voice (e.g., Erin threw the ball to Kelli.) and then switch to passive voice (e.g., The ball was thrown to Kelli by Erin.).

12. Point out the use of the word by as a clue to the actor in a passive voice sentence (e.g., Ice cream was eaten by the girl.).

13. Provide the student with a simple paragraph or story and have him/her change some of the active voice sentences into passive voice.

14. Have the student change active voice sentences into passive voice (e.g., The man kicked the football. - The football was kicked by the man. The boy chased the girl. - The girl was chased by the boy.).

15. Have the student change passive voice sentences into active voice (e.g., The ball was kicked by the boy. - The boy kicked the ball. The mouse was chased by the cat. - The cat chased the mouse.).

16. Have the student rearrange scrambled words into an appropriate passive voice sentence (e.g., flowers, by, picked, the, her, were).

17. Point out passive voice sentences to the student when they appear in his/her textbooks. Have him/her change these sentences to active voice to demonstrate comprehension.

18. Choose a peer to model appropriate comprehension and use of passive voice sentences for the student. Have the peer work with the student to improve his/her abilities in this area.

19. Provide the student with a series of active and passive voice sentence pairs and have him/her determine whether the meanings are the same or different (e.g., The girl gave a party. - A party was given by the girl. The girl was hit by the boy. - The boy hit the girl.).

20. Video the student and his/her classmates performing various actions. Play the video without the sound and have the student narrate what is happening using a variety of active and passive voice sentences (e.g., Matt is reading a book to Ryan. Kelli is being helped by Erin.). This activity could be modified by using a prerecorded video.

21. While the class is engaged in various activities, describe your observations using active and passive voice sentences interchangeably.

148 Has difficulty comprehending picture and/or verbal absurdities

Goal:

1. The student will improve his/her critical thinking and reasoning skills.

Objectives:

1. The student will identify absurdities in visual material in _____ out of _____ trials.
2. The student will explain absurdities in visual material in _____ out of _____ trials.
3. The student will identify absurdities in verbal material in _____ out of _____ trials.
4. The student will explain absurdities in verbal material in _____ out of _____ trials.

Interventions:

1. Have the student's hearing checked if it has not been recently checked.

2. Explain the importance of comprehending absurdities in visual and verbal information (i.e., humor and the ability to determine the plausibility of a situation are often based on the ability to determine whether or not something is absurd).

3. Reinforce the student for demonstrating comprehension of absurdities: (a) give the student a tangible reward (e.g., classroom privileges, line leading, passing out materials, five minutes free time, etc.) or (b) give the student an intangible reward (e.g., praise, fist bump, smile, etc.).

4. Determine whether or not the student has a limited expressive and/or receptive vocabulary which would influence his/her ability to comprehend absurdities.

5. Use concrete examples of absurdities (e.g., wear different colored shoes, put socks on your hands instead of gloves, etc.) before introducing visual and verbal absurdities.

6. Tell the student that you will be doing or saying some unusual things during the day and have him/her tell you when he/she notices something silly. When he/she identifies an absurdity, have him/her explain why it is silly and what would be appropriate. (If the student fails to notice something, specifically draw his/her attention to it and explain the absurdity.)

7. Reinforce those students in the classroom who demonstrate comprehension of absurdities.

8. Help the student heighten his/her awareness of the differences between fantasy and reality by discussing stories, movies, TV programs, etc., that are familiar to him/her. Point out specific aspects that are realistic and make-believe.

9. Choose a peer to model appropriate comprehension of absurdities for the student to improve his/her ability to understand absurdities.

10. Determine whether or not the student comprehends and uses antonyms which are often used in absurdities.

11. Have the student and his/her peers generate true and false statements about nouns presented verbally, in writing, or visually (e.g., A bird can fly. A bird can drive a car.).

12. Have the student identify which of his/her peers' statements are true and which are false.

13. Provide the student with an adjective and have him/her list nouns that could and could not go with it (e.g., Sweet could apply to candy, ice cream, sugar, etc.; but could not apply to pickle, lemon, etc. Ask him/her to tell you what is silly, absurd, or wrong with a statement, such as the lemon is sweet.).

14. Provide the student with a noun and have him/her list verbs that could and could not go with it (e.g., Bird could apply to sing, fly, etc.; but could not apply to cook, paint, roller skate, etc. Ask him/her to tell you what is silly, absurd, or wrong with the statement, the bird was roller skating.).

15. Provide the student with a verb and have him/her list nouns that could and could not go with it (e.g., Runs could apply to dog, person, car, stocking, etc.; but could not apply to table, chair, candy, glass, etc. Ask him/her to tell you what is silly, absurd, or wrong with the statement, the table runs fast.).

16. Have the student raise a hand or clap hands each time he/she hears an absurd/silly statement about a designated topic (e.g., dogs have 4 legs, fly airplanes, bark, etc.).

17. Have the student try to perform extremely difficult or impossible actions to facilitate his/her comprehension of sensible vs. nonsense situations.

18. Use simple comic strips that focus on absurdities and have the student identify what could or couldn't really happen and why it is funny.

19. Use seasons of the year or a time of the day and have the student tell or write sentences that would be true and some that would not be true (e.g., It is hot in the summer./It snows in the summer. The stars shine at night./The sun shines at night.).

20. Have the student use concept words to produce accurate and inaccurate sentences (e.g., Stars are up in the sky./Stars are down in the sky. Tuesday comes after Monday./Tuesday comes after Wednesday.).

21. Have the student identify absurdities in math word problems (e.g., John had 6 apples and gave 3 of them to Sue. Now John has 8 apples left.).

22. Provide the student with the outline of the body of an animal and have him/her add parts to the picture based on instructions from you and/or the rest of the class. Use a combination of accurate and inaccurate possibilities (e.g., for a horse, add five legs, two tails, two ears, one eye, a hat, and color it brown with purple polka dots.) After he/she finishes the drawing, have him/her identify the correct attributes as well as the absurdities.

23. Have the student make up accurate and inaccurate statements about how musical instruments and sports equipment are used (e.g., You play hockey with a tennis racquet. You hit a ball with a bat. You play a violin with a bow. You blow into a drum. etc.).

24. Describe situations that could happen and situations that could not happen (e.g., a man carrying a briefcase and a penguin flying a kite). Have the student identify the possible situations and change the silly ones to make them realistic.

25. Teach the student the difference between impossible and improbable (e.g., a doctor could wear his bathing suit to the hospital, but it is improbable).

26. Point out absurdities in poetry, short stories, articles, etc., and have him/her explain what makes the situations silly.

27. Provide the student with newspapers or magazines to find articles or pictures of real-life situations that are unusual or improbable (e.g., a cat and a mouse who are friends).

28. Point out that some TV commercials and magazine ads use absurdities to get attention. Have the student identify the absurdities in specific examples.

29. Make up a silly sentence to begin a story. Have the student correct your sentence and add another silly sentence of his/her own which, in turn, will be corrected by a classmate who will add another silly sentence, etc., until the story is completed.

30. Read stories that combine reality and fantasy to the class (e.g., *Peter Pan*, science fiction, etc.). Discuss the aspects of reality and fantasy during and after the reading.

Goals:

1. The student will improve his/her articulation skills.
2. The student will improve his/her conversational speech.
3. The student will improve his/her discrimination of speech sounds.
4. The student will improve his/her grammatical speech.
5. The student will improve his/her production of speech sounds.
6. The student will improve his/her production of speech sounds in isolation.
7. The student will improve his/her production of speech sounds in sentences.
8. The student will improve his/her production of speech sounds in syllables.
9. The student will improve his/her production of speech sounds in words.
10. The student will improve his/her production of speech sounds in spontaneous speech.
11. The student will improve the ability to express himself/herself verbally.
12. The student will improve the fluency of his/her speech.

Objectives:

1. The student will discriminate between correct and incorrect production of the target sound in words in _____ out of _____ trials.
2. The student will imitate correct production of the target sound in isolation in _____ out of _____ trials.
3. The student will imitate correct production of the target sound in words in _____ out of _____ trials.
4. The student will imitate correct production of the target sound in sentences in _____ out of _____ trials.
5. The student will imitate speech sounds independently with _____% accuracy.
6. The student will imitate speech sounds with verbal prompting and assistance with _____% accuracy.
7. The student will recognize speech sounds with _____% accuracy.

Interventions:

1. Be sure that the student can hear the difference between the target sound the way it should be made and the way it sounds when incorrectly produced.

2. Have the student keep a list of all the words he/she can think of which contain sounds he/she has difficulty producing accurately.

3. During oral reading, underline words containing the target sound and reinforce the student for correct productions.

4. Evaluate the appropriateness of requiring the student to accurately produce certain sounds (e.g., developmentally, certain sounds may not be produced accurately until the age of 8 or 9).

5. Have the student cut out pictures of items containing the target sound or word. Display them where they can be practiced each day.

6. Make cards with the target sound and cards with vowels. Have the student combine a target sound card with a vowel card to make a syllable that he/she can produce (e.g., *ra, re, ro,* and *ar, er, or*).

7. Have the student keep a notebook of difficult words encountered each day. These can be practiced by the student with teacher or peer assistance.

8. Have the student read simple passages and audio record them. Have him/her listen to the recording and mark error and/or correct productions.

9. Play a board game that requires the student to name pictures containing the target sound. The student has to produce the target sound correctly before he/she can move on the game board. (This activity can be simplified or expanded based on the level of success of the student.)

10. Have the student's hearing checked if it has not been recently checked.

11. Use a drawing as a visual aid to show the student how the mouth looks during production of the target sound.

12. Have the student stand up each time he/she hears the target sound produced accurately as contrasted with inaccurate productions (e.g., /s/, /th/, /s/, /s/, /th/, etc.).

13. Provide the student with a list of words containing the target sound. Have him/her practice the words daily. As the student masters the word list, add more words. (Using words from the student's everyday vocabulary, reading lists, spelling lists, etc., will facilitate transfer of correct production of the target sound into everyday speech.)

14. Have the student tally the number of correct productions of the targeted sound when the teacher or a peer reads a list of words.

15. Have the student use fun phonics sheets to practice pronouncing his/her target sounds. These are also good for home practice.

16. Tell the student what to listen for when requiring him/her to imitate speech sounds.

17. Have the student write sentences using words containing the target sound.

18. Choose a peer to model correctly producing targeted words for the student.

19. Initially, each correct production may need reinforcement. As the student progresses, random reinforcement may be adequate.

20. Have the student make up sentences using words containing the target sound.

21. Involve parents by asking them to rate their child's speech for a specific length of time (e.g., during dinner count no errors, a few errors, or many errors).

22. Make sure the student is attending to the source of information (e.g., eye contact is being made, hands are free of materials, etc.).

23. Play a game, such as *Simon Says* in which the student tries to reproduce correct productions of targeted words.

24. Have the student show thumbs up each time the target sound is produced accurately when pictures are named and thumbs down if the target sound is produced inaccurately.

25. Provide the student with verbal reminders or prompts when he/she requires help imitating speech sounds.

26. Reinforce the student for correct productions of the target sound: (a) give the student a tangible reward (e.g., classroom privileges, line leading, passing out materials, five minutes free time, etc.) or (b) give the student an intangible reward (e.g., praise, fist bump, smile, etc.).

27. Speak to the student to explain what he/she needs to do differently (e.g., make the sound like you do). The teacher should be careful to use the sound that is being targeted and not the letter name (e.g., /s/ not *s*).

28. Have the student use a carrier phrase combined with a word containing the target sound (e.g., I like _____. I see a _____.).

29. Audio record a spontaneous monologue given by the student. Listen to the recording with him/her and tally error and/or correct productions. The teacher and the student should compare their analyses of the productions.

30. Have the student raise a hand or clap hands when he/she hears the target sound produced during a series of isolated sound productions (e.g., */s/, /sh/, /r/, /m/, /r/, /t/, /k/, /r/, /z/, /w/, /n/, /r/,* etc.).

31. Use a puppet to produce the target sound correctly and incorrectly. The student earns a sticker for correctly distinguishing a set number of correct/incorrect productions the puppet makes.

32. Present the student with a list of topics. Have the student select a topic and then give a spontaneous speech for a specific length of time. Count errors and suggest ways for him/her to improve.

33. Use pictures of similar sounding words (e.g., if the student says /sh/ for /ch/, use pictures of /sh/ and /ch/ words such as *ships* and *chips*). As the teacher says the words, the student points to the appropriate picture, then the student takes a turn saying the words as the teacher points.

34. Have the student read a list of words and rate his/her production after each word.

150 Has difficulty recognizing and using multiple-meaning words

Goals:

1. The student will improve his/her vocabulary skills.
2. The student will demonstrate understanding and use of multiple-meaning words.

Objectives:

1. The student will point to objects/pictures or perform actions which represent the different meanings of the target vocabulary in _____ out of _____ trials.
2. The student will label objects/pictures or perform actions with appropriate target vocabulary in _____ out of _____ trials.
3. The student will demonstrate comprehension of multiple-meaning words by stating the word when both definitions are given with _____% accuracy.
4. The student will provide more than one definition for multiple-meaning words in _____ out of _____ trials.
5. The student will demonstrate comprehension of multiple-meaning words by drawing a cartoon showing each of the multiple meanings of the given word with _____% accuracy.
6. The student will appropriately use multiple-meaning words in verbal/written sentences in _____ out of _____ trials.
7. The student will use multiple-meaning words appropriately in everyday speaking situations in _____ out of _____ trials.
8. The student will demonstrate comprehension of multiple-meaning words by creating a sentence using two or more uses of the word with _____% accuracy.

Interventions:

1. Have the student's hearing checked if it has not been recently checked.

2. Reinforce the student for using multiple-meaning words accurately: (a) give the student a tangible reward (e.g., classroom privileges, line leading, passing out materials, five minutes free time, etc.) or (b) give the student an intangible reward (e.g., praise, fist bump, smile, etc.).

3. Teach the student the meanings of same and different as they relate to multiple-meaning words. Emphasize similarities and differences between concrete objects, pictures, actions, etc., to facilitate the understanding of these word relationships before targeting new vocabulary.

4. Have the student illustrate, cut out pictures of, or physically demonstrate different meanings of multiple-meaning words.

5. Reinforce those students in the classroom who use multiple-meaning words appropriately.

6. Have the student draw or cut out pictures to illustrate as many meanings of a homograph as he/she can in one scene/cartoon (e.g., an elephant with its trunk wrapped around a tree trunk beside a car with a trunk in/on its trunk).

7. Give the student several definitions of the word and have him/her match definitions with sentences that contain the word in various contexts (e.g., Mary locked her groceries in the trunk; He moved the log with his trunk; Sue put her trunk on the plane; (a) a piece of luggage, (b) part of a car, (c) an elephant's nose).

8. Choose a peer who comprehends multiple-meaning words to work with the student to discover alternate meanings of words. Have them write sentences together to demonstrate the various meanings.

9. Teach the student to use context clues and known vocabulary to determine the meaning of multiple-meaning words (i.e., listening to or looking at the surrounding words and determining what type of word would be appropriate).

10. Explain to the student where he/she can find word meanings in the classroom library (e.g., dictionary, thesaurus, encyclopedia, etc.).

11. Have the student maintain a vocabulary notebook with all the various definitions of homographs.

12. Prepare a list of homographs which the student will encounter before reading a given assignment. Help him/her, or choose a peer to help him/her, look up each word and identify the definitions that are new to him/her.

13. Have the class apply homographs to their personal experiences in written and verbal work.

14. Have the student write sentences using a homograph more than once to convey its various meanings (e.g., The mean witch didn't mean to look so mean.).

15. Have the student write paragraphs or short stories to convey the various meanings of one or more homographs.

16. Encourage the student to be creative in his/her use of multiple-meaning words to foster generalization of the various meanings into his/her everyday life (e.g., make board games using homographs, make collages illustrating various homographs, select teams or partners for games based on the collection of meanings for a homograph, design bulletin boards depicting various meanings of a homograph, make greeting cards that include several meanings of a homograph, etc.).

17. Send home new definitions of homographs and encourage parents to use them in activities and general conversation.

18. Point out various meanings of words as they apply to the student's five senses (e.g., The icing tastes too sweet. The baby looks sweet. The flowers smell sweet.).

19. Post *Today's Homograph* and have the class identify different meanings of the word by listening for different uses of the word throughout the day.

20. Have the student underline or highlight examples of multiple-meaning words in newspaper or magazine articles.

21. Highlight or underline homographs in sentences and have the student tell or write the meaning based on the context.

22. Identify multiple-meaning words throughout the day as they are used in various classes (e.g., The men will scale the mountain. One inch on a map of this scale equals 50 miles. We will be looking at fish scales in science today. Try to sing up the musical scale.). Ask teachers of music, art, P.E., etc., to point out this information during their classes as well.

23. Use visual aids whenever possible when introducing new definitions for homographs.

Goals:

1. The student will improve his/her articulation skills.
2. The student will improve his/her discrimination of speech sounds.
3. The student will improve his/her production of speech sounds in isolation.
4. The student will improve his/her production of speech sounds in syllables.
5. The student will improve his/her production of speech sounds in words.
6. The student will improve his/her production of speech sounds in sentences.
7. The student will improve his/her production of speech sounds in spontaneous speech.

Objectives:

1. The student will identify the number of syllables in a multisyllabic word in _____ out of _____ trials.
2. The student will imitate multisyllabic words at a slowed rate of speech in _____ out of _____ trials.
3. The student will imitate multisyllabic words at a normal rate of speech in _____ out of _____ trials.
4. The student will produce multisyllabic words at a slowed rate of speech in a sentence in _____ out of _____ trials.
5. The student will produce multisyllabic words at a normal rate of speech in a sentence in _____ out of _____ trials.
6. The student will produce multisyllabic words at a slowed rate of speech in conversation in _____ out of _____ trials.
7. The student will produce multisyllabic words at a normal rate of speech in conversation in _____ out of _____ trials.

Interventions:

1. Have the student's hearing checked if it has not been recently checked.

2. Provide the student with an appropriate model for targeted speech sounds.

3. Evaluate the appropriateness of requiring the student to accurately produce certain sounds (e.g., developmentally, certain sounds may not be produced accurately until the age of 8 or 9). These sounds will naturally be difficult for a child to accurately sequence.

4. Speak to the student to explain what he/she needs to do differently (e.g., sequence the sounds correctly, /el/ - /e/ - /phant/, not /ef/ - /e/ - /lant/).

5. Be sure that the student can hear the difference between the target word when the sounds are correctly sequenced and when the sounds are sequenced incorrectly.

6. Reinforce the student for correctly sequencing sounds in target words: (a) give the student a tangible reward (e.g., classroom privileges, line leading, passing out materials, five minutes free time, etc.) or (b) give the student an intangible reward (e.g., praise, fist bump, smile, etc.). Initially, each correctly sequenced production may need reinforcement. As the student progresses, random reinforcement may be adequate.

7. Use a puppet to produce words with the sounds sequenced correctly and incorrectly. The student earns a sticker for correctly distinguishing a set number of correct/incorrect productions the puppet makes.

8. Have the student stand up each time he/she hears targeted words with sounds sequenced accurately contrasted with inaccurate productions (e.g., elephant not ephelant).

9. During a picture-naming activity, have the student show thumbs up each time targeted words are produced with accurate sequencing and thumbs down if the targeted words are sequenced inaccurately.

10. Have the student tally the number of correct productions of targeted words when the teacher or peer reads a list of words.

11. Have the student read simple passages while audio recording them, listen to the recording, and mark errors and/or correct productions.

12. Audio record a spontaneous monologue given by the student. Listen to the recording with him/her and tally error and/or correct productions. The teacher and the student should compare their analyses of the productions.

13. If the student can read, have him/her practice syllables by underlining the syllables of a word as he/she reads them.

14. Have the student read a list of words and rate his/her production after each word.

15. Have the student place vertical lines between the syllables of targeted words as he/she reads the words aloud.

16. Have the student identify the number of syllables in a word. Begin with two-syllable words, then three-syllable words, etc.

17. Teach the student that each syllable must have a vowel. Have him/her identify the vowels as the syllables are repeated aloud.

18. Divide targeted words into syllables and print them on a sheet of poster board. Have the student flip an object on the paper, and then say the syllable the object lands on. Have the student say the entire word.

19. Find the first syllable in a word in which an error exists and practice that syllable first.

20. Have the student practice nonsense words using a list of the phonograms that correspond to the syllables in the mispronounced word (e.g., elephant = bell - a - pant, dell - a - rant, jell - a - slant).

21. Have the student sit in one of three chairs which represent the number of syllables in a targeted word (e.g., three-syllable word = three chairs). Choose a word card from a prepared box and say it aloud. Have the student repeat the word and tell what syllable is represented by the chair in which he/she is sitting (e.g., for spaghetti, if the student is sitting in the second chair, he/she says spaghetti - get). Have the student change chairs and continue with another card.

22. Help the student correctly pronounce a word by slowing down his/her speech. Have him/her repeat each syllable after you and then put the first two syllables together. Add the third syllable (and fourth, etc.) when the previous ones are correct.

23. Play a game such as *Simon Says* in which the student tries to accurately imitate the sequencing in targeted words when the words are first produced by the teacher or peers.

24. Play a board game that requires the student to name pictures containing targeted words. The student has to produce the target word correctly before he/she can move on the game board. (This activity can be simplified or expanded based on the level of success of the student.)

25. Have the student cut out pictures of items containing the target sound or word. Display them where they can be practiced each day.

26. Provide the student with a word list containing targeted words. Have him/her practice the words daily. As the student masters the word list, add more words. (Using words from the student's everyday vocabulary, reading lists, spelling lists, etc., will facilitate transfer of correct production of the targeted words into everyday speech.)

27. Have the student keep a notebook of words encountered each day which contain difficult sequencing for him/her. These can be practiced by the student with teacher or peer assistance

28. Have the student keep a list of all the words he/she can think of which contain sequences of sounds which are difficult for him/her to produce.

29. Have the student use a carrier phrase combined with targeted words (e.g., I like _____. I see a _____.).

30. Have the student make up sentences using targeted words.

31. Present the student with a list of topics. Have the student select a topic and then give a spontaneous speech for a specific length of time. Count errors and suggest ways for him/her to improve.

32. Involve parents by asking them to rate their child's speech for a specific length of time (e.g., during dinner count no errors, a few errors, or many errors).

33. During oral reading, underline targeted words and reinforce the student for correct productions.

152 Has difficulty understanding nonliteral forms of speech such as idioms, proverbs, similes, metaphors, jokes, puns, and riddles

Goals:

1. The student will improve his/her critical thinking and reasoning skills.
2. The student will improve his/her vocabulary skills.
3. The student will demonstrate comprehension of nonliteral forms of speech.

Objectives:

1. The student will identify absurdities in visual or verbal material in _____ out of _____ trials.
2. The student will explain absurdities in visual or verbal material in _____ out of _____ trials.
3. The student will categorize objects, pictures, or events by similarities in _____ out of _____ trials.
4. The student will provide associations for target vocabulary in _____ out of _____ trials.
5. The student will define target vocabulary in _____ out of _____ trials.
6. The student will differentiate between literal and nonliteral meanings of idioms, proverbs, similes, etc., in _____ out of _____ trials.
7. The student will restate nonliteral forms of speech in his/her own words in _____ out of _____ trials.
8. The student will use nonliteral forms of speech in everyday speaking situations in _____ out of _____ trials.
9. The student will differentiate between similes and metaphors in _____ out of _____ trials.
10. The student will demonstrate the ability to comprehend an idiom by providing a one-word translation with _____% accuracy.
11. The student will demonstrate the ability to create a simile by producing one when given the first part of a phrase with _____% accuracy.
12. The student will demonstrate the ability to create a metaphor by changing a simile to a metaphor with _____% accuracy.
13. The student will demonstrate understanding of the difference between a simile and a metaphor by identifying whether phrases are one or the other with _____% accuracy.
14. The student will demonstrate comprehension of the meaning of proverbs by paraphrasing them with _____% accuracy.

Interventions:

1. Have the student's hearing checked if it has not been recently checked.

2. Reinforce the student for demonstrating comprehension of figurative language: (a) give the student a tangible reward (e.g., classroom privileges, line leading, passing out materials, five minutes free time, etc.) or (b) give the student an intangible reward (e.g., praise, fist bump, smile, etc.).

3. Explain to the student that nonliteral forms of language make communication more interesting, but they never mean exactly what they say. Identify the concept of playing with language through nonliteral forms.

4. Reinforce those students in the classroom who demonstrate comprehension of nonliteral forms of language.

5. Choose a peer to model comprehension of figurative language for the student. Have the peer work with the student to improve his/her comprehension of nonliteral forms of language.

6. Teach a unit on figurative language. Have the student choose the more interesting of sentence pairs (e.g., Joe talks too much. - Joe is always shooting off his mouth.).

7. Have the student match idioms, similes, metaphors, etc., to their definitions.

8. Have the student keep a vocabulary or figurative language notebook in which he/she can list new vocabulary and nonliteral forms of language accompanied by definitions for reference.

9. Point out idioms, similes, metaphors, etc., that are contained in the student's everyday reading materials. Help him/her determine the meaning from context by providing two or three choices, including the literal translation.

10. Have the student identify idioms, similes, metaphors, etc., in his/her everyday reading material and determine the meaning from context. Provide choices of definitions, including the literal translation, when necessary.

11. Point out to the student that a simile uses as or like and a metaphor does not. Emphasize that neither form of figurative language is meant to be interpreted literally.

12. Have the student list things which possess a specific quality (e.g., blue things: October sky, cornflower, sapphire; hot things: oven, sun, firecracker; etc.). Then have him/her complete a statement with an appropriate simile or metaphor (e.g., Her eyes were as blue as _____. On a summer day, the front seat of the car was as hot as _____.).

13. Have the student choose an idiom, simile, metaphor, etc., from a list to complete a sentence, paragraph, story, etc.

14. Have the student illustrate the literal translation and true meaning of an idiom, simile, metaphor, etc., (e.g., raining cats and dogs, mad as a hornet, feeling blue, etc.).

15. Draw attention to idioms, similes, metaphors, etc., used throughout the day and have the student explain his/her interpretation of their meanings.

16. Divide the class into teams and have one team illustrate an idiom, simile, metaphor, etc., according to its literal translation while the other team guesses what it is and uses it appropriately in a sentence.

17. Have the student illustrate both meanings of proverbs, puns, etc.

18. Have the class design greeting cards, posters, ads, bulletin boards, etc., using idioms, similes, metaphors, etc.

19. Point out that some TV commercials and magazine ads use figurative language to get attention. Have the student identify idioms, similes, puns, etc., in specific commercials or ads.

20. Have the students ask parents/grandparents to provide examples of figurative language used when they were younger (e.g., out of sight, far out, etc.).

21. Post an *Idiom for the Day* and have the class use it in as many contexts as possible to reinforce its meaning (e.g., seeing eye to eye, clear as mud, etc.). Similes and metaphors could be posted and used in the same way.

22. Point out proverbs in context, as in *Aesop's Fables, Poor Richard's Almanac*, etc. Have the student use the context of the story to help him/her choose an appropriate moral from two options.

23. Have the student match a list of proverbs with their definitions.

24. Have the student find matches for proverbs that have been cut into two parts (e.g., money burns a hole/in your pocket; do not kill the goose that lays/the golden egg; etc.).

25. Post a *Proverb for the Day* and use it throughout the day. Have the class identify its meaning whenever it is used.

26. Point out that nonverbal communication can serve as a cue that a joke is being made (e.g., smile, wink, nudge, etc.).

27. Have the student choose a punch line for a riddle (e.g., What has four wheels and flies? - a car, an airplane, or a garbage truck).

28. Have the class design greeting cards, bulletin boards, posters, ads, etc., using proverbs, puns, etc.

Goal:

1. The student will improve his/her verbal sentence structure.

Objectives:

1. The student will differentiate between grammatically complete and incomplete sentences in _____ out of _____ trials.
2. The student will imitate grammatically complete sentences in _____ out of _____ trials.
3. The student will use grammatically complete sentences during structured language activities in _____ out of _____ trials.
4. The student will spontaneously use grammatically complete sentences in _____ out of _____ trials.
5. The student will use grammatically complete sentences in conversational speech in _____ out of _____ trials.
6. The student will use auxiliary verbs correctly (e.g., The boy is walking.) in _____ out of _____ trials.
7. The student will use linking verbs correctly (e.g., The boy is happy.) in _____ out of _____ trials.
8. The student will correctly use the articles a, an, the, or some with the appropriate nouns in phrases in _____ out of _____ trials.
9. The student will correctly use the articles a, an, the, or some with the appropriate nouns in sentences in _____ out of _____ trials.

Interventions:

1. Have the student's hearing checked if it has not been recently checked.

2. Speak to the student to explain that he/she is using grammatically incomplete sentences by omitting the function words. Explain the importance of speaking in grammatically complete sentences.

3. Determine the type of grammatical model to which the student is exposed at home. Without placing negative connotations on his/her parents' grammatical style, explain the difference between standard and nonstandard grammar. Explain the importance of function words.

4. Model speaking in complete statements or thoughts (e.g., speak clearly, slowly, concisely, and in complete sentences, including all function words) for the student.

5. Allow the student to speak without being interrupted or hurried.

6. Reduce the emphasis on competition. Competitive activities may cause the student to hurry and not include appropriate function words.

7. Have the student keep a list of times and/or situations in which he/she is nervous, anxious, etc., and has more trouble with speech than usual. Help the student identify ways to feel more confident in those situations.

8. Reinforce the student for using grammatically complete sentences and including appropriate function words in his/her speech: (a) give the student a tangible reward (e.g., classroom privileges, line leading, passing out materials, five minutes free time, etc.) or (b) give the student an intangible reward (e.g., praise, fist bump, smile, etc.).

9. Demonstrate correct and incorrect speech. Use grammatically complete/incomplete sentences, including/excluding appropriate function words, and have the student critique each example and make appropriate modifications.

10. When the student has difficulty during a conversation, remind him/her that this occasionally happens to everyone.

11. Choose a peer to model the appropriate use of function words for the student.

12. If the student omits articles, have him/her point to items in a catalog or book while naming the item with an appropriate article (e.g., a shoe, a book, an apple, the car, etc.).

13. When the student does not use complete sentences with appropriate function words (e.g., He sits on box.), expand on what he/she said (e.g., He sits on the box.). This provides a model for more complete sentences with appropriate function words.

14. Make sure the student understands the use of function words by pointing out that grammatically complete sentences contain certain types of words such as articles (the, an, a), auxiliary verbs (is, are, was, were) used with other verbs, copular verbs (is, are, was, were) used alone, etc. An analysis of the specific types of words the student is omitting may be necessary for this activity.

15. Increase the student's awareness of the omissions by audio recording the student while he/she is speaking with another student who uses grammatically complete sentences which include appropriate function words. Play the recording for the student to see if he/she can identify statements which include the appropriate function words.

16. Make note of the student's most common errors and write out some of the sentences. Go over the list with the student and teach which articles go with specific nouns.

17. Make a practice sheet of nouns and articles for the student to match.

18. Have the student supply omitted function words in verbal and written activities (e.g., The bird _____ flying. _____ bird is flying.).

19. Use a puppet to produce statements which omit function words, similar to those omitted by the student. Have the student correct the puppet's errors.

20. Provide the student with simple scrambled sentences which contain appropriate function words. Have the student unscramble the words to make a complete sentence.

21. Provide the student with noun cards, verb cards, article cards, and helping verb cards. Have him/her create sentences using one of each (e.g., A cat is running.).

22. Have the student practice the use of articles by having him/her rapidly name pictures or objects with an appropriate article. Include some nouns that begin with vowel sounds to facilitate the use of an.

23. Have the student name objects in the classroom using an appropriate article before each one.

24. Have the student act out specific verbs while saying what he/she is doing (e.g., I am running, walking, jumping, etc.).

25. Play *I am going on a trip and I am taking _____.* Add a logical item with each successive turn. Require correct usage of auxiliary verbs and articles.

26. Use a private signal (e.g., touching earlobe, raising index finger, etc.) to remind the student to use grammatically complete sentences containing appropriate function words.

27. Routinely audio record the student's speech and point out grammatically incomplete sentences that lack appropriate function words. With each recording, reinforce the student as his/her use of grammatically complete sentences improves.

28. After audio recording the student's speech, have him/her identify the grammatically incomplete sentences and make appropriate modifications by including function words where omitted.

29. Have the student complete worksheets in which he/she must choose between sentences which contain appropriate function words and sentences which do not. Have him/her make appropriate modifications.

30. During the day, write down examples of the student's sentences in which appropriate function words are omitted. Read the sentences to the student and have him/her make appropriate corrections verbally.

31. Make a list of the most common sentences in which the student omits function words. Spend time with the student practicing how to make these sentences complete.

32. Have the student verbally construct grammatically complete sentences when provided with subject and verb forms. Emphasize the use of appropriate function words.

33. When speaking privately with the student, restate his/her incomplete sentence with a rising inflection (e.g., Ball under table?) to assess if the student recognizes errors and spontaneously makes appropriate corrections.

34. Using a book without words, have the student tell the story with grammatically complete sentences containing appropriate function words. Audio record the story and play it for the student. Have the student listen for complete/incomplete sentences and make appropriate corrections.

35. Make a list of the attributes which are likely to help a person become a good speaker (e.g., takes his/her time, thinks of what to say before speaking, etc.).

36. Ask the parents to encourage the student's use of grammatically complete sentences at home by praising him/her when complete sentences are used and appropriate function words are included.

37. Video the student and his/her classmates performing various actions. Play the video without the sound and have the student narrate in grammatically complete sentences which contain all appropriate function words. A prerecorded video could also be used for this activity.

38. Use simple comic strips with captions deleted and have the student describe what the characters are doing in complete sentences containing appropriate function words.

39. Have the student practice descriptive statements or thoughts he/she can use when speaking, with an emphasis on the inclusion of function words.

40. Have the student role-play various situations in which speaking well is important (e.g., during a job interview).

Goal:

1. The student will improve his/her usage of the present progressive.

Objectives:

1. The student will differentiate between sentences containing correct and incorrect present progressive verb forms in _____ out of _____ trials.
2. The student will imitate appropriate present progressive verbs in sentences in _____ out of _____ trials.
3. The student will utilize appropriate present progressive verbs in sentences in _____ out of _____ trials.
4. The student will spontaneously produce appropriate present progressive verbs during conversational speech in _____ out of _____ trials.

Interventions:

1. Have the student's hearing checked if it has not been recently checked.

2. Determine the type of grammatical model to which the student is exposed at home. Without placing negative connotations on his/her parents' grammatical style, explain the difference between standard and nonstandard grammar.

3. Determine if the student's errors are the result of dialectical differences (the omission of present progressive tense may not be atypical within his/her social group).

4. Reinforce the student for using present progressive tense correctly: (a) give the student a tangible reward (e.g., classroom privileges, line leading, passing out materials, five minutes free time, etc.) or (b) give the student an intangible reward (e.g., praise, fist bump, smile, etc.).

5. Reinforce those students in the classroom who use present progressive tense correctly.

6. Increase the student's awareness of the problem by audio recording the student while he/she is speaking with another student who uses present progressive tense correctly. Play the recording back for the student to see if he/she can identify correct/incorrect verb usage.

7. Choose a peer to model present progressive tense correctly for the student.

8. Use a private signal (e.g., touching earlobe, raising index finger, etc.) to remind the student to use present progressive tense.

9. Audio record the student's speech to point out present progressive tense errors. With each recording, reinforce the student as his/her use of present progressive tense improves.

10. After audio recording the student's speech, have him/her identify the incorrect present progressive verbs and make appropriate corrections.

11. Have the student complete worksheets in which he/she must choose the appropriate verb to use in sentences (e.g., She (is walking/walk) to school.).

12. Have the student change sentences on worksheets to present progressive tense (e.g., She walks to school. - She is walking to school.).

13. During the day, write down specific present progressive tense errors produced by the student. Read the sentences to the student and have him/her make corrections verbally.

14. Give the student a sentence and have him/her change it from present tense to present progressive tense (e.g., I walk. - I am walking.).

15. Ask open-ended questions which stimulate use of present progressive tense (e.g., What is that boy doing?).

16. Ask the parents to encourage the student's correct use of present progressive tense at home by praising him/her for correct usage.

17. While the class is engaged in various activities, describe your observations using present progressive tense. Have students do likewise.

18. Video the student and his/her classmates performing various actions. Play the video without the sound and have the student narrate what is happening using present progressive tense. A prerecorded video could also be used for this activity.

19. When speaking privately with the student, restate his/her present progressive tense errors with a rising inflection (e.g., She walk?) to assess if the student recognizes errors and spontaneously makes corrections.

155 Voice pitch is too high or too low for age and gender

Goals:

1. The student will correctly discriminate vocal quality in himself/herself and others.
2. The student will demonstrate appropriate pitch.
3. The student will demonstrate appropriate vocal quality.

Objectives:

1. The student will identify appropriate and inappropriate pitch levels in _____ out of _____ trials.
2. The student will identify personal situations during which appropriate and inappropriate pitch levels occur.
3. The student will utilize appropriate pitch levels during productions of words in _____ out of _____ trials.
4. The student will utilize appropriate pitch levels during productions of sentences in _____ out of _____ trials.
5. The student will utilize appropriate pitch levels while reading in _____ out of _____ trials.
6. The student will utilize appropriate pitch levels during conversation in _____ out of _____ trials.

Interventions:

1. Have the student's hearing checked if it has not been recently checked.

2. Speak to the student and explain that he/she is using a pitch level that is too high/low. Explain the importance of using an appropriate pitch level.

3. Provide the student with an appropriate voice model.

4. Reinforce the student for appropriate voice quality: (a) give the student a tangible reward (e.g., classroom privileges, line leading, passing out materials, five minutes free time, etc.) or (b) give the student an intangible reward (e.g., praise, fist bump, smile, etc.).

5. Increase the student's awareness of the problem by audio recording him/her while he/she is speaking with a peer who exhibits an appropriate pitch level. Play the recording to see if the student can hear the difference between the pitch levels.

6. Demonstrate laryngeal tension by having the student vocalize (e.g., say eee or ah) while trying to lift himself/herself up from a sitting position in a hard chair.

7. Discuss with the student the negative connotations which are sometimes attached to people who use a pitch level that is too high or too low. Unusual pitch levels may be interpreted to mean that the person is overly weak or possesses low self-esteem. Discussion of these negative connotations may motivate the student to make changes in his/her pitch.

8. Select simple reading materials and have the student read aloud with varying levels of pitch while you record the reading. Have the student listen and decide which levels are most appropriate.

9. Have the student differentiate between tension and relaxation by first tensing his/her body and then relaxing. (Feel the student's neck and shoulders to determine the presence or absence of tension.)

10. Have the student use relaxation exercises (e.g., tensing and then relaxing specific muscle groups, head rotation exercises, imagery, etc.).

11. To facilitate understanding of a voice problem (pitch too high/low), develop a short unit on vocal quality to be taught to the class.

12. Have the student describe animal voices that are low/high (e.g., lion - low; mouse - high) and compare them with his/her own pitch level.

13. Have the student describe the pitch level of famous people, cartoon characters, people at school or home, etc. Have him/her differentiate between pitch levels that sound low and those that are high.

14. Use puppets to demonstrate different levels of pitch. Have the student attempt to match the pitch levels.

15. Encourage good posture while sitting, standing, walking, etc. Poor posture can obstruct good breath support which facilitates normal levels of pitch.

16. Have the student demonstrate proper breath support for speaking using his/her diaphragm.

17. If the student's pitch level changes while he/she is under stress, bring this information to the attention of the student.

18. Have the student rank, hierarchically, the situations in which his/her pitch level is too high or too low. Discuss these situations to facilitate the student's awareness of when he/she is using inappropriate pitch levels and the variance in the situations.

19. Involve the parents by asking them to rate their child's pitch level (e.g., appropriate, too high, too low) for a specific length of time and/or in a specific situation (e.g., during playtime, at dinner, at bedtime; inside or outside; in the presence of family members, peers, or authority figures; etc.).

20. Check to see if the child is taking part in activities which could strain his/her voice. Pitch changes can occur as a result of vocal abuse. If the child is involved in situations where he/she abuses his/her voice, alternatives to these situations should be introduced.

21. Have the student list school activities during which his/her voice is too high or too low. Discuss ways the student could use a more moderate pitch level during these situations.

22. Work on downward and upward inflectional shifts of the same word, initially exaggerating the extent of pitch change.

23. Have the student take part in short plays or skits which require a lower/higher pitch level (e.g., *Goldilocks and the Three Bears*).

24. Fill two glasses with varying amounts of water and tap them with a spoon. Have the student identify which is higher/lower. Have him/her try to match the pitch levels.

25. Have the student demonstrate pitch differences by stretching and plucking rubber bands that he/she pulls to different lengths. Discuss with the students that this is how the vocal cords perform: the tighter they are stretched, the higher the resulting pitch.

26. Play a high/low note on a pitch pipe. If the pitch is low, the student responds in a low voice; if the pitch is high, the student responds in a high voice. As a class activity, the student will benefit from hearing pitch changes in the voices of other students.

27. Have the student list all the different sound effects that he/she and his/her friends make while playing and their pitch levels (e.g., motor noises, monster noises, etc.).

28. Discuss the effect on their voices. Suggest alternatives to voices that use extremely low or high pitches or are too loud.

29. Have the student list occasions when he/she uses a volume level that is too loud or too soft or a pitch level that is too high or too low. Discuss alternative ways to communicate in these situations (e.g., walk over to a person instead of shouting across the room, blow a whistle outside to get someone's attention instead of yelling, talk at a normal volume level as opposed to a whisper, etc.).

30. Have the student identify occasions when he/she uses good vocal quality vs. a voice that is too high or too low in pitch. Discuss ways to improve vocal quality during these situations.

31. Have the student demonstrate his/her best (optimal) pitch level.

32. Have the student tally the number of times he/she uses a pitch level that is too high or too low (e.g., during recess, while speaking to a teacher, etc.).

33. When the student has a cold, sore throat, laryngitis, etc.; discuss how the throat might look and encourage the student to talk as little as possible. Do not encourage whispering as an alternative as it may also irritate his/her voice.

34. When the student is about to engage in an activity that facilitates vocal abuse, have him/her wear a string bracelet, sticker, etc., to remind him/her to use alternative strategies, good vocal quality, and appropriate volume levels.

35. Establish a method that you can use to remind the student to use good vocal quality when he/she is speaking too loud/soft or too high/low (e.g., thumbs up to raise pitch, thumbs down to lower pitch).

36. Remind the student to use proper breathing techniques and a relaxed voice during music class, which can be a period of vocal stress.

37. Discuss with the student how temperature and humidity can influence his/her vocal quality.

38. Discuss how a person's voice changes when they are nervous, tired, angry, etc.

Goals:

1. The student will improve his/her articulation skills.
2. The student will improve his/her discrimination of speech sounds.
3. The student will improve his/her production of speech sounds in isolation.
4. The student will improve his/her production of speech sounds in syllables.
5. The student will improve his/her production of speech sounds in words.
6. The student will improve his/her production of speech sounds in sentences.
7. The student will improve his/her production of speech sounds in spontaneous speech.

Objectives:

1. The student will recognize a too fast (or too slow) rate of speech when samples are presented in _____ out of _____ trials.
2. The student will imitate sentences at an appropriate rate of speech in _____ out of _____ trials.
3. The student will read sentences at an appropriate rate of speech in _____ out of _____ trials.
4. The student will spontaneously produce sentences at an appropriate rate of speech in _____ out of _____ trials.

Interventions:

1. Have the student's hearing checked if it has not been recently checked.

2. Audio record your own speech and time the recording. Divide the number of words by the time elapsed to determine words per minute. If slower or faster than 160-170 words per minute, adjust your own rate of speaking to provide the student with an appropriate model.

3. Evaluate the appropriateness of requiring the student to speak at a certain rate (e.g., the student may have difficulty processing information or experience word-finding difficulties which slow his/her speech).

4. Speak to the student to explain what he/she needs to do differently (e.g., speak slower or faster).

5. Reinforce the student for speaking at an appropriate rate: (a) give the student a tangible reward (e.g., classroom privileges, line leading, passing out materials, five minutes free time, etc.) or (b) give the student an intangible reward (e.g., praise, fist bump, smile, etc.). Initially, consistent reinforcement may be needed. As the student progresses, random reinforcement may be adequate.

6. Develop a signal between you and the student to indicate that he/she needs to slow down/speed up.

7. Determine the student's rate of speech by having him/her read a passage with which he/she is comfortable while you time the reading. Divide the number of words in the passage by the time elapsed to determine the words per minute or rate. A good rate is 160 to 170 words per minute. Discuss this with the student and then time him/her at weekly intervals for six weeks. Chart his/her progress.

8. Audio record the student and play a portion of the recording back to him/her to determine if he/she can recognize the inappropriate rate of speech. If the student does not identify an appropriate rate, play recordings that demonstrate an appropriate rate of speech for practice.

9. Have the student practice saying a sentence at an appropriate rate and then at an inappropriate rate. Have the student listen and compare, then identify which sentence is better. Audio recording may facilitate this activity.

10. Have the student recite the alphabet with short/fast duration of each consonant. Repeat this exercise with average duration and long/slow duration.

11. Have the student read a list of one-syllable words with exaggerated short/fast duration of each word. Repeat this exercise with average duration and long/slow duration.

12. Have the student read an easy passage at 100 wpm and then at 200 wpm. Discuss his/her success or lack of success.

13. Have the student read an easy passage of approximately 1000 words that has been marked off into blocks of 160-170 words. Time the student while he/she is reading this passage and signal at one-minute intervals so that the student becomes aware of the appropriate rate of speech.

14. Have the student practice saying the same sentence over and over with emphasis on a different word each time (e.g., **You** went home late. You went **home** late. You went home **late**.).

15. Tape a reminder (e.g., to slow down or speed up) to the student's desk to make him/her aware of his/her rate of speech.

16. Use a metronome and have the student read or repeat words at an appropriate rate of speech. Turn the metronome off to check if the student can match the practiced rate.

17. Have the student take part in short skits or plays which require him/her to use a voice which is slower/faster.

18. Tap a finger lightly as the student is speaking to facilitate his/her awareness of his/her rate of speech.

19. Consult with the student's music teacher about rhythm exercises/games which can be implemented in the classroom or the music room. The student's rate may improve with his/her awareness of rhythm.

Goals:

1. The student will decrease his/her stuttering behavior.
2. The student will decrease his/her secondary stuttering characteristics.

Objectives:

1. The student's stuttering behavior, including secondary characteristics, will decrease by _____%.
2. The student will use slow, easy speech in a controlled one-to-one environment in _____ out of _____ trials.
3. The student will use slow, easy speech in the presence of peers in _____ out of _____ trials.
4. The student will use slow, easy speech in the presence of authority figures in _____ out of _____ trials.
5. The student will imitate echo speech correctly _____% of the time.
6. The student will demonstrate control by fluent stuttering to break pseudo-block with _____% accuracy.
7. The student will monitor his/her speech _____% of the time.

Interventions:

1. Have the student's hearing checked if it has not been recently checked.

2. Reinforce the student for speaking fluently: (a) give the student a tangible reward (e.g., classroom privileges, line leading, passing out materials, five minutes free time, etc.) or (b) give the student an intangible reward (e.g., praise, fist bump, smile, etc.).

3. Familiarize yourself and the student with the terms fluency, dysfluency, stuttering, easy speech, etc. Keep these words as neutral as possible, without negative connotations.

4. Evaluate the appropriateness of requiring the student to speak without dysfluency (e.g., developmentally, young children experience normal dysfluency in their speech and all persons are occasionally dysfluent).

5. Provide the student with an appropriate model of slow, easy speech. Lengthen the pauses between words, phrases, and sentences.

6. Choose a peer to model appropriate speech for the student. Pair the students to sit together, perform assignments together, etc.

7. During conversations, calmly delay your verbal responses by one or two seconds.

8. Audio record the student so he/she may listen to and evaluate his/her own speech.

9. Have the student identify a good speaker and give the reasons he/she thinks that person is a good speaker.

10. Develop a list of the attributes which are likely to help a person become a good speaker. Have the student practice each attribute.

11. During oral reading, underline or highlight words which are difficult for the student to say and provide reinforcement when he/she says them fluently.

12. Have the student keep a list of times and/or situations in which he/she has particular difficulty with speech (e.g., times when he/she is nervous, embarrassed, etc.). Discuss the reasons for this and seek solutions to the difficulty experienced.

13. Have the student practice techniques for relaxing (e.g., deep breathing, tensing and relaxing muscles, etc.) which he/she can employ when he/she starts to become dysfluent.

14. Have the student identify the specific words or phrases on which he/she becomes dysfluent and practice those particular words or phrases.

15. Encourage the student to maintain eye contact during all speaking situations. If the student is noticeably more fluent when eye contact is averted, attempt to facilitate eye contact on a gradual basis.

16. Have the student speak in unison with you while you are modeling slow, easy speech.

17. Reinforce the student's moments of relative fluency. Emphasize that these occurred during moments when he/she was speaking slowly and easily.

18. Empathize with the student and explain that he/she is not less valuable as a person because of dysfluency. Emphasize the student's positive attributes.

19. Empathize with feelings of anger which the student may be experiencing.

20. When the student is speaking fluently, try to extend the positive experience by allowing him/her to continue speaking.

21. Reinforce the student each time he/she answers a question or makes a spontaneous comment in class.

22. If the student is speaking too rapidly, remind him/her to slow down and take his/her time. Develop a private signal (e.g., raising one finger, touching earlobe, etc.) to avoid calling too much attention to his/her speech in front of the whole class.

23. Give the student your undivided attention when he/she is speaking to you so he/she will not feel a need to hurry or compete with others for attention.

24. If the student is more dysfluent when he/she is involved in another activity at the same time he/she is talking, encourage him/her to stop the other activity.

25. If the student is highly excited, wait until he/she is calmer before requiring any verbal explanations or interactions. A high level of excitement often interferes with fluency.

26. During moments of dysfluency, use non-verbal activities to relax the student.

27. Do not interrupt or finish the student's sentences even if you think you can anticipate what the student is going to say. This can be extremely frustrating and may decrease the student's willingness to engage in future communicative interactions.

28. Help the student learn to identify periods of dysfluency and periods of slow, easy speech.

29. Help the student identify situations in which he/she is more fluent or less fluent. Determine the features of the fluent situations that seem to facilitate fluency and transfer those features to the less fluent situations.

30. When the student is dysfluent during conversation, explain to him/her that this happens to everyone at times.

31. Do not force the student to interact with others if it causes dysfluency.

32. Point out to the student that he/she is capable of fluent speech and is in control of his/her speech in many situations.

33. Model slow, easy speech for the student and encourage him/her to speak at a similar rate. Practice with the student for a short time each day until he/she is able to match the rate.

34. Provide the student with a list of sentences and encourage him/her to read these at a slow rate.

35. Prepare simple verbal reading passages in written form in which phrases are separated by large spaces (indicating a pause). Have the student practice reading the passages aloud.

36. Use a private cue (e.g., raise a finger, touch earlobe, etc.) to encourage the student to answer questions at a slow rate of speech.

37. Use a private cue (e.g., raise a finger, touch earlobe, etc.) to encourage the student to use a slow speaking rate during classroom activities.

38. Reduce the emphasis on competition. Competitive activities may increase the student's anxiety and cause him/her to be more dysfluent.

39. Do not require the student to speak in front of other students if he/she is uncomfortable doing so. Have the student speak to the teacher or another student privately if he/she would be more comfortable.

40. As the student is able to speak fluently in more situations (e.g., delivering messages to the office, speaking with the counselor, etc.), gradually increase those experiences as long as the student continues to be successful.

41. Meet with the student's parents to determine his/her level of dysfluency at home, parental reactions to the dysfluency, and successful strategies the parents have employed when dealing with the dysfluent behavior.

42. Teach the student ways to restate or rephrase a misunderstood message rather than continuing to repeat the original message with the same error pattern.

43. Take time to listen to the student when he/she displays frustration/anger. Talk to the student about appropriate ways of dealing with these feelings.

44. Determine whether or not the student avoids certain situations because of his/her perception of increased dysfluency. Discuss with the student the aspects of those situations that seem to cause increased anxiety. Examine possible modifications that could be implemented in the classroom to facilitate frustration tolerance (e.g., if speaking in front of the whole class causes stress, reduce the number of listeners and gradually increase the size of the group as the student's frustration tolerance increases).

45. Discuss and role-play with the entire class different disabilities and the accompanying frustrations they might feel if they were experiencing similar difficulties. Include speech problems in this discussion.

46. When the student seems extremely frustrated by a stuttering episode, react calmly with a reassuring statement (e.g., Sometimes words do not come out easily, do they? You worked hard on that word.).

47. When the student experiences a severe episode of dysfluency, respond by paraphrasing/repeating the content of his/her message to communicate that the message has been understood.

48. Provide the student with as many social and academic successes as possible.

Goals:

1. The student will decrease his/her secondary stuttering characteristics.
2. The student will decrease his/her stuttering behavior.
3. The student will improve his/her conversational speech.
4. The student will improve his/her frustration tolerance level.
5. The student will improve his/her grammatical speech.
6. The student will improve his/her production of speech sounds.
7. The student will improve the ability to express himself/herself verbally.
8. The student will improve the fluency of his/her speech.

Objectives:

1. The student will correctly pause between words, phrases, and sentences on _____out of _____occasions.
2. The student will identify listener behaviors which indicate that his/her message was not fully understood in _____ out of _____ trials.
3. The student will restate a misunderstood message in _____ out of _____ trials.
4. The student will speak at a rate that can be understood by a listener _____% of the time.
5. The student will speak at a rate with repetitions and corrections to be understood by a listener _____% of the time.
6. The student will use slow, easy speech with decreased signs of frustration in the presence of authority figures in _____ out of _____ trials.
7. The student will use slow, easy speech with decreased signs of frustration in the presence of peers in _____ out of _____ trials.
8. The student will use slow, easy speech with decreased signs of frustration in a controlled one-to-one environment in _____ out of _____ trials.

Interventions:

1. As the student is able to speak fluently in more situations (e.g., delivering messages to the office, speaking with the counselor, etc.), gradually increase those experiences as long as the student continues to be successful.

2. Determine whether or not the student avoids certain situations because of his/her perception of increased dysfluency. Discuss with the student the aspects of those situations that seem to cause increased anxiety. Examine possible modifications that could be implemented in the classroom to facilitate frustration tolerance (e.g., if speaking in front of the whole class causes stress, reduce the number of listeners and gradually increase the size of the group as the student's frustration tolerance increases).

3. Have the student keep a list of times and/or situations in which speech is difficult (e.g., times when he/she is nervous, embarrassed, etc.). Discuss the reasons for this and consider possible solutions to the difficulty experienced.

4. Discuss and role-play with the entire class different disabilities and the accompanying frustrations they might feel if they were experiencing similar difficulties. Include speech problems in this discussion.

5. Do not interrupt or finish the student's sentences even if you think you can anticipate what the student is going to say. This can be extremely frustrating and may decrease the student's willingness to participate in future communicative interactions.

6. During conversations, calmly delay your verbal responses by one or two seconds.

7. If the student is speaking too rapidly, remind him/her to slow down. Develop a private signal (e.g., raising one finger, touching earlobe, etc.) to avoid calling too much attention to the student's speech in front of the whole class.

8. During oral reading, underline or high-light words which are difficult for the student to say and provide reinforcement when he/she says them fluently.

9. Empathize with feelings of anger which the student may be experiencing due to speaking dysfluently.

10. Encourage the student to maintain eye contact during all speaking situations. If the student is noticeably more fluent when eye contact is averted, attempt to facilitate eye contact on a gradual basis.

11. When the student is speaking fluently, try to extend the positive experience by allowing him/her to continue speaking.

12. Evaluate the appropriateness of requir-ing the student to speak without dysfluency (e.g., developmentally, young children experi-ence normal dysfluency in their speech and all persons are occasionally dysfluent).

13. Develop a list of the attributes which are likely to help a person become a good speaker. Have the student practice each attribute.

14. Familiarize yourself and the student with the terms fluency, dysfluency, stuttering, easy speech, etc. Keep these words as neutral as pos-sible, without negative connotations.

15. Have the student identify a good speaker and give the reasons he/she thinks that person is a good speaker.

16. If the student is more dysfluent when involved in another activity at the same time he/she is talking, encourage the student to stop the other activity.

17. Have the student identify the specific words or phrases on which he/she becomes dysfluent and practice those particular words or phrases.

18. When the student seems extremely frus-trated by a stuttering episode, react calmly with a reassuring statement (e.g., Sometimes words do not come out easily, do they? You worked hard on that word.).

19. Have the student speak in unison with you while you are modeling slow, easy speech.

20. Do not require the student to speak in front of other students if he/she is uncomfortable doing so. Have the student speak to the teacher or another student privately if the student would be more comfortable doing so.

21. Provide the student with as many social and academic successes as possible.

22. Help the student learn to identify periods of dysfluency and periods of slow, easy speech.

23. Choose a peer to model appropriate speech for the student. Pair the students to sit together, perform assignments together, etc.

24. If the student is highly excited, wait until he/she is calmer before requiring any verbal explanations or interactions. A high level of excitement often interferes with fluency.

25. During moments of dysfluency, use non-verbal activities to relax the student.

26. Reinforce the student for speaking flu-ently: (a) give the student a tangible reward (e.g., classroom privileges, line leading, passing out materials, five minutes free time, etc.) or (b) give the student an intangible reward (e.g., praise, fist bump, smile, etc.).

27. Have the student's hearing checked if it has not been recently checked.

28. Meet with the student's parents to determine his/her level of dysfluency at home, parental reactions to the dysfluency, and suc-cessful strategies the parents have employed when dealing with the dysfluent speech.

29. Help the student identify situations in which he/she is more fluent or less fluent. Determine the features of the fluent situations that seem to facilitate fluency and transfer those features to the less fluent situations.

30. Model slow, easy speech for the student and encourage him/her to speak at a similar rate. Practice with the student for a short time each day until he/she is able to match the rate.

31. Give the student your undivided attention when he/she is speaking to you so he/she will not feel a need to hurry or compete with others for attention.

32. Point out to the student that he/she is capable of fluent speech and is in control of speech in many situations.

33. Reduce the emphasis on competition. Competitive activities may increase the student's anxiety and cause him/her to speak more dysfluently.

34. Prepare simple verbal reading passages in written form in which phrases are separated by large spaces (indicating a pause). Have the student practice reading the passages aloud.

35. Use a private cue (e.g., raise a finger, touch earlobe, etc.) to encourage the student to answer questions at a slow rate of speech.

36. Provide the student with an appropriate model of slow, easy speech. Lengthen the pauses between words, phrases, and sentences.

37. Reinforce the student each time he/she answers a question or makes a spontaneous comment in class.

38. Take time to listen to the student when he/she displays frustration/anger. Talk to the student about appropriate ways of dealing with these feelings.

39. Teach the student ways to restate or rephrase a misunderstood message rather than continuing to repeat the original message with the same error patterns.

40. Provide the student with a list of sentences and encourage him/her to read these at a slow rate.

41. Do not force the student to interact with others if it causes dysfluency.

42. When the student is dysfluent during conversation, explain that this happens to everyone at times.

43. Reinforce the student's moments of relative fluency. Emphasize that these occurred during moments when he/she was speaking slowly and easily.

44. Use a private cue (e.g., raise a finger, touch earlobe, etc.) to encourage the student to use a slow speaking rate during classroom activities.

45. Audio record the student so he/she may listen to and evaluate his/her own speech.

46. Empathize with the student and explain that he/she is not less valuable as a person because of his/her dysfluency. Emphasize the student's positive attributes.

47. Have the student practice techniques for relaxing (e.g., deep breathing, tensing and relaxing muscles, etc.) which can be employed when he/she starts to speak dysfluently.

48. When the student experiences a severe episode of dysfluency, respond by paraphrasing/repeating the content of his/her message to communicate that the message has been understood.

159 Speaks in an unnatural voice

Goals:

1. The student will speak in a natural voice.
2. The student will use a natural tone of voice when speaking.

Objectives:

1. The student will speak in a natural voice on _____ out of _____ trials.
2. The student will use a natural tone of voice when speaking on _____ out of _____ trials.

Interventions:

1. Avoid topics, situations, etc., (e.g., death, divorce, unemployment, alcoholism, etc.) which cause the student to speak in an unnatural voice.

2. Choose a peer to model using a natural voice when speaking.

3. Write a contract with the student specifying what behavior is expected (e.g., using a natural voice) and what reinforcement will be made available when the terms of the contract have been met.

4. Communicate with parents, agencies, or the appropriate parties to inform them of the problem, determine the cause of the problem, and consider possible solutions to the problem.

5. Do not force the student to interact with others.

6. Reinforce those students in the classroom who use a natural voice when speaking.

7. Evaluate the appropriateness of the task to determine (a) if the task is too easy, (b) if the task is too difficult, or (c) if the length of time scheduled to complete the task is adequate.

8. Give the student a predetermined signal when he/she begins to use an unnatural voice.

9. Ignore the student's unnatural voice if it occurs infrequently or only in stimulating situations.

10. Make sure that all adults (e.g., school and home) require the student to speak in a natural voice.

11. Reinforce the student for speaking in a natural voice based on the length of time he/she can be successful. As the student demonstrates success, gradually increase the length of time required for reinforcement.

12. Do not reinforce inappropriate behavior by laughing when the student talks in an unnatural voice.

13. Make sure that the student's unnatural voice is not inadvertently reinforced by over-attending to it (i.e., the student may speak in an unnatural voice because of the constant attention given to him/her).

14. Express your feelings in a socially acceptable way.

15. Place the student in situations in which he/she is comfortable and most likely to use a natural voice.

16. Reinforce the student for speaking in a natural voice: (a) give the student a tangible reward (e.g., classroom privileges, line leading, passing out materials, five minutes free time, etc.) or (b) give the student an intangible reward (e.g., praise, fist bump, smile, etc.).

17. Speak to the student to explain (a) what he/she is doing wrong (e.g., using an unnatural voice) and (b) what he/she should be doing (e.g., using a natural voice).

18. Teach the student appropriate ways to communicate displeasure, anger, frustration, etc.

19. Communicate with parents (e.g., notes home, phone calls, etc.) to share information about the student's progress. The parents may reinforce the student at home for using a natural voice at school.

20. Have the student use a natural voice at all times in the classroom.

160 Speaks incoherently

Goals:

1. The student will speak in a natural voice.
2. The student will speak coherently.

Objectives:

1. The student will make comments that are intelligible on _____ out of _____ trials.
2. The student will make statements that are connected on _____ out of _____ trials.
3. The student will make statements that are related on _____ out of _____ trials.
4. The student will speak coherently on _____ out of _____ trials.
5. The student will speak in a natural voice on _____ out of _____ trials.
6. The student will use a natural tone of voice when speaking on _____ out of _____ trials.

Interventions:

1. Allow the student to speak without being interrupted or hurried.

2. Model speaking coherently (e.g., speak clearly, slowly, concisely, and in complete sentences, statements, and thoughts) for the student.

3. Have the student identify who he/she thinks is a good speaker and why.

4. Break down the qualities a good speaker possesses (e.g., rate, diction, volume, vocabulary, etc.) and have the student evaluate himself/herself on each quality. Set a goal for improvement in only one or two areas at a time.

5. Demonstrate coherent and incoherent speech. Use complete/incomplete statements and thoughts and have the student critique each example.

6. Have the student practice descriptive statements or thoughts he/she can use when speaking.

7. Do not require the student to speak in front of other students if he/she is uncomfortable doing so. Have the student speak to the teacher or another student privately if he/she would be more comfortable.

8. Choose a peer to model speaking in complete statements or thoughts. Assign the students to work together, perform assignments together, etc.

9. When the student has difficulty during a conversation, remind the student that this occasionally happens to everyone and he/she should not become upset.

10. Verbally correct the student when he/she does not use complete sentences or thoughts when speaking so he/she can hear the correct version of what is being said.

11. Do not force the student to interact with others.

12. Have the student practice techniques for relaxing (e.g., deep breathing, tensing and relaxing muscles, etc.) which the student can employ when he/she starts to become dysfluent.

13. Reinforce those students in the classroom who use complete statements or thoughts when speaking.

14. If the student is speaking too rapidly, remind him/her to slow down and take his/her time. Be sure to give him/her undivided attention so he/she will not feel a need to hurry or compete with others for attention.

15. Write a contract with the student specifying what behavior is expected (e.g., using coherent statements or thoughts when speaking) and what reinforcement will be made available when the terms of the contract have been met.

16. Have the student role-play various situations in which speaking coherently is important (e.g., during a job interview).

17. Make a list of the attributes that are likely to help a person become a good speaker (e.g., takes his/her time, thinks of what to say before starting, etc.).

18. Prepare simple verbal reading passages in written form in which phrases are separated by large spaces (indicating a pause). Have the student practice reading the passages aloud.

19. Teach the student appropriate ways to communicate displeasure, anger, frustration, etc.

20. Have the student keep a list of times and/or situations in which he/she is nervous, anxious, etc., and has more trouble with speech than usual. Help the student identify ways to feel more successful with those situations.

21. When the student does not use complete sentences (e.g., points to a ball and names it), elaborate on what he/she said, (e.g., ask him/her if he/she wants to play with the ball). This provides a model for more complete statements and thoughts.

22. Have the student read simple passages and audio record them. Have him/her listen and underline words or phrases that were omitted, added, substituted, or rearranged.

23. Reinforce the student for using complete statements or thoughts when speaking: (a) give the student a tangible reward (e.g., classroom privileges, line leading, passing out materials, five minutes free time, etc.) or (b) give the student an intangible reward (e.g., praise, fist bump, smile, etc.).

24. Audio record a spontaneous monologue given by the student. Listen to the recording with him/her and tally error and/or correct productions. The teacher and the student should compare their analyses of the productions.

25. Make a list of the most common incomplete statements or thoughts the student uses. Spend time with the student practicing how to make these statements or thoughts complete.

26. Reduce the emphasis on competition. Competitive activities may increase the student's anxiety and reduce the student's ability to complete statements or thoughts.

161 Speaks slowly, pauses when speaking, speaks softly, speaks monotonously, speaks less than previously, etc.

Goal:

1. While expressing thoughts and feelings, the student will engage the listener's interest.

Objectives:

1. The student will express thoughts and feelings in a manner that engages the listener's interest on _____ out of _____ trials.
2. The student will demonstrate successful verbal communication skills on _____ out of _____ trials.

Interventions:

1. Reinforce the student for communicating thoughts and feelings in a way that appropriately engages the listener's attention: (a) give the student a tangible reward (e.g., classroom privileges, line leading, passing out materials, five minutes free time, etc.) or (b) give the student an intangible reward (e.g., praise, fist bump, smile, etc.).

2. Provide the student time, support (e.g., counseling, speech therapy, etc.) and encouragement to establish rapport. Any significant change in behavior, such as a student speaking less than previously or experiencing speech problems may warrant the need of additional support.

3. Make sure the student receives appropriate attention/screening to rule out factors which would frustrate the student's ability to progress.

4. Do not force the student to talk. It is more important to give positive reinforcement for voluntary speech.

5. Determine what will be positive reinforcement for the student. Social praise from an instructor or an authority source may decrease socializing behavior due to fear of embarrassment. Through a reinforcer survey, interviews with the student and parents, and observations, develop a list of positive reinforcers specific to that student.

6. Speak with the student to explain (a) what he/she has done correctly (e.g., attempting to interact during class, etc.) and (b) what he/she might be doing to improve his/her response (e.g., talking with more expression and fewer pauses, etc.).

7. Write a contract with the student specifying what behavior is expected (e.g., verbally communicating in group activities) and what reinforcement will be available when the terms of the contract have been met.

8. Communicate with parents (e.g., notes home, phone calls, etc.) to share information about the student's progress. The parents may reinforce the student at home for verbally communicating in group activities or special events at school.

9. Evaluate the appropriateness of the task to determine (a) if the task is too easy, (b) if the task is too difficult, or (c) if the length of time the student is expected to verbally communicate in an interesting, expressive manner is adequate.

10. Choose a peer to sit/work directly with the student (e.g., in different settings or activities such as art, music, P.E., on the bus, tutoring, group projects, running errands in the building, recess, etc.). Reinforce the peer for his/her positive communication during activities. Reinforce the student when he/she models the peer's positive activity response.

11. Provide the student with many opportunities for social and academic successes.

12. Give the student the responsibility of helping another in the group if the student expresses interest and confidence in the subject area.

13. Emphasize individual success or progress over winning or beating others.

14. The student may benefit from developing and achieving short-term goals and objectives addressing a concern. The following may be helpful:

- Help the student identify a short-term goal (e.g., within three to five days) related to class work to be completed.
- Develop a few objectives with the student to attain the short-term goal. Provide the student with assistance to follow the plans and achieve the goal.
- Provide the student with positive reinforcement for his/her attempts to attain the goal.
- Use the success experienced by the student in this situation to build toward replacing poor communication skills.

15. Let the student know you value his/her thoughts and opinions. The student needs to know you hear, understand, and appreciate him/her regardless of how well his/her thoughts are communicated.

16. When the student expresses concern over his/her communication skills, discuss with him/her positive steps he/she may choose to take to improve his/her skills. Reinforce the student when he/she takes positive action.

17. Teach the student to identify situations which cause him/her to speak in a boring or monotonous way. For example, the student may identify a social event, such as a dance, as a situation which results in monotonous speech. The student could then consider how he/she could initiate communication at the event.

18. When the student's worries or concerns affect his/her ability to verbally respond in stressful situations, modifying expectations may be necessary. Permitting students to develop and present verbal reports in pairs or small groups may be a more productive learning experience than expecting everyone to work alone.

19. Encourage friendship building in the classroom (e.g., students may wish to attend extracurricular activities in small groups, etc.). The opportunity to work with friends on projects may help the student overcome his/her unwarranted fears or concerns.

20. Encourage the student to communicate:
- Listen to the student.
- Help the student formulate a positive, productive approach to the concern.
- Provide the student with assistance for his/her initial attempts at using the approach to promote success.
- Provide the student with positive reinforcement for his/her efforts.
- Provide the student with input for making changes to better meet activity expectations.

21. Ask the student to record his/her thoughts and feelings in a diary or private notebook to facilitate self-expression.

22. Do not let the student's poor communication skills become a means of activity avoidance. Make sure the student participates according to expectations once fears have been addressed and there are no other factors (e.g, illness, unusual environmental stressors, etc.) that preclude regular activity involvement.

23. Ask the student to be the leader of a small-group activity if he/she possesses mastery of skills or an interest in that area.

24. Reduce the emphasis on competition. Frequent or continuous failure may result in an increase in poor communication skills.

25. Provide the student with positive feedback to indicate he/she is successfully communicating thoughts and feelings in an interesting manner.

26. The student may avoid activity participation by not going to school. Make sure the student receives support to assure his/her timely presence at school.

27. Reinforce other students for facilitating the student's self-esteem. Provide a classroom environment which includes noncompetitive small-group learning experiences and promotes the self-esteem of all students.

28. Provide success-oriented special events or activities (e.g., opportunity to be a charter member of a reading or hobby club, etc.) to develop the student's interests and the opportunity for meaningful participation.

29. Help the student build toward a desired goal in small, nonthreatening steps (e.g., small-group lunches might build toward a class party, then a picnic involving two classes, etc.).

30. Allow the student to choose peers with whom he/she feels comfortable for small-group projects.

31. Assign outgoing, nonthreatening peers to help the student participate in classroom activities.

32. Supervise classroom activities closely so peers with whom the student interacts do not stimulate inappropriate behavior or ridicule.

33. Be specific and positive when providing the student constructive criticism.

34. When the student has difficulty with verbal communication during particular situations or activities, adjust behavioral and/or activity expectations to his/her strengths and needs. As the student demonstrates success, gradually increase expectations based on his/her performance.

35. Teach the student problem-solving skills (e.g., talking, walking away, calling upon an arbitrator, compromising, etc.). This will facilitate the student being able to manage stressful times when he/she experiences difficulty with communication skills.

36. Make sure the student is able to successfully participate in activities (e.g., understands the rules, is familiar with the activity, will be compatible with peers engaged in the activity, etc.).

37. Assign responsibilities related to activities (e.g., being a leader, passing out materials, being a peer tutor, etc.) which will facilitate the student's successful verbal communication.

38. The student may appreciate constructive remarks and verbal praise in conversations away from the group. Loud, open remarks may do more harm than good regarding facilitating the social skills for the student.

39. Encourage students to give each other positive feedback for small-group contributions and other forms of positive verbal exchange.

40. Provide the student with a variety of ways to develop rapport with the instructor(s) (e.g., writing notes, talking about concerns privately, etc.).

41. Identify situations when the student will have difficulty with communication skills due to fear or worry. Discuss coping mechanisms and other choices with the student for these situations (e.g., going to a restroom if the student needs to cry; developing concise, organized notes for public speaking; etc.). Reinforce the student for his/her attempts at using such coping mechanisms.

42. Do not expect the student to directly confront the feared situation. Provide opportunities for his/her success in activities which resemble the feared situation (e.g., role-play, simulation experiences, etc.).

43. Encourage the student to work on positive, nonthreatening approaches to fearful situations (e.g., using coping skills to manage difficult situations).

44. Build positive self-concept among students by including the following approaches:
- Offer opportunities for students to work together noncompetitively on class projects.
- Identify and compliment each student's unique contribution to group work.
- Organize time to speak with students individually.

45. The student who has poor communication skills due to worry, fear, or embarrassment may be his/her own worst critic. Make sure the student has the necessary support (e.g., speech therapy, counseling, working in concert with the student and his/her family, etc.) to build self-esteem.

46. Help the student develop more interesting, positive verbal communication skills by recording him/her. Have the student watch the recording and discuss his/her communication skills.

47. Give the student opportunities to rehearse communication skills during role-play and other simulation experiences.

48. Encourage the student to use nonverbal forms of communication (e.g., achieving eye contact, holding head and shoulders up, etc.) when talking with others.

49. Focus on the subject of conversation rather than the student. He/she may become more motivated to use positive communication skills when given the opportunity to become inspired about the subject.

50. Provide experiences in communication through the arts (e.g., writing, acting, singing, painting, etc.).

51. Have the student role-play various situations in which speaking well is important (e.g., during a job interview).

52. Involve parents by asking them to rate their child's speech for a specific length of time (e.g., during dinner count no errors, a few errors, or many errors).

53. Develop a list of the attributes which will help a person become a good speaker. Have the student practice each attribute.

54. Choose a peer to model appropriate speech for the student. Pair the students to sit together, perform assignments together, etc.

55. Ask questions which stimulate language. Avoid those which can be answered by yes/no or a nod of the head (e.g., ask the student what he/she did at recess instead of asking if he/she played on the slide, ask the student what he/she did on vacation instead of asking if he/she stayed home over the holidays, etc.).

Goals:

1. The student will improve his/her articulation skills.
2. The student will improve his/her discrimination of speech sounds.
3. The student will improve his/her production of speech sounds in isolation.
4. The student will improve his/her production of speech sounds in syllables.
5. The student will improve his/her production of speech sounds in words.
6. The student will improve his/her production of speech sounds in sentences.
7. The student will improve his/her production of speech sounds in spontaneous speech.

Objectives:

1. The student will identify listener behaviors that indicate an unfavorable reaction to his/her speech in _____ out of _____ trials.
2. The student will restate an unintelligible statement in _____ out of _____ trials.
3. The student will differentiate between correct and incorrect productions of sounds or words in _____ out of _____ trials.
4. The student will imitate the correct production of words containing the target sound in the initial, final, and medial positions with _____% accuracy.
5. The student will spontaneously produce age-appropriate speech sounds in words in _____ out of _____ trials.
6. The student will spontaneously produce age-appropriate speech sounds in sentences in _____ out of _____ trials.
7. The student will spontaneously produce age-appropriate speech sounds in conversational speech in _____ out of _____ trials.

Interventions:

1. Have the student's hearing checked if it has not been recently checked.

2. Provide the student with an appropriate model for targeted speech sounds.

3. Evaluate the appropriateness of requiring the student to accurately produce certain sounds (e.g., developmentally, certain sounds may not be produced accurately until the age of 8 or 9).

4. Speak to the student to explain what he/she needs to do differently (e.g., using the /r/ sound instead of the /w/ sound). The teacher should be careful to use the sound that is being targeted and not the letter name (e.g., /r/ not *ar*).

5. Have the student raise a hand or clap hands when he/she hears the target sound produced during a series of isolated sound productions (e.g., /s/, /sh/,/r/, /m/, /r/, /t/, /k/, /r/, /z/, /w/, /n/, /r/, etc.).

6. Reinforce the student for correct productions of the target sound: (a) give the student a tangible reward (e.g., classroom privileges, line leading, passing out materials, five minutes free time, etc.) or (b) give the student an intangible reward (e.g., praise, fist bump, smile, etc.). Initially, each correct production may need reinforcement. As the student progresses, random reinforcement may be adequate.

7. Be sure that the student can hear the difference between the sounds as they should be made (target sounds) and the way he/she is incorrectly producing them (error sounds).

8. Use a puppet to produce the error and target sounds. The student earns a sticker for correctly distinguishing a set number of correct/incorrect productions the puppet makes.

9. Have the student stand up each time he/she hears the target sound produced accurately in contrast to the error sound (e.g., /w/, /r/, /r/, /w/, /w/ /w/, /r/, /r/, etc.).

10. Show the student a picture and name it. Have the student show thumbs up each time the target sound is produced accurately and thumbs down if the target sound is produced inaccurately.

11. Using pictures of similar sounding words, say each word and have the student point to the appropriate picture (e.g., *run* and *one*, *bat* and *back*).

12. Have the student tally the number of correct productions of the target sound when the teacher or a peer reads a list of words.

13. Have the student read simple passages and audio record them. Have him/her listen to the recordings and mark error and/or correct productions.

14. Audio record a spontaneous monologue given by the student. Listen to the recording with him/her and tally error and/or correct productions. The teacher and the student should compare their analyses of the productions.

15. Have the student read a list of words and rate his/her production after each word.

16. Play a game such as *Simon Says* in which the student tries to imitate the target sounds/words when produced by the teacher or peers.

17. Use a drawing as a visual aid to show the student how the mouth looks during production of the target sound.

18. Make cards with the target sound and cards with vowels. Have the student combine a target sound card with a vowel card to make a syllable that he/she can produce (e.g., *ra, re, ro,* and *ar, er, or*).

19. Play a board game that requires the student to name pictures containing the targeted words. The student has to pronounce the target words correctly before he/she can move on the game board. (This activity can be simplified or expanded based on the level of success of the student.)

20. Have the student cut out pictures of items containing targeted words and display them where they can be practiced each day.

21. Provide the student with a word list containing targeted words. Have him/her practice the words daily. As the student masters the word list, add more words. (Using words from the student's everyday vocabulary, reading lists, spelling lists, etc., will facilitate transfer of correct production of the targeted words into everyday speech.)

22. Have the student keep a notebook of difficult words encountered each day. These can be practiced by the student with the teacher or peer assistance.

23. Have the student use a carrier phrase combined with a targeted word (e.g., I like _____. I see a _____.).

24. Have the student make up sentences using targeted words.

25. During oral reading, underline targeted words and reinforce the student for correct productions.

26. Involve parents by asking them to rate their child's speech for a specific length of time (e.g., during dinner count no errors, a few errors, or many errors).

27. Present the student with a list of topics. Have the student select a topic and then give a spontaneous speech for a specific length of time. Count errors and suggest ways for him/her to improve.

28. Share with the student a time in your life when you were frustrated to let him/her know that you understand his/her feelings.

29. Teach the student ways to restate or rephrase a misunderstood message rather than continuing to repeat the original message with the same error pattern.

30. Discuss and role-play with the entire class different disabilities and the accompanying frustrations the students might feel if they were experiencing similar difficulties. Include speech problems in this discussion.

31. As the student works on specific sounds, make a list of the sounds, syllables, words, phrases, etc., that the student can articulate correctly and easily. When frustration occurs or an unfavorable reaction is perceived, have him/her repeat the list so that he/she can see the progress that has been made.

32. Make a short list of words in the student's regular curriculum which contain the target sound and which he/she can articulate intelligibly. Ask the student questions which will require one or more of these words as an answer.

163 Substitutes one sound for another sound

Goals:

1. The student will improve his/her articulation skills.
2. The student will improve his/her discrimination of speech sounds.
3. The student will improve his/her production of speech sounds in isolation.
4. The student will improve his/her production of speech sounds in syllables.
5. The student will improve his/her production of speech sounds in words.
6. The student will improve his/her production of speech sounds in sentences.
7. The student will improve his/her production of speech sounds in spontaneous speech.

Objectives:

1. The student will discriminate between correct and incorrect production of the target sound in _____ out of _____ trials.
2. The student will imitate correct production of the target sound in isolation in _____ out of _____ trials.
3. The student will imitate correct production of the target sound in words in _____ out of _____ trials.
4. The student will spontaneously produce the target sound in words in _____ out of _____ trials.
5. The student will spontaneously produce the target sound in sentences in _____ out of _____ trials.
6. The student will spontaneously produce the target sound in conversational speech in _____ out of _____ trials.

Interventions:

1. Have the student's hearing checked if it has not been recently checked.

2. Evaluate the appropriateness of requiring the student to accurately produce certain sounds (e.g., developmentally, certain sounds may not be produced accurately until the age of 8 or 9).

3. Speak to the student to explain what he/she needs to do differently (e.g., use the /r/ sound instead of the /w/ sound). The teacher should be careful to use the sound that is being targeted and not the letter name (e.g., /r/ not *ar*).

4. Reinforce the student for correct productions of the target sound: (a) give the student a tangible reward (e.g., classroom privileges, line leading, passing out materials, five minutes free time, etc.) or (b) give the student an intangible reward (e.g., praise, fist bump, smile, etc.). Initially, each correct production may need reinforcement. As the student progresses, random reinforcement may be adequate.

5. Be sure that the student can hear the difference between the sound as it should be produced (target sound) and the way he/she is incorrectly producing it (error sound).

6. Have the student raise a hand or clap hands when he/she hears the target sound produced during a series of isolated sound productions (e.g., /s/, /sh/, /r/, /m/, /r/, /t/, /k/, /r/, /z/, /w/, /n/, /r/, etc.).

7. Use a puppet to produce the target and error sounds. The student earns a sticker for correctly distinguishing a set number of correct/incorrect productions the puppet makes.

8. Have the student stand up each time he/she hears the target sound produced accurately in contrast to the error sound (e.g., /w/, /r/, /r/, /r/, /w/, /w/, /w/, /r/, /r/, etc.).

9. Show the student a picture and name it. Have the student show thumbs up each time the target sound is produced accurately and thumbs down if the target sound is produced inaccurately.

10. Using pictures of similar sounding words, say each word and have the student point to the appropriate picture (e.g., *run* and *one*, or *bat* and *back*).

11. Have the student tally the number of correct productions of the target sound when the teacher or a peer reads a list of words.

12. Have the student read simple passages and audio record them. Have him/her listen to the recording and mark error and/or correct productions.

13. Audio record a spontaneous monologue given by the student. Listen to the recording with him/her and tally error and/or correct productions. The teacher and the student should compare their analyses of the productions.

14. Have the student read a list of words and rate his/her production of the target sound after each word.

15. Choose a peer to model correctly producing the target sound for the student.

16. Play a game such as *Simon Says* in which the student tries to imitate the target sound when produced by the teacher or peers.

17. Use a diagram as a visual aid to show the student how the mouth looks during production of the target sound.

18. Make cards with the target sound and cards with vowels. Have the student combine a target sound card with a vowel card to make a syllable that he/she can produce (e.g., *ra, re, ro,* and *ar, er, or*).

19. Have the student make up sentences using the target sound.

20. Have the student cut out pictures of items containing the target sound and display them where they can be practiced each day.

21. Present the student with a list of topics. Have the student select a topic and then give a spontaneous speech for a specific length of time. Count errors and suggest ways for him/her to improve.

22. Provide the student with a list of words containing the target sound. (The student will probably be able to produce the target sound more easily at the beginning or end of a word than in the middle.) Have him/her practice the words daily. As the student masters the word list, add more words. (Using words from the student's everyday vocabulary, reading lists, spelling lists, etc., will facilitate transfer of correct production of the target sound into everyday speech.)

23. Have the student use fun phonics sheets to practice pronouncing his/her target sounds. These are also good for home practice.

24. Have the student keep a notebook of difficult words encountered each day. These can be practiced by the student with teacher or peer assistance.

25. Have the student use a carrier phrase combined with a word containing the target sound (e.g., I like _____. I see a _____.).

26. Have the student keep a list of all the words he/she can think of which contain sounds he/she has difficulty producing accurately.

27. During oral reading, underline targeted sounds and reinforce the student for correct sound production.

28. Involve parents by asking them to rate their child's speech for a specific length of time (e.g., during dinner, count no errors, a few errors, or many errors).

29. Play a board game that requires the student to name pictures containing the target sound. The student has to produce the target sound correctly before he/she can move on the game board. (This activity can be simplified or expanded based on the level of success of the student.)

164 Uses inappropriate verb tenses when speaking

Goals:

1. The student will improve his/her conversational speech.
2. The student will improve his/her grammatical speech.
3. The student will improve his/her usage of verb tenses.
4. The student will improve the ability to express himself/herself verbally.

Objectives:

1. The student will differentiate between sentences containing correct and incorrect verb tenses in _____ out of _____ trials.
2. The student will imitate appropriate verb tense in sentences in _____ out of _____ trials.
3. The student will spontaneously produce appropriate verb tenses during conversational speech in _____ out of _____ trials.
4. The student will state if the action of a verb represents the present, past, or future with _____% accuracy.
5. The student will use the future verb tense correctly when speaking with _____% accuracy.
6. The student will use the past verb tense correctly when speaking with _____% accuracy.
7. The student will use the present verb tense correctly when speaking with _____% accuracy.

Interventions:

1. After audio recording the student's speech, have him/her identify the incorrect verb tenses and make appropriate corrections.

2. Determine the type of grammatical model to which the student is exposed at home. Without placing negative connotations on the parents' grammatical style, explain the difference between standard and nonstandard grammar.

3. Have the student select a verb to master using correctly as a goal. As the student masters the correct use of the verb, he/she puts it on a list with a star and selects another verb to master.

4. Ask the parents to encourage the student's correct use of verb tenses at home by praising him/her when appropriate verb tenses are used.

5. Copy a simple paragraph which is in the present tense. Highlight the verbs and have the student change all the verbs to past and/or future tense. This activity could be completed verbally or in written form.

6. Determine if the student's errors are the result of dialectical differences (i.e., the pattern of verb tense usage may not be atypical within his/her social group).

7. Reinforce those students in the classroom who use verb tenses correctly.

8. Use a private signal (e.g., hand over shoulder/past tense, pointing forward/future tense, etc.) to remind the student to use correct verb tense.

9. During the day, write down specific verb tense errors produced by the student. Read the sentences to the student and have him/her make appropriate corrections verbally.

10. Explain that changes must be made in a verb to indicate when an event happened (e.g., past, present, future).

11. Give the student a sentence and have him/her change it from present to past, past to present, future to past, etc.

12. While the class is engaged in various activities, describe your observations using present tense. Have students do likewise. Expand this activity to include past and future tenses by asking appropriate questions (e.g., What just happened? What were you doing? What will you do next?).

13. Choose a peer to practice verb tenses with the student. Each tense should be used in a sentence rather than only conjugating the verbs.

14. Have the student assist in correcting other students' written work, looking for errors in verb tenses.

15. Determine whether the student has appropriate sequencing skills. The concept of sequencing influences comprehension of verb tensing (e.g., Can the student answer questions using first, next, then, etc.? Does he/she use such vocabulary when speaking even though verb tenses are incorrect?).

16. Have the student list activities he/she did when little, activities the student can do now, and things he/she will be able to do when grown up. Emphasize appropriate verb tenses throughout this activity.

17. Have the student make corrections for incorrect verb tenses on worksheets.

18. When speaking privately with the student, restate his/her verb tense error with a rising inflection (e.g., Yesterday he plays?) to assess if the student recognizes errors and spontaneously makes appropriate corrections.

19. Choose a peer to model correct verb tenses for the student.

20. Increase the student's awareness of the problem by audio recording the student while he/she is speaking with another student who uses verb tenses correctly. Play the recording for the student to see if he/she can identify correct/incorrect verb tensing.

21. Make a list of those verb tenses the student most commonly uses incorrectly. This list will become the guide for identifying the verb tenses which the student should practice each day.

22. Have the student's hearing checked if it has not been recently checked.

23. Make the conjugation of verbs a daily activity.

24. Make headings entitled yesterday, today, and tomorrow under which the class can list activities they were doing, are doing, or will do. The following day, change the today heading to yesterday and the tomorrow heading to today. Emphasize appropriate verb tenses throughout this activity.

25. Have the student make up sentences with given verbs in the past, present, and future tenses.

26. Make sure the student understands the concept of verb tenses by demonstrating what is happening, what already happened, and what will happen through the use of objects, pictures, and/or written sentences (depending on the student's abilities).

27. Reinforce the student for using verb tenses correctly: (a) give the student a tangible reward (e.g., classroom privileges, line leading, passing out materials, five minutes free time, etc.) or (b) give the student an intangible reward (e.g., praise, fist bump, smile, etc.).

28. Have the student complete worksheets in which he/she must supply the correct verb tense in each sentence (e.g., Yesterday I _____ to school.).

29. Audio record the student's speech to point out errors in verb tenses. With each recording, reinforce the student as his/her use of verb tenses improves.

30. Determine whether the student understands the concept of time which influences comprehension of verb tensing (e.g., Can he/she answer questions using yesterday, today, tomorrow, before, later, etc.? Does he/she use such vocabulary when speaking even though the verb tense is incorrect?).

31. Video the student and his/her classmates performing various actions. Play the video without the sound and have the student narrate what is happening in present tense, what happened in past tense, and/or what will happen in future tense. A prerecorded video could also be used for this activity.

32. Write down specific verb tense errors made by the student during the day. Give the written sentences to the student and have him/her make appropriate corrections. At first, mark the errors for him/her to correct. As the student becomes more proficient with this task, have him/her find and correct the errors independently.

33. Give the student a series of written and verbal sentences and have him/her identify the ones which demonstrate appropriate verb tensing. Have him/her make appropriate modifications for those sentences which demonstrate inappropriate verb tensing.

165 Uses inappropriate verbal and/or nonverbal language in social situations or interactions with peers and/or adults

Goal:

1. The student will improve his/her verbal and/or nonverbal language skills.

Objectives:

1. The student will choose an appropriate response (from multiple choices) to use in given situations in _____ out of _____ trials.
2. The student will decide whether a statement begins, maintains, or finishes a conversation in _____ out of _____ trials.
3. The student will demonstrate the ability to correctly introduce himself/herself to a peer _____ % of the time.
4. The student will demonstrate the ability to correctly introduce himself/herself to an adult _____ % of the time.
5. The student will utilize appropriate statements to begin, maintain, or finish a conversation during everyday speaking activities in _____ out of _____ trials.

Interventions:

1. Have the student's hearing checked if it has not been recently checked.

2. Reinforce the student for using appropriate verbal and/or nonverbal language in social situations or interactions with peers and/or adults: (a) give the student a tangible reward (e.g., classroom privileges, line leading, passing out materials, five minutes free time, etc.) or (b) give the student an intangible reward (e.g., praise, fist bump, smile, etc.).

3. Reinforce other students in the classroom for appropriate verbal and/or nonverbal interactions.

4. Model appropriate verbal and nonverbal language in social situations and in interactions with peers and adults.

5. Speak with the student to explain that he/she is using inappropriate verbal and/or nonverbal language. Be specific about the types of language the student is using and the situation(s) in which they are occurring.

6. Choose a peer to model appropriate verbal and nonverbal language in social situations and in interactions with peers and adults for the student.

7. Acknowledge the student's attempts to communicate his/her needs (e.g., facial expressions, gestures, inactivity, self-deprecating comments, etc.).

8. Communicate to the student that he is a worthwhile individual.

9. Encourage appropriate eye contact in all communicative situations.

10. To understand the student's needs and to provide opportunities for appropriate verbal interactions, communicate with the student as often as possible.

11. Provide the student with many academic and social successes.

12. Determine an individual(s) in the school environment with whom the student would most want to engage in a conversation (e.g., custodian, librarian, resource teacher, principal, older student, etc.). Allow the student to spend time carrying on a conversation with the individual(s) each day.

13. Spend time each day talking with the student on an individual basis about his/her interests.

14. Pair the student with an outgoing student who engages in appropriate verbal interactions on a frequent basis.

15. Provide opportunities for appropriate interactions within the classroom.

16. Reduce stimuli which contribute to the student's inappropriate language.

17. Allow the student to be a member of a group without requiring active participation.

18. Have the student show visitors and new students around the school.

19. Be sure to greet or acknowledge the student as often as possible (e.g., greet him/her in the hallways or cafeteria, welcome him/her to class, acknowledge a job done well, etc.). Encourage him/her to acknowledge you in return.

20. Have the student run errands which will require verbal and/or nonverbal interactions with other students, teachers, administrators, etc.

21. Experiment with various groupings to determine the group in which the student is most comfortable carrying on conversations with peers and adults.

22. Have the student play games which require carrying on conversations with others.

23. Teach the student social interaction skills (e.g., ways in which to appropriately respond to others' attempts to be friendly, complimentary, sympathetic, etc.).

24. Prompt the student to help him/her utilize more appropriate verbal/nonverbal language (e.g., Teacher: How are you? Student: Fred. Teacher: How are you feeling, Fred?).

25. Teach the student conversational phrases (e.g., How are you? How's it going? See you later.) to use when speaking to peers and adults.

26. Teach the student conversational rules (e.g., explain that it is appropriate to greet a person when you're seeing him/her for the first time of the day but not when it's been only five minutes since the last encounter).

27. Teach the student appropriate verbal and nonverbal responses to common everyday situations.

28. Have the student engage in simulated conversational activities with feedback designed to teach conversational skills (e.g., greetings, questions, topics of conversations, etc.).

29. Teach the student appropriate body language and explain the effect it can have on communication.

30. Explain to the student that inflectional patterns, loudness, pitch rate, etc., can influence the communicative message. Have the student practice different statements while varying these parameters, then discuss the influence on meaning.

31. Teach the student that he/she should respond differently depending on the person to whom he/she is talking. Discuss how age, position, and/or familiarity can change the form of the greeting/closing used (e.g., What's happening? How are you doing?).

32. Help the student develop social awareness (e.g., people may be embarrassed by what you say, feelings can be hurt by comments, tact is the best policy, remember interactions which have made you feel good and treat others in the same manner, etc.).

33. Use a private signal (e.g., holding up a finger, etc.) to remind the student to use appropriate verbal and/or nonverbal language.

34. Audio record the student. Have him/her listen to the recording to determine instances in which he/she is using inappropriate verbal language.

35. Rephrase the student's words to assist the student in utilizing more appropriate verbal interactions.

36. Teach a unit centered around finding examples of language which are appropriate for use in various situations.

37. Point out examples of appropriate language usage (both verbal and nonverbal) as they occur during the day.

38. Encourage the whole class to wait quietly for any student to respond to a question.

39. Make a list of emotions (e.g., sad, scared, happy, etc.) and have the student express each of them in a sentence.

40. Create a *Feeling Box* and place an unseen item in the box. Have the student describe what it feels like while another student tries to guess what it is.

41. Use puppets to retell a story or act out an activity. Have the student do the same by following your model.

42. Have the student practice being someone else in a specific situation (e.g., talking on the phone, being a cashier in a grocery store, etc.).

43. Have the student watch a video or television program. Have him/her tell you what he/she thinks might have happened before or after the story.

44. Have the student practice taking written messages to different persons in the school setting (e.g., librarian, school counselor, principal, etc.) and later delivering the messages verbally.

45. Have the student practice saying what you or another student has said. Teach the student to imitate inflectional patterns and facial expressions as well as to repeat the words. Video record this activity and have the student analyze his/her success at this activity.

46. Choose a peer to deliberately make mistakes while conveying a message (e.g., leaving out the place or time when a date is being made). Have the student identify the errors and ask for clarification.

47. Teach the student to be aware of listener response to determine if the meaning of a message has been received accurately.

48. Provide immediate feedback and cues for the student when his/her message has not been received accurately.

49. Ask the student to provide pictures of himself/herself at various ages. Help the student to explain what his/her reactions to certain situations might have been at those particular ages. Then ask the student to guess what his/her reaction might be in ten years.

50. Have the student draw a picture of himself/herself and then narrate a story in which he/she is the main character.

51. Set up fictitious situations in the classroom (e.g., restaurant, gas station, grocery store, etc.). Have the student role-play working in each situation. Have him/her change roles often.

52. Provide the student with a wordless picture book and have him/her narrate the story.

53. Help the student create and perform a short skit which revolves around a topic that is interesting to him/her.

54. Pair the student with a peer. Have them take turns interviewing and being interviewed. This may be done with the students being themselves or pretending to be another person or a fictitious character.

166 Uses incorrect word order when speaking

Goals:

1. The student will use correct word order when speaking.
2. The student will improve his/her verbal sentence structure.

Objectives:

1. The student will differentiate between grammatically correct and incorrect sentences in _____ out of _____ trials.
2. The student will imitate a grammatically correct sentence in _____ out of _____ trials.
3. The student will rearrange words to form a grammatically correct sentence in _____ out of _____ trials.
4. The student will spontaneously formulate grammatically correct sentences during conversational speech in _____ out of _____ trials.

Interventions:

1. Have the student's hearing checked if it has not been recently checked.

2. Speak to the student to explain that he/she is using incorrect word order in his/her sentences. Explain the importance of speaking with words in the correct order in sentences.

3. Determine the type of grammatical model to which the student is exposed at home. Without placing negative connotations on the parents' grammatical style, explain the difference between standard and nonstandard grammar.

4. Model speaking in complete statements (e.g., speak clearly, slowly, concisely; and use complete sentences, statements and thoughts) for the student.

5. Allow the student to speak without being interrupted or hurried.

6. Reduce the emphasis on competition. Competitive activities may cause the student to hurry and not use correct word order when speaking.

7. Have the student keep a list of times and/or situations in which he/she is nervous, anxious, etc., and has more trouble than usual with speech. Help the student identify ways to feel more comfortable in those situations.

8. Choose a peer to model correct word order for the student.

9. Reinforce the student for using correct word order when speaking: (a) give the student a tangible reward (e.g., classroom privileges, line leading, passing out materials, five minutes free time, etc.) or (b) give the student an intangible reward (e.g., praise, fist bump, smile, etc.).

10. Demonstrate acceptable and unacceptable speech. Use correct/incorrect word order and have the student critique each example.

11. When the student has difficulty during a conversation, remind him/her that this occasionally happens to everyone.

12. Increase the student's awareness of the problem by audio recording the student while he/she is speaking with another student who uses correct word order. Play the recording for the student to see if he/she can identify correct/incorrect order.

13. Teach the student the components of a complete sentence (i.e., subject, verb, and an object). Point out the components using objects, pictures, sentences, etc., depending on the student's abilities.

14. Make sure the student understands that sentences express thoughts about a subject and what the subject is or does.

15. Use a private signal (e.g., touching earlobe, raising index finger, etc.) to remind the student to use correct word order when speaking.

16. Routinely audio record the student's speech and point out incorrect word order in sentences. With each recording, reinforce the student as his/her use of correct word order improves.

17. After audio recording the student's speech, have him/her identify instances of incorrect word order in sentences and make appropriate modifications.

18. Have the student complete worksheets in which he/she must identify sentences with correct/incorrect word order.

19. During the day, write down examples of the student's incorrect word order. Read the sentences to the student and have him/her make appropriate corrections verbally.

20. Make a list of the student's most common errors in word order. Spend time with the student practicing how to correct the word order when speaking.

21. Video the student and his/her classmates performing various actions. Play the video without the sound and have the student narrate in grammatically correct sentences. A prerecorded video could also be used for this activity.

22. Have the student practice descriptive statements or thoughts containing correct word order which he/she can use when speaking (e.g., describe an object, picture, activity, etc., using correct word order).

23. When speaking privately with the student, restate his/her error pattern with a rising inflection (e.g., Got me my mom a new bike?) to assess if the student recognizes errors and spontaneously makes appropriate corrections.

24. Give the student a series of written and verbal sentences and have him/her identify the ones which demonstrate incorrect word order. Have him/her make appropriate corrections.

25. Present the student with a series of scrambled words in written and verbal form. Have him/ her rearrange the words to form grammatically correct sentences.

26. Have the student role-play various situations in which proper speech is important (e.g., during a job interview).

27. Make a list of the attributes which are likely to help a person become a good speaker (e.g., takes his/her time, thinks of what to say before starting, etc.).

28. Ask the parents to encourage the student's use of correct word order at home by praising him/her for using grammatically correct sentences.

29. Have the student verbally construct grammatically correct sentences when provided with subject and verb forms.

30. Use simple comic strips with captions deleted and have the student describe in correct word order what the characters are doing.

31. Have the student identify and correct errors after listening to examples of sentences containing incorrect word order.

32. Using a book without words, have the student tell the story using grammatically correct sentences. Audio record the story and play it for the student to listen for incorrect word order and make appropriate corrections.

Goal:

1. The student will improve his/her use of negation when speaking.

Objectives:

1. The student will differentiate between sentences containing correct and incorrect forms of negation in _____ out of _____ trials.
2. The student will imitate negatives in sentences in _____ out of _____ trials.
3. The student will use appropriate negation during structured language activities in _____ out of _____ trials.
4. The student will spontaneously use negation appropriately in sentences in _____ out _____ trials.
5. The student will use negation appropriately in conversational speech in _____ out of _____ trials.

Interventions:

1. Have the student's hearing checked if it has not been recently checked.

2. Speak to the student and explain that he/she is using negation inappropriately and explain the importance of speaking in grammatically correct sentences.

3. Determine the type of grammatical model to which the student is exposed at home. Without placing negative connotations on his/her parents' grammatical style, explain the difference between standard and nonstandard grammar.

4. Determine if the student's errors are the result of dialectical differences (i.e., the pattern of negation usage may not be atypical within his/her social group).

5. Reinforce the student for appropriate use of negation: (a) give the student a tangible reward (e.g., classroom privileges, line leading, passing out materials, five minutes free time, etc.) or (b) give the student an intangible reward (e.g., praise, fist bump, smile, etc.).

6. Increase the student's awareness of the problem by audio recording the student while he/she is speaking with another student who exhibits appropriate use of negation. Play the recording for the student to see if he/she can identify correct/incorrect usage.

7. Choose a peer to model the appropriate use of negation for the student.

8. Make sure the student understands the appropriate use of negation. Demonstrate through the use of objects, pictures, and/or written sentences.

9. Provide the student with numerous correct examples of the appropriate use of negation (e.g., He is not coming to my house. - He does not come to my house.).

10. Use a private signal (e.g., touching earlobe, raising index finger, etc.) to remind the student to use negation appropriately.

11. Make a list of those forms of negation the student most commonly uses incorrectly. This list will become the guide for learning activities for correct use of negation.

12. Routinely audio record the student's speech and point out errors in the use of negation. With each recording, reinforce the student as his/her use of negation improves.

13. After audio recording the student's speech, have him/her identify errors involving the use of negation and have him/her make appropriate corrections.

14. Have the student complete worksheets in which he/she must choose the correct use of negation (e.g., He (no/is not) _____ my friend. I (don't never/don't ever) _____ go fishing.).

15. Provide the student with written sentences for which he/she needs to make changes from incorrect use of negation to correct use (e.g., They didn't never leave. No one never comes to my house.).

16. During the day, write down specific instances of incorrect use of negation. Read the sentences to the student and have him/her make appropriate corrections verbally.

17. Write down specific instances of inappropriate use of negation made by the student during the day. Give the written sentences to the student and have him/her make appropriate corrections. At first, mark the errors for him/her to correct. As the student becomes more proficient with this task, have him/her find and correct the errors independently.

18. Have the student verbally construct sentences in which negation is used appropriately.

19. When you are discussing categories, make up a list that indicates inclusion or exclusion in a category (e.g., An apple is a fruit. It is not a _____.). Have the student fill in the blank with other categories where it does not belong.

20. Using category cards, have the student determine which card doesn't belong and why it does not (e.g., The dog doesn't belong because it is not a zoo animal.).

21. Have the student find several objects in the room that can be described by one adjective (round, heavy, red, etc.). Choose a matching number of objects that cannot be described using the same adjectives and have the student describe those objects.

22. Using pictures from an old yearbook, have the student look at the pictures. When the student sees a picture of someone he/she does not know, have him/her state that he/she does not know that person.

23. Ask the parents to encourage the student's correct use of negation at home by praising him/her when appropriate use occurs.

24. Have the class play guessing games which facilitate the use of negation (e.g., Is it a vegetable?). Make sure the responses are complete statements (e.g., No, it's not a vegetable.).

25. Have the student look through a catalog with a classmate and have each one identify all the things he/she doesn't like. Have the student state what he/she doesn't like as well as the dislikes of the classmate (e.g., I don't like . . . and Bob doesn't like . . .).

26. Using an absurd statement or picture, have the student explain, in a complete sentence, why it doesn't make sense (e.g., The cat barked. Student responds: Cats don't bark.).

27. Ask general knowledge questions and assist the student in answering appropriately (e.g., Is the sun shaped like a box?). Have the student answer in a complete sentence (e.g., No, the sun isn't shaped like a box.).

28. Ask situational questions and assist the student in answering appropriately (e.g., Would you put chocolate on spaghetti?). Have the student answer in a complete sentence (e.g., No, I wouldn't.).

29. Using audio recordings of environmental sounds, assist the student in responding appropriately to questions about the sounds (e.g., Is that the sound of water running? Student responds: No, it isn't. It sounds like wind.).

30. Have the student make a list of things he/she does not like. Assist the student in using negation appropriately, using a carrier phrase (e.g., I don't like . . .) while responding. This activity can be done both verbally and in writing.

31. When speaking privately with the student, restate his/her incorrect use of negation with a rising inflection (e.g., He not my friend?) to assess if the student recognizes errors and spontaneously makes appropriate corrections.

32. Give the student a series of written and verbal sentences and have him/her identify whether or not negation has been used correctly. Have him/her make appropriate changes to the incorrect uses.

168 Uses plurality incorrectly in noun and verb forms

Goals:

1. The student will improve his/her verbal sentence structure.
2. The student will improve his/her use of plural forms.

Objectives:

1. The student will differentiate between sentences containing correct and incorrect noun/verb plural forms in _____ out of _____ trials.
2. The student will imitate sentences containing correct noun/verb plural forms in _____ out of _____ trials.
3. The student will use correct noun/verb plural forms in sentences during structured language activities in _____ out of _____ trials.
4. The student will spontaneously use correct noun/verb plural forms in sentences in _____ out of _____ trials.
5. The student will use correct noun/verb plural forms during conversational speech in _____ out of _____ trials.

Interventions:

1. Have the student's hearing checked if it has not been recently checked.

2. Speak to the student and explain that he/she is using plurality incorrectly and explain the importance of speaking in grammatically correct sentences.

3. Determine the type of grammatical model to which the student is exposed at home. Without placing negative connotations on his/her parents' grammatical style, explain the difference between standard and nonstandard grammar.

4. Provide the student with an appropriate model of correct plurality.

5. Evaluate the appropriateness of requiring the student to speak with correct plurality (e.g., developmentally, a child may not utilize correct plurality for some irregular noun/verb forms until the age of 6 or 7).

6. Determine if the student's errors are the result of dialectical differences (the pattern of plurality usage may not be atypical within his/her social group).

7. Choose a peer to model correct plurality in noun and verb forms for the student.

8. Reinforce the student for appropriate use of plurality: (a) give the student a tangible reward (e.g., classroom privileges, line leading, passing out materials, five minutes free time, etc.) or (b) give the student an intangible reward (e.g., praise, fist bump, smile, etc.).

9. Increase the student's awareness of the problem by audio recording him/her while he/she is speaking with a student who exhibits appropriate use of plurality. Play the recording for the student to see if he/she can identify correct/incorrect forms.

10. Make sure the student understands the concept of plurality (e.g., cat - cats).

11. Provide a written model for the student to see how the *s* moves in the third person present tense. A singular subject has an *s* at the end of the verb (e.g., The cat eats.) and a plural subject has an *s* at the end of the noun (e.g., The cats eat.).

12. Have the student demonstrate the concept of plurality through the use of objects or pictures. Have him/her describe what the objects are doing or what is happening in the pictures. Assist the student in using plurality correctly.

13. Have the student verbally construct sentences with specific noun/verb plural forms.

14. Explain that certain forms of verbs go with certain subjects and that correct use of plurality requires the appropriate match of subject and verb (e.g., There is a cat. There are two cats.). Be sure that the student knows the various possibilities of subject-verb agreement and how to select the correct one.

15. Provide the student with examples of correct plurality for those combinations he/she most commonly uses incorrectly.

16. Give the student specific nouns/verbs and have him/her supply the appropriate plurals for each one.

17. Use a private signal (e.g., touching earlobe, raising index finger, etc.) to remind the student to use correct plurality.

18. Routinely audio record the student's speech and point out errors in plurality. With each recording, reinforce the student as his/her use of correct plurality improves.

19. After audio recording the student's speech, have him/her identify the errors involving plurality and make appropriate corrections.

20. Have the student complete worksheets in which he/she must choose the correct verb to go with a plural subject (e.g., The boys (is/are) climbing the tree.).

21. Have the student complete worksheets in which he/she must choose the correct subject to go with a verb (e.g., The (boy/boys) eat.).

22. Ask the parents to encourage the student's correct use of plurality at home by praising him/her when correct plurality is used.

23. Have the student make corrections for incorrect plural forms on worksheets (e.g., There are two gooses. They is my friends.).

24. During the day, write down specific plurality errors produced by the student. Read the sentences to the student and have him/her make appropriate corrections verbally.

25. Write down specific plurality errors made by the student during the day. Give the written sentences to the student and have him/her make appropriate corrections. At first, mark the errors for him/her to correct. As the student becomes more proficient with this task, have him/her find and correct the errors independently.

26. Have the student identify a noun or verb as a goal to master using in the correct plural form. As the student masters the correct use of the noun/verb, he/she puts it on a list with a star and identifies another noun/verb to master.

27. Make a list of those nouns/verbs the student most commonly uses incorrectly. This list will become the guide for learning activities in correct use of plurality.

28. When the student makes plurality errors in written work, mark the errors and provide the appropriate form or have the student make the appropriate corrections. Have the student read the corrected sentences aloud.

29. When speaking privately with the student, restate his/her plurality error with a rising inflection (e.g., Two gooses?) to assess if the student recognizes errors and spontaneously makes appropriate corrections.

30. Give the student a series of written and verbal sentences and have him/her identify which contain correct and incorrect plural forms and make appropriate modifications.

31. Identify the plural forms with which the student has the most difficulty. Provide a list of the correct forms which the student can keep at his/her desk for a reference when doing written work.

169 Uses pronouns incorrectly

Goal:

1. The student will improve his/her pronoun usage.

Objectives:

1. The student will differentiate between sentences containing grammatically correct and incorrect pronouns in _____ out of _____ trials.
2. The student will imitate appropriate pronoun usage in sentences in _____ out of _____ trials.
3. The student will utilize appropriate subject pronouns in sentences in _____ out of _____ trials.
4. The student will utilize appropriate object pronouns in sentences in _____ out of _____ trials.
5. The student will utilize appropriate possessive pronouns in sentences in _____ out of _____ trials.
6. The student will spontaneously produce appropriate pronoun forms during conversational speech in _____ out of _____ trials.

Interventions:

1. Have the student's hearing checked if it has not been recently checked.

2. Speak to the student to explain that he/she is using pronouns incorrectly. Explain the importance of speaking in grammatically correct sentences.

3. Determine the type of grammatical model to which the student is exposed at home. Without placing negative connotations on the parents' grammatical style, explain the difference between standard and nonstandard grammar.

4. Choose a peer to model the appropriate use of pronouns for the student.

5. Evaluate the appropriateness of requiring the student to use all pronouns correctly (e.g., developmentally, possessive pronoun usage may be in the emergent stage between the ages of 5 and 6 years; reflexive pronouns may not emerge until the age of 7 years).

6. Determine if the student's errors are the result of dialectical differences (i.e., the pattern of pronoun usage may not be atypical within his/her social group).

7. Reinforce the student for appropriate pronoun usage: (a) give the student a tangible reward (e.g., classroom privileges, line leading, passing out materials, five minutes free time, etc.) or (b) give the student an intangible reward (e.g., praise, fist bump, smile, etc.).

8. Increase the student's awareness of the problem by audio recording the student while he/she is speaking with another student who exhibits appropriate pronoun usage. Play the recording for the student to see if he/she can identify correct/incorrect forms.

9. Make sure the student understands the different pronoun forms as they are used in sentences. Demonstrate through the use of objects, pictures, and/or written sentences (e.g., He is wearing a shirt. The shirt belongs to him. His shirt is red. The shirt is his. He bought the shirt for himself.).

10. Provide the student with numerous correct examples of pronoun usage for those forms he/she most commonly uses incorrectly.

11. Use a private signal (e.g., touching earlobe, raising index finger, etc.) to remind the student to use appropriate pronoun forms.

12. Make a list of those pronouns the student most commonly uses incorrectly. This list will become the guide for learning activities for correct pronoun usage.

13. Have the student verbally construct sentences with specific pronoun forms.

14. Routinely audio record the student's speech and point out errors in pronoun usage. With each taping, reinforce the student as his/her pronoun usage improves.

15. After audio recording the student's speech, have him/her identify incorrect pronoun usage and make appropriate corrections.

16. Have the student complete worksheets in which he/she must choose the correct pronoun forms (e.g., (He/Him) _____ is my friend. (I/Me) _____ like to go fishing.).

17. To reinforce the concept that pronouns need a referent, have the student describe an individual or individuals using the appropriate pronouns (e.g., Randy is a boy. He is tall. He is laughing. His shirt is blue.).

18. During the day, write down specific pronoun errors produced by the student. Read the sentences to the student and have him/her make appropriate corrections verbally.

19. To reinforce the appropriate use of I, frequently ask the student to tell you what he/she is doing in a complete sentence.

20. Have the student make corrections for incorrect pronoun forms on worksheets (e.g., Her is my friend. - She is my friend.).

21. Provide the student with written sentences for which he/she needs to make changes from a proper noun to a pronoun (e.g., Randy is my friend. - He is my friend.).

22. Give the student a series of written and verbal sentences and have him/her identify whether or not appropriate pronoun forms are used. Have him/her make appropriate corrections.

23. Use simple comic strips with the captions deleted and have the student describe the characters and what they are doing by using appropriate pronouns.

24. Ask the parents to encourage the student's correct usage of pronouns at home by praising him/her when correct pronoun forms are used.

25. Have the student identify a single pronoun (e.g., I, it, etc.) or a pair of pronouns (e.g., he/she, his/hers, his/her, we/they, etc.) as a goal to master using correctly. As the student masters the correct use of the pronoun(s), he/she puts it/them on a list with a star and identifies another pronoun or pronoun pair to master.

26. To teach the correct pronoun form, point to an individual in the classroom or one in a picture and have the student tell what he/she is doing, with emphasis on the pronoun form. Instruct the student to start his/her descriptive sentence using that pronoun (e.g., He/She is doing math.).

27. Video the student and his/her classmates performing various actions. Play the video without the sound and have the student narrate by using appropriate pronoun forms. This activity could be modified by using a pre-recorded video.

28. Using a book without words, have the student tell the story, emphasizing appropriate pronoun usage. Audio record the story and play it for the student to listen for incorrect pronoun usage. Have him/her make appropriate modifications.

29. When speaking privately with the student, restate his/her pronoun error with a rising inflection (e.g., Him is my friend?) to assess if the student recognizes errors and spontaneously makes appropriate corrections.

30. Write down specific pronoun errors made by the student during the day. Give the written sentences to the student and have him/her make appropriate corrections. At first, mark the errors for him/her to correct. As the student becomes more proficient with this task, have him/her find and correct the errors independently.

170 Uses sentences which are grammatically incomplete when speaking

Goals:

1. The student will use grammatically complete sentences when speaking.
2. The student will improve his/her verbal sentence structure.

Objectives:

1. The student will differentiate between grammatically complete and incomplete sentences in _____ out of _____ trials.
2. The student will imitate grammatically complete sentences in _____ out of _____ trials.
3. The student will use grammatically complete sentences during structured language activities in _____ out of _____ trials.
4. The student will spontaneously use grammatically complete sentences in _____ out of _____ trials.
5. The student will use grammatically complete sentences in conversational speech in _____ out of _____ trials.

Interventions:

1. Have the student's hearing checked if it has not been recently checked.

2. Speak to the student to explain that he/she is using grammatically incomplete sentences. Explain the importance of speaking in grammatically complete sentences.

3. Determine the type of grammatical model to which the student is exposed at home. Without placing negative connotations on his/her parents' grammatical style, explain the difference between standard and nonstandard grammar.

4. Model speaking in complete statements or thoughts (e.g., speak clearly, slowly, and concisely; and use complete sentences, statements, and thoughts) for the student.

5. When the student does not use complete sentences (e.g., points to a ball and names it), expand on what he/she said, (e.g., ask him/her if he/she wants to play with the ball). This provides a model for more complete statements and thoughts.

6. Allow the student to speak without being interrupted or hurried.

7. Reduce the emphasis on competition. Competitive activities may cause the student to hurry and not speak in complete statements or thoughts.

8. Have the student keep a list of times and/or situations in which he/she is nervous, anxious, etc., and has more trouble than usual with speech. Help the student identify ways to feel more comfortable in those situations.

9. Reinforce the student for using grammatically complete sentences: (a) give the student a tangible reward (e.g., classroom privileges, line leading, passing out materials, five minutes free time, etc.) or (b) give the student an intangible reward (e.g., praise, fist bump, smile, etc.).

10. Use complete/incomplete statements and thoughts and have the student critique each example.

11. When the student has difficulty during a conversation, remind him/her that this occasionally happens to everyone.

12. Increase the student's awareness of the problem by audio recording the student while he/she is speaking with a peer who uses grammatically complete sentences. Play the recording for the student to see if he/she can identify complete/incomplete forms.

13. Choose a peer to model how to use grammatically complete sentences for the student.

14. Teach the student the components of a complete sentence (i.e., subject, verb, and an object). Point out the components using objects, pictures, sentences, etc., depending on the student's abilities.

15. Make sure the student understands that complete sentences express thoughts about a subject and what that subject is or does.

16. Use a private signal (e.g., touching earlobe, raising index finger, etc.) to remind the student to use grammatically complete sentences.

17. Routinely audio record the student's speech and point out grammatically incomplete sentences. With each taping, reinforce the student as his/her use of grammatically complete sentences improves.

18. After audio recording the student's speech, have him/her identify the grammatically incomplete sentences and make appropriate modifications.

19. Have the student complete worksheets in which he/she must choose sentences which are grammatically complete/incomplete. Have him/her make changes to the grammatically incomplete sentences to make them complete.

20. During the day, write down examples of the student's incomplete sentences. Read the sentences to the student and have him/her make appropriate corrections.

21. Make a list of the most common incomplete statements the student uses. Spend time with the student practicing how to make these statements complete.

22. Have the student verbally construct grammatically complete sentences when provided with a subject and verb.

23. Have the student practice descriptive statements he/she can use when speaking (e.g., describe objects, pictures, activities, etc., in grammatically complete statements).

24. When speaking privately with the student, restate his/her incomplete sentence with a rising inflection (e.g., Ball under table?) to assess if the student recognizes errors and spontaneously makes appropriate corrections.

25. Give the student a series of written and verbal sentences and have him/her identify which are grammatically complete and incomplete.

26. Have the student identify and correct errors after listening to examples of grammatically complete/incomplete sentences.

27. Have the student role-play various situations in which speaking well is important (e.g., during a job interview).

28. Make a list of the attributes which are likely to help a person become a good speaker (e.g., takes his/her time, thinks of what to say before starting, etc.).

29. Ask the parents to encourage the student's use of grammatically complete sentences at home by praising him/her when complete sentences are used.

30. Have the student describe himself/herself and/or his/her classmates in grammatically complete sentences.

31. Video the student and his/her classmates performing various actions. Play the video without the sound and have the student narrate in grammatically complete sentences. A prerecorded video could also be used for this activity.

32. Use simple comic strips with captions deleted and have the student describe what the characters are doing in complete sentences.

33. Using a book without words, have the student tell the story using grammatically complete sentences. Audio record the story and play it for the student to listen for incomplete sentences and make appropriate corrections.

Goals:

1. The student will correctly discriminate vocal quality in himself/herself and others.
2. The student will demonstrate appropriate vocal quality.

Objectives:

1. The student will identify appropriate and inappropriate vocal qualities in _____ out of _____ trials.
2. The student will identify listener behaviors which indicate an unfavorable reaction to his/her message in _____ out of _____ trials.
3. The student will restate a misunderstood message in _____ out of _____ trials.
4. The student will identify personal situations and vocal behaviors that might cause harsh, breathy, or hoarse vocal quality in _____ out of _____ trials.

Interventions:

1. Have the student's hearing checked if it has not been recently checked.

2. Provide the student with an appropriate voice model.

3. Reinforce the student for appropriate voice quality: (a) give the student a tangible reward (e.g., classroom privileges, line leading, passing out materials, five minutes free time, etc.) or (b) give the student an intangible reward (e.g., praise, fist bump, smile, etc.).

4. Discuss with the student the negative connotations which are sometimes attached to a person who uses a voice that is too loud/soft or too high/low. Loud voices may be interpreted to mean that the person is angry, arrogant, etc., while soft voices may be associated with a person who is shy, timid, lacking self-confidence, etc. Discussion of these negative connotations may motivate the student to make changes in his/her voice.

5. Speak to the student to explain what he/she needs to do differently (e.g., use a quiet voice vs. a loud voice, whistle or clap vs. yelling, talk less, etc.).

6. Be sure the student can hear the difference between appropriate voice quality and voice quality that is harsh, breathy, or hoarse.

7. Use puppets to demonstrate appropriate voice quality and voice quality that is harsh, breathy, or hoarse.

8. Audio record the student while he/she is speaking with another student who exhibits appropriate voice quality. Play the recording to see if the student can hear the difference between voice qualities.

9. Have the student read a list of words and rate his/her productions as appropriate or harsh, breathy, hoarse, etc. If it is too difficult for the student to rate his/her own live voice, audio record the reading and play it for him/her to rate.

10. Show a model or diagram of the location of the larynx to the student and discuss how it works.

11. Demonstrate the larynx under tension by having the student push against your chin while you resist. Push against the student's chin while he/she resists. Vocalize while doing this activity (e.g., say eee or count).

12. Demonstrate laryngeal tension by having the student vocalize (e.g., say eee or ah) while trying to lift himself/herself up from a sitting position in a hard chair.

13. Have the student differentiate between tension and relaxation by first tensing his/her body and then relaxing. (Feel the student's neck and shoulders to determine the presence or absence of tension.)

14. Choose relaxation exercises to be used by the student (e.g., tensing and relaxing specific muscle groups, head rotation exercises, imagery, etc.).

15. Establish a quiet time during the day when no one speaks except in an emergency. Soft music could be played in the background.

16. To facilitate understanding of a voice problem caused by vocal abuse, teach a short unit on vocal quality to the class.

17. Have the student describe animal voices that sound abusive (e.g., lion - roar; mouse - squeaky) and compare them with his/her own voice quality.

18. Have the student describe the vocal quality of famous people, cartoon characters, people at school or home, etc. Have him/her differentiate between vocal qualities that sound pleasant and those that sound harsh, breathy, and/or hoarse.

19. Encourage good posture while sitting, standing, walking, etc. Poor posture can obstruct good breath support which facilitates vocal quality.

20. Have the student demonstrate proper breath support for speaking using his/her diaphragm.

21. Discuss how a person's voice changes when they are nervous, tired, angry, etc.

22. If the student is speaking with an unusually tight or closed mouth, increase his/her awareness of such behavior by having him/her tally the occurrences during a specified period of time.

23. Have the student rank, hierarchically, the situations in which his/her voice is too loud. Discuss these situations to facilitate the student's awareness of when he/she is using inappropriate vocal quality.

24. Involve parents by asking them to rate their child's voice quality (e.g., too loud, harsh, breathy, etc.) for a specific length of time and/or in a specific location (e.g., during playtime, at dinner, at bedtime, inside, outside, etc.).

25. Have the student list reasons why people might yell or talk very loudly (e.g., when angry, in a crowd, at a football game, etc.).

26. Have the student describe reactions listeners have to a voice that is too loud, harsh, hoarse, breathy, or hyper/hyponasal (e.g., annoyance at someone who appears to be yelling, asking to have something repeated, etc.).

27. Have the student list all the different sound effects that he/she and his/her friends make while playing (e.g., motor noises, monster noises, etc.). Discuss the effect on their voices. Suggest alternatives to throat noises (e.g., sounds made at the front of the mouth with tongue and lips).

28. Have the student list school activities that result in vocal abuse. Discuss ways that the student could avoid misusing his/her voice in these situations (e.g., clapping hands at recess vs. yelling).

29. Have the student list occasions when he/she abuses his/her voice. Discuss alternative ways to communicate in these situations (e.g., walk over to a person instead of shouting across the room, blow a whistle outside to get someone's attention instead of yelling, etc.).

30. If the student uses shouting to gain attention, have him/her practice alternative methods of gaining attention (e.g., stressing a specific word in a sentence, using pitch variation, pausing before an important word, using gestures, etc.).

31. Have the student identify words that have a soft or loud connotation in stories that he/she reads (e.g., soft = shiver, warm, gentle, luminous; loud = bang, hate, stop, gang).

32. Have the student identify occasions when he/she uses good vocal quality vs. vocal abuse. Discuss ways to improve vocal quality during abusive situations.

33. Have the student demonstrate his/her best vocal quality.

34. Discuss how clearing the throat irritates the throat. Encourage the student to get a drink instead.

35. Have the student tally the number of times he/she abuses his/her voice during a designated time (e.g., during recess). Encourage him/her to decrease the number of abuses from one occasion to the next.

36. When the student has a cold, sore throat, laryngitis, etc.; discuss how the throat might look and encourage the student to talk as little as possible. Do not encourage whispering as an alternative, as it may also irritate his/her larynx.

37. Remind the student to use proper breathing techniques and a relaxed voice during music class, which can be a period of vocal stress.

38. Involve the entire class in the development of a self-improvement unit in which each student adopts a goal (e.g., exercising regularly, keeping a neat desk, etc.). For the student with a voice problem, working on good vocal quality can be his/her goal.

39. When the student is about to engage in an activity that facilitates vocal abuse, have him/her wear a string bracelet, sticker, etc., to remind him/her to use alternate strategies and/or good vocal habits.

40. Discuss with the student how temperature and humidity can influence his/her vocal quality.

41. Discuss and role-play with the entire class different disabilities and the accompanying frustrations they might feel if they were experiencing similar difficulties. Include voice problems in this discussion.

42. Establish a method that you can use to remind the student to use good vocal quality when he/she is abusing his/her voice (e.g., pointing to your throat, index finger to lips as for the quiet sign, etc.).

Goals:

1. The student will correctly discriminate vocal quality in himself/herself and others.
2. The student will demonstrate appropriate vocal quality in daily communication.

Objectives:

1. The student will identify appropriate and inappropriate vocal qualities in _____ out of _____ trials.
2. The student will identify listener behaviors which indicate an unfavorable reaction to his/her message in _____ out of _____ trials.
3. The student will restate a misunderstood message in _____ out of _____ trials.
4. The student will identify personal situations and vocal behaviors that might cause harsh, breathy, or hoarse vocal quality in _____ out of _____ trials.

Interventions:

1. Have the student's hearing checked if it has not been recently checked.

2. Provide the student with an appropriate voice model.

3. Reinforce the student for appropriate voice quality: (a) give the student a tangible reward (e.g., classroom privileges, line leading, passing out materials, five minutes free time, etc.) or (b) give the student an intangible reward (e.g., praise, fist bump, smile, etc.).

4. Discuss with the student the negative connotations which are sometimes attached to a person who uses a voice that is too loud/soft or too high/low. Loud voices may be interpreted to mean that the person is angry, arrogant, etc., while soft voices may be associated with a person who is shy, timid, lacking self-confidence, etc. Discussion of these negative connotations may motivate the student to make changes in his/her voice.

5. Speak to the student to explain what he/she needs to do differently (e.g., use a quiet voice vs. a loud voice; whistle or clap vs. yelling; talk less; make the /m/, /n/, and /ng/ sounds come through his/her nose when speaking, but don't let any other sounds come through his/her nose; etc.).

6. Be sure the student can hear the difference between appropriate voice quality and voice quality that is harsh, breathy, hoarse, hypernasal, hyponasal, etc.

7. Use puppets to demonstrate appropriate voice quality and voice quality that is harsh, breathy, hoarse, hypernasal, hyponasal, etc.

8. Audio record the student while he/she is speaking with a peer who exhibits appropriate voice quality. Play the recording to see if the student can hear the difference between voice qualities.

9. If the student exhibits a hypernasal vocal quality, audio record the student while he/she reads sentences which do not contain nasal sounds (e.g., Both cats have fleas. Chris has three cookies.). Have the student listen to the recording and mark words which contain nasality.

10. If the student exhibits a hyponasal vocal quality, audio record the student while he/she reads sentences which contain nasal sounds (e.g., My mama moved my hammer. Nan is numb.). Have the student listen to the recording and mark words which lack appropriate nasality.

11. Have the student read a list of words and rate his/her productions as appropriate or harsh, breathy, hoarse, etc. If it is too difficult for the student to rate his/her own live voice, audio record the reading and play it for him/her to rate.

12. Have the student demonstrate proper breath support for speaking using his/her diaphragm.

13. If the student is hyper/hyponasal, have him/her read a list that contains words without nasal sounds (e.g., bat, shoe, rug, etc.) or with nasal sounds (e.g., none, money, ping, etc.) and rate his/her productions as appropriately non-nasal or nasal.

14. Show a model or diagram of the location of the larynx to the student and discuss how it works.

15. Demonstrate the larynx under tension by having the student push against your chin while you resist. Push against the student's chin while he/she resists. Vocalize while doing this activity (e.g., say eee or count).

16. Demonstrate laryngeal tension by having the student vocalize (e.g., say eee or ah) while trying to lift himself/herself up from a sitting position in a hard chair.

17. Have the student differentiate between tension and relaxation by first tensing his/her body and then relaxing. (Feel the student's neck and shoulders to determine the presence or absence of tension.)

18. Choose relaxation exercises to be used by the student (e.g., tensing and relaxing specific muscle groups, head rotation exercises, imagery, etc.).

19. Establish a quiet time during the day when no one speaks except in an emergency. Soft music could be played in the background.

20. To facilitate understanding of a voice problem caused by vocal abuse, teach a short unit on vocal quality to the class.

21. Have the student describe animal voices that sound abusive (e.g., lion - roar; mouse - squeaky) and compare them with his/her own voice quality.

22. Have the student describe the vocal quality of famous people, cartoon characters, people at school or home, etc. Have him/her differentiate between vocal qualities that sound pleasant and those that sound harsh, breathy, and/or hoarse.

23. Encourage good posture while sitting, standing, walking, etc. Poor posture can obstruct good breath support which facilitates vocal quality.

24. Discuss how a person's voice changes when they are nervous, tired, angry, etc.

25. If the student is speaking with an unusually tight or closed mouth, increase his/her awareness of such behavior by having him/her tally the occurrences during a specified period of time.

26. If the student is hypernasal, have him/her demonstrate and practice open verbal resonance during speaking to decrease hypernasality. (When the student exaggerates his/her mouth opening during speaking, more sound typically exits the mouth vs. the nasal cavity.)

27. Have the student rank, hierarchically, the situations in which his/her voice is too loud. Discuss these situations to facilitate the student's awareness of when he/she is using inappropriate vocal quality.

28. Have the student identify occasions when he/she uses appropriate nasal resonance. Discuss ways to facilitate occasions of appropriate resonance.

29. Involve parents by asking them to rate their child's voice quality (e.g., too loud, harsh, breathy, nasal, etc.) for a specific length of time and/or in a specific location (e.g., during playtime, at dinner, at bedtime, inside, outside, etc.).

30. Have the student list reasons why people might yell or talk very loudly (e.g., when angry, in a crowd, at a football game, etc.).

31. Have the student describe reactions listeners have to a voice that is too loud, harsh, hoarse, breathy, or hyper/hyponasal (e.g., annoyance at someone who appears to be yelling, asking to have something repeated, etc.).

32. Discuss how clearing the throat irritates the throat. Encourage the student to get a drink instead.

33. Have the student list all the different sound effects that he/she and his/her friends make while playing (e.g., motor noises, monster noises, etc.). Discuss the effect on their voices. Suggest alternatives to throat noises (e.g., sounds made at the front of the mouth with tongue and lips).

34. Have the student list school activities that result in vocal abuse. Discuss ways that the student could avoid misusing his/her voice in these situations (e.g., clapping hands at recess vs. yelling).

35. Have the student list occasions when he/she abuses his/her voice. Discuss alternative ways to communicate in these situations (e.g., walk over to a person instead of shouting across the room, blow a whistle outside to get someone's attention instead of yelling, etc.).

36. If the student uses shouting to gain attention, have him/her practice alternative methods of gaining attention (e.g., stressing a specific word in a sentence, using pitch variations, pausing before an important word, using gestures, etc.).

37. Have the student identify words that have a soft or loud connotation in stories that he/she reads (e.g., soft = shiver, warm, gentle, luminous; loud = bang, hate, stop, gang).

38. Have the student identify occasions when he/she uses good vocal quality vs. vocal abuse. Discuss ways to improve vocal quality during abusive situations.

39. Have the student tally the number of times he/she abuses his/her voice during a designated time (e.g., during recess). Encourage him/her to decrease the number of abuses from one occasion to the next.

40. When the student has a cold, sore throat, laryngitis, etc.; discuss how the throat might look and encourage the student to talk as little as possible. Do not encourage whispering as an alternative as it may also irritate his/her voice.

41. Remind the student to use proper breathing techniques and a relaxed voice during music class, which can be a period of vocal stress.

42. Establish a method that you can use to remind the student to use good vocal quality when he/she is abusing his/her voice (e.g., pointing to your throat, index finger to lips as for the quiet sign, etc.).

43. When the student is about to engage in an activity that facilitates vocal abuse, have him/her wear a string bracelet, sticker, etc., to remind him/her to use alternate strategies and/or good vocal habits.

44. For the hypernasal student, establish a method that you can use to remind him/her to use appropriate open verbal resonance during class activities (e.g., cupping one hand in the shape of a C by your mouth).

45. For the hyponasal student, establish a method that you can use to remind him/her to use appropriate nasal resonance during class activities (e.g., pointing to your nose).

46. Have the student demonstrate his/her best vocal quality.

47. Teach the student ways to restate or rephrase a misunderstood message rather than continuing to repeat the original message with the same error pattern.

173 Voice quality sounds harsh, breathy, and/or hoarse

Goals:

1. The student will improve his/her voice quality.
2. The student will correctly discriminate vocal quality in himself/herself and others.
3. The student will demonstrate appropriate pitch.
4. The student will demonstrate appropriate voice volume.
5. The student will demonstrate appropriate nasality.
6. The student will demonstrate appropriate vocal quality.

Objectives:

1. The student will identify appropriate and inappropriate vocal qualities in _____ out of _____ trials.
2. The student will identify personal situations and vocal behaviors that might cause harsh, breathy, or hoarse vocal quality in _____ out of _____ trials.
3. The student will demonstrate proper breathing technique for phonation in _____ out of _____ trials.
4. The student will demonstrate proper breathing technique during therapy sessions in _____ out of _____ trials.
5. The student will maintain proper breathing during conversation in _____ out of _____ trials.
6. The student will demonstrate the difference between a hard glottal attack and easy onset of phonation during therapy in _____ out of _____ trials.
7. The student will maintain easy onset of phonation during conversation in _____ out of _____ trials.
8. The student will reduce instances of vocal abuse by _____% as measured against a baseline number of instances at the beginning of therapy.

Interventions:

1. Have the student's hearing checked if it has not been recently checked.

2. Provide the student with an appropriate voice model.

3. Reinforce the student for appropriate voice quality: (a) give the student a tangible reward (e.g., classroom privileges, line leading, passing out materials, five minutes free time, etc.) or (b) give the student an intangible reward (e.g., praise, fist bump, smile, etc.).

4. Speak to the student to explain what he/she needs to do differently (e.g., use a quiet voice vs. a loud voice, whistle or clap vs. yelling, talk less, etc.).

5. Be sure the student can hear the difference between appropriate voice quality and voice quality that is harsh, breathy, hoarse, etc.

6. Use puppets to demonstrate appropriate voice quality and voice quality that is harsh, breathy, hoarse, etc.

7. Audio record the student while he/she is speaking with another student who exhibits appropriate voice quality. Play the recording to see if the student can hear the difference between voice qualities.

8. Have the student read a list of words and rate his/her productions as appropriate or harsh, breathy, hoarse, etc. If it is too difficult for the student to rate his/her own live voice, audio record and play for him/her to rate.

9. Show a model or diagram of the location of the larynx to the student and discuss how it works.

10. Demonstrate the larynx under tension by having the student push against your chin while you resist. Push against the student's chin while he/she resists. Vocalize while doing this activity (e.g., say eee or count).

11. Discuss how a person's voice changes when they are nervous, tired, angry, etc.

12. Demonstrate laryngeal tension by having the student vocalize (e.g., say eee or ah) while trying to lift himself/herself up from a sitting position in a hard chair.

13. Have the student differentiate between tension and relaxation by first tensing his/her body and then relaxing. (Feel the student's neck and shoulders to determine the presence or absence of tension.)

14. Choose relaxation exercises to be used by the student (e.g., tensing and relaxing specific muscle groups, head rotation exercises, imagery, etc.).

15. Establish a quiet time during the day when no one speaks except in an emergency. Soft music could be played in the background.

16. To facilitate understanding of a voice problem caused by vocal abuse, teach a short unit on vocal quality to the class.

17. Have the student describe animal voices that sound abusive (e.g., lion - roar; mouse - squeaky) and compare them with his/her own voice quality.

18. Have the student describe the vocal quality of famous people, cartoon characters, people at school or home, etc. Have him/her differentiate between vocal qualities that sound pleasant and those that sound harsh, breathy, and/or hoarse.

19. Encourage good posture while sitting, standing, walking, etc. Poor posture can obstruct good breath support which facilitates vocal quality.

20. Have the student demonstrate proper breath support for speaking using his/her diaphragm.

21. Have the student rank, hierarchically, the situations in which his/her voice is too loud. Discuss these situations to facilitate the student's awareness of when he/she is using inappropriate vocal quality.

22. Have the student list reasons why people might yell or talk very loudly (e.g., when angry, in a crowd, at a football game, etc.).

23. Have the student describe reactions listeners have to a voice that is too loud, harsh, hoarse, breathy, hyper/hyponasal (e.g., annoyance at someone who appears to be yelling, asking to have something repeated, etc.).

24. Have the student list all the different sound effects that he/she and his/her friends make while playing (e.g., motor noises, monster noises, etc.). Discuss the effect of those sounds on their voices. Suggest alternatives to throat noises (e.g., sounds made at the front of the mouth with tongue and lips).

25. Help the student determine if he/she is participating in any activities during which his/her voice might be strained (e.g., gym, recess, cheerleading, drama, vocal music, baseball, soccer, etc.). Discuss ways that the student could avoid misusing his/her voice in these situations (e.g., clapping hands vs. yelling, walking over to a person vs. shouting at the person, performing actions vs. yelling, etc.).

26. Help the student determine the times and circumstances when his/her voice quality is better/worse (e.g., after gym, early in the morning, late in the day, on Mondays, etc.).

27. Involve parents by asking them to rate their child's voice quality (e.g., appropriate, too loud, harsh, breathy, etc.) for a specific length of time and/or in a specific situation (e.g., during playtime, at dinner, at bedtime; inside or outside; in the presence of family members, peers, or authority figures; etc.).

28. Have the student list occasions when he/she abuses his/her voice. Discuss alternative ways to communicate in these situations (e.g., walk over to a person instead of shouting across the room, blow a whistle outside to get someone's attention instead of yelling, etc.).

29. If the student uses shouting to gain attention, have him/her practice alternative methods of gaining attention (e.g., stressing a specific word in a sentence, using pitch variations, pausing before an important word, using gestures, etc.).

30. Have the student demonstrate his/her best vocal quality.

31. Have the student identify words that have a soft or loud connotation in stories that he/she reads (e.g., soft = shiver, warm, gentle, luminous; loud = bang, hate, stop, gang).

32. Have the student tally the number of times he/she abuses his/her voice during a designated time (e.g., during recess). Encourage him/her to decrease the number of abuses from one occasion to the next.

33. Discuss how clearing the throat irritates the throat. Encourage the student to get a drink instead.

34. When the student is about to engage in an activity that facilitates vocal abuse, have him/her wear a string bracelet, sticker, etc., to remind him/her to use alternate strategies and/or good vocal habits.

35. When the student has a cold, sore throat, laryngitis, etc.; discuss how the throat might look and encourage the student to talk as little as possible. Do not encourage whispering as an alternative as it may also irritate his/her voice.

36. Remind the student to use proper breathing techniques and a relaxed voice during music class, which can be a period of vocal stress.

37. Have the student identify occasions when he/she uses good vocal quality vs. vocal abuse. Discuss ways to improve vocal quality during abusive situations.

38. Establish a method that you can use to remind the student to use good vocal quality when he/she is abusing his/her voice (e.g., pointing to your throat, index finger to lips as for the quiet sign, etc.).

174 Voice quality sounds hypernasal (e.g., sounds like the student is talking through his/her nose) or hyponasal (e.g., sounds like the student has a cold)

Goals:

1. The student will improve his/her voice quality.
2. The student will correctly discriminate vocal quality in self and others.
3. The student will demonstrate appropriate pitch.
4. The student will demonstrate appropriate voice volume.
5. The student will demonstrate appropriate nasality.
6. The student will demonstrate appropriate vocal quality.

Objectives:

1. The student will identify appropriate and inappropriate vocal qualities in _____ out of _____ trials.
2. The student will repeat 10 words with appropriate nasal emission on the /m/, /n/,and /ng/ sounds with _____% accuracy.
3. The student will exaggerate open verbal movements during productions of words with _____% accuracy.
4. The student will exaggerate open verbal movements during productions of sentences with _____% accuracy.
5. The student will exaggerate open verbal movements while reading with _____% accuracy.
6. The student will exaggerate open verbal movements during conversation with _____% accuracy.

Interventions:

1. Have the student's hearing checked if it has not been recently checked.

2. Provide the student with an appropriate voice model.

3. Reinforce the student for appropriate voice quality: (a) give the student a tangible reward (e.g., classroom privileges, line leading, passing out materials, five minutes free time, etc.) or (b) give the student an intangible reward (e.g., praise, fist bump, smile, etc.).

4. Speak to the student to explain what he/she needs to do differently (e.g., make the /m/, /n/,and /ng/ sounds come through his/her nose when speaking, but don't let any other sounds come through his/her nose).

5. Have the student demonstrate his/her best verbal resonance.

6. Use puppets to demonstrate appropriate voice quality and voice quality with too much or too little nasal resonance.

7. Audio record the student while he/she is speaking with another student who exhibits appropriate voice quality. Play the recording to see if the student can hear the difference between voice qualities.

8. Be sure the student can hear the difference between appropriate voice quality and voice quality with too much or too little nasal resonance.

9. Audio record the student while he/she reads sentences which do not contain nasal sounds (e.g., Both cats have fleas. Chris has three cookies. Skipper eats cheese with chopsticks.). Have the student listen to the recording and mark the words he/she hears which contain nasality.

10. Have the student read a list that contains words with no nasal sounds (e.g., bat, shoe, rug, hat, etc.) and rate his/her productions as appropriate or nasal. If it is too difficult for the student to rate his/her own live voice, audio record the reading and play it for him/her to rate.

11. Audio record the student while he/she reads sentences which contain nasal sounds (e.g., My mama moved my hammer. Nan is numb. The Ming ring is mine.). Have the student listen to the recording and mark the words he/she hears which lack appropriate nasality.

12. Have the student demonstrate proper breath support for speaking using his/her diaphragm.

13. Establish a method that you can use to remind the hypernasal student to use open verbal resonance during class activities (e.g., cupping one hand in the shape of a C by your mouth).

14. Have the student read a list that contains words with nasal sounds (e.g., none, money, Ming, etc.) and rate his/her productions as appropriate or lacking in nasality.

15. Have the student keep a list of words he/she can think of which contain nasal/nonnasal sounds for practice.

16. Involve parents by asking them to rate their child's voice quality (e.g., too much nasality, appropriate resonance, too little nasality) for a specific length of time and/or during a specific situation (e.g., during dinner, during play, while reading, etc.).

17. Discuss how a person's voice changes when they are nervous, tired, angry, etc.

18. Have the student identify occasions when he/she uses appropriate nasal resonance. Discuss ways to facilitate occasions of appropriate resonance.

19. Establish a method that you can use to remind the hyponasal student to use appropriate verbal/nasal resonance during class activities (e.g., pointing to your nose).

20. Use words in vocabulary and spelling lists or in classroom subjects that can be used to practice improving hypernasality or hyponasality. (Using words from academic subject matter will facilitate transfer of appropriate verbal/nasal resonance into everyday speech.)

21. Highlight some of the nasal sounds in a paragraph copied from the student's reading book or textbook. Have the student practice reading it aloud and reinforce instances of appropriate nasal resonance.

22. Have the student demonstrate and practice open verbal resonance during speaking to decrease hypernasality. (When the student exaggerates his/her mouth opening during speaking, more sound typically exits the mouth vs. the nasal cavity.)

23. If the student is speaking with an unusually tight or closed mouth, increase his/her awareness of such behavior by having him/her tally the occurrences during a specified period of time.

Goals:

1. The student will correctly discriminate vocal quality in himself/herself and others.
2. The student will demonstrate appropriate voice volume.
3. The student will demonstrate appropriate vocal quality.

Objectives:

1. The student will identify appropriate and inappropriate vocal volume levels in _____ out of _____ trials.
2. The student will identify personal situations during which appropriate and inappropriate vocal volume levels occur in _____ out of _____ trials.
3. The student will utilize appropriate vocal volume levels during productions of words in _____ out of _____ trials.
4. The student will utilize appropriate vocal volume levels during productions of sentences in _____ out of _____ trials.
5. The student will utilize appropriate vocal volume levels while reading in _____ out of _____ trials.
6. The student will utilize appropriate vocal volume levels during conversation in _____ out of _____ trials.

Interventions:

1. Have the student's hearing checked if it has not been recently checked.

2. Speak to the student and explain that he/she is using an inappropriately loud/soft voice and explain the importance of using an appropriate vocal volume to match different situations.

3. Provide the student with an appropriate voice model.

4. Reinforce the student for appropriate voice quality: (a) give the student a tangible reward (e.g., classroom privileges, line leading, passing out materials, five minutes free time, etc.) or (b) give the student an intangible reward (e.g., praise, fist bump, smile, etc.).

5. Increase the student's awareness of the problem by audio recording him/her while he/she is speaking with a peer who exhibits appropriate vocal volume. Play the recording to see if the student can hear the difference between the volumes.

6. Have the student differentiate between tension and relaxation by first tensing his/her body and then relaxing. (Feel the student's neck and shoulders to determine the presence or absence of tension.)

7. Discuss with the student the negative connotations which are sometimes attached to a person who uses a voice that is too loud/soft. Loud voices may be interpreted to mean that the person is angry, arrogant, etc., while soft voices may be associated with a person who is shy, timid, lacking self-confidence, etc. Discussion of these negative connotations may motivate the student to make changes in his/her voice.

8. Select simple reading materials and have the student read aloud at varying volume levels while you record the reading. Have the student listen and decide which volume levels are most appropriate for the classroom setting.

9. Demonstrate laryngeal tension by having the student vocalize (e.g., say eee or ah) while trying to lift himself/herself up from a sitting position in a hard chair.

10. Choose relaxation exercises to be used by the student (e.g., tensing and then relaxing specific muscle groups, head rotation exercises, imagery, etc.).

11. Establish a quiet time during the day when no one speaks except in an emergency. Soft music could be played in the background.

12. To facilitate understanding of a voice problem caused by a voice that is too loud/soft, teach a short unit on vocal quality to the class.

13. Have the student describe animal voices that sound abusive (e.g., lion - loud; mouse - quiet) and compare them with his/her own vocal volume.

14. Have the student write a short story about animals and then narrate it, switching between loud and soft voices.

15. Have the student describe vocal volumes of famous people, cartoon characters, people at school or home, etc. Have him/her differentiate between vocal volumes that sound quiet/soft and those that sound loud.

16. Encourage good posture while sitting, standing, walking, etc. Poor posture can obstruct good breath support which facilitates vocal quality.

17. Have the student demonstrate proper breath support for speaking using his/her diaphragm.

18. Discuss how a person's voice changes when they are nervous, tired, angry, etc.

19. Have the student rank, hierarchically, the situations in which his/her voice is too loud or too soft. Discuss these situations to facilitate the student's awareness of when he/she is using inappropriate volume and the variance in these situations.

20. Involve parents by asking them to rate their child's voice quality (e.g., appropriate, too loud, harsh, hoarse, breathy, etc.) for a specific length of time and/or in a specific situation (e.g., during playtime, at dinner, at bedtime; inside or outside; in the presence of family members, peers, authority figures; etc.).

21. If the student is speaking with an unusually tight or closed mouth, increase his/her awareness of such behavior by having him/her tally the occurrences during a specified period of time.

22. Have the student demonstrate and practice open verbal resonance when speaking to facilitate volume.

23. Establish a method that you can use to remind the student to use open verbal resonance during class activities (e.g., cupping one hand in the shape of a C by your mouth).

24. Have the student list reasons that might cause people to yell or talk very loudly (e.g., when angry, in a crowd, at a football game, etc.). Talk about how the voice feels after these situations.

25. Have the student describe reactions listeners have to a voice that is too loud or too soft (e.g., annoyance at someone who appears to be yelling, asking to have something repeated, etc.).

26. Have the student list all the different sound effects that he/she and his/her friends make while playing (e.g., motor noises, monster noises, etc.). Discuss the effect on their voices. Suggest alternatives to loud noises.

27. Help the student determine the times and circumstances when his/her voice quality is better/ worse (e.g., after gym, early in the morning, late in the day, on Mondays, etc.).

28. Help the student determine if he/she is participating in any activities during which his/her voice might be strained (e.g., gym, recess, drama, cheerleading, vocal music, baseball, soccer, etc.). Discuss ways that the student could avoid misusing his/her voice in these situations (e.g., clapping hands vs. yelling, walking over to a person vs. shouting at the person, performing actions vs. yelling, etc.).

29. Have the student list occasions when he/she uses a volume level that is too loud or too soft. Discuss alternative ways to communicate in these situations (e.g., walk over to a person instead of shouting across the room, blow a whistle outside to get someone's attention instead of yelling, talk at a normal volume level as opposed to a whisper, etc.).

30. Have the student identify occasions when he/she uses good vocal quality vs. a voice that is too loud or too soft. Discuss ways to improve vocal quality during these situations.

31. If the student uses shouting to gain attention, have him/her practice alternative methods of gaining attention (e.g., stressing a specific word in a sentence, using pitch variations, pausing before an important word, using gestures, etc.).

32. Remind the student to use proper breathing techniques and a relaxed voice during music class, which can be a period of vocal stress.

33. Have the student identify words that have a soft or loud connotation in stories that he/she reads (e.g., soft = shiver, warm, gentle, luminous; loud = bang, hate, stop, gang).

34. Have the student tally the number of times he/she uses a vocal volume level that is too soft or too loud (e.g., during recess, while speaking to a teacher, etc.).

35. When the student has a cold, sore throat, laryngitis, etc.; discuss how the throat might look and encourage the student to talk as little as possible. Do not encourage whispering as an alternative as it may also irritate his/her voice.

36. Have the student take part in short plays or skits that require a voice that is softer/louder.

37. Establish a method that you can use to remind the student to use good vocal quality when he/she is speaking too loud or too soft.

38. Have the student demonstrate his/her best volume level.

39. With younger children, use puppets to practice appropriate volume.

40. When the student is about to engage in an activity that fosters loud/soft speaking, have him/her wear a string bracelet, sticker, etc., to remind him/her to use alternative strategies, good vocal quality, and appropriate volume levels.

176 Cannot identify an object that is different from others in a group

Goal:

1. Identifies an object that is different from others in a group.

Objectives:

1. Identifies one different item out of a group of four similar items, given _____ (visual, tactile, auditory cue) from an adult, _____ out of _____ times.
2. Identifies one different item out of a group of four similar items, given _____ (%, minimal, moderate, maximum, etc.) assistance from an adult, _____ out of _____ times.
3. Identifies one different item out of a group of four similar items _____ out of _____ times.
4. Groups items according to color, given _____ (visual, tactile, auditory cue) from an adult, _____ out of _____ times.
5. Groups items according to color, given _____ (%, minimal, moderate, maximum, etc.) assistance from an adult, _____ out of _____ times.
6. Groups items according to color, _____ out of _____ times.
7. Groups items according to similarities (color, usage, concept, etc.), given _____ (visual, tactile, auditory cue) from an adult, _____ out of _____ times.
8. Groups items according to similarities (color, usage, concept, etc.), given _____ (%, minimal, moderate, maximum, etc.) assistance from an adult, _____ out of _____ times.
9. Groups items according to similarities (color, usage, concept, etc.), _____ out of _____ times.

Interventions:

1. Use a group of items familiar to the child. For example, use alphabet letters and include one item that is different (e.g., a cup, a ball, etc.) Ask the child to identify the item that is different from the others in the group.

2. Work with the child on creating groups so he/she understands the concept of a group (e.g., sort red shapes into a red cup, etc.).

3. Create flash cards of objects and have the child match objects that go together (e.g., eating utensils, same shape, same color, etc.).

4. Be sure the child is able to perform the prerequisite skills of comparing, sorting/ classifying and matching with manipulatives and concrete objects.

5. Begin with only a few objects. Increase the number as the child develops understanding.

6. Begin grouping objects that are exactly the same (e.g., apples) and one that is very different (e.g., a banana). Have the child identify the object that is different.

7. Ask the child guiding questions about the objects. For example, How are these things alike? What rule do these things follow? Then ask how the same objects are different.

8. Help the child work through identifying the object that is different. Have him/her look at each object one by one and point out what is alike and what is different aloud (e.g., This is an apple. This is a banana. This is an apple. They are all fruits, but the banana is different because is it long and yellow.).

9. Begin with visuals, such as sorting mats or cards with pictures. Fade the pictures out to help the child sort the objects. Next, find the object that is sitting by itself.

10. Demonstrate the concept of thinking out loud to solve a problem. Work the problem out while describing the thought processes being used to find the answer.

11. Focus on only one attribute (e.g., color, shape, etc.) and ask the child to identify the one that is different.

12. Focus on the concept of same or alike, by presenting small groups of objects that are similar, then add one object that is not related in any way and discuss how that object is different.

13. With young children, use manipulatives and concrete objects with which the child is familiar. Do not use worksheets.

14. Start with at least three objects that are identical and one that is obviously different. Have the child take the one that is different out of the group. Say, That is not the same. It is different.

15. Sort colors by making a red box using an empty cereal box with a piece of red construction paper taped to the front. Cut out pictures of red objects (e.g., a red boat, ball, car, etc.) matching the same red as the construction paper so that the color will be identical. Tell the child that only red things can go in the red box. Hold a red object against the front of the red box. Say, Yes, this is the same. It is red. This can go in the red box. or No, this is not the same. It is different. This cannot go in the red box.

16. Use plastic dishes and silverware. Hand the child one plate at a time and have him/her stack the dishes saying, These are the same. Periodically give the child a spoon instead of a plate. Say, No that doesn't go on the pile. It is different.

17. Sort shapes using a shape sorter. When the shape fits, say, Yes, this is the same. When it does not fit, say, No, this is different.

18. Sort socks comparing each pair of socks. Say, These are the same. or These are different.

19. Use three or four pictures each of different farm animals. Line up several pictures of the same animal and one that is different. Go down the line saying each animal's sound as you point to each picture (e.g., moo, moo, moo, quack). Have the student tell which animal is different.

20. Collect objects from outdoors (e.g., small rocks, flowers, acorns, etc.) Place two acorns on the table and add acorns one at a time saying, This is the same. Periodically place a flower or a rock in the group of acorns and ask if it goes with the acorn.

21. Match shapes beginning with a circle. Place another circle beside it and say, Circle. This is the same. After placing three or four circles in a row, place a triangle next in line. Say, Triangle. Is this the same? No, this is different. Remove it. Place a few more circles in a row, and then place a square next in line. The child should say, No, that is different.

22. Find foods that are the same at snack time and one that is different (e.g., grape, grape, grape, apple, etc.) Have the student identify which one is different.

Goals:

1. Displays an understanding of one or more prepositions by placing an object appropriately.
2. Displays an understanding of two or more prepositions by placing an object appropriately.
3. Displays an understanding of three or more prepositions by placing an object appropriately.

Objectives:

1. Displays understanding of one preposition by placing an object appropriately, given _____ (visual, tactile, auditory cue) from an adult, _____ out of _____ times.
2. Displays understanding of one preposition by placing an object appropriately, given _____ (%, minimal, moderate, maximum, etc.) assistance from an adult, _____ out of _____ times.
3. Displays understanding of one preposition by placing an object appropriately _____ out of _____ times.
4. Displays understanding of two prepositions by placing an object appropriately, given _____ (visual, tactile, auditory cue) from an adult, _____ out of _____ times.
5. Displays understanding of two prepositions by placing an object appropriately, given _____ (%, minimal, moderate, maximum, etc.) assistance from an adult, _____ out of _____ times.
6. Displays understanding of two prepositions by placing an object appropriately _____ out of _____ times.
7. Displays understanding of three prepositions by placing an object appropriately, given _____ (visual, tactile, auditory cue) from an adult, _____ out of _____ times.
8. Displays understanding of three prepositions by placing an object appropriately, given _____ (%, minimal, moderate, maximum, etc.) assistance from an adult, _____ out of _____ times.
9. Displays understanding of three prepositions by placing an object appropriately, _____ out of _____ times.
10. Displays understanding of prepositions by positioning himself/herself according to the preposition, given _____ (visual, tactile, auditory cue) from an adult, _____ out of _____ times.
11. Displays understanding of prepositions by positioning himself/herself according to the preposition, given _____ (%, minimal, moderate, maximum, etc.) assistance from an adult, _____ out of _____ times.
12. Displays understanding of prepositions by positioning himself/herself according to the preposition _____ out of _____ times.
13. Correctly answers a question from a preposition picture card (i.e., is the cat on or under the table?) _____ out of _____ times.

Interventions:

1. Practice prepositions through body movements. Give the child directions using prepositions and assist the child in following the directions (e.g., put the ball on the table, under the table, beside the table, etc.).

2. Have the child place his/her favorite stuffed animals in the requested positions.

3. Read books and ask questions using prepositions. Have the child answer the questions (e.g., Is the cat on the couch or under the couch?). Create a song about prepositions. Sing the song as you and the child perform the movements with your bodies.

4. Have the child cut and paste pictures of objects or cutouts in different positions (beside, beneath, above, etc.) on a piece of paper with a picture of a large square or other shape.

5. Create an obstacle course in the classroom or playground. Have the child perform various movements using prepositions (e.g., stand next to the chair, walk around the chair two times, sit under the slide, etc.).

6. Create a treasure hunt by hiding various items in the classroom. Give clues to finding the items using prepositions.

7. Play a game of *Simon Says* using prepositions. Use one, then two, then three prepositions to check the child's understanding.

8. Have the child place objects in different positions (e.g., beside, beneath, above, etc.) using pom-poms and a container (e.g., cup, bowl, etc.).

9. Have the child hide something from you and direct you to it by using prepositions.

Goal:

1. Matches two colors.

Objective:

1. Identifies one color, given _____ (visual, tactile, auditory cue) from an adult, _____ out of _____ times.
2. Identifies one color, given _____ (%, minimal, moderate, maximum, etc.) assistance from an adult, _____ out of _____ times.
3. Identifies one color _____ out of _____ times.
4. Identifies two colors, given _____ (visual, tactile, auditory cue) from an adult, _____ out of _____ times.
5. Identifies two colors, given _____ (%, minimal, moderate, maximum, etc.) assistance from an adult, _____ out of _____ times.
6. Identifies two colors _____ out of _____ times.
7. Finds a matching colored card (begin with only two cards on the table), given _____ (visual, tactile, auditory cue) from an adult, _____ out of _____ times.
8. Finds a matching colored card (begin with only two cards on the table), given _____ (%, minimal, moderate, maximum, etc.) assistance from an adult, _____ out of _____ times.
9. Finds a matching colored card (begin with only two cards on the table) _____ out of _____ times.

Interventions:

1. Use colored flash cards and demonstrate matching two that are the same.

2. Match items of the same color (e.g., two shoes, two hair clips, pair of socks, etc.).

3. Be sure the child is able to name every color presented. Begin with a choice of two colors. Frequently children struggle with finding the correct word when they know the color. When given a choice, it is easier to determine if the child knows the color.

4. Create a matching game using a magnetic surface (e.g., cookie sheet, etc.) and two colors of construction paper cards with magnets glued to the back. Ask the child to place cards on the matching color.

5. Cut out colored bird shapes and feathers from construction paper. Have the child glue feathers on the matching bird.

6. Place colored bears into matching cups, cups with a picture of a colored bear on the side, etc.

7. Use edible items. Have five different candy beans on the table. Hand one to the child and tell him/her to match it with one that is the same color. Reward the child with the matching candy beans.

8. Teach the concept of matching by matching similar shaped items (e.g., balls, pretzels, spoons, etc.).

9. Using three flash cards, place one card in front of the child. Tell him/her one of the two cards you have matches his/her card. Place both cards on the table and ask, Does this card match your card or does this one?

10. Use colored chutes made from paper tubes. Have the child drop colored pom-poms through the chute that is the same color as the pom-poms (i.e., matches).

179 Cannot identify pictures that go together

Goal:

1. Identifies pictures that go together.

Objectives:

1. Identifies pictures of items on flash cards, given _____ (visual, tactile, auditory cue) from an adult, _____ out of _____ times.
2. Identifies pictures of items on flash cards, given _____ (%, minimal, moderate, maximum, etc.) assistance from an adult, _____ out of _____ times.
3. Identifies pictures of items on flash cards _____ out of _____ times.
4. Identifies two out of three pictures that go together, given _____ (visual, tactile, auditory cue) from an adult, _____ out of _____ times.
5. Identifies two out of three pictures that go together, given _____ (%, minimal, moderate, maximum, etc.) assistance from an adult, _____ out of _____ times.
6. Identifies two out of three pictures that go together _____ out of _____ times.
7. Identifies pictures that go together, given _____ (visual, tactile, auditory cue) from an adult, _____ out of _____ times.
8. Identifies pictures that go together, given _____ (%, minimal, moderate, maximum, etc.) assistance from an adult, _____ out of _____ times.
9. Identifies pictures that go together _____ out of _____ times.
10. Identifies two out of three items that go together when items are placed in front of him/her, given _____ (visual, tactile, auditory cue) from an adult, _____ out of _____ times.
11. Identifies two out of three items that go together when items are placed in front of him/her, given _____ (%, minimal, moderate, maximum, etc.) assistance from an adult, _____ out of _____ times.
12. Identifies two out of three items that go together when items are placed in front of him/her _____ out of _____ times.

Interventions:

1. Use a group of items familiar to the child. For example, use alphabet letters and include one item that is different (e.g., a cup, a ball, etc.) Ask the child to identify the item that is different from the others in the group.

2. Work with the child on creating groups to increase his/her understanding of a group (e.g., sort colored shapes into same colored cups, etc.).

3. Create flash cards of groups of objects (e.g., eating utensils, bathing articles, same shapes, colors, etc.) and have the child match objects that go together.

4. Using three flash cards, place one card in front of the child. Tell him/her one of the two cards you have matches his/her card. Place both cards on the table and ask, Does this card match your card or does this one?

5. Label and name objects at home that go together.

6. Put objects on a table and match them. Let the child touch the objects.

7. Enlarge pictures and materials for the child. Visual association is very important.

8. Present a series of objects and have the child identify the one that does not belong in the same category (e.g., fork, spoon, cup, sock; sock, shoe, shirt, plate; etc.).

9. Be sure the child understands that objects, people, and ideas can be grouped based on how they are alike.

10. Present a few objects and ask the child to verbally identify the objects that belong.

11. Play a game such as, *I'm thinking of an object which goes with* _____ (e.g., toothpaste, soap, bath towel, etc.). Ask the child to name an object that goes with that object.

12. Have the child practice grouping pictures that go together by drawing pictures that go together or cutting out pictures that go together from a magazine.

13. Reinforce the child for correctly identifying pictures that go together: (a) give him/her a tangible reward (e.g., an edible treat, a special item, etc.) or (b) give him/her an intangible reward (e.g., praise, smile, hug, etc.).

14. Reinforce the child for attempting to identify pictures that go together. As the child demonstrates success, increase the requirement for reinforcement.

180 Cannot correctly point to a penny, nickel, and dime

Goals:

1. Correctly points to a penny.
2. Correctly points to a nickel.
3. Correctly points to a dime.
4. Correctly points to two coins (penny, nickel and/or dime).
5. Correctly points to three coins (penny, nickel, and dime).

Objectives:

1. Identifies one coin _____ out of _____ times.
2. Identifies two coins _____ out of _____ times.
3. Identifies three coins _____ out of _____ times.
4. Removes all pennies out of a stack of coins and puts them into a piggy bank _____ out of _____ times.
5. Removes all nickels out of a stack of coins and puts them into a piggy bank _____ out of _____ times.
6. Removes all dimes out of a stack of coins and puts them into a piggy bank _____ out of _____ times.

Interventions:

1. Have the child practice matching the coins by placing pennies on pictures of pennies, nickels on pictures of nickels, and dimes on pictures of dimes.

2. Have the child practice counting the pennies by 1s, nickels by 5s and dimes by 10s to help him/her identify the difference.

3. Explain to the child how each coin is different. Use descriptions of color, picture, and size of the coins.

4. Play store with the child by placing pictures of a coin on each object. Have the child give you the coin that matches the picture while naming the coin. Next, remove the picture and tell the child how much the item costs (e.g., one penny, one nickel, or one dime). Have the child hand you the correct coin for the object.

5. Have the child practice recognizing coins by their size. Draw circles that match the different coin sizes. Have the child place coins in the blank circles that are the same size as the coin.

6. Use two coins that are different in size and/or color (e.g., a penny and a nickel). Explain the differences in the coins while the child is observing (e.g., looking at coins on a table, holding coins in his/her hand, etc.).

7. Have the child practice handling coins and identifying their differences by sorting pennies and nickels into separate cups.

8. Reinforce the child for correctly pointing to a penny, nickel, and dime: (a) give him/her a tangible reward (e.g., an edible treat, a special item, etc.) or (b) give him/her an intangible reward (e.g., praise, smile, hug, etc.).

9. Reinforce the child for attempting to point to a penny, nickel, and dime. As the child demonstrates success, increase the requirement for reinforcement.

10. Have the child place coins in the matching column of a labeled graph.

11. Use a coin matching strip to sort pennies, nickels, and dimes.

181 Cannot point to a square, circle, and triangle

Goals:

1. Points to a square.
2. Points to a circle.
3. Points to a triangle.
4. Points to two shapes when asked to identify them.
5. Points to three shapes when asked to identify them.

Objectives:

1. When given a simple shape insert puzzle (square, circle and triangle), correctly inserts one shape _____ out of _____ times.
2. When given a simple shape insert puzzle (square, circle and triangle), correctly inserts two shapes _____ out of _____ times.
3. When given a simple shape insert puzzle (square, circle and triangle), correctly inserts all three shapes _____ out of _____ times.
4. When given a simple shape insert puzzle (square, circle and triangle) with two pieces already inserted, correctly inserts one shape _____ out of _____ times.
5. When given a simple shape insert puzzle (square, circle and triangle) with one piece already inserted, correctly inserts two shapes, _____ out of _____ times.
6. While in the community, identifies one circle _____ out of _____ times.
7. While in the community, identifies _____ (#) circle(s) _____ out of _____ times.
8. While in the community, identifies one triangle _____ out of _____ times.
9. While in the community, identifies _____ (#) triangle(s) _____ out of _____ times.
10. While in the community, identifies one square _____ out of _____ times.
11. While in the community, identifies _____ (#) square(s) _____ out of _____ times.

Interventions:

1. Using simple insert puzzles with a square, circle, and triangle; name each shape as the child removes it. As the child inserts the pieces, help him/her name the shapes again.

2. Using a simple insert puzzle with two shapes removed (e.g., a circle and another shape), ask the child to place the circle in the puzzle. Provide assistance in choosing the correct piece if necessary.

3. Look for squares, circles, and triangles while out in the community (e.g., on a walk, shopping, etc.). Take time to stop and identify each shape. Choose simple items so that the child will be able to identify a square, circle, and triangle. Trace the item with your finger to show the child the shape.

4. Practice identifying the shapes by sorting each shape into a container marked with the shape.

5. Name each shape as the child is playing with them, sorting them, placing them in puzzles, etc.

6. Play games that incorporate the shapes. Use various board games as well as computer games that teach shape recognition.

7. Read books about shapes.

8. Place four to six circles around the room. Have the child search for the circles. As the child masters looking for circles, add another shape to the game. To help the child identify the shapes, make each shape a different color (e.g., circles - red, squares - blue, etc.). As the child masters the ability to identify the shapes, make the game more difficult by making all of the shapes the same color.

9. Allow the child to master identification of one shape before additional shapes are added. Add shapes one at a time, as the child masters recognition of each shape.

10. Reinforce the child for correctly pointing to a square, circle, and triangle: (a) give him/her a tangible reward (e.g., an edible treat, a special item, etc.) or (b) give him/her an intangible reward (e.g., praise, smile, hug, etc.).

11. Reinforce the child for attempting to point to a square, circle, and triangle. As the child demonstrates success, increase the requirement for reinforcement.

182 Cannot identify the numbers one to four and cannot count a specified quantity (1-4) when asked

Goals:

1. Identifies the numeral one when asked and/or given a visual of the number.
2. Identifies the numerals one and two when asked and/or given a visual of the number.
3. Identifies the numerals one, two and three when asked and/or given a visual of the number.
4. Identifies the numerals one, two, three, and four when asked and/or given a visual of the number.
5. Picks up one object from a group when asked.
6. Picks up two objects from a group when asked.
7. Picks up three objects from a group when asked.
8. Picks up four objects from a group when asked.

Objectives:

1. Identifies _____ number(s) from flash cards _____ out of _____ times.
2. Counts _____ number of items _____ out of_____ times.
3. Places _____ number of items into a cup when asked _____ out of _____ times.

Interventions:

1. Practice counting from one through four.

2. Practice counting items slowly and deliberately as you touch each item and say a number. Help the child to touch each item while counting. Ask the child to count the items on his/her own.

3. Play games that incorporate numbers. Use board games as well as computer games that teach number recognition.

4. Read books that teach number recognition.

5. Using counting items (e.g., bears, etc.), count each one as it is placed in a cup. Help the child count to four, then have the child count alone.

6. Sing songs with numbers, such as *One little, two little, three little bumble bees*, etc. Demonstrate the numbers with your fingers as you sing.

7. Use flash cards to identify numbers 1-4.

8. Ask the child to show you a specified quantity and hand you the number of items requested (e.g., Show me three cotton balls. Hand me one cotton ball.).

9. Reinforce the child for correctly retrieving a specific quantity: (a) give him/her a tangible reward (e.g., an edible treat, a special item, etc.) or (b) give him/her an intangible reward (e.g., praise, smile, hug, etc.).

10. Reinforce the child for attempting to give you a specific quantity. As the child demonstrates success, increase the requirement for reinforcement.

183 Cannot classify objects according to size, shape, color, category, etc.

Goals:

1. Classifies objects by grouping them according to size.
2. Classifies objects by grouping them according to shape.
3. Classifies objects by grouping them according to color.
4. Classifies objects by grouping them according to category (i.e., cats vs. dogs, etc.).

Objectives:

1. Identifies various colors of objects _____ out of _____ times.
2. Places sorting bears in the correct colored cup, with less than _____ errors, _____ out of _____ times.
3. Sorts various shapes in a sorting toy, with maximal (75%) verbal cues, _____ out of _____ times.
4. Sorts various shapes in a sorting toy, with moderate (50%) verbal cues, _____ out of _____ times.
5. Sorts various shapes in a sorting toy, with minimal (25% or less) verbal cues, _____ out of _____ times.
6. Sorts various shapes in a sorting toy, with less than _____ errors, _____ out of _____ times.
7. Identifies big versus little _____ out of _____ times.
8. Identifies and classifies pictures of different types of cats and dogs into appropriately marked jars _____ out of _____ times.

Interventions:

1. Practice grouping items according to color. Use sorting bears and place the bears into the matching color cup. Say: These match, these are the same color.

2. Demonstrate the concept of big and little. Have similar items with one being big and one being little. Ask the child to give you the big one (as you show him/her your arms stretched out very wide). Then ask the child for the one that is little (as you show him/her a small space between your thumb and index finger).

3. Reinforce the child for correctly grouping objects: (a) give him/her a tangible reward (e.g., an edible treat, a special item, etc.) or (b) give him/her an intangible reward (e.g., praise, smile, hug, etc.).

4. Demonstrate the skill for the child before asking him/her to perform the skill independently.

5. Be sure the child understands the concept of various colors or shapes prior to sorting.

6. Practice sorting shapes with a shape sorter toy.

7. Use many different index cards with animals on them (two to three different animal types). Ask the child to place the cat cards in the jar with the cat picture on it. Repeat for each animal.

8. Practice acting like various animals so that the child understands the characteristics of the animals.

9. Reinforce the child for attempting to group objects. As the child demonstrates success, increase the requirement for reinforcement.

10. Use index cards with pictures of articles of clothing on them. Ask the child to place the articles of clothing that are alike in a stack together (e.g., hats, shoes, shirts, etc.).

184 Cannot point to a group of objects that has more or less

Goals:

1. Points to a group of objects that has more.
2. Points to a group of objects that has less.
3. Points to a group of objects that has more or less.

Objectives:

1. When given a group of two items and a group of ten items, identifies the group with more or less _____ out of _____ times.
2. Identifies which card from a deck of playing cards has more or less _____ out of _____ times.
3. Counts items in a group and marks a number line _____ out of _____ times.
4. Counts items in a group and marks a number line to determine which group has more _____ out of _____ times.
5. Counts items in a group and marks a number line to determine which group has less _____ out of _____ times.

Interventions:

1. Use a number line to indicate where numbers fall. Mark the line toward the zero with the word less and toward the higher numbers with the word more. Show the child two groups of objects. Have the child count then circle the number of objects in each group on the number line. Show the child how to determine which number means more.

2. Use a deck of cards to practice more or less. Randomly pull two cards from the deck. Count the number of items on the card. Ask the child to tell you which card has more items and which card has less.

3. Use animal shapes. Line the animals up in a row for one group. Line the second group up directly under the first group. Ask the child to identify which one has more/less.

4. Reinforce the child for correctly identifying groups of more or less: (a) give him/her a tangible reward (e.g., an edible treat, a special item, etc.) or (b) give him/her an intangible reward (e.g., praise, smile, hug, etc.).

5. Use giant dice to play a game. When the dice are rolled, have the child point to the one that has more or less dots than the other.

6. Use pictures with groups of more and less. Have the child circle the group with more/less.

7. Using candy pieces, have a group that is significantly less than the other. Ask the child which group he/she would want and why. Help the child identify the group that has more and the group that has less. Count the candy pieces to show the number association. Reward the child with a candy piece. Practice this again with groups that are closer in size. Reward the child each time with a candy piece for the correct answer.

8. Practice with items that are motivators for the child (e.g., use cars with kids that love to play with cars, etc.).

9. Place a group of three large beads beside a group of two large beads. Ask the child to point to the group with more. Vary the objects and quantities presented so that the child has the opportunity to practice recognizing more and less.

10. Reinforce the child for attempting to identify groups of more or less. As the child demonstrates success, increase the requirement for reinforcement.

11. During snack time, fill two plates with snacks (e.g., cookies, crackers, etc.), one plate containing more than the other. Have the children discuss which plate has more and which plate has less. As the children begin to take a snack from one of the plates, continue the lesson of more vs. less.

185 Cannot point to a one dollar bill and a five dollar bill

Goals:

1. Identifies a one dollar bill.
2. Identifies a five dollar bill.

Objectives:

1. Identifies the numbers one and five _____ out of _____ times.
2. Identifies a one and five dollar bill by explaining _____ (#) differences _____ out of _____ times.
3. Points to a one dollar bill _____ out of _____ times.
4. Points to a five dollar bill _____ out of _____ times.

Interventions:

1. Practice identifying numbers 1, 5, 10, 20, 100. As the child is able to identify the numbers, ask the child to identify a one dollar bill from two choices.

2. Explain to the child how to identify paper money by using the numbers.

3. Explain to the child the differences between a one dollar bill and a five dollar bill. Point out the pictures of George Washington and Abraham Lincoln, etc.

4. Use play money with prominently displayed numbers on the face of each bill. Ask the child to identify the one and the five.

5. Play a sorting game with play money where the child makes a stack of one dollar bills and a stack of five dollar bills.

6. When the child is successful at identifying the numbers displayed on play money, ask him/her to identify authentic bills.

7. Reinforce the child for correctly identifying a one dollar bill and a five dollar bill: (a) give him/her a tangible reward (e.g., an edible treat, a special item, etc.) or (b) give him/her an intangible reward (e.g., praise, smile, hug, etc.).

8. Reinforce the child for attempting to identify a one dollar bill and a five dollar bill. As the child demonstrates success, increase the requirement for reinforcement.

9. Play store with objects priced either $1 or $5.

10. Play a money matching game using cards picturing a $1 or $5 bill. As the child demonstrates success, gradually increase the number of cards to include all denominations of bills and coins.

186 Does not use several pronouns correctly in conversation

Goals:
1. Uses at least one pronoun correctly in conversation.
2. Uses more than one pronoun correctly in conversation.
3. Uses several pronouns correctly in conversation.

Objectives:
1. Uses _____ (#) pronouns during conversation, given _____ (#) verbal cues from an adult, _____ out of _____ times.
2. Uses correct pronouns during conversation when corrected by an adult _____ out of _____ times.
3. Uses _____ (#) pronouns during conversation _____ out of _____ times.

NOTE:
Developmentally appropriate ages for pronoun usage are:
- Three years - I, me, you, mine
- Four years - he, she, they, we, your
- Five years - his, her, him, yours, our, ours, their, theirs.

Interventions:

1. Use the correct pronouns during conversation with the child (e.g., I need a drink vs. Mommy needs a drink.). Ask the child to repeat the correct phrase. Be sure to be at the child's level when speaking to him/her while maintaining eye contact.

2. Practice he/she by identifying others in the community/school that the child may know. Have the child identify the person by he or she.

3. Use pronouns during dramatic play. Use puppets or other characters to practice pronouns.

4. Use picture cards or illustrated books that show children and adults in action. Phrase the actions in multiple formats (e.g., The mother is stirring with the spoon. She is stirring with it.).

5. Use direct, specific questions to increase pronoun usage (e.g., What did the girl do? or What happened to the boy?). Give immediate feedback to correct errors.

6. Use natural interactions with emphasis on the multiple formats of nouns/pronouns (e.g., While putting away toys say, Eli, this is your truck. You pick it up. He will put it away.).

7. Use patterned story books for early learners (e.g., *Brown Bear, Brown Bear, What do You See?*, *Polar Bear, Polar Bear, What do You Hear?*, *If You Give a Mouse a Cookie*.).

8. Familiarize the child with pronouns for both genders.

9. When a child confuses pronouns such as saying, hold you for hold me, use the child's hand to point to himself/herself or the appropriate object of the pronoun while stating the correct phrase, hold me while pointing to him/her.

10. In groups, use modeling with repetition. For example, ask each child in the group, What is your name? while pointing at the child. Prompt or model pointing at himself/herself while responding, My name is _____.

11. Whisper the appropriate pronoun usage to the child while he/she is interacting with another peer or adult.

12. Use present tense with one to two-year olds when teaching correct pronoun usage. Toddlers are better at acquiring new information in the present tense due to limited memory capacity.

187 Cannot correctly answer how and where questions

Goals:

1. Correctly answers how questions.
2. Correctly answers where questions.
3. Correctly answers how and where questions.

Objectives:

1. Answers how questions during conversation, given _____ (#) verbal cues from an adult, _____ out of _____ times.
2. Answers how questions during conversation, when corrected by an adult, _____ out of _____ times.
3. Answers how questions during conversation _____ out of _____ times.
4. Answers where questions during conversation, given _____ (#) verbal cues from an adult, _____ out of _____ times.
5. Answers where questions during conversation, when corrected by an adult _____ out of _____ times.
6. Answers where questions during conversation _____ out of _____ times.
7. Answers how and where questions during conversation, given _____ (#) verbal cues from an adult, _ out of _____ times.
8. Answers how and where questions during conversation, when corrected by an adult, _____ out of _____ times.
9. Answers how and where questions during conversation _____ out of _____ times.

Interventions:

1. Play *Where is it?*. Ask the child to find something simple in the environment. When asking, Where is it?, be sure to use an inquisitive look on your face, look around the room, and use your index finger to point around the room. Have the child look for the item. Praise him/her for attempting or giving the correct answer.

2. Have the child hide an item and ask you, Where is it? Play find the item.

3. Use the word where when playing hide and seek. Have the child hide. Ask, Where is _____? Where could he/she be? When found, say, There you are! or Here you are!

4. Play a game by hiding a favorite item under a blanket. Ask the child, Where is _____? Have the child find the item.

5. Determine whether the child knows the difference between telling and asking. Young children frequently confuse these concepts and launch into a lengthy narrative about some personal experience when asked if they have any questions.

6. Have the child's hearing checked if it has not been recently checked.

7. Reinforce the child for correctly answering questions involving how and where: (a) give him/her a tangible reward (e.g., an edible treat, a special item, etc.) or (b) give him/her an intangible reward (e.g., praise, smile, hug, etc.).

8. Reinforce the child for attempting to answer how and where questions. As the child demonstrates success, increase the requirement for reinforcement.

9. Choose a peer to model responding correctly to how and where questions for the child.

10. Restate questions in a simpler form when necessary to facilitate comprehension (e.g., When do you go to bed? could be restated as What time do you go to bed?).

11. Use visual aids or demonstrations whenever possible to facilitate comprehension of questions.

Goal:

1. Correctly uses an object.

Objectives:

1. Correctly uses an object that is provided to him/her, given _____(#) verbal cues from an adult, _____ out of _____ times.
2. Correctly uses an object that is provided to him/her, given hand over hand assistance from an adult, _____ out of _____ times.
3. Correctly uses an object that is provided to him/her, given only initial hand over hand assistance from an adult, _____ out of _____ times.
4. Correctly uses an object that is provided to him/her, once its use is demonstrated, _____ out of _____ times.
5. Correctly uses an object that is provided to him/her _____ out of _____ times.

Interventions:

1. Provide the child with opportunities to experiment with objects. Allow for engagement with other children to help the child learn how to use an object.

2. Demonstrate how an object is to be used. Allow the child time to practice using the object correctly.

3. Allow the child to interact with you as you use an object, (e.g., stir with a spoon, dig with a plastic shovel, pour from a small pitcher, etc.).

4. Practice using objects during role-play with puppets or dolls.

5. Using real objects, describe your actions as you use the object (e.g., demonstrate using a wash cloth to wash your face, say, A wash cloth is used to wash your face.).

6. Use toys to demonstrate how an object is used (e.g., demonstrate using a toy screwdriver to tighten a toy screw, say, The screwdriver is used to tighten a screw.).

7. Hand the child a toy and ask him/her to show you how to use it (e.g., a toy spoon with a toy mixing bowl, a toy hammer with a peg board, etc.). Ask the child to tell you what he/she is doing.

8. Reinforce the child for correctly using an object: (a) give him/her a tangible reward (e.g., an edible treat, a special item, etc.) or (b) give him/her an intangible reward (e.g., praise, smile, hug, etc.).

9. Reinforce the child for attempting to correctly use an object. As the child demonstrates success, increase the requirement for reinforcement.

10. Play a matching game with cards. Have the child match an object card with its intended use card (e.g., comb - hair, toothbrush - teeth, shoes - feet, etc.) As the child demonstrates success, gradually increase the complexity of the cards and their intended uses.

189 Does not use the past tense of verbs

Goal:

1. Uses the past tense of verbs during conversation.

Objectives:

1. Uses the past tense of verbs during conversation, given _____(#) verbal cues from an adult, _____ out of _____ times.
2. Uses the past tense of verbs during conversation, given occasional reminders from an adult, _____ out of _____ times.
3. Uses the past tense of verbs during conversation, given only initial verbal assistance from an adult, _____ out of _____ times.
4. Uses the past tense of verbs during conversation _____ out of _____ times.

Interventions:

1. Have the child practice using the past verb tense. Correct his/her verb tense and ask him/her to repeat what was said using the past tense of the verb.

2. Use the past tense during conversations with the child.

3. Reinforce the child for attempting to use the past verb tense. As the child demonstrates success, increase the requirement for reinforcement.

4. Determine whether the child understands the concept of time which influences comprehension of verb tensing (i.e., Can he/she answer questions using yesterday, today, tomorrow, before, later, etc.? Does he/she use such vocabulary when speaking even though the verb tense is incorrect?).

5. Determine whether the child has appropriate sequencing skills. The concept of sequencing influences comprehension of verb tensing (i.e., Can he/she answer questions using first, next, then, etc.? Does he/she use such vocabulary when speaking even though verb tenses are incorrect?).

6. Have the child's hearing checked if it has not been recently checked.

7. Correct the child's verb tense so that he/she will become accustomed to hearing the correct verb tense.

8. Reinforce the child for using the past verb tense correctly: (a) give him/her a tangible reward (e.g., an edible treat, a special item, etc.) or (b) give him/her an intangible reward (e.g., praise, smile, hug, etc.).

9. Use before and after pictures of an event or situation (e.g., picture of child holding a glass and picture of child standing beside the broken glass on the floor). Ask questions prompting the child to explain what happened while encouraging correct verb tense usage.

10. Use actions to demonstrate past tense verbs. Have the child act out the verb in different tenses (e.g., jump/jumping/jumped; hop/hopping/hopped; clap/clapping/clapped).

Goal:

1. Answers why questions correctly.

Objectives:

1. Answers why questions correctly during conversation, given _____(#) verbal cues from an adult, _____ out of _____ times.
2. Answers why questions correctly during conversation, given occasional reminders from an adult, _____ out of _____ times.
3. Answers why questions correctly during conversation, given only initial verbal assistance from an adult, _____ out of _____ times.
4. Answers why questions correctly during conversation, when given a story board (visual) to help him/her explain, _____ out of _____ times.
5. Answers why questions correctly during conversation _____ out of _____ times.

Interventions:

1. Ask the child why when he/she can answer correctly. Build on this concept by asking why at times that he/she may need help to answer.

2. Reinforce the child for correctly answering why questions: (a) give him/her a tangible reward (e.g., an edible treat, a special item, etc.) or (b) give him/her an intangible reward (e.g., praise, smile, hug, etc.).

3. Reinforce the child for attempting to answer why questions. As the child demonstrates success, increase the requirement for reinforcement.

4. Use visual aids or demonstrations whenever possible to facilitate comprehension of questions.

5. Have the child's hearing checked if it has not been recently checked.

6. Determine whether the child knows the difference between telling and asking. Young children frequently confuse these concepts and launch into a lengthy narrative about some personal experience when asked if they have any questions.

7. Restate questions when necessary to facilitate comprehension (e.g., Why are you crying? could be restated as, What happened to cause you to cry?).

8. Use pictures which depict cause/effect information in conjunction with why questions (e.g., a picture of a broken cookie jar and a little boy crying, paired with the question, Why is the boy crying?).

9. Ask the child questions using *what*, where, who, when, how, and finally why (e.g., What did you eat for breakfast?; Where did you eat breakfast?; Who did you sit with at breakfast?).

10. Use a story board and ask why questions.

191 Cannot count by rote memory from one to fifteen

Goals:

1. Identifies the number(s) _____ (e.g., one through fifteen) when asked and/or given a visual of the number.
2. Identifies the number(s) _____ (e.g., one through fifteen) when asked.
3. Counts from _____ to _____ from memory.

Objectives:

1. Identifies number(s) from flash cards _____ out of _____ times.
2. Counts _____ number of items _____ out of _____ times.
3. Places _____ number of items into a cup when asked _____ out of _____ times.
4. Places _____ number of items into a cup when asked, given hand over hand assistance from an adult, _____ out of _____ times.
5. Counts from _____ to _____, from memory, _____ out of _____ times.

Interventions:

1. Sing counting songs.

2. Use electronic learning devices that teach counting skills.

3. Reinforce the child for attempting to rote count from one to fifteen. As the child demonstrates success, increase the requirement for reinforcement.

4. Reinforce the child for correctly counting from one to fifteen: (a) give him/her a tangible reward (e.g., an edible treat, a special item, etc.) or (b) give him/her an intangible reward (e.g., praise, smile, hug, etc.).

5. Practice counting one to fifteen pieces of candy. When the child succeeds, reward him/her with a piece of the candy.

6. Practice counting with things that are interesting to the child (e.g., cars, bugs, flowers, etc.).

7. Practice counting while out in the community or riding in the car.

8. Help the child count by moving blocks from the floor into a box, one at a time.

9. Practice counting one to fifteen by saying a number each time you pick up an item and place it in a box.

10. Read counting books and encourage the child to count the objects on each page. When the story is finished, repeat the numbers aloud with the child (e.g., one, two, three, etc.).

11. Play a ball toss game. When the ball is tossed to a child, have the children count. Repeat until they can count from 1-15.

12. Write numbers 1-5; 6-10; 10-15, etc., on separate lines on a board. Practice reciting each row of numbers. As the child demonstrates success, add the next row. Continue adding rows until he/she can recite numbers 1-15.

Goals:

1. Tells a story using pictures.
2. Tells a story using a book.
3. Tells a story using pictures or a book.

Objectives:

1. Tells what is happening in a picture when given two or more sequence cards, given occasional verbal cues, _____ out of _____ times.
2. Tells what is happening in a picture when given two or more sequence cards _____ out of _____ times.
3. Tells what is happening in a picture when given two sequence cards, given occasional verbal cues, _____ out of _____ times.
4. Tells what is happening in a picture when given two sequence cards _____ out of _____ times.
5. Tells what is happening in a picture when given one sequence card, given occasional verbal cues, _____ out of _____ times.
6. Tells what is happening in a picture when given one sequence card _____ out of _____ times.
7. Tells a story from a familiar book, given occasional verbal cues, _____ out of _____ times.
8. Tells a story from a familiar book _____ out of _____ times.

Interventions:

1. Begin with a book that the child knows very well. Have the child take a turn reading/telling the story to a group of stuffed animals, favorite items, or friends. Once mastered, have the child use books/pictures that are not as familiar to him/her.

2. Read books to the child on a regular basis.

3. Have the child talk about a piece of artwork to help him/her tell a story from a picture.

4. Practice telling a story with sequence pictures. Begin with two to three pictures. Once mastered, add other pictures to make the story longer.

5. Ask the child to tell a story using a simple board book. As the child demonstrates success, introduce paper books.

6. Use puppets and dolls during playtime to make up stories.

7. Place various objects in a story telling bag. Begin with a starter sentence and ask a child to pull one item out of the bag. Each time an object is pulled out, it eats the next one (e.g., There once was a giraffe who ate a... , who ate a ..., who ate a ....). As the child demonstrates success, have him/her make up a story each time he/she pulls an object from the bag.

8. Using rolled newsprint paper, create a story telling pathway. As the children make their way down the path, have them use the items or pictures in their path to tell their story.

9. Have the children create a story. Begin with a starting sentence and have each child add on to the story (e.g., Once upon a time, a tiny mouse...).

10. Use a story telling board game.

193 Cannot rhyme words

Goal:

1. Rhymes words.

Objectives:

1. Finds _____ (#) word(s) that rhyme, when given simple three-letter words, _____ out of _____ times.
2. Uses the alphabet to find rhyming words _____ out of _____ times.
3. Finds one rhyming word for a complex word _____ out of _____ times.
4. Finds one rhyming word when using flash cards _____ out of _____ times.
5. Understands that the ending sound of a word is what makes it rhyme _____ out of _____ times.

Interventions:

1. Sing songs with rhyming words. Point out the words that rhyme and how they sound similar.

2. Explain to the child that he/she can use different letters in the alphabet to find words that rhyme. Begin with a word family, such as -at. Start with the letter a and place it in front of at. Say the word. If it doesn't work, move on to the next letter until a word that rhymes is found (e.g., bat, cat, fat, etc.).

3. Show the child that rhyming words frequently have different beginning letters and the same letters at the end. (e.g., hat - bat; blue - glue; etc.).

4. Read books that have rhyming words. Point out the words that rhyme emphasizing that they sound very similar.

5. Recite traditional nursery rhymes while doing corresponding movements.

6. Play a rhyming basket/box/bucket game. Place various objects in a basket/box/ bucket. Make up nonsense rhyming words for the objects that will give children clues to each item (e.g., fizzers - scissors; lencil - pencil; etc.).

7. Play a rhyming word game similar to musical chairs that involves walking around the chairs when words rhyme and finding a chair to sit down in when words do not rhyme (e.g., can - man, dog - frog, dog - log, dog - cat).

8. Play *I Spy* using rhyming words as clues (e.g., I spy something that rhymes with look.).

9. Play rhyming bingo.

10. Play games using word families (e.g., -op, -am, and -at families).

Goal:

1. Describes the weather outside.

Objectives:

1. Observes weather from the window and chooses the appropriate felt shape to depict the weather outside, given two choices, _____ out of _____ times.
2. Observes weather from the window and chooses the appropriate felt shape to depict the weather outside, given occasional verbal cues, _____ out of _____ times.
3. Observes weather from the window and chooses the appropriate felt shape to depict the weather outside _____ out of _____ times.
4. Explains the weather seen on flash cards with a simple word or words when given two or more choices, _____ out of _____ times.
5. Explains the weather seen on flash cards with a simple word or words when given two choices, _____ out of _____ times.
6. Explains the weather seen on flash cards with a simple word or words _____ out of _____ times.
7. Observes weather from the window and chooses the appropriate picture from a picture list to depict the weather outside _____ out of _____ times.
8. Accurately describes the weather _____ out of _____ times.

Interventions:

1. Use a felt board with different pictures to display the weather outside. Have the child go to the window, look outside, and pick the correct felt picture that represents the weather (e.g., sun, cloud, rain, snow, etc.).

2. Using flash cards with different weather pictures, have the child explain the weather represented in the picture.

3. Find different types of weather pictures in magazines to represent the various weather patterns.

4. Provide dress-up clothing for different kinds of weather. Children may take turns choosing a weather picture from a bucket and dressing in the appropriate clothing. The other children try to guess the weather word.

5. Make sure the child is able to identify different types of weather and weather pictures (e.g., sunny, cloudy, snowing, raining, foggy, etc.).

6. Use a weather doll to discuss the weather outside each morning. Allow the child to dress the doll in appropriate clothing for the weather.

7. Reinforce the child for correctly describing the weather outside: (a) give him/her a tangible reward (e.g., an edible treat, a special item, etc.) or (b) give him/her an intangible reward (e.g., praise, smile, hug, etc.).

8. Reinforce the child for attempting to describe the weather outside. As the child demonstrates success, gradually increase the requirement for reinforcement.

9. Create a weather journal. Each day, have the child glue a picture on a page that describes the weather or draw a picture of the weather.

10. Watch the news reports about weather.

III. Appendix

CONTRACT

I, _____,

HEREBY DECLARE THAT I WILL _____

_____

_____.

THIS JOB WILL BE CONSIDERED SUCCESSFUL _____

_____.

NAME: _____,

FOR THE SUCCESSFUL COMPLETION OF THE ABOVE JOB,

YOU MAY _____

_____

DATE SIGNED: _____

DATE COMPLETED: _____

_____
SIGNED

Outline Form

Subject: _____

Topic: _____

	General	Specific
Who:		
What:		
Where:		
When:		
How:		
Why:		
Vocabulary:		

Outline Form (Alternative)

Subject: _____

Topic: _____

<u>**General**</u>   <u>**Specific**</u>

What:

Why:

How:

Vocabulary:

Example:

Mapping Form

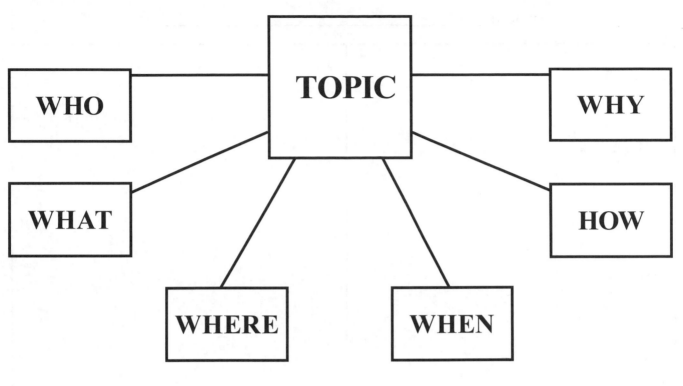

WHO

WHAT

TOPIC

WHERE

WHEN

WHY

HOW

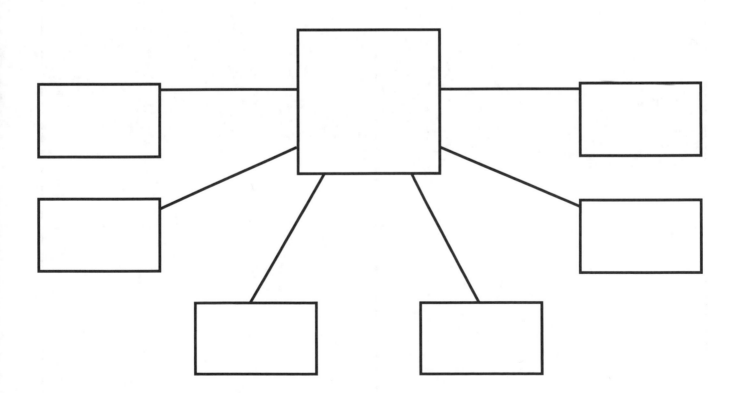

Double-Column Form

Subject: _____

Who:

What:

Where:

When:

How:

Why:

Assignment Form

Subject: _____

	General	Specific
What:		
How:		
Materials:		
When:		

Subject: _____

	General	Specific
What:		
How:		
Materials:		
When:		

Assignment Sheet

ASSIGNMENT SHEET

DATE _____

SUBJECT	ASSIGNMENT	DUE DATE	TEACHER INITIALS

Comments:

_____

PARENT SIGNATURE

ASSIGNMENT SHEET

DATE _____

SUBJECT	ASSIGNMENT	DUE DATE	TEACHER INITIALS

Comments:

_____

PARENT SIGNATURE

2-Week Project Outline

DAY 1   **Determine the exact assignment**

- Identify due date

DAY 2-4   **Project preparation**

- Read assigned materials
- Research related materials
- Gather necessary materials

DAY 5   **Summarize reading material**

- Answer: Who, What, Where, When, How, Why

DAY 6   **Preliminary project construction**

- Make sketches, determine scale, make revisions

DAY 7-11   **Project construction**

- Lay out all materials
- Prepare materials to scale
- Draw/color
- Cut
- Glue
- Paint

DAY 12   **Touch up work**

- Label, check that all items are secure, etc.

DAY 13   **Write paragraph from summary (Day 5)**

DAY 14   **Turn in!**

Test-Taking Skills

1. Survey entire test for the kinds of items that are included (e.g., true-false, multiple-choice, fill-in-the-blank, etc.).

2. Read all directions.

3. Underline or circle all key words or phrases in the directions (e.g., locate, write, choose the best answer, identify the main idea, etc.).

4. Do not answer any items until the directions are thoroughly understood (i.e., ask the teacher for clarification if directions are not thoroughly understood).

5. Respond to all items for which the answer is known; skip remaining items to answer later.

6. For those items which are difficult to answer, underline the key words (e.g., who, what, where, when, how, why) and then respond.

7. For those items still not understood, ask the teacher for clarification.

8. Go back and check all answers for accuracy (e.g., followed directions, proper use of math operations, no careless errors).

ADDITIONAL SUGGESTIONS

- In order for a statement to be true, all of the statement must be true (e.g., note words such as all, never, always, etc.).

- When matching, first answer items that are known. Cross off answers that are used; then go back to remaining items and make the best choice.

- Some items may provide clues or reminders for items that could not be answered the first time through the test.

- When writing an essay answer, construct the answer around Who, What, Where, When, How, and Why.

- On multiple-choice items, read all choices before responding. If any of the choices look new or different, they are probably not the correct answer.

- If a true-false item looks new or different, it is probably false.

Studying for a Test

1. Identify the information to be covered on the test.

2. Identify and collect all necessary materials (e.g., textbook, notebook, etc.).

3. Identify major topics.

4. Under each topic, identify major headings.

5. Under each heading, use the Outline Form to identify Who, What, Where, When, How, and Why or underline/highlight.

6. Make study aids such as flash cards. (See Forms.)

7. Memorize information using the Outline Form and/or mnemonic strategies.

ADDITIONAL SUGGESTIONS

- Study with a friend.

- Write practice questions from the Outline Form and answer the questions.

- If study questions are provided, answer all questions.

- Make sure that all information in the summary is thoroughly understood.

Flash Card Study Aid

Topic: _____

Who:

What:

Where:

When:

How:

Why:

Topic: _____

Who:

What:

Where:

When:

How:

Why:

Fiction Frame

Title: _____

Author: _____

This story takes place _____.

An important character in this story is _____

who _____.

A problem occurs when _____

_____.

Next, _____

_____.

The problem is solved when _____

_____

_____.

At the end of the story, _____

_____

_____.

Parent Letter Sample

Dear Parent(s):

Your child will be bringing home an assignment sheet each day. This assignment sheet will indicate the assignments that are to be completed at home and when they are due.

Please check for this sheet every day in order to monitor homework completion. After all assignments are completed, please sign the sheet and return it to school with your child. Thank you for your support.

Sincerely,

Note Taking

- **Outline Form**
  (e.g., Who, What, Where, When, How, Why)

- **Mapping Form**
  (e.g., Who, What, Where, When, How, Why)

- **Double-Column Form**
  (e.g., Who, What, Where, When, How, Why)

- **Assignment Form**
  (e.g., What, How, Materials, When)

- **Assignment Sheet**

- **2-Week Project Outline**

Selected Abbreviations and Symbols

ab.	about		qt.	quart
addn.	addition		rd.	road
bk.	book		rep.	representative
bldg.	building		Rev.	Reverend
c/o	in care of		s.s.	social studies
cap.	capital		S.S.#	social security number
cent.	century		sc.	science
ch., chap.	chapter		sch.	school
cm	centimeter		sig.	signature
co.	company		sp.	spelling
cont.	continent		sq.	square
cont.	continued		subj.	subject
corp.	corporation		subt.	subtraction
D.O.B.	date of birth		syn.	synonym
DB	database		T	ton
dept.	department		temp.	temporary
dict.	dictionary		treas.	treasurer
doz.	dozen		univ.	university
educ.	education		US, USA	United States of America
enc.	encyclopedia		v.	verb
Eng.	English		VP	vice president
etc.	et cetera, and so forth		vs.	versus
fig.	figure		w/	with
g	gram		wk.	week
geog.	geography		wt.	weight
gov., govt.	government		yd.	yard
hist.	history		yr.	year
ht., hgt.	height		&	and
ill., illus.	illustration		@	at
in.	inch		¢	cents
intro.	introduction		$	dollars
lab.	laboratory		#	number or pound
lang.	language		☠	poison
lat.	latitude		♻	recycle
lb.	pound			
leg.	legislature			
lib.	library			
liq.	liquid			
max.	maximum			
meas.	measure			
mi.	mile			
min.	minute			
misc.	miscellaneous			
mo.	month			
natl.	national			
no.	number			
oz.	ounce			
p., pg.	page			
par.	paragraph			
PC	personal computer			
pd.	paid			
pop.	population			
Pres.	president			
pt.	pint			

The above list only serves as an example. The student should further develop his/her own list.

References:

Cormier, R.A. (1995). *Error-free writing: A lifetime guide to flawless business writing.* Englewood Cliffs, NJ: Prentice-Hall.

Merriam-Webster's collegiate dictionary (11th ed.). (2003). Springfield, MA: Merriam-Webster.

The new york public library™ desk reference (4th ed.). (2002) New York, NY: Hyperion.

University of Chicago Press. (2003). *The chicago manual of style (15th ed.).* Chicago: Author.

Typical Methods of Modifying Academic Tasks

- Reduce the number of problems on a page (e.g., five problems to a page; the student may be required to do four pages of five problems on each page throughout the day if necessary).

- Use a highlight marker to identify key words, phrases, or sentences for the student to read.

- Remove pages from workbooks or reading material and present these to the student one at a time rather than allowing the student to become anxious with workbooks or texts.

- Outline reading material for the student at his/her reading level, emphasizing main ideas.

- Record material for the student to listen to as he/she reads along.

- Read tests/quizzes aloud for the student.

- Record tests/quizzes for the student.

- Make a bright construction paper border for the student to place around reading material to maintain his/her attention to the task.

- Make a reading window from construction paper which the student places over sentences or paragraphs to maintain attention.

- Provide manipulative objects for the student to use in solving math problems.

- Rearrange problems on a page (e.g., if crowded, create more space between the problems).

- Use graph paper for math problems, handwriting, etc.

- Rewrite directions at an appropriate reading level.

- Record directions.

- Have peers deliver directions or explanations.

- Allow more time to take tests or quizzes.

Preventing Behavior Problems

- Determine reinforcer preferences.

- Determine academic ability levels.

- Determine social interaction skills.

- Determine ability to remain on task.

- Determine group behavior.

- Monitor and limit contemporary determinants of inappropriate behavior such as having to wait, task length, task difficulty, peer involvement, etc.

- Base seating arrangements on behavior.

- Base group involvement on behavior.

- Maintain teacher mobility in the classroom.

- Maintain teacher/student contact: visual, verbal, and physical.

- Use criteria for expectations based on observed behavior and performance.

- Use shaping, fading, and imitation procedures to gradually change behavior.

- Maintain variety in reinforcers.

- Use the *Premack Principle* in arranging the schedule (i.e., a more desirable task can be used to reinforce the completion of a less desirable task).

- Use curriculum as reinforcement.

- Use rules, point cards, and schedules of daily events as discriminative stimuli.

- Use contracting to individualize, specify expected behavior, and identify reinforcers.

- Arrange seating so all students have visibility to and from the teacher, and the teacher can scan the entire class.

- Maintain a full schedule of activities.

- Use language that is positive and firm, not demeaning, insulting, or harassing.

- Intervene early when any form of conflict occurs.

- Do not ignore behavior as an excuse for not intervening.

- Use time-out to help the student resolve problem behavior.

- Use removal to prevent contagion, destruction of property, and danger to others.

- Communicate and coordinate with other teachers.

- Communicate with home to prevent students playing one adult against another.

Elementary Reinforcer Survey

Name: _____ Age: _____ Date: _____

1. The things I like to do after school are _____
   _____

2. If I had ten dollars, I would _____
   _____

3. My favorite TV programs are _____
   _____

4. My favorite game at school is _____
   _____

5. My best friends are _____
   _____

6. My favorite time of day is _____
   _____

7. My favorite toys are _____
   _____

8. My favorite music is _____
   _____

9. My favorite subject at school is _____
   _____

10. I like to read about _____
    _____

11. The places I like to go in town are _____
    _____

12. My favorite foods are _____
    _____

13. My favorite inside activities are _____
    _____

14. My favorite outside activities are _____
    _____

15. My hobbies are _____
    _____

16. My favorite animals are _____
    _____

17. The three things I like to do most are _____
    _____

The Reinforcer Survey may be given to one student or a group of students. If the students cannot read, the survey is read to them. If they cannot write their answers, the answers are given verbally.

Secondary Reinforcer Survey

Name: _____ Age: _____ Date: _____

1. The things I like to do after school are _____
   _____

2. If I had ten dollars, I would _____
   _____

3. My favorite TV programs are _____
   _____

4. My best friends are _____
   _____

5. My favorite time of day is _____
   _____

6. My favorite music is _____
   _____

7. My favorite subject at school is _____
   _____

8. I like to read about _____
   _____

9. The places I like to go in town are _____
   _____

10. My favorite foods are _____
    _____

11. My favorite inside activities are _____
    _____

12. My favorite outside activities are _____
    _____

13. My hobbies are _____
    _____

14. My favorite animals are _____
    _____

15. The three things I like to do most are _____
    _____

The Reinforcer Survey may be given to one student or a group of students. If the students cannot read, the survey is read to them. If they cannot write their answers, the answers are given verbally.

Elementary Classroom Reinforcers

Name: _____   **Date:** _____

☐ Activity/game sheets	☐ Leave shoes off in the room for a day
☐ Be a helper in another classroom	☐ Drop lowest test score
☐ Be the classroom helper	☐ Listen to an audio book
☐ Solve brainteasers	☐ Listen to music while working
☐ Bring a drink to class	☐ *No Homework* pass
☐ Bring a snack/candy to class	☐ *No Assignment* pass
☐ Bring a stuffed animal to school for the day	☐ *No Quiz* pass
☐ Chew gum in class	☐ *No Test* pass
☐ Classroom helper	☐ *No Morning Work* pass
☐ Earn tokens for privileges	☐ Open book test
☐ Dance to favorite music in the classroom	☐ Earn pencils, pens, and markers
☐ Draw on the whiteboard for 5 minutes	☐ Permission to use teacher's special pen or pencil for the day
☐ Earn a food day for individuals or whole class	☐ Private lunch in the classroom with a friend
☐ Eat lunch outdoors	☐ Put a puzzle together
☐ Eat lunch with the teacher or principal	☐ Earn raffle tickets for donated prize
☐ Extra art time	☐ Read to the class
☐ Computer time	☐ Reduced homework
☐ Extra credit / extra credit pass / extra credit points	☐ Remove a tardy
☐ Extra reading time	☐ Bring an item for Show and Tell
☐ Extra recess	☐ Sit by friends
☐ Field trip	☐ Sit in a unique spot or chair for the day (e.g., rocking chair)
☐ Special dress day - option to wear a fun hat or no uniform	☐ Sit with a buddy at lunch
☐ Time to listen to music, mingle w/friends, read	☐ Earn stickers
☐ Early to lunch / front of lunch line pass	☐ Library time
☐ Game time	☐ Take a fun physical activity break
☐ Hall pass	☐ Teach class
☐ 5 minutes of free time	☐ Teacher performs a special skill (e.g., singing, cartwheel, etc.)
☐ Teacher's assistant for the day	☐ Earn trinkets (e.g., magnets, frisbees, etc.)
☐ Positive note sent home to parents	☐ Turn in an assignment late
☐ Free time doing an activity of choice	☐ Walk with the principal or teacher
☐ Lunch or breakfast in the classroom	☐ Watch a fun video
☐ Help design/put up a bulletin board	
☐ Leave class 1 minute early	

This Elementary Classroom Reinforcers list may be used in special or regular education classes. Teachers and/or students can check those reinforcers most appropriate.

Secondary Classroom Reinforcers

Name: _____   **Date:** _____

- ☐ Activity/game sheets
- ☐ Assemblies
- ☐ Be a helper in another classroom
- ☐ Be the classroom helper
- ☐ Solve brainteasers
- ☐ Bring a drink to class
- ☐ Bring a snack/candy to class
- ☐ Bring a stuffed animal to school for the day
- ☐ Chew gum in class
- ☐ Classroom helper
- ☐ Earn tokens for privileges or video stores, music stores, or movies
- ☐ Dance to favorite music in the classroom
- ☐ Draw on the whiteboard for 5 minutes
- ☐ Drawings for donated prizes
- ☐ Earn a food day for individuals or whole class
- ☐ Eat lunch outdoors
- ☐ Eat lunch with the teacher or principal
- ☐ Extra art time
- ☐ Computer time
- ☐ Extra credit / extra credit pass / extra credit points
- ☐ Extra reading time
- ☐ Extra recess
- ☐ Field trip
- ☐ Special dress day - option to wear a fun hat or no uniform
- ☐ Time to listen to music, use cell phone, mingle w/ friends, read
- ☐ Early to lunch / front of lunch line pass
- ☐ Game time
- ☐ Hall pass
- ☐ 5 minutes of free time
- ☐ Teacher's assistant for the day
- ☐ Positive note sent home to parents
- ☐ Free time doing an activity of choice
- ☐ Lunch or breakfast in the classroom
- ☐ Help design/put up a bulletin board
- ☐ Journal share
- ☐ Leave class 1 minute early
- ☐ Leave shoes off in the room for a day
- ☐ Drop lowest test score
- ☐ Listen to an audio book
- ☐ Listen to music while working
- ☐ *No Homework* pass
- ☐ *No Assignment* pass
- ☐ *No Quiz* pass
- ☐ *No Test* pass
- ☐ *No Morning Work* pass
- ☐ Open book test
- ☐ Permission to use teacher's special pen or pencil for the day
- ☐ Private lunch in the classroom with a friend
- ☐ Put a puzzle together
- ☐ Earn raffle tickets for donated prize
- ☐ Read to the class
- ☐ Reduced homework
- ☐ Remove a tardy
- ☐ Bring an item for Show and Tell
- ☐ Sit by friends
- ☐ Sit in a unique spot or chair for the day (e.g., rocking chair)
- ☐ Sit with a buddy at lunch
- ☐ Earn stickers
- ☐ Library time
- ☐ Take a fun physical activity break
- ☐ Teach class
- ☐ Teacher performs a special skill (e.g., singing, cartwheel, etc.)
- ☐ Earn trinkets (e.g., magnets, frisbees, etc.)
- ☐ Turn in an assignment late
- ☐ Walk with the principal or teacher
- ☐ Watch a fun video

This Secondary Classroom Reinforcers list may be used in special or regular education classes. Teachers and/or students can check those reinforcers most appropriate.

Elementary Reinforcer Menu

Reinforcer Menu

Reinforcer	Points Needed
Delivering Messages	15
Feeding Pets	20
Emptying Wastebasket	20
Passing out Materials	20
Peer Tutoring	25
Leading the Class Line	25
Using a Computer	25
Working with Clay	30
Using Colored Markers	30
Using Colored Marker	30
Playing a Board Game	35

Class Reinforcer Menu

Reinforcer	Points Needed
Share Music	15
Lunch Outdoors	20
Class Visitor	25
Put on a Play	25
See a Movie	30
Write and Mail Letters	30
Field Trip	30
Take Class Pictures	30
Have Adults in for Lunch	30
Pop Popcorn	35

The Reinforcer Menu is compiled from information gathered by having a student or students respond to the Reinforcer Survey.

Secondary Reinforcer Menu

Reinforcer Menu

Reinforcer	Points Needed
Reading	15
Watch a Movie	20
Assistant	20
Snack or Beverage	20
Peer Tutoring	25
Leading the Class Line	25
Using a Computer	25
Work on Hobby	30
Food or Drink Coupon	30
Extra Credit	30
No Assignment/Homework Pass	35

Class Reinforcer Menu

Reinforcer	Points Needed
Do Nothing	15
Listen to Music	20
Picnic Lunch	25
Have Class Outside	25
Field Trip	30
Watch TV	30
Play a Game	30
Go to a Movie	35

The Reinforcer Menu is compiled from information gathered by having a student or students respond to the Reinforcer Survey.

Point Card

Name: _____

Time	Days of Week				
	M	T	W	TH	F
8:00 - 8:50					
9:00 - 9:50					
10:00 - 10:50					
11:00 - 11:20					
11:30 - 12:20					
12:30 - 1:20					
1:30 - 2:20					
2:30 - 3:20					

This is a Point Card for secondary level students and may be used in special or regular education classes. Teachers assign points, give checks, or sign initials for appropriate behavior demonstrated by the student while in the classroom. These points are relative to rules of the classroom, expected behavior, a contract developed with the student, etc. A 3 x 5 inch index card is easily kept in a shirt pocket and small enough to reduce embarrassment for students who would prefer to keep their behavioral support program confidential.

Point Record

Academic Points

Monday	1	2	3	4	5	6	7	8	9	10	11	12	13	14

Tuesday	1	2	3	4	5	6	7	8	9	10	11	12	13	14

Wednesday	1	2	3	4	5	6	7	8	9	10	11	12	13	14

Thursday	1	2	3	4	5	6	7	8	9	10	11	12	13	14

Friday	1	2	3	4	5	6	7	8	9	10	11	12	13	14

Social Points

Monday														

Tuesday														

Wednesday														

Thursday														

Friday														

The Point Record is for recording Academic Points, top section, for each task completed with criteria met; and Social Points, bottom section, for demonstrating appropriate behavior in and around the classroom. The Point Record is kept with the student at all times, wherever he/she may be, in order that points may be given for following any school rules.

Rules for School Environments

GENERAL SOCIAL RULES. . . .

- BE QUIET.
- REMAIN IN YOUR SEAT.
- WORK ON ASSIGNED TASK.
- RAISE YOUR HAND.

HALLWAY RULES. . . .

- WALK IN THE HALL.
- WALK IN A LINE.
- WALK ON THE RIGHT.
- WALK QUIETLY.

CAFETERIA RULES. . . .

- BE QUIET IN THE CAFETERIA LINE.
- WALK TO YOUR TABLE.
- TALK QUIETLY.
- REMAIN SEATED.

OUTDOOR RULES. . . .

- TAKE PART IN AN ACTIVITY.
- TAKE TURNS.
- BE FRIENDLY.
- LINE UP WHEN IT IS TIME.

ACADEMIC RULES. . . .

- FINISH ONE TASK.
- MEET THE CRITERIA TO EARN 5 POINTS.

These rules, except for perhaps the outdoor rules, are applicable to all grade levels and have been used in public schools for general behavioral expectations.

Student Conference Report

Student's Name: _____ Grade Level: _____ Date: _____

School Personnel Involved and Titles: _____

_____

Initiation of Conference:

Regularly Scheduled Conference ☐   Teacher Initiation ☐   Other Personnel Initiation ☐

Student Initiation ☐   Parent Initiation ☐

Nature of Communication:

Information Sharing ☐   Progress Update ☐   Problem Identification ☐   Other ☐

Conference Summary (attach copies of written communications):

_____

_____

_____

_____

Expectations Based on Conference:

_____

_____

_____

Signatures of Conference Participants:

_____

_____

_____

The Student Conference Report is used for recording conferences held with the student to identify problems, concerns, progress, etc.

Parent Communication Form

Student's Name: _____ Grade Level: _____ Date: _____

Teacher's Name: _____ Class: _____

Parent(s): _____

Other School Personnel: _____

Type of Communication:

Parent Visit to School ☐   Teacher Visit to Home ☐   Out-of-School Location ☐

Letter ☐   Note ☐   Phone Call ☐   Email ☐   Other ☐

Initiation of Communication:

School Scheduled Meeting ☐   Teacher Initiation ☐   Parent Initiation ☐   Other ☐

Nature of Communication:

Information Sharing ☐   Progress Update ☐   Problem Identification ☐   Other ☐

Communication Summary (attach copies of written communications):

_____

_____

_____

_____

Expectations for Further Communication:

_____

_____

_____

Signatures of Participants (If Communication Made in Person):

_____

_____

   The Parent Communication Form is a record of communication made with parents in person, by phone, or by notes or letters.

Schedule of Daily Events

Schedule of Daily Events

Name:

	#1	#2	#3	#4	#5	#6	#7	#8	#9	#10
Monday										
Tuesday										
Wednesday										
Thursday										
Friday										

Schedule of Daily Events

Name:

	#1	#2	#3	#4	#5	#6	#7	#8	#9	#10
Tuesday										

Each individual student's Schedule of Daily Events is developed for him/her and attached to his/her desk for a week at a time or for one day at a time. This schedule identifies each activity/task the student is assigned for the day, and the schedule is filled in by the teacher one day at a time. Students tend to know what they are to do next when the schedule is provided, and teachers can expect fewer interruptions for directions when students refer to their schedules.